THE COMPLETE IDIOT'S GUIDE® TO

40,000 Baby Names

Second Edition

by Marcia Layton Turner

ALPHA

A member of Penguin Group (USA) Inc.

ALPHA BOOKS

Published by the Penguin Group

Penguin Group (USA) Inc., 375 Hudson Street, New York, New York 10014, USA

Penguin Group (Canada), 90 Eglinton Avenue East, Suite 700, Toronto, Ontario M4P 2Y3, Canada (a division of Pearson Penguin Canada Inc.)

Penguin Books Ltd., 80 Strand, London WC2R 0RL, England

Penguin Ireland, 25 St. Stephen's Green, Dublin 2, Ireland (a division of Penguin Books Ltd.)

Penguin Group (Australia), 250 Camberwell Road, Camberwell, Victoria 3124, Australia (a division of Pearson Australia Group Pty. Ltd.)

Penguin Books India Pvt. Ltd., 11 Community Centre, Panchsheel Park, New Delhi—110 017, India

Penguin Group (NZ), 67 Apollo Drive, Rosedale, North Shore, Auckland 1311, New Zealand (a division of Pearson New Zealand Ltd.)

Penguin Books (South Africa) (Pty.) Ltd., 24 Sturdee Avenue, Rosebank, Johannesburg 2196, South Africa

Penguin Books Ltd., Registered Offices: 80 Strand, London WC2R 0RL, England

International Standard Book Number: 978-1-59257-841-2
Library of Congress Catalog Card Number: 2008935066

11 10 09   8 7 6 5 4 3 2 1

Interpretation of the printing code: The rightmost number of the first series of numbers is the year of the book's printing; the rightmost number of the second series of numbers is the number of the book's printing. For example, a printing code of 09-1 shows that the first printing occurred in 2009.

Printed in the United States of America

Note: This publication contains the opinions and ideas of its author. It is intended to provide helpful and informative material on the subject matter covered. It is sold with the understanding that the author and publisher are not engaged in rendering professional services in the book. If the reader requires personal assistance or advice, a competent professional should be consulted.

The author and publisher specifically disclaim any responsibility for any liability, loss, or risk, personal or otherwise, which is incurred as a consequence, directly or indirectly, of the use and application of any of the contents of this book.

Most Alpha books are available at special quantity discounts for bulk purchases for sales promotions, premiums, fund-raising, or educational use. Special books, or book excerpts, can also be created to fit specific needs.

For details, write: Special Markets, Alpha Books, 375 Hudson Street, New York, NY 10014.

Publisher: *Marie Butler-Knight*
Editorial Director/Acquisitions Editor: *Mike Sanders*
Senior Managing Editor: *Billy Fields*
Senior Development Editor: *Christy Wagner*
Production Editor: *Megan Douglass*

Copy Editor: *Michael Dietsch*
Cover/Book Designer: *Kurt Owens*
Layout: *Brian Massey*
Proofreader: *Laura Caddell*

To Amanda and Grant.

Contents at a Glance

Part 1: Ideas and Inspiration: The Lists   1

   1   Fame and the Name Game   3
*From legends of the silver screen to TV stars to today's—and
yesterday's—top crooners, for a name with star power, here's
where to look.*

   2   Noteworthy Names   35
*For an unusual and unique name, this chapter provides
plenty of options, including cartoon-character names, initial
names, and … let's just say "unique" names.*

   3   Winners, Winners, and More Winners   45
*To get your child a head-start in life, why not consider a
name that's already a winner? Check out these names of winning athletes, playwrights, musicians, and thinkers.*

   4   Money Monikers   75
*If you hope your baby will be a corporate leader, the lists of
Fortune 1000 CEOs, entrepreneurs, and brands in this chap-
ter will provide plenty of name possibilities.*

   5   Political Names   81
*For names of world leaders, presidents, first ladies, patriots,
warriors, civil rights leaders and activists, and peacemakers,
check out this political chapter.*

   6   Scientific Suggestions   95
*In this chapter you'll find names with a scientific bent, such
as Nobel Prize winners, well-known scientists throughout history, inventors, pilots, and astronauts.*

   7   Pure and Natural Possibilities   101
*For a close-to-nature name, try these names of stars, planets,
mountains, rivers, jewels, gems, animals, flowers, fruits, and
colors.*

   8   Artistic Appellations   111
*To inspire creativity in your child, try one of these names of
artists, authors, poets, dancers, composers, and other artsy
folks.*

9   Naming Nationwide   135
     Here you'll find lists of names popular over the years, sorted
     by decade, as well as popular names by country, region, state,
     and major city. The top 100 girl and boy names are also
     listed.

10   Cultural Cachet   149
     Prefer a name based on your cultural heritage? This chapter
     contains names from a wide variety of backgrounds.

11   Hunting Through History   181
     For a name from ancient times, mythology, legends, or his-
     torical firsts, you can't go wrong with this chapter.

12   Names from Religion   195
     Turn to this chapter for faith-based names from Judaism,
     Christianity, Buddhism, Hindu, Islam, Wicca, and more.

Part 2:   Giant Alphabetical List of Names, Origins, and Meanings   215

     Girl Names   217
     This comprehensive A-to-Z listing of girl names helps you
     consider all your options before settling on the perfect choice.

     Boy Names   325
     Whether you're looking for ideas or are pretty sure what you
     want to call your son, the tens of thousands of boy names here
     is all you need.

Appendix

     Online Resources   427

Contents

Part 1: Ideas and Inspiration: The Lists   **1**

  1 Fame and the Name Game   **3**

Silver Screen Legends 4
Movie Stars 5
Movie Characters 6
Movie Directors 8
Child Stars 9
Celebrities' Babies 10
Dramatic Designations 13
Soap Opera Hunks and Hussies 16
Sitcom Sweethearts 18
Comedians and Comediennes 20
TV Talk Show Hosts 21
Game Show Hosts and Hostesses 22
Newscasters/Journalists 23
Rock Kings and Queens 25
Country Stars 27
Gospel Singers 28
Rappers and Hip-Hop Heroes 29
Pop Princes and Princesses 30
American Idol Finalists 30
Names from Songs 31

  2 Noteworthy Names   **35**

Cartoon Characters 36
Disney Characters 37
Secret Identities of Superheroes 38
Before They Were Famous—Name Changers 39
Alliterative Names 40
Double Names 41
Initial Names 42
Unusual Names 42
Gothic/Vampire Names 43
Traditional Names 43

3 Winners, Winners, and More Winners **45**

Pulitzer Prize Winners 46
Nobel Prize Winners 48
Oscar Winning Actors and Actresses 49
Tony Winners 52
Emmy Winners 54
Grammy Winners 57
Olympic Medalists 60
Heisman Trophy Winners 61
Series MVPs 62
NBA/NCAA All-Stars 64
Hockey Hunks and Babes 66
Gymnast Guys and Gals 68
Spinners and Stunners—Ice Skaters 69
Grand Slammers—Tennis Players 70
Golf Pros 71
NASCAR Names 73

4 Money Monikers **75**

CEOs 76
Entrepreneurs 77
Heirs and Heiresses 78
Brand Names 79

5 Political Names **81**

World Leaders, Past and Present 82
Kings and Queens 84
Princes and Princesses 85
Dukes, Duchesses, and Other Royalty 86
U.S. Presidents 86
First Ladies 87
Presidents' Kids 88
Patriots/Military Leaders 91
Warriors 91
Peacemakers 92
Black History/Civil Rights Leaders 93
Activists 94

6 Scientific Suggestions **95**

Scientists 96

Inventors and Discoverers............................... 98

Sky-High Names—Astronauts and Aviators 99

7 Pure and Natural Possibilities **101**

Stars and Planets 102

Mountains and Valleys 102

Lakes and Rivers.. 103

Jewels, Gems, and Minerals............................ 104

Birds and Animals...................................... 105

Flowers and Trees....................................... 107

Fruits.. 108

Food Names 108

Colors 109

Moods 109

Hair Color Names....................................... 110

Unisex Names.. 110

8 Artistic Appellations **111**

Artists... 112

Favorite Children's Book/Show Characters 113

Literary Characters 115

Romance Heroes and Heroines........................... 116

Science-Fiction/Fantasy Names 119

Best-Selling Authors.................................... 120

Names from Shakespeare................................ 123

Poets.. 126

Composers 127

Opera Singers 129

Dancers 130

Fashion Designers 131

Chefs 132

Architects 133

9 Naming Nationwide **135**

Top Baby Names by Country 136

Top Five Baby Names by U.S. State for 2007 137

Most Popular Names by Major U.S. City................ 140

Named for Cities 141
Named for States 143
Top 100 Most Popular Names for 2007 143
Most Popular Names by Year 145
Most Popular Names by Decade 146
Most Popular Twin Names 147
Up-and-Coming Names 148

10 Cultural Cachet   149

African/African American Names 150
Arabic Names 151
Australian Names 152
Chinese Names 153
Czech Names 154
Dutch Names 155
English Names 155
French Names 157
German Names 158
Greek Names 160
Hawaiian Names 161
Hispanic/Latino Names 162
Indian Names 163
Irish Names 164
Italian Names 165
Jamaican Names 166
Japanese Names 167
Korean Names 169
Native American Names 170
Persian Names 171
Polish Names 172
Portuguese Names 173
Russian/Eastern European Names 174
Scandinavian Names 175
Scottish/Welsh Names 177
Swedish Names 177
Turkish Names 178
Ukrainian Names 178

11 Hunting Through History 181

Ancient Names 182

Names from Mythology 183

Names from Arthurian Legend 184

Victorian Names 185

Heroes and Heroines 187

Pioneers/Explorers 188

Cowboys and Cowgirls 189

Hippie Names 189

Calendar-Based Names 190

Historical Firsts 190

Historical Family Surnames 192

Occupations Throughout History 193

Historical Landmarks 193

12 Names from Religion 195

Greek and Roman Gods 196

Angels 197

Biblical Names 198

Saints 200

Religious Leaders 202

Popes 203

Catholic Names 204

Jewish/Hebrew Names 206

Buddhist Names 208

Hindu Names 209

Muslim Names 211

Wiccan Names 212

Virtues 213

Part 2: Giant Alphabetical List of Names, Origins, and Meanings 215

Girl Names 217

Boy Names 325

Appendix

Online Resources 427

Foreword

First names are fun. It's hard to pass up reading about such facets of our own name as its origin, meaning, usage in different countries, popularity at present and in the past, variations in spelling, spin-offs, diminutives, and the important people—as well as the notorious ones (hopefully not too many of the latter)—who share the name. Aside from the calories involved, reading about names is no different from eating popcorn—it is difficult to stop without dipping into the book for the same information about our parents, spouse, siblings, friends, and others.

An ironic feature of our name is that it says more about our parents and the period when we were born than it does about us. We had nothing to do with the choice; it was our parents (influenced by a variety of factors) who made a decision that the vast majority of us accept for the rest of our life. Parents often struggle over the choice they make. It is particularly easy for parents to torture themselves if they try to figure out what image their child's name will have and—in turn—how others will respond to the name. Yes, names do differ in their imagery. (If you have any doubts about this, compare the names of performers who have changed their names, and consider how the shift in image fits in with the performer's niche.) Seeking to make a good choice and avoid a disastrous one, many turn to books such as this one to get ideas and inspiration.

The fascination we have with names has an unfortunate consequence: it is easy to overlook special features of names that allow us to understand how our culture changes, to say nothing of the mechanisms that generate fashion and tastes. We live in a world in which our tastes in foods, cars, clothing, beverages, movies, music, and the like are affected by manufacturers, retailers, and industries that use high-powered advertising, subtle selling techniques, consumer research, and subliminal devices to affect our choices. Names, however, are refreshingly free of these efforts—there are no commercial efforts to influence the choices made by parents. An infant's name matters not at all to diaper manufacturers—I leave it to your imagination what does matter to them.

A second important feature is that names are free: you may or may not be able to afford a fancy car or an expensive home or take a cruise (unless we include rowboat rentals), but naming choices are not restricted by income. (Yet the classes differ in their tastes even though there is no economic restriction on their choices.) Fashions occur not only in such matters as clothing and names and music; fashions and tastes are also observed in scientific topics, school curriculums, political campaigns, corporate administration, views of the role of government, tax policies and priorities, and even our manners and choice of words. The study of names helps us discover not only the pure mechanisms of fashion and taste, but also how our society and culture have changed through the centuries.

Here are a few illustrations of these broader considerations. In many nations, names first became a matter of fashion and taste only in the latter part of the nineteenth century. Previously, choices were much less a matter of *liking* or *disliking* a name, but rather meeting obligations (naming a child after grandparents or other relatives, and following traditional practices). And whereas parents now worry if the name they choose will be *too* popular, at one point it was common for the five most popular names for each sex to be given to 50 percent or more of the infants born in a given year. Distinctiveness was once not a virtue. Although fashions in names may seem idiosyncratic and haphazard, often they follow orderly processes. Tastes are affected by parental education, other features of social class, race, ethnic origin, immigration status, region, and the like. On the other hand, just to whet your appetite, sociologists now know of a variety of special mechanisms that operate to change tastes in names without necessarily reflecting any social processes or having any special meaning. In effect, popular explanations of cultural changes are often way off the mark—seeking meaning when there is none.

Stanley Lieberson
Abbott Lawrence Lowell Professor of Sociology
Harvard University
Author, *A Matter of Taste: How Names, Fashions, and Culture Change* (Yale University Press, 2000)

Introduction

Choosing a baby name is hard work! It's also a lot of fun, but unless you decided long ago what to name your children and your spouse or partner agreed, you may want some support. Perhaps a book with tens of thousands of exciting possibilities? You're in luck, because you're holding such a book. I'm here to help you find the name that fits your little one like a glove.

However, before you even start scanning the many names here, you might want to take a step back and discuss with your partner exactly what kind of name you're going for. Do you want a cool and edgy name, or a more traditional and preppy moniker? Perhaps artsy is more your style. Or were you thinking you'd like a name befitting a future jock? If you can decide up front the kind of name you want, you'll probably have an easier time narrowing your list to a manageable number of possibilities.

One approach is to choose a name from one of your families—perhaps a parent, grandparent, or favorite aunt or uncle. Some families have standing traditions of naming children after certain relatives, which you may want to consider. Or maybe you could use a surname—a last name—as a first for your baby. It can be a great way to keep a family name alive.

As you start to create a list of "possibles"—names that may work—it's always a good idea to check on the names' original meanings. Although the importance of meanings isn't as prominent today as it was years ago, considering a name's meaning may help you whittle down your list. You'd hate to saddle your child with a name that means "loser" or suggests he or she has a problem right from the get-go!

In addition to looking into the meanings of names, sounding them out is also smart. How does each name sound in conjunction with your last name or with the middle name you plan to use? Is it alliterative, with both names beginning with the same vowel or consonant sound? Or is it hard to pronounce? Or worse, does it create a phrase with its own meaning, such as "Jean Poole" or "Ivy Leaf"?

Although many of us want distinctive names, there's a fine line between "distinctive" and "disaster." Come elementary school, your child may become the butt of some very painful jokes if you select a name that suggests an unflattering nickname.

And if you have your heart set on a particular name that just isn't working as a first name, there's always the middle name, which has become more and more common since the 1950s.

But the most important factor of all is whether you like it. Beyond how it sounds, what it means, how cool or uncool it is, how many other kids have the same name, whether it will irritate your relatives, or if it breaks with a long-standing family tradition, you and your significant other need to feel good about it. You need to love it. I hope this book helps you find a name that fits your baby to a T.

How This Book Is Organized

This book is presented in two parts:

In **Part 1, "Ideas and Inspiration: The Lists,"** you'll find more than 150 lists to help you brainstorm possible names. You can narrow your choices by the type of list presented, such as science-oriented or biblical, for instance, or read through them all for more alternatives.

Part 2, "Giant Alphabetical List of Names, Origins, and Meanings," is both a cross-reference tool for the lists in Part 1 and a resource for researching the origins, meanings, and spelling variations for names of interest—more than 40,000 of them!

Acknowledgments

As you'll see once you start flipping through the pages filled with thousands of names, this book took a lot of hard work to compile and research. I'm indebted to Jessica and Alexandra Assimon for their assistance. Diane Chichelli, in particular, was a lifesaver in researching lists and name origins.

I also appreciate the guidance and wisdom of my editor, Mike Sanders, and my agent, Marilyn Allen, as well as the production team, who were faced with a particularly challenging project. Thank you all.

I also want to thank my husband, Charlie, who pitched in at various stages of the project to be sure I included more than the 40,000 names promised.

Special Thanks to the Technical Reviewer

The Complete Idiot's Guide to 40,000 Baby Names, Second Edition, was reviewed by an expert who double-checked the accuracy of what you'll learn here, to help us ensure that this book gives you everything you need to know about finding the perfect name for your baby. Special thanks are extended to Linda Saracino.

Trademarks

All terms mentioned in this book that are known to be or are suspected of being trademarks or service marks have been appropriately capitalized. Alpha Books and Penguin Group (USA) Inc. cannot attest to the accuracy of this information. Use of a term in this book should not be regarded as affecting the validity of any trademark or service mark.

Part 1

Ideas and Inspiration: The Lists

You're going to have a baby! Congratulations! Now what will you call him or her? To jump-start the process of finding the perfect name for your baby, Part 1 is filled with more than 150 lists of names organized by category. From celebrities' baby names to names based on cultural heritage to names of presidents, popes, first ladies, astronauts, famous criminals, and lots more, the following chapters give you tons of possibilities for your new little one.

Fame and the Name Game

Your child is, in many ways, a reflection of you—your hopes and dreams, your likes and dislikes, your personality, your quirks. So why not look to the names of people who have influenced your life in some way—celebrities, TV stars, musicians, even criminals—not that you want to name your kid after Jack the Ripper—when thinking about your baby's name?

The names in this chapter are celebrities, from the silver screen and TV, to music and musicians, from yesterday and today. If you're a rock 'n' roll fan, you'll find plenty of inspiration from the names of rock stars past and present in these pages. Or if country is more your speed, you'll see many familiar names listed here as a starting point for your baby name search.

Silver Screen Legends

Girl Names

Anne Bancroft
Audrey Hepburn
Barbara Stanwyck
Bette Davis
Claudette Colbert
Cloris Leachman
Debbie Reynolds
Dolores del Rio
Donna Reed
Elizabeth Taylor
Ellen Burstyn
Eva Marie Saint
Faye Dunaway

Gena Rowlands
Geraldine Page
Ginger Rogers
Grace Kelly
Greer Garson
Hedy Lamarr
Helen Hayes
Ingrid Bergman
Jane Wyman
Jessica Tandy
Jo Van Fleet
Joan Crawford
Joanne Woodward

Judi Dench
Julie Christie
June Allyson
Katharine
  Hepburn
Lee Grant
Loretta Young
Louise Fletcher
Martha Raye
Mary Pickford
Mercedes
  McCambridge
Myrna Loy

Norma Shearer
Olivia de
  Havilland
Patty Duke
Phyllis Diller
Rita Moreno
Sandy Dennis
Shelley Winters
Sophia Loren
Teresa Wright
Vanessa Redgrave
Vivien Leigh

Boy Names

Alan Alda
Alec Guinness
Anthony Quinn
Art Carney
Basil Rathbone
Bing Crosby
Broderick
  Crawford
Burl Ives
Burt Lancaster
Cary Grant

Charlton Heston
Clark Gable
David Niven
Don Ameche
Edmund Gwenn
Ernest Borgnine
Errol Flynn
Frank Sinatra
Gary Cooper
George C. Scott
Gregory Peck

Henry Fonda
Humphrey Bogart
Jack Lemmon
James Cagney
James Stewart
John Houseman
Laurence Olivier
Lionel Barrymore
Marlon Brando
Maximilian Schell
Peter Finch

Peter Ustinov
Ray Milland
Red Buttons
Robert Duvall
Rod Steiger
Sidney Poitier
Spencer Tracy
Victor McLaglen
William Holden
Yul Brynner

Movie Stars

Girl Names

Angelina Jolie	Glenn Close	Lindsay Lohan	Renée Zellweger
Anne Hathaway	Halle Berry	Liv Tyler	Sandra Bullock
Ashley Tisdale	Helen Mirren	Maggie Gyllenhaal	Scarlett Johansson
Brittany Murphy	Jennifer Connelly		Sienna Miller
Cameron Diaz	Jodie Foster	Megan Fox	Sophia Bush
Charlize Theron	Julia Roberts	Meryl Streep	Uma Thurman
Demi Moore	Kate Winslet	Natalie Portman	Vanessa Hudgens
Drew Barrymore	Kirsten Dunst	Nicole Kidman	Whoopi Goldberg
Elisha Cuthbert	Kyra Sedgwick	Reese Witherspoon	Winona Ryder

Boy Names

Adam Sandler	Derek Luke	Johnny Depp	Pierce Brosnan
Al Pacino	Don Cheadle	Kal Penn	Robert De Niro
Ben Affleck	Edward Norton	Kevin Spacey	Russell Crowe
Brad Pitt	Ewan McGregor	Kurt Russell	Samuel L. Jackson
Christian Bale	George Clooney	Leonardo DiCaprio	Seth Rogen
Colin Farrell	Harrison Ford		Shia LaBeouf
Dane Cook	Heath Ledger	Liam Neeson	Steve Carell
Daniel Craig	Jake Gyllenhaal	Matt Damon	Tobey Maguire
Danny Glover	James McAvoy	Mel Gibson	Tom Cruise
Denzel Washington	Jim Sturgess	Orlando Bloom	Val Kilmer

Movie Characters

Girl Names

Character	Actor	Movie
Ada Monroe	Nicole Kidman	*Cold Mountain*
Alicia Nash	Jennifer Connelly	*A Beautiful Mind*
Aurora Greenway	Shirley MacLaine	*Terms of Endearment*
Beatrix Kiddo	Uma Thurman	*Kill Bill*
Birdee Pruitt	Sandra Bullock	*Hope Floats*
Bree Davis	Helen Hunt	*Dr. T and the Women*
Charlotte Hollis	Olivia de Havilland	*Hush, Hush Sweet Charlotte*
Clarice Starling	Jodie Foster	*The Silence of the Lambs*
Clementine Kruczynski	Kate Winslet	*Eternal Sunshine of the Spotless Mind*
Dolly Pelliker	Cher	*Silkwood*
Elise Elliot	Goldie Hawn	*The First Wives Club*
Elle Wood	Reese Witherspoon	*Legally Blonde*
Erica Barry	Diane Keaton	*Something's Gotta Give*
Erin Brockovich	Julia Roberts	*Erin Brockovich*
Francesca Johnson	Meryl Streep	*The Bridges of Madison County*
Gracie Hart	Sandra Bullock	*Miss Congeniality*
Ilsa Laszlo	Ingrid Bergman	*Casablanca*
Jacy Farrow	Cybill Shepherd	*The Last Picture Show*
Jenny Cavilleri	Ali McGraw	*Love Story*
Jo March	Katharine Hepburn	*Little Women*
Juno MacGuff	Ellen Page	*Juno*
Kate McKay	Meg Ryan	*Kate and Leopold*
Lace Pennamin	Kyra Sedgwick	*Phenomenon*
Lee Holloway	Maggie Gyllenhaal	*Secretary*
Lilia Herriton	Helen Mirren	*Where Angels Fear to Tread*
Maggie Fitzgerald	Hilary Swank	*Million Dollar Baby*
Marge Gunderson	Frances McDormand	*Fargo*
Matty Walker	Kathleen Turner	*Body Heat*
Muriel Pritchett	Geena Davis	*The Accidental Tourist*
Penny Lane	Kate Hudson	*Almost Famous*
Regan MacNeil	Linda Blair	*The Exorcist*
Rose Dewitt Bukater	Kate Winslet	*Titanic*
Ruth Wonderly	Bebe Daniels	*The Maltese Falcon*

Character	Actor	Movie
Samantha Stanton	Mary-Kate Olsen	*Switching Goals*
Susanna Kaysen	Winona Ryder	*Girl, Interrupted*
Tess McGill	Melanie Griffith	*Working Girl*
Velvet Brown	Elizabeth Taylor	*National Velvet*
Winnifred "Winnie" Foster	Alexis Bledel	*Tuck Everlasting*

Boy Names

Character	Actor	Movie
Allan Quatermain	Sean Connery	*The League of Extraordinary Gentlemen*
Amos Calloway	Danny DeVito	*Big Fish*
Ben Marco	Denzel Washington	*The Manchurian Candidate*
Boyd Redding	Morgan Freeman	*The Shawshank Redemption*
Butch Cassidy	Paul Newman	*Butch Cassidy and the Sundance Kid*
Catcher Block	Ewan McGregor	*Down with Love*
Charlie Mackenzie	Mike Myers	*So I Married an Axe Murderer*
Doyle Gipson	Samuel L. Jackson	*Changing Lanes*
Elliott	Henry Thomas	*E.T. the Extra-Terrestrial*
Finnegan Bell	Ethan Hawke	*Great Expectations*
Forrest Gump	Tom Hanks	*Forrest Gump*
Frank Abagnale	Leonardo DiCaprio	*Catch Me If You Can*
Garth Algar	Dana Carvey	*Wayne's World*
Gordon Bombay	Emilio Estevez	*D3: The Mighty Ducks*
Herman Boone	Denzel Washington	*Remember the Titans*
Holden McNeil	Ben Affleck	*Chasing Amy*
Indiana Jones	Harrison Ford	*Indiana Jones*
Jack Aubrey	Russell Crowe	*Master and Commander*
Jason Bourne	Richard Chamberlain/ Matt Damon	*The Bourne Identity*
Jerry Fletcher	Mel Gibson	*Conspiracy Theory*
Joel Barish	Jim Carrey	*Eternal Sunshine of the Spotless Mind*
Julian Kaye	Richard Gere	*American Gigolo*
Karl Childers	Billy Bob Thornton	*Sling Blade*
Lloyd Dobler	John Cusack	*Say Anything*
Max Baron	James Spader	*White Palace*

continues

Movie Characters continued

Boy Names

Character	Actor	Movie
Mickey O'Neill	Brad Pitt	*Snatch*
Mitch Albom	Hank Azaria	*Tuesdays with Morrie*
Norman Bates	Anthony Perkins	*Psycho*
Oskar Schindler	Liam Neeson	*Schindler's List*
Pete Monash	Topher Grace	*Win a Date with Tad Hamilton*
Ray Kinsella	Kevin Costner	*Field of Dreams*
Ren McCormack	Kevin Bacon	*Footloose*
Ricky McKinney	Jon Bon Jovi	*Pay It Forward*
Robert Clayton Dean	Will Smith	*Enemy of the State*
Roger Murtaugh	Danny Glover	*Lethal Weapon*
Ron Burgundy	Will Ferrell	*Anchorman*
Samuel Gerard	Tommy Lee Jones	*U.S. Marshals*
Shelly Kaplow	Alec Baldwin	*The Cooler*
Stu Shepard	Colin Farrell	*Phone Booth*
Sy Parrish	Robin Williams	*One Hour Photo*
Tom Booker	Robert Redford	*The Horse Whisperer*
Will Hunting	Matt Damon	*Good Will Hunting*
Willie Beaman	Jamie Foxx	*Any Given Sunday*
Wyatt	Peter Fonda	*Easy Rider*

Movie Directors

Girl Names

Cherie Nowlan	Kirsten Sheridan	Lourdes Portillo	Samira Makhmalbaf
Jane Campion	Lena Wertmuller	Mimi Leder	Shari Springer Berman
Julie Delpy	Leni Riefenstahl	Miranda July	
Kassi Lemmons	Louise Brooks	Robin Swicord	Sofia Coppola

Boy Names

Abbas Kiarostami	Billy Wilder	David Lynch	Francis Ford Coppola
Aki Kaurismäki	Busby Berkeley	Elia Kazan	Fritz Lang
Alfred Hitchcock	Buster Keaton	Errol Morris	Godfrey Reggio
Andy Warhol	Dario Argento	Ethan Coen	

Hayao Miyazaki	M. Night Shyamalan	Quentin Tarantino	Theo van Gogh
Jim Henson	Martin Scorsese	Rob Zombie	Werner Herzog
Joel Coen	Michael Moore	Spike Jonze	Wong Kar-wai
Kevin Smith	Orson Welles	Steven Soderbergh	Woody Allen
King Vidor	Preston Sturges	Steven Spielberg	Yale Strom
			Yash Chopra

Child Stars

Girl Names

Actor	TV Show/ Movie/ Claim to Fame	Actor	TV Show/ Movie/ Claim to Fame
Abigail Breslin	*Little Miss Sunshine*	Lisa Loring	*The Addams Family*
Alexis Fields	*Moesha*	Mackenzie Phillips	*One Day at a Time*
Anissa Jones	*Family Affair*	Mary-Kate Olsen	*Full House*
Ashley Olsen	*Full House*	Melissa Sue Anderson	*Little House on the Prairie*
Candace Cameron	*Full House*		
Dakota Fanning	*Charlotte's Web*	Miley Cyrus	*Hannah Montana*
Dana Plato	*Diff'rent Strokes*	Miranda Cosgrove	*iCarly*
Danica McKellar	*The Wonder Years*	Nicole Eggert	*Charles in Charge*
Emma Roberts	*Nancy Drew*	Quinn Cummings	*The Goodbye Girl*
Gaby Hoffman	*This Is My Life*	Sally Field	*The Flying Nun*
Heather Ripley	*Chitty Chitty Bang Bang*	Sheila Hames	*The Many Loves of Dobie Gillis*
Inger Nilsson	*Pippi Longstocking*	Sidney Greenbush	*Little House on the Prairie*
Jamie Lynn Spears	*Zoey 101*	Tatyana Ali	*The Fresh Prince of Bel-Air*
Jodie Sweetin	*Full House*		
Kim Richards	*Escape to Witch Mountain*	Tempestt Bledsoe	*The Cosby Show*
		Tiffany Amber Thiessen	*Saved by the Bell*
Kristy McNichol	*Little Darlings*		
Lark Voorhies	*Saved by the Bell*	Valerie Bertinelli	*One Day at a Time*
Lindsay Greenbush	*Little House on the Prairie*		

continues

Child Stars

Boy Names

Actor	TV Show/ Movie/ Claim to Fame	Actor	TV Show/ Movie/ Claim to Fame
Adam Rich	*Eight Is Enough*	Haley Joel Osment	*Sixth Sense*
Andrew Lawrence	*Brotherly Love*	Henry Thomas	*E.T. the Extra-Terrestrial*
Barry Williams	*The Brady Bunch*		
Billy Mumy	*Lost in Space*	Ilan Mitchell-Smith	*Weird Science*
Butch Patrick	*The Munsters*	Jaleel White	*Family Matters*
Claude Jarman Jr.	*The Yearling*	Jonathan Taylor Thomas	*Home Improvement*
Cole Sprouse	*Suite Life of Zack and Cody*	Leif Garrett	*Tiger Beat* pinup
Corey Feldman	*The Goonies*	Macauley Culkin	*Home Alone*
Corin Nemec	*Parker Lewis Can't Lose*	Michael Oliver	*Problem Child*
		Noah Hathaway	*The NeverEnding Story*
Dan Frischman	*Head of the Class*	Peter Billingsley	*A Christmas Story*
Drake Parker	*Drake and Josh*	Ricky Segall	*The Partridge Family*
Dustin Diamond	*Saved by the Bell*		
Dylan Sprouse	*Suite Life of Zack and Cody*	Sean Astin	*The Goonies*
Emmanuel Lewis	*Webster*	Taran Noah Smith	*Home Improvement*
Fred Savage	*The Wonder Years*	Wil Wheaton	*Stand by Me*
		Zachery Ty Bryan	*Home Improvement*

Celebrities' Babies

Girl Names

Child	Parent(s)	Child	Parent(s)
Apple	Gwyneth Paltrow and Chris Martin	Bella	Billy Bob Thornton and Connie Angland
Aquinnah	Tracy Pollan and Michael J. Fox	Brea	Eddie Murphy
Ava	Reese Witherspoon and Ryan Phillippe	Brooke	Chynna Phillips and Billy Baldwin
Bailey	Melissa Etheridge	Camera	Arthur Ashe

Child	Parent(s)	Child	Parent(s)
Carys	Catherine Zeta-Jones and Michael Douglas	Langley	Mariel Hemingway
Chelsea	Steven Tyler	Leni	Heidi Klum and Flavio Briatore
Clementine	Claudia Schiffer and Matthew Vaughn	Lola	Kelly Ripa and Mark Consuelos
Coco	Courtney Cox and David Arquette	Lourdes	Madonna
		Mackenzie	J. K. Rowling
Dannielynn	Anna Nicole Smith and Larry Birkhead	MaKena'lei	Helen Hunt
Deva	Monica Bellucci and Vincent Cassel	Marina	Matt LeBlanc
		Mattea	Mira Sorvino
Dree	Mariel Hemingway	Mia	Kate Winslet
Elinor	Katie Couric	Natasha	Alex Rodriguez
Emme	Jennifer Lopez and Marc Anthony	Nico	Thandie Newton
		Paloma	Emilio Estevez
Ensa	Bill and Camille Cosby	Piper Maru	Gillian Anderson
Ever	Milla Jovovich and Paul Anderson	Puma	Erykah Badu
Frances	Kate and Andy Spade	Rainbow	Ving Rhames
Gabrielle	Donna Karan	Rowan	Brooke Shields
Gaia	Emma Thompson and Greg Wise	Rumer	Demi Moore and Bruce Willis
Georgia	Mick Jagger and Jerry Hall	Sam Alexis	Tiger Woods
		Schuyler	Tracy Pollan and Michael J. Fox
Harlow	Nicole Richie and Joel Madden	Scout	Demi Moore and Bruce Willis
Hazel	Julia Roberts		
Honor	Jessica Alba	Shea	John Grisham
Ireland	Kim Basinger and Alec Baldwin	Shiloh	Angelina Jolie and Brad Pitt
Iris	Jude Law and Sadie Frost	Siobhan	Rebecca Lobo and Steve Rushin
Isabella	Nicole Kidman and Tom Cruise	Sosie	Kyra Sedgwick and Kevin Bacon
Ivanka	Donald and Ivanna Trump	Suri	Tom Cruise and Katie Holmes
Jasmine	Michael Jordan		
Jordan	Bono	Tallulah	Demi Moore and Bruce Willis
Kaia	Cindy Crawford and Randy Gerber	Taylor	Garth Brooks
Katia	Denzel Washington		

continues

Celebrities' Babies continued

Girl Names

Child	Parent(s)	Child	Parent(s)
Violet	Jennifer Garner and Ben Affleck	Willow	Will Smith and Jada Pinkett Smith
Vivienne Marcheline	Angelina Jolie and Brad Pitt	Zahra	Chris Rock
		Zola	Eddie Murphy

Boy Names

Child	Parent(s)	Child	Parent(s)
Aidan	Lou Rawls	Jett	Kelly Preston and John Travolta
Aurelius	Elle MacPherson	Kal-El	Nicolas Cage
Austin	Tommy Lee Jones	Kit	Jodie Foster
Banjo	Rachel Griffiths	Knox Léon	Angelina Jolie and Brad Pitt
Beckett	Melissa Etheridge		
Boston	Kurt Russell	Maddox	Angelina Jolie
Brawley	Nick Nolte	Magnus	Will Ferrell
Brody	Gabrielle Reece and Laird Hamilton	Marston	Hugh Hefner
Brooklyn	Victoria and David Beckham	Max	Christina Aguilera; Jennifer Lopez and Marc Anthony
Caspar	Claudia Schiffer	Milo	Ricki Lake; Liv Tyler and Royston Langdon
Cosimo	Beck and Marissa Ribisi		
Cruz	Victoria and David Beckham	Oliver	Bridget Fonda and Danny Elfman
Damian	Liz Hurley and Steve Bing	Owen	Kevin Kline
Dylan	Catherine Zeta-Jones and Michael Douglas	Phinneaus	Julia Roberts
		Pilot Inspektor	Jason Lee
Ellery	Laura Dern	Pirate	Jonathan Davis
Finley	Holly Marie Combs	Presley	Cindy Crawford
Freedom	Ving Rhames	Rafferty	Jude Law and Sadie Frost
Holden	Brendan Fraser	Rebel	Robert Rodriguez
Indiana	Casey Affleck and Summer Phoenix	Ripley	Thandie Newton
Jaden	Will Smith and Jada Pinkett Smith	Rocco	Madonna and Guy Ritchie

Child	Parent(s)	Child	Parent(s)
Rocket	Robert Rodriguez	Trey	Will Smith
Roman	Debra Messing; Holly Robinson Peete and Rodney Peete	True	Kirstie Alley and Parker Stevenson
Rudy	Jude Law and Sadie Frost	Truman	Rita Wilson and Tom Hanks
Ryder	Kate Hudson and Chris Robinson	Ty	Pam Dawber and Mark Harmon
Satchel	Spike Lee; Woody Allen	Weston	Nicolas Cage
Sawyer	Kate Capshaw and Steven Spielberg	Will	Mel Gibson
		Wolfgang	Eddie Van Halen and Valerie Bertinelli
Sebastian	James Spader	Wyatt	Goldie Hawn and Kurt Russell
Seven	Erykah Badu		
Speck	John Mellencamp and Elaine Irwin-Mellencamp	Yusef	Jesse Jackson
Taj Monroe	Steven Tyler	Zen	Corey Feldman

Dramatic Designations

Girl Names

Character	Actor	TV Show
Abigail Bartlett	Stockard Channing	*The West Wing*
Adrianna La Cerva	Drea de Matteo	*The Sopranos*
Allison DuBois	Patricia Arquette	*Medium*
Bette Porter	Jennifer Beals	*The L Word*
Blair Waldorf	Leighton Meester	*Gossip Girl*
Bree Van De Kamp	Marcia Cross	*Desperate Housewives*
Bridget DuBois	Maria Lark	*Medium*
Buffy Summers	Sarah Michelle Gellar	*Buffy the Vampire Slayer*
Callie Torres	Sara Ramirez	*Grey's Anatomy*
Catherine Willows	Marg Helgenberger	*CSI*
Chloe O'Brian	Mary Lynn Rajskub	*24*
Claire Bennet	Hayden Panettiere	*Heroes*
Connie McDowell	Charlotte Ross	*NYPD Blue*
Cordelia Chase	Charisma Carpenter	*Angel*
Edie Britt	Nicollette Sheridan	*Desperate Housewives*

continues

Dramatic Designations continued

Girl Names

Character	Actor	TV Show
Elle Bishop	Kristen Bell	*Heroes*
Felicity Porter	Keri Russell	*Felicity*
Gabrielle Solis	Eva Longoria	*Desperate Housewives*
Gillian Gray	Jessica Tuck	*Judging Amy*
Grace Santiago	Valerie Cruz	*Nip/Tuck*
Isobel "Izzie" Stevens	Katherine Heigl	*Grey's Anatomy*
Jing-Mei (Deb) Chen	Ming-Na	*ER*
Jordan Cavanaugh	Jill Hennessy	*Crossing Jordan*
Katherine Anne "Kate" Austen	Evangeline Lilly	*Lost*
Kerry Weaver	Laura Innes	*ER*
Lauren Reed	Melissa George	*Alias*
Lilly Rush	Kathryn Morris	*Cold Case*
Lorelai Gilmore	Lauren Graham	*Gilmore Girls*
Lyla Garrity	Minka Kelly	*Friday Night Lights*
Marissa Cooper	Mischa Barton	*The O.C.*
Maxine Gray	Tyne Daly	*Judging Amy*
Miranda Bailey	Chandra Wilson	*Grey's Anatomy*
Natalie Teeger	Traylor Howard	*Monk*
Niki Sanders	Ali Larter	*Heroes*
Nora Lewin	Dianne Wiest	*Law and Order*
Paige Halliwell	Rose McGowan	*Charmed*
Piper Halliwell	Holly Marie Combs	*Charmed*
Prudence Halliwell	Shannen Doherty	*Charmed*
Rayanne Graff	A. J. Langer	*My So-Called Life*
Rory Gilmore	Alexis Bledel	*Gilmore Girls*
Ruth Fisher	Frances Conroy	*Six Feet Under*
Samantha Taggart	Linda Cardellini	*ER*
Sara Sidle	Jorja Fox	*CSI*
Serena van der Woodsen	Blake Lively	*Gossip Girl*
Shane McCutcheon	Katherine Moennig	*The L Word*
Sharona Fleming	Bitty Schram	*Monk*

Character	Actor	TV Show
Simone Deveaux	Tawny Cypress	*Heroes*
Sydney Bristow	Jennifer Garner	*Alias*
Veronica Mars	Kristen Bell	*Veronica Mars*
Vivian Johnson	Marianne Jean-Baptiste	*Without a Trace*
Willow Rosenberg	Alyson Hannigan	*Buffy the Vampire Slayer*

Boy Names

Character	Actor	TV Show
Adrian Monk	Tony Shaloub	*Monk*
Anthony (A. J.) Soprano	Robert Iler	*The Sopranos*
Arvin Sloan	Ron Rifkin	*Alias*
Brad Chase	Mark Valley	*Boston Legal*
Bruce Van Exel	Richard T. Jones	*Judging Amy*
Carlos Solis	Ricardo Antonio Chivira	*Desperate Housewives*
Christian Troy	Julian McMahon	*Nip/Tuck*
Cole Turner	Julian McMahon	*Charmed*
Dexter Morgan	Michael C. Hall	*Dexter*
Duncan Cane	Teddy Dunn	*Veronica Mars*
Eric Weiss	Greg Grunberg	*Alias*
Frederico Diaz	Freddy Rodriguez	*Six Feet Under*
Garrett Macy	Miguel Ferrer	*Crossing Jordan*
Gil Grissom	William Petersen	*CSI*
Graham Chase	Tom Irwin	*My So-Called Life*
Gregory House	Hugh Laurie	*House M.D.*
Hiro Nakamura	Masi Oka	*Heroes*
Horatio Cane	David Caruso	*CSI: Miami*
Jack Bristow	Victor Garber	*Alias*
Jordan Catalano	Jared Leto	*My So-Called Life*
Joshua Lyman	Bradley Whitford	*The West Wing*
Kyle McCarty	Kevin Rahm	*Judging Amy*
Leland Stottlemeyer	Ted Levine	*Monk*
Logan Echolls	Jason Dohring	*Veronica Mars*
Logan Huntzberger	Matt Czuchry	*Gilmore Girls*

continues

Dramatic Designations continued

Boy Names

Character	Actor	TV Show
Luke Danes	Scott Patterson	*Gilmore Girls*
Luke Girardi	Michael Welch	*Joan of Arcadia*
Lyle Bennet	Randall Bentley	*Heroes*
Marshall Flinkman	Kevin Weisman	*Alias*
Martin Fitzgerald	Eric Close	*Without a Trace*
Micah Sanders	Noah Gray-Cabey	*Heroes*
Nate Archibald	Chace Crawford	*Gossip Girl*
Ned Riley	Thomas McCarthy	*Boston Public*
Nick Vera	Jeremy Ratchford	*Cold Case*
Noah Bennet	Jack Coleman	*Heroes*
Orson Hodge	Kyle MacLachlan	*Desperate Housewives*
Pacey Witter	Joshua Jackson	*Dawson's Creek*
Parker Scavo	Joshua Moore	*Desperate Housewives*
Paul Young	Mark Moses	*Desperate Housewives*
Randall Disher	Jason Gray-Stanford	*Monk*
Rex Van de Kamp	Steven Culp	*Desperate Housewives*
Russell Corwin	Ben Foster	*Six Feet Under*
Sayid Jarrah	Naveen Andrews	*Lost*
Seth Cohen	Adam Brody	*The O.C.*
Tristan DuGray	Chad Michael Murray	*Gilmore Girls*
Vincent Gray	Dan Futterman	*Judging Amy*
Wallace Fennell	Percy Daggs III	*Veronica Mars*
Zach Young	Cody Kasch	*Desperate Housewives*

Soap Opera Hunks and Hussies

Girl Names

Hussy	Soap Opera	Hussy	Soap Opera
Ambrosia Moore	*The Bold and the Beautiful*	Calliope Jones	*Days of Our Lives*
		Cricket Blair	*The Young and the Restless*
Belle Black	*Days of Our Lives*		
Billie Reed	*Days of Our Lives*	Dahlia Ventura	*As the World Turns*

Hussy	Soap Opera	Hussy	Soap Opera
Drucilla Winters	*The Young and the Restless*	Marah Lewis	*Guiding Light*
		Marlena Black	*Days of Our Lives*
Eden August	*Guiding Light*	Nikki Munson	*As the World Turns*
Felicia Jones Scorpio	*General Hospital*	Olivia Winters	*The Young and the Restless*
Frannie Hughes	*As the World Turns*	Opal Cortlandt	*All My Children*
Hope Brady	*Days of Our Lives*	Pilar Santos	*Passions*
Jennifer Devereaux	*Days of Our Lives*	Rosanna Cabot	*As the World Turns*
Katie Pereti Coleman	*As the World Turns*	Sage Snyder	*As the World Turns*
Kendall Hart	*All My Children*	Sheridan Crane Lopez-Fitzgerald	*Passions*
Lahoma Vale Lucas	*Another World*	Skye Chandler	*All My Children*
Lien Hughes	*As the World Turns*	Tara Martin	*All My Children*

Boy Names

Hunk	Soap Opera	Hunk	Soap Opera
Abe Carver	*Days of Our Lives*	Keemo Volien Abbott	*The Young and the Restless*
Blade Bladeson	*The Young and the Restless*	Lucas Roberts	*Days of Our Lives*
Brock Reynolds	*The Young and the Restless*	Marcus Taggert	*General Hospital*
		Mateo Santos	*All My Children*
Burke Donovan	*As the World Turns*	Neil Winters	*The Young and the Restless*
Damon Porter	*The Young and the Restless*	Niko Kelly	*All My Children*
Deacon Sharpe	*The Bold and the Beautiful*	Pierce Riley	*All My Children*
Dillon Quartermaine	*General Hospital*	Ridge Forrester	*The Bold and the Beautiful*
Emilio Ramirez	*Days of Our Lives*	Royce Keller	*As the World Turns*
Evan Webster	*Another World*	Snapper Foster	*The Young and the Restless*
Frisco Jones	*General Hospital*	Sven Petersen	*Another World*
Harlan Barrett	*General Hospital*	Tad Martin	*All My Children*
Holden Snyder	*As the World Turns*	Trey Kenyon	*All My Children*
Jagger Cates	*General Hospital*	Wade Larson	*As the World Turns*
Jory Andros	*Guiding Light*	Walker Daniels	*As the World Turns*
Judge Grange	*Another World*	Zander Smith	*General Hospital*

Sitcom Sweethearts

Girl Names

Character	Actor	Sitcom
Amy McDougal-Barone	Monica Horan	*Everybody Loves Raymond*
Angela Martin	Angela Kinsey	*The Office*
Angie Palmero Lopez	Constance Marie	*George Lopez*
Beatriz "Betty" Suarez	America Ferrera	*Ugly Betty*
Berta	Conchatta Ferrell	*Two and a Half Men*
Blair Warner	Lisa Welchel	*The Facts of Life*
Carmen Consuelo Lopez	Stacey Haglund	*George Lopez*
Carrie Heffernan	Leah Remini	*The King of Queens*
Corky Sherwood	Faith Ford	*Murphy Brown*
Daphne Moon Crane	Jane Leeves	*Frasier*
Dylan Messinger	Ashley Williams	*Good Morning, Miami*
Elizabeth "Liz" Lemon	Tina Fey	*30 Rock*
Ethel Mertz	Vivian Vance	*I Love Lucy*
Grace Adler	Debra Messing	*Will and Grace*
Heidi Keppert	Debbe Dunning	*Home Improvement*
Hillary Banks	Karyn Parsons	*The Fresh Prince of Bel-Air*
Jackie Burkhart	Mila Kunis	*That '70s Show*
Karen Filippelli	Rashida Jones	*The Office*
Kitty Forman	Debra Jo Rupp	*That '70s Show*
Kyra Hart	Scarlett Pomers	*Reba*
Lily Aldrin	Alyson Hannigan	*How I Met Your Mother*
Lindsay Bluth Fünke	Portia DeRossi	*Arrested Development*
Lucille Bluth	Jessica Walter	*Arrested Development*
Mallory Keaton	Justine Bateman	*Family Ties*
Marni Fliss	Jennifer Finnigan	*Committed*
Phoebe Buffay	Lisa Kudrow	*Friends*
Rachel Green	Jennifer Aniston	*Friends*
Sophia Spirelli Petrillo-Weinstock	Estelle Getty	*The Golden Girls*
Syndey Hughley	Ashley Monique Clark	*The Hughleys*
Tess	Tammy Lynn Michaels	*Committed*
Vanessa "Nessa" Thomkins	Camille Winbush	*The Bernie Mac Show*
Vivian Banks	Daphne Maxwell Reid	*The Fresh Prince of Bel-Air*

Character	Actor	Sitcom
Wilhelmina Slater	Vanessa Williams	*Ugly Betty*
Willona Woods	Ja'net Dubois	*Good Times*
Yvonne Hughley	Elise Neal	*The Hughleys*

Boy Names

Character	Actor	Sitcom
Alan Harper	Jon Cryer	*Two and a Half Men*
Alex P. Keaton	Michael J. Fox	*Family Ties*
Bernie "Mac" McCullough	Bernie Mac	*The Bernie Mac Show*
Bowie James	Darius McCrary	*Committed*
Brock Hart	Christopher Rich	*Reba*
Chandler Bing	Matthew Perry	*Friends*
Chris Peterson	Chris Elliott	*Get a Life*
Creed Bratton	Creed Bratton	*The Office*
Darryl Hughley	D. L. Hughley	*The Hughleys*
Deacon Palmer	Victor Williams	*The King of Queens*
Dewey Wilkerson	Erik Per Sullivan	*Malcolm in the Middle*
Douglas Heffernan	Kevin James	*The King of Queens*
Dwight Schrute	Rainn Wilson	*The Office*
Eric Forman	Topher Grace	*That '70s Show*
Francis Wilkerson	Christopher Masterson	*Malcolm in the Middle*
George-Michael Bluth	Michael Cera	*Arrested Development*
Heathcliff Huxtable	Bill Cosby	*The Cosby Show*
Jack McFarland	Sean Hayes	*Will and Grace*
Jacob David "Jake" Harper	Angus Jones	*Two and a Half Men*
John Francis "Jack" Donaghy	Alec Baldwin	*30 Rock*
Jonas Grumby ("Skipper")	Alan Hale Jr.	*Gilligan's Island*
Josh Girard	Lonny Ross	*30 Rock*
Keith Anderson	Ben Powers	*Good Times*
Malcolm Wilkerson	Frankie Muniz	*Malcolm in the Middle*
Marshall Eriksen	Jason Segel	*How I Met Your Mother*
Michael Bluth	Jason Bateman	*Arrested Development*
Reese Wilkerson	Justin Berfield	*Malcolm in the Middle*
Richard Gilmore	Edward Herrmann	*Gilmore Girls*
Robert Barone	Brad Garrett	*Everybody Loves Raymond*

continues

Sitcom Sweethearts continued

Boy Names

Character	Actor	Sitcom
Ted Mosby	Josh Radnor	*How I Met Your Mother*
Tobias Fünke	David Cross	*Arrested Development*
Tracy Jordan	Tracy Morgan	*30 Rock*
Van Montgomery	Steve Howey	*Reba*
Vic Palmero	Emiliano Diez	*George Lopez*

Comedians and Comediennes

Girl Names

Ellen DeGeneres	Lucille Ball	Shelley Berman
Gilda Radner	Phyllis Diller	Tina Fey
Gracie Allen	Roseanne Barr	Tracey Ullman
Janeane Garofalo	Ruth Buzzi	Whoopi Goldberg
Lily Tomlin	Sarah Silverman	

Boy Names

Al Franken	George Burns	Milton Berle
Arj Barker	Jack Benny	Moe Howard
Bernie Mac	Jason Alexander	Richard Belzer
Bud Abbott	Jerry Seinfeld	Robin Williams
Cheech Marin	John Belushi	Roscoe "Fatty" Arbuckle
Chris Rock	John Byner	Rowan Atkinson
Dan Aykroyd	John Candy	Sid Caesar
Don Adams	Lenny Bruce	Steve Carell
Eddie Izzard	Mel Brooks	Woody Allen
Flip Wilson		

TV Talk Show Hosts

Girl Names

Host	Show
Asha Blake	*Later Today*
Barbara Walters	*The View*
Cybill Shepherd	*Men Are from Mars, Women Are from Venus*
Ellen DeGeneres	*The Ellen DeGeneres Show*
Iyanla Vanzant	*Iyanla*
Joan Rivers	*Still Talking*
Jodi Applegate	*Later Today*
Joy Browne	*Dr. Joy Browne Show*
Katie Couric	*Today Show*
Kelly Ripa	*Live with Regis and Kelly*
Leeza Gibbons	*Leeza*
Oprah Winfrey	*The Oprah Winfrey Show*
Queen Latifah	*Queen Latifah in the House*
Ricki Lake	*Ricki Lake*
Rosie O'Donnell	*The Rosie O'Donnell Show*
Ruth Westheimer (Dr.)	*Dr. Ruth*
Sam Phillips	*Men Are from Mars, Women Are from Venus*
Sarah Ferguson, Duchess of York	*Larry King Live*
Star Jones	*The View*
Tyra Banks	*Tyra*
Vickie Gabereau	*Vickie Gabereau Live*

Boy Names

Host	Show
Adam Carolla	*The Man Show*
Andy Richter	*Late Night*
Arsenio Hall	*Arsenio*
Bill Maher	*Politically Incorrect*
Carson Daly	*Last Call*
Chris Rock	*The Chris Rock Show*
Craig Ferguson	*The Late, Late Show*
Ernie Kovacs	*The Tonight Show*
Garry Shandling	*The Larry Sanders Show*
Geraldo Rivera	*Rivera Live*
Howard Stern	*The Howard Stern Show*
Jay Leno	*The Tonight Show*
Jesse Ventura	*Jesse Ventura Show*
Jimmy Kimmel	*The Man Show; Jimmy Kimmel Live!*
Joey Bishop	*The Joey Bishop Show*
Jon Stewart	*The Daily Show*
Keenen Wayans	*Vibe*
Mario Lopez	*The Other Half*
Matt Lauer	*Today Show*
Montel Williams	*The Montel Williams Show*
Morton Downey Jr.	*Morton Downey Jr. Show*

continues

TV Talk Show Hosts continued

Boy Names

Host	Show	Host	Show
Regis Philbin	Live with Regis and Kelly	Sinbad	Vibe
		Stephen Colbert	The Colbert Report
Richard Simmons	Dreammaker	Tavis Smiley	The Tavis Smiley Show
Rondell Sheridan	Men Are from Mars, Women Are from Venus	Tom Green	The Tom Green Show
RuPaul	The RuPaul Show	Wayne Brady	The Wayne Brady Show
Rush Limbaugh	The Rush Limbaugh Show		

Game Show Hosts and Hostesses

Girl Names

Host	Show	Host	Show
Anne Robinson	The Weakest Link	Summer Sanders	Figure It Out
Gina St. John	Who Knows You Best?	Vera Vague	Follow the Leader
Meredith Viera	Who Wants to Be a Millionaire?	Vicki Lawrence	Win, Lose or Draw

Boy Names

Host	Show	Host	Show
Alex Trebek	Jeopardy!	Ed McMahon	Who Do You Trust?
Allen Ludden	Password	Garry Moore	To Tell the Truth
Art Fleming	Jeopardy!	Gene Wood	Card Sharks
Art Linkletter	People Are Funny	Groucho Marx	You Bet Your Life
Ben Stein	Win Ben Stein's Money	Gene Rayburn	Tic Tac Dough
		Hal March	The $64,000 Question
Bill Cullen	The $25,000 Pyramid	Howie Mandel	Deal or No Deal
Bob Barker	The Price Is Right	Jack Barry	The Joker's Wild
Bob Eubanks	The Newlywed Game	Jeff Foxworthy	Are You Smarter than a Fifth Grader?
Chuck Woolery	Love Connection		
Dick Clark	The $10,000 Pyramid	Jim Lange	The Dating Game
Drew Carey	The Price Is Right	Joey Fatone	Singing Bee

Host	Show	Host	Show
Johnny Carson	*Earn Your Vacation*	Phil Keoghan	*The Amazing Race*
Monty Hall	*Let's Make a Deal*	Richard Dawson	*Family Feud*
Pat Sajak	*Wheel of Fortune*	Ryan Seacrest	*Gladiators 2000*
Peter Marshall	*Hollywood Squares*	Wink Martindale	*What's This Song?*

Newscasters/Journalists

Girl Names

Newscaster	Network	Newscaster	Network
Alex Witt	MSNBC	Greta Van Susteren	FOX
Alexis Glick	CNBC	Heidi Collins	CNN
Alisha Davis	CNN	Jamie Colby	FOX
Alisyn Camerota	FOX	Jessica Yellin	MSNBC
Anita Vogel	FOX	Josie Burke	CNN
Ashleigh Banfield	NBC	Juliet Huddy	FOX
Barbara Walters	ABC	Kara Henderson	CNN
Bertha Coombs	CNBC	Katie Couric	CBS
Bianca Solorzano	MSNBC	Kelly Arena	CNN
Brigitte Quinn	FOX	Kiran Chetry	FOX
Campbell Brown	MSNBC	Kitty Pilgrim	CNN
Christiane Amanpour	CNN	Kristine Johnson	CNN
Claudia Cowan	FOX	Leslie Laroche	CNBC
Claudia DiFolco	MSNBC	Linda Stouffer	CNN
Connie Chung	NBC	Lis Wiehl	FOX
Contessa Brewer	MSNBC	Lisa Ling	National Geographic
Dagen McDowell	FOX	Maria Bartiromo	MSNBC/CBC
Dari Alexander	FOX	Maya Kulycky	CNBC
Daryn Kagan	MSNBC	Megyn Kendall	FOX
Dawna Friesen	NBC	Mercedes Colwin	MSNBC
Elizabeth Cohen	CNN	Meredith Vieira	NBC
Erica Hill	CNN	Milissa Rehberger	NBC
Flavia Colgan	MSNBC	Molly Henneberg	FOX
Fredricka Whitfield	CNN		
Gerri Willis	CNN		

continues

Newscasters/Journalists continued

Girl Names

Newscaster	Network	Newscaster	Network
Nanette Hansen	MSN	Sibila Vargas	CNN
Natalie Allen	NBC	Soledad O'Brien	CNN
Norah O'Donnell	NBC	Sumi Das	MSNBC
Page Hopkins	FOX	Tracye Hutchins	CNN
Rebecca Gomez	FOX	Uma Pemmaraju	FOX
Rosey Edeh	MSNBC	Veronica De La Cruz	CNN
Rudi Bakhtiar	CNN	Whitney Casey	CNN
Sachi Koto	CNN	Willow Bay	NBC
Shanon Cook	CNN		

Boy Names

Newscaster	Network	Newscaster	Network
Aaron Brown	CNN	Harris Whitbeck	CNN
Adam Housley	FOX	Jack Cafferty	CNN
Anderson Cooper	CNN	James Rosen	FOX
Bill O'Reilly	FOX	Jason Carroll	CNN
Bob Simon	CBS	Jerry Nachman	MSNBC
Brad Goode	CNBC	Jesse Ventura	MPR News
Brian Kilmeade	FOX	Joe Kernen	CNBC
Brit Hume	FOX	John Gibson	FOX
Carl Quintanilla	MSNBC	Julian Phillips	FOX
Charlie Rose	CBS	Keith Olbermann	MSNBC
Chip Reid	NBC	Kendis Gibson	CNN
Chris Matthews	MSNBC	Kevin Sites	NBC
Dan Abrams	MSNBC	Kris Osborn	CNN
Dan Rather	CBS	Larry King	CNN
David Faber	MSNBC	Leon Harris	FOX
Dennis Miller	CNBC	Lester Holt	MSNBC
Ed Bradley	CBS	Lou Dobbs	CNN
Geraldo Rivera	FOX	Matt Lauer	MSNBC
Greg Palkot	FOX	Maurice DuBois	MSNBC

Newscaster	Network	Newscaster	Network
Miguel Marquez	CNN	Sanjay Gupta	CNN
Mike Galanos	CNN	Sean McLaughlin	MSNBC
Miles O'Brien	CNN	Shepard Smith	FOX
Morley Safer	ABC	Steve Doocy	FOX
Neil Cavuto	FOX	Stone Phillips	NBC
Nic Robertson	CNN	Thomas Roberts	CNN
Peter Jennings	ABC	Tom Brokaw	NBC
Randy Meier	MSNBC	Tony Snow	FOX
Reney Miguel	CNN	Trace Gallagher	FOX
Richard Engel	MSNBC	Tucker Carlson	PBS
Rick Sanchez	MSNBC	Walter Cronkite	CBS
Rob Marciano	CNN	William La Jeunesse	FOX
Sam Shane	MSNBC	Wolf Blitzer	CNN

Rock Kings and Queens

Girl Names

Alanis Morissette

Ani DiFranco

Annie Lennox, Eurythmics

Aretha Franklin

Belinda Carlisle, Go-Gos

Billie Holiday

Brenda Lee

Carly Simon

Carole King

Cass Elliot, The Mamas and the Papas

Chan Marshall, Cat Power

Chrissie Hynde, Pretenders

Cindy Wilson, B-52s

Cleotha Staples, The Staple Singers

Deborah Harry, Blondie

Diana Ross, The Supremes

Donna Godchaux, Grateful Dead

Dusty Springfield

Etta James

Gladys Knight, Gladys Knight and the Pips

Grace Slick, Jefferson Airplane

Janis Joplin

Joan Armatrading

Joni Mitchell

Linda Ronstadt

Martha Reeves, Martha and the Vandellas

Maureen Tucker, Velvet Underground

Meg White, The White Stripes

Michelle Phillips, The Mamas and the Papas

Natalie Merchant, 10,000 Maniacs

Neko Case

Pat Benatar

continues

Rock Kings and Queens continued

Girl Names

Patti LaBelle, LaBelle

Polly Jean Harvey

Sade

Sam Phillips

Stevie Nicks, Fleetwood Mac

Susanna Hoffs, The Bangles

Tina Turner

Tina Weymouth, Talking Heads

Boy Names

Ace Frehley, Kiss

Alice Cooper

Axl Rose, Guns 'n' Roses

Billy Idol

Bo Diddley

Bob Dylan

Bob Marley

Bono, U2

Bruce Springsteen

Buck Roeser, Blue Oyster Cult

Buddy Holly

Carlos Santana, Santana

Cesar Rosas, Los Lobos

Chuck Berry

David Bowie

Dewey Martin, Buffalo Springfield

Don Henley, The Eagles

Eddie Vedder, Pearl Jam

Elton John

Elvis Costello

Elvis Presley

Eric Clapton

Frank Zappa

Freddie Mercury, Queen

Gene Simmons, Kiss

George Harrison, The Beatles

Hilton Valentine, The Animals

Isaac Hayes

Jack White, The White Stripes

James Brown

Jerry Garcia, Grateful Dead

Jim Morrison, The Doors

Jimi Hendrix

Joe Strummer, The Clash

John Lennon, The Beatles

Jon Bon Jovi, Bon Jovi

Mick Jagger, Rolling Stones

Neil Young, Crosby, Stills, Nash and
  Young

Otis Redding

Paul McCartney, The Beatles

Pete Townshend, The Who

Phil Rudd, AC/DC

Phillard Williams, Earth, Wind and Fire

Ray Charles

Ric Ocasek, The Cars

Ringo Starr, The Beatles

Robert Plant, Led Zeppelin

Rod Stewart

Roger Daltrey, The Who

Simon Gallup, The Cure

Steven Tyler, Aerosmith

Sting, The Police

Syd Barrett, Pink Floyd

Tom Petty, Tom Petty and the
Heartbreakers

Van Morrison

Woody Guthrie

Country Stars

Girl Names

Alison Krauss

Amber Dotson

Anne Murray

Barbara Mandrell

Becky Hobbs

Bonnie Raitt

Brenda Lee

Carlene Carter

Carrie
Underwood

Caryl Mack
Parker

Chalee Tennison

Claudia Church

Connie Smith

Crystal Gayle

Danni Leigh

Dolly Parton

Dottie West

Emmylou Harris

Faith Hill

Gretchen Wilson

Jamie O'Neal

Jennifer Day

Jessi Alexander

Jo Dee Messina

Julie Harris

June Carter Cash

Kasey Chambers

Kathy Mattea

Kippi Brannon

Kylie Harris

Lari White

LeAnn Rimes

Lee Ann Womack

Loretta Lynn

Lynn Anderson

Martina McBride

Mary Chapin
Carpenter

Mindy McCready

Miranda Lambert

Patsy Cline

Patsy Montana

Patty Loveless

Reba McEntire

Rebecca Lynn
Howard

Rheanne Rivers

Sara Evans

Shania Twain

Shelly Fairchild

Sherrié Austin

Suzanne
Alexander

Tammy Wynette

Tanya Tucker

Tara Lyn Hart

Trisha Yearwood

Wynonna Judd

Boy Names

Aaron Lines

Alan Jackson

Bill Anderson

Billy Dean

Billy Ray Cyrus

Blaine Larsen

Blake Shelton

Brad Paisley

Buck Owens

Charley Pride

Charlie Daniels

Charlie Rich

Chet Atkins

Clint Black

Conway Twitty

Damon Gray

Davis Daniel

Deryl Dodd

Dierks Bentley

Don Williams

Dusty Drake

Dwight Yoakam

Earl Thomas
Conley

Eddie Rabbitt

Eddy Arnold

Ernest Tubb

Garth Brooks

Gary Allan

Gene Autry

Gene Watson

George Jones

George Strait

Glen Campbell

Hank Snow

Hank Williams

Jerry Jeff Walker

Johnny Cash

Keith Anderson

Keith Whitely

Keni Thomas

Kenny Chesney

Kenny Rogers

Kix Brooks

Larry Gatlin

continues

Country Stars continued

Boy Names

Leroy Van Dyke	Randy Travis	Royal Wade Kimes	Trini Triggs
Marty Robbins	Rhett Akins	Sammy Kershaw	Ty Herndon
Mel Tillis	Ricky Scaggs	Shane Minor	Vern Gosdin
Merle Haggard	Roger Miller	Tim McGraw	Vince Gill
Mickey Gilley	Ronnie Dun	Toby Keith	Waylon Jennings
Noah Kelley	Ronnie Milsap	Trace Adkins	Willie Nelson
Paul Overstreet	Roy Acuff		

Gospel Singers

Girl Names

Albertina Walker	Cleotha Staples	Jan Buckner	Miggie Lewis
Amy Grant	Doris Akers	Janis Lewis Phillips	Nelly Griesen
Anna Carter	Dorothy Norwood	Jerri Morrison	Polly Lewis
Annie Herring	Dottie Rambo	Lena "Mom" Speer	Reba Rambo
Bertha Lee	Ethel Waters	Lonnie McIntorsh	Rose Carter
Bessie Johnson	Eva Mae LeFevre	Mahalia Jackson	Sallie Martin
Blind Mamie Forehand	Evie Tornquist	Mary Ann Gaither	Sandi Patty
Cassietta George	Fanny Crosby	Mary Nelson	Sherrill Nielsen
Cece Winans	Frances Preston	Maude LeFevre	Shirley Ceasar
Clara Ward	Gloria Gaither	Mavis Staples	Vestal Goodman
Clarice Baxter	Inez Andrews		Wendy Bagwell

Boy Names

Adger Pace	Asa Brooks Everett	Bob Hartman	Charley Patton
Al Green	Austin Coleman	Bobby Butler	Clarence Fountain
Albert Brumley	Ben Speer	Booker White	Cleavant Derricks
Alphus LeFevre	Bentley Ackley	Brock Speer	Cliff Barrows
Andrae Crouch	Billy Graham	Bryan Hutson	Connor Hall
Andrew Ishee	Blind Willie Davis	Buck Rambo	D. P. "Dad" Carter
Anthony Burger	Bo Weavil Jackson	Buddy Liles	Danny Gaither
Armond Morales		Bukka White	

Dennis Crumpton
Denver Crumpler
Derrell Stewart
Don Breland
Doyle Blackwood
Eddie Head
Edward Clayborn
Edwin Hawkins
Elvis Presley
Frank Palmes
G. T. "Dad" Speer
Gary McSpadden
George Scott
Glen Payne
Greg Hough
Haldor Lillenas
Herman Harper
Hobart Evans
Homer Rodeheaver

Hovie Lister
Ira Stanphill
J. D. Sumner
Jake Hess
James Cleveland
Jarrell McCracken
Jaybird Coleman
Jerry Martin
Jimmy Carter
Joe Taggart
Joey Williams
John DeGroff Petra
Keith Green
Kirk Franklin
Kurt Kaiser
Larry Norman
Lee Roy Abernathy
Les Beasley
Lewis Phillips

"Little" Roy Lewis
Lloyd Orrell
Lon "Deacon" Freeman
Lou Hildreth
Lowell Mason
Mark Ellerbee
Marvin Norcross
Matthew Ward
Mosie Lister
Noel Fox
Oliver Cooper
Oren Parris
Otis Jones
P. P. Bliss
Parker Jonathan
Pat Boone
Perry Morgan
Powell Hassell
Ralph Carmichael

Ray Dean Reese
Rex Humbard
Ricky McKinnie
Robert Summers
Roger Breeland
Ron Page
Roosevelt Graves
Smitty Gatlin
Steve Sanders
Stuart Hamblen
Tennessee Ernie Ford
Tim Lovelace
Thomas Dorsey
Tommy Fairchild
Tony Brown
Urias LeFevre
Versey Smith
Wally Fowler
William Smith
Willie Wynn

Rappers and Hip-Hop Heroes

Girl Names

Beyoncé
Da Brat
Eve

Lil' Kim
Mary J. Blige
MC Lyte

Missy Elliott
Queen Latifah
Remy Ma

Roxanne Shante
Salt-n-Pepa
Yo-yo

Boy Names

50 Cent
André 3000
AZ
Beane Sigel
Big Daddy Kane

Bun B
Busta Rhymes
Common
Cool Keith
Emcee Lynx

Eminem
Heavy D
Jay Z
Kanye West
Lil Jon

Little Wayne
LL Cool J
Nas
P. Diddy
Rick Ross

continues

Rappers and Hip-Hop Heroes continued

Boy Names

Saigon	Snoop Dogg	T. I.	Young Jeezy
Skyzoo	Spoonie Gee	Tupac	

Pop Princes and Princesses

Girl Names

Aaliyah	Faith Evans	Kelly Clarkson	Missy Elliott
Alicia Keys	Fantasia Barrino	Kylie	Natalie Imbruglia
Amerie	Gwen Stefani	Leona Lewis	Natasha Bedingfield
Ashanti	Hilary Duff	Lindsay Lohan	Nina Sky
Ashlee Simpson	Janet Jackson	Madonna	Nivea
Avril Lavigne	Jennifer Lopez	Mandy Moore	Rihanna
Beyoncé Knowles	Jessica Simpson	Mariah Carey	Shakira
Britney Spears	JoJo	Mary J. Blige	Vanessa Carlton
Christina Aguilera	Joss Stone	Michelle Branch	
Christina Milian	Katy Perry	Miley Cyrus	

Boy Names

Baby Bash	Jay-Z	Mario	Ryan Cabrera
Babyface	Jesse McCartney	Michael Jackson	Sean "P. Diddy" Combs
Eminem	John Mayer	Nick Carter	Usher
Frankie J.	Justin Timberlake	Papa Roach	Will Smith
Gavin DeGraw	Kanye West	R. Kelly	Wyclef Jean
Howie Day	Ludacris	Rob Thomas	

American Idol Finalists

Girl Names

Amanda Overmyer	Christina Christian	Jordin Sparks
Brooke White	Diana DeGarmo	Katharine Hope McPhee
Carly Smithson	Fantasia Barrino	Kellie Dawn Pickler
Carrie Underwood	Haley Scarnato	Kelly Clarkson

Kristy Lee Cook

Lisa Gabrielle Tucker

Mandisa Lynn Hundley

Melissa Christine
  McGhee

Nikki McKibbin

Paris Ana'is Bennett

Ramiele Malubay

Ryan Starr

Syesha Mercado

Tamyra Gray

Boy Names

A. J. Gil

Blake Lewis

Bo Bice

Brett Asa "Ace" Young

Chikezie Eze

Christopher Adam
  "Chris" Daughtry

Clay Aiken

David Archuleta

David Cook

David Hernandez

Efraym Elliott Yamin

EJay Day

Jason Castro

Jim Verraros

Justin Guarini

Kevin Patrick Covais

Michael Johns

RJ Helton

Ruben Studdard

Taylor Reuben Hicks

William Joel "Bucky"
  Covington III

Names from Songs

Girl Names

Name	Artist	Song
Adia	Sarah McLachlan	"Adia"
Adrienne	The Calling	"Adrienne"
Alethea	Robin Trower	"Alethea"
Angie	The Rolling Stones	"Angie"
Arabella	The Kinks	"Wicked Arabella"
Beth	Kiss	"Beth"
Black Betty	Ram Jam	"Black Betty"
Billie Jean	Michael Jackson	"Billie Jean"
Carrie	Dr. Hook and the Medicine Show	"Carry Me Carrie"
Charlotte	The Cure	"Charlotte Sometimes"
Cynthia	Blue Rodeo	"Cynthia"
Darlene	Led Zepplin	"Darlene"
Diane	John Mellencamp	"Jack and Diane"
Elvira	Oak Ridge Boys	"Elvira"
Emma	Hot Chocolate	"Emma"
Felicia	Blues Traveler	"Felicia"

continues

Names from Songs continued

Girl Names

Name	Artist	Song
Francine	ZZ Top	"Francine"
Georgia	Ray Charles	"Georgia on My Mind"
Glynis	Smashing Pumpkins	"Glynis"
Guinnevere	Crosby, Stills and Nash	"Guinnevere"
Iris	Goo Goo Dolls	"Iris"
Isabel	John Denver	"Isabel"
Jamie	Van Halen	"Jamie's Crying"
Jenny	Tommy Tutone	"867-5309/Jenny"
Josephine	George Thorogood	"Ride on Josephine"
Kim	Concrete Blonde	"Songs for Kim"
Layla	Eric Clapton	"Layla"
Lily	The Who	"Pictures of Lily"
Lola	The Kinks	"Lola"
Mabel	Goldfinger	"Mabel"
Maggie May	The Beatles	"Maggie May"
Mandy	Barry Manilow	"Mandy"
Mariah	The Kingston Trio	"They Call the Wind Mariah"
Nancy	Frank Sinatra	"Nancy with the Laughing Face"
Natalie	The Killers	"Believe Me Natalie"
Ophelia	The Band	"Ophelia"
Peggy Sue	Buddy Holly	"Peggy Sue"
Penny	Hanson	"Penny and Me"
Rebecca	The Bee Gees	"Rebecca"
Rhiannon	Fleetwood Mac	"Rhiannon"
Rhonda	The Beach Boys	"Help Me Rhonda"
Rosalinda	Billy Joel	"Rosalinda's Eyes"
Rosanna	Toto	"Rosanna"
Roxanne	The Police	"Roxanne"
Sara	Fleetwood Mac	"Sara"
Sheila	Ready for the World	"Oh, Sheila"
Sherry	The Four Seasons	"Sherry"
Virginia	Tori Amos	"Virginia"
Wendy	The Beach Boys	"Wendy"

Boy Names

Name	Artist	Song
Achilles	Led Zeppelin	"Achilles Last Stand"
Adam	Aerosmith	"Adam's Apple"
Al	Paul Simon	"You Can Call Me Al"
Andy	The Killers	"Andy You're a Star"
Billy	Bo Donaldson and the Heywoods	"Billy Don't Be a Hero"
Boris	The Who	"Boris the Spider"
Brian	Barenaked Ladies	"Brian Wilson"
Casey	Grateful Dead	"Casey Jones"
Charlie	The Coasters	"Charlie Brown"
Daniel	Elton John	"Daniel"
Dave	The Roches	"Uncle Dave"
Earl	Dixie Chicks	"Goodbye Earl"
Eddie	The Teen Queens	"Eddie My Love"
Edmund	Gordon Lightfoot	"The Wreck of the *Edmund Fitzgerald*"
Frankie	Connie Francis	"Frankie"
Henry	Lowest of the Low	"Henry Needs a New Pair of Shoes"
Jack	John Mellencamp	"Jack and Diane"
Jeremy	Pearl Jam	"Jeremy"
Jesse	Carly Simon	"Jesse"
Joe	Frank Zappa	"Joe's Garage"
Johnny	Bruce Springsteen	"Johnny Bye Bye"
Kenneth	R.E.M.	"What's the Frequency Kenneth?"
Leroy	Jim Croce	"Bad, Bad Leroy Brown"
Louie	The Kingsmen	"Louie, Louie"
Mickey	Toni Basil	"Mickey"
Nathan	The Supremes	"Nathan Jones"
Neil	Carole King	"Oh, Neil"
Noah	Harry Belafonte	"Noah"
Norman	Sue Thompson	"Norman"
Oliver	Elvis Costello	"Oliver's Army"
Oskar	Our Lady Peace	"Hello Oskar"

continues

Names from Songs continued

Boy Names

Name	Artist	Song
Peter	XTC	"Ballad of Peter Pumpkinhead"
Quinn	Bob Dylan	"Mighty Quinn"
Ray	Aimee Mann	"Ray"
Sam	Olivia Newton-John	"Sam"
Shane	Liz Phair	"Shane"
Simon	Lifehouse	"Simon"
Steve	Sheryl Crow	"Steve McQueen"
Sue	Johnny Cash	"A Boy Named Sue"
Wayne	Chantal Kreviazuk	"Wayne"
Willie Joe	The Mystery Trio	"Willie Joe"

Noteworthy Names

When choosing a name for your baby, you might decide to imbue him or her with a powerful superhero name such as those featured in this chapter's list of superheroes' secret identities. Or maybe you feel like going silly with one of the names featured in the cartoon-character name lists.

In this chapter, you'll also find lists of actors' and actresses' "before and after" names. If you're looking for an alliterative or initialed moniker, you'll find those in this chapter as well.

In addition, you'll find some nicknames you can bestow upon your newborn and classic names that have been around for decades.

Cartoon Characters

Girl Names

Character	Cartoon	Character	Cartoon
Angelica Pickles	*Rugrats*	Lilo	*Lilo and Stitch*
Aurora	*Sleeping Beauty*	Lois Griffin	*Family Guy*
Belle	*Beauty and the Beast*	Luanne Platter	*King of the Hill*
Bianca	*The Rescuers*	Marge Simpson	*The Simpsons*
Clementine	*Caillou*	Marianne Thornberry	*The Wild Thornberrys*
Daisy Duck	*Donald Duck*		
Daphne Blake	*Scooby-Doo*	Megan Griffin	*Family Guy*
Daria	*Beavis and Butt-head*	Melody Valentine	*Josie and the Pussycats*
Dora	*Dora the Explorer*	Nala	*The Lion King*
Dory	*Finding Nemo*	Nora	*Pete's Dragon*
Esmeralda	*The Hunchback of Notre Dame*	Pearl	*Finding Nemo*
		Pocahontas	*Pocahontas*
Jasmine	*Aladdin*	Trixie	*Speed Racer*
Josie McCoy	*Josie and the Pussycats*	Veronica Lodge	*Archie*
Kim Possible	*Kim Possible*		

Boy Names

Character	Cartoon	Character	Cartoon
Aladdin	*Aladdin*	Dylan "Dil" Pickles	*Rugrats*
Albert	*Fat Albert*		
Arthur	*The Sword in the Stone*	Elmer Fudd	*Looney Tunes*
		Elroy Jetson	*The Jetsons*
Bart Simpson	*The Simpsons*	Fred Flintstone	*The Flintstones*
Bernard	*The Rescuers*	Gaston	*Beauty and the Beast*
Casper	*Casper the Friendly Ghost*	Hank Hill	*King of the Hill*
		Linus van Pelt	*Peanuts*
Dennis Mitchell	*Dennis the Menace*	Marlin	*Finding Nemo*
Dexter	*Dexter's Laboratory*	Mickey Mouse	*Mickey Mouse*
Diego	*Dora the Explorer*	Nemo	*Finding Nemo*
Dudley Do-Right	*Rocky and Bullwinkle*	Nigel Thornberry	*The Wild Thornberrys*

Character	Cartoon	Character	Cartoon
Rocket J. Squirrel	*Rocky and Bullwinkle*	Theodore	*Alvin and the Chipmunks*
Simba	*The Lion King*	Timmy Turner	*The Fairly OddParents*

Disney Characters

Girl Names

Character	Cartoon	Character	Cartoon
Alice	*Alice in Wonderland*	Katrina	*The Adventures of Ichabod and Mr. Toad*
Ariel	*The Little Mermaid*	Lucy	*101 Dalmatians*
Carlotta	*The Little Mermaid*	Marian	*Robin Hood*
Dinah	*Alice in Wonderland*	Minnie	*Mickey Mouse*
Ena	*Bambi*	Olivia	*The Great Mouse Detective*
Felicia	*The Great Mouse Detective*	Thalia	*Hercules*
Hyacinth	*Fantasia*	Vanessa	*The Little Mermaid*
Jessie	*Toy Story 2*	Wendy	*Peter Pan*

Boy Names

Character	Cartoon	Character	Cartoon
Akela	*The Jungle Book*	Gus	*Cinderella*
Alonzo	*102 Dalmatians*	Horace	*101 Dalmatians*
Bartholomew	*The Great Mouse Detective*	Hugo	*The Hunchback of Notre Dame*
Basil	*The Great Mouse Detective*	Jafar	*Aladdin*
Cody	*The Rescuers Down Under*	Jake	*The Rescuers Down Under*
Demetrius	*Hercules*	Luke	*The Rescuers Down Under*
Dewey	*Donald Duck*	Maurice	*Beauty and the Beast*
Eric	*The Little Mermaid*	Max	*The Little Mermaid*
Fenton	*Atlantis: the Lost Empire*	Otto	*Robin Hood*
Gideon	*Pinocchio*	Pedro	*Lady and the Tramp*
		Winston	*Oliver and Company*

Secret Identities of Superheroes

Girl Names

Superhero	Secret Identity	Superhero	Secret Identity
Batgirl	Barbara Gordon	Queen of Swords	Maria Teresa Alvarado
Bionic Woman	Jaime Sommers	Supergirl	Linda Danvers
Black Scorpion	Darcy Walker	Witchblade	Sara Pezzini
Catwoman	Selina Kyle	Wonder Girl	Drusilla Prince
The Girl from U.N.C.L.E.	April Dancer	Wonder Woman	Yeoman Diana Prince
Oracle	Barbara Gordon		

Boy Names

Superhero	Secret Identity	Superhero	Secret Identity
Batman	Bruce Wayne	Mr. Terrific	Stanley Beamish
Captain America	Steve Rogers	Penguin	Oswald Chesterfield Cobblepot
Captain Marvel	Billy Batson	Phantom	Kit Walker Jr.
Captain Midnight	Captain Jim "Red" Albright	Riddler	Edward "E" Nigma
Captain Nice	Carter Nash	Robin, Boy Wonder	Dick Grayson
The Crow	Eric Draven	Robin Hood	Sir Robin of Loxley
The Flash	Barry Allen	The Saint	Simon Templar
Gemini Man	Sam Casey	Scarlet Pimpernel	Sir Percy Blakeney
Green Hornet	Britt Reid	Six Million Dollar Man	Col. Steve Austin
Incredible Hulk	Dr. Bruce Banner	Spider-Man	Peter Parker
Invisible Man	Daniel Westin	Sub-Mariner	Lord Namor
Iron Man	Tony Stark	Superman	Clark Kent
Jetman	Oscar North	Tarzan	John Clayton III, Lord Greystoke
Jon Sable	Nicholas Flemming	Ultra Man	Andrew Clements
Lone Ranger	John Reid	Zorro	Don Diego de la Vega
Man from Atlantis	Mark Harris		
The Mighty Thor	Dr. Don Blake		
Mr. Fantastic	Reed Richards		

Before They Were Famous–
Name Changers

Girl Names

Celebrity Name	Original Name	Celebrity Name	Original Name
Alicia Keys	Alicia Cook	Julianne Moore	Julie Anne Smith
Anna Nicole Smith	Vickie Lynn Hogan	Kate Capshaw	Kathleen Sue Nail
Carmen Electra	Tara Patrick	Kelly Preston	Kelly Smith
Cher	Cherilyn La Piere	Lauren Bacall	Betty Joan Perske
		Leelee Sobieski	Liliane Sobieski
Courtney Love	Michelle Harrison	Macy Gray	Natalie McIntyre
Demi Moore	Demetria Guynes	Marilyn Monroe	Norma Jeane Mortensen
Elle Macpherson	Eleanor Gow	Michelle Phillips	Holly Gilliam
Faith Hill	Audrey Faith Perry	Pink	Alecia Moore
		Portia de Rossi	Amanda Rogers
Goldie Hawn	Goldie Jean Studlendegehawn	Queen Latifah	Dana Owens
		Shania Twain	Eileen Regina Edwards
Jodie Foster	Alicia Christian Foster	Tina Turner	Anna Mae Bullock
		Winona Ryder	Winona Horowitz

Boy Names

Celebrity Name	Original Name	Celebrity Name	Original Name
Alan Alda	Alphonso D'Abruzzo	Christian Slater	Christian Michael Hawkins
Bernie Mac	Bernard Jeffery McCullough	Coolio	Artis Ivey Jr.
Bill Clinton	William Jefferson Blythe IV	Elton John	Reginald Kenneth Dwight
Bono	Paul Hewson	Eminem	Marshall Mathers III
Brad Pitt	William Bradley Pitt	Jay Leno	James Leno
Chad Lowe	Charles Lowe	Jon Bon Jovi	Jon Bongiovi

continues

Before They Were Famous–Name Changers continued

Boy Names

Celebrity Name	Original Name	Celebrity Name	Original Name
Kareem Abdul-Jabbar	Ferdinand Lewis Alcindor Jr.	Sylvester Stallone	Michael Stallone
Moby	Richard Melville Hall	Taye Diggs	Scott Diggs
		Tim McGraw	Samuel Timothy Smith
Muhammad Ali	Cassius Clay	Tom Cruise	Thomas Cruise Mapother IV
Nicolas Cage	Nicholas Kim Coppola	Vin Diesel	Mark Vincent
Rodney Dangerfield	Jacob Cohen	Warren Beatty	Henry Warren Beaty
Snoop Dogg	Calvin Broadus		
Spike Lee	Shelton Jackson Lee	Woody Allen	Allen Stewart Konigsberg
Sting	Gordon Matthew Sumner		

Alliterative Names

Girl Names

Name	Claim to Fame	Name	Claim to Fame
Barbara Bush	First lady	Janet Jackson	Singer
Brigitte Bardot	Actress	Katie Couric	*Today Show* host
Brooke Burns	Actress	Kim Cattrall	Actress
Courteney Cox	Actress	Laura Linney	Actress
Cybill Shepherd	Actress	Lucy Liu	Actress
Dana Delany	Actress	Martina McBride	Country singer
Dominique Dawes	Gymnast	Michael Michele	Actress
Dorothy Dandridge	Actress	Parker Posey	Actress
Faith Ford	Actress	Rachael Ray	Chef
Farrah Fawcett	Actress	Rene Russo	Actress
Greta Garbo	Actress	Susan Sarandon	Actress
Holly Hunter	Actress	Tina Turner	Singer

Boy Names

Name	Claim to Fame	Name	Claim to Fame
Arthur Ashe	Tennis pro	Lyle Lovett	Singer
Barry Bonds	Baseball pro	Mark McGuire	Baseball pro
Ben Barnes	Actor	Matthew McConaughey	Actor
Benjamin Bratt	Actor	Mike Myers	Actor
Björn Borg	Tennis pro	Nick Nolte	Actor
Calvin Coolidge	U.S. president	Ozzy Osbourne	Rock 'n' roller
Chevy Chase	Actor	Pablo Picasso	Artist
Clark Kent	Superman	Paul Prudhomme	Chef
David Duchovny	Actor	Sammy Sosa	Baseball pro
Ernie Els	Golf pro	Sylvester "Sly" Stallone	Actor
Gilbert Gottfried	Actor	Ted Turner	Entrepreneur/ CNN founder
Hubert Humphrey	U.S. vice president		
James Joyce	Author	Travis Tritt	Country musician
Jesse Jackson	Clergyman	Walt Whitman	Poet
Kirk Cameron	Actor	Zig Ziglar	Business consultant
Lennox Lewis	Boxer		

Double Names

Girl Names

Carrie-Anne Moss	Julia Louis-Dreyfus	Sarah Jessica Parker
Catherine Mary Stewart	Mary-Kate Olsen	Summer Joy Phoenix
Eva Marie Saint	Mary-Louise Parker	Tammy Faye Bakker
Hallie Kate Eisenberg	Penelope Ann Miller	Tiffany Amber Thiessen
Joey Lauren Adams	Rachael Leigh Cook	

Boy Names

Anthony Michael Hall	Jan-Michael Vincent	Neil Patrick Harris
Billy Bob Thornton	Jason James Richter	Richard Dean Anderson
Brian Austin Green	Jean-Claude Van Damme	Scott William Winters
David James Elliot	Jonathan Taylor Thomas	Sean Patrick Flanery
Edward James Olmos	Michael Thomas Dunn	Tommy Lee Jones
Haley Joel Osment		

Initial Names

Girl Names

Name	Claim to Fame	Name	Claim to Fame
C. C. Bloom	*Beaches* character	J. B. Fletcher	*Murder, She Wrote* character
C. J. Cregg	*The West Wing* character	K. D. Lang	Singer
		P. J. Soles	Actress

Boy Names

Name	Claim to Fame	Name	Claim to Fame
D. B. Sweeney	Actor	J. C. Chasez	*NSYNC singer
E. E. Cummings	Poet	LL Cool J	Rapper
F. Lee Bailey	Attorney	P. T. Barnum	Showman
I. M. Pei	Architect		

Unusual Names

Girl Names

Apple Martin

Blue Angel Evans

Chastity Bono

Daisy Boo Oliver

Diva Zappa

Fifi Trixibelle Geldof

Heavenly Hirani Tigerlilly Hutchence

Ima Hogg

Ione Skye

Justice Mellencamp

Liberty Kasem

Moon Unit Zappa

Nell Marmalade Eliot

Peaches Honeyblossom Geldof

Pia Zadora

Pixie Geldof

Rumer Willis

Sistine Stallone

Soleil Moon Frye

Starlite Berenson

Boy Names

Audio Science Sossamon

Banjo Griffiths

Denim Kole Braxton Lewis

Dweezil Zappa

Edsel Ford

ESPN ("Espen") Malachi McCall

Fuddy Wayans

Hud Mellencamp

Ib Melchior

Moses Martin

Mumtaz Wonder

Pirate Inspector Davis

Rock Brynner

Rolan Bolan

Speck Mellencamp

Tara Gabriel Galaxy Gramophone Getty

Taro Hart

Topo McGuire

Zowie Bowie

Gothic/Vampire Names

Girl Names

Bela	Claudia	Karayan	Nicki
Bianca	Estelle	Lucine	Pandora
Bronwen	Gabrielle	Madeleine	Wynn
Celeste			

Boy Names

Akasha	Asphar	Eamen	Rashid
Aleron	Athan	Enkil	Raven
Amadeo	Avicus	Flavius	Rune
Amarande	Blaine	Kern	Santiago
Ambrose	Carden	Lestat	Tainn
Andros	Damian	Louis	Tariq
Arjun	Danton	Merrick	Vega
Armand			

Traditional Names

Girl Names

Ann (Russell)	Elsa (Lanchester)	Juliet (Mills)	Ruth (Hale)
Bette (Davis)	Estelle (Getty)	Kim (Novak)	Sarah (Whitney)
Carrie (Abrams)	Ethel (Waters)	Maggie (Riley)	Tabitha (Whitney)
Deborah (Kerr)	Jane (Marple)	Patricia (Neal)	Vanessa (Redgrave)
Donna (Reed)			

Traditional Names

Boy Names

Andrew (Turck)

Anthony (Flynn)

David (Wideman)

Donald (Sutherland)

Edmund (Trebus)

Elliott (Andrus)

Garrett (Kinney)

Gene (Hackman)

George (Blair)

Ira (Prosser)

Isaac (Newton)

James (Joyce)

Joel (Stebbins)

John (Baker)

Joseph (Johnson)

Levi (Stainton)

Orrin (Reed)

Paul (Newman)

Phillip (Crane)

Quincy (Whitney)

Robert (Smith)

Ronald (Ferguson)

Russell (Squier)

Sean (Connery)

William (Price)

Winners, Winners, and More Winners

Every parent wants his or her little girl or boy to be successful. You're probably already having dreams of your baby making it big. Whatever your passion—whether it's a hobby, a sport, a form of entertainment, or an indulgence—you're sure to find it here, followed by a long list of winners in that area.

In the following pages, you'll find names of great thinkers such as Pulitzer prize and Nobel Prize winners, as well as names of performers, including Oscar, Tony, Emmy, and Grammy winners. Among sports greats, you'll spot everyone from golfers to football players, Olympic medalists, NASCAR racers, gymnasts, basketball and baseball heavy-hitters, and much more.

Pulitzer Prize Winners

Girl Names

Winner	Category	Winner	Category
Amy Lowell	Poetry	Linda Greenhouse	Beat reporting
Annalyn Swan	Biography	Lisa Pollak	Feature writing
Carol Guzy	Photography	Liz Balmaseda	Commentary
Carolyn Cole	Photography	Louise Glück	Poetry
Cheryl Diaz Meyer	Photography	Margaret Widdemer	Poetry
Connie Schultz	Commentary	Margo Jefferson	Criticism
Cornelia Grumman	Editorial writing	Marilynne Robinson	Fiction
Deanne Fitzmaurice	Photography	Martha Rial	Photography
Diana Sugg	Beat reporting	Maureen Dowd	Commentary
Doris Kearns Goodwin	History	Melinda Wagner	Music
		Michiko Kakutani	Criticism
Dorothy Rabinowitz	Commentary	Natasha Trethewey	Poetry
Edith Wharton	Novel	Paula Vogel	Drama
Edna St. Vincent Millay	Poetry	Renée Byer	Feature photography
Eileen McNamara	Commentary	Samantha Power	General non-fiction
Gail Caldwell	Criticism		
Gretchen Morgenson	Beat reporting	Sara Teasdale	Poetry
Isabel Wilkerson	Feature writing	Sari Horwitz	Investigative reporting
Jo Becker	National reporting	Sonia Nazario	Feature writing
Joan Hedrick	Biography	Stacy Schiff	Biography
Julia Keller	Feature writing	Stephanie Welsh	Photography
Katharine Graham	Biography or autobiography	Tina Rosenberg	General non-fiction
Kim Murphy	International reporting	Usha Lee McFarling	Explanatory reporting
Laura E. Richards	Biography	Willa Cather	Novel
Leonora Speyer	Poetry	Zona Gale	Drama

Boy Names

Winner	Category	Winner	Category
Aaron Jay Kernis	Music	Hamlin Garland	Biography
Adrees Latif	Photography	Harold Littledale	Reporting
Albert Beveridge	Biography	Horton Foote	Drama
Alex Raksin	Editorial writing	Ian Johnson	International reporting
Alva Johnston	Reporting	Jared Diamond	General non-fiction
Angelo Henderson	Feature writing		
Barry Bearak	International reporting	Jesse Lynch Williams	Drama
Barton Gellman	National reporting	Joel Pett	Editorial cartooning
Bernard Stein	Editorial writing	Junot Diaz	Fiction
Booth Tarkington	Novel	Justin Smith	History
Brett Blackledge	Investigative reporting	Kai Bird	Biography or autobiography
Burton Hendrick	History	Kevin Helliker	Explanatory reporting
Byron Acohido	Beat reporting		
Carl Sandburg	Poetry	Kirke Simpson	Reporting
Chuck Philips	Beat reporting	Leon Dash	Explanatory journalism
Clarence Williams	Photography	Leonard Pitts Jr.	Commentary
Clifford Levy	Investigative reporting	Lloyd Schwartz	Criticism
		Louis Seibold	Reporting
Colbert King	Commentary	Magner White	Reporting
Cormac McCarthy	Fiction	Matt Davies	Editorial cartooning
Daniel Golden	Beat reporting		
Dele Olojede	International reporting	Morton Gould	Music
		Nelson Harding	Editorial cartooning
Edwin Arlington Robinson	Poetry	Nicholas Kristof	Commentary
Emory Holloway	Biography	Nigel Jaquiss	Investigative reporting
Eugene O'Neill	Drama	Nilo Cruz	Drama
Frank O'Brien	Editorial writing	Ornette Coleman	Music
Franz Wright	Poetry	Owen Davis	Drama
Gareth Cook	Explanatory reporting	Philip Roth	Fiction
Gunther Schuller	Music		

continues

Pulitzer Prize Winners   continued

Boy Names

Winner	Category	Winner	Category
Preston Gannaway	Photography	Sinclair Lewis	Novel
Robert Frost	Poetry	Steven Stucky	Music
Rollin Kirby	Editorial cartooning	Thelonius Monk	Special citation
Samuel Flagg Bemis	History	Walt Handelsman	Editorial cartooning
Saul Friedländer	General non-fiction	William Cabell Bruce	Biography
		Wynton Marsalis	Music
Sidney Howard	Drama		

Nobel Prize Winners

Girl Names

Winner	Category	Winner	Category
Alva Myrdal	Peace	Mairead Corrigan	Peace
Aung San Suu Kyi	Peace	Marie Curie	Physics; Chemistry
Barbara McClintock	Medicine	Nadine Gordimer	Literature
Bertha von Suttner	Peace	Nelly Sachs	Literature
Betty Williams	Peace	Pearl Buck	Literature
Christiane Nüsslein-Volhard	Medicine	Rigoberta Menchú Tum	Peace
Doris Lessing	Literature	Rosalyn Sussman Yalow	Medicine
Elfriede Jelinek	Literature	Selma Lagerlöf	Literature
Emily Balch	Peace	Shirin Ebadi	Peace
Gabriela Mistral	Literature	Sigrid Undset	Literature
Gertrude Elion	Medicine	Mother Teresa	Peace
Gerty Radnitz Cori	Medicine	Toni Morrison	Literature
Grazia Deledda	Literature	Wangari Maathai	Peace
Irène Joliot-Curie	Chemistry	Wislawa Szymborska	Literature
Jody Williams	Peace		
Linda Buck	Medicine		

Boy Names

Winner	Category	Winner	Category
Aaron Ciechanover	Chemistry	Koichi Tanaka	Chemistry
Al Gore	Peace	Kurt Wüthrich	Chemistry
Alexei Abrikosov	Physics	Leland Hartwell	Medicine
Arvid Carlsson	Medicine	Masatoshi Koshiba	Physics
Avram Hershko	Chemistry	Orhan Pamuk	Literature
Clive Granger	Economics	Peter Agre	Chemistry
Daniel Kahneman	Economics	Riccardo Giacconi	Physics
David Gross	Physics	Richard Axel	Medicine
Edward Prescott	Economics	Roderick MacKinnon	Chemistry
Finn Kydland	Economics	Ryoji Noyori	Chemistry
Frank Wilczek	Physics	Sydney Brenner	Medicine
Gao Xingjian	Medicine	Theodor Hänsch	Physics
Gerhard Ertl	Chemistry	Tim Hunt	Medicine
Grameen Bank	Peace	Vernon Smith	Economics
Imre Kertész	Medicine	Vitaly Ginzburg	Physics
Irwin Rose	Chemistry	Wolfgang Ketterle	Physics
Joseph Stiglitz	Economics	Zhores Alferov	Physics
Kofi Annan	Peace		

Oscar Winning Actors and Actresses*

Girl Names

Winner	Character	Movie
Angelina Jolie	Lisa Rowe	*Girl, Interrupted*
Barbra Streisand	Fanny Brice	*Funny Girl*
Cate Blanchett	Katharine Hepburn	*The Aviator*
Catherine Zeta-Jones	Velma Kelly	*Chicago*
Charlize Theron	Aileen Wuornos	*Monster*
Dianne Wiest	Holly	*Hannah and Her Sisters*
Emma Thompson	Margaret Schlegel	*Howards End*
Estelle Parsons	Blanche Barrow	*Bonnie and Clyde*
Faye Dunaway	Diana Christensen	*Network*

*Information from 1964 through 2007.

continues

Oscar Winning Actors and Actresses* continued

Girl Names

Winner	Character	Movie
Geena Davis	Muriel	*The Accidental Tourist*
Gwyneth Paltrow	Viola De Lesseps	*Shakespeare in Love*
Halle Berry	Leticia Musgrove	*Monster's Ball*
Helen Mirren	The Queen	*The Queen*
Hilary Swank	Brandon Teena/ Teena Brandon	*Boys Don't Cry*
	Maggie Fitzgerald	*Million Dollar Baby*
Holly Hunter	Ada McGrath	*The Piano*
Jennifer Hudson	Effie White	*Dreamgirls*
Jessica Lange	Carly Marshall	*Blue Sky*
	Julie Nichols	*Tootsie*
Jodie Foster	Clarice Starling	*The Silence of the Lambs*
	Sarah Tobias	*The Accused*
Julia Roberts	Erin Brockovich	*Erin Brockovich*
Katharine Hepburn	Queen Eleanor of Aquitane	*The Lion in Winter*
Kim Basinger	Lynn Bracken	*L.A. Confidential*
Lee Grant	Felicia Carr	*Shampoo*
Marion Cotillard	Edith Piaf	*La Vie en Rose*
Marisa Tomei	Mona Lisa Vito	*My Cousin Vinny*
Marlee Matlin	Sarah Norman	*Children of a Lesser God*
Mercedes Ruehl	Anne	*The Fisher King*
Mira Sorvino	Linda Ash	*Mighty Aphrodite*
Nicole Kidman	Virginia Woolf	*The Hours*
Olympia Dukakis	Rose Castorini	*Moonstruck*
Rachel Weisz	Tessa Quayle	*The Constant Gardener*
Reese Witherspoon	June Carter	*Walk the Line*
Renée Zellweger	Ruby Thewes	*Cold Mountain*
Shirley MacLaine	Aurora Greenway	*Terms of Endearment*
Sissy Spacek	Loretta Lynn	*Coal Miner's Daughter*
Susan Sarandon	Sister Helen Prejean	*Dead Man Walking*
Tatum O'Neal	Addie Loggins	*Paper Moon*
Tilda Swinton	Karen Crowder	*Michael Clayton*
Vanessa Redgrave	Julia	*Julia*

Boy Names

Winner	Character	Movie
Adrien Brody	Wladyslaw Szpilman	*The Pianist*
Al Pacino	Lt. Col. Frank Slade	*Scent of a Woman*
Alan Arkin	Grandpa	*Little Miss Sunshine*
Anthony Hopkins	Dr. Hannibal Lecter	*The Silence of the Lambs*
Ben Kingsley	Mahatma Gandhi	*Ghandi*
Benicio Del Toro	Javier Rodriguez	*Traffic*
Christopher Walken	Nick	*The Deer Hunter*
Cuba Gooding Jr.	Rod Tidwell	*Jerry Maguire*
Daniel Day Lewis	Christy Brown Daniel Plainview	*My Left Foot* *There Will Be Blood*
Denzel Washington	Alonzo	*Training Day*
Dustin Hoffman	Raymond Babbitt Ted Kramer	*Rain Man* *Kramer vs. Kramer*
Forest Whitaker	Idi Amin	*The Last King of Scotland*
Gene Hackman	Jimmy "Popeye" Doyle Little Bill Daggett	*The French Connection* *Unforgiven*
George Clooney	Bob Barnes	*Syriana*
Gig Young	Rocky	*They Shoot Horses, Don't They?*
Haing S. Ngor	Dith Pran	*The Killing Fields*
Jamie Foxx	Ray Charles	*Ray*
Javier Bardem	Anton Chigurh	*No Country for Old Men*
Jeremy Irons	Claus Von Bulow	*Reversal of Fortune*
Jon Voight	Luke Martin	*Coming Home*
Kevin Spacey	Lester Burnham	*American Beauty*
Louis Gossett Jr.	Sgt. Emil Foley	*An Officer and a Gentleman*
Marlon Brando	Don Vito Corleone	*The Godfather*
Michael Caine	Elliot	*Hannah and Her Sisters*
Morgan Freeman	Eddie Scrap-Iron Dupris	*Million Dollar Baby*
Nicolas Cage	Ben Sanderson	*Leaving Las Vegas*
Philip Seymour Hoffman	Truman Capote	*Capote*
Rex Harrison	Professor Henry Higgins	*My Fair Lady*
Richard Dreyfuss	Elliot Garfield	*The Goodbye Girl*
Roberto Benigni	Guido Orefice	*Life Is Beautiful*

continues

Oscar Winning Actors and Actresses* continued

Boy Names

Winner	Character	Movie
Robin Williams	Sean McGuire	*Good Will Hunting*
Russell Crowe	Maximus Decimus Meridius	*Gladiator*
Sean Penn	Jimmy Markum	*Mystic River*
Tim Robbins	Dave Boyle	*Mystic River*
Tom Hanks	Andrew Beckett Forrest Gump	*Philadelphia Forrest Gump*
William Hurt	Luis Molina	*Kiss of the Spider Woman*

Tony Winners

Girl Names

Winner	Category	Play
Adriane Lenox	Actress, play	*Doubt*
Anita Waxman	Revival, play	*The Real Thing*
Audra McDonald	Actress, play	*Master Class*
Bebe Neuwirth	Actress, musical	*Chicago*
Bernadette Peters	Actress, musical	*Annie Get Your Gun*
Cady Huffman	Actress, musical	*The Producers*
Charlene Marshall	Play, revival	*Long Day's Journey into Night*
Cherry Jones	Actress, play	*Doubt*
Cynthia Nixon	Actress, play	*Rabbit Hole*
Florence Klotz	Costume designer	*Show Boat*
Frances de la Tour	Actress, play	*The History Boys*
Frances Edelstein	Tony Honors for Excellence in Theater	
Gillian Gregory	Choreographer	*Me and My Girl*
Harriet Harris	Actress, musical	*Thoroughly Modern Millie*
Heather Headley	Actress, musical	*Aida*
Idina Menzel	Actress, musical	*Wicked*
Kara Medoff	Play, revival	*Long Day's Journey into Night*
Kristin Chenoweth	Actress, musical	*You're a Good Man, Charlie Brown*

Winner	Category	Play
LaChanze	Actress, musical	*The Color Purple*
Lillias White	Actress, musical	*The Life*
Lindsay Duncan	Actress, play	*Private Lives*
Margo Lion	Producer, musical	*Hairspray*
Marissa Jaret Winokur	Actress, musical	*Hairspray*
Natasha Katz	Lighting designer	*Aida*
Phylicia Rashad	Actress, play	*A Raisin in the Sun*
Robyn Goodman	Producer, musical	*Avenue Q*
Rondi Reed	Actress, play	*August: Osage County*
Sutton Foster	Actress, musical	*Thoroughly Modern Millie*
Twyla Tharp	Choreographer	*Movin' Out*
Uta Hagen	Actress, drama	*Who's Afraid of Virginia Woolf*
Viola Davis	Actress, play	*King Hedley II*
Yasmina Reza	Writer, play	*Art*
Zoe Caldwell	Actress, play	*Master Class*

Boy Names

Winner	Category	Play
Alfred Uhry	Book, musical	*Parade*
André Bishop	Producer, musical	*Contact*
Bernard Gersten	Producer, revival	*Our Town*
Billy Crudup	Actor, play	*The Coast of Utopia*
Billy Joel	Orchestrations	*Movin' Out*
Boyd Gaines	Actor, musical	*Gypsy*
Christian Hoff	Actor, musical	*Jersey Boys*
Christopher Plummer	Actor, play	*Barrymore*
Darren Bagert	Producer, revival	*Long Day's Journey into Night*
Dick Latessa	Actor, musical	*Hairspray*
Douglas Besterman	Orchestration	*Fosse*
Duncan Sheik	Score	*Spring Awakening*
Ellis Rabb	Director, play	*The Royal Family*
Elton John	Original musical score	*Aida*
Frank Langella	Actor, play	*Fortune's Fool*

continues

Tony Winners　continued

Boy Names

Winner	Category	Play
Garth Fagan	Choreographer	The Lion King
Hugh Jackman	Actor, musical	The Boy from Oz
Ian McDiarmid	Actor, play	Faith Healer
Jefferson Mays	Actor, play	I Am My Own Wife
Jules Fisher	Lighting designer	Bring in 'da Noise/ Bring in 'da Funk
Ken Billington	Lighting designer	Chicago
Liev Schreiber	Actor, play	Glengarry Glen Ross
Lloyd Richards	Director, play	Fences
Mark Rylance	Actor, play	Boeing-Boeing
Maury Yeston	Original musical score	Titanic
Nathan Lane	Actor, musical	The Producers
Nigel Levings	Lighting designer	La Boheme
Norbert Leo Butz	Actor, musical	Dirty Rotten Scoundrels
Owen Teale	Actor, play	A Doll's House
Rick Steiner	Producer, musical	Hairspray
Ruben Santiago-Hudson	Actor, play	Seven Guitars
Shuler Hensley	Actor, musical	Oklahoma!
Stuart Malina	Orchestrations	Movin' Out
Tharon Musser	Lighting designer	Dreamgirls
Trevor Nunn	Director, musical	Les Misérables
Wilson Jermaine Heredia	Actor, musical	Rent

Emmy Winners

Girl Names

Winner	Category	Show
Aisha Wagle	Coordinating producer	A Baby Story
Audrey Jones	Producer	The View
Candice Bergen	Actress	Murphy Brown
Casey Childs	Director	All My Children
Cloris Leachman	Actress	Malcolm in the Middle
Cynthia Nixon	Actress	Sex and the City

Winner	Category	Show
Dana Goodman	Producer	*The View*
Dava Waite Peaslee	Casting	*How I Met Your Mother*
Erin Irwin	Producer	*The Wayne Brady Show*
Felicity Huffman	Actress	*Desperate Housewives*
Frances Reid	Actress	*Days of Our Lives*
Gaynelle Evans	Executive producer	*Before the Dinosaurs*
Gena Rowlands	Actress	*Hysterical Blindness*
Haleigh Safran	Producer	*The View*
Isabel Sanford	Actress	*The Jeffersons*
Jakki Taylor	Coordinating producer	*The View*
Kirstie Alley	Actress	*Cheers; David's Mother*
Krysia Plonka	Supervising producer	*The Wayne Brady Show*
Libby Goldstein	Casting	*Ugly Betty*
Lindsay Wagner	Actress	*The Bionic Woman*
Liz Naylor	Producer	*A Baby Story*
Lorri Leighton	Producer	*A Baby Story*
Maria Notaras	Producer	*The Wayne Brady Show*
Mariska Hargitay	Actress	*Law & Order: Special Victims Unit*
Mary-Louise Parker	Actress	*Angels in America*
Nan Schwieger	Producer	*Reading Rainbow*
Nicole Silver	Producer	*Reading Rainbow*
Rachel Ames	Actress	*General Hospital*
Roseanne Arnold	Actress	*Roseanne*
Samantha Horn	Costume	*Elizabeth I*
Sarah Jessica Parker	Actress	*Sex and the City*
Shelly Moore	Writer	*General Hospital*
Sudie Anning	Producer	*Reading Rainbow*
Tamara Grady	Stage manager	*All My Children*
Twila Liggett	Director	*Reading Rainbow*
Tyne Daly	Actress	*Judging Amy*
Vanessa Marcil	Actress	*General Hospital*
Vivian Gundaker	Producer	*As the World Turns*

Emmy Winners

Boy Names

Winner	Category	Show
Albert Finney	Actor	*The Gathering Storm*
Alik Sakharov	Cinematography	*Rome*
Beau Bridges	Actor	*The Second Civil War*
Bill Geddie	Executive producer	*The View*
Bradley Whitford	Actor	*The West Wing*
Burt Reynolds	Actor	*Evening Shade*
Carroll O'Connor	Actor	*All in the Family; In the Heat of the Night*
Craig T. Nelson	Actor	*Coach*
Don Hastings	Actor	*As the World Turns*
Ed Wiseman	Producer	*Reading Rainbow*
Freddy Rodriguez	Supporting actor	*Six Feet Under*
Garin Wolf	Writer	*General Hospital*
Glenn Davish	Producer	*The View*
Grenville Horner	Production designer	*Jane Eyre*
Hal Holbrook	Actor	*Sandburg's Lincoln*
James Spader	Actor	*Boston Legal*
Jerry Pilato	Associate director	*All My Children*
Jordi Vilasuso	Actor	*Guiding Light*
Josh Gilbert	Producer	*The Wayne Brady Show*
Judd Hirsch	Actor	*Taxi*
Kelsey Bay	Coordinating producer	*As the World Turns*
Kiefer Sutherland	Actor	*24*
Lee Farber	Producer	*The Wayne Brady Show*
Levar Burton	Executive producer	*Reading Rainbow*
Maurice Benard	Actor	*General Hospital*
Michael Loman	Executive producer	*Sesame Street*
Neil Cohen	Executive producer	*A Baby Story*
Orly Wiseman	Producer	*Reading Rainbow*
Ray Liotta	Actor	*ER*
Ricky Gervais	Actor	*Extras*
Rocky Schmidt	Senior producer	*Jeopardy!*
Rusty Swope	Stage manager	*All My Children*

Winner	Category	Show
Shane Farley	Producer	*The Wayne Brady Show*
Shia Labeouf	Actor	*Even Stevens*
Sid Caesar	Actor	*Caesar's Hour*
Telly Savalas	Actor	*Kojak*
Trey Parker	Executive producer	*South Park*
Wade Robson	Choreographer	*So You Think You Can Dance*
Wayne Brady	Actor	*Whose Line Is It Anyway?*

Grammy Winners

Girl Names

Musician	Category	Musician	Category
Alannah Myles	Rock	Dee Dee Bridgewater	Jazz
Alicia Keys	R&B	Dianne Reeves	Jazz
Amy Grant	Gospel	Dionne Warwick	Pop
Amy Winehouse	Pop	Donna Summer	Pop
Ani DiFranco	Packaging	Emmylou Harris	Country
Anita Baker	R&B	Enya	New Age
Anne Sofie von Otter	Classical	Faith Hill	Country
Barbra Streisand	Pop	Fiona Apple	Rock
Bette Midler	Pop	Gloria Estefan	Latin
Beyoncé	R&B	Irene Cara	Pop
Brandy	R&B	Janet Jackson	Pop
Carrie Underwood	Country	Joan Sebastian	Latin
CeCe Winans	Gospel	Jody Watley	Pop
Cecilia Bartoli	Classical	Joni Mitchell	Pop
Celia Cruz	Latin	Juice Newton	Country
Celine Dion	Pop	June Carter Cash	Country
Chaka Khan	R&B	K. D. Lang	Traditional pop
Cher	Pop	Kathy Mattea	Country
Christina Aguilera	Pop	Kelly Clarkson	Pop
Cissy Houston	Gospel	Lauryn Hill	R&B
Cyndi Lauper	Pop	Lena Horne	Jazz
Debby Boone	Gospel	Macy Gray	Pop

continues

Grammy Winners continued

Girl Names

Musician	Category	Musician	Category
Madonna	Pop	Pink	Rock
Mariah Carey	R&B	Queen Latifah	Rap
Mary Youngblood	Folk	Renée Fleming	Classical
Melissa Etheridge	Rock	Rihanna	Rap
Missy Elliott	Rap	Sarah McLachlan	Pop
Monica	R&B	Shawn Colvin	Folk
Mya	Pop	Sheena Easton	Pop
Naomi Judd	Country	Shelby Lynne	Country
Natalie Cole	Jazz	Sheryl Crow	Rock
Nelly Furtado	Pop	Shirley Horn	Jazz
Norah Jones	Pop	Susan Graham	Classical
Pam Tillis	Country	Thelma Houston	R&B
Patti Page	Traditional pop	Toni Braxton	R&B
Paula Cole	Rock	Tracy Chapman	Rock
		Whitney Houston	R&B

Boy Names

Musician	Category	Musician	Category
Aaron Neville	Country	Dave Matthews	Rock
Al Jarreau	R&B	David Russell	Classical
André Previn	Classical	Dominick Argento	Classical
Art Neville	Rock	Donald Fagen	Pop
Barry White	R&B	Elvis Costello	Pop
Beck	Rock	Emanuel Ax	Classical
Billy Joel	Rock	Enrique Iglesias	Latin
Bobby Brown	R&B	George Winston	New Age
Bruce Hornsby	Pop	Gnarls Barkley	Alternative
Bruce Springsteen	Rock	Grover Mitchell	Jazz
Burt Bacharach	Composing	Harry Connick Jr.	Jazz
Chick Corea	Jazz	Herbie Hancock	Jazz
Christopher Cross	Arranging	Jack White	Rock
Coolio	Rap	James Taylor	Pop

Musician	Category	Musician	Category
Jeff Beck	Rock	Murray Perahia	Classical
Jimmy Page	Rock	Nat "King" Cole	Pop
Jimmy Sturr	Polka	Nelly	Rap
Joe Jackson	Pop	Ozzy Osbourne	Rock
John Fogerty	Rock	Pat Metheny	New Age
Jon Secada	Latin	Paul Simon	Pop
José Feliciano	Latin	Peabo Bryson	Pop
Joshua Bell	Classical	Pete Seeger	Folk
Julio Iglesias	Latin	Peter Gabriel	Music video
Justin Timberlake	Pop	Phil Collins	Composing
Kanye West	Rap	Quincy Jones	Jazz
Keith Urban	Country	R. Kelly	R&B
Kenny Loggins	Pop	Randy Brecker	Jazz
Kurt Cobain	Alternative	Ricky Skaggs	Country
LL Cool J	Rap	Robert Palmer	Rock
Lenny Kravitz	Rock	Rubén Blades	Latin
Les Paul	Pop	Seal	Pop
Lionel Richie	Pop	Sergio Mendes	World
Lou Rawls	R&B	Stevie Wonder	R&B
Ludacris	Rap	Tito Puente	Latin
Luis Miguel	Latin	Tony Bennett	Traditional pop
Luther Vandross	R&B	Travis Tritt	Country
Lyle Lovett	Country	Warren Zevon	Folk
Marvin Gaye	R&B	Waylon Jennings	Country
McCoy Tyner	Jazz	Willie Nelson	Country
Michael Bolton	Pop	Wynton Marsalis	Jazz
Michael Bublé	Pop	Yo-Yo Ma	Classical
Miles Davis	Jazz		

Olympic Medalists

Girl Names

Winner	Sport	Winner	Sport
Amanda Beard	Swimming	Jill Kintner	Cycling
Angel Martino	Swimming	Katarina Witt	Figure skating
Beezie Madden	Equestrian	Katie Hoff	Swimming
Bente Skari	Cross-country skiing	Katja Seizinger	Alpine skiing
		Kristi Yamaguchi	Figure skating
Cappie Pondexter	Basketball	Mariel Zagunis	Fencing
Carly Patterson	Gymnastics	Mary Lou Retton	Gymnastics
Claudia Boyarskikh	Cross-country skiing	Merlene Ottey	Track and field
Daniela Ceccarelli	Alpine skiing	Misty May-Treanor	Beach volleyball
Dara Torres	Swimming	Nadia Comaneci	Gymnastics
Diann Roffe-Steinrotter	Alpine skiing	Nastia Liukin	Gymnastics
Ecaterina Szabo	Gymnastics	Natalie Coughlin	Swimming
Ethelda Bleibtrey	Swimming	Nikki Stone	Freestyle skiing
Florence Griffith-Joyner	Track and field	Oksana Baiul	Figure skating
Galina Kulakova	Cross-country skiing	Picabo Street	Alpine skiing
		Sada Jacobson	Fencing
Gwen Torrence	Track and field	Shannon Miller	Gymnastics
Hyleas Fountain	Heptathalon	Shawn Johnson	Gymnastics
Jackie Joyner-Kersee	Track and field	Tara Lipinski	Figure skating
Janica Kostelic	Alpine skiing	Valerie Brisco-Hooks	Track and field
Jennie Finch	Softball	Wilma Rudolph	Track and field

Boy Names

Winner	Sport	Winner	Sport
Aaron Piersol	Swimming	Derek Parra	Speed skating
Alberto Tomba	Alpine skiing	Dick Button	Figure skating
Alexei Yagudin	Figure skating	Eric Heiden	Speed skating
Brian Boitano	Figure skating	Fritz Strobl	Alpine skiing
Carl Lewis	Track and field	Gary Hall Jr.	Swimming
Carmelo Anthony	Basketball	Georg Hackl	Luge
Casey FitzRandolph	Speed skating	Ilia Kulik	Figure skating

Winner	Sport	Winner	Sport
Irving Jaffee	Speed skating	Mclain Ward	Equestrian
Jason Lezak	Swimming	Michael Johnson	Track and field
Jean-Claude Killy	Alpine skiing	Michael Phelps	Swimming
Jesse Owens	Track and field	Neil Walker	Swimming
Kerron Clement	Track and field	Oscar De La Hoya	Boxing
LaShawn Merritt	Track and field	Pernell Whitaker	Boxing
Lasse Kjus	Alpine skiing	Ryan Lochte	Swimming
Lenny Krayzelburg	Swimming	Scott Hamilton	Figure skating
Matt Biondi	Swimming	Tommy Moe	Alpine skiing
Matti Nykanen	Ski jumping	Viktor Petrenko	Figure skating
Maurice Greene	Track and field	Walton Eller	Shooting

Heisman Trophy Winners

Girl Names

Not applicable.

Boy Names

Winner	School	Winner	School
Andre Ware	University of Houston	Desmond Howard	University of Michigan
Angelo Bertelli	University of Notre Dame	Doak Walker	Southern Methodist University
Bo Jackson	Auburn University	Earl Campbell	University of Texas
Bruce Smith	University of Minnesota	Eric Crouch	University of Nebraska
Carson Palmer	University of Southern California	Ernie Davis	Syracuse University
		Felix Blanchard	Army
Charles White	University of Southern California	Frank Sinkwich	University of Georgia
Chris Weinke	Florida State University	Gary Beban	University of California-Los Angeles
Clint Frank	Yale University		
Danny Wuerffel	University of Florida	George Rogers	University of South Carolina
Davey O'Brien	Texas Christian University	Gino Torretta	University of Miami

continues

Heisman Trophy Winners continued

Boy Names

Winner	School	Winner	School
Glenn Davis	Army	Nile Kinnick	University of Iowa
Herschel Walker	University of Georgia	Peter Dawkins	Army
Howard Cassady	Ohio State University	Rashaan Salaam	University of Colorado
Jason White	University of Oklahoma	Reggie Bush	University of Southern California
Jay Berwanger	University of Chicago	Ricky Williams	University of Texas
Jim Plunkett	Stanford University	Roger Staubach	Navy
Joe Bellino	Navy	Steve Spurrier	University of Florida
John Huarte	University of Notre Dame	Terry Baker	Oregon State University
Johnny Rodgers	University of Nebraska	Tim Brown	University of Notre Dame
Larry Kelley	Yale University	Tim Tebow	University of Florida
Leon Hart	University of Notre Dame	Troy Smith	Ohio State
Les Horvath	Ohio State University	Ty Detmer	Brigham Young University
Marcus Allen	University of Southern California	Vic Janowicz	Ohio State University
Matt Leinart	University of Southern California	Vinny Testaverde	University of Miami
Mike Garrett	University of Southern California		

Series MVPs

Girl Names

MVP	Sport	MVP	Sport
Ashley Earley	Basketball	Jillian Robbins	Basketball
Crystal Kelly	Basketball	Khara Smith	Basketball
Dee-Dee Wheeler	Basketball	Kiera Hardy	Basketball
Elisha Turek	Basketball	Lauren Jackson	Basketball
Eva Cunningham	Basketball	Leilani Mitchell	Basketball
Jazz Covington	Basketball	Lisa Leslie	Basketball

MVP	Sport	MVP	Sport
Meg Bulger	Basketball	Shay Doron	Basketball
Milena Tomova	Basketball	Sheryl Swoopes	Basketball
Ofa Wright	Basketball	Sugiery Monsac	Basketball
Reka Cserny	Basketball	Tan White	Basketball
Rolanda Monroe	Basketball	Tanisha Wright	Basketball
Sancho Lyttle	Basketball	Tori Talbert	Basketball

Boy Names

MVP	Sport	MVP	Sport
Bart Starr	Football	Manny Ramirez	Baseball
Bucky Dent	Baseball	Marcus Allen	Football
Charles Barkley	Basketball	Mariano Rivera	Baseball
Darrell Porter	Baseball	Mike Lowell	Baseball
David Eckstein	Baseball	Moses Malone	Basketball
Desmond Howard	Football	Orel Hershiser	Baseball
Dexter Jackson	Football	Oscar Robertson	Basketball
Dirk Nowitzki	Basketball	Pedro Guerrero	Baseball
Emmitt Smith	Football	Peyton Manning	Football
Franco Harris	Football	Phil Simms	Football
Gene Tenace	Baseball	Randy White	Football
Hakeem Olajuwon	Basketball	Reggie Jackson	Baseball
Harvey Martin	Football	Roberto Clemente	Baseball
Jake Scott	Football	Roger Staubach	Football
Jermaine Dye	Baseball	Rollie Fingers	Baseball
Jose Rijo	Baseball	Sandy Koufax	Baseball
Julius Erving	Basketball	Scott Brosius	Baseball
Kareem Abdul-Jabbar	Basketball	Shaquille O'Neal	Basketball
Karl Malone	Basketball	Shaun Alexander	Football
Kobe Bryant	Basketball	Steve Nash	Basketball
Kurt Warner	Football	Terrell Davis	Football
LaDainian Tomlinson	Football	Tom Brady	Football
Lew Burdette	Baseball	Troy Aikman	Football
Livan Hernandez	Baseball	Whitey Ford	Baseball
Lynn Swann	Football	Willis Reed	Basketball
		Wilt Chamberlain	Basketball

NBA/NCAA All-Stars

Girl Names

All-Star	Team	All-Star	Team
Alison Bales	Duke University Blue Devils	Janese Hardrick	University of Georgia Lady Bulldogs
Amber Flynn	Bowling Green State University Falcons	Johannah Leedham	Franklin Pierce University Ravens
Anna Chappell	University of Arizona Wildcats	Joy Hollingsworth	University of Arizona Wildcats
Brie Madden	Kansas State University Wildcats	Karly Chesko	Canisius College Golden Griffins
Brittney Keil	College of the Holy Cross Crusaders	Kelly Killion	Holy Family University Tigers
Caprice Smith	DePaul University Blue Demons	Kelsey Simonds	Stonehill College Skyhawks
Casmir Patterson	DePaul University Blue Demons	Kenisha Daniels	Alcorn State University Lady Braves
Catherine Carr	Holy Family University Tigers	Kia Alexander	Alcorn State University Lady Braves
Cavanaugh Hagen	Canisius College Golden Griffins	Kymira Woodberry	Molloy College Lions
Chelsea Whitaker	Baylor University Bears	Lashawn Johnson	Illinois State University Redbirds
Corinne Turner	George Washington University Colonials	Leisel Harry	Coppin State College Lady Eagles
Cyndi Valentin	Indiana University Hoosiers	Margaret DeCiman	Louisiana Tech Lady Techsters
Danielle Adefeso	University of Arizona Wildcats	Monique Currie	Duke University Blue Devils
Daphne Andre	University of Houston Lady Cougars	Natasha Dennis	Alcorn State University Lady Braves
Denita Plain	Coppin State College Lady Eagles	Nia Capuano	Canisius College Golden Griffins
Ebony Franklin	Alcorn State Lady Braves	Nina Simokes	University of Louisville Cardinals
Erica Taylor	Louisiana Tech University Lady Techsters	Patrika Barlow	University of Louisville Cardinals
Jaci McCormack	Illinois State University Redbirds	Quianna Chaney	Louisiana State University Lady Tigers
		Rachael Carney	DePaul University Blue Demons

All-Star	Team	All-Star	Team
Sakima Smith	Bowling Green State University Falcons	Talia Sutton	Coppin State College Lady Eagles
Sarah Placek	College of the Holy Cross Crusaders	Tanika Price	University of Hartford Hawks
Sherill Baker	University of Georgia Lady Bulldogs	Tosha Christmas	Louisiana Tech Lady Techsters
Sophia White	Baylor University Bears	Wanisha Smith	Duke University Blue Devils
Stephanie Blanton	Ohio State Buckeyes	Whitney Taylor	Bowling Green University Falcons
Sylvia Fowles	Louisiana State University Lady Tigers		

Boy Names

All-Star	Team	All-Star	Team
Allen Iverson	Philadelphia 76ers	Derek Fisher	Golden State Warriors
Alonzo Mourning	Miami Heat	Dikembe Mutombo	Houston Rockets
Amare Stoudemire	Phoenix Suns	Dirk Nowitzki	Dallas Mavericks
Antoine Walker	Boston Celtics	Dolph Schayes	New York Knicks
Baron Davis	Golden State Warriors	Earvin "Magic" Johnson	Los Angeles Lakers
Brad Miller	Sacramento Kings	Eddy Curry	Chicago Bulls
Brandon Roy	Portland Trail Blazers	Emanuel Ginobili	San Antonio Spurs
Bryon Russell	Denver Nuggets		
Carlos Boozer	Utah Jazz	Gilbert Arenas	Washington Wizards
Carmelo Anthony	Denver Nuggets	Glen Rice	Charlotte Bobcats
Chauncey Billups	Detroit Pistons	Hakeem Olajuwon	Toronto Raptors
Christopher Paul	New Orleans Hornets	Hersey Hawkins	New Orleans Hornets
Clyde Drexler	Portland Trail Blazers	Isiah Thomas	Detroit Pistons
Dale Davis	Indiana Pacers	Jerome Kersey	San Antonio Spurs
Darryl Dawkins	Detroit Pistons	Jo Jo White	Boston Celtics
David West	New Orleans Hornets	Joe Johnson	Atlanta Hawks
		Josh Howard	Dallas Mavericks

continues

NBA/NCAA All-Stars continued

Boy Names

All-Star	Team	All-Star	Team
Julius Erving	Philadelphia 76ers	Ricky Davis	Boston Celtics
Kareem Abdul-Jabbar	Los Angeles Lakers	Robert Parish	Chicago Bulls
		Sam Perkins	Indiana Pacers
Karl Malone	Los Angeles Lakers	Scottie Pippen	Chicago Bulls
Kenyon Martin	Denver Nuggets	Shaquille O'Neal	Miami Heat
Kevin Garnett	Minnesota Timberwolves		
		Shareef Abdur-Rahim	Portland Trail Blazers
Kiki Vandeweghe	Denver Nuggets		
Kobe Bryant	Los Angeles Lakers	Stephon Marbury	New York Knicks
Larry Bird	Boston Celtics	Terry Porter	San Antonio Spurs
LeBron James	Cleveland Cavaliers	Toni Kukoc	Milwaukee Bucks
Manu Ginóbili	San Antonio Spurs	Tony Parker	San Antonio Spurs
Mehmet Okur	Utah Jazz	Tracy McGrady	Houston Rockets
Michael Jordan	Chicago Bulls	Tree Rollins	Indiana Pacers
Moses Malone	Portland Trail Blazers	Tyson Chandler	Chicago Bulls
Otis Thorpe	New Orleans Hornets	Vern Mikkelsen	Minneapolis Lakers
		Vince Carter	New Jersey Nets
Pau Gasol	Los Angeles Lakers	Vlade Divac	Los Angeles Lakers
Peja Stojakovic	Sacramento Kings	Wes Unseld	Baltimore Bullets
Radoslav Nesterovic	San Antonio Spurs	Willis Reed	New York Knicks
		Yao Ming	Houston Rockets
Rashard Lewis	Orlando Magic	Zydrunas Ilgauskas	Cleveland Cavaliers
Reggie Miller	Indiana Pacers		

Hockey Hunks and Babes

Girl Names

Hockey Babe	Team	Hockey Babe	Team
Annika Ahlen	Sweden	Cassie Campbell	Canada
Bettina Evers	Germany	Danielle Goyette	Canada
Cammie Granato	USA	Emma Bowles	Great Britain

Hockey Babe	Team	Hockey Babe	Team
Fiona Smith	Canada	Kristina Bergstrand	Sweden
Geraldine Heaney	Canada	Lina Huo	China
Gillian Apps	Canada	Manon Rheume	Canada
Gretchen Ulion	USA	Nancy Drolet	Canada
Isabelle Minier	Canada	Natalie Darwitz	USA
Jayna Hefford	Canada	Nina Gall	Germany
Jeanine Sobek	USA	Robyn Ann Armour	Australia
Jennifer Botterill	USA	Sabine Schumacher	Switzerland
Karyn Bye	USA	Yuka Oda	Japan

Boy Names

Hockey Hunk	Team	Hockey Hunk	Team
Aaron Ward	Carolina Hurricanes	Francis Lessard	Atlanta Thrashers
Alex Ovechkin	Washington Capitals	Guillaume Lefebvre	Pittsburg Penguins
Andreas Lilja	Florida Panthers	Henrik Zetterberg	Detroit Red Wings
Ari Ahonen	New Jersey Devils		
Brett Lysak	Carolina Hurricanes	Ian Laperriere	Los Angeles Kings
Brooks Laich	Washington Capitals	Jarome Iginla	Calgary Flames
Bryce Lampman	New York Rangers	Jere Lehtinen	Dallas Stars
Cam Ward	Carolina Hurricanes	Jesse Wallin	Detriot Red Wings
Chad Wiseman	New York Rangers	Joe Thornton	San Jose Sharks
Chris Osgood	Detroit Red Wings	Jozef Balej	Montreal Canadiens
Christian Backman	St. Louis Blues	Kevyn Adams	Boston Bruins
Claude Lapointe	Philadelphia Flyers	Kip Brennan	Los Angeles Kings
Daymond Langkow	Phoenix Coyotes	Lance Ward	Anaheim Mighty Ducks
Dominik Hasek	Detroit Red Wings	Marek Zidlicky	Nashville Predators
Drake Berehowsky	Toronto Maple Leafs	Mattias Weinhandl	New York Islanders
Duvie Westcott	Columbus Blue Jackets	Mikko Luoma	Edmonton Oilers
		Neil Little	Philadelphia Flyers
Emmanuel Legace	Detroit Red Wings	Nikita Alexeev	Tampa Bay Lightning
Evgeni Malkin	Pittsburgh Penguins		

continues

Hockey Hunks and Babes continued

Boy Names

Hockey Hunk	Team	Hockey Hunk	Team
Nolan Baumgartner	Vancouver Canucks	Sebastien Aubin	Pittsburg Penguins
Pascal Leclaire	Columbus Blue Jackets	Stu Barnes	Dallas Stars
Pavel Datsyuk	Detroit Red Wings	Trevor Letowski	Columbus Blue Jackets
Quintin Laing	Chicago Blackhawks	Vincent Lecavalier	Tampa Bay Lightning
Ramzi Abid	Pittsburg Penguins	Wes Waltz	Minnesota Wild
Ryan Barnes	Detroit Red Wings	Zac Bierk	Phoenix Coyotes

Gymnast Guys and Gals

Girl Names

Gymnast	Country	Gymnast	Country
Alicia Sacramone	USA	Lilia Podkopayeva	Ukraine
Anastasia (Nastia) Liukin	USA	Marcia Frederick	USA
Aurelia Dobre	Romania	Mohini Bhardwaj	USA
Brandy Johnson	USA	Nadia Comaneci	Romania
Carly Patterson	USA	Nelli Kim	Soviet Union
Catalina Ponor	Romania	Oksana Omeliantchik	Soviet Union
Chellsie Memmel	USA	Olga Bicherova	Soviet Union
Dominique Dawes	USA	Pearl Perkins	USA
Ecaterina Szabo	Romania	Rachel Tidd	USA
Elise Ray	USA	Shannon Miller	USA
He Kexin	China	Shawn Johnson	USA
Hollie Vise	USA	Svetlana Boginskaia	Soviet Union
Jaycie Phelps	USA	Svetlana Khorkina	Soviet Union
Jiang Yuyuan	China	Tatiana Gutsu	Soviet Union
Julianne McNamara	USA	Terin Humphrey	USA
Kerri Strug	USA	Vera Caslavska	Czechoslovakia
Kim Zmeskal	USA	Yang Bo	China
		Yelena Mukhina	Soviet Union
		Zhu Zheng	China

Boy Names

Gymnast	Country	Gymnast	Country
Alexander Artemev	USA	Kerry Huston	USA
Alexei Nimov	Russia	Kip Simons	USA
Bart Conner	USA	Kurt Thomas	USA
Blaine Wilson	USA	Lance Ringnald	USA
Boris Shakhlin	Soviet Union	Leon Stukelj	Slovenia
Brett McClure	USA	Li Xiaopeng	China
Chainey Umphrey	USA	Marshall Avener	USA
Conrad Voorsanger	USA	Mihai Bagiu	USA
Ed Hennig	USA	Mitch Gaylord	USA
Frank Cumiskey	USA	Morgan Hamm	USA
Georges Miez	Switzerland	Nikolay Andrianov	Soviet Union
Guard Young	USA	Paul Hamm	USA
Guillermo Alvarez	USA	Raj Bhavsar	USA
Hiroyuki Tomita	Japan	Ross Brewer	Great Britain
Huang Xu	China	Rusty Mitchell	USA
Jair Lynch	USA	Scott Keswick	USA
Jarrod Hanks	USA	Trent Dimas	USA
Jordan Jovtchev	Bulgaria	Vitaly Scherbo	Soviet Union
Josh Stein	USA	Yang Wei	China
		Yann Cucherat	France

Spinners and Stunners–Ice Skaters

Girl Names

Andrea Ehrig

Barbara Ann Scott

Beatrix Schuba

Bonnie Blair

Carol Heiss

Catriona Le May Doan

Cecilia Colledge

Christa Luding-Rothenburger

Christina Kaiser

Claudia Pechstein

Connie Carpenter

Dagmar Lurz

Debi Thomas

Dianna Holum

Dorothy Hamill

Ekaterina Gordeeva

Elizabeth Manley

Ethel Mukelt

Eva Pawlik

Gabriele Seyfert

Gunda Niemann-Stirnemann

Ingrid Wendl

Irina Rodnina

Jacqueline du Bief

Jayne Torvill

Jeanne Ashworth

Jill Trenary

Karin Kania

Katarina Witt

continues

Spinners and Stunners-Ice Skaters continued

Girl Names

Kira Ivanova	Maribel Vinson	Radka Kovarikova	Tara Lipinski
Kristi Yamaguchi	Michelle Kwan	Regine Heitzer	Tenley Albright
Lee-Kyung Chun	Nancy Kerrigan	Rosalynn Sumners	Theresa Weld
Lidiva Skoblikova	Nicole Bobek	Sarah Hughes	Vivi-Anne Hulten
Linda Fratianne	Oksana Baiul	Sonja Henie	Yvonne Van Gennip
Madge Syers	Peggy Fleming	Tai Babilonia	

Boy Names

Alain Calmat	Georges Gautschi	Martin Stixrud	Robin Cousins
Aleksey Urmanov	Gillis Grafstrom	Montgomery Wilson	Ronnie Robertson
Andreas Krogh	Hans Gerschwiler	Ondrej Nepela	Scott Hamilton
Arthur Cumming	Hayes Alan Jenkins	Patrick Pera	Sergey Chetveroukhin
Brian Boitano	Helmut Seibt	Paul Wylie	Tim Wood
Charles Tickner	Ilya Kulik	Philippe Candeloro	Toller Cranston
David Jenkins	James Grogan	Rene Novotny	Ulrich Salchow
Dick Button	John Curry	Richard Johannson	Viktor Petrenko
Elvis Stojko	Josef Sabovcik	Robert Van Zeebroeck	Vladimir Kovalev
Ernst Baier	Karl Schafer		Willy Bockl
Felix Kaspar	Manfred Schnelldorfer		Wolfgang Schwarz
Geoffrey Hall-Say			

Grand Slammers-Tennis Players

Girl Names

Abigail Spears	Anna Kournikova	Elena Dementieva	Iva Majoli
Alicia Molik	Arantxa Sanchez Vicario	Elena Likhovtseva	Jana Novotna
Amelie Mauresmo	Billie Jean King	Evonne Goolagong Cawley	Jelena Jankovic
Amy Frazier	Chris Evert	Gabriela Sabatini	Jennifer Capriati
Ana Ivanovic	Conchita Martinez	Hana Mandlikova	Jill Craybas
Anastasia Myskina	Elena Bovina	Helena Sukova	Justine Henin
Anke Huber			Kim Clijsters

Lindsay Davenport

Maria Sharapova

Marion Bartoli

Marissa Irvin

Martina Hingis

Martina Navratilova

Mary Jo Fernandez

Mary Pierce

Monica Seles

Nadia Petrova

Natasha Zvereva

Nathalie Dechy

Pam Shriver

Patty Schnyder

Serena Williams

Steffi Graf

Svetlana Kuznetsova

Tatiana Golovin

Tracy Austin

Venus Williams

Vera Zvonareva

Virginia Wade

Boy Names

Adriano Panatta

Andre Agassi

Andy Roddick

Arthur Ashe

Björn Borg

Bobby Riggs

Boris Becker

Carlos Moya

David Nalbandian

Dominik Hrbaty

Gaston Gaudio

Goran Ivanisevic

Guillermo Canas

Guillermo Coria

Guillermo Vilas

Gustavo Kuerten

Ilie Nastase

Ivan Lendl

Ivan Ljubicic

Jan Kodes

Jim Courier

Jimmy Connors

Joachim Johansson

Johan Kriek

John McEnroe

John Newcombe

Lleyton Hewitt

Manuel Orantes

Marat Safin

Mario Ancic

Mats Wilander

Michael Chang

Michael Stich

Nikolay Davydenko

Pat Cash

Patrick Rafter

Pete Sampras

Petr Korda

Radek Stepanek

Rafael Nadal

Richard Krajicek

Rod Laver

Roger Federer

Sergi Bruguera

Stan Smith

Stefan Edberg

Thomas Johansson

Thomas Muster

Tim Henmen

Tommy Robredo

Vitas Gerulaitis

Yannick Noah

Yevgeny Kafelnikov

Golf Pros

Girl Names

Angela Park

Annika Sorenstam

Beth Bauer

Beth Daniel

Birdie Kim

Brandie Burton

Candie Kung

Carin Koch

Catriona Matthew

Christina Kim

Cristie Kerr

Danielle Ammaccapane

Dawn Coe-Jones

Deb Richard

Dorothy Delasin

Emilee Klein

Eun-Hee Ji

Gloria Park

Grace Park

Heather Bowie

Hee-Won Han

Helen Alfredsson

Inbee Park

Janice Moodie

Jennifer Rosales

Jeong Jang

Jill McGill

Jimin Kang

Joo Mi Kim

Juli Inkster

Karen Stupples

continues

Golf Pros   continued

Girl Names

Karine Icher	Lorena Ochoa	Nicole Perrot	Shi Hyun Ahn
Karrie Webb	Lorie Kane	Pat Hurst	Silvia Cavalleri
Katherine Hull	Maria Hjorth	Paula Creamer	Stacy Prammanasudh
Kim Saiki	Meg Mallon	Rachel Hetherington	Suzann Pettersen
Kristi Albers	Mi Hyun Kim	Reilley Rankin	Tina Barrett
Laura Davies	Michele Redman	Rosie Jones	Wendy Ward
Laura Diaz	Michelle Wie	Se Ri Pak	Yani Tseng
Leta Lindley	Moira Dunn	Seon Hwa Lee	Young Kim
Liselotte Neumann	Natalie Gulbis		

Boy Names

Adam Scott	Duffy Waldorf	José Maria Olazabal	Rod Pampling
Angel Cabrera	Ernie Els	Justin Leonard	Rory Sabbatini
Anthony Kim	Fred Couples	K. J. Choi	Scott Verplank
Arnold Palmer	Fred Funk	Kenny Perry	Sergio Garcia
Bart Bryant	Geoff Ogilvy	Kirk Triplett	Shaun Micheel
Bernhard Langer	Graeme McDowell	Lee Westwood	Shigeki Maruyama
Bob Tway	Greg Norman	Luke Donald	Stephen Ames
Bobby Jones	Hal Sutton	Mark Hensby	Stewart Cink
Boo Weekley	Hank Kuehne	Miguel Jimenez	Stuart Appleby
Brett Quigley	Harrison Frazar	Mike Weir	Tag Ridings
Camilo Villegas	Ian Poulter	Nick O'Hern	Thomas Bjorn
Carl Pettersson	Jack Nicklaus	Padraig Harrington	Tiger Woods
Chad Campbell	Jaxon Brigman	Paul Casey	Tim Clark
Chris DiMarco	Jay Haas	Per-Ulrik Johansson	Titch Moore
Colin Montgomerie	Jeff Maggert	Peter Lonard	Todd Hamilton
Corey Pavin	Jesper Parnevik	Phil Mickelson	Tom Lehman
Craig Parry	Jim Furyk	Pierre Fulke	Trevor Immelman
Darren Clarke	Joey Sindelar	Retief Goosen	Vaughn Taylor
David Toms	John Daly	Robert Allenby	Vijay Singh
Davis Love III	Jonathan Kaye		Zach Johnson

NASCAR Names

Girl Names

Ann Bunselmeyer

Christine Beckers

Erin Crocker

Ethel Mobley

Fifi Scott

Goldie Parsons

Janet Guthrie

Lella Lombardi

Louise Smith

Marian Pagan

Patty Moise

Robin McCall

Sara Christian

Shawna Robinson

Stacy Compton

Teresa Earnhardt

Boy Names

A. J. Allmendinger

Allan Grice

Alton Jones

Andy Belmont

Austin Cameron

Baxter Price

Blair Aiken

Bobby Allison

Bobby Labonte

Boris Said

Brandon Ash

Brent Elliott

Brett Bodine

Brian Vickers

Buck Baker

Buddy Arrington

Cale Yarborough

Carl Adams

Carl Edwards

Casey Atwood

Casey Mears

Chad Blount

Charlie Rudolph

Chet Fillip

Chuck Wahl

Clark Dwyer

Clay Young

Clint Bowyer

Christian Fittipaldi

Dale Earnhardt Jr.

Dale Jarrett

Darrell Waltrip

Dave Blaney

Davey Allison

David Gilliland

David Ragan

David Reutimann

Denny Hamlin

Derrike Cope

Dick Whalen

Doc Faustina

Donnie Allison

Doug Wheeler

Earl Ross

Edward Cooper

Eldon Dotson

Elliott Forbes-Robinson

Elliott Sadler

Ernie Cline

Fonty Flock

Frank Warren

Gary Baker

George Wiltshire

Gil Roth

Glen Francis

Gordon Johncock

Graham Taylor

Grant Adcox

Greg Biffle

Harry Goularte

Henley Gray

Hermie Sadler

Howard Rose

Hut Stricklin

Ivan Baldwin

J. J. Yeley

Jack Donohue

Jamie McMurray

Jason Hedlesky

Jeff Burton

Jeff Gordon

continues

NASCAR Names continued

Boy Names

Jeremy Mayfield	Marv Acton	Roland Wlodyka
Jerry Nadeau	Matt Kenseth	Ruben Garcia
Jimmie Johnson	Maurice Randall	Rusty Wallace
Jimmy Walker	Michael McDowell	Ryan Newman
Joe Nemechek	Michael Waltrip	Salt Walther
Joey Arrington	Mickey Gibbs	Sam Ard
John Alexander	Mike Alexander	Sam Hornish Jr.
Johnny Sauter	Morgan Shepard	Satch Worley
Jon Wood	Neil Bonnett	Scott Autrey
Juan Montoya	Nelson Oswald	Scott Riggs
Kasey Kahne	Norm Palmer	Shane Hall
Keith Davis	Oma Kimbrough	Stanley Smith
Kenny Wallace	Pancho Carter	Strout Wayne
Kerry Earnhardt	Patrick Carpentier	Ted Fritz
Kevin Harvick	Paul Dean Holt	Terry Labonte
Kirk Bryant	Paul Menard	Terry Ryan
Klaus Graf	Phil Barkdoll	Tom Williams
Kurt Busch	Ralph Jones	Tony Ave
Kyle Busch	Randy Renfrow	Tony Raines
Kyle Petty	Ray Elder	Tony Stewart
Lake Speed	Reed Sorenson	Travis Kvapil
Laurent Rioux	Regan Smith	Trevor Boys
Lee Raymond	Richard White	Vince Giamformaggio
Loy Allen	Robby Gordon	Walter Wallace
Mark Martin	Rodney Combs	Ward Burton
Martin Truex Jr.	Roger McCluskey	Wayne Watercutter
Marty Robbins		

Money Monikers

If you fancy your son or daughter as a future corporate leader, take a look at some of the names of today's CEOs of the Fortune 1000 for name ideas. You'll find names of all the women currently heading U.S. corporations, as well as a mix of men holding the same top spot.

Or scan the names of some of the world's best-known entrepreneurs. Important historical figures such as Andrew Carnegie and John D. Rockefeller are here, too, as are some of today's hot-shot entrepreneurs, such as Jeff Bezos and Liz Lange.

For even more fun, peek at some of the brand names some parents have given their kids. From liqueur to cars to shoes, you'll see quite a variety to choose from. Or you may be inspired to use one of your own favorite brands.

CEOs

Girl Names

CEO	Company	CEO	Company
Andrea Jung	Avon	Mary Agnes Wilderotter	Citizens Communications
Angela Braly	Wellpoint	Mary Forté	Zale Corporation
Anne Mulcahy	Xerox	Mary Sammons	Rite Aid
Brenda Barnes	Sara Lee	Patricia Gallup	PC Connection
Cindy Taylor	Oil States International	Patricia Russo	Alcatel-Lucent
Dona Davis Young	The Phoenix Companies	Patricia Woertz	Archer Daniels Midland
Dorrit Bern	Charming Shoppes	Paula Rosput	AGL Resources
Eileen Scott	Pathmark Stores	S. Marce Fuller	Mirant
Janet Robinson	*The New York Times*	Shelly Lazarus	Olgilvy & Mather
Kathleen Ligocki	Tower Automotive	Stephanie Streeter	Banta
Marion Sandler	Golden West Financial Corp.	Susan Ivey	Reynolds American

Boy Names

CEO	Company	CEO	Company
Alan Lafley	Procter and Gamble	Edward Rust Jr.	State Farm Insurance Companies
Aldo Zucaro	Old Republic International	Elden Smith	Fleetwood Enterprises
Antonio Perez	Eastman Kodak Co.	Eli Harari	SanDisk
August Busch	Anheuser-Busch	Francisco D'Souza	Cognizant Technology Solutions
Bernard Poussot	Wyeth	G. Richard Wagoner Jr.	General Motors
Bharat Masrani	Commerce Bancorp		
Blake Nordstrom	Nordstrom	Gabriel Tirador	Mercury General
Burke Whitman	Health Management Associates	H. Lee Scott	Wal-Mart Stores
Burton Tansky	Neiman Marcus	Harris DeLoach Jr.	Sonoco Products
Claiborne Deming	Murphy Oil	Henri Termeer	Genzyme
Clarence Otis	Darden Restaurants	Heywood Wilansky	Retail Ventures
Dale Wolf	Coventry Health Care	Jay Fishman	St. Paul Travelers Cos.
Dinesh Paliwal	Harman International Industries		

CEO	Company	CEO	Company
Jeffrey Immelt	General Electric	Rex Tillerson	Exxon Mobil
Jose Maria Alapont	Federal-Mogul	Robert Iger	Disney
		Samuel Palmisano	IBM
Kelcy Warren	Energy Transfer Equity	Seymour Sternberg	New York Life Insurance
Kendall Powell	General Mills	Sherrill Hudson	TECO Energy
Kenneth Chenault	American Express	Steven Ballmer	Microsoft
Kent Thiry	DaVita	Theodore Solso	Cummins
Lew Frankfort	Coach	Vikram Pandit	Citigroup
Marijn Dekkers	Thermo Electron	Warren Buffett	Berkshire Hathaway
Mark Hurd	Hewlett-Packard	Wendell Weeks	Corning
Myron Ullman	J.C. Penney	Wesley von Schack	Energy East
Nolan Archibald	Black and Decker	William Perez	William Wrigley Jr.
Phillippe Dauman	Viacom	Zev Weiss	American Greetings
Rajiv Gupta	Rohm and Haas		

Entrepreneurs

Girl Names

Entrepreneur	Company/Industry	Entrepreneur	Company/Industry
Anita Roddick	The Body Shop	Lillian Vernon	Lillian Vernon
Betsey Johnson	Betsey Johnson	Liz Lange	Liz Lange Maternity
Coco Chanel	Chanel		
Debbi Fields Rose	Mrs. Fields	Martha Stewart	Martha Stewart Living Omnimedia
Donna Karan	Donna Karan Corp.		
Estée Lauder	Estée Lauder	Mary Kay Ash	Mary Kay Cosmetics
Jenny Craig	Jenny Craig International	Oprah Winfrey	Harpo, Inc.
		Rachel Ashwell	Shabby Chic
Josie Natori	Natori Lingerie	Vera Wang	Vera Wang
Kimora Lee Simmons	Baby Phat		

Entrepreneurs

Boy Names

Entrepreneur	Company/Industry	Entrepreneur	Company/Industry
Andrew Carnegie	Steel industry	Ray Kroc	McDonald's
Donald Burr	People Express	Richard Branson	Virgin
George Lucas	Lucasfilm Ltd.	Sam Walton	Wal-Mart
Howard Schultz	Starbucks	Sean "P. Diddy" Combs	Sean Jean
Jeff Bezos	Amazon.com		
Jerry Yang	Yahoo!	Steve Jobs	Apple Computer
Leon Leonwood "L.L." Bean	L.L. Bean	Sumner Redstone	Viacom
		Ted Turner	Turner Broadcasting
Michael Dell	Dell Computer		
Milton Hershey	Hershey's	Walt Disney	The Walt Disney Co.
Paul Allen	Microsoft	Will Keith Kellogg	Kellogg's
Pierre Omidyar	eBay		

Heirs and Heiresses

Girl Names

Name	Relationship
Aerin Lauder	Granddaughter of cosmetic maven Estée Lauder
Amanda Hearst	Great-granddaughter of publishing legend William Randolph Hearst
Anna Anisimova	Daughter of Russian metals businessman Vassily Anisimov
Dylan Lauren	Daughter of fashion designer Ralph Lauren
Georgina Bloomberg	Daughter of New York City mayor and entrepreneur Michael Bloomberg
Ivanka Trump	Daughter of real estate mogul Donald Trump
Julia Louis-Dreyfus	Daughter of French billionaire Gerard Louis-Dreyfus
Lydia Hearst-Shaw	Great-granddaughter of publishing legend William Randolph Hearst
Nicky Hilton	Family owns Hilton hotels
Paris Hilton	Family owns Hilton hotels

Boy Names

Name	Relationship
Aditya Mittal	Son of Lakshmi Mittal (of steel firm Arcelor Mittal), the fourth-richest person in the world
Barron Hilton	Family owns Hilton hotels
Brandon Davis	Grandson of oil magnate Marvin Davis
David Lauren	Son of designer Ralph Lauren
Fabian Basabe	Son of Ecuadorian businessman and Martina Borgomanero, heiress to La Perla lingerie
James Murdoch	Son of media mogul Rupert Murdoch
Jamie Johnson	Great-grandson of Johnson & Johnson founder
Jeffrey Jordan	Son of basketball great Michael Jordan
John Elkann	Grandson of automaker Gianni Agnelli
Sam Branson	Son of Virgin Airlines owner Sir Richard Branson
Stavros Niarchos III	Grandson of shipping tycoon Stavros Niarchos

Brand Names

Girl Names

Name	Product	Name	Product	Name	Product
Alize	Fruity wine	Cristal	Champagne	L'Oréal	Cosmetics
Armani	Fashion designer	Dakota	Truck	Lexus	Car
		Dannon	Yogurt	Melitta	Coffee filter
Breck	Shampoo	Delta	Airline	Mercedes	Car
Cambria	Car	Dior	Fashion designer	Meridian	Phone products
Camry	Car				
Catera	Car	Eternity	Perfume	Nautica	Clothing
Celica	Car	Evian	Water	Nivea	Skin cream
Chanel	Fashion designer	Fanta	Soft drink	Porsche	Car
		Halston	Fashion designer	Shasta	Soda
Chloe	Perfume			Skyy	Vodka
Clinique	Cosmetics	Infiniti	Car	Tiffany	Jewelery

Brand Names

Boy Names

Name	Product	Name	Product
Acura	Car	Guinness	Beer
Armani	Fashion designer	Harley	Motorcycle
Avis	Car rental	Hennessy	Liqueur
Baxter	Health care	Hyatt	Hotel
Canon	Camera	Ikea	Furniture
Cartier	Jewelery	Jaguar	Car
Corvette	Car	Jameson	Whiskey
Courvoisier	Liqueur	Killian	Beer
Delmonte	Fruits and vegetables	Ronrico	Rum
Denim	Cologne	Skyy	Vodka
Disney	Corporation	Stetson	Cologne
Elgin	Watch	Timberland	Shoes
Ford	Car		

Political Names

You might relate to a famous leader from the past, be it a president, world leader, or an activist. If you're thinking of honoring someone political by naming your child after him or her, this is the chapter to check out.

The lists in this chapter open up a world of possibilities for baby names, from president and first lady names to the names of their children. Names of peacemakers and patriots are also featured in this historical, politically active chapter.

World Leaders, Past and Present

Girl Names

Leader	Title	Country
Adrienne Clarkson	Governor-General	Canada
Angela Merkel	Chancellor	Germany
Benazir Bhutto	Prime Minister	Pakistan
Cristina Fernandez de Kirchner	President	Argentina
Gloria Macapagal-Arroyo	President	Philippines
Golda Meir	Prime Minister	Israel
Gro Harlem Brundtland	Prime Minister	Norway
Helen Clark	Prime Minister	New Zealand
Indira Gandhi	Prime Minister	India
Ivy Dumont	Governor-General	The Bahamas
Khaleda Zia	Prime Minister	Bangladesh
Lidia Gueiler	Prime Minister	Bolivia
Margaret Thatcher	Prime Minister	United Kingdom
Mary Eugenia Charles	Prime Minister	Dominica
Mary McAleese	President	Ireland
Mary Robinson	President	Ireland
Megawati Sukarnoputri	President	Indonesia
Michaëlle Jean	Governor-General	Canada
Michelle Bachelet	President	Chile
Pearlette Louisy	Governor-General	Saint Lucia
Tarja Halonen	President	Finland
Vaira Vike-Freiberga	President	Latvia
Vigdis Finnbogadottir	President	Iceland
Violeta Barrios de Chamorro	President	Nicaragua

Boy Names

Leader	Title	Country
Abel Pacheco	President	Costa Rica
Adolf Hitler	Chancellor	Germany
Alfredo Palacio	President	Ecuador

Leader	Title	Country
Ariel Sharon	Prime Minister	Israel
Charlemagne	Emperor	Europe
Colville Young	Governor-General	Belize
Felipe Calderón	President	Mexico
Festus Mogae	President	Botswana
Hamid Karzai	President	Afghanistan
Heinz Fischer	President	Austria
Horst Koehler	President	Germany
Hugo Chavez	President	Venezuela
Jacques Chirac	President	France
Jintao Hu	President	China
Junichiro Koizumi	Prime Minister	Japan
Karolos Papoulias	President	Greece
Leonel Fernandez	President	Dominican Republic
Macky Sall	Prime Minister	Senegal
Manmohan Singh	Prime Minister	India
Martin Torrijos	President	Panama
Michael Jeffery	Governor-General	Australia
Nestor Kirchner	President	Argentina
Nicolas Sarkozy	President	France
Nuri al-Maliki	Prime Minister	Iraq
Omar Karami	Prime Minister	Lebanon
Patrick Manning	Prime Minister	Trinidad and Tobago
Paul Biya	President	Cameroon
Ricardo Lagos	President	Chile
Samuel Schmid	President	Switzerland
Silvio Berlusconi	Prime Minister	Italy
Soe Win	Prime Minister	Burma
Thabo Mbeki	President	South Africa
Tony Blair	Prime Minister	United Kingdom
Vaclav Klaus	President	Czech Republic
Vicente Fox	President	Mexico
Viktor Yushchenko	President	Ukraine
Vladimir Putin	President	Russia
Winston Churchill	Prime Minister	United Kingdom

Kings and Queens

Girl Names

Queen	Title	Country	Queen	Title	Country
Anne	Queen	England	Julianna	Queen	Netherlands
Beatrix	Queen	Netherlands	Margaret of Anjou	Queen	England
Catherine of Aragon	Queen	England	Margrethe II	Queen	Denmark
Cleopatra	Queen	Egypt	Mary	Queen	England
Elizabeth I	Queen	England	Matilda	Queen	England
Emma	Queen	Hawaii	Nefertiti	Queen	Kemet (Ancient Egypt)
Henrietta Maria	Queen	England			
Jane Grey	Queen	England	Victoria	Queen	England

Boy Names

King	Title	Country	King	Title	Country
Alfred the Great	King	England	George Augustus	King	England
Athelstan	King	England	Hardicanute	King	England, Denmark
Canute the Dane	King	England	Harold	King	England
Charles (1st)	King	England	Henry	King	England
Eadred	King	England	Ina	King of the West Saxons	England
Eadwig	King	England			
Edgar	King	Scotland	James	King	England
Edmund	King	England	John	King	England
Edward	King	England	Malcolm III	King	Scotland
Egbert	King of Wessex	England	Moshoeshoe	King	Present-day Lesotho
Ethelbert	King of Kent	England			
Ethelwolf	King	England	Offa	King of Mercia	England
Edwin	King of Northumbria	England	Oswald	King of Northumbria	England

King	Title	Country	King	Title	Country
Penda	King of Mercia	England	Stephen	King	England
Rama	King of Ayodhya	India	Sven	King	Denmark
Richard	King	England	William	King	England, Ireland, Scotland

Princes and Princesses

Girl Names

Princess	Country	Princess	Country
Alexandra	England, Denmark	Isabella	France, Denmark
Alexia	Netherlands	Marie-Christine von Reibnitz	England
Amalia	Netherlands	Mary	Denmark
Anne Elizabeth Alice Louise	England	Michael	England
Ariane	Netherlands	Philomela	Greece
Beatrice Elizabeth Mary	England	Roxanne	Azerbaijan
Diana Frances Spencer	England	Saisha	India
Eugenie Victoria Helena	England	Victoria	Sweden
		Zara	England

Boy Names

Prince	Country	Prince	Country
Albert	England	Frederik	Denmark
Andrew	England	George	Canada
Charles Philip Arthur George	England	Henry Charles Albert Davis	England
Christian	Denmark	Philip	Scotland
Edward	England	Richard	England
Felipe	Asturias/ Spain	William Arthur Philip Louis	England

Dukes, Duchesses, and Other Royalty

Girl Names

Royalty	Title	Country
Alexandra Feodorovna	Empress	Russia
Anastasia Romanov	Grand Duchess	Russia
Birgitte Eva van Deurs	Duchess of Gloucester	England
Camilla Rosemary Shand	Duchess of Cornwall	England
Candace	Empress	Ethiopia
Maria-Feodorovna	Empress	Russia
Olga Nicholaevna Romanova	Grand Duchess	Russia
Sarah Ferguson	Duchess of York	England
Sophia August Frederika	Empress Catherine II ("Catherine the Great")	Russia
Sophie Rhys-Jones	Countess of Wessex	England
Tatiana Romanov	Grand Duchess	Russia

Boy Names

Royalty	Title	Country
Aleksey Romanov	Tsar	Russia
Alexander	Emperor	Russia
Angus Ogilvy	Earl of Airlie	England
Augustus Henry Fitzroy	Duke of Grafton	England
Edward Anthony Richard Lewis	Earl of Wessex	England
Frederick "Lord North"	Earl of Guildford	England
Godwin	Earl of Kent	England
Piers Gaveston	Earl of Cornwall	England
Richard Alexander Walter George	Duke of Gloucester	England
Simon de Montfort	4th Count Earl of Liecester	England

U.S. Presidents

Girl Names

Not applicable.

Boy Names

Abraham Lincoln

Andrew Jackson

Andrew Johnson

Barack Obama

Benjamin Harrison

Calvin Coolidge

Chester Arthur

Dwight Eisenhower

Franklin Pierce

Franklin Roosevelt

George Herbert Walker Bush

George Walker Bush

George Washington

Gerald Ford

Grover Cleveland

Harry S. Truman

Herbert Hoover

Hiram Ulysses S. Grant

James Buchanan

James Garfield

James Madison

James Monroe

James Polk

Jimmy Carter

John Adams

John Fitzgerald Kennedy

John Quincy Adams

John Tyler

Lyndon Baines Johnson

Martin van Buren

Millard Fillmore

Richard Nixon

Ronald Reagan

Rutherford Birchard Hayes

Theodore Roosevelt

Thomas Jefferson

Warren Harding

William Jefferson Clinton

William Henry Harrison

William Howard Taft

William McKinley

Woodrow Wilson

Zachary Taylor

First Ladies

Girl Names

Abigail Powers Fillmore

Abigail Smith Adams

Anna Eleanor Roosevelt

Anna Tuthill Symmes Harrison

Barbara Pierce Bush

Caroline Lavinia Scott Harrison

Claudia "Lady Bird" Taylor Johnson

Dolley Payne Todd Madison

Edith Bolling Galt Wilson

Edith Kermit Carow Roosevelt

Eleanor Rosalynn Smith Carter

Eliza McCardle Johnson

Elizabeth "Bess" Virginia Wallace Truman

Elizabeth "Betty" Bloomer Warren Ford

Elizabeth "Eliza" Kortright Monroe

Ellen Lewis Herndon Arthur

Florence Kling DeWolf Harding

Frances Folsom Cleveland

Grace Anna Goodhew Coolidge

Hannah Hoes van Buren

Helen Herron Taft

Hillary Rodham Clinton

Ida Saxton McKinley

Jacqueline Lee Bouvier Kennedy

Jane Means Appleton Pierce

Julia Dent Grant

Julia Gardiner Tyler

Laura Welch Bush

continues

First Ladies continued

Girl Names

Lou Henry Hoover

Louisa Catherine Johnson Adams

Lucretia Rudolph Garfield

Lucy Ware Webb Hayes

Margaret Mackall Smith Taylor

Martha Dandridge Custis Washington

Martha Wayles Skelton Jefferson

Mary "Mamie" Geneva Doud Eisenhower

Mary Todd Lincoln

Michelle LaVaugh Robinson Obama

Nancy Davis Reagan

Rachel Donelson Robards Jackson

Sarah Childress Polk

Thelma Patricia "Pat" Catherine Ryan Nixon

Boy Names

Not applicable.

Presidents' Kids

Girl Names

First Kid	Father
Abigail "Nabby" Adams Smith	John Adams
Alice Lee Roosevelt Longworth	Theodore Roosevelt
Amy Carter Wentzel	James Carter Jr.
Anna Tuthill Harrison Taylor	William Henry Harrison
Anne Margaret Mackall Taylor Wood	Zachary Taylor
Barbara Pierce Bush	George W. Bush
Caroline Kennedy Schlossberg	John F. Kennedy
Chelsea Victoria Clinton	William Clinton
Dorothy "Doro" Bush Koch	George Herbert Walker Bush
Eleanor "Nellie" Randolph Wilson McAdoo	Woodrow Wilson
Eliza Arabella "Trot" Garfield	James A. Garfield
Elizabeth "Lizzie" Tyler Waller	John Tyler
Ellen Wrenshall "Nellie" Grant Sartoris Jones	Ulysses S. Grant
Esther Cleveland Bosanquet	Grover Cleveland
Ethel Carow Roosevelt Derby	Theodore Roosevelt
Fanny Hayes Smith	Rutherford B. Hayes
Helen Herron Taft Manning	William Howard Taft

First Kid	Father
Ida McKinley	William McKinley
Jane Randolph Jefferson	Thomas Jefferson
Jenna Welch Bush	George W. Bush
Jessie Woodrow Wilson Sayre	Woodrow Wilson
Julia Tyler Spencer	John Tyler
Julie Nixon Eisenhower	Richard M. Nixon
Katherine "Katie" McKinley	William McKinley
Letitia (Letty) Tyler Semple	John Tyler
Louisa Catherine Adams	John Quincy Adams
Luci Baines Johnson Turpin	Lyndon Baines Johnson
Lucy Elizabeth Jefferson	Thomas Jefferson
Lynda Bird Johnson Robb	Lyndon Baines Johnson
Malia Ann Obama	Barack Obama
Maria Hester Monroe Gouverneur	James Monroe
Margaret Woodrow Wilson	Woodrow Wilson
Martha "Patsy" Parke Custis	George Washington
Mary Abigail "Abby" Fillmore	Millard Fillmore
Maureen Reagan Revell	Ronald Reagan
Natasha "Sasha" Obama	Barack Obama
Octavia Pannel Taylor	Zachary Taylor
Patricia "Patti Davis" Ann Reagan	Ronald Reagan
Pauline Robinson "Robin" Bush	George Herbert Walker Bush
Pearl Tyler Ellis	John Tyler
Ruth Cleveland	Grover Cleveland
Sarah Knox Taylor Davis	Zachary Taylor
Susan Ford Vance Bales	Gerald Ford
Susanna Adams	John Adams
Tricia Nixon Cox	Richard M. Nixon

Boy Names

First Kid	Father
Abraham van Buren	Martin van Buren
Abram Garfield	James A. Garfield
Allan Henry Hoover	Herbert Clark Hoover
Andrew Jackson Jr.	Andrew Jackson

continues

Presidents' Kids continued

Boy Names

First Kid	Father
Archibald "Archie" Bulloch Roosevelt	Theodore Roosevelt
Benjamin Pierce	Franklin Pierce
Birchard Austin Hayes	Rutherford B. Hayes
Calvin Coolidge Jr.	Calvin Coolidge
Carter Bassett Harrison	William Henry Harrison
Charles Adams	John Adams
David Gardiner "Gardie" Tyler	John Tyler
Donnell Jeffrey "Jeff" Carter	James Carter Jr.
Doud Dwight "Ikky" Eisenhower	Dwight D. Eisenhower
Edward Baker "Eddie" Lincoln	Abraham Lincoln
Elliott Roosevelt	Franklin Delano Roosevelt
Eugene Marshall "Pete" DeWolfe	Warren G. Harding
Francis Grover Cleveland	Grover Cleveland
Frank Robert Pierce	Franklin Pierce
Franklin Roosevelt	Franklin Delano Roosevelt
Fredrick Dent Grant	Ulysses S. Grant
George Washington Adams	John Quincy Adams
Harry Augustus "Hal" Garfield	James A. Garfield
Herbert Hoover Jr.	Herbert Clark Hoover
Irvin McDowell Garfield	James A. Garfield
James Earl "Chip" Carter III	James Carter Jr.
James Rudolf Garfield	James A. Garfield
Jesse Root Grant	Ulysses S. Grant
John Alexander "Alex" Tyler	John Tyler
Kermit Roosevelt	Theodore Roosevelt
Lachlan Tyler	John Tyler
Lyon Gardiner Tyler	John Tyler
Manning Force Hayes	Rutherford B. Hayes
Marion Cleveland Dell Amen	Grover Cleveland
Marshall Polk	James K. Polk
Martin Van Buren Jr.	Martin Van Buren
Marvin Pierce Bush	George H. W. Bush
Michael Gerald Ford	Gerald Ford
Millard Powers Fillmore	Millard Fillmore

First Kid	Father
Neil Mallon Bush	George H. W. Bush
Oscar Folsom Cleveland	Grover Cleveland
Patrick Bouvier Kennedy	John F. Kennedy
Quentin Roosevelt	Theodore Roosevelt
Richard Folsom "Dick" Cleveland	Grover Cleveland
Robert Alphonso Taft	William Howard Taft
Ronald Prescott Reagan	Ronald Reagan
Russell Benjamin Harrison	Benjamin Harrison
Rutherford Platt Hayes	Rutherford B. Hayes
Smith Thompson van Buren	Martin van Buren
Steven Meigs Ford	Gerald Ford
Tazewell Tyler	John Tyler
Theodore "Ted" Roosevelt Jr.	Theodore Roosevelt
Thomas Boylston Adams	John Adams
Ulysses Simpson "Buck" Grant Jr.	Ulysses S. Grant
William Henry Harrison Jr.	William Henry Harrison
William Lewis Arthur Chester	Alan Arthur

Patriots/Military Leaders

Girl Names

Abigail Adams	Betsy Ross	Martha Washington	Mercy Otis-Warren
Anna Comnena	Deborah Sampson		Phillis Wheatley

Boy Names

Ben Franklin	George Washington	John Adams	Stonewall Jackson
Colin Powell		Nelson Mandela	Thomas Jefferson
David Petraeus	H. Norman Schwarzkopf	Patrick Henry	William Fallon

Warriors

Girl Names

Eleanor of Castile	Hippolyte	Thyra, Queen of Denmark
Emma, Countess of Norfolk	Marguerite de Provence	Xianthippe

Warriors

Boy Names

Atilla the Hun   Vernon Baker   William Carney

Peacemakers

Girl Names

Peacemaker	Area of Work	Peacemaker	Area of Work
Alva Myrdal	Sweden	Jody Williams	International Campaign to Ban Landmines
Aung San Suu Kyi	Burma		
Bertha von Suttner	Austria		
Betty Williams	United Kingdom	Kathy Kelly	United States
		Mairead Corrigan	Northern Ireland
Emily Balch	United States		
Helen Caldicott	Australia	Mother Teresa	India
Jane Addams	United States	Rigoberta Menchu Tum	Guatemala
Jane Hamilton-Merritt (Dr.)	United States	Shirin Ebadi	Iran
		Wangari Maathai	Kenya

Boy Names

Peacemaker	Area of Work	Peacemaker	Area of Work
Abuna Elias Chacour	Israel	David Trimble	Northern Ireland
Adolfo Perez Esquivel	Argentina		
Albert Lutuli	South Africa	Desmond Tutu	South Africa
Alfonso Garcia Robles	Mexico	Elie Wiesel	United States
Andrei Sakharov	USSR	Elihu Root	United States
Aristide Briand	France	Elisaku Sato	Japan
Carlos Filipe Belo (Archbishop)	East Timor	Gerson Perez	Colombia
		Henry Kissinger	United States
Cordell Hull	United States	Jimmy Carter	United States
Craig Kielburger	United States	Jose Ramos Horta	East Timor
Dag Hammarskjold	Sweden	Joseph Rotblat	Canada

Peacemaker	Area of Work	Peacemaker	Area of Work
Kim Dae-jung	South Korea	Nelson Mandela	South Africa
Kofi Annan	United Nations	Norman Borlaug	United States
		Oscar Arias Sanchez	Costa Rica
Lars Olaf Soderblom	Sweden	Ralph Bunche	United States
Lech Walesa	Poland	Rene Cassin	France
Leon Jouhaux	France		
		Sean MacBride	Ireland
Linus Pauling	United States	Shimon Peres	Israel
Mahatma Ghandi	India		
		Tenzin Gyatso	Tibet
Martin Luther King Jr.	United States	(Dalai Lama)	
Menachem Begin	Israel	Tobias Asser	Netherlands
Michael Scharf	United States	Willy Brandt	Germany
Mikhail Gorbachev	Russia	Yasser Arafat	Palestine
Mohamed Anwar al-Sadat	Egypt	Yitzhak Rabin	Israel

Black History/Civil Rights Leaders

Girl Names

Bessie Coleman	Eliza Bryant	Mary McLeod Bethune
Biddy Mason	Ella Fitzgerald	Maya Angelou
Billie Holiday	Fannie Lou Hamer	Rita Dove
Cathay Williams	Harriet Tubman	Rosa Parks
Charlotte Forten Grimke	Ida Wells Barnett	Sally Hemings
Diana Fletcher	Josephine Baker	Sojourner Truth
Dorothy Dandridge	Mahalia Jackson	Susan McKinney
Edmonia Lewis	Marian Anderson	Zelma Watson George

Boy Names

Asa Philip Randolph	Ernest Just	Jesse Owens
Benjamin Banneker	Erroll Garner	Jim Beckwourth
Carter Woodson	Eubie Blake	Jim Crow
Charles Drew	Frederick Douglass	Langston Hughes
Duke Ellington	George Washington Carver	Louis Armstrong
Eldridge Cleaver		

continues

Black History/Civil Rights Leaders continued

Boy Names

Louis Farrakhan	Nat "King" Cole	Scott Joplin
Malcolm X	Paul Laurence Dunbar	Thelonious Monk
Marcus Garvey	Percy Lavon Julian	Whitney Moore Young
Martin Luther King Jr.	Ralph Bunche	William Edward Burghardt (W. E. B.) DuBois
Matthew Henson	Salem Poor	

Activists

Girl Names

Name	Cause	Name	Cause
Heather Mills	Anti–land mines	Kaisha Atakhanova	Nuclear waste reform
Jane Akre	Milk safety		
Julia Bonds	Anti–mountaintop removal mining	Melissa Poe	Clean environment
		Stephanie Roth	Anti–gold mining in Romania

Boy Names

Name	Cause	Name	Cause
Adam Werbach	Conservationist	John Corkill	Environmental
Corneiele Ewango	Environmental protection	Jose Andres Cortez (Father)	Environmental
Dailan Pugh	Environmental	Peter Rawlinson	Forests
Isidro Baldenegro Lopez	Forestry reform activist	Robert Hunter	Eco-crusader
		Steve Wilson	Milk safety

Scientific Suggestions

If science is your thing, or you'd like your little one to be inspired by the subject, the following lists should generate some ideas. In these pages, you'll find world-renowned scientists, celebrated inventors, and scientists who shoot for the stars—astronauts and pilots, that is.

Whether you hope your baby will make a mark on history or you'd like to honor someone in the scientific community who already has, the lists in this chapter are sure to provide some suggestions.

Scientists

Girl Names

Name	Science	Time Period
Anna Atkins	Botany	1799–1871
Augusta Lovelace	Inventor of early computer	1815–1852
Caroline Herschel	Discovered comet	1750–1848
Celia Borromeo	Natural philosopher	Middle Ages
Clemence Royer	Encyclopedist	1830–?
Cornelia Clapp	Zoology	1849–1934
Dorotea Bucca	Physician	Middle Ages
Eliza Pinckney	Agriculture	1723–1766
Emilie de Breteuil	Physicist	1706–1749
Florence Nightingale	Nurse statistician	1820–1910
Georgia Rooks	Physician	20th century
Grace Hopper	Mathematician	1906–1992
Henrietta Leavitt	Astronomer	1868–1921
Hertha Ayrton	Physicist	1854–1923
Ida Tacke	Physicist	20th century
Josephine Kablick	Botanist	18th century
Kate Gleason	Engineer	1865–1933
Laura Bassi	Physicist	1711–1778
Lise Meitner	Physicist	1878–1968
Lucy Hobbs Taylor	Dentist	1833–1910
Martha Logan	Horticulturist	1702–1779
Maud Menten	Biologist	20th century
Nettie Stevens	Biologist	1861–1912
Nor Mahal	Inventor	17th century
Olive Beech	Aviation	1920–1986
Patsy Sherman	Inventor	20th century
Rosalind Franklin	Chemist	1920–1957
Sadie Delany	Home economics	1891–1999
Sethanne Howard	Astronomer	1944–
Sophia Brahe	Astronomer	1556–1643
Themista	Natural philosopher	Ancient Greece
Williamina Fleming	Astronomer	1857–1911

Boy Names

Name	Science	Time Period
Albert Einstein	Father of modern science	1879–1955
Alessandro Volta	Battery inventor	1745–1827
Amedeo Avogadro	Chemist	1776–1856
Blaise Pascal	Mathematician	1623–1662
Carl Sagan	Astronomer	1934–1996
Christiaan Huygens	Mathematician	1629–1695
Daniel Bernoulli	Mathematician	1700–1782
Edme Mariotte	Physicist	1620–1684
Ernst Haeckel	Biologist	1843–1919
Evangelista Torricelli	Physicist	1608–1647
Francis Crick	Molecular biologist	1916–2004
Friedrich Wohler	Chemist	1800–1882
Galileo Galilei	Astronomer	1564–1642
Giovanni Venturi	Physicist	1745–1822
Gregor Mendel	Anthropologist	1822–1884
Gustav Hertz	Physicist	1887–1975
Hannes Olof Alfven	Physicist	1908–1995
Humphry Davy	Chemist	1778–1829
Isaac Newton	Mathematician and physicist	1642–1727
Jacques Charles	Aeronaut	1746–1823
Johannes Kepler	Astronomer	1571–1630
Konrad Lorenz	Ethologist	1903–1989
Leonardo da Vinci	Artist and engineer	1452–1519
Max Planck	Physicist	1858–1947
Nicolas Copernicus	Astronomer	1473–1543
Nikola Tesla	Inventor	1856–1943
Niels Bohr	Physicist	1885–1962
Pierre Curie	Radiologist	1859–1906
René Descartes	Mathematician	1596–1650
Stephen Hawking	Physicist	1942–
Thomas Edison	Inventor	1847–1931
Tycho Brahe	Astronomer	1546–1601
Wilhelm Roentgen	Physicist	1845–1923

Inventors and Discoverers

Girl Names

Inventor	Invention/Discovery	Inventor	Invention/Discovery
Alice Parker	Gas furnace	Lillian Russell	Dresser trunk
Ann Moore	Snugli baby carrier	Margaret Knight	Flat-bottom bags
Anna Keichline	Combined sink and washtub; first female architect	Marion Donovan	Disposable diapers
		Marjorie Joyner	Permanent hair-styling system
Barbara Askins	Film processing system	Martha Coston	Signal flares
		Mary Dixon Kies	Weaving process
Bette Graham	Liquid Paper	Mary Phelps Jacob	Bra
Beulah Henry	Bobbinless sewing machine	Patricia Bath	Medical improvement
Carol Wior	Slimming swimsuit		
Frances Gabe	Self-cleaning house	Patsy Sherman	Scotchgard
Gertrude Elion	Leukemia-fighting drug	Ruth Handler	Barbie doll
		Sarah Boone	Ironing board improvement
Grace Hopper	Computing improvements	Stephanie Kwolek	Kevlar
Harriet Tracy	Safety elevator	Sybilla Masters	Corn mill
Josephine Cochran	Dishwasher	Virginia Apgar	Newborn screening system
Julie Newmar	Ultra-sheer pantyhose		

Boy Names

Inventor	Invention/Discovery	Inventor	Invention/Discovery
Albert Einstein	Theory of relativity	Earle Dickson	Band-Aids
Alexander Graham Bell	Telephone	Edwin Land	Polaroid photography
Art Fry	Post-it Notes	Elias Howe	Sewing machine
Benjamin Rubin	Vaccination needle	Galileo Galilei	Planets revolve around sun
Carl Sontheimer	Cuisinart		
Chester Carlson	Photocopying	George Washington Carver	Peanut butter; agriculture improvements
Clarence Birdseye	Commercial frozen food		

Inventor	Invention/ Discovery	Inventor	Invention/ Discovery
Henry Ford	Assembly line auto production	Ole Evinrude	Outboard motor
		Percy Spencer	Microwave oven
Sir Isaac Newton	Telescope; the three laws of physics	Pierre Lorillard	Tuxedo
		Ralph Samuelson	Waterskiing
Jerome Lemelson	Bar code readers; cassette players	Samuel Morse	Telegraph
Johannes Gutenberg	Moveable type	Schulyer Wheeler	Electric fan
		Thomas Edison	Phonograph
Jonas Salk	Polio vaccine	Tim Berners-Lee	World Wide Web
Levi Strauss	Blue jeans	Walt Disney	Feature-length animated films
Louis Pasteur	Discovered germs; pasteurization process	Whitcomb Judson	Early zipper
Martin Cooper	Modern cell phone	Willis Carrier	Air conditioning

Sky-High Names—Astronauts and Aviators

Girl Names

Agnes Firth	Ellen Baker	Kathryn Sullivan	Pamela Melroy
Amelia Earhart	Ellen Ochoa	Laurel Clark	Peggy Whitson
Amelie Beese	Enid Hibbard	Leda Richberg Hornsby	Roberta Bondar
Anna Fisher	Ester Vietta		Rosina Ferrario
Bessie Coleman	Eugenia Shakhovskaya	Lydia V. Zvereva	Sally Ride
Bonnie Dunbar		Mae Jemison	Sandra Magnus
Catherine Coleman	Florence Seidel	Margaret Rhea Seddon	Shannon Lucid
	Helen Sharman		Susan Kilrain
Cheridah de Beauvoir Stocks	Helene Dutrieu	Marie Marvingt	Suzanne Bernard
	Hilda Beatrice Hewlitt	Marie-Louise Driancourt	Tamara Jernigan
Christa McAuliffe		Marsha Ivins	Valentina Tereshkova
Claudie Haignere	Jeanne Herveux	Mary Cleave	
E. Lilian Todd	Julia Clark	Nancy Currie	Willa Beatrice Brown
Eileen Collins	Kalpana Chawla		

Sky-High Names—Astronauts and Aviators

Boy Names

Alan Shepard

Arch Hoxsey

Armstrong Drexel

Bentfield Hucks

Bernard Harris Jr.

Beryl Williams

Bill Anders

Bruce McCandless

Buzz Aldrin

Calbraith Rodgers

Chauncy Vought

Curtis Brown

Dale Gardner

David Scott

Dirk Frimont

Donn Eisele

Duane Carey

Emile Dubonnet

Frank Borman

Franklin Chang-Diaz

Fred Haise

Guion Bluford

Gus Grissom

Hans Grade

Hubert Latham

James Irwin

Jerome Apt

Jerry Ross

Jim Lovell

Joe Walker

John Glenn

John Swigert

Jules Vedrines

Ladis Lewkowicz

Leroy Gordon Cooper

Loren Acton

Max Lillie

Michael Anderson

Neil Armstrong

Norman Thagard

Orville Wright

Osbert Edwin Williams

Otto Brodie

Owen Garriott

Patrick Baudry

Pete Conrad

Raymond Saulnier

Rene Barrier

Rexford Smith

Rick Husband

Ronald McNair

Silas Christofferson

St. Croix Johnstone

Story Musgrave

Taylor Wang

Wally Schirra

Weldon Cooke

Wilbur Wright

Pure and Natural Possibilities

For parents who want their child to be in touch with the earth, the planet, and its ultimate possibility, the lists in this chapter offer name choices from the world in which we live—from the stars and planets that hover above us to the mountains, valleys, rivers, and lakes that make up the world's geography.

If you want your child's name to embrace the minerals, jewels, and gems mined from the earth's surface, you'll find lists of those names here as well. Names for flowers, fruits, animals, and colors also abound. If you're looking for a name that speaks to your connection to the earth, you're sure to find something here.

Stars and Planets

Girl Names

Adhara	Cassiopeia	Jana	Rishima
Amaris	Celine	Luna	Shaula
Andromeda	Chandrama	Moon	Soleil
Antlia	Columba	Nokomis	Tainn
Apus	Dyan	Norma	Vega
Ara	Hina	Polaris	Venus
Badriya	Hydra	Rigel	Virgo
Bellatrix	Indu		

Boy Names

Altair	Centaurus	Leo	Procyon
Antares	Cepheus	Lupus	Regulus
Aquarius	Cetus	Mars	Sagittarius
Aquila	Charon	Mercury	Saturn
Arcturus	Circinus	Orion	Shivendu
Aries	Corvus	Pavo	Sirius
Auriga	Cygnus	Pegasus	Som
Bootes	Draco	Perseus	Sun
Caelum	Eridanus	Phoenix	Taurus
Cancer	Hadar	Pluto	Uranus
Capricornus	Hydrus	Pollux	Vikesh
Castor			

Mountains and Valleys

Girl Names

Aase	Dale	Denver	Glyn
Alba	Dallon	Elam	Hallam
Ashland	Deanna	Gayora	Hollace
Aspen	Deena	Gelilah	Kalinda
Cyd	Deiondre	Glenna	Kendall

Kia	Marcy	Orea	Vail
Kiona	Montana	Peri	Whitney
Kiri	Odina	Sierra	Yama
Kirima	Olympia	Tarin	Zaltana
Madison			

Boy Names

Aaron	Clifford	Everest	Mitchell
Adams	Craig	Geordi	Montana
Alban	Crawford	Gibbes	Montego
Arlo	Cyd	Glen	Montenegro
Banagher	Dale	Hallam	Montgomery
Bartholomew	Dallon	Hamilton	Ogden
Belden	Dalton	Heaton	Orestes
Berg	Deiondre	Holden	Percival
Blackburn	Denver	Kendall	Rainier
Braden	Dix	Knox	Roden
Brent	Doane	Lamont	Sheldon
Buckley	Elam	Lincoln	Tarin
Camden	Elbert	McKinley	Vail

Lakes and Rivers

Girl Names

Afton	Hachi	Naiyah	Shannon
Arnon	Ivria	Narmada	Tamesis
Avon	Jamuna	Nile	Tanginika
Avonmora	Jordan	Nimiani	Tapati
Belisma	Kaveri	Ohio	Tarangini
Blaine	Lake	Rhea	Teleri
Carey	Laken	Riva	Triveni
Clodagh	Lindsay	Ryo	Tyne
Darya	Mallow	Sarita	Varana
Delta	Manda	Saryu	Yamuna
Guadalupe			

Lakes and Rivers

Boy Names

Afram	Chilton	Kelby	Ohio
Afton	Clifford	Kelvin	Orrin
Annan	Clyde	Lachlan	Redford
Arnon	Deverell	Laken	Rio
Avon	Douglas	Mallow	River
Avonmore	Ford	Mansfield	Romney
Ballinamore	George	Marland	Ryo
Blaine	Guadalupe	Max	Severin
Caldwell	Inis	Melborn	Tarik
Cameron	Jafar	Merton	Tiberius
Carlow	Jiang	Monroe	Tyne
Cary	Johnavon	Moses	Vytharana
Chad	Jordan	Niger	Wade

Jewels, Gems, and Minerals

Girl Names

Agate	Cameo	Garnet	Mauve
Alexandrite	Cara	Gemma	Moonstone Adularia
Allirea	Carnelian	Ghita	Moss Agate
Amethyst	Chalcedony	Goldie	Noire
Aquamarine	Cinnabar	Greta	Olivine
Auburn	Citrine	Hazel	Onyx
Azure	Coral	Heliotrope	Opal
Basalt	Crisiant	Iolite	Pearl
Beryl	Crystal	Ivory	Peridot
Biana	Cyanite	Jacinth	Prunella
Blanca	Diamond	Jade	Quartz
Blanche	Ebony	Jewel	Rose Quartz
Bloodstone	Emerald/	Lilac	Sapphire
Beryl	Emeraude	Madge	Sienna
Calcite	Fawn	Malachite	

Spodumene	Teal	Tourmaline	Violet
Tangerine	Topaz	Turquoise	Zoisite
Tawny			

Boy Names

Almas	Flint	Jet	Sterling
Bernstein	Geode	Mica	Stone
Bronze	Gold	Obsidian	Ulexite
Bruno	Indigo	Platinum	Yahto
Carnelian	Jasper	Slate	Zircon
Copper			

Birds and Animals

Girl Names

Name	Derivation/ Meaning	Name	Derivation/ Meaning
Alouette	Bird	Hinda	Female deer
Aqualina	Like an eagle	Jemima	Dove
Ariella	God's lioness	Jena	Little bird
Arva	Eagle	Kanara	Canary
Ava	Little bird	Lark	Skylark
Ayala	Deer	Leandra	Lion woman
Brena	Raven	Leona	Lioness
Brenda	Small raven	Loni	Lion
Bunny	Rabbit	Melissa	Honeybee
Calandra	Lark	Merle	Blackbird
Chenoa	White dove	Merlyn	Falcon
Columbine	Dove	Mink	Weasel
Danuta	Little deer	Orpah	Fawn
Deborah	Bee	Orsa	Female bear
Delphine	Dolphin	Paloma	Dove
Dorcas	Gazelle	Penelope	Duck
Fawn	Young deer	Rachel	Ewe

continues

Birds and Animals   continued

Girl Names

Name	Derivation/Meaning	Name	Derivation/Meaning
Raven	Blackbird	Una	Lamb
Robin	Bird	Ursula	Female bear
Rosalind	From word for horse	Ushi	Ox
Rosamond	From word for horse	Wren	Bird
Starling	Bird	Yona	Dove
Tabitha	Doe	Zera	Wolf
Teal	Water bird	Zippora	Bird

Boy Names

Name	Derivation/Meaning	Name	Derivation/Meaning
Adelard	Old eagles	Conall	Strong wolf
Adler	Eagle	Corbett	Raven
Adolphus	Noble wolf	Dolf	Noble wolf
Andor	Thundering eagle	Dov	Bear
Ari	Lion	Drake	Dragon
Aries	Ram	Dyani	Deer
Arno	Eagle-wolf	Eachan	Brown horse
Barend	Firm bear	Eden	Bear cub
Barrett	Bear strength	Falk	Falcon
Berend	Bearlike	Finch	Songbird
Bertram	Bright raven	Fox	Fox
Bram	Raven	Gawain	Battle hawk
Brock	Badger	Giles	Young goat
Bronco	Wild horse	Harshul	Deer
Buck	Male deer	Hart	Red deer
Castor	Beaver	Hawk	Bird
Colin	Young animal	Hawkins	Little hawk
Colt	Young horse	Herring	Small fish

Name	Derivation/Meaning	Name	Derivation/Meaning
Hershel	Deer	Raynard	Fox
Jackal	Wild dog	Reno	Reindeer
Jay	Jaybird	Rodolf	Famous wolf
Jonah	Dove	Roe	Small deer
Kaleb	Dog	Roebuck	Male deer
Leo	Lion	Roswald	Mighty horse
Lionel	Young lion	Rudi	Famous wolf
Lowell	Young wolf	Tahatan	Hawk
Merle	Blackbird	Tiger	Tiger
Newt	Small salamander	Tod	Fox
Oisin	Little deer	Ursel	Bear
Orsen	Little bear	Wolfe	Wolf
Osborn	Divine bear	Yonas	Dove
		Zvi	Deer

Flowers and Trees

Girl Names

Alona	Cocoa	Ivy	Petunia
Ashley	Daisy	Jasmine	Phyllis
Ayana	Daphne	Juniper	Poppy
Azalea	Fauna	Laura	Raisa
Azhaar	Fern	Laurel	Rhoda
Blossom	Flora	Lian	Rose
Bryony	Florence	Lily	Sage
Burnet	Gardenia	Linnea	Sugar
Calendula	Ginger	Magnolia	Susan
Calla	Hana	Marigold	Varda
Camillia	Hazel	Myrtle	Viola
Carmel	Heather	Narcissus	Violet
Cerise	Holly	Nawar	Willow
Cherise	Hyacinth	Olive	Yasmeen
Cherry	Ione	Olivia	Yolanda
Cheryl	Iris	Pansy	Zinnia

Flowers and Trees

Boy Names

Aiken	Elder	Hickory	Lennox
Alder	Ellery	Hollis	Lyndon
Aster	Elmore	Ivo	Oakes
Basil	Forrest	Jacek	Oliver
Berry	Garth	Kai	Oren
Birch	Glanville	Keith	Perry
Boyce	Grover	Landon	Shelly
Cedar	Hawthorne	Lee	Vernon
Cochise	Heath		

Fruits

Girl Names

Alani	Cherry	Jana	Tangerine
Anzu	Clementine	Minaku	Tao
Apple	Elma	Mora	Xiu Mei
Cam	Eustacia	Prunella	Zabrina
Carmen	Evelina	Sabra	Zerdali
Cherise			

Boy Names

Berry	Frasier	Perry	Ringo
Ephraim			

Food Names

Girl Names

Ambra	Cookie	Sugar
Candy	Dory	Suzy Q
Cherry	Salsa	

Boy Names

Barry	Marlin	Quince
Galina	Monk	Tom
Kale		

Colors

Girl Names

Affera	Flavia	Kala	Scarlet
Afra	Garnet	Lilia	Silver
Amber	Ginger	Midori	Talutah
Azure	Hong	Nelia	Violet
Debbani	Hyacinth	Ornat	Xantha
Devaki	Jacinta	Ruby	Zukra
Ebony	Jette		

Boy Names

Adham	Donovan	Hinto	Nila
Al-Ashab	Dwyer	Jet	Odhran
Blake	Earc	Kadir	Porfio
Bruno	Flavian	Kieran	Rad
Cerny	Floyd	Lloyd	Roy
Conroy	Gorman	Matlal	Russell
Cronan	Harkin	Mustanen	Zeleny

Moods

Girl Names

Bliss	Menuha	Serene
Hope	Merry	Stormy
Joy	Saja	Sunny

Moods

Boy Names

Blue	Galen	Stille
Chipper	Jazz	

Hair Color Names

Girl Names

Name	Derivation/ Meaning	Name	Derivation/ Meaning
Blondelle	Blond	Keira	Black-haired
Finola	White-haired	Nuala	White-haired
Gwendolyn	Fair-haired	Rufina	Red-haired
Gwenllian	White-haired	Zanthe	Light-haired
Juliette	Soft-haired		

Boy Names

Name	Derivation/ Meaning	Name	Derivation/ Meaning
Bayard	With red-brown hair	Grayson	Son of the gray-haired
Bowie	Yellow-haired	Maurizio	Dark-haired
Dewitt	Blond	Read	Red-haired
Dolan	Dark-haired	Rufus	Redhead
Findlay	Blond-haired soldier	Russell	Redhead
Finley	Fair-haired one	Sherlock	Fair-haired
Flavian	Yellow/blond	Xanthus	Blond
Flynn	Heir to the redhead	Xanto	Blond-haired

Unisex Names

Alex	Corey	Hillary/Hilary	Morgan	Taylor
Avery	Devon	Jordan	Nicky	Val
Bailey	Frances/ Francis	Kelly	Quincy	Wynne
Cameron		Kiley	Robin	Young
Chase	Gene/Jeanne	Logan	Shannon	Zane

Artistic Appellations

Many of you likely grew up admiring an author, or perhaps you saw a painting in an art gallery and became enamored of that artist's work. This chapter offers names of famous artists, best-selling authors, and characters from literature as well as names of those immortal characters who have peopled William Shakespeare's works.

For those of you interested in science fiction and fantasy, I've also included a section of names with sci-fi/fantasy flair. For parents who have never given up their love of children's literature, you'll find a list of the boys and girls who filled the pages of your favorite books. And for other artistic endeavors from food to fashion, you'll find those names here, too.

Artists

Girl Names

Andrea Mantegna

Anna Atkins

Anna Mary Robertson Moses

Berenice Abbott

Berthe Morisot

Doris Ulmann

Dorothea Tanning

Elizabeth Butler

Evelyn de Morgan

Francesca della Piero

Georgia O'Keeffe

Judith Lyster

Leonora Carrington

Marie Bracquemond

Mary Cassatt

Rita Angus

Rosa Bonheur

Simone Martini

Tilly Kettle

Boy Names

Adam Elsheimer

Albrecht Altdorfer

Alexandre Cabanel

Alfred Sisley

Alonso Cano

Antonio Allegri Corregio

Auguste Rodin

Balthasar van der Ast

Benjamin West

Benvenuto Cellini

Camille Pissarro

Caspar David Friedrich

Charles Le Brun

Claude Monet

Dante Gabriel Rossetti

David Hockney

Dirck van Baburen

Domenico Ghirlandaio

Edgar Degas

Edvard Munch

Edward Hopper

El Greco

Eugene Boudin

Federico Barocci

Fra Angelico

Francis Bacon

Franz Marc

Gerard Davis

Giovanni Bellini

Gustave Caillebotte

Hendrick Avercamp

Henri Matisse

Henri Rousseau

Hieronymus Bosch

Honore Daumier

Jackson Pollock

James Tissot

Jan Vermeer

Jasper Cropsey

Jeanne-Baptiste Simeon Chardin

Jesse Trevino

Joan Miro

John Constable

Joseph Cornell

Joshua Shaw

Leonardo da Vinci

Lorenzo di Piero de' Medici

Luca Della Robbia

Lucian Freud

Michelangelo Buonarroti

Nehemiah Partridge

Nicholas Hilliard

Norman Rockwell

Odilon Redon

Paul Cézanne

Peter Paul Rubens

Pierre-Auguste Renoir

Pieter Bruegel

Raffaello Sanzio Raphael

Rembrandt van Rijn

Robert Campin

Ron Kitaj

Salvadore Dali

Sandro Botticelli

Stuart Davis

Theodore Chasseriau

Thomas Cole

Titian

Vincent van Gogh

Wassily Kandinsky

William Blake

Yves Tanguy

Zacharie Astruc

Favorite Children's Book/Show Characters

Girl Names

Character	Children's Book/Show	Character	Children's Book/Show
Alanna	*Alanna: The First Adventure*	Jenny Linsky	*Jenny and the Cat Club*
Alice	*Alice in Wonderland*	Judy	*Runaway Pony*
Amanda	*Amanda Pig and Her Big Brother Oliver*	Laura Ingalls	*Little House on the Prairie*
Amelia Bedelia	*Amelia Bedelia* series	Lizzie	*Berenstain Bears*
Anastasia	*Anastasia Krupnik*	Lucy Pevensie	*The Chronicles of Narnia*
Anne Shirley	*Anne of Green Gables*	Luna Lovegood	*Harry Potter* series
Arrietty	*The Borrowers*	Madeline	*Mad About Madeline*
Barbie	*Barbie Fairytopia*	Manyara	*Mufaro's Beautiful Daughters*
Beezus	*Beezus and Ramona*	Nan Bobbsey	*Bobbsey Twins Go to the Seashore*
Betsy	*Betsy-Tacy* books		
Caitlin Seeger	*Caitlin's Way*	Nancy Drew	*Nancy Drew Mysteries*
Candy Quackenbush	*Abarat: Days of Magic, Nights of War*	Nina	*Runaway Pony*
		Olivia	*Olivia*
Charlotte	*Charlotte's Web*	Sam Bangs	*Sam Bangs and Moonshine*
Clarissa	*Clarissa Explains It All*		
Claudia	*From the Mixed-Up Files of Mrs. Basil E Frankweiler*	Sophie	*When Sophie Gets Angry—Really, Really Angry*
Dorothy	*The Wizard of Oz*	Sunny Baudelaire	*Lemony Snicket's A Series of Unfortunate Events*
Ella Sarah	*Ella Sarah Gets Dressed*		
Ellen	*Edgar and Ellen*	Tacy	*Betsy-Tacy* books
Eloise	*Eloise*	Violet Baudelaire	*Lemony Snicket's A Series of Unfortunate Events*
Emily Elizabeth	*Clifford the Big Red Dog*		
Fern	*Charlotte's Web*	Wanda	*The Hundred Dresses*
Flossie Bobbsey	*Bobbsey Twins Go to the Seashore*	Wednesday Addams	*The Addams Family*
Ginny Weasley	*Harry Potter* series	Willa	*Tell Me Something Before I Go to Sleep*
Hermione Granger	*Harry Potter* series		
Jane	*Fun with Dick and Jane*		

Favorite Children's Book/Show Characters

Boy Names

Character	Children's Book/Show	Character	Children's Book/Show
Alec	*The Black Stallion*	Gordon	*Thomas the Tank Engine*
Alexander Cold	*City of the Beasts*	Harold	*Harold and the Purple Crayon*
Artemis Fowl	*Artemis Fowl*		
Arthur	*Arthur*	Harry Potter	*Harry Potter* series
Bo	*The Thief Lord*	Jack	*Magic Tree House #14: Day of the Dragon King*
Bert Bobbsey	*Bobbsey Twins Go to the Seashore*	James	*James and the Giant Peach*
Braid Beard	*How I Became a Pirate*	Jeremy Jacob	*How I Became a Pirate*
Caspian	*Chronicles of Narnia*	Joaquin Murieta	*Bandit's Moon*
Charlie Bucket	*Charlie and the Chocolate Factory*	Joe	*Time Warp Trio*
Christopher Robin	*Winnie the Pooh*	Marshall Teller	*Eerie, Indiana*
Clifford	*Clifford the Big Red Dog*	Max	*Where the Wild Things Are*
Crispin	*Crispin: Cross of Lead*	Mickey	*In the Night Kitchen*
Damian Cray	*Eagle Strike: An Alex Rider Adventure*	Mike Mulligan	*Mike Mulligan and His Steam Shovel*
Danny	*Danny and the Dinosaur*	Milo	*The Phantom Tollbooth*
David	*No, David!*	Omri	*Indian in the Cupboard*
Dennis	*Dennis the Menace*	Pete Wrigley	*The Adventures of Pete and Pete*
Dexter	*Dexter's Laboratory*		
Dick	*Fun with Dick and Jane*	Prosper	*The Thief Lord*
Eddie McDowd	*100 Deeds for Eddie McDowd*	Ron Weasley	*Harry Potter* series
		Sam	*Time Warp Trio*
Edgar	*Edgar and Ellen*	Stuart	*Stuart Little*
Edmund Pevensie	*Chronicles of Narnia*	Thomas	*Thomas the Tank Engine*
Freddie Fernortner	*Fearless First Grader*		

Literary Characters

Girl Names

Character	Book	Character	Book
Ántonia Shimerda	*My Ántonia*	Josephine "Jo" March	*Little Women*
Celie	*The Color Purple*	Lily Bart	*House of Mirth*
Clarissa Dalloway	*Mrs. Dalloway*	Lolita	*Lolita*
Claudine	*Claudine at School*	Margaret Schlegel	*Howards End*
Daisy Buchanan	*The Great Gatsby*	Mary Katherine Blackwood	*We Have Always Lived in the Castle*
Frankie Addams	*The Member of the Wedding*	Molly Bloom	*Ulysses*
Hana	*The English Patient*	Nora Charles	*The Thin Man*
Hazel Motes	*Wise Blood*	Phoebe Caulfield	*The Catcher in the Rye*
Holly Golightly	*Breakfast at Tiffany's*	Scout Finch	*To Kill a Mockingbird*
Jane Eyre	*Jane Eyre*	Sula Peace	*Sula*
Janie Crawford	*Their Eyes Were Watching God*		
Jean Brodie	*The Prime of Miss Jean Brodie*		

Boy Names

Character	Book	Character	Book
Alden Pyle	*The Quiet American*	Clyde Griffiths	*An American Tragedy*
Alex Portnoy	*Portnoy's Complaint*	Dean Moriarty	*On the Road*
Arthur "Boo" Radley	*To Kill a Mockingbird*	Eugene Henderson	*Henderson the Rain King*
Atticus Finch	*To Kill a Mockingbird*	Geoffrey Firmin	*Under the Volcano*
Augustus McCrae	*Lonesome Dove*	George Smiley	*Tinker, Tailor, Soldier, Spy*
Aureliano Buendia	*One Hundred Years of Solitude*	Gregor Samsa	*The Metamorphosis*
Benjy	*The Sound and the Fury*	Henry Chinaski	*Post Office*
Bigger Thomas	*Native Son*	Holden Caulfield	*The Catcher in the Rye*
Binx Bolling	*The Moviegoer*	Humbert	*Lolita*
Charles Kinbote	*Pale Fire*	Ignatius Reilly	*A Confederacy of Dunces*
Christopher Tietjens	*Parade's End*	Jake Barnes	*The Sun Also Rises*

continues

Literary Characters continued

Boy Names

Character	Book	Character	Book
James Bond	*Casino Royale*	Rabbit Angstrom	*Rabbit, Run*
Jay Gatsby	*The Great Gatsby*	Sam Spade	*The Maltese Falcon*
Jeeves	*My Man Jeeves*	Santiago	*The Old Man and the Sea*
Joseph K.	*The Trial*	Sebastian Flyte	*Brideshead Revisited*
Lennie Small	*Of Mice and Men*	Seymour Glass	*Nine Stories*
Leopold Bloom	*Ulysses*	Sherlock Holmes	*The Hound of the Baskervilles*
Maurice Bendrix	*The End of the Affair*		
Nathan Zuckerman	*My Life as a Man*	Stephen Dedalus	*A Portrait of the Artist as a Young Man*
Neddy Merrill	*The Swimmer*		
Newland Archer	*The Age of Innocence*	Tarzan	*Tarzan of the Apes*
Nick Adams	*In Our Time*	Tom Ripley	*The Talented Mr. Ripley*
Oskar Matzerath	*The Tin Drum*		
Peter Pan	*The Little White Bird*	Willie Stark	*All the King's Men*
Philip Marlowe	*The Big Sleep*	Yossarian	*Catch-22*
Quentin Compson	*The Sound and the Fury*	Yuri Zhivago	*Dr. Zhivago*

Romance Heroes and Heroines

Girl Names

Heroine	Romance
Aloysia Weber	*Marrying Mozart* by Stephanie Cowell
Althea Almott	*Picking Up the Pieces* by Barbara Gale
Ardys Trevallon	*The Queen's Fencer* by Caitlin Scott Turner
Beatrix Carmichael	*Our Husband* by Stephanie Bond
Caitlan Claiborne	*Irish Fire* by Jeanette Baker
Callie Quinn	*Callie's Convict* by Heidi Betts
Camryn O'Brien	*From Boardwalk with Love* by Nina Bangs
Dani Strauss	*The Mommy Fund* by Madeline J. Jacob
Deidre Doyle	*Silver Wedding* by Maeve Binchy
Eden Beckett	*A Man of Affairs* by Ann Barbour

Heroine

Romance

Heroine	Romance
Elspeth Stewart	*Ride the Fire* by Pamela Clare
Emmaline Denford	*Something About Emmaline* by Elizabeth Boyle
Felicity Chambeau	*Her Forever Man* by Leanne Banks
Fonda Blayne	*Spotlight* by Carole Bellacera
Georgiana Escott	*One Night of Passion* by Elizabeth Boyle
Hester Poitevant	*The Bridemaker* by Rexanne Becnel
Jillian Fitzgerald	*Nell* by Jeanette Baker
Jo Beth Jensen	*The Cowboy Way* by Candace Schuler
Kaylynn Summers	*Spirit's Song* by Madeline Baker
Kirby Greenland	*I Am Not Esther* by Fleur Beale
Lacey O'Neill	*Kiss River* by Diane Chamberlain
Lauren Remington	*Born to Be Wild* by Patti Berg
Madeline Breton	*The Bride Finder* by Susan Carroll
Margrete Trewsbury	*The Maiden's Heart* by Julie Beard
Olivia FitzDurham	*Glass Houses* by Stella Cameron
Piper Devon	*Hush* by Jo Leigh
Prudence Reynolds	*Texas Star* by Elaine Barbieri
Quinn McKenzie	*Crazy for You* by Jennifer Crusie
Ripley Logan	*Private Investigations* by Tori Carrington
Sierra Lavotini	*Drag Strip* by Nancy Bartholomew
Sophia Armitage	*Irresistible* by Mary Balogh
Tempe Walsh	*Hot Stuff* by Flo Fitzpatrick
Thea Garrett	*Swear by the Moon* by Shirlee Busbee
Tru Van Dyne	*Unraveled* by C. J. Barry
Vivianna Greentree	*Lessons in Seduction* by Sara Bennett
Zoe Beckett	*A Man of Affairs* by Ann Barbour

Boy Names

Hero

Romance

Hero	Romance
Adrian Hawke	*The Bridemaker* by Rexanne Becnel
Aiden Flynn	*Glass Houses* by Stella Cameron
Anatole St. Leger	*The Bride Finder* by Susan Carroll
Britt Cameron	*Cameron* by Beverly Barton
Brock Logan	*Her Forever Man* by Leanne Banks

continues

Romance Heroes and Heroines continued

Boy Names

Hero	Romance
Caldwell Star	*Texas Star* by Elaine Barbieri
Ciaran Tamberlane	*My Forever Love* by Marsha Canham
Clay O'Neill	*Kiss River* by Diane Chamberlain
Desmond Doyle	*Silver Wedding* by Maeve Binchy
Devlin McCloud	*Leaping Hearts* by Jessica Bird
Donal O'Flaherty	*Nell* by Jeanette Baker
Gideon Cole	*To Love a Thief* by Julie Ann Long
Grayson St. Cyre	*Mad Jack* by Catherine Coulter
Harry Benson	*Picking Up the Pieces* by Barbara Gale
Ian Rufford	*The Companion* by Susan Squires
Jake Bannister	*Western Rose* by Lynna Banning
Lex Tanner	*The Countdown* by Ruth Wind
Max Wilde	*Born to Be Wild* by Patti Berg
Morgan Farrell	*Looking for a Hero* by Patti Berg
Neil Ellsworth	*Shadows on the Lake* by Leona Karr
Nicholas Devoncroix	*The Passion* by Donna Boyd
Oliver Montegomery	*Lessons in Seduction* by Sara Bennett
Patrick Blackburne	*Swear by the Moon* by Shirlee Busbee
Rayce Coburne	*Unraveled* by C. J. Barry
Roan Benedict	*Roan* by Jennifer Blake
Seth Lindow	*A Man of Affairs* by Ann Barbour
Shane Jeffrey	*Ashes of Dreams* by Ruth Ryan Langan
Stuart Chesterton	*Kiss the Bride* by Patricia Cabot
Tobin de Clare	*Wicked* by Jill Barnett
Trace Winslow	*Hush* by Jo Leigh
Tucker Johnston	*Inventing Savannah* by Susan Shapiro Barash/Joanne Lara
Vic Drummond	*Do You Believe?* by Ann Lawrence
Wade Mason	*Callie's Convict* by Heidi Betts

Science-Fiction/Fantasy Names

Girl Names

Aari	Duenna	Jesmin	Mala	Renora
Alandra	Elani	Jira	Marayna	Salia
Allaya	Eliann	K'Rene	Marna	Sayana
Anara	Eowyn	Kambrea	Merla	Shenna
Ariana	Eudana	Karana	Narra	Tayna
Arissa	Fayla	Katarra	Neema	Tendra
Arwen	Fiolla	Kierra	Nevala	Tierna
Ayala	Gaeriel	Kilana	Nori	Umali
Beata	Galadriel	Latika	Onaya	Vima
Brixie	Gilora	Leosa	Philana	Wrenn
Chalan	Hela	Lisea	Qatai	Yareena
Deila	Isela	Losira	Ravis	Zarabeth
Demma	Jaya	Lysia		

Boy Names

Adin	Brin	Faramir	Lohden	Rondon
Alzen	Cindel	Farran	Macias	Sarin
Amanin	Corin	Haldir	Mavek	Sauron
Amaros	Darod	Hogan	Mordock	Tabris
Aragorn	Dathan	Inyri	Narik	Talar
Arturis	Dillard	Ishan	Odan	Tarquin
Athan	Doran	Kainon	Orlando	Theoden
Azen	Draylan	Kalin	Parell	Valen
Balin	Droe	Kir	Peregrin	Vima
Batai	Dwalin	Larell	Quarren	Webb
Belar	Elrond	Lidell	Ramsey	Yareth
Berik	Eris	Liko	Rivan	Zolan
Boromir	Ezral			

Best-Selling Authors

Girl Names

Author	Work	Author	Work
Agatha Christie	The Mysterious Mr. Quin	Jean Auel	Clan of the Cave Bear
Alice Sebold	The Lovely Bones	Jennifer Crusie	Charlie All Night
Amy Tan	The Joy Luck Club	Jennifer Weiner	Good in Bed
Ann Rule	Every Breath You Take	Joan Collins	Misfortune's Daughters
Anna Quindlen	A Short Guide to a Happy Life	Jodi Picoult	My Sister's Keeper
Anne Rice	Interview with the Vampire	Joyce Carol Oates	We Were the Mulvaneys
Ayn Rand	Atlas Shrugged	Karen Robards	Superstition
Barbara Delinsky	The Summer I Dared	Kate Douglas Wiggin	Rebecca of Sunnybrook Farm
Beatrix Potter	The Tale of Peter Rabbit	Kate White	If Looks Could Kill
Charlotte Brontë	Jane Eyre	Kitty Kelley	The Family: The Real Story of the Bush Dynasty
Danielle Steel	Safe Harbour		
Debbie Macomber	Angels Everywhere	Laura Ingalls Wilder	The Little House series
Edith Wharton	The House of Mirth	Laurell Hamilton	A Stroke of Midnight
Evelyn Waugh	Scoop	Lilian Jackson Braun	The Cat Who Talked Turkey
Fern Michaels	Pretty Woman	Louisa May Alcott	Little Women
Flannery O'Connor	The Complete Stories of Flannery O'Connor	Lucy Maud Montgomery	Anne of Green Gables
Frances Hodgson Burnett	Little Lord Fauntleroy	Maeve Binchy	Nights of Rain and Stars
Gertrude Stein	Three Lives and Tender Buttons	Margaret Atwood	The Handmaid's Tale
Harper Lee	To Kill a Mockingbird	Margaret Mitchell	Gone with the Wind
Harriet Beecher Stowe	Uncle Tom's Cabin	Margery Williams	Velveteen Rabbit
Heidi Murkoff	What to Expect the First Year	Marietta Holley	Around the World with Josiah Allen's Wife
Iris Johansen	Countdown	Marilynne Robinson	Housekeeping
J. K. Rowling	Harry Potter series	Mary Higgins Clark	No Place Like Home
Jane Austen	Pride and Prejudice		
Janet Evanovich	Back to the Bedroom		

Author	Work
Maya Angelou	*I Know Why the Caged Bird Sings*
Nicole Krauss	*The History of Love: A Novel*
Nora Roberts	*Black Rose*
Patricia Cornwell	*Predator*
Rebecca Wells	*Divine Secrets of the YA-YA Sisterhood*
Sandra Brown	*White Hot*
Sarah Vowell	*Assassination Vacation*
Sojourner Truth	*Book of Life*
Sue Grafton	*R Is for Ricochet*

Author	Work
Sue Monk Kidd	*The Secret Life of Bees*
Susan Orlean	*The Orchid Thief*
Suze Orman	*The Money Book for the Young, Fabulous and Broke*
Sylvia Plath	*The Bell Jar*
Toni Morrison	*Beloved*
Virginia Woolf	*Mrs. Dalloway*
Willa Cather	*My Ántonia*
Zora Neale Hurston	*Their Eyes Were Watching God*

Boy Names

Author	Work
Alexander McCall Smith	*The No. 1 Ladies' Detective Agency*
Arthur Agatston	*The South Beach Diet Good Fats/Good Carbs Guide*
Buzz Bissinger	*Three Nights in August: Strategy, Heartbreak and Joy: Inside the Mind of a Manager*
Charles Dickens	*Great Expectations*
Clive Cussler	*Polar Shift*
Dan Brown	*The Da Vinci Code*
Dave Barry	*Big Trouble*
David Baldacci	*Split Second*
David McCullough	*1776*
Dean Koontz	*Velocity*
Deepak Chopra	*The Book of Secrets: Unlocking the Dimensions of Your Life*
Don Miguel Ruiz	*The Four Agreements* (*Toltec Wisdom* series)

Author	Work
Douglas Adams	*Ultimate Hitchhiker's Guide to the Galaxy*
Edgar Allan Poe	*The Murders in the Rue Morgue*
Ernest Hemingway	*The Old Man and the Sea*
F. Scott Fitzgerald	*The Great Gatsby*
Gregg Hurwitz	*Do No Harm*
Harlan Coben	*Just One Look*
Henry James	*The Portrait of a Lady*
Herman Melville	*Moby Dick*
Ian McEwan	*Atonement*
Jack London	*The Call of the Wild*
James Patterson	*The Lake House*
Jared Diamond	*Collapse: How Societies Choose to Fail or Succeed*
Jim Collins	*Built to Last: Successful Habits of Visionary Companies*
John Gray	*Men Are from Mars: Women Are from Venus*

continues

Best-Selling Authors continued

Boy Names

Author	Work	Author	Work
John Grisham	*The Broker*	Rick Warren	*The Purpose Driven Life: Why on Earth Am I Here For?*
John Irving	*Until I Find You*		
John le Carré	*The Constant Gardener*	Ridley Pearson	*Cut and Run*
John Saul	*Perfect Nightmare*	Robert Fulghum	*All I Really Needed to Know I Learned in Kindergarten*
Jon Stewart	*The Daily Show with Jon Stewart Presents America (The Book): A Citizen's Guide to Democracy Inaction*		
		Robert Kiyosaki	*The ABC's of Real Estate Investing: What the Rich Invest in That The Poor and Middle Class Do Not!*
Jonathan Kellerman	*Rage*		
Joseph Wambaugh	*The Onion Field*	Robert Louis Stevenson	*Treasure Island*
Ken Follett	*Pillars of the Earth*	Robert Ludlum	*The Bourne Identity*
Khaled Hosseini	*The Kite Runner*	Scott Turow	*Reversible Errors*
Leo Tolstoy	*Anna Karenina*	Sinclair Lewis	*Babbitt*
Malcolm Gladwell	*Blink: The Power of Thinking Without Thinking*	Spencer Johnson	*Who Moved My Cheese?*
		Stephen King	*The Shining*
Mark Twain	*The Adventures of Huckleberry Finn*	Steven Levitt	*Freakonomics: A Rogue Economist Explores the Hidden Side of Everything*
Michael Connelly	*The Closers*		
Michael Crichton	*Jurassic Park*		
Mitch Albom	*The Five People You Meet in Heaven*	Tom Clancy	*The Teeth of the Tiger*
		Upton Sinclair	*The Jungle*
Nathaniel Hawthorne	*The Scarlet Letter*	Wally Lamb	*She's Come Undone*
		Washington Irving	*Legend of Sleepy Hollow*
Nelson DeMille	*Night Fall*		
Nicholas Sparks	*The Notebook*	William Bernhardt	*Hate Crime: A Novel of Suspense*
Oscar Wilde	*The Picture of Dorian Gray*	William Shakespeare	*Hamlet*
Philip McGraw	*Family First*		

Names from Shakespeare

Girl Names

Character	Play
Adriana	The Comedy of Errors
Aemilia	The Comedy of Errors
Alice	Henry IV
Andromache	Troilus and Cressida
Anne Page	The Merry Wives of Windsor
Audrey	As You Like It
Beatrice	Much Ado About Nothing
Bianca	The Taming of the Shrew; Othello
Calpurnia	Julius Caesar
Cassandra	Troilus and Cressida
Celia	As You Like It
Ceres	The Tempest
Charmian	Antony and Cleopatra
Cleopatra	Antony and Cleopatra
Constance	King John
Cordelia	King Lear
Cressida	Troilus and Cressida
Desdemona	Othello
Diana	All's Well That Ends Well; Pericles
Dionyza	Pericles
Dorcas	The Winter's Tale
Emilia	The Winter's Tale; Othello
Francisca	Measure for Measure
Gertrude	Hamlet
Goneril	King Lear
Helen	Troilus and Cressida; Cymbeline
Helena	A Midsummer Night's Dream; All's Well That Ends Well

Character	Play
Hermia	A Midsummer Night's Dream
Hermione	The Winter's Tale
Hero	Much Ado About Nothing
Hippolyta	A Midsummer Night's Dream
Imogen	Cymbeline
Iras	Antony and Cleopatra
Iris	The Tempest
Isabella	Measure for Measure
Jessica	The Merchant of Venice
Julia	The Two Gentlemen of Verona
Juliet	Romeo and Juliet; Measure for Measure
Juno	The Tempest
Katharina	The Taming of the Shrew
Lavinia	Titus Andronicus
Luce	The Comedy of Errors
Lucetta	The Two Gentlemen of Verona
Luciana	The Comedy of Errors
Lychorinda	Pericles
Margaret	Much Ado About Nothing
Maria	Twelfth Night
Mariana	All's Well That Ends Well; Measure for Measure
Marina	Pericles
Miranda	The Tempest
Mopsa	The Winter's Tale
Nerissa	The Merchant of Venice
Octavia	Antony and Cleopatra

continues

Names from Shakespeare continued

Girl Names

Character	Play
Olivia	*Twelfth Night*
Ophelia	*Hamlet*
Patience	*Henry VIII*
Paulina	*The Winter's Tale*
Perdita	*The Winter's Tale*
Phebe	*As You Like It*
Phrynia	*Timon of Athens*
Portia	*The Merchant of Venice; Julius Caesar*
Regan	*King Lear*
Rosalind	*As You Like It*
Rosaline	*Romeo and Juliet*

Character	Play
Silvia	*The Two Gentlemen of Verona*
Tamora	*Titus Andronicus*
Thaisa	*Pericles*
Timandra	*Timon of Athens*
Titania	*A Midsummer Night's Dream*
Ursula	*Much Ado About Nothing*
Valeria	*Coriolanus*
Viola	*Twelfth Night*
Violenta	*All's Well That Ends Well*
Virgilia	*Coriolanus*
Volumnia	*Coriolanus*

Boy Names

Character	Play
Abraham	*Romeo and Juliet*
Adam	*As You Like It*
Adriano	*Love's Labor's Lost*
Agamemnon	*Troilus and Cressida*
Alonso	*The Tempest*
Amiens	*As You Like It*
Angus	*Macbeth*
Archidamus	*The Winter's Tale*
Balthazar	*The Comedy of Errors*
Bardolph	*The Merry Wives of Windsor; Henry V*
Bassanio	*The Merchant of Venice*
Bassett	*King Henry VI*
Bates	*Henry V*
Benedick	*Much Ado About Nothing*
Boyet	*Love's Labor's Lost*

Character	Play
Caius	*Titus Andronicus*
Camillo	*The Winter's Tale*
Cassio	*Othello*
Cato	*Julius Caesar*
Chiron	*Titus Andronicus*
Cicero	*Julius Caesar*
Claudio	*Much Ado About Nothing; Measure for Measure*
Cleon	*Pericles*
Conrade	*Much Ado About Nothing*
Costard	*Love's Labor's Lost*
Cromwell	*Henry VIII*
Curan	*King Lear*
Curtis	*The Taming of the Shrew*
Dion	*The Winter's Tale*
Donalbain	*Macbeth*

Character	Play
Dromio	*The Comedy of Errors*
Dumaine	*Love's Labor's Lost*
Duncan	*Macbeth*
Edgar	*King Lear*
Escanes	*Pericles*
Fabian	*Twelfth Night*
Falstaff (Sir John)	*Henry IV; The Merry Wives of Windsor*
Fenton	*The Merry Wives of Windsor*
Ferdinand	*The Tempest; Love's Labor's Lost*
Feste	*Twelfth Night*
Ford	*The Merry Wives of Windsor*
Francisco	*Hamlet; The Tempest*
Gallus	*Antony and Cleopatra*
Gremio	*The Taming of the Shrew*
Griffith	*Henry VIII*
Guildenstern	*Hamlet*
Hamlet	*Hamlet*
Hector	*Troilus and Cressida*
Horatio	*Hamlet*
Iachima	*Cymbeline*
Iago	*Othello*
Jamy	*Henry V*
Julius Caesar	*Julius Caesar*
Laertes	*Hamlet*
Launce	*The Two Gentlemen of Verona*
Laurence (Friar)	*Romeo and Juliet*
Lennox	*Macbeth*
Leontes	*The Winter's Tale*
Longaville	*Love's Labor's Lost*
Lorenzo	*The Merchant of Venice*

Character	Play
Lucio	*Measure for Measure*
Lysander	*A Midsummer Night's Dream*
Macbeth	*Macbeth*
Macduff	*Macbeth*
Macmorris	*Henry V*
Marcellus	*Hamlet*
Mardian	*Antony and Cleopatra*
Mark Antony	*Antony and Cleopatra*
Menelaus	*Troilus and Cressida*
Montague	*Romeo and Juliet*
Montano	*Othello*
Nathaniel	*Love's Labor's Lost*
Nestor	*Troilus and Cressida*
Oberon	*A Midsummer Night's Dream*
Octavius	*Julius Caesar*
Orlando	*As You Like It*
Osric	*Hamlet*
Othello	*Othello*
Pandarus	*Troilus and Cressida*
Philo	*Antony and Cleopatra*
Pindarus	*Julius Caesar*
Priam	*Troilus and Cressida*
Proteus	*The Two Gentlemen of Verona*
Quince	*A Midsummer Night's Dream*
Quintus	*Titus Andronicus*
Reynaldo	*Hamlet*
Romeo	*Romeo and Juliet*
Ross	*Macbeth*
Rugby	*The Merry Wives of Windsor*

continues

Names from Shakespeare continued

Boy Names

Character	Play	Character	Play
Sampson	*Romeo and Juliet*	Titus	*Coriolanus; Timon of Athens*
Sebastian	*The Tempest; Twelfth Night*	Tranio	*The Taming of the Shrew*
Seyton	*Macbeth*	Tybalt	*Romeo and Juliet*
Strato	*Julius Caesar*	Ulysses	*Troilus and Cressida*
Theseus	*A Midsummer Night's Dream*	Varrius	*Antony and Cleopatra*
		Verges	*Much Ado About Nothing*
Timon	*Timon of Athens*	William	*As You Like It*

Poets

Girl Names

Alice Cary	Gwendolyn Bennett	Michelle Cliff
Anne Sexton	Gwendolyn Brooks	Norma Cole
Barbara Guest	Janet Frame	Pam Ayres
Carol Ann Duffy	Joanna Baillie	Penelope Fitzgerald
Diane DiPrima	Joy Harjo	Phoebe Cary
Dorothy Auchterlonie	June Jordan	Rae Armantrout
Elaine Feinstein	Lisa Jarnot	Rita Dove
Elizabeth Bishop	Lucille Clifton	Sandra Cisneros
Emily Dickinson	Margaret Atwood	Susanne Blamire
Erica Jong	Mary Wedderburn Cannon	Sylvia Plath
Ethel Anderson	Mathilde Blind	Thea Astley
Fanny Howe	Maura Dooley	Tina Darragh
Felicia Hemans	Maya Angelou	Wanda Coleman
Fleur Adcock		

Boy Names

Alexander Hume	Anselm Berrigan	Ben Jonson
Albert Gordon Austin	Arthur Henry Adams	Bernard Barton
Allen Fisher	Asa Benveniste	Bob Cobbing
Allen Ginsberg	Austin Clarke	Brian Coffey

Bruce Andrews
Carl Sandburg
Charles Causely
Constantine Cavafy
David Ball
Denis Devlin
Douglas Dunn
E. E. Cummings
Ebenezer Elliot
Edmund Blunden
Edward Dorn
Edwin Atherstone
Elijah Fenton
Ezra Pound
Geoffrey Chaucer
George Chapman
Gilbert Adair

Harold Acton
Henry Carey
Jack Clarke
Jack Kerouac
James Tate
Jesse Ball
John Ashbery
Joseph Addison
Keith Douglas
Ken Barratt
Lawrence Ferlinghetti
Leigh Hunt
Lewis Carroll
Lex Banning
Mark Akenside
Matthew Arnold
Maurice Biggs

Michael Davidson
Miles Champion
Oliver Wendell Holmes
Peter Bladen
Ralph Waldo Emerson
Randall Jarrell
Ray DiPalma
Richard Caddel
Robert Frost
Samuel Bishop
Simon Armitage
Stanley Kunitz
Theodore Roethke
Thomas Ashe
Trevor Joyce
Wendell Berry
William Carlos Williams

Composers

Girl Names

Agathe Backer Grondahl
Angela Morley
Anne Boleyn
Annette von Droste-Hülshoff
Barbara White
Beth Anderson
Bunita Marcus
Carla Bley
Caroline Sheridan Norton
Caterina Assandra
Cécile Chaminade
Cecilia Maria Barthelemon

Clara Schumann
Eleanor Hovda
Elisabeth Lutyens
Ellen Wright
Elodie Lauten
Ethel Smyth
Eve Beglarian
Fanny Mendelssohn
Frances Allitsen
Francesca Caccini
Germaine Tailleferre
Gertrude van den Bergh
Grace Williams
Helene de Montgeroult

Joan La Barbara
Johanna Mathieux Kinkel
Josephine Lang
Julia Wolfe
Kaija Saariaho
Laurie Spiegel
Lili Boulanger
Lois Vierk
Louise Talma
Maddalena Cassulana
Madeleine Dring
Maria Teresa Agnesi
Marion Bauer
Maryanne Amacher

continues

Composers continued

Girl Names

Meredith Monk	Ruth Crawford-Seeger	Tekla Badarzewska
Nadia Boulanger	Settimia Caccini	Thea Musgrave
Pauline Oliveros	Shulamit Ran	Usha Khanna
Rebecca Clarke	Sofia Gubaidulina	Wendy Carlos

Boy Names

Aaron Copland	Franz Liszt	Johann Pachelbel
Alexander Scriabin	Franz Schubert	Johann Sebastian Bach
Andrew Lloyd Webber	Frederic Chopin	Johannes Brahms
Antonín Dvorák	Gabriel Fauré	John Philip Sousa
Antonini Vivaldi	Georg Telemann	Joseph Haydn
Archangelo Corelli	George Gershwin	Kurt Weill
Arnold Schoenberg	George Handel	Leonard Bernstein
Arthur Sullivan	Giacomo Puccini	Ludwig van Beethoven
Béla Bartók	Gian Carlo Menotti	Manuel de Falla
Benjamin Britten	Gioacchino Rossini	Maurice Ravel
Carl von Weber	Giovanni Gabrieli	Nicolo Paganini
Charles Gounod	Giuseppe Verdi	Piotr Ilyitch Tchaikovsky
Christoph Gluck	Gustav Mahler	Ralph Vaughan Williams
Claude Debussy	Hector Berlioz	Richard Wagner
Claudio Monteverdi	Heinrich Schütz	Robert Schumann
Dmitri Shostakovich	Henry Purcell	Samuel Barber
Dominick Argento	Igor Stravinsky	Serge Prokofiev
Edvard Grieg	Jean Sibelius	Sergei Rachmaninoff
Felix Mendelssohn	Jean-Baptiste Lully	Wolfgang Amadeus Mozart
François Couperin	Jean-Philippe Rameau	

Opera Singers

Girl Names

Adria Firestone	Dolora Zajick	Karen Parks	Mirella Freni
Alessandra Marc	Edita Gruberova	Kathleen Battle	Patricia Caicedo
Angela Brown	Ellen Denham	Kirsten Flagstad	Renata Tebaldi
Anna Netrebko	Eva Marton	Leontyne Price	Renée Fleming
Beverly Sills	Fabiana Bravo	Lesley Garrett	Rosemary Wagner-Scott
Birgit Nilsson	Felicity Lott	Lotte Lehmann	
Catherine Hayes	Frederica von Stade	Luana DeVol	Ruth Ann Swenson
Cecilia Bartoli		Lucia Aliberti	Stella Scott
Chon Wolson	Hayley Westenra	Mara Kelley	Suzanne Mentzer
Christine Brewer	Hildegard Behrens	Marcella Sembrich	Tania Melanie Marsh
Dagmar zum Hingst	Jane Eaglen	Maria Callas	Teresa Zykus-Gara
Deborah Voigt	Janice Baird	Marilyn Horne	
Denyce Graves	Jennifer Larmore	Mary Bella	Vivica Genaux
	Joan Sutherland		

Boy Names

Andrea Bocelli	Fredrick Redd	Jussi Bjorling	Placido Domingo
Bryn Terfel	Fritz Wunderlich	Louis Quilico	Richard Tucker
David Faircloth	Gerard Edery	Luciano Pavarotti	Robert Sims
Dennis Jesse	Giovanni Meoni	Mark Evans	Russell Watson
Dietrich Fisher-Dieskau	Grant Doyle	Matthias Goerne	Ryan Taylor
	Ian Gray	Miguel Velasquez	Samuel Ramsey
Dmitri Hvorostovsky	James Anest	Nathaniel Watson	Scott Russell
Enrico Caruso	Jerry Hadley	Nicolai Gedda	Stuart Neill
Ezio Pinza	John Davies	Nolan Van Way	Thomas Hampson
Franco Corelli	José Carreras	Paul Carey Jones	Warren Leonard
François le Roux	Joseph Shore	Peter Schreier	William Warfield
	Josh Groban	Phillip Mentor	

Dancers

Girl Names

Dancer	Dance	Dancer	Dance
Adeline Genée	Ballet	Jennifer Lopez	Hip-hop
Agnes Letestu	Ballet	Karen Kain	Ballet
Alicia Markova	Ballet	Kathrine Dunham	Jazz
Ann Miller	Tap	Lucile Grahn	Ballet
Anna Pavlova	Ballet	Margot Fonteyn	Ballet
Aurelie Dupont	Ballet	Maria Alexandrova	Ballet
Britney Spears	Hip-hop	Mathilde Kschessinska	Ballet
Christina Aguilera	Hip-hop	Melissa Hayden	Ballet
Cyd Charisse	Ballet	Missy Elliot	Hip-hop
Darcey Bussell	Ballet	Olga Preobrajenska	Ballet
Devora Canario	Hip-hop	Patricia McBride	Ballet
Eleanor Powell	Tap	Ruby Keeler	Tap
Elisabeth Maurin	Ballet	Suzanne DiNunzio	Hip-hop
Fanny Cerito	Ballet	Suzanne Farrell	Ballet
Gwen Verdon	Jazz	Sylvie Guillem	Ballet
Janet Jackson	Hip-hop	Vera Ellen	Tap

Boy Names

Dancer	Dance	Dancer	Dance
Anton Dolin	Ballet	Gene Kelly	Tap
Barry Lather	Hip-hop	Gregory Hines	Tap
Bill "Bojangles" Robinson	Tap	Gus Giordano	Jazz
Bob Fosse	Jazz	Howard "Sandman" Sims	Tap
Charles Jude	Ballet	Jean-Pierre Bonnefous	Ballet
Cyril Atanassoff	Ballet	Jeremie Belingard	Ballet
Darrin Henson	Hip-hop	Joe Frisco	Jazz
Emmanuel Thibault	Ballet	John Bubbles	Tap
Erik Bruhn	Ballet	Jose Manuel Carreno	Ballet
Ethan Stiefel	Ballet	Justin Timberlake	Hip-hop
Fred Astaire	Tap	Marcelo Gomes	Ballet

Dancer	Dance	Dancer	Dance
Michael Vester	Ballet	Rudolf Nureyev	Ballet
Mikhail Baryshnikov	Ballet	Sammy Davis Jr.	Tap
Nicolas Lerich	Ballet	Savion Glover	Tap
Nino Ananiashvili	Ballet	Seth Stewart	Hip-hop
Pavel Gerdt	Ballet	Yuri Soloviev	Ballet
Rolando Sarabia	Ballet		

Fashion Designers

Girl Names

Anna Sui	Donatella Versace	Norma Kamali
Betsey Johnson	Donna Karan	Stella McCartney
Cate Coles	Elsa Schiaparelli	Vera Wang
Chloe Dao	Kimora Lee Simmons	Vivienne Westwood
Coco Chanel	Nicole Miller	

Boy Names

Alexander McQueen	Issey Miyake	Stefano Gabbana
Christian Dior	Jared Gold	Sully Bonnelly
Christian Lacroix	Jean Paul Gaultier	Thierry Mugler
Domenico Dolce	Oscar de la Renta	Todd Oldham
Dries Van Noten	Osmany Laffita	Tommy Hilfiger
Emilio Pucci	Paul Smith	Wolfgang Joop
Gianfranco Ferre	Pierre Cardin	Yves Saint Laurent
Giorgio Armani	Ralph Lauren	Zang Toi
Helmut Lang	Santino Rice	

Chefs

Girl Names

Alexandra Ewald
Alice Waters
Amy Scherber
Anita Lo
Ann Nurse
Anne Rosenzweig
Barbara Kafka
Barbara Lynch
Biba Caggiano
Caprial Pence
Carrie Nahabedian
Cat Cora
Diane Forley
Giada De Laurentiis
Helene Darroze

Jody Adams
Julia Child
Katy Sparks
Lidia Bastianich
Madeleine Kamman
Marion Cunningham
Martha Stewart
Mary Bergin
Mary Sue Milliken
Maryann Esposito
Melissa Kelly
Mina Newman
Mindy Segal
Mollie Katzen
Monique Barbeau

Nathalie Dupree
Nigella Lawson
Odette Fada
Patricia Yeo
Paula Deen
Rachael Ray
Roxanne Klein
Sara Moulton
Sarah Stegner
Sue Torres
Susan Feniger
Susan O'Rourke
Zarela Martines
Zov Karamardian

Boy Names

Alain Ducasse
Allen Susser
Alton Brown
Anthony Bourdain
Antoine Careme
Bobby Flay
Charlie Palmer
Charlie Trotter
Daniel Boulud
David Burke
David Ruggerio
Emeril Lagasse
Fritz Maytag
Gordon Ramsay
Graham Kerr

Guy Fieri
Jacques Pepin
James Beard
Jamie Oliver
Jean-Georges
 Vongerichten
Jeff Smith
Jody Denton
José Andrés
Marcel Desaulniers
Marcus Samuelsson
Mario Batali
Michael Ginor
Michael Lomonaco
Michael McCarty
Ming Tsai

Morgan Larsson
Nobu Matsuhisa
Norman Van Aken
Paul Prudhomme
Reed Hearon
Rick Bayless
Roberto Donna
Rocco DiSpirito
Sanford D'Amato
Steve Johnson
Thomas Keller
Todd English
Todd Gray
Tyler Florence
Wolfgang Puck

Architects

Girl Names

Anna Keichline

Denise Scott Brown

Elizabeth Plater-Zyberk

Julia Morgan

Marion Mahony Griffin

Zaha Hadid

Boy Names

Adolf Loos

Albert Kahn

Aldo Rossi

Alvar Aalto

Andres Duany

Antonio Gaudi

Arne Jacobsen

Bouke Albada

Carlo Scarpa

Cass Gilbert

Cesar Pelli

Charles Eames

Charles Edouard Jeanneret

Eero Saarinen

Frank Furness

Frank Gehry

Frank Lloyd Wright

Fumihiko Maki

Horace Trumbauer

Joze Plecnik

Kenzo Tange

Leon Battista Alberti

Louis Sullivan

Ludwig Mies van der Rohe

Makoto Watanabe

Mauro Codussi

Michael Graves

Moshe Safdie

Otto Wagner

Philippe Starck

Pierre Koenig

Pietro Belluschi

Rem Koolhaas

Renzo Piano

Victor Horta

Naming Nationwide

It's funny: choosing a baby name is such a personal decision, yet many parents often choose the same name for their child their neighbors, friends, and family members chose for their child. Take a look at this chapter's lists of the most popular baby names world-wide, as well as some of the frequent choices by region, state, and city in the United States.

You may also find inspiration by checking out popular names from the past, such as in the lists of top baby names by decade. Or skim the list of the top 100 names nationwide for more recent hot picks.

Top Baby Names by Country

Note: Following each country name are the top three most popular names, in descending order of popularity.

Girl Names

Australia	Ella, Emily, Olivia	Ireland	Katie, Grace, Sophie
Austria	Lena, Leonie, Sarah	Israel	Noa, Roni, Yael
Belgium	Lotte, Julie, Emma	Italy	Guila, Alessia, Alice
Brazil	Julia, Givanna, Maria	Japan	Hina, Yui, Miu
Canada	Emma, Sophia, Olivia	Mexico	Gabriela, Maria, Carmen
Chile	Martina, Constanza, Catalina	Netherlands	Sanne, Emma, Anna
China	Bao, Min, Zan	New Zealand	Ella, Sophie, Olivia
Croatia	Lana, Lucija, Petra	Nigeria	Fabayo, Abagbe, Chinue
Czech Republic	Jana, Petra, Lenka	Norway	Thea, Emma, Sara
Denmark	Sofie, Laura, Freja	Philippines	Maricel, Michelle, Jennifer
England/ Wales	Ruby, Emily, Sophie	Poland	Anna, Maria, Katarzyna
Finland	Maria, Emilia, Sofia	Russia	Alesandra, Alina, Anastasia
France	Emma, Lea, Manon	Scotland	Sophie, Emma, Lucy
Germany	Maria, Sophia, Katharina	Spain	Lucia, Maria, Paula
Greece	Sappho, Eugina, Calliope	Sweden	Emma, Maja, Agnes
Hungary	Anna, Viktoria, Reka	Turkey	Elif, Zeynep, Irem
Iceland	Guðrún, Sigríður, Kristín	United States	Emily, Isabella, Emma
		Vietnam	Thu, Nhung, Kim

Boy Names

Africa	Harun, Muhhamad, Salim	Croatia	Luka, Ivan, Marko
Australia	Jack, Lachlan, Thomas	Czech Republic	Jan, Jakub, Tomas
Austria	Lukas, Tobias, David	Denmark	Lucas, Mikkel, Magnus
Belgium	Milan, Wout, Senne	England/ Wales	Jack, Thomas, Oliver
Brazil	Gabriel, Gustavo, Giulherme	Finland	Juhani, Johannes, Matias
Canada	Aidan, Ethan, Jacob	France	Enzo, Mathis, Lucas
Chile	Benjamin, Vicente, Matias	Germany	Leon, Maximilian, Lukas
China	Aoyun, An, Quon		

Greece	Diokles, Arcadicus, Hippias	Nigeria	Abiade, Madu, Danjuma
Hungary	Bence, Máté, Balázs	Norway	Markus, Mathias, Jonas
Iceland	Sigríður, Guðmundur, Jón	Poland	Marcin, Adam, Marek
Ireland	Jack, James, Matthew	Russia	Alexandr, Andrey, Daniil
Israel	Uri, Ro'l, Amit	Scotland	Lewis, Jack, Ryan
Italy	Andrea, Lorenzo, Simone	Spain	Alejandro, Daniel, Pablo
Japan	Yuuki, Haruto, Souta	Sweden	Lucas, Oscar, William
Mexico	Alejandro, Juan Carlos, Migel	Turkey	Arda, Yusu, Mehmet
Netherlands	Dan, Sem, Thomas	United States	Jacob, Michael, Ethan
New Zealand	Jack, James, Joshua	Vietnam	Due, Quang, Minh

Top Five Baby Names by U.S. State for 2007

Note: 2007 is the latest year for which information was available at the time of printing.

Girl Names

Alabama	Emma, Madison, Emily, Hannah, Elizabeth	Florida	Isabella, Sophia, Emily, Madison, Ava
Alaska	Isabella, Madison, Ava, Abigail, Emily	Georgia	Madison, Emily, Emma, Ava, Abigail
Arizona	Isabella, Emily, Mia, Sophia, Ashley	Hawaii	Sophia, Ava, Chloe, Isabella, Emma
Arkansas	Madison, Emma, Emily, Addison, Olivia	Idaho	Emma, Emily, Olivia, Hannah, Abigail
California	Emily, Isabella, Sophia, Ashley, Samantha	Illinois	Isabella, Olivia, Emily, Ava, Sophia
Colorado	Isabella, Sophia, Emma, Olivia, Abigail	Indiana	Emma, Ava, Olivia, Madison, Addison
Connecticut	Isabella, Olivia, Ava, Emma, Emily	Iowa	Ava, Emma, Addison, Olivia, Grace
Delaware	Sophia, Ava, Emily, Madison, Abigail	Kansas	Addison, Emma, Ava, Madison, Emily
District of Columbia	Ashley, Sophia, Katherine, Elizabeth, Caroline	Kentucky	Madison, Emma, Emily, Addison, Olivia

continues

Top Five Baby Names by U.S. State for 2007 continued

Girl Names

Louisiana	Madison, Ava, Emma, Isabella, Olivia	North Dakota	Emma, Ava, Olivia, Madison, Abigail
Maine	Madison, Abigail, Olivia, Emma, Ava	Ohio	Ava, Madison, Olivia, Emma, Isabella
Maryland	Madison, Emily, Ava, Olivia, Abigail	Oklahoma	Emma, Madison, Emily, Addison, Hannah
Massachusetts	Ava, Isabella, Sophia, Olivia, Emma	Oregon	Emma, Sophia, Isabella, Emily, Olivia
Michigan	Ava, Madison, Emma, Olivia, Isabella	Pennsylvania	Ava, Olivia, Emma, Madison, Isabella
Minnesota	Ava, Olivia, Emma, Addison, Sophia	Rhode Island	Sophia, Ava, Isabella, Madison, Olivia
Mississippi	Madison, Emma, Chloe, Hannah, Addison	South Carolina	Madison, Emma, Emily, Abigail, Ava
Missouri	Emma, Madison, Ava, Addison, Olivia	South Dakota	Ava, Emma, Olivia, Addison, Hannah
Montana	Emma, Madison, Olivia, Addison, Emily	Tennessee	Emma, Madison, Emily, Addison, Abigail
Nebraska	Addison, Emma, Ava, Elizabeth, Emily	Texas	Emily, Mia, Isabella, Madison, Abigail
Nevada	Emily, Sophia, Isabella, Madison, Ava	Utah	Olivia, Emma, Abigail, Elizabeth, Ava
New Hampshire	Olivia, Abigail, Ava, Emma, Madison	Vermont	Ava, Emma, Abigail, Olivia, Ella
New Jersey	Isabella, Emily, Sophia, Ava, Olivia	Virginia	Madison, Abigail, Emily, Olivia, Emma
New Mexico	Isabella, Sophia, Emily, Nevaeh, Alyssa	Washington	Olivia, Emily, Emma, Sophia, Isabella
New York	Isabella, Sophia, Emily, Olivia, Ava	West Virginia	Madison, Emma, Emily, Abigail, Hannah
North Carolina	Madison, Emma, Emily, Ava, Abigail	Wisconsin	Ava, Emma, Olivia, Sophia, Addison
		Wyoming	Madison, Emma, Abigail, Taylor, Alexis

Boy Names

Alabama	William, James, Christopher, John, Jacob
Alaska	Aiden, Logan, Alexander, Ethan, Jacob
Arizona	Angel, Jose, Daniel, Anthony, Jacob
Arkansas	William, Jacob, Ethan, Jackson, Christopher
California	Daniel, Anthony, Angel, Jacob, David
Colorado	Jacob, Daniel, Alexander, Ethan, Joshua
Connecticut	Michael, Ryan, Matthew, Joseph, Anthony
Delaware	Michael, Ryan, Alexander, Christopher, John
District of Columbia	William, John, Christopher, Michael, Anthony
Florida	Anthony, Michael, Christopher, Joshua, Daniel
Georgia	William, Joshua, Christopher, Jacob, Michael
Hawaii	Noah, Ethan, Joshua, Isaiah, Elijah
Idaho	Jacob, Ethan, Logan, Isaac, Michael
Illinois	Daniel, Anthony, Jacob, Alexander, Michael
Indiana	Jacob, Ethan, Noah, Logan, Andrew
Iowa	Ethan, Jacob, Logan, Noah, Jackson
Kansas	Ethan, Jacob, Alexander, Jackson, Noah
Kentucky	Jacob, William, Ethan, James, Logan
Louisiana	Jacob, Ethan, Joshua, Michael, Christopher
Maine	Ethan, Jacob, Noah, William, Logan
Maryland	Michael, Christopher, Joshua, Jacob, William
Massachusetts	Matthew, Michael, Ryan, William, Jacob
Michigan	Jacob, Ethan, Michael, Logan, Noah
Minnesota	Jacob, Ethan, Logan, Jack, Samuel
Mississippi	William, James, Christopher, John, Joshua
Missouri	Jacob, Ethan, Logan, Andrew, Noah
Montana	Ethan, Logan, Jacob, Noah, Mason
Nebraska	Jacob, Alexander, Jackson, William, Ethan
Nevada	Anthony, Angel, Christopher, Daniel, Jacob
New Hampshire	Jacob, Logan, Ryan, Connor, Ethan
New Jersey	Michael, Matthew, Anthony, Daniel, Joseph
New Mexico	Jacob, Joshua, Michael, Isaiah, Gabriel
New York	Michael, Matthew, Anthony, Joseph, Daniel
North Carolina	William, Jacob, Christopher, Joshua, Ethan
North Dakota	Logan, Ethan, Jacob, Jack, Alexander
Ohio	Jacob, Michael, Ethan, Andrew, Logan
Oklahoma	Ethan, Jacob, Joshua, Noah, William
Oregon	Jacob, Alexander, Logan, Daniel, Ethan

continues

Top Five Baby Names by U.S. State for 2007 continued

Boy Names

Pennsylvania	Michael, Jacob, Ryan, Logan, Matthew	Vermont	Logan, Jacob, Alexander, Mason, Noah
Rhode Island	Michael, Anthony, Jacob, Nicholas, Ethan	Virginia	William, Jacob, Christopher, Joshua, Michael
South Carolina	William, James, Christopher, Michael, Joshua	Washington	Jacob, Ethan, Alexander, Daniel, Logan
South Dakota	Ethan, Mason, Jacob, Gavin, Noah	West Virginia	Jacob, Ethan, Logan, Austin, Hunter
Tennessee	William, Jacob, Ethan, James, Joshua	Wisconsin	Ethan, Jacob, Logan, Mason, Alexander
Texas	Jose, Jacob, Daniel, Christopher, Angel	Wyoming	Ethan, James, Gavin, William, Logan
Utah	Ethan, Jacob, Benjamin, Joshua, Samuel		

Most Popular Names by Major U.S. City

Girl Names

Boston	Isabella, Mia, Megan, Ava, Madison	New York	Ashley, Emily, Isabella, Sarah, Kayla
Chicago	Sophia, Olivia, Emily, Mia, Emma	Philadelphia	Madison, Ava, Gabriella, Mia, Jasmine
Dallas	Emily, Isabella, Abigail, Madison, Emma	Portland	Ella, Madison, Abigail, Emily, Lucy
Denver	Sophia, Elizabeth, Natalie, Olivia, Alexis	San Francisco	Isabella, Emily, Alexis, Hannah, Sofia
Los Angeles	Samantha, Ashley, Sophia, Natalie, Mia		

Boy Names

Boston	Joseph, James, Henry, Ryan, John	Denver	Elijah, Angel, Noah, Ryan, Daniel
Chicago	Michael, Jack, John, Adrian, Anthony	Los Angeles	Anthony, Jonathan, Daniel, Nathan, David
Dallas	Jayden, Jacob, Jeremiah, Joshua, William	New York	Michael, Daniel, Matthew, Joshua, Justin

Philadelphia	Michael, Jayden, Christopher, Anthony, Ryan	San Francisco	Joshua, Ethan, Joseph, Alexander, Aaron
Portland	Jacob, Jayden, Joshua, Aiden, William		

Named for Cities

Don't see your city listed here? Find the top baby names in your locale at www.our365.com/Wisdom/BabyNameScape/default.aspx.

Girl Names

City	State or Country	City	State or Country
Acadia	Canada	Lee	Massachusetts
Adeline	Illinois	Leslie	Michigan
Adena	Ohio	London	England
Allison	Ohio	Lourdes	France
Aspen	Colorado	Madison	Wisconsin
Atlanta	Georgia	Marion	Ohio
Bethany	Delaware (Beach)	Melba	Idaho
Brooklyn	New York	Milan	Italy
Cameron	Missouri	Morgan	Louisiana
Carmel	California	Olympia	Washington
Catalina	California	Paris	France
Charlotte	North Carolina	Portland	Oregon; Maine
Chelsea	Massachusetts; Michigan	Raleigh	North Carolina
Cheyenne	Wyoming	Salem	Massachusetts
Devon	England	Savannah	Georgia
Eden	North Carolina	Selma	Alabama
Florence	Italy	Sharon	Massachusetts
Geneva	Switzerland	Shelby	North Carolina
Hailey	Idaho	Siena	Italy
Helena	Montana	Sierra	California
Jersey	New Jersey	Sydney	Australia
Jordan	Utah	Valencia	Spain
Kelsey	England	Venice	Italy
Kennedy	Minnesota	Victoria	Canada
Kingston	Jamaica		

Named for Cities

Boy Names

City	State or Country	City	State or Country
Abbott	Texas	Diego (San)	California
Acton	Massachusetts	Douglas	Wyoming
Aiken	South Carolina	Durand	Wisconsin
Albany	New York	Edmond	Oklahoma
Alden	Michigan	Eugene	Oregon
Alton	Illinois	Flint	Michigan
Amory	Mississippi	Garrett	Indiana
Austin	Texas	Gary	Indiana
Baden	Germany	Gibson	Illinois
Baldwin	Kansas	Hamilton	Bermuda
Beaumont	Texas	Harlem	New York
Blair	Nebraska	Houston	Texas
Boston	Massachusetts	Hudson	New York
Brandon	Canada	Hunter	North Dakota
Brighton	Colorado	Jackson	Mississippi
Camden	Maine; New Jersey	Kent	England
Camillus	New York	Kyle	Texas
Carson	Nevada	Logan	Utah
Charleston	West Virginia	Melbourne	Australia
Chase	Virginia	Ogden	Utah
Chester	Pennsylvania	Owen	Canada
Cleveland	Ohio	Phoenix	Arizona
Clyde	Ohio	Quincy	Massachusetts
Cody	Wyoming	Riley	Kansas
Cortez	Colorado	Stamford	Connecticut
Dallas	Texas	Trenton	New Jersey
Dalton	Georgia	Troy	New York
Davis	California	Tyler	Texas
Denver	Colorado	Wyatt	Indiana

Named for States

Girl Names

Alabama	Dakota	Montana
Caroline	Georgia	Virginia

Boy Names

Arizona	Texas	Wyoming
Indiana		

Top 100 Most Popular Names for 2007

Note: These are listed in order of popularity.

Girl Names

Emily	Ella	Destiny	Madeline
Isabella	Brianna	Jessica	Maya
Emma	Hailey	Morgan	Kylie
Ava	Taylor	Kaitlyn	Jennifer
Madison	Anna	Brooke	Mackenzie
Sophia	Kayla	Allison	Claire
Olivia	Lily	Makayla	Gabrielle
Abigail	Lauren	Avery	Leah
Hannah	Victoria	Alexandra	Aubrey
Elizabeth	Savannah	Jocelyn	Arianna
Addison	Nevaeh	Audrey	Vanessa
Samantha	Jasmine	Riley	Trinity
Ashley	Lillian	Kimberly	Ariana
Alyssa	Julia	Maria	Faith
Mia	Sofia	Evelyn	Katelyn
Chloe	Kaylee	Zoe	Haley
Natalie	Sydney	Brooklyn	Amelia
Sarah	Gabriella	Angelina	Megan
Alexis	Katherine	Andrea	Isabelle
Grace	Alexa	Rachel	Melanie

continues

Top 100 Most Popular Names for 2007 continued

Girl Names

Sara	Isabel	Autumn	Gracie
Sophie	Nicole	Mariah	Molly
Bailey	Stephanie	Mary	Valeria
Aaliyah	Paige	Michelle	Caroline
Layla	Gianna	Jada	Jordan

Boy Names

Jacob	Benjamin	Thomas	Jaden
Michael	Aiden	Aaron	Jesus
Ethan	Gabriel	Lucas	Bryan
Joshua	Dylan	Aidan	Chase
Daniel	Elijah	Connor	Carter
Christopher	Brandon	Owen	Brian
Anthony	Gavin	Hunter	Nathaniel
William	Jackson	Diego	Eric
Matthew	Angel	Jason	Cole
Andrew	Jose	Luis	Dominic
Alexander	Caleb	Adrian	Kyle
David	Mason	Charles	Tristan
Joseph	Jack	Juan	Blake
Noah	Kevin	Brayden	Liam
James	Evan	Adam	Carson
Ryan	Isaac	Julian	Henry
Logan	Zachary	Jeremiah	Caden
Jayden	Isaiah	Xavier	Brady
John	Justin	Wyatt	Miguel
Nicholas	Jordan	Carlos	Cooper
Tyler	Luke	Hayden	Antonio
Christian	Robert	Sebastian	Steven
Jonathan	Austin	Alex	Kaden
Nathan	Landon	Ian	Richard
Samuel	Cameron	Sean	Timothy

Most Popular Names by Year

Girl Names

2007 Emily, Isabella, Emma, Ava, Madison, Sophia, Olivia, Abigail, Hannah, Elizabeth

2006 Emily, Emma, Madison, Isabella, Ava, Abigail, Olivia, Hannah, Sophia, Samantha

2005 Emily, Emma, Madison, Abigail, Olivia, Isabella, Hannah, Samantha, Ava, Ashley

2004 Emily, Emma, Madison, Olivia, Hannah, Abigail, Isabella, Ashley, Samantha, Elizabeth

2003 Emily, Emma, Madison, Hannah, Olivia, Abigail, Alexis, Ashley, Elizabeth, Samantha

2002 Emily, Madison, Hannah, Emma, Alexis, Ashley, Abigail, Sarah, Samantha, Olivia

2001 Emily, Madison, Hannah, Ashley, Alexis, Sarah, Samantha, Abigail, Elizabeth, Olivia

2000 Emily, Hannah, Madison, Ashley, Sarah, Alexis, Samantha, Jessica, Taylor, Elizabeth

1999 Emily, Hannah, Alexis, Sarah, Samantha, Ashley, Madison, Taylor, Jessica, Elizabeth

1998 Emily, Hannah, Samantha, Ashley, Sarah, Alexis, Taylor, Jessica, Madison, Elizabeth

1997 Emily, Jessica, Ashley, Sarah, Hannah, Samantha, Taylor, Alexis, Elizabeth, Madison

1996 Emily, Jessica, Ashley, Sarah, Samantha, Taylor, Hannah, Alexis, Rachel, Elizabeth

1995 Jessica, Ashley, Emily, Samantha, Sarah, Taylor, Hannah, Brittany, Amanda, Elizabeth

1994 Jessica, Ashley, Emily, Samantha, Sarah, Taylor, Brittany, Amanda, Elizabeth, Megan

1993 Jessica, Ashley, Sarah, Samantha, Emily, Brittany, Taylor, Amanda, Elizabeth, Stephanie

1992 Ashley, Jessica, Amanda, Brittany, Sarah, Samantha, Emily, Stephanie, Elizabeth, Megan

1991 Ashley, Jessica, Brittany, Amanda, Samantha, Sarah, Stephanie, Jennifer, Elizabeth, Emily

1990 Jessica, Ashley, Brittany, Amanda, Samantha, Sarah, Stephanie, Jennifer, Elizabeth, Lauren

Boy Names

2007 Jacob, Michael, Ethan, Joshua, Daniel, Christopher, Anthony, William, Matthew, Andrew

2006 Jacob, Michael, Joshua, Ethan, Matthew, Daniel, Christopher, Andrew, Anthony, William

2005 Jacob, Michael, Joshua, Matthew, Ethan, Andrew, Daniel, Anthony, Christopher, Joseph

2004 Jacob, Michael, Joshua, Matthew, Ethan, Andrew, Daniel, William, Joseph, Christopher

2003 Jacob, Michael, Joshua, Matthew, Andrew, Ethan, Joseph, Daniel, Christopher, Anthony

2002 Jacob, Michael, Joshua, Matthew, Ethan, Andrew, Joseph, Christopher, Nicholas, Daniel

continues

Most Popular Names by Year continued

Boy Names

2001 Jacob, Michael, Matthew, Joshua, Christopher, Nicholas, Andrew, Joseph, Daniel, William

2000 Jacob, Michael, Matthew, Joshua, Christopher, Nicholas, Andrew, Joseph, Daniel, Tyler

1999 Jacob, Michael, Matthew, Joshua, Christopher, Nicholas, Andrew, Joseph, Tyler, Daniel

1998 Michael, Jacob, Matthew, Joshua, Christopher, Nicholas, Brandon, Tyler, Andrew, Austin

1997 Michael, Jacob, Matthew, Christopher, Joshua, Nicholas, Brandon, Andrew, Austin, Tyler

1996 Michael, Matthew, Jacob, Christopher, Joshua, Nicholas, Tyler, Brandon, Austin, Andrew

1995 Michael, Matthew, Christopher, Jacob, Joshua, Nicholas, Tyler, Brandon, Daniel, Austin

1994 Michael, Christopher, Matthew, Joshua, Tyler, Brandon, Jacob, Daniel, Nicholas, Andrew

1993 Michael, Christopher, Matthew, Joshua, Tyler, Brandon, Daniel, Nicholas, Jacob, Andrew

1992 Michael, Christopher, Matthew, Joshua, Andrew, Brandon, Daniel, Tyler, James, David

1991 Michael, Christopher, Matthew, Joshua, Andrew, Daniel, James, David, Joseph, John

1990 Michael, Christopher, Matthew, Joshua, Daniel, David, Andrew, James, Justin, Joseph

Most Popular Names by Decade

Girl Names

2000s Emily, Madison, Hannah, Emma, Ashley, Alexis, Samantha, Sarah, Abigail, Olivia

1990s Jessica, Ashley, Emily, Samantha, Sarah, Amanda, Brittany, Elizabeth, Taylor, Megan

1980s Jessica, Jennifer, Amanda, Ashley, Sarah, Stephanie, Melissa, Nicole, Elizabeth, Heather

1970s Jennifer, Amy, Melissa, Michelle, Kimberly, Lisa, Angela, Heather, Stephanie, Nicole

1960s Lisa, Mary, Susan, Karen, Kimberly, Patricia, Linda, Donna, Michelle, Cynthia

1950s Mary, Linda, Patricia, Susan, Deborah, Barbara, Debra, Karen, Nancy, Donna

1940s Mary, Linda, Barbara, Patricia, Carol, Sandra, Nancy, Sharon, Judith, Susan

1930s Mary, Betty, Barbara, Shirley, Patricia, Dorothy, Joan, Margaret, Nancy, Helen

1920s Mary, Dorothy, Helen, Betty, Margaret, Ruth, Virginia, Doris, Mildred, Frances

1910s Mary, Helen, Dorothy, Margaret, Ruth, Mildred, Anna, Elizabeth, Frances, Virginia

1900s Mary, Helen, Margaret, Anna, Ruth, Elizabeth, Dorothy, Marie, Florence, Mildred

| 1890s | Mary, Anna, Margaret, Helen, Elizabeth, Ruth, Florence, Ethel, Emma, Marie | 1880s | Mary, Anna, Emma, Elizabeth, Margaret, Minnie, Ida, Bertha, Clara, Alice |

Boy Names

2000s	Jacob, Michael, Joshua, Matthew, Andrew, Christopher, Joseph, Nicholas, Daniel, William
1990s	Michael, Christopher, Matthew, Joshua, Jacob, Nicholas, Andrew, Daniel, Tyler, Joseph
1980s	Michael, Christopher, Matthew, Joshua, David, James, Daniel, Robert, John, Joseph
1970s	Michael, Christopher, Jason, David, James, John, Robert, Brian, William, Matthew
1960s	Michael, David, John, James, Robert, Mark, William, Richard, Thomas, Jeffrey
1950s	James, Michael, Robert, John, David, William, Richard, Thomas, Mark, Charles

1940s	James, Robert, John, William, Richard, David, Charles, Thomas, Michael, Ronald
1930s	Robert, James, John, William, Richard, Charles, Donald, George, Thomas, Joseph
1920s	Robert, John, James, William, Charles, George, Joseph, Richard, Edward, Donald
1910s	John, William, James, Robert, Joseph, George, Charles, Edward, Frank, Thomas
1900s	John, William, James, George, Charles, Robert, Joseph, Frank, Edward, Thomas
1890s	John, William, James, George, Charles, Joseph, Frank, Robert, Edward, Henry
1880s	John, William, James, George, Frank, Joseph, Henry, Robert, Thomas

Most Popular Twin Names

Girl Names

Ella, Emma	Faith, Hope	Isabella, Sophia
Madison, Morgan	Mackenzie, Madison	Olivia, Sophia
Gabriella, Isabella	Hailey, Hannah	Ava, Emma

Boy Names

Jacob, Joshua	Landon, Logan	Ethan, Evan
Matthew, Michael	Brandon, Bryan	Alexander, Benjamin
Daniel, David	Christian, Christopher	Hayden, Hunter
Isaac, Isaiah	Andrew, Matthew	Nathan, Noah
Taylor, Tyler		**continues**

Most Popular Twin Names   continued

Girl and Boy Names

Madison, Matthew	Jayden, Jordan	Emma, Ethan
Emily, Ethan	Madison, Mason	

Up-and-Coming Names

Girl Names

Addison	Boston	Emme	London
Adeline	Briton	Grace	Olympia
Alma	Cordelia	Heatherly	Paris
Athena	Dresden	Ireland	Rebecca
Ava	Easton	Jameson	Willow
Blessing			

Boy Names

Alston	Bishop	Indigo	Randolph
Ashton	Brooklyn	Lian	Story
Atlantis	Cairo	Logan	Tyler
Beckham	Hudson		

Cultural Cachet

Giving your baby a name that reflects your cultural heritage puts your child in touch with his or her roots and is a wonderful way to proclaim your identity and honor your family's tradition.

This chapter gives you an overview of names that cross cultural lines. Whether you're honoring your own heritage or looking to embrace another, the lists in this chapter help you choose the name that best reflects your child's identity.

African/African American Names

Girl Names

Aba	Kadija	Moesha	Sukutai
Abeni	Kambo	Monisha	Takiyah
Abiba	Kanene	Muncel	Tale
Afric	Kapera	Nabelung	Talisa
Aissa	Karimah	Nakeisha	Talisha
Anada	Kasinda	Narkeasha	Tamika
Arziki	Keisha	Nichelle	Tamira
Baako	Kendis	Niesha	Tamyra
Beyonce	Kesia	Pemba	Tandice
Caimile	Lakeesha	Quanda	Tanginika
Catava	Lakin	Rashida	Taniel
Chipo	Lanelle	Raziya	Tanisha
Corentine	Laqueta	Safiya	Tapanga
Dericia	Laquinta	Saidah	Tariana
Ebere	Latanya	Salihah	Temima
Faizah	Lateefah	Shandi	Timberly
Femi	Latisha	Shandra	Tyrell
Fola	Latoya	Shantell	Tyronica
Gaynelle	Limber	Shaquana	Yetty
Habika	Maizah	Shasmecka	Zabia
Halima	Malika	Shateque	Zalika
Isoke	Mandisa	Sibongile	Zarina
Jariah	Marjani	Sidone	Zina
Jendayi	Mekell	Sitembile	

Boy Names

Africa	Deion	Faraji	Jevonte
Aitan	Denzel	Ibeamaka	Juma
Chata	Deshawn	Jabari	Kendis
Chiamaka	Dewayne	Jamar	Khalon
Chike	Duante	Jayvyn	Lakin
Dakarai	Essien	Jelani	Mablevi

Mykelti	Shaquille	Tavarius	Ulan
Nabulung	Sulaiman	Tavon	Vashon
Naeem	Tabansi	Terrel	Yobachi
Obiajulu	Tabari	Tevin	Zabia
Razi	Tamarr	Trory	Zaid
Roshaun	Tameron	Tyrell	Zareb
Runako	Taurean	Uba	Zeshawn
Salim			

Arabic Names

Girl Names

Akilah	Fatima	Leila	Saida
Ali	Fatin	Lina	Salwa
Alima	Hala	Mahala	Samirah
Aliya	Hana	Majida	Samma
Almira	Hasna	Malak	Sana
Altair	Hayfa	Malika	Saree
Alzena	Helima	Nabila	Sawsan
Amala	Imam	Nada	Shahira
Amani	Iman	Nadira	Shakira
Basimah	Isra	Nafeeza	Shammara
Bibi	Israt	Noy	Siham
Cala	Jala	Oma	Sultana
Cantara	Jamal	Peridot	Sumehra
Carna	Kadira	Qadira	Tahira
Dirran	Kalila	Qamra	Thana
Fadila	Kamil	Rabi	Thara
Faiza	Khalidah	Saffron	Ulima
Farah	Latifa	Safia	Unaiza
Farida	Layla	Sahar	Vega

Arabic Names

Boy Names

Aladdin	Faysal	Majid	Tamir
Aleser	Ghassan	Malik	Tariq
Ali	Ginton	Mansoor	Thabit
Alim	Givon	Mansur	Umar
Altair	Habib	Masud	Usamah
Amal	Hadi	Mohammed	Usman
Amin	Idris	Nassir	Wahib
Amir	Imam	Omar	Walid
Ansari	Jabir	Osman	Waseem
Anwar	Jaleel	Qadir	Xavier
Ashraf	Jalen	Qasim	Yasar
Burhan	Jamal	Rafi	Yasir
Cemal	Jibril	Rafiq	Yazid
Coman	Kadin	Rahman	Yusuf
Ebrahim	Kadir	Sabir	Zafar
Emir	Kalb	Sadik	Zahir
Fadil	Latif	Salah	Zaki
Faisal	Leron	Salim	Zia
Farid	Mahmood	Salman	Zolta
Farook	Mahomet		

Australian Names

Girl Names

Abbey	Ava	Chelle	Hailey
Adaline	Becka	Corrie	Honour
Addison	Bindi	Cristin	Idalia
Adelaide	Brianna	Dale	Jaelynn
Aly	Brooke	Ellie	Janaya
Angelina	Cali	Ember	Jania
Ashley	Carley	Francine	Jewel
Audrianna	Charlotte	Gabriella	Jiya

Jolene	Magdalena	Rae	Tahlia
Jordana	Martika	Sharonda	Tasha
Libbi	Melba	Sheila	Tayla
Lilac	Myla	Sherline	Valmai
Lilli	Nakia	Sibelle	Xara
Lucinda	Narelle	Sukie	Xavia
Madelein	Nyree		

Boy Names

Ashton	Gavin	Kieron	Mikel
Baz	Harrison	Kira	Noah
Bernard	Ivan	Kylie	Norbert
Bert	Jalon	Lachlan	Riley
Braylon	Janica	Landon	Samuel
Bruno	Jase	Larry	Shane
Caleb	Jaylen	Lawson	Sydney
Canna	Jeremey	Lester	Terence
Darnell	Jimm	Logan	Tyler
Dominick	Jodie	Malcom	Wynter
Dylan	Kaelan	Melbourne	Xaviar
Evan	Kiel	Merwin	

Chinese Names

Girl Names

Ah lam	Da xia	Jin	Mei xing
An	Fang	Jing wei	Mei zhen
Bo	Fang hua	Jun	Mingmei
Chow	Genji	Lian	Sun
Chu hua	Guanyin	Lien	Tao
Chun	Hua	Ling	Xiao
Chyou	Hui fang	Mee/Mei	Yin

Chinese Names

Boy Names

An	Gan	Li	Sun
Bo	Ho	Liang	Tung
Chan	Hsin	Manchu	Wang
Chen	Huang fu	Ming	Wen
Chung	Jin˙	Quon	Yu
Cong	Jing	Shen	Yuan
Deshi	Kong	Shing	Zhong

Czech Names

Girl Names

Acedia	Ivana	Marjeta	Ryba
Anezka	Kamil	Milena	Verushka
Beta	Kamila	Nadezda	Viera
Dana	Kate	Rayna	Zdenka
Dusana	Katerine	Reina	Zelenka
Eliska	Lida	Rickena	

Boy Names

Bedrich	Jiri	Milan	Vaclav
Ctirad	Josef	Milos	Vavrin
Damek	Karel	Oldrich	Vavrinec
Dusan	Kazimir	Radek	Viktor
Evzen	Kornel	Strom	Vilem
Jakub	Miklos	Tomas	

Dutch Names

Girl Names

Brandie	Kaatje	Marieke	Schuyler
Brandy	Kalie	Nelleke	Sofie
Dorothea	Karel	Saskia	Tryne
Gisela	Lene		

Boy Names

Arend	Hugo	Kyler	Thijs
Arje	Izaak	Maarten	Van
Arne	Jakob	Piet	Veit
Barend	Jeremias	Roosevelt	Wagner
Carel	Joost	Rutger	Waldemar
Claus	Josef	Schuyler	Wim
Deman	Kees	Skipper	Wolter
Dirk	Klaas	Thies	Zeeman

English Names

Girl Names

Addison	Cady	Eppie	Jannie
Afton	Charla	Faren	Jemma
Alden	Chenelle	Floris	Jolene
Alvina	Clare	Georgie	Karsen
Arden	Corliss	Gilda	Kendra
Arleigh	Dale	Haiden	Kimber
Artis	Dana	Halsey	Kirby
Ashlin	Deisy	Haven	Landon
Berlynn	Delsie	Henna	Laury
Berti	Dixie	Hollyn	Leeza
Binney	Edie	Iolanthe	Liana
Blythe	Effie	Jamey	Lolly
Bonnie	Ellen	Janeth	Lynell

continues

English Names continued

Girl Names

Mada	Piper	Stacia	Torri
Maggie	Primrose	Starleen	Twyla
Maretta	Quinn	Starr	Tyne
Maribel	Ragine	Stockard	Udele
Marlo	Rennie	Sybella	Waverly
May	Rowan	Taci	Weslee
Nara	Rue	Taite	Willie
Odella	Sable	Tanner	Winifred
Ona	Sebrina	Tatum	Yudelle
Osma	Sela	Taya	Zeta
Paiton	Sheldon	Tinble	

Boy Names

Adney	Blake	Davis	Grant
Ahearn	Booker	Dean	Gresham
Alcott	Bradshaw	Denham	Hagley
Aldrich	Bramwell	Derward	Halbert
Alford	Brigham	Diamond	Halsey
Arledge	Buckley	Draper	Hedley
Arundel	Burleigh	Dunley	Hurst
Ashford	Burris	Dyson	Hutton
Atley	Byrd	Edward	Jagger
Atwell	Calvert	Egerton	Jarett
Ayers	Carlton	Ellison	Kelton
Bancroft	Chance	Ewing	Kenley
Barker	Churchill	Farnell	Kidd
Barnes	Clifton	Farold	Kirkland
Barric	Colter	Fielding	Kolton
Beacher	Corwin	Fiske	Laird
Bell	Crandall	Ford	Lathrop
Birkitt	Dalbert	Fuller	Lawford
Bishop	Darby	Geary	Layton

Lewin	Paden	Rockwell	Tate
Lindell	Palmer	Royce	Thorley
Locke	Penn	Rudyard	Tilford
Mick	Pierson	Saxon	Tucker
Miller	Radbert	Shaw	Vance
Mitchell	Raine	Sidwell	Walker
Niles	Rayburn	Snowden	Ward
Norwood	Reed	Spalding	Wesley
Ogden	Rigby	Storm	Will
Onslow	Rochester	Stuart	Zane
Orrick			

French Names

Girl Names

Alair	Déja	Ivette	Oralia
Amarante	Desi	Jae	Orane
Amélie	Dominique	Jardena	Page
Ami	Elita	Jenay	Pippi
Ariane	Eloise	Joelle	Rayna
Babette	Emmaline	Juliet	Remi
Bedelia	Etoile	Lacy	Rue
Berneta	Evonne	Liana	Sarotte
Blaise	Faye	Lisette	Sharice
Brie	Felicity	Lyla	Solange
Brienne	Fontanna	Mallory	Sorrel
Cami	Françoise	Manon	Susette
Camille	Frederique	Mardi	Sylvie
Caron	Gaby	Marguerite	Talia
Chantal	Geneva	Merane	Tayce
Charlotte	Genevieve	Miette	Tempest
Cherelle	Gigi	Mignon	Valerie
Colette	Helene	Monique	Virginie
Daryl	Isabeau	Noelle	

French Names

Boy Names

Alain	Clement	Herve	Prewitt
Alaire	Cornell	Holland	Raynard
Amando	Coyne	Jacques	Renny
Andre	Darcy	Jules	Ross
Antoine	Dax	Lamar	Saber
Aramis	Delano	Lance	Sargent
Averill	Demont	Laurent	Sennett
Beau	Destin	Luc	Simeon
Belden	Donatien	Marc	Sully
Benoit	Edouard	Mason	Telford
Bernard	Fabron	Maxime	Thayer
Boden	Ferrand	Montrell	Thibault
Boone	Gage	Neville	Trent
Borden	Garrison	Norris	Troy
Cassius	Geraud	Olivier	Vardon
Chaney	Giles	Pascal	Verrill
Chante	Gregoire	Pembroke	Victoir
Chase	Hackett	Phillippe	Wyatt
Clark	Harbin	Pierre	Yves

German Names

Girl Names

Adalia	Aubrey	Chay	Emily
Adelina	Ava	Chloris	Emma
Adolfina	Berit	Clay	Erika
Agneta	Bernadette	Dagmar	Ernestine
Alberta	Berta	Dagna	Faiga
Amara	Bluma	Dame	Frederika
Antje	Callan	Ebba	Frieda
Arabelle	Carleigh	Edwina	Gerda

Giselle	Lorelei	Norberta	Ulrika
Gretchen	Lorraine	Odelia	Ulva
Heidi	Louise	Orlantha	Unna
Henrietta	Madison	Pepin	Uta
Idonia	Mallory	Richelle	Viveka
Ilse	Marlene	Roderica	Wanda
Jarvia	Mathilda	Senta	Zelda
Jenell	Minna	Serilda	Zelinda
Leyna	Morgen	Ula	Zelma
Liese	Nixie		

Boy Names

Abelard	Dieter	Imre	Penrod
Adelfried	Dutch	Johann	Raynard
Adelino	Eberhard	Kellen	Redmond
Adelmo	Eldwin	Kiefer	Ritter
Adler	Ellery	Lamar	Roderick
Adolph	Emery	Lance	Rudolph
Alaric	Emil	Leopold	Stein
Albert	Ernest	Loring	Strom
Alger	Ferdinand	Louis/Lewis	Tab
Arnold	Frederick	Luther	Ulbrecht
Baldwin	Fremont	Madison	Varick
Barend	Garin	Manfred	Verner
Bergen	Gerard	Merrill	Vilhelm
Blaz	Gilbert	Nevin	Warner
Brandeis	Hackett	Norbert	Yale
Burke	Hahn	Odell	Yohann
Conrad	Heller	Otis	Zelig
Derek	Herman		

Greek Names

Girl Names

Adara	Damaris	Kairos	Phillippa
Agnes	Daphne	Kalliope	Phoebe
Alessa	Daria	Kyra	Rita
Alexandra	Delfina	Leanore	Saba
Amari	Demetria	Lydia	Sibley
Andrea	Dionne	Magdalen	Sofi
Astra	Elana	Maris	Stefania
Athena	Elisha	Medora	Sula
Basha	Eudora	Melinda	Tahlia
Beryl	Fantasia	Nyssa	Tassos
Calla	Galen	Ola	Thaddea
Callista	Gemini	Olympia	Triana
Carissa	Hera	Ophelia	Trina
Casandra	Hermione	Pallas	Ursula
Charis	Hilary	Pandora	Vanna
Cleo	Iona	Peri	Xena
Colette	Irene	Petra	Yolie
Corrina	Jacey		

Boy Names

Adonis	Colson	Giles	Kyros
Ajax	Corydon	Gregorios	Lazarus
Alec	Cyril	Hamon	Lex
Apollo	Damen	Hector	Makis
Ares	Darius	Hermes	Maron
Arion	Deion	Iakobos	Myron
Aristo	Elias	Icarus	Nicholas
Avram	Erastus	Isaak	Orion
Basil	Eros	Jason	Otis
Carsten	Euclid	Julius	Panos
Christos	Feodore	Kit	Paris
Cohn	Gale	Kostas	Pello

Petar	Strom	Topher	Yanni
Rastus	Tad	Ulysses	Yorick
Rouvin	Talos	Urian	Zenon
Sandro	Thanos	Vassos	Zeus
Stavros	Tibalt	Xenos	Zorba
Stefanos	Titus		

Hawaiian Names

Girl Names

Akela	Iolana	Kekona	Mily
Alana	Kai	Kiana	Nalani
Aloani	Kaili	Kiele	Noelani
Aloha	Kalama	Lana	Okelani
Alohi	Kalea	Lani	Oliana
Anani	Kalia	Lanikai	Peni
Aulii	Kamea	Lokelani	Roselani
Edena	Kane	Makani	Ululani
Haimi	Keandra	Malu	Wanika
Haleigha	Keilana		

Boy Names

Akamu	Kalei	Kimo	Malo
Analu	Kale	Konala	Mauli
Aulii	Kane	Leilani	Meka
Bane	Kanoa	Liko	Moke
Havika	Kapono	Loe	Nalani
Kahoku	Keahi	Maik	Oke
Kai	Keanu	Makaio	Palani
Kaili	Kelii	Makan	Pekelo
Kalani	Keon		

Hispanic/Latino Names

Girl Names

Abril	Gotzone	Marietta	Seina
Adella	Gustava	Mercedes	Teodora
Aidia	Hermosa	Neiva	Terciero
Beatriz	Honoria	Nina	Trella
Benita	Hortensia	Noemi	Ursulina
Brigida	Ines/Inez	Olinda	Usoa
Camila	Irene	Ora	Valentina
Carisa	Isabel	Osana	Veta
Carola	Jacinta	Paquita	Vina
Daria	Jimena	Pepita	Xalbadora
Devera	Joaquina	Pia	Xaviera
Dulce	Karmen	Querida	Xevera
Elena	Kasandra	Quinta	Yadra
Emilie	Katia	Regina	Yoana
Enriqua	Lara	Ria	Yolanda
Fe	Leya	Rocio	Zanetta
Flor	Linda	Sabana	Zita
Friera	Lupe	Sancia	Zurine
Gitana	Maitea		

Boy Names

Abran	Edgardo	Hugo	Mario
Adan	Efraim	Iago	Monte
Adriano	Eloy	Ignado	Neron
Beltran	Fanuco	Ivan	Nicolas
Berto	Felix	Javier	Oliverio
Carlos	Fraco	Jerrold	Orlan
Casimiro	Gaspar	Joaquin	Oro
Cesar	Gervasio	Kemen	Pablo
Dario	Guido	Lazaro	Pedro
Delmar	Hector	Leonel	Ponce
Donatello	Hilario	Lisandro	Rafael

Ramon	Tabor	Urbano	Xabat
Reyes	Timo	Veto	Xalvador
Salvadore	Turi	Vicente	Yago
Senon	Ulises	Vidal	Zacarias
Stefano			

Indian Names

Girl Names

Abha	Gunwanti	Nitya	Tamasa
Aishwarya	Hedy	Nityapriya	Ujwala
Bhamini	Heera	Olena	Ulka
Bhanumati	Iccha	Omana	Vatsala
Chitralekha	Iha	Panna	Vedi
Chitrali	Jalaja	Parama	Wamika
Dhanishta	Jamini	Quarrtulain	Wamil
Dhanya	Kanaka	Quasar	Xena
Ela	Kanakabati	Ragamaya	Yashawini
Elena	Lalita	Ragini	Yashila
Fawiza	Lalitya	Sahila	Zahra
Fayyim	Mahubala	Sai	Zarine
Gunjana	Maina	Tamanna	

Boy Names

Abdul-Jabaar	Harley	Naayantara	Talleen
Abheek	Harmendra	Nabarun	Tamal
Balaaditya	Idris	Omprakash	Utsav
Balachandra	Iham	Omrao	Uttam
Chudamani	Japesh	Palak	Vachan
Duff	Jasbeer	Palash	Vaibhav
Dulal	Kabir	Quasim	William
Erman	Kailas	Quintin	Wiqar
Ervar	Latafat	Rafael	Yashwant
Faraz	Latif	Rafat	Yatin
Farhad	Magan	Sacchidananda	Zarir
Girish	Mahabahu	Sachet	Ziya
Glen			

Irish Names

Girl Names

Adan	Ennis	Keara	Richael
Ailey	Eveleen	Kelsey	Rory
Aislinn	Fallon	Kerri	Ryann
Akaisha	Farran	Leena	Shae
Brea	Fiona	Leila	Shanessa
Breen	Gale	Liadan	Shannon
Brenna	Gladys	Maeve	Sheena
Bridget	Glenna	Moira	Sinead
Cacey	Hiolair	Muriel	Tara/Tari/Taryn
Caitlynn	Hisolda	Nelda	Teagan
Cassidy	Honour/Honoria	Noreen	Treasa/Treise
Ciannait	Ida	Nuala	Unity
Ciar	Ilene	Ohnicio	Uny
Darnell	Ina	Oma	Vevila
Doreen	Jana	Orla	Vevina
Duvessa	Kacey	Padraigin	Zaira
Eileen	Kallie		

Boy Names

Abban	Cormack	Griffin	Liam
Adare	Daire	Hagan	Maclean
Aeary	Daman	Haley	Miles
Aiden	Darby	Hurley	Moriarty
Bain	Devlin	Inerney	Murphy
Beacan	Eman	Inis/Innes	Neilan
Blaine	Evin	Jarlath	Nevan
Braden	Ewan	Justin	Nolyn
Cahir	Fallon	Loaghaire	Odell
Carey	Farren	Kagan	Odran
Carrick	Finnegan	Kean	Ossian
Colm	Galvin	Laughlin	Padric
Conroy	Gannon	Lorcan	Peyton

Pierce	Rearden	Shane	Tiernan
Quigley	Rian	Shea	Torrence
Quinlan	Roark	Sheridon	Uistean
Quinn	Shamus	Teague	Ward

Italian Names

Girl Names

Alessandra	Cornelia	Ines	Oriana
Angela	Dalia	Jovanna	Paola
Anna	Delinda	Justina	Pia
Artemia	Diana	Karah	Priscilla
Aryana	Donatella	Lia	Renata
Benedetta	Elena	Lilla	Rita
Berenice	Emilia	Lucia	Rosa
Bianca	Enza	Luisa	Serafina
Candida	Ester	Marcella	Silvia
Carmela	Eva	Maria	Simona
Carmelina	Felicita	Marta	Tamara
Carola	Franca	Matilde	Teresa
Capri	Francesca	Maura	Valeria
Caprice	Gema	Mia	Vedette
Carla	Ghita	Mila	Venecia
Caterina	Gioia	Miriam	Vera
Colomba	Giovanna	Nicola	Zola
Concetta	Gisella		

Boy Names

Aldo	Boris	Cristoforo	Enrico
Angelo	Bruno	Dante	Ermanno
Antonio	Carlo	Dino	Fabiano
Armando	Carmine	Domenico	Federico
Arturo	Claudio	Donato	Flavio
Bartolomeo	Cola	Edoardo	Francesco
Benito	Corrado	Emanuele	**continues**

Italian Names continued

Boy Names

Franco	Ivo	Nino	Santo
Furio	Jacopo	Oscar	Sergio
Gaspare	Lanz	Otello	Siro
Genovese	Lazaro	Paco	Taddeo
Geraldo	Leonardo	Paolo	Tazio
Giancarlo	Luca	Pietro	Tulio
Gianni	Luigi	Raimondo	Uberto
Gino	Marco	Raul	Ugo
Giorgio	Milan	Renardo	Vito
Guido	Napoleon	Ruggerio	Walter
Indro	Nicolo	Salvatore	

Jamaican Names

Girl Names

Aiesha	Drusilla	Kina	Raca
Aleale	Durene	Lanecia	Raeni
Althea	Earlene	Lateia	Santianna
Alvita	Evie	Latreece	Shalonna
Amoy	Ezola	Lora	Taniyah
Ayana	Francelle	Louella	Tany
Bertena	Freya	Mabinty	Tegan
Breeon	Gelisa	Maisie	Tye
Bryah	Imogen	Maurita	Vea
Cantrice	Jacinta	Mishon	Veruca
Chemier	Jalissa	Necie	Wyndolyn
Corine	Janeka	Ornella	Yasmin
Desreta	Kea	Poppy	Zola
Dorsey			

Boy Names

Adrian	Casim	Edgerin	Mancel
Alizabeth	Chante	Ernard	Montez
Alphonse	Cleavant	Ferric	Nero
Alwan	Cordell	Jamaall	Radd
Amos	Dallen	Janard	Reggis
Andre	Damerae	Jimar	Rhashan
Anthone	Dante	Jomo	Roscoe
Bartt	Daquain	Keyair	Sayon
Bastiaan	Dejohn	Khenan	Serek
Bevaun	Demery	Laron	Sidell
Booker	Deole	Lavon	Treven
Bowie	Duron	Lovell	Vishon
Calbert	Eason	Major	Wyclef

Japanese Names

Girl Names

Ai	Hachi	Kei	Machi
Aiko	Hama	Keiko	Mai
Akako	Hana	Kiaria	Maiko
Aki	Hanako	Kiku	Mari
Akina	Haya	Kimi	Mariko
Amaya	Hisa	Kioko	Masago
Aneko	Hoshi	Kita	Masako
Asa	Ima	Kiwa	Matsuko
Ayame	Ishi	Kohana	Michi
Chika	Iva	Koko	Midori
Chiyo	Jin	Koto	Mieko
Cho	Kaede	Kuma	Mika
Dai	Kagami	Kumiko	Miki
Etsu	Kaiya	Kuri	Mina
Gen	Kameko	Kyoko	Mine
Gin	Kami	Leiko	Mio

continues

Japanese Names continued

Girl Names

Miwa	Rini	Suki	Tora
Miya	Rui	Sumi	Tori
Miyuki	Ruri	Suzu	Toshi
Morie	Ryo	Taka	Uma
Mura	Sachi	Takara	Umeko
Nami	Sada	Taki	Usagi
Naomi	Saki	Tamaka	Uta
Nara	Sakura	Tamiko	Wakana
Nishi	Sasa	Tanaka	Washi
Nori	Sato	Tani	Yasu
Noriko	Sawa	Taree	Yayoi
Nozomi	Sayo	Tazu	Yei
Nyoko	Seki	Tera	Yoko
Rai	Sen	Tetsu	Yoi
Raku	Shika	Toki	Yumi
Rei	Shina	Tomi	Yuri
Ren	Sorano		

Boy Names

Akemi	Jiro	Ken	Masato
Akira	Jo	Kentaro	Michio
Benjiro	Joben	Kin	Miki
Botan	Joji	Kioshi	Minoru
Danno	Jomei	Kisho	Montaro
Fujita	Jun	Kiyoshi	Morio
Goro	Kado	Makoto	Naoko
Haru	Kana	Mamoru	Raidon
Hideaki	Kanaye	Manzo	Renjiro
Hiromasa	Kane	Mareo	Ringo
Hiroshi	Kaori	Maro	Ronin
Hisoka	Kazuo	Masahiro	Saburo
Hoshi	Keitaro	Masao	Samuru

Sen	Taro	Udo	Yoshi
Shiro	Tomi	Yasashiku	Yukio
Takeo	Tomo	Yasuo	Zen
Tani	Toyo	Yogi	

Korean Names

Girl Names

Ae Cha	Ho Sook	Min Hee
Ae Sook	Hwa Young	Min Jung
Bong Cha	Hy	Myung Hee
Cho Hee	Hye Su	Sang Hee
Chun Hei	Hyun Jae	Soo Min
Chung Ae	Hyun Ok	Soo Yun
Chung Cha	Jae Hwa	Soon Bok
Eun	Jin Ae	Sun
Eun Ae	Jin Kyong	Sun Hi
Eun Kyung	Jung	Sun Jung
Eun Mi	Kyung Mi	Young Il
Eun Sun	Kyung Soon	Young Mi
Hana	Mi Cha	Young Soon
Hea Jung	Mi Hi	Yun
Hea Woo	Mi Kyong	Yun Hee
Hei Ryung		

Boy Names

Bae	Hyun Su	Jung-Hwa
Chin Ho	Hyun-Shik	Kang-Dae
Chung-Hee	Il Sung	Kwan
Dae-Ho	In Ho	Kwang-Sun
Dae-Hyun	In-Su	Kyu Bok
Dong-Min	Jae-Hwa	Kyu Bong
Du-Ho	Jae-Sun	Kyung Boy
Hyo	Jin-Sang	Kyung-Sam
Hyun Ki	Jung Hee	Min Ki

continues

Korean Names continued

Boy Names

Mun-Hee	Sang Kyu	Tae-Hyun
Myung-Dae	Shin	Yong Sook
Myung-Ki	Shin-Il	Young Ho
Nam-Kyu	Suk-Chul	Young Ja

Native American Names

Girl Names

Abey	Eyota	Migisi	Sokanon
Adoette	Fala	Muna	Suleta
Alameda	Galilahi	Nadie	Tablita
Alawa	Genesee	Nascha	Tadewi
Aleshanee	Honovi	Nata	Talulah
Amitola	Hurit	Nova	Tiponi
Aponi	Huyana	Nuna	Tiva
Awendela	Ituha	Nuttah	Tuwa
Ayita	Kachina	Odina	Una
Bena	Kai	Olathe	Unega
Bly	Kay	Onida	Urika
Chapawee	Kwanita	Opa	Usdi
Chenoa	Leotie	Pelipa	Utina
Doli	Lulu	Peta	Wachiwi
Donoma	Luyu	Poloma	Weayaya
Dyani	Magena	Quanah	Wyanet
Elu	Mai	Sihu	Zonta
Enola			

Boy Names

Adahy	Atohi	Chogan	Dyami
Ahanu	Bemossed	Cochise	Elan
Alo	Bidziil	Dakotah	Elsu
Ashkii	Chayton	Dichali	Etu

Gad	Langundo	Nitis	Tokala
Gosheven	Lenno	Nodin	Tyee
Hania	Lusio	Ogima	Viho
Hassun	Mahkah	Paco	Waban
Helaku	Maska	Patwin	Wahkan
Holata	Mikasi	Rowtag	Wamblee
Huritt	Misu	Sakima	Wapi
Illanipi	Mohe	Shilah	Wicasa
Kele	Mojag	Tadi	Wuliton
Keme	Nahele	Taima	Wynono
Kitchi	Napayshni	Takoda	Yahto
Koi	Nashoba	Tatonga	Yas
Kwahu	Nigan	Tawa	Yuma
Lallo	Nikan		

Persian Names

Girl Names

Alea	Gita	Leila	Nahid
Armani	Haleh	Lila	Narda
Ayesha	Hawa	Mahubeh	Pari
Aylin	Hester	Manoush	Peri
Azarin	Hestia	Marjan	Roxana
Bibiyana	Jaleh	Mehri	Sadira
Bita	Jasmin	Melika	Soraya
Cyra	Jessamine	Melody	Souzan
Dana	Khina	Mila	Taraneh
Donya	Kira	Mina	Yasmin
Esther	Ladan	Mitra	Zenda
Fila	Laleh	Nadia	Zohreh
Gatha			

Persian Names

Boy Names

Aban	Borna	Hafez	Nasim
Abbas	Cass	Hamid	Omid
Adar	Cyrus	Hassan	Rami
Ahmad	Dareh	Jafar	Rasheed
Akbar	Davood	Jalal	Reza
Amir	Ebi	Javed	Rohan
Aram	Eskander	Kamal	Said
Arash	Faraz	Karim	Sami
Arman	Farhad	Kasper	Shah
Asad	Fazel	Kaveh	Sohrab
Atash	Feroz	Kian	Tabor
Azad	Firouz	Masoud	Taher
Bahram	Ghadir	Mehdi	Xerxes
Behdad	Habib	Mohsen	Zakaria
Bijan	Hadi	Nard	

Polish Names

Girl Names

Alka	Jadwiga	Rayna
Aniela	Jolanta	Reina
Anusia	Kamila	Roza
Basha	Kamilia	Tesia
Basia	Karol	Tola
Brygid	Klaudia	Valeska
Celestyn	Klementyna	Zofia
Danuta	Marian	Zosia
Ewa	Olesia	Zotia
Felcia	Polish	Zuzanna
Filipina	Rasine	

Boy Names

Antoni	Jarek	Marcin
Aurek	Jedrek	Nelek
Bazyli	Jerzy	Pavel
Bialy	Jozef	Stefan
Dobry	Kasper	Szymon
Erek	Konrad	Tanek
Filip	Kornel	Tomasz
Gerik	Lech	Tytus
Jacek	Ludwik	Viktor
Jakub	Mandek	Walenty

Portuguese Names

Girl Names

Armonda	Elisabete	Leticia	Manuelita
Arsenia	Fortunata	Madalena	Pabiola
Cecília	Iracema	Manuela	Sancha

Boy Names

Aemiliano	Davi	Hieronimo	Patrício
Aleixo	Demetrio	Hilario	Reinaldo
Almeida	Eduardo	Lino	Renaldo
Armando	Emilio	Manel	Rodrigo
Arsenio	Faro	Manuel	Ronaldo
Aurelio	Feliciano	Marcelo	Sancho
Branco	Filipe	Mateus	Tadeu
Carlos	Fortunato	Matheus	Thiago
Chavez	Henrique	Miguel	Virgilio
Cristovao			

Russian/Eastern European Names

Girl Names

Alka	Ivanna	Marjeta	Talia
Ana	Jadwiga	Mila	Tanya
Anastasia	Jelena	Nadezda	Tesia
Anezka	Jolanta	Natalya	Tola
Aniela	Julya	Natasha	Valeska
Anstice	Kamila	Natasia	Vania
Avel	Karel/Karol	Nika	Vanka
Basha	Kate/Katerina	Nikita	Vanya
Beta	Kisa	Oksana	Vera
Bohdana	Kiska	Olesia	Verushka
Celestyn	Klementyna	Olga	Viera
Cyzarine	Kludia	Olien	Yalena
Danuta	Lacey	Raisa	Yeva
Dusana	Lara	Rasien	Yuri
Ekaterina	Larissa	Rayna/Reina	Zasha
Eliska	Lida	Ryba	Zdenka
Ewa	Lilia	Sasha	Zelenka
Felicia	Luba	Sashenka	Zilya
Feodora	Marian	Savina	Zofia
Filipina	Marina	Sonia/Sonya	Zotia
Galina	Marinka	Svetlana	Zuzana
Helina			

Boy Names

Akim	Damek	Filip	Jarek
Anstice	Dana	Fyodor	Josef
Antoni	Demyan	Gavrie	Karel
Aurek	Dobry	Gavril	Kaspar
Avel	Dusan	Gerik	Kazimir
Bazyli	Egor	Ilya	Kirill
Bedrich	Erek	Ivan	Kliment
Boris	Evzen	Jakub	Konrad

Konstantin	Nelek	Semyon	Vanya
Kostya	Nikita	Sevastian	Vasily
Lesta	Oldrich	Stefan	Viktor
Lev	Oleg	Strom	Vilem
Maksim	Osip	Tanek	Walenty
Marcin	Pavel	Tomas	Yakov
Mikhail	Radek	Uri/Uriah/Urie	Yerik
Milos	Rurik	Ustin	Yevgeni
Naum	Sacha	Vadim	

Scandinavian Names

Girl Names

Abbellonna	Freja	Lena/Lene
Agata	Freya	Lisabet/Lisbet
Agneta	Gala	Louisa/Lovisa
Amalia	Gisela	Marcy
Anke	Greet/Gret/Greta	Margareta/Margit
Anneliese	Guro	Matilda/Matilde
Barbro	Hanna	Mia
Beatrix	Hedda/Hedvig	Monika
Birgit/Birgitta/Birgitte	Helena	Nissa
Brynhild	Hildegard	Oda
Carina	Idonea/Idony/Idun	Ola
Celia	Ingrid	Petrine
Charlotta	Irena	Petronilla
Cornelia	Janna/Jesine	Quenby
Dagmar	Jette	Rae
Dania	Johanna/Jonna	Rakel
Dorothea	Karen/Karin	Rebekka
Ebba	Karita	Runa
Elke	Katrine	Sanna
Erika	Klara	Sibella/Sibilla/Sibylla
Eva	Laila	Sigrid

continues

Scandinavian Names continued

Girl Names

Sonja/Sonje	Ulla	Vega
Susanna	Ulrika	Vera
Thora	Ulrike	Vilhemina/Wilhelmina
Tilda	Unn	Viveka
Tova/Tove	Vanja	Ylwa

Boy Names

Aksel	Georg	Peder/Pieter
Amund	Greger/Gregor	Per
Anders	Haakon	Quinby
Anton	Hendrik	Ragnar
Balder	Igor	Rikard
Benedikt	Ingmar	Roth
Bjorn	Ivar	Rurik
Borg	Jakob	Sigmund
Canute	Jorgen	Soren
Carolus	Josef	Stefan
Claus	Karl	Sven
Cornelis	Konstantin	Tait
Dag	Kristoffer	Thorwald
Davin	Larson	Torgeir
Diederik/Dierk/Dirk	Ludvig	Ulf
Dyre	Maarten	Ulrik
Edvard	Matheu	Urban
Egil	Michiel	Uwe
Emil	Morten	Valdermar
Erik	Natanael	Verner
Filip	Nels	Viktor
Fiske	Niklaus	Von
Frans	Odin	Waldemar
Fredrik	Olaf/Olav/Olof	Werner
Gamel	Ove	Willem
Garth	Pal/Pavel	

Scottish/Welsh Names

Girl Names

Aileen	Bryce	Leslie
Blair	Christal	Meredith
Briton	Elspeth	Paisley
Bronwyn	Guinevere	Tegan

Boy Names

Alistair	Calen	Rance
Angus	Fife	Rhys
Bowen	Hamish	Ross
Boyd		

Swedish Names

Girl Names

Becka	Gunilla	Karina	Marna
Bibi	Henrika	Linnaea	Naima
Dahlia	Hulda	Malin	Vada
Edla	Inger	Marit	

Boy Names

Algot	Kaj	Mans	Sten
Arvid	Kalle	Marten	Ström
Arwed	Kettil	Nilsson	Sture
Elof	Lindberg	Olander	Torell
Gjord	Lindell	Petter	Torger
Hilmar	Loffe	Sigbjörn	Torrell
Jöns	Malin	Sigge	

Turkish Names

Girl Names

Adalet	Beste	Feyza	Renan
Afet	Bikem	Gunce	Saadet
Ahsen	Birsen	Hamiyet	Sarila
Ahu	Cansu	Hulya	Sema
Asuman	Cemile	Katife	Umay
Aydan	Deniz	Kutlay	Yelda
Aysel	Ekin	Manolya	Yesim
Azime	Elma	Melis	Yildiz
Bahar	Esin	Neylan	Zerdali
Behice	Fehime	Pervin	Zerrin
Beria			

Boy Names

Abi	Bedir	Kahil	Ozturk
Acar	Berk	Kahraman	Sener
Adli	Cahil	Kemal	Sevilen
Ahir	Duman	Kerem	Sukru
Akar	Emre	Khan	Tabib
Asad	Enver	Kiral	Umit
Asker	Erol	Mesut	Uner
Ayden	Halil	Murat	Yunus
Azad	Husamettin	Ohannes	Zeheb
Baris	Ihsan	Onan	Zeki
Basir	Kabil	Osman	

Ukrainian Names

Girl Names

Alla	Kalyna	Mariya	Valentyna
Dariya	Levina	Masha	Vesna
Daryna	Lyuba	Odessa	Zenovia
Hanna	Lyudmyla	Olena	

Boy Names

Andriy	Kyrylo	Oleksandr	Theodosius
Bohdan	Luka	Oleksiy	Valentyn
Dmytro	Marko	Petro	Yuriy
Fedir	Mykhailo	Taras	Zenon
Grigor	Mykola		

Hunting Through History

Names taken from ancient times can carry a lot of weight and history. And who knows—maybe naming your baby after a mythological character or pioneer may up the ante for his or her greatness! If your penchant is toward the more modern, you'll find choices from the Old West for your modern-day cowboy or cowgirl. Or perhaps your child was born on a day that holds significance. Why not name him or her after that day, time, month, or week?

Hang on, because this chapter covers a lot of history.

Ancient Names

Girl Names

Name	Origin	Name	Origin
Abtin	Persian	Indira	Sanskrit
Ahmose	Egyptian	Isis	Egyptian
Anis	Romany/Gypsy	Jaya	Sanskrit
Ardeshir	Persian	Kasra	Persian
Aria	Persian	Khety	Egyptian
Aruna	Sanskrit	Leela	Sanskrit
Asha	Sanskrit	Meena	Sanskrit
Bameket	Egyptian	Nebta	Egyptian
Deva	Sanskrit	Neferu	Egyptian
Djab	Egyptian	Peneli	Romany/Gypsy
Eir	Old Norse	Priya	Sanskrit
Emmanaia	Romany/Gypsy	Rennefer	Egyptian
Everilda	Romany/Gypsy	Saga	Old Norse
Freya	Old Norse	Senen	Egyptian
Frigg	Old Norse	Sif	Old Norse
Gerd	Old Norse	Signy	Old Norse
Gita	Sanskrit	Sigrun	Old Norse
Grid	Old Norse	Siv	Old Norse
Gudrun	Old Norse	Talaitha	Romany/Gypsy
Heidrun	Old Norse	Tetisheri	Egyptian
Hekenu	Egyptian	Valkryie	Old Norse

Boy Names

Name	Origin	Name	Origin
Abtin	Persian	Behrooz	Persian
Alvis	Old Norse	Caspar	Romany/Gypsy
Ambrosius	Romany/Gypsy	Cyrus	Persian
Ankhhaf	Egyptian	Darius	Persian
Ardalan	Persian	Dipak	Sanskrit
Balder	Old Norse	Djau	Egyptian
Banefre	Egyptian	Emaus	Romany/Gypsy

Name	Origin	Name	Origin
Frey	Old Norse	Othi	Romany/Gypsy
Freyr	Old Norse	Persepolis	Persian
Gagino	Romany/Gypsy	Prakash	Sanskrit
Gandale	Old Norse	Rahotep	Egyptian
Gunnar	Old Norse	Rama	Sanskrit
Hormoz	Persian	Ranjit	Sanskrit
Huni	Egyptian	Sanjay	Sanskrit
Imhotep	Egyptian	Sigurd	Old Norse
Ing	Old Norse	Sindri	Old Norse
Jarl	Old Norse	Sohrab	Persian
Kourosh	Persian	Tem	Romany/Gypsy
Krishna	Sanskrit	Thor	Old Norse
Kumar	Sanskrit	Tobar	Romany/Gypsy
Lakshmi	Sanskrit	Tyr	Old Norse
Loki	Old Norse	Unas	Egyptian
Mahesh	Sanskrit	Vidar	Old Norse
Nataraj	Sanskrit	Volund	Old Norse
Nedes	Egyptian	Xerxes	Persian
Njord	Old Norse	Zindel	Romany/Gypsy
Odin	Old Norse		

Names from Mythology

Girl Names

Acantha	Cassandra	Guinevere	Polyhymnia
Aegle	Ceridwen	Iblis	Rhiannon
Aella	Clarine	Isolde	Tanith
Agaue	Clio	Lachesis	Tara
Aglaia	Clotho	Lynelle	Terpsichore
Agrona	Cotovatre	Melpomene	Thalia
Atropos	Diana	Mnemosyne	Tryamon
Avalon	Dido	Nimaine/Nineve	Urania
Bedegrayne	Erato	Ourania	Venus
Branwen	Euphrosyne	Pandora	Viviane
Calliope	Euterpe	Phoebe	Ysolde

Names from Mythology

Boy Names

Ahura Mazda	Charon	Leander	Rion
Aleyn	Coeus	Marrock	Rivalen
Atlas	Dagonet	Merlin	Robin (Hood)
Awarnach	Damon	Octha	Ryons
Balduf	Dionysus	Odysseus	Uther
Beowulf	Drystan	Parsifal	Valkyrie
Blaise	Enki	Pelleas	Vidar
Breri	Frollo	Percival	Vortigem
Cabal	Hermes	Prometheus	Zephyr
Cavalon	Lancelot		

Names from Arthurian Legend

Girl Names

Acheflour	Dindrane	Igraine	Morgane
Angharad	Elain	Iseult	Morgause
Angharat	Enid	Isolde	Morvydd
Avalon	Ettard	Laudine	Nimue
Belakane	Ganieda	Lausanne	Nineve
Blancheflour	Guinevere	Lisanor	Olwen
Brangaine	Gwenevak	Llamrei	Sabelle
Branwen	Gyneth	Lynette	Shalott
Clarissant	Herzeloyde	Lyonesse	Vivian
Condwiramurs	Iblis	Modron	Ygraine
Cundrie			

Boy Names

Accalon	Ban	Bors	Caradoc
Aglovale	Bedivere	Bran	Catigern
Agravain	Bilis	Breunor	Claudas
Arthur	Bleoberis	Cador	Constantine
Balin	Bliant	Calogrenant	Culhwch

Custennin	Geraint	Lionel	Percival
Dagonet	Gingalain	Llyr	Rience
Daniel	Goreu	Loholt	Sagramor
Dinadan	Gorlois	Lot	Segwarides
Drystan	Griflet	Lucan	Teithi
Ector	Gwalltafwyn	Lucius	Tom
Erbin	Gwyn	Maleagant	Tor
Erec	Halwn	Marrok	Trevrizent
Evelake	Hector	Meliadus	Tristan
Feirefiz	Hoel	Menw	Turquine
Frollo	Ironside	Merlin	Uchdryd
Gaheris	Ither	Mordred	Urien
Gahmuret	Kay	Morholt	Uther
Galahad	Kilydd	Palamedes	Valerin
Galehot	Lamorak	Pelleas	Vortigern
Gareth	Lancelot	Pelles	Vortimer
Gawain	Leodegrance	Pellinore	Ywain

Victorian Names

Girl Names

Abigale	Bess	Ethel	Hannah
Ada	Charity	Eudora	Hattie
Adella	Charlotte	Eva	Helen
Agnes	Chastity	Fanny	Helene
Allie	Claire	Fidelia	Henrietta
Almira	Constance	Flora	Hester
Alva	Cynthia	Florence	Hope
Amelia	Dorothy	Frances	Hortence
America	Edith	Geneve	Jane
Ann	Edna	Genevieve	Jessamine
Arrah	Eleanor	Georgia	Josephine
Beatrice	Elizabeth	Gertrude	Julia
Becky	Emma	Gladys	Juliet
Bernice	Esther	Grace	Katherine

continues

Victorian Names continued

Girl Names

Laura	Mary	Peggy	Sarah
Leah	Matilda	Permelia	Savannah
Lenora	Maude	Philomena	Selina
Letitia	Maxine	Phoebe	Sophronia
Lila	Mildred	Polly	Stella
Lorena	Minerva	Rachel	Theodosia
Lottie	Molly	Rebecca	Vertiline
Louisa	Natalie	Rhoda	Virginia
Lucy	Nellie	Rowena	Vivian
Lulu	Nettie	Ruth	Winnifred
Lydia	Nora	Sally	Zona
Margaret	Orpha	Samantha	Zylphia
Martha			

Boy Names

Aaron	Benjamin	Edmund	Harland
Abraham	Bennet	Edwin	Harrison
Alan	Bernard	Eldon	Harvey
Albert	Bertram	Elijah	Henry
Alexander	Buford	Enoch	Hiram
Alonzo	Byron	Ezekiel	Horace
Ambrose	Calvin	Ezra	Hugh
Amon	Charles	Francis	Isaac
Andrew	Christopher	Franklin	Isaiah
Archibald	Clarence	Frederick	Jacob
Arnold	Clement	Gabriel	James
Asa	Clinton	Garrett	Jasper
August	Cole	George	Jedediah
Barnabas	Columbus	Gideon	Jefferson
Bartholomew	Daniel	Gilbert	Jesse
Benedict	David	Granville	Joel

John	Mark	Orville	Simon
Jonathan	Martin	Oscar	Stanley
Joseph	Matthew	Owen	Stephen
Joshua	Maurice	Patrick	Thaddeus
Josiah	Maxwell	Paul	Theodore
Julian	Merrill	Perry	Thomas
Julius	Meriwether	Peter	Timothy
Lafayette	Micajah	Ralph	Ulysses
Lawrence	Mordecai	Raymond	Uriah
Leander	Morgan	Reuben	Victor
Lester	Morris	Richard	Walter
Lewis	Nathaniel	Robert	Warren
Levi	Ned	Roderick	Washington
Louis	Newton	Rudolph	Wilfred
Lucas	Nicholas	Rufus	William
Lucian	Ninian	Samuel	Zachariah
Luke	Obediah	Seth	Zebulon
Luther	Octavius	Silas	Zedock
Marcellus	Ora		

Heroes and Heroines

Girl Names

Amelia Earhart	Harriet Beecher Stowe	Mary Wollstonecraft
Anne Hutchinson	Helen Keller	Molly Pitcher
Clara Barton	Jane Addams	Penina Moise
Deborah Sampson	Lucretia Mott	Rebecca Gratz
Dolley Madison	Lucy Stone	Rosa Parks
Elizabeth Cady Stanton	Margaret Corbin	Sojourner Truth
Emma Lazarus	Maria Weston Chapman	Susan B. Anthony
Florence Nightingale	Marie Curie	Zora Neale Hurston
Gloria Steinem		

Heroes and Heroines

Boy Names

Aaron Lopez

Adolphus Simeon
  Solomons

Charles Calistus Burleigh

Crispus Attucks

Edward Rosewater

Francis Salvador

Frederick Douglass

George Washington
  Carver

John Calhoun

Leon Dyer (Col.)

Leopold Karpeles

Levi Strauss

Louis Pasteur

Nathan Hale

Paul Revere

Robert E. Lee

Sam Houston

Solomon Bush

Theodore Parker

Thomas Jefferson

Ulysses S. Grant

Wendell Phillips

William Lloyd Garrison

Pioneers/Explorers

Girl Names

Christa McAuliffe

Elizabeth I (Queen)

Isabella Eberhardt

Louise Boyd

Mae Jemison

Martha Ballard

Mary Kingsley

Roberta Bondar

Sacajawea

Sally Ride

Sue Hendrickson

Sylvia Earle

Valentina Tereshova

Boy Names

Alexander Mackenzie

Amerigo Vespucci

Bartolomeu Dias

Christopher Columbus

Daniel Boone

David Thompson

Edmund Hillary

Eric the Red

Ferdinand Magellan

Francis Drake

Henry Hudson

Hernán Cortés

Jacques Cousteau

James Cook

Jedediah Smith

John Cabot

Juan de Cartegena

Kit Carson

Leif Eriksson

Marco Polo

Matthew Henson

Meriwether Lewis

Ponce de Leon

Samuel de Champlain

Sebastian Cabot

Walter Raleigh

William Clark

Zebulon Pike

Cowboys and Cowgirls

Girl Names

Annie Oakley	Helen Hunt Jackson	Patsy Montana
Belle Starr	Lucille Mulhall	Pauline Cushman
Dale Evans	Martha "Calamity Jane" Cannary	Rose Maddox
Diane Fletcher		

Boy Names

Allen "Rocky" Lane	Eddie Dean	Monte Hale
Bill Pickett	Gene Autry	Nat Love
Bob Leavitt	George Glenn	Roy Rogers
Buffalo Bill	Jay "Tonto" Silverheels	Sunset Carson
Buster Crabbe	Jesse James	Tagg Oakley
Butch Cassidy	John Henry "Doc" Holliday	Tom Mix
Cooper Smith	John Wayne	Will Rogers
		Wyatt Earp

Hippie Names

Girl Names

Autumn	Flower	Love	Sky/Skye
Butterfly	Grace	Meadow	Star
Charity	Harmony	Moon	Stardust
China	Hope	Ocean	Starlight
Crystal	Jade	Opal	Summer
Daisy	Janis	Peace	Sunflower
Dharma	Joy	Rain	Sunny
Faith	Karma	Rainbow	Sunshine
Feather	Lilly	Rose	Willow

Boy Names

Blue	Quinn	Stone	Ziggy
Dylan	River	Storm	Zoe
Ethan	Sage	Timothy	
Lennon	Sebastian	Xavier	

Calendar-Based Names

Girl Names

Aba	Brook	Kesa	Spring
Abmaba	Cerelia	Koleyn	Summer
Aki	Chyou	Kudio	Tuesday
Akiyama	Easter	Kwaku	Verda
Akosua	Ekua	Kwashi	Vernice
Ajua	Epua	Laverne	Wednesday
April	February	May	Welya
Arbor	January	Season	Winter
Autumn	Jesen	Sorley	Zima
Aviva	June		

Boy Names

Abeeku	Dack	Koffi	Sarngin
Arley	Daren	Koleyn	Somerton
Arslan	Edan	Kwaku	Theron
August	Equinox	Kwamin	Ver
Averil	Estio	Kwau	Verano
Badar	Hiemo	Leo	Wen
Botan	Hurley	Noel	Yule
Cam	Jarek	Quillan	Zeeman
Cerella	Kell	Ramadan	Zenos
Chand	Kevat		

Historical Firsts

Girl Names

Historical Name	Year	Noteworthiness
Anne Bradstreet	1650	First female American published writer
Annie Moore	1892	First immigrant to pass through Ellis Island
Antonia Novello	1990	First female U.S. surgeon general
Arabella Mansfield	1869	First woman lawyer
Barbara Walters	1976	First female network TV newscaster

Historical Name	Year	Noteworthiness
Diane Crump	1970	First female Kentucky Derby jockey
Emily Warner	1973	First female commercial airline pilot
Geraldine Ferraro	1984	First female vice presidential nominee in a major party (Democrat)
Gertrude Ederle	1926	First woman to swim the English Channel
Henrietta Johnson	1707	First female professional American artist
Jacqueline Means	1977	First female ordained Episcopal priest
Janet Guthrie	1986	First woman to race in the Indy 500
Mary Kies	1809	First woman issued a U.S. patent
Nellie Tayloe Ross	1925	First female U.S. governor (Wyoming)
Sally Jean Priesand	1972	First female ordained rabbi in the United States
Sandra Day O'Connor	1981	First female Supreme Court justice
Susanna Medora Salter	1887	First female elected mayor in the United States
Tenley Albright	1953	First American to win Women's World Figure Skating Championship
Victoria Woodhull	1872	First woman to run for U.S. president
Wallis Simpson	1936	First *Time* magazine "Woman of the Year"
Wilma Mankiller	1983	First woman to lead a major Native American tribe (Cherokee)

Boy Names

Historical Name	Year	Noteworthiness
Al Jolson	1927	Played lead role in first talking picture, *The Jazz Singer*
Alan Shepard Jr.	1961	First American in space
Benjamin Franklin	1753	First U.S. postmaster
Chadwick Haheo Rowan	1993	First non-Japanese sumo wrestler
Charles Lindbergh	1927	First man to fly solo across the Atlantic Ocean
Christiaan Barnard	1967	Performed first human heart transplant
Chuck Yaeger	1947	First person to break the sound barrier
David Farragut	1866	First U.S. Navy admiral
Edmund Hillary (Sir)	1953	First climber to reach top of Mt. Everest
Elias Haskett Derby	1805	America's first millionaire
John Jay	1789	First U.S. Supreme Court Justice
John McDermott	1897	First Boston Marathon winner

continues

Historical Firsts continued

Boy Names

Historical Name	Year	Noteworthiness
Neil Armstrong	1969	First man to walk on the moon
Maurice Garin	1903	First Tour de France winner
Roald Amundsen	1911	First man to reach the South Pole
Roger Bannister	1954	First person to break the 4-minute mile
Samuel Hopkins	1790	Awarded U.S. patent #1
Steve Fossett	2002	First balloonist to fly solo around the world
Tim Hyer	1841	First boxing champion
Yuri Alekseyevich Gagarin	1961	First human in space

Historical Family Surnames

Girl Names

Ali	Harper	Peyton
Avery	Hayden	Reagan
Blake	Lindsay	Reese
Campbell	McKenzie	Simone
Delaney	Paige	Whitney

Boy Names

Armstrong	Emerson	Moore
Bowen	Grant	Price
Brown	Kendall	Pritchard
Clark	Kennedy	Reilly
Crippen	Logan	Russell

Occupations Throughout History

Girl Names

Name	Occupation	Name	Occupation
Bailey	Bailiff	Piper	Pipe player
Bernice	Skilled warrior	Taylor	Tailor
Fallon	Textile worker	Tinker	Mender of pots and pans
Lavender	Washer woman	Yvonne	Archer

Boy Names

Name	Occupation	Name	Occupation
Archer	Archer	Hunter	Hunter
Brewster	Brewer	Marshal	Marshal
Chandler	Candle maker	Mason	Stone worker
Clark	Scholar	Miller	Grain grinder
Cohen	Priest	Ranger	Warden/Gamekeeper
Collier	Coal miner	Sawyer	Wood worker
Crocker	Maker of pots	Tanner	Cures animal hides
Fisher	Fisherman	Tucker	Cleans cloth
Gunner	Battle warrior		

Historical Landmarks

Girl Names

Everest	Pisa	Sydney
Liberty	Shea	Victoria

Boy Names

Alamo	Mahal	Tabor
Brooklyn	Niagara	Vinson
Lincoln	Panama	

Names from Religion

Some parents look to their religion for guidance when choosing a more spiritual name for their baby. In this chapter, you'll find a wide range of choices, from Greek and Roman gods; to angel names; to names of virtues; to historical names such as those of popes, saints, and religious leaders. You'll also find names with Christian, Jewish, Buddhist, Hindu, Muslim, and Wiccan backgrounds.

And even if you've chosen a name already, this chapter can fill you in on its history or religious significance.

Greek and Roman Gods

Girl Names

Goddess	Reign	Goddess	Reign
Amphitrite	Sea goddess	Hera	Goddess of marriage
Aphrodite	Goddess of love and beauty	Hestia	Goddess of the hearth
		Iris	Goddess of the rainbow
Artemis	Goddess of the moon; huntress	Istra	Goddess of psyche
		Juno	Goddess of fidelity
Athena	Goddess of wisdom	Lucina	Goddess of childbirth
Bellona	Goddess of war	Minerva	Goddess of wisdom
Demeter	Goddess of agriculture	Mnemosyne	Goddess of memory
Dione	Titan goddess	Nike	Goddess of victory
Eos	Goddess of the dawn	Nyx	Goddess of the night
Eris	Goddess of discord	Pales	Goddess of shepherds and herdsmen
Flora	Goddess of flowers		
Fortuna	Goddess of fortune	Selene	Moon goddess
Gaea	Goddess of the earth	Terra	Earth goddess
Hebe	Goddess of youth	Venus	Goddess of love
Hecate	Goddess of sorcery and witchcraft		

Boy Names

God	Reign	God	Reign
Apollo	God of beauty	Hypnos	God of sleep
Atlas	Titan god	Janus	God of gates and doors
Baccus	God of wine	Momus	God of ridicule
Cronus	God of harvests	Morpheus	God of dreams
Dionysus	God of wine	Pluto	God of the underworld
Eros	God of love	Plutus	God of wealth
Hades	God of the underworld	Pontus	Sea god
Helios	God of the sun	Poseidon	Sea god
Hephaestus	God of fire	Proteus	Sea god
Hercules	Hero (son of Zeus)	Quirinus	War god
Hermes	God of physicians and thieves	Silvanus	God of the woods and fields
Hyman	God of marriage	Terminus	God of boundaries and landmarks

God	Reign	God	Reign
Thanatos	God of death	Vulcan	God of the forge
Vertumnus	God of fruits and vegetables	Zeus	King of the gods

Angels

Girl Names

Angel	Reign	Angel	Reign
Amriel	Angel of May	Muriel	Angel of June
Arael	Angel of birds	Nitika	Angel of precious stones
Cassiel	The earthly mother	Oriel	Angel of destiny
Dabria	One of five angels who transcribed books Ezra dictated	Pariel	Angel who wards off evil
		Sofiel	Angel of fruits and vegetables
Dara	Angel of rains and rivers	Talia	Angel who escorts the sun on its daily course
Dina	Guardian angel of wisdom		
Hariel	Angel of tame animals	Tariel	Angel of summer
Laila	Angel who guides spirits at their birth		

Boy Names

Angel	Reign	Angel	Reign
Aban	Angel of October	Gabriel	Angel who sits at left hand of God
Arel	Angel of fire		
Asasiel	One of five angels who transcribed books Ezra dictated	Geron	Angel called during magic-based prayer
		Hamal	Angel of water
Asmodel	Angel of April	Hamaliel	Angel of August
Azar	Angel of November	Irin	An exalted angel; twin of Qaddis
Barchiel	Angel of February		
Dai	Angel of December	Javan	Guardian angel of Greece
Elijah	Legendary prophet-turned-angel	Joel	Archangel who suggested Adam name things
Ethan	One of five angels who transcribed books Ezra dictated	Kadi	Angel who presides over Friday
		Lucifer	Angel of the morning star
Farris	Angel who oversees second hour of the night	Malchidiel	Angel of March

continues

Angels continued

Boy Names

Angel	Reign	Angel	Reign
Manuel	Angel who oversees the Cancer zodiac sign	Uriel	Inspiration of writers and teachers
Michael	Angel who holds the keys to the kingdom of heaven	Yahriel	Angel of the moon
Murdad	Angel of July	Yale	Angel who attends throne of God
Raphael	Angel of healing	Zachriel	Angel of memory
Sauriel	One of five angels who transcribed books Ezra dictated	Zamael	Angel of joy
		Zaniel	Angel of Monday and the Libra zodiac sign
Seleucia	One of five angels who transcribed books Ezra dictated	Zazel	Angel summoned for love invocations

Biblical Names

Girl Names

Aaliyah	Candace	Gilana	Joakima
Abira	Carmel	Hadassah	Joan
Abital	Cassia	Hali	Joelle
Ada	Chanah	Hana	Jonina
Adalia	Dara	Helah	Jora
Ahava	Dayla	Ideh	Jordane
Amissa	Delilah	Ilana	Josephine
Apphia	Dinah	Ivah	Judith
Ascah	Eden	Ivana	Justine
Asenath	Edna	Jale	Kadisha
Atarah	Eleora	Jane	Keturah
Athaliah	Ellen	Janna	Keziah
Aviva	Esther	Japhia	Leah
Bathsheba	Eunice	Jedida	Lemuela
Bethany	Eve	Jemima	Lois
Beulah	Galya	Jensine	Lydia
Bracha	Geva	Jerusha	Mahalath

Marsena

Martha

Mehitabel

Miriam

Moriah

Myra

Naomi

Neriah

Peninnah

Persis

Phoebe

Rachel

Rebekah

Rhoda

Ruth

Salome

Samaria

Sapphira

Sela

Seraphina

Shera

Shobi

Susanna

Tabitha

Talitha

Tamar

Tirza

Tryphena

Vashti

Zillah

Zilpah

Zipporah

Zoe

Boy Names

Aaron

Abel

Abijah

Abner

Abraham

Absolom

Achan

Adam

Adlai

Allon

Alphaeus

Alvah

Amal

Ammiel

Amon

Amos

Amram

Ananias

Anath

Ara

Archelaus

Asa

Asher

Azariah

Barnabas

Bartholomew

Baruch

Benaiah

Bethuel

Boaz

Caesar

Cain

Carmi

Carpus

Cephus

Cyrus

Daniel

Darius

David

Demetrius

Ebenezer

Edom

Ehud

Elam

Elazar

Elihu

Elijah

Elkanah

Emanuel

Enoch

Eran

Esau

Ethan

Ezekiel

Ezra

Felix

Gabriel

Garrison

Gershon

Gideon

Goliath

Gomer

Haggai

Haran

Heber

Hillel

Hiram

Hosea

Ira

Isaiah

Ishmael

Israel

Ithamar

Jabez

Jabin

Jachin

Jacob

Jadon

Jairus

James

Japhet

Jared

Jason

Javan

Jeremiah

Jericho

Jesse

Job

Joel

Jonah

Jonathan

Joram

Joseph

Joshua

Josiah

Judah

continues

Biblical Names continued

Boy Names

Julius	Nathan	Raphael	Simon
Kenan	Nehemiah	Reuben	Solomon
Laban	Nicodemus	Reuel	Timothy
Lamech	Noah	Rufus	Tiras
Levi	Obadiah	Samson	Tobias
Luke	Omar	Samuel	Uri
Madai	Oren	Saul	Uriel
Malachi	Pallu	Seth	Uzi
Mark	Paul	Shadrach	Zachariah
Meshach	Peter	Shiloh	Zalmon
Micah	Phares	Silas	Zared
Moses	Pontius	Simeon	Zebulon
Nahum			

Saints

Girl Names

Adela	Brigid	Hilda
Agape	Catherine of Siena	Hyacintha Mariscotti
Agatha	Cecilia	Irene
Agnes	Chionia	Ita
Alice	Christina	Joan Delanoue
Anastasia Patricia	Clare of Assisi	Julia Billiart
Angela Merici	Colette	Juliana Falconieri
Antonia	Dymphna	Julitta of Caesarea
Anysia	Eulalia of Merida	Kateri Tekakwitha
Audrey	Eve	Lilian
Aurea	Felicity	Lucy of Syracuse
Barbara	Flora of Beaulieu	Madeleine Sophie Barat
Basilissa	Gemma Galgani	Matilda
Beatrice	Genevieve	Maura of Troyes
Bertilla Boscardin	Gertrude of Helfta	Melania the Younger

Mercedes

Monica

Nonnita

Patricia

Raphaela Mary Porras

Rita of Cascia

Rose of Lima

Rufina

Sabina

Scholastica

Seraphina

Solangia

Sunniva

Ursula

Veronica Giuliana

Zita

Boy Names

Adalbert

Aedan

Albert the Great

Aloysius

Amator

Ambrose

Anselm

Apollo

Arsenius the Great

Austin of Canterbury

Bairre

Barnabas

Benedict

Benen

Blaan

Boris

Brendan

Bruno

Caedmon

Cajetan

Canice

Castor

Chad

Charles Borromeo

Ciaran

Clement

Colm

Conrad

Cyprian

Damian

Denis

Dewi

Dominic of Silos

Donatus

Dunstan

Eadbert

Edmund the Martyr

Elmo

Fabian

Fergus

Francis of Assisi

Frederick of Utrecht

Gatian

George the Great

Gerard Majella

Gerlac

Germanus

Gildas the Wise

Giles

Gleb

Godfrey

Guy of Cortona

Harvey

Henry of Cocket

Hervé

Hugh of Rouen

Ivo of Chartres

James

Jerome

Joachim

Jordan of Saxony

Jude

Julian the Hospitaller

Julius

Justus

Kenneth

Landry

Laserian

Laurence

Leger

Leonard

Lucius

Luke

Macartan

Marcellus

Marius

Mark

Martin

Maximilian

Medard

Modan

continues

Saints continued

Boy Names

Montanus	Quentin	Timothy
Nicholas	Radbod	Tobias
Nino	Raymund	Tutilo
Norbert	Roderic	Urban V
Odo of Cluny	Romanus	Victor Maurus
Oliver Plunket	Rupert of Salzburg	Vincent de Paul
Otto	Silvin	Walter of L'Esterp
Owen	Stephen of Hungary	Wenceslaus
Patrick	Tarasius	Wolstan
Paul Miki	Teilo	Wulfstan
Peter Canisius	Ternan	Zachary
Philip Neri	Theodore	

Religious Leaders

Girl Names

Agnes	Helen Prejean (Sister)	Mother Cabrini
Aimee Semple McPherson	Jeanette Rankin	Mother Seton
	Joan of Arc	Mother Teresa
Barbara Harris	Marianne Williamson	Suzanne Langer
Elizabeth Fry	Mary Baker Eddy	Sylvia Pankhurst
Harriet Martineau	Mary Daly	Tammy Faye Bakker

Boy Names

Al Sharpton (Reverend)	Confucius	Frederick Buechner
Augustine (Saint)	Desmond Tutu (Bishop)	Fulton Sheen
Bertrand Russell	Dietrich Bonhoeffer	George Fox
Billy Graham	Edwin Chapin	Gordon B. Hinckley (president, Church of Latter Day Saints)
Brigham Young	Emanuel Swedenborg	
Buddha	Ernest Dimnet	Harry Fosdick
Charles Spurgeon	Ezra Taft Benson	Henry Ward Beecher
Chatam Sofer (Rabbi)	Francis of Assisi (Saint)	Ignatius Loyola (Saint)

Immanuel Kant

Isaac Watts

Prophet Isaiah

Jeremy Collier

Jerry Falwell

Jesse Jackson Sr. (Reverend)

Jesus Christ

Jim Bakker

Jimmy Swaggart

John the Baptist

John Wesley

Joseph Alois Ratzinger (Pope Benedict XVI)

Joseph Smith

Karol Wojtyla (Pope John Paul II)

Lao-Tzu

Li Hongzhi (Master)

Louis Farrakhan

Mahatma Gandhi

Martin Luther

Martin Luther King Jr. (Dr.)

Max Weber

Mohammed

Moses

Norman Vincent Peale

Pat Robertson (Reverend)

Paul (Saint)

Paul Tillich

Peter Marshall

Phillips Brooks

Reinhold Niebuhr

Robert Schuller

Ron L. Hubbard

Rowan Williams (Archbishop of Canterbury)

Ruhollah Khomeini (Ayatollah)

Siddha Nagarjuna

Tenzin Gyatso (Dalai Lama)

Thomas Aquinas

W. Deen Mohammed (Imam)

William Channing

Zoroaster

Popes

Girl Names

Not applicable.

Boy Names

Adeodatus	Callistus	Eusebius	Innocent
Adrian	Celestine	Eutychian	John
Agapetus	Clement	Evaristus	John Paul
Agatho	Conon	Fabian	Julius
Alexander	Constantine	Felix	Lando
Anacletus	Cornelius	Formosus	Leo
Anastasius	Damasus	Gelasius	Liberius
Anicetus	Deusdedit	Gregory	Linus
Anterus	Dionysius	Hilarius	Lucius
Benedict	Donus	Honorius	Marcellinus
Boniface	Eleutherius	Hormisdas	Marcellus
Caius	Eugene	Hyginus	Marcus

continues

Popes continued

Boy Names

Marinus	Pontain	Sisinnius	Urban
Martin	Romanus	Sixtus	Valentine
Miltiades	Sabinian	Soter	Victor
Nicholas	Sergius	Stephen	Vigilius
Paschal	Severinus	Sylvester	Vitalian
Paul	Silverius	Symmachus	Zachary
Pelagius	Simplicius	Telesphorus	Zephyrinus
Peter	Siricius	Theodore	Zosimus
Pius			

Catholic Names

Girl Names

Ada	Cleopatra	Hilary	Lucilla
Adelaide	Daria	Hope	Lucretia
Adele	Donata	Ingrid	Lydia
Alena	Dorothy	Isabel	Marcella
Alexandra	Edith	Isidore	Margaret
Alexis	Elizabeth	Jan	Maria
Anna	Emily	Jane	Mariana
Anne	Emma	Jean	Marie
Augustine	Eve	Jessica	Marina
Ava	Fabiola	Joanna	Martha
Beatrix	Faith	Jordan	Martina
Bernadette	Florentina	Judith	Mary
Bernardine	Gabriel	Julie	Natalia
Bertha	Gabriella	Justina	Olga
Bridget	Georgia	Katharine	Paula
Camilla	Gladys	Kiara	Philomena
Carmen	Gwen	Laura	Priscilla
Celestine	Helen	Laurentia	Regina
Claudia	Helena	Lea	Rene

Rosalia	Tabitha	Theresa	Vivian
Serena	Teresa	Therese	Winifred
Sofia	Thea	Victoria	Zoe
Sylvia			

Boy Names

Aaron	Christopher	Hilary	Moses
Abel	Cletus	Hubert	Myron
Abraham	Colman	Isaac	Nathanael
Adam	Conan	Jacob	Octavius
Adolf	Constantine	Jason	Olaf
Adolphus	Cornelius	Jeremiah	Osmund
Adrian	Cyrus	Jeremy	Philemon
Aidan	Daniel	John	Ralph
Alexander	Darius	Jonas	Raphael
Alfred	David	Joseph	Richard
Amedeus	Donald	Juan	Robert
Andrew	Edward	Judas	Roger
Angelo	Elian	Justin	Ronald
Angus	Elias	Kevin	Rufus
Anthony	Emmanuel	Lazarus	Salomon
Aquila	Engelbert	Leopold	Samson
Arian	Erhard	Linus	Silas
Arnold	Ernest	Lorenzo	Simon
Augustus	Eugene	Louis	Stephen
Baldwin	Felix	Lucian	Sylvester
Bartholomew	Ferdinand	Luke	Thomas
Basil	Frances	Magnus	Ulrich
Benjamin	Gabriel	Manuel	Valentine
Bernard	Gerald	Mark	Vladimir
Blane	Gervase	Mathias	Wilfrid
Brandan	Gilbert	Matthew	William
Brice	Gregory	Matthias	Wolfgang
Cain	Harold	Maurice	Zachariah
Christian	Herbert	Michael	

Jewish/Hebrew Names

Girl Names

Aaliyah	Azalia	Hali	Maria
Abie	Bara	Hana	Marisha
Abira	Basha	Hanne	Netta
Abra	Bethesda	Hava	Nisi
Achazia	Bettina	Heba	Odelia
Ada	Bracha	Hedia	Raphaela
Adalia	Carmel	Hedva	Rena
Adamina	Chanah	Ideh	Sadie
Adelaide	Chaya	Ilana	Saloma
Adena	Daba	Iva	Samara
Aderes	Dalia	Ivana/Ivy	Shira
Adie	Damaris	Jael	Simona
Adina	Daniela	Jaen	Soshannah
Adine	Dara	Jamee	Tamara
Ahava	Davan	Jardena	Thadine
Ailsa	Davine	Jensine	Thomasina
Akiva	Daya	Jezebel	Tivona
Aliza	Dayla	Jobey	Tove
Alumit	Delilah	Joelle	Uma
Amissa	Edria	Jora	Varda
Anke	Efrosini	Jordane	Vidette
Araminta	Eilis	Kazia	Yachne
Arashel	Eleora	Kefira	Yadira
Arella	Else	Lailie	Ydel
Ariel/Ariella	Emanuela	Lexine	Yesmina
Asa	Endora	Lia	Yoninah
Asenka	Evelina	Lilith	Zahar
Asisa	Galya	Magda	Zehava
Astera	Gana	Magdalene	Zerlinda
Atara	Genesis	Malca	Zila
Aviva	Geva	Malina	Zisel
Ayala	Hadara	Mangena	Zita
Ayla	Hadassa	Mara	Zuriel

Boy Names

Aaron	Britt	Jacob	Nehemiah
Abbott	Cain	Jarlath	Nirel
Abdiel	Caleb	Jaron	Nisi
Abel	Chaika	Jedidiah	Noadiah
Abie	Chaim	Jeremiah	Noah
Abijah	Dagan	Jesus	Obadiah
Abner	Daniel	Jonah	Omar
Abraham	Doron	Jonas	Oran
Abrahsa	Dov	Jorgen	Oren
Abram	Eban	Joseph	Osaze
Acacio	Ebenezer	Joshua	Osborne
Adam	Eden	Josiah	Palti
Addai	Eisig	Jude	Ranen
Adlai	Eli	Kabos	Raphael
Adley	Elias	Kaniel	Ravid
Admon	Elijah	Laban	Reuben
Adon	Ely	Label	Reuel
Ahab	Emanuel	Lazarus	Rishon
Ahmik	Ephraim	Lemuel	Roni
Aitan	Ethan	Leshem	Sachiel
Amiel	Ethel	Levi	Sagiv
Amos	Ezekiel	Lot	Saloman
Ardon	Ezio	Malachi	Saul
Ari	Ezra	Matai	Seff
Armon	Gabai	Matthew	Seraphim
Arnon	Gabriel	Mehetable	Seth
Asher	Genesis	Mendel	Shulamith
Axel	Gersham	Michael	Simon
Barnabas	Gideon	Mihaly	Sivan
Barnaby	Hosea	Mordecai	Solomon
Bartholomew	Hyman	Moses	Talman
Baruch	Ichabod	Nachmanke	Teman
Benjamin	Isaac	Nadav	Thaddeus
Benson	Israel	Nathan	Timur
Brighton	Itzak	Nathaniel	Tivon

continues

Jewish/Hebrew Names continued

Boy Names

Tobias	Yadon	Zabulon	Zebediah
Tovi	Yakov	Zaccheo	Zedekiah
Udeh	Yan	Zachariah	Zephan
Uriah	Yanis	Zakai	Zev
Uzi	Yarin	Zane	Ziff
Vered	Yaron	Zared	Ziv
Yadid	Yehudi	Zazu	

Buddhist Names

Girl Names

An	Da Shin	Hiten	Myoki
Anzan	Dainin	Ishu	Roshin
Bankei	Eido	Jakushitsu	Saiun
Chen-chio	Etsudo	Jimin	Shinjo
Chen-tao	Fuyo	Koge	Showa
Chinshu	Gyo Shin	Mu Ji Yo	Taido
Chorei	Hakue	Myo Ka	Tennen

Boy Names

Abhaya	Doryo	Itsu Ro	Nanruy
Ana	Engu	Jikai	Niao-ka
Bankei	Enmei	Jiryu	Nyogen
Banko	Eryu	Kakumyo	Quang Tu
Banzan	Fo-hai	Kando	Reiju
Bassui	Fo-hsing	Kogen	Ryushin
Chan Khong	Fudoki	Kozan	Sariputra
Chimon	Genjo	Lung-t'an	Seido
Chotan	Genko	Ma-tzu	Seigan
Daeshim	Hakaku	Mu-nan	Seiko
Daido	Hui K'o	Mugen	Seiryu
Dai-In	Hui-chao	Nan Shin	Seung Sahn

Shisen	T'su Yu	Unkan	Zanchu
Shoju Rojin	Tamon	Wu-pen	Zendo
Suriak	Tan Gong	Ya'o Xia'ng	Zuiki

Hindu Names

Girl Names

Akuti	Hina	Marisa	Priti
Anjali	Indira	Matangi	Priya
Anuradha	Indu	Medha	Punita
Anusha	Jahnavi	Meena	Purandhri
Aparna	Jamuna	Menaka	Purnima
Aruna	Jaya	Mohini	Pusti
Asha	Jayani	Nalini	Radhika
Banu	Juhi	Nanda	Rani
Basanti	Jyoti	Narmada	Rati
Bhama	Kala	Neelam	Reena
Bharati	Kanchana	Neerja	Rekha
Bina	Kanya	Nidhi	Revati
Bindiya	Kausalya	Nidra	Rima
Charu	Kavita	Nira	Roshni
Chhaya	Kirti	Nirmala	Rudrani
Chitra	Komal	Nirupa	Rupali
Chitrangda	Kriti	Nisha	Sabita
Darshana	Kshama	Nitya	Sachi
Deepa	Lakshmi	Padma	Sangita
Devaki	Lalita	Padmini	Sanjna
Dipti	Lolaksi	Pallavi	Sapna
Divya	Madhu	Parnika	Sarasvati
Dristi	Madhur	Parvati	Sarmistha
Ekta	Mala	Pavani	Saryu
Gayatri	Malati	Pivari	Savarna
Gita	Mallika	Pooja	Savita
Gopi	Malti	Prachi	Seema
Harhsa	Mamta	Prisha	Shanti
Hema	Manushi	Pritha	Shobha

continues

Hindu Names continued

Girl Names

Shreya	Sunita	Tulasi	Vasanta
Shubha	Suravinda	Tusti	Vasumati
Smirti	Surotama	Uma	Vidya
Somatra	Surya	Urmila	Vimala
Sraddha	Susila	Urvasi	Vinata
Subhadra	Suvrata	Uttara	Vineeta
Subhaga	Tapi	Vanita	Visala
Subhuja	Taruna	Varsha	Yaksha
Sudevi	Tejal	Varuni	Yauvani

Boy Names

Abhay	Balavan	Iravan	Mohan
Abhijit	Bharat	Jaideep	Mohit
Achyuta	Bhudev	Jayant	Mukul
Aditya	Bramha	Jeevan	Nachik
Ajatashatru	Chandra	Jimuta	Nagesh
Ajay	Cholan	Jitendra	Namdev
Akaash	Dattatreya	Kalidas	Nandin
Akshay	Devarsi	Kamadev	Narayana
Amal	Dhananjay	Kapil	Naresh
Amar	Dharuna	Kartikeya	Narsi
Amit	Dhatri	Kavi	Navin
Anand	Dilip	Keshav	Neel
Anay	Dinesh	Kirit	Nimai
Anoop	Duranjaya	Kusagra	Nimish
Arjun	Durjaya	Kush	Niramitra
Aseem	Eknath	Lokesh	Omprakash
Asija	Gajendra	Madhav	Pandya
Asuman	Ganesh	Mahabala	Paramartha
Asvin	Girish	Mahesh	Parnab
Atharvan	Gopal	Maitreya	Prabhakar
Atul	Hari	Mandhatri	Prabhu
Badal	Harsh	Manik	Pradeep
Balaji	Hitesh	Mehul	Pramath

Pramsu	Rantidev	Siddharth	Varun
Pranav	Ravi	Srinivas	Vasava
Prasata	Rohit	Sudesha	Vasuman
Prasoon	Sagar	Sudeva	Veer
Pravin	Sahadev	Sukumar	Vidvan
Prem	Samrat	Sumit	Vijay
Prithu	Samudra	Suresh	Vikram
Privrata	Sandeep	Surya	Vimal
Purujit	Sanjay	Taksa	Vinay
Pusan	Sanjeev	Tarang	Vinod
Raj	Sarat	Tushar	Virat
Rajeev	Satrujit	Udai	Visvajit
Rakesh	Saunak	Upendra	Vivatma
Ram	Shalabh	Urjavaha	Yashodhara
Ramanuja	Shashwat	Vairaja	Yogendra
Randir	Shiv	Variya	

Muslim Names

Girl Names

Abia	Jamila	Maritza	Saree
Akilah	Janan	Maysa	Shakera
Alea	Jarita	Mouna	Skye
Alima	Jenna	Nadira	Sommer
Aliye	Kadejah	Nekia	Talitha
Amina	Kaela	Nima	Tara
Anan	Karida	Omaira	Thana
Anisa	Laela	Polla	Ulima
Bibi	Lakia	Qadira	Vega
Callie	Lateefah	Rafa	Waheeda
Emani	Lila	Rana	Walad
Faizah	Lina	Rida	Yaminah
Fatima	Lucine	Rukan	Yesenia
Ghada	Lydia	Saba	Zahra
Habiba	Mahala	Safiya	Zia
Hana	Manar	Sana	Zulima
Hayfa			

Muslim Names

Boy Names

Abbud	Fatin	Lateef	Salam
Abdulaziz	Ferran	Mahdi	Samman
Aden	Gamal	Mahmoud	Seif
Adham	Ghazi	Malcolm	Shakir
Ahmad	Haddad	Malek	Sharif
Akil	Haidar	Marwan	Suhail
Alam	Hakim	Mohammed/	Syed
Ali	Hamza	Muhammad	Tahir
Altair	Hasan	Munir	Tamir
Amar	Hilel	Mustafa	Tarik
Asadel	Hussain	Nabil	Wahid
Azeem	Imad	Nadim	Waleed
Basam	Isam	Nadir	Wasim
Borak	Jabir	Naji	Xavier
Boutros	Jakeem	Nasser	Yasir
Caleb	Jawhar	Nuri	Yusuf
Coman	Jumah	Omar	Zahir
Dekel	Kadar	Qamar	Zaid
Fahd	Kadeem	Rahul	Zaki
Faisal	Kale	Rasheed	Zimraan
Fakih	Kasib	Reyhan	Zuhayr
Faris	Khalid	Riyad	

Wiccan Names

Girl Names

Abiona	Alina	Aurora	Esme
Adalia	Alivia	Brietta	Evadne
Ailis	Alleta	Candra	Fai
Alanna	Aludra	Chanda	Farica
Alcina	Anais	Cindeigh	Feronia
Aldora	Aruna	Ella	Fulvia

Githa	Kisa	Milliani	Ryanne
Hekt	Kisha	Nimue	Sheera
Idalis	Llewellyn	Pamphile	Tala
Jana	Louhi	Qiana	Talia
Jocosa	Marinette	Radella	Talitha
Kachina	Medea	Rae Beth	Vanita
Kalinda	Meroe	Rhiannon	Xandria
Keelin	Morgan		

Boy Names

Barrett	Charles	Mabon	Paul Beyerl
Blaise	Colborn		

Virtues

Girl Names

Adore	Courtesy	Honesty	Patience
Affinity	Delight	Honor	Peacefulness
Amiable	Desire	Hope	Pity
Amity	Destiny	Humbleness	Pleasance
Amour	Divinity	Humility	Providence
Beauty	Essence	Infinity	Prudence
Bliss	Eternal	Integrity	Purity
Blythe	Ethereal	Joy	Sacrifice
Bonny	Faith	Kindness	Serena
Chance	Felicity	Knowledge	Sobriety
Charisma	Fidelity	Liberty	Solace
Charity	Fortitude	Love	Spirituality
Chastity	Fortune	Mercy	Sympathy
Cherish	Freedom	Merry	Temperance
Compassion	Gentle	Mirth	Tranquility
Concord	Glory	Modesty	Truth
Constance	Grace	Muse	Winsome
Courage	Harmony	Noble	Wisdom

Virtues

Boy Names

Chance	Justice	Merit	Valor
Chivalry	Loyal	Tenacious	Verity
Gallant	Lucky	True	Wisdom
			Zeal

Part 2

Giant Alphabetical List of Names, Origins, and Meanings

After you've gathered some possible names for your baby, you can turn to Part 2, which lists the historical origins, meanings, and spelling variations of all the names in Part 1—plus thousands of others. When you know what the names actually mean, you may find some that just "fit" better than others.

Or if you're impatient, you can skip ahead to this part, without having looked at Part 1, and start scanning the A-to-Z master list for possible name candidates. Happy hunting!

Girl Names

A

Aaliyah (Hebrew) Exalted. *Alea, Aleah, Aleaseya, Aleeya, Alia, Aliya, Aliyah, Allyiah*

Aamoir Origin and meaning unknown.

Aari (Hebrew) Like a beautiful melody. *Aarie, Aariel, Aaries, Aree, Arey, Aria, Ariana, Arie, Ariealla, Ariel, Ary*

Aase (Hebrew) Flower of the Lord. *Asaella*

Aasta (Nordic) Love. *Aastah, Asta, Astah*

Aba (African) Born on Thursday.

Abagbe (African) Child who was desired.

Abauro (Greek) Sunlit sky.

Abbellonna (Hebrew) Exhalation of breath; form of Abel.

Abby (Latin) Head of a monastery; nickname for Abigail. *Abbe, Abbey, Abbie, Abey*

Abelarda (Arabic) Servant of Allah.

Abeni (African) Prayed for. *Abena, Abina, Abinah*

Abeque (Native American) Stays at home. *Abequa*

Abey (Native American) Leaf.

Abeytu (Native American) Green leaf.

Abha (Sanskrit) Splendor.

Abia (Arabic) Great. *Abbia, Abbiah, Abiah*

Abiba (African) Child born after grandmother died.

Abida (Arabic) Worshipper. *Abedah, Abidah*

Abie (Hebrew) Mother of many.

Abiel (Hebrew) God is my father.

Abigail (Hebrew) A father's joy. *Abagail, Abbagail, Abbagale, Abbagayle, Abbegail, Abbegale, Abbegayle, Abbeygale, Abbie, Abbiegail, Abbiegayle, Abbigael, Abbigail, Abby, Abbygail, Abbygale, Abbygayle, Abegail, Abegale, Abegayle, Abigale, Abigayle, Gail*

Abinaya (American) Combination of Abby and Ann. *Abenaa, Abeneya, Abinayan*

Abiona (Yoruban) Born on a journey.

Abira (Hebrew) My strength. *Abbira, Abeera, Abeerah, Abeir, Aberah, Abiir, Abir*

Abital (Hebrew) My father is night dew.

Abmaba (African) Born on Thursday.

Abra (Hebrew) Mother of many nations; feminine form of Abraham. *Abree, Abri, Abria*

Abriana (Italian) Mother of nations. *Abbrienna, Abbryana, Abreana, Abreanna, Abreanne, Abreeana, Abreona, Abreonia, Abriann, Abrianna, Abrien, Abrienna, Abrienne, Abrion, Abryanna*

Abril (French) Secure, protected. *Abreal, Abrial, Abriale, Abrielle, Abrille*

Abtin (Persian) Character from *Shahnameh*; Fereidoun's father.

Abundia (Latin) Abundance.

Acacia (Greek) Thorny. *Acaciah, Acasha, Acatia, Accassia*

Acadia (Canadian) Place name. *Caddie, Cadie*

Acalia (Latin) Name for adoptive mother of Romulus and Remus.

Acantha (Greek) Thorny.

Acedia (Native American) Place of plenty.

Achazia (Hebrew) The Lord holds.

Acheflour (Scottish) White flower in Arthurian legend.

Acima (Illyrian) Praised by God. *Acimah, Acyma, Acymah*

Ada (Hebrew) Adorned. (Latin) Of noble birth. *Adah, Adailia, Adalee, Adara, Adda, Addah, Addi, Addiah, Addie, Addy, Ade, Auda, Eda, Etta*

Adalcira (Spanish) Combination of Ada and Alcira.

Adalgisa (German) Noble hostage.

Adalia (Spanish) Noble. *Adal, Adala, Adalea, Adaleah, Adali, Adalie, Adaly*

Adalsinda (German) Noble strength.

Adamina (Hebrew) Daughter of the earth.

Adan (Irish) Warm.

Adana (Spanish) Form of Adama. *Adanah, Adania, Adanya*

Adara (Greek) Beauty. *Adair, Adaire, Adar, Adarah, Adare, Adarra*

Adawna (Latin) Beautiful sunrise. *Adawnah*

Adaya (American) Form of Ada. *Adayah, Addiah*

Addie (German) Form of Adelaide. *Adde, Addey, Addi, Adei, Attie*

Addison (English) Daughter of Adam. *Addisen, Addisson, Addyson, Adisen, Adison, Adysen, Adyson*

Adelaide (German) Noble, kind. *Adalia, Adaline, Addie, Adela, Adelae, Adele, Adeleana, Adelena, Adelia, Adelina, Adeline, Adella, Adelle, Adelynn, Adelynne, Adie, Adilenna, Adiline, Adlin, Adlynn, Aline, Della*

Adelma (Teutonic) Protector of the needy.

Adelpha (Greek) Dear sister. *Adelfa, Adelfah, Adelphah, Adelphie*

Adena (Hebrew) Delicate. *Adeena, Aden, Adenna, Adina, Adine, Adinna*

Aderes (Latin) One who protects.

Adhara (Arabic) Maiden; star.

Adia (Swahili) Gift. *Addia, Adea, Adiah*

Adoette (Native American) Large tree. *Adooeette*

Adolfina (German) Noble wolf.

Adonia (Spanish) Beautiful. *Adoniah, Adonica, Adonya*

Adora (Latin) Beloved. *Adore, Adoree, Adoria, Dora*

Adriana (Italian) Dark; rich.

Adrielle (Hebrew) Member of God's flock. *Adriel, Adrielli, Adryelle*

Adrienne (Greek) Rich. (Latin) Dark. Feminine form of Adrian. *Adrea, Adreah, Adrean, Adreana, Adreanah, Adreane, Adreann, Adreanna, Adreannah, Adreanne, Adreena, Adreenah, Adreene, Adria, Adriah, Adrian, Adrianah, Adriane, Adrianne, Adrien, Adriena, Adrienah, Adriene, Adrienn, Adrienna, Adriennah, Adrina, Adrinah, Adrine, Adryan, Adryana, Adryanah, Adryane, Adryann, Adryannah*

Adsila (Native American) Blossom.

Adya (Hindi) Sunday. *Adia*

Ae Cha (Korean) Love and daughter.

Ae Sook (Korean) Love and purity.

Aegle (Greek) Illuminated.

Aella (Irish) From Ireland. *Aellyn*

Aelwyd (Welsh) From the chimney.

Aemilia (Latin) Rival. (German) Hard-working. Feminine form of Aemilius.

Aerona (Welsh) Berry. *Aeronah, Aeronna*

Affera (Hebrew) Young deer. *Affery, Aphra*

Affinity (Latin) Relationship by marriage.

Afilia (German) Noble.

Afina (Hebrew) Young doe. *Afinah, Afynah, Aphina*

Afra (Hebrew) Female deer. (Arabic) Color of the earth. *Affra, Affrey*

Afric (Irish) Pleasant. *Africa*

Afrodite (Greek) Goddess of love and beauty. *Afrodita*

Afton (Old English) From the Afton River. *Aftan, Aftona, Aftone, Aftonia*

Agalia (Spanish) Joy.

Agape (Greek) Love of the next.

Agata (Greek) Good. *Agace, Agacia, Agafa, Agafia, Agase, Agath, Agatha, Agathi, Agathia, Agathie, Agatka, Agaue, Agethe, Aggie, Aggy, Agota, Agotha, Agueda, Akta*

Aglaia (Greek) Wisdom. *Aglae, Aglaya*

Agnes (Greek) Pure. *Adneda, Agenta, Aggie, Aggy, Agna, Agnella, Agnelle, Agnesa, Agnesca, Agnese, Agnessa, Agnesse, Agnessija, Agneta, Agnete, Agnetha, Agnetis, Agnette, Agnies, Agnieszka, Agnizica, Agnizika, Agnizka, Agnola, Agytha, Aigneis, Ameyce, Anis, Annais, Annes, Anneys, Anneyse, Annice, Annot, Annys, Ina, Ines, Inesila, Inessa, Inez, Nancy, Nesa, Nesta, Neza, Neziko, Ynes, Ynez*

Agrona (Old English) Goddess of strife and slaughter.

Ah Lam (Chinese) Like an orchid. (Arabic) Witty; one who has pleasant dreams.

Ahava (Hebrew) Cherished one. *Ahave, Ahivia*

Ahlam (Arabic) Witty.

Ahmose (Hebrew) Mother of Hatshepsut.

Ai (Japanese) Love.

Aida (Old English) Joyful. *Aidah, Aide, Aidee*

Aidia (Spanish) Help.

Aiko (Japanese) Little loved one.

Ailani (Hawaiian) Chief. *Aelani, Ailana*

Aileen (Greek) Light; form of Helen. *Aila, Ailean, Aileana, Aileanah, Aileane, Ailee, Ailena, Ailenah, Ailene, Ailey, Alean, Aleana, Aleanah, Aleane, Aleen, Aleena, Aleenah, Aleene, Alena, Alene, Alina, Aline, Eilean, Eileana, Eileane, Eileen, Eileena, Eileene, Eilleen, Eleana, Eleanah, Eleane, Elena, Elenah, Elene, Ileana, Ileane, Ilina, Ilinah, Iline, Illean, Illeana, Illeanah, Illeane, Illian, Illiana, Illianah, Illiane, Illianna, Illiannah, Illianne, Leana, Leanah, Leane, Lena, Liana, Lianah, Lyan, Lyana, Lyann, Lyanna, Lyannah, Lyanne, Lynah*

Aili (Scottish) Form of Alice. *Ailee, Ailey, Ailie*

Ailis (Irish) Honest. *Ailesh, Ailish*

Ailsa (Scottish) Island dweller; island of Alfsigr. *Ailis, Ailsha, Aylsah, Elsa, Elsha, Elshe*

Aimee (Latin) Beloved. *Ami, Amia, Amie, Amity*

Aina (Hebrew) Form of Anna.

Ainsley (Scottish) My meadow. *Ainslee, Ainsleigh, Ainslie, Ainsly, Ainsworth, Aynsley*

Airleas (Irish) Promise. *Airleah, Ayrleas, Ayrlee, Ayrly*

Aisha (Arabic) Life. *Aieshah, Aishah, Aisia, Ayeesha, Ayeisha, Ayisha*

Aishwarya (Sanskrit) Wealth.

Aislinn (Old English) Dream; form of Ashlyn. *Aislin, Aislyn, Aislynn, Aissah, Ayslin, Ayslinn, Ayslyn, Ayslynn, Ayssa, Ayssah*

Aissa (African) Grateful.

Aiyana (Native American) Eternal blossom. *Aiyanah, Aiyona*

Aja (Hindi) Goat. *Aija, Aijah, Ajha, Ajyah*

Ajua (African) Born on Monday.

Akaisha (Irish) The akaisha flower.

Akako (Japanese) Red.

Akanah (Japanese) Red. *Akae, Akaho, Akane, Akari*

Akelah (Russian) She of fair skin.

Aki (Japanese) Autumn. *Akee, Akeeye*

Akilah (Arabic) Intelligent. *Akeela, Akeelah, Akeila, Akeilah*

Akina (Japanese) Spring flower.

Akiva (Hebrew) Protect.

Akiyama (Japanese) Autumn mountain.

Akosua (African) Born on Sunday.

Akuti (Hindi) Princess.

Alabama (Native American) Tribal town.

Alaia (Arabic) Happy.

Alair (French) Cheerful; version of Hillary. *Alaira, Allaire*

Alamea (Hawaiian) Precious. *Alameah, Alameya*

Alameda (Native American) Grove of cottonwood.

Alana (Irish) Attractive; peaceful. (Hawaiian) Offering. Feminine form of Alan. *Alaina, Alani, Alania, Alanis, Alanna, Allanah, Allannah, Allyn, Alyn*

Alandra (Spanish) Form of Alexandra. *Alantrah*

Alani (Irish) Form of Alana. *Alaini, Alanee, Alaney, Alanya*

Alaqua (Native American) Sweet gum tree.

Alarice (German) Ruler of all. *Alaricia, Alarisa, Alarise*

Alawa (Native American) Pea.

Alba (Latin) Thick or mass vegetation; feminine form of Albin. *Albah, Albani, Albany, Albine, Elba*

Alberta (German) Noble. (French) Bright. Feminine form of Albert. *Albertina, Albertyna*

Albreanna (American) Combination of Alberta and Breanna. *Albreanna, Albreona*

Alcina (Greek) Strong-minded; name of a Greek enchantress. *Alceena, Alcine, Alsinia, Alzina*

Alcott (Old English) Old cottage. *Alcot, Walcot, Walcott*

Aldegunda (German) Famous leader.

Alden (Old English) Wise protector. *Aldan, Aldon, Alldyn*

Aldora (Greek) Winged gift. *Aldorah*

Alea (Arabic) Exalted. *Allea, Alleah, Alleea*

Aleela (Swahili) She cries. *Aleaia, Aleelah, Alila*

Alegria (Spanish) Cheerful. *Aleggra, Alegra*

Alena (Russian) Form of Helen. *Aleena, Aleni, Alenia, Alenya*

Aleshanee (Native American) She plays all the time.

Alethea (Greek) Truthful one. *Alethia, Aletta, Alettah, Alithea, Alitheah, Alithiah, Allathea, Allatheah, Allathia, Allathiah, Allethea, Alletheah, Allethia, Allethiah, Allethya, Allethyah, Allythea, Allytheah, Allythia, Allythiah, Allythya, Allythyah, Alythea, Alytheah, Alythia, Alythiah, Alythya, Alythyah*

Alette (Latin) Wing. *Aletta, Alettah*

Alexandra (Greek) Defender of mankind; feminine form of Alexander. *Alandra, Alejanda, Aleka, Aleksey, Alesandra, Alessa, Alessandra, Alex, Alexa, Alexandria, Alexandrina, Alexia, Alexine, Alexis, Aliki, Allesandra, Alya, Lexie, Lexy, Sandra, Sandy, Sanie, Zandra*

Alexandrite (Russian) Gemstone with special optical effects; named after Czar Alexander II.

Alexius (Greek) Form of Alexis. *Allexius*

Alfreda (English) Wise counselor. *Alfredda, Alfreeda, Alfrida, Alfrieda*

Algoma (Native American) Valley of flowers.

Alhertina (Spanish) Noble.

Alice (German) Noble. (Greek) Truth. *Addala, Adelice, Adelicia, Ailis, Aleece, Aleese, Aletta, Alexis, Ali, Aliceie, Alicia, Aliciedik, Alicija, Aliedik, Alika, Aliki, Alina, Aline, Alisa, Alisan, Alise, Alisen, Alisin, Alison, Alissa, Alisun, Alisyn, Aliza, Allie, Allisan, Allisen, Allisin, Allison, Allisun, Allisyn, Ally, Allyce, Allyse, Alodia, Alse, Alyce, Alys, Alyse, Alyssa, Elice, Elisan, Elise, Elisen, Elisin, Elison, Elisun, Elisyn, Elsje, Ilyssa*

Alida (Greek) Beautifully dressed. *Aleda, Aletta, Alette, Alidia, Allida, Allidia, Lida*

Alika (Hawaiian) Truthful. *Aleca, Alikah, Alyka*

Alima (Arabic) Dancer. *Aleema, Aleemah, Alimah, Alyma, Alymah*

Alina (Slavic) Bright. *Aleana, Aleina, Aliana, Alinna*

Alisha (Greek) Truthful. (German) Noble. *Aliscia, Alisea, Alishah, Alishay, Alishaye, Alishya, Alisyia, Alitsha, Allisia*

Alison (Irish) Of noble birth. *Aleason, Aleeson, Aleighson, Aleison, Alisan, Alisana, Alisanah, Alisen,* *Alisena, Alisenah, Alisin, Alisina, Alisinah, Alissa, Alissah, Alisson, Alissun, Alissyn, Alisun, Alisyn, Alisyna, Alisynah, Alisyne, Allisa, Allisah, Allisan, Allisanah, Allisen, Allisena, Allisenah, Allisin, Allisina, Allisinah, Allisine, Allison, Allisona, Allisonah, Allisone, Alliss, Allissa, Allisun, Allisuna, Allisyn, Allysna, Allysyne, Alson, Alsona, Alsonah, Alsone, Alysan, Alysen, Alysena, Alysenah, Alysene, Alysin, Alysina, Alysinah, Alysine, Alyson, Alysonah, Alysone, Alyssa, Alyssah, Alysse, Alysun, Alysyn, Alysyn, Alysyna, Alysynah, Alysyne, Alyzan, Alyzana, Alyzane, Alyzen, Alyzena, Alyzene, Alyzin, Alyzina, Alyzine, Alyzyn, Alyzyna, Alyzyne*

Alivia (English) Peace; form of Olivia. *Alivah*

Alixia (Greek) Defender of mankind; form of Alex. *Alix, Alixe, Allix, Alyx*

Aliya (Hebrew) Ascender. *Aliyiah, Alliyha*

Aliye (Arabic) Noble. *Aliyeh*

Aliza (Hebrew) Joyous. *Aliezah, Aliz, Alizah, Alizee*

Alize (French) Gentle trade wind; name of a cognac.

Alka (Hindi) Girl with lovely hair. *Alaka*

Alla (Ukrainian) Form of Ella. *Ala, Alah, Alya*

Allaya (English) Highly exalted.

Allegra (Latin) Brisk and cheerful; a musical marking for a fast tempo. *Allegrah, Allegria*

Alleta (Scandinavian) Heroine; form of Halle.

Allie (English) Form of Allison. *Aley, Ali, Alley, Alli*

Allirea (Aboriginal) Quartz.

Alma (Latin) Soul or nourishing. *Almah, Almar*

Almeda (Arabic) Ambitious. *Allmeda, Almedah, Almeta*

Almira (Arabic) Aristocratic princess. *Allmeera, Allmerah, Almeeria, Almyrah*

Almodis (German) Animated.

Aloani (Hindi) Cloud from heaven. (Hawaiian) Bright sky. Variation of Aolani. *Alohilani*

Alodie (English) Rich. *Alodee, Alodey, Alodi, Alodia, Alody*

Aloha (Hawaiian) Love; Hawaiian form of "hello" and "good-bye."

Alohi (Hawaiian) Brilliant.

Alona (Hawaiian) Beautiful. *Alonnah, Alonya*

Aloysia (Old German) Famous in war.

Alsoomse (Native American) Independent.

Alta (Latin) Tall. *Allta, Altah, Alto*

Altair (Greek) Star. *Altaira, Altayre, Alteyra, Altyr*

Althea (Greek) Healer. *Alethea, Alithea, Allie, Altheah, Altheda, Althedah, Althia, Althiah, Althya, Althyah, Thea*

Altrina (Science fiction) Character from *Star Trek: Deep Space Nine.*

Aludra (Greek) Virgin.

Alumit (Hebrew) Secret.

Alva (Spanish) Fair complexion. *Alvah, Alvana*

Alvarita (Spanish) Speaker of truth.

Alverah (Latin) Honest. *Alverah, Alveryah*

Alvina (Old English) Wise companion; feminine version of Alvin. *Alveen, Alveena, Alveenia, Alvenea, Alvinae, Alvine, Alvinea, Alvinia, Alvinna, Alvita, Alvyna, Alwin, Alwyn*

Alyssa (Arabic) Moon goddess. *Ahlyssa, Alaysia, Alaysieh, Alissa, Allissa, Allyssa, Alyesa, Alyissa, Lasine*

Alzena (Arabic) Woman. *Alsena, Alzenah, Alzina, Alzinah*

Amadahy (Native American) Forest water.

Amadea (Latin) Loves God. *Amadeah, Amadia, Amadya, Amadyah*

Amadis (Latin) The great love.

Amala (Arabic) Hope. *Amahl, Amahla, Amal, Amel*

Amanda (Latin) Love. *Amanada, Amandah, Amandi, Amandy, Mandie, Mandy*

Amani (Arabic) Form of Imani. *Aamani, Ahmani, Amanee, Amaney*

Amara (Greek) Eternal beauty. *Amaria, Amar, Amarah, Amari, Amariah*

Amarante (Japanese) Flower that never fades.

Amari (Hindi) Immortal. *Amarta*

Amarie (English) Gracious under adversity.

Amarina (Australian) Rain. *Amarinah, Amarine, Amaryn, Amaryne*

Amaris (English) Child of the moon. *Amariss, Amarissa, Amarys, Maris*

Amaya (Japanese) Night rain. *Amaia, Amayah*

Amber (Arabic) Jewel. *Ambar, Ambarlea, Ambarlee, Ambarlei, Ambarleigh, Ambarley, Ambarli, Ambarlie, Ambarlina, Ambarline, Amberlea, Amberlee, Amberlei, Amberleigh, Amberley, Amberli, Amberlia, Amberliah, Amberlie, Amberlina, Amberline, Amberly, Amberlyah, Ambur, Amburlea, Amburlee, Amburleigh, Amburley, Amburli, Amburlia, Amburliah, Amburlie, Amburlina, Amburline, Amburly, Amburlya*

Ambra (American) Form of Amber.

Ambrosia (Greek) Immortal; food of the gods. *Ambrosa, Ambrosiah*

Amelia (German) Industrious. *Amala, Amalah, Amalburga, Amalea, Amaleah, Amalee, Amaleigh, Amaleta, Amali, Amalia, Amalie, Amalita, Amalitah, Amela, Amelie, Amelija, Amelina, Amelinda, Amelindah, Ameline, Amelita, Amelitah, Amelynda, Amelyndah, Amilia, Amiliah, Amilina, Amilinda, Amiline, Amilita, Amilitah, Ammileine, Ammilina, Amylaya, Amylia, Amyliah, Amylyah, Emelia, Emelin, Emelina, Emeline, Emelita, Emelitah, Emmelina, Emmeline, Emmilyn, Emmilyna, Emmilyne*

America (Teutonic) Industrious. *Amarica, Amaricka, Americka, Amerique*

Amerie (German) Industrious leader.

Amethyst (Greek) Wine; purple-violet gemstone believed to prevent drunkenness.

Ami (Hindi) Nectar. *Aami, Amii*

Amiable (Middle English) Good natured, likable.

Amilia (Latin) Form of Amelia. *Amiliah, Amillia*

Amina (Arabic) Trustworthy. *Aamena, Aamina, Aaminah, Ameena, Ameenah, Aminah, Aminda*

Aminta (Greek) The protector.

Amira (Hebrew) Speech. *Amyra, Amyrah*

Amissa (Hebrew) Friend. *Amisah, Amisia, Amissah, Amiza*

Amitola (Native American) Rainbow.

Amity (Latin) Friendly. *Amitee, Amitey, Amiti, Amitie, Amytee, Amytey, Amyti, Amytie, Amyty*

Amlika (Hindi) Mother. *Amlikah, Amlyka*

Amorette (Latin) Beloved. *Amoreta, Amoretta, Amorettah, Amorytt*

Amorina (Spanish) She falls in love easily.

Amory (Latin) Loving; for girl or boy. *Emery, Emory*

Amour (French) Love.

Amoy (Jamaican) Beautiful goddess.

Amphitrite (Greek) Sea goddess.

Amriel (Latin) Angel of the month of May.

Amunet (Egyptian) Guardian goddess of the pharaohs.

Amy (Latin) Beloved. *Aime, Aimee, Aimey, Aimi, Aimia, Aimiah, Aimie, Aimy, Aimya, Aimyah, Amata, Amatah, Ame, Amee, Amei, Amey, Ami, Amia, Amiah, Amice, Amie, Amity, Amorett, Amoretta, Amorita, Amoritta, Amorittah, Amoritte, Amoryt, Amoryta, Amorytah, Amoryte, Amorytta, Amoryttah, Amorytte*

An (Chinese) Peaceful.

Anaba (Native American) She turns from battle. *Anabah*

Anais (pronounced *AH-na-ees*) (Hebrew) Gracious. *Anaise*

Anala (Hindi) Fine. *Analah*

Analicia (English) Form of Analisa. *Analisia*

Anan (Arabic) Clouds.

Ananda (Hindi) Blissful. *Anandah*

Anani (Hawaiian) Orange blossoms. *Nani*

Anara (Arabic) Pomegranate flower. *Anargu*

Anastasia (Greek) Resurrection. *Anastace, Anastacia, Anastacya, Anastacyah, Anastas, Anastase, Anastasee, Anastasie, Anastassia, Anastatia, Anastazia, Anastazya, Anastiaciah, Anastice, Anastise, Anastziah, Anestasia, Annestas, Annestasia, Annnestassia, Anstace, Ansteece, Ansteese, Anstes, Anstey, Anstice, Anstis, Natasha, Tasha, Tasia*

Andrea (Greek) Strong and brave; feminine form of Andrew. *Abdryann, Adrinah, Aindrea, Anderea, Andra, Andrah, Andreana, Andreanah, Andreane, Andreann, Andreanna, Andreannah, Andreanne, Andree, Andreean, Andreeana, Andreeanah, Andreeane, Andrel, Andrela, Andrelah, Andrell, Andrella, Andrellah, Andrelle, Andrena, Andretta, Andrette, Andria, Andriah, Andrian, Andriann, Andrianna, Andriannah, Andrianne, Andrina, Andrya, Andryah, Andryan, Andryana, Andryanah, Andryane, Andryanem, Andryanna, Andryannah, Andryanne*

Andromache (Greek) In mythology, the wife of Hector who became Queen of Epirius. (Shakespearean) Character from *Troilus and Cressida*.

Andromeda (Greek) Beautiful maiden rescued by Perseus.

Anechka (Russian) Grace.

Aneesa (Arabic) Of good company. *Aneesa, Aneesah, Aneese*

Aneko (Japanese) Older sister.

Anela (Hawaiian) Angel. *Anel, Anelah, Anella, Anellah*

Anezka (Slavic) Pure.

Angela (Greek) Heavenly messenger. *Agnola, Aindrea, Ancela, Ange, Angel, Angele, Angelica, Angelika, Angelin, Angelina, Angelinah, Angeline, Angeliqua, Angeliquah, Angelique, Angelita, Angell, Angella, Angellah, Angelle, Angelo, Angiola, Aniela, Anja, Anjah,*

Anjal, Anjala, Anjalah, Anjel, Anjela, Anjelah, Anjella, Anjelle, Engel, Engela, Engelah, Engelchen, Engelica, Engelika, Engeliqua, Engeliquah, Engelique, Engell, Engella, Engellah, Engelle, Engelyca, Engelycka, Engelyka, Enjel, Enjela, Enjelah, Enjele, Enjell, Enjella, Enjellah, Enjelle, Enjelliqua, Enjelliquah, Enjellique, Enjellyca, Enjellycah, Enjellycka, Enjellyka, Enjellyqua, Enjellyquah, Enjellyque

Angeni (Native American) Spirit. *Angeeny, Angenia*

Angharad (African) Much loved.

Angharat (Scottish) Peredur's beloved in Arthurian legend.

Anh (Vietnamese) Peace; safety.

Ani (Hawaiian) Beautiful. *Aanye, Anee, Anie*

Aniela (Polish) Form of Anna. *Anielah, Aniella, Aniellah, Annielah*

Anisa (Arabic) Friendly.

Anita (Hebrew) Graceful. *Anitta, Anittah, Anitte, Annita, Annitah, Annite, Annitt, Annitta, Annittah, Annitte, Annyta, Annytah, Annytta, Annyttah, Annytte*

Anjali (Hindi) Offering with both hands.

Ann (Hebrew) Gift of God's favor. *Anabel, Anca, Ani, Anica, Anicah, Anika, Anikah, Aniqua, Aniquah, Anita, Anke, Ann, Anna, Annabel, Annabella, Annabelle, Annchen, Anne, Anneka, Annette, Annia, Annice, Annie, Annis,*

Annuska, Annys, Anya, Anyca, Anycah, Anyka, Anykah, Anyqua, Anyquah, Bella, Hannah

Annabeth (English) Favor. A devout woman who saw infant Jesus presented at the temple in Jerusalem. Combination of Anna and Beth. *Anabeth*

Annalynn (English) Beautiful daughter; combination of Anna and Lynn. *Analyn, Analynne, Annalynne*

Anneliese (German) Graceful satisfaction. *Analiese, Analisa, Analise, Anetta, Annalisa, Annalise, Annalyca, Annalyce, Annalys, Annalysa, Annalyse, Anneliese, Anneliesel, Annelys, Annelysa, Annelyse*

Annina (Hebrew) Graceful. *Anina, Aninah, Anninah*

Annipe (Egyptian) Daughter of the Nile.

Annora (Latin) Honor. *Annorah, Annore, Annoria*

Anstice (Greek) One who will rise again.

Anthea (Greek) Flower. *Antea, Anthe, Anthia, Anthiah*

Antigua (Spanish) Old.

Antje (German) Grace.

Antlia (Latin) Air pump; constellation.

Antonia (Greek) Flourishing. (Latin) Praiseworthy. Feminine form of Anthony. *Antoinette, Antonett, Antonetta, Antonette, Antoni, Antoniah, Antonias, Antonica, Antonicah, Antonie, Antonietta, Antoninas, Antonnia, Antonniah,*

Antonya, Antonyah, Toinetta, Toinette, Toni, Tonia, Tonya, Toynetta, Toynette, Tuanetta, Tueanette

Anuncia (Latin) Messenger.

Anuradha (Hindi) Name of a star.

Anusha (Hindi) Beautiful morning.

Anusia (Greek) Grace.

Anya (Russian) Form of Anna. *Aaniyah, Aniya, Aniyah, Anja*

Anysia (Greek) Complete.

Anzan (Japanese) Quiet mountain.

Anzu (Japanese) Apricot.

Aoi (Japanese) Hollyhock.

Aparna (Hindi) Goddess Parvati.

Aphrodite (Greek) Goddess of love. *Afrodita, Afrodite, Aphrodita, Aphrodyta, Aphrodytah, Aphrodyte*

Aponi (Native American) Butterfly.

Apphia (Hebrew) Fruitful.

Apple (American) Fruit.

April (Latin) Blooming. *Aprel, Aprela, Aprelah, Aprella, Aprelle, Aprila, Aprilah, Aprilett, Apriletta, Aprilette, Aprill, Aprilla, Aprillah, Aprille, Apryl, Apryla, Aprylah, Apryll, Aprylla, Aprylle, Ava, Avril, Avrilett, Avriletta, Avrilette, Avryl, Avryla, Avrylah, Avryle, Avryleett, Avryletta, Avryll, Avrylla, Avryllah, Avrylle, Avryllettah, Avryllette*

Apus (Greek) Footless; constellation.

Aqualina (Latin) Tender waters.

Aquamarine (Latin) Gemstone; color.

Aquene (Native American) Peace.

Ara (Arabic) Embellishing. *Aara, Aira, Arae, Arah, Araya*

Arabelle (German) Beautiful eagle. *Arabel, Arabela, Arabele, Arabella*

Arali (Greek) Name for the netherworld.

Arama (Spanish) Reference to the Virgin Mary.

Araminta (English) Character in *The Man Who Laughs* by eighteenth-century playwright Victor Hugo. (Hebrew) Lofty. Combination of Arabella and Aminta.

Arantxa (Old English) Thornbush.

Arashel (Hebrew) Strong and protected.

Arbor (Latin) Herb garden.

Arden (Latin) Passionate; for girl or boy. *Ardelia, Ardi, Ardis, Ardon*

Ardeshir (Persian) A character in *Shanameh*, eleventh-century *Epic of Kings* by Firdowski.

Ardith (Hebrew) Flowering field. *Ardyth, Ardythe*

Ardys (English) Warm.

Arella (Hebrew) Angel messenger. *Arela, Arellah, Arelle*

Aretha (Greek) Virtuous. *Areata, Areatah, Areatha, Areathah, Areathia, Areathiah, Areeta, Areetah, Areetha, Areethah, Areethia, Areethiah, Areta, Aretah, Arethia, Arethiah, Aretta, Arettah, Arette, Aritha,*

Arithah, Arytha, Arythah, Arythia, Arythiah, Arythya, Arythyah, Retha, Rethah

Aria (German) Melody. *Ari, Ariah, Ariann, Arianna, Ariannah, Arianne, Arya, Aryah, Aryan, Aryana, Aryanah, Aryane, Aryann, Aryanna, Aryannah, Aryanne*

Ariadne (Greek) Mythological daughter of King Minos of Crete. *Aria, Arianna, Arianne*

Ariana (Old English) Silver. (Greek) Holy. *Ariadne, Ariane, Arianne, Arionna, Arriana*

Ariel (Hebrew) Lion of God. *Arael, Ari, Arial, Ariela, Ariella, Ario, Aryel*

Arietta (Italian) Melody. *Arieta, Ariete, Ariettah*

Aril (Latin) Bright seed cover.

Arissa (Greek) Best. *Arista, Aristen*

Arleigh (Old English) Meadow of the hare.

Arlene (Irish) Pledge. *Arleen, Arleine, Arlette, Arline, Arlyn, Arlynn*

Arlington (American) Place name.

Armani (African) Faith.

Armonda (German) Man in the army.

Arnette (English) Little eagle. *Arneta, Arnetta, Arnettah*

Arnon (Hebrew) Rushing stream; also boy's name.

Aroa (German) Good person.

Arrah Origin and meaning unknown.

Arrietty (German) Home ruler; version of Harriet. *Arietta*

Arsenia (Spanish) Masculine. *Arcenia, Arsania, Arsemia*

Artemia (Greek) Gift from Artemis. *Artemesia*

Artemis (Greek) Moon goddess.

Artis (Scottish) Bear. *Arthea, Arthelia, Arthette, Artice, Artina*

Aruna (Hindi) Dawn. *Aruni*

Arva (Latin) From the seashore.

Arziki (African) Prosperity.

Asa (Japanese) Born in the morning.

Ascah (Hebrew) Anklet.

Asenath (Hebrew) She belongs to her father.

Asenka (Hebrew) Graceful.

Asha (African) Life.

Ashanti (African) Thank you. *Achante, Achanti, Asante, Ashantae, Ashante, Ashantee, Ashantie, Ashaunta, Ashauntae, Ashaunti, Ashonti, Ashuntae, Ashunti*

Ashland (English) Place name.

Ashley (Old English) Ash tree; for girl or boy. *Ash, Ashby, Ashe, Ashford, Ashia, Ashiah, Ashla, Ashlana, Ashlanah, Ashlane, Ashlaney, Ashlea, Ashleah, Ashlee, Ashlei, Ashleigh, Ashlen, Ashlena, Ashlenah, Ashlene, Ashli, Ashlia, Ashliah, Ashlie, Ashlin, Ashlina, Ashlinah, Ashline, Ashling, Ashly, Ashlya, Ashlyah*

Asisa (Hebrew) Ripe.

Aspen (Old English) Tree. *Aspin, Aspyn*

Astrid (Greek) Star. (Old Norse) Super strength. *Asta, Astera, Astra, Astrah, Astrea, Astreah, Astred, Astree, Astrey, Astriah, Astrya, Astryah, Astyr*

Atara (Hebrew) Crown. *Atarah, Ataree*

Athaliah (Biblical) The time of the Lord.

Athena (Greek) Goddess of war. *Atheana, Atheanah, Athenah, Athenais, Athene, Atherlea, Atherleah, Atherlee, Atherlei, Atherleigh, Atherley, Atherli, Atherlia, Atherliah, Atherlie, Atherly, Atherlya, Atherlyah*

Atlanta (American) Place name; immoveable. *Atalanta*

Atropos (Greek) One of the three Moirae, the Fates, the female deities who supervised fate rather than determined it. Atropos was the Fate who cut the thread or web of life.

Aubrey (German) Elf rule. *Aubary, Auberi, Aubery, Aubray, Aubre, Aubrea, Aubree, Aubrei, Aubreigh, Aubri, Aubria, Aubrie, Aubry, Aubury*

Auburn (Latin) Fair. *Alban, Aubin*

Audrey (Old English) Noble strength. *Audey, Audie, Audra, Audrah, Audre, Audrea, Audree, Audri, Audria, Audriah, Audrie, Audry, Audrya, Audryah, Audrye, Etheldreda*

Audrianna (English) Combination of Audrey and Anna. *Audreanna, Audrienna, Audryana, Audryanna*

Augusta (Latin) Exalted. *Augie, Augusta, Augustina, Augustine, Augustus, Gus, Gussie, Gussy, Gusta*

Aulii (Hawaiian) Exquisite.

Aung Sun (Burmese) For father.

Aurelia (Latin) Gold. *Aurea, Aurelie, Aurora, Aurore*

Aureliano (Spanish) Golden.

Aurora (Greek) Goddess of the dawn. *Aurorah, Aurore, Aurure, Ora, Orah*

Autumn (Latin) Of woods. *Autum*

Ava (Latin) Birdlike. *Avada, Avae, Avalee, Aveen, Avelina, Aveline, Avelyn, Avis, Avlynn*

Avalon (Latin) Island. *Avalona, Avalonah, Avaloni, Avalonia, Avaloniah, Avalonie, Avalony, Avalonya, Avalonyah*

Avel (Greek) Breath.

Avery (English) Counselor.

Aviva (Hebrew) Springtime. *Avi, Avia, Avital, Avivah*

Avon (Old English) The river.

Avril (French) Month of April. *Averel, Averell, Averil, Averyl*

Awendela (Native American) Morning.

Ayala (Hebrew) Gazelle.

Ayame (Japanese) Iris.

Ayana (African) Beautiful flower. (Hindi) Innocent. *Ahyana, Ayan, Ayania, Ayanna, Ayna*

Ayasha (Arabic) Mohammed's wife. (Native American) Little one. *Ayesha*

Ayita (Native American) Worker.

Ayla (Hebrew) Oak tree. *Aylah, Aylana, Aylanah, Aylanna, Aylannah, Aylea, Aylee, Ayleena, Aylena, Aylene*

Aylin (Turkish) Moon halo.

Ayn (Hebrew) Prayer.

Azalea (Arabic) Democracy.

Azarin (Persian) Chamomile flower.

Azura (Persian) Sky blue. *Azure*

Azure (Biblical) He who assists; also boy's name.

B

Baako (African) First-born.

Babette (French) Stranger. *Babbette, Babbie, Babet, Babeta, Babetah, Babett, Babetta, Babettah, Babidjana, Babita, Babittah, Babs*

Badriya (Muslim) Resembling the full moon.

Bailey (French) Bailiff. (Old English) Fortification. *Bailea, Baileah, Bailee, Bailei, Bailli, Baily, Baylee, Bayley*

Bakana (Australian) Guardian. *Bakanah, Bakanna, Bakannah*

Bakari (Swahili) Noble promise. *Bakarie, Bakary*

Balbina (Latin) Stammerer. *Balbinah, Balbine, Balbyna, Balbynah*

Bambi (Italian) Child; little doll. *Bambea, Bambee, Bambia, Bambiah, Bambie, Bambino, Bamby, Bambya*

Bameket Origin and meaning unknown.

Bankei (Japanese) Ten thousand blessings.

Banon (Welsh) Queen.

Banu (Turkish) Woman. *Bano*

Bao (Chinese) Treasure; precious.

Baptista (Latin) Baptizer. *Baptisa, Baptiste, Batista*

Bara (Hebrew) To choose. *Barah, Barra, Barrah, Bára*

Barbada (Arabic) Blessing.

Barbara (Latin) Foreign, strange. *Babette, Babs, Bararella, Barb, Barbie, Barbra, Barbro, Barbs, Barby, Bobbie*

Barika (Swahili) Bloom. *Barikah, Baryka, Barykah*

Barran (Russian) Ram. *Baran, Barana, Baranah, Barein, Bareina*

Barrett (German) Strong as a bear.

Basalt (Greek) Hard, dark, igneous rock.

Basanti (Hindi) Spring.

Basha (Hebrew) Daughter of God. *Bashiah, Bashya, Bashyah, Basia, Basiah, Basya, Basyah, Bathia, Batia, Batya, Batyah*

Bashira (Arabic) Joyful, happy. *Basheera, Bashiga, Bashirah*

Basilissa (Greek) Regal; feminine form of Basil. *Basile, Basilla*

Basillia (Latin) Queenly. *Basilia, Basiliah, Basilie, Basilla, Basillah*

Basimah (Arabic) Smile. *Basmah*

Bathsheba (Hebrew) Daughter of the oath.

Bathshua, Batsheva, Batshevah, Batya, Bersaba, Bethsabee, Bethsheba, Sheba

Beata (Latin) Blessed. *Beatah, Beatta, Beeta, Beetah, Beita, Beitah, Beyta, Beytah*

Beatrice (Latin) Happy. *Bea, Beah, Beate, Beatirsa, Beatrix, Beatriz, Beattie, Beatty, Beezus, Trixie*

Becky (Hebrew) To tie, bind; enchantingly beautiful. *Becca, Becka, Becki, Beckie, Bekki, Reba, Rebeca, Rebecca, Rebeka, Rebekah, Ree, Reeba, Riba, Riva, Rivalee, Rivi, Rivkah, Rivy*

Bedegrayne (English) The castle and forest where Arthur fought his battle against 11 kings in Arthurian legend. *Bedgraine*

Bedelia (French) Strength; might. (Irish) High goddess. *Bedeelia, Bedeliah, Bedelya, Bedelyah, Biddy, Bidelia*

Bela (Czech) White. (Hungarian) Bright. *Belah, Belau, Belia, Beliah, Biela*

Belakane (Scottish) Arthurian legend. (African) Queen.

Belicia (Spanish) Dedicated to God. *Bela, Beliciah, Belysia*

Belinda (Spanish) Beautiful. *Balina, Balinah, Balinda, Ballinda, Ballindah, Beauty, Belita, Bell, Belladonna, Belle, Bellini, Belva, Belvia, Belynda, Linda*

Bella (Latin) Beautiful. *Bellah, Belle, Bellina*

Bellona (Latin) Roman goddess of war.

Belva (Latin) Beautiful view. *Belvia, Belviah, Belvyah*

Bena (Hebrew) One of wisdom. *Benah, Benay, Benea, Benna, Bennah*

Benazir (Muslim) Incomparable.

Benedetta (Latin) Blessed. *Benetta, Benita, Bente*

Berdine (German) Glorious. *Berdina, Berdinah, Birdeen, Birdenie*

Berit (German) Glorious, splendid; strength. *Beret, Berete, Berette, Biret*

Berkley (Scottish) Meadow. *Berkeley, Berkly*

Berlynn (German) Bear. *Berla, Berlin, Berlinda, Berline, Berling, Berlinn, Berlyn, Berlyne, Berlynne*

Bernadette (French) Brave as a bear. (English) Intelligent. Feminine version of Bernard. *Bern, Berna, Bernadete, Bernadina, Bernadine, Berneta, Bernetta, Berni, Bernie, Burnette, Burney, Burnice*

Bernice (Greek) Bringer of victory. *Berenice, Bernica, Bernicia, Bernise, Bernyc, Bernyce, Bernyse, Berry, Berta, Berti, Bunny*

Berry (English) Berry. *Berce, Beri, Berri, Bery*

Bertha (Saxon) Glorious; beautiful. *Berti, Bertie, Bertina, Birtha, Birthe, Byrth, Byrtha, Byrthah*

Berwyn (Welsh) White-haired. *Berwin, Berwina, Berwinah, Beryne*

Beryl (Hebrew) Jewel. *Berel, Beril, Berila, Berile, Berill, Berille, Berylla, Berylle*

Bess (Hebrew) God's oath; dedicated. *Babette, Belita, Besse, Bessie, Bessy, Bestey,*

Bet, Beta, Beth, Betta, Bette, Betti, Bettina, Bettine, Betty, Ealasidde, Eilise, Elisa, Elisabeth, Elisabetta, Elise, Elissa, Eliza, Elizabet, Elizabeth, Elsa, Elsabet, Elsbeth

Bethany (Hebrew) House of mercy. *Bethani, Bethanie, Bethel, Betheny, Bethesda, Bethnie*

Betsy (American) Form of Elizabeth. *Betsee, Betsey, Betsi, Betsye*

Bettina (Hebrew) House of God. (Spanish) Majestic. Combination of Beth and Tina. *Betina, Betine, Bettyne, Betyne*

Betty (Hebrew) Consecrated to God. *Beti, Betti, Bettie*

Beulah (Hebrew) Married. *Beula, Beulla, Beullah*

Bevanne (Welsh) Child of Evan. *Bevann, Bevin, Bevina, Bevine*

Beverly (Old English) Meadow of beavers. *Bev, Beverely, Beverle, Beverlea, Beverleah, Beverlee, Beverleigh, Beverley*

Beyonce (African American) Beyond others.

Bhamini (Sanskrit) Beautiful.

Bhanumati (Sanskrit) Luminous.

Bharati (Hindi) Goddess of knowledge and arts.

Bhuma (Hindi) Earth. *Bhoomi*

Bian (Vietnamese) Hidden. *Biann, Bianne, Byan, Byann*

Bianca (Italian) White; fair. *Biancca, Biancha, Biancia, Bianco, Blake, Blanca,*

Blanch, Blancha, Blanche, Branca

Bibi (Arabic) Lady. *BeBe, Beebee, Bibiana, Bibiyana, Byby*

Bibiana (Latin) Lively. *Bibiane, Bibiann, Bibianne*

Billie (English) Resolution; wise. *Bilee, Bilei, Bileigh, Biley, Bille, Billea, Billeah, Billy, Billye, Byli, Bylli, Bylly, Byly*

Bina (Hindi) Musical instrument. (Hebrew) Intelligence; understanding. *Binah, Binney, Binta, Bintah, Byna, Bynah, Sabina*

Bindi (Latin) Beautiful serpent.

Bindiya (Hindi) Drop or point.

Binney (German) From the name Bingham; kettle-shape hollow. *Bin, Bing, Binnee, Binni, Binnie, Binny*

Birdee (English) Birdlike. *Bird, Birde, Birdea, Birdella, Birdena, Birdey, Birdi, Birdie, Birdy*

Birgit (Irish) Defender. *Bergeta, Birget, Birgita, Birgitt, Birgitta, Birgitte, Birkita*

Bisa (African) Greatly loved.

Bjorg (Scandinavian) Salvation. *Bjorga*

Bladina (Latin) Friendly. *Bladeen, Bladene, Bladine, Bladyna*

Blaine (Gaelic) Lean. (Old English) Source of a river. *Blain, Blane, Blayne*

Blair (Gaelic) Plain. *Blaire, Blare, Blayr, Blayre*

Blake (English) Dark. *Blaik, Blaike, Blayke*

Blakely (English) Dark meadow. *Blaiklee, Blaikleigh, Blakeley, Blakelie*

Blanche (French) White. *Blanca, Blanch, Blancha*

Blancheflour (Scottish) White flower.

Blase (Latin) One who stammers. *Blais, Blaise, Blaisia, Blaiz, Blaize, Blasha, Blasia, Blayse, Blayze, Blaza, Blaze, Blazena, Blazia*

Blessing (English) Consecration.

Bliss (English) Perfect joy. *Blis, Blisa, Blisasa, Blisse, Blys, Blysa, Blyss, Blyssa, Blysse*

Blodwyn (Welsh) Flower. *Blodwen, Blodwin, Blodwinah, Blodwynn*

Blondelle (French) Blond-haired. *Blondel, Blondela, Blondelia, Blondell, Blondie*

Bloodstone (Greek) Green with red spots; the martyr's stone.

Blossom (Old English) Lovely.

Blue Angel (American) Sad angel.

Bluma (German) Flower. *Blooma*

Bly (Native American) Tall child.

Blythe (Old English) Joyous. *Bligh, Bliss, Blithe*

Bo (Norse) To live or dwell. (Hebrew) Strong and fast. (Scandinavian) Commanding. *Beau, Bow*

Bobette (American) Form of Roberta. *Bobbet, Bobinette*

Bodil (Norwegian) Mighty ruler. *Bodila, Bodilah, Bodyl, Bodyla*

Bohdana (Russian) From God.

Bong Cha (Korean) Superior daughter.

Bonita (Spanish) Pretty. *Bonitah, Bonitta, Bonittah, Bonnitah, Bonyta*

Bonnie (Scottish) Good. *Bonea, Bonee, Boney, Boni, Boniface, Bonifacy, Bonita, Bonne, Bonnell, Bonney, Bonni, Bonniah, Bonnibel, Bonnin, Bonny*

Boston (American) Place name.

Bracha (Hebrew) Blessing.

Brady (Irish) Spirited. *Bradey, Bradie, Braidee, Braidey*

Braeden (English) Broad hill. *Bradyn, Bradynn, Braedan, Braidan, Braydon*

Braelyn (American) Combination of Braeden and Lynn. *Braelin, Braelle, Braelon, Brailey*

Brandie (Dutch) Fiery spirit distilled from wine. (American) Sweet nectar. *Branddeece, Brandea, Brandee, Brandei, Brandi, Brandis, Brandise, Brandy, Brandyse, Branwen, Bronwen, Bronwyn*

Brangaine (Scottish) Arthurian legend, character from *Isolde*.

Brea (Old English) Thin broth. *Breah, Bree, Breeah, Bri*

Breck (Irish) Freckled. *Brec, Breca, Breckin, Brecklyn, Brecklynn*

Bree (English) Broth. *Breay, Brei, Breigh, Brey, Brie*

Breena (Irish) Fairy land. *Breenah, Breene, Breenea, Breenia, Breeniah, Breina, Breinah*

Brena (Irish) Raven; maiden with dark hair. *Brenah, Brenie, Brenin, Brenn, Brenna, Brennah, Brennaugh, Brenne*

Brenda (Old English) Sword. (Irish) Little raven. Fiery hill. Feminine of Brandon. *Branda, Bren, Brendah, Brendie, Brendyl, Brennda, Brenndah, Breonna, Brinda, Brindah, Brynna, Brynnda, Brynndah*

Bret (Irish) Form of Britany. *Brett, Bretta, Brettah, Brette, Brettin, Bretton*

Brianna (Irish) Strong, virtuous. *Breeann, Briana, Briann, Briannah, Briannon*

Briar (French) Heather. *Brier, Bryar*

Brice (Irish) Swift. (English) Son of a nobleman. *Brick, Bristol, Brixey, Brixie, Bryce*

Bridget (Irish) Resolute, strong. *Biddy, Birgit, Birgitta, Breanna, Bree, Briana, Brianna, Brianne, Brid, Brie, Brienne, Brietta, Brigada, Brigetta, Brigette, Brighid, Brigid, Brigida, Brigita, Brigitte, Brit, Brita, Britta, Britte, Bryanne*

Brighton (English) Bright town. *Breighton, Brightin, Bryton*

Brina (Latin) Form of Sabrina. *Brinah, Brinlee, Brinly*

Brisa (Spanish) Beloved. *Breza, Brisah, Brissa, Brysa*

Briton (English) Form of Britain.

Brittany (English) Place name; anglicized version of Bretagne, a section of France; from Britain. *Brita, Britain, Britaney, Britannia, Britany, Britnee, Britny, Britt, Britta, Brittania, Brittney, Brittny*

Bronwyn (Welsh) White-breasted. *Bronwin, Bronwine, Bronwynn*

Brook (Old English) Stream. *Bhrooke, Brooke, Brookee, Brookelle, Brookes, Brookia, Brookie, Brooks, Burne*

Bruna (German) Brunette. (Yiddish) Brown. *Brona*

Brygid (Irish) Strong.

Bryn (Welsh) Hill. *Brunhild, Brunhilde, Brynhil, Brynne*

Bryony (English) Vine with small blossoms. *Brionie, Bryonee, Bryoney, Bryoni, Bryonia*

Buffy (Old English) Consecrated to God. *Bufee, Bufey, Buffee, Buffey, Buffi, Buffie, Buffye, Bufi, Bufie, Bufy*

Bunita (Australian) Meaning unknown.

Bunny (English) Little rabbit. *Buni, Bunney, Bunni, Bunnie*

Burnet (Modern English) Burnette.

Butterfly (American) Flying insect.

C

Cacey (Irish) Vigilant. (African) Favorite. Form of Casey. *Cace, Cacee, Cacia, Cacie, Cacy, Casee, Kacey, Kaci, Kacie, Kacy, Kasey, Kasie, Kassie, Kaycee,*

Kecia, Keesha, Keisha, Kesha, Keshia, Kesia, Kisha, Kizzy

Cachay (African American) Prestigious. *Caché, Cashay, Kachay, Kashay*

Cadence (Latin) Rhythmic. *Cadena, Cadenza, Kadena, Kadenza*

Cady (American) Simple happiness. (Old English) Rhythmic flow of sounds. Possible combination of Katy and Cody. *Cade, Cadee, Cadey, Cadi, Cadie, Cadye, Caidie, Kade, Kadee, Kadi, Kadie, Kady, Kayde*

Cailida (Spanish) Adoring.

Cailin (Scottish) Triumphant people. *Caelan, Caileen, Cailyn, Calunn, Cauleen, Caulin*

Caitlin (Irish) Pure beauty; form of Catherine. *Caitlan, Caitlyn, Caitlynn, Catalina, Catelyn, Kaitlin, Kaitlyn, Katelyn, Kaytlin*

Caiwen (Welsh) Blessed fair one. *Ceinwen, Kayne, Keyne*

Cala (Arabic) Castle.

Calandra (Greek) Lark; Calinda and Calynda are contemporary variants or blends with Linda. *Cal, Calandia, Calandre, Calandria, Calendre, Calinda, Callee, Calley, Cally, Calynda, Cayla, Ceil, Celia, Cielo, Cleo, Kalandra*

Calantha (Greek) Beautiful blossoms. *Calanthe, Callee, Kalantha*

Calatea (Greek) Ancient mythological creature. *Calatee*

Calcite (Latin) Burnt lime; gray; colorless.

Calendula (Latin) Flower that blooms every month of the year.

Cali (Greek) Form of Callie. *Calia, Caliah*

Calida (Spanish) Affectionate. *Callida*

Calista (Greek) Most beautiful. *Cala, Calesta, Calissa, Calisto, Calla, Callesta, Callia, Callista, Calliste, Callysta, Calyssa, Calysta, Celeste, Celestine, Kala, Kalesta, Kalista, Kalla, Kallesta, Kalli, Kallie, Kallista, Kally, Kallysta*

Callan (German) Chatter. (Irish) Powerful in battle. *Callen, Calynn, Kallan*

Calliope (Greek) Beautiful voice. *Callia, Callyope, Kalliope*

Callis (Latin) Cup. *Callys*

Calpurnia (Shakespearean) Character from *Julius Caesar*.

Cambria (Latin) From Wales. *Cambaria, Cambree, Cambrie, Kambria*

Camelia (Italian) Evergreen shrub. *Camalia, Camela, Cameliah, Camillia, Kamelia*

Cameo (English) Engraved gem. *Camio, Cammeo, Camyo, Kamea*

Camera (American) Photographic device. *Cameri, Cameria*

Cameron (Old English) Bent nose. *Cam, Cami, Camm, Cammie, Camryn, Camyron*

Camesha (American) Form of Camisha. *Cameesha, Camesa, Cameshia, Kameska*

Camille (Latin) Attendant at a religious ceremony. *Caimile, Camelia, Camila,*

Camilla, Camillia, Cammie, Cammilla, Cammy, Kamilla, Kamille, Mila

Camira (Aboriginal) Of the wind.

Campbell (Latin) Beautiful field. (Scottish) Crooked mouth. *Cambel, Cambell, Kampbell*

Camry (Brand name) Model of Toyota car. *Camree, Camrey, Camri*

Candace (Ethopian) Brilliantly white. (Greek) White-hot. *Candaice, Candase, Candayce, Candee, Candi, Candice, Candie, Candis, Candiss, Candy, Candyce, Candys, Dace, Dacee, Dacey, Dacie, Dacy, Kandace, Kandice, Kandiss, Kandy*

Candela (Spanish) Fire. *Candelas*

Candida (Latin) Bright; glowing white. *Candi, Candide, Candie, Candy*

Candra (Latin) Luminescent. (Greek) Pure and chaste. Form of Candace. *Candrah, Candrea, Candria, Candriah*

Canela (Latin) Cinnamon.

Cantara (Arabic) Small crossing. *Cantarah*

Cantrelle (French) Song. *Cantrel, Cantrela, Cantrele, Cantrella*

Capri (Anglo-Saxon) Unpredictable, whimsical; form of Caprice. *Capree, Caprey, Caprie, Capry*

Caprial Origin and meaning unknown.

Caprice (Italian) Fanciful. *Capreece, Capri, Capriana, Capricia, Caprise, Capryce*

Cara (Latin) Dear. (Irish) Friend. (Italian) Beloved one. (Vietnamese) Diamond. *Caera, Canna, Caragh, Carah, Caralie, Careen, Carine, Carita, Carra, Kara, Karra*

Caralee (Irish) Form of Cara. *Caralea, Caraleigh, Caralia, Caralie*

Carenza (Cornish) Loving, affectionate. *Caranza, Caranzah, Caranzia, Carenzah*

Caresse (French) Touch. *Caress, Caressa*

Carey (Latin) Dear. (Irish) Pure. (Spanish) Dear. (Welsh) Near the castle. *Cari, Carie, Carrey, Carrie, Carry, Cary, Kerrie, Kerry*

Carin (Irish) Friend. (Italian) Beloved one. *Caren, Caryn, Karena, Karin, Karina, Karine, Karyn*

Carina (Greek) Pure. (Latin) Little darling. Form of Catherine. *Caaren, Careena, Careenna, Cariana, Carinna, Caryna, Carynna, Kareena*

Carisa (Latin) Most beloved one. (Greek) Grace. *Caresa, Caressa, Carissa, Carisse, Carita, Carrisa, Charissa, Karisa, Karissa, Kharissa*

Carisma (Greek) Divinely favored. *Carismah, Carismara, Carysma, Carysmah*

Carita (Latin) Charitable. *Caritah, Caritta, Carittah, Carytah*

Carla (Latin) Strong one. (Old German) Freeholder. Feminine form of Carl. *Carilla, Carlah, Carlana, Carlee, Carleen, Carleigh,*

Carlena, Carlene, Carletta, Carlette, Carley, Carlia, Carlina, Carlisa, Carlita, Carlla, Carlyn, Karla, Karleen, Karlie, Karlla, Karly

Carlin (Irish) Little champion. *Carlan, Carlana, Carlanah, Carrlin*

Carlissa (American) Combination of Carla and Lissa. *Carlisa, Carliss, Carlissah, Carlisse*

Carlotta (Italian) Valiant; strong; free. (Spanish) Little and womanly. Form of Charlotte or Caroline. *Carlota, Charley, Charlie, Charlotta, Karlotte, Lotta, Lottie, Lotty, Tottie, Totty*

Carly (English) Form of Caroline. *Carlea, Carlee, Carley, Carli, Carlia*

Carlyle (English) Carla's island. *Carlyse, Carlysle*

Carmel (Hebrew) Garden or field of fruit. *Canneline, Cannella, Carma, Carmela, Carmelina, Carmeline, Carmelita, Carmella, Carmelle, Carmen, Carmia, Carmiel, Carmina, Carmine, Carmita, Kamelit, Karmel, Karmela, Karmelita, Karmelle, Karmen, Lina, Lita, Melina, Mell, Melli, Mellie, Melly*

Carmina (Latin) Song. *Carmen, Carminah, Carmine, Carmynah*

Carna (Latin) Horn. *Carniela, Karniela, Karnyella*

Carnelian (Latin) Red gem. *Carnelia, Carneliah, Carnelya, Carnelyan, Cornelian*

Carol (English) Song. (Old German) Freeholder. English feminine form of Carolus; originally a short form of Caroline;

feminine form of Charles. *Carel, Carline, Caro, Carola, Carole, Caroll, Caroly, Carri, Carrie, Carrola, Carroll, Caryl, Caryll, Karel, Kari, Karla, Karleen, Karli, Karlie, Karlina, Karlinka, Karlote, Karlotta, Karol, Karola, Karole, Karryl, Karryll, Karyl, Karyll, Kerril, Kerryl, Keryl*

Caroline (French) Little and strong; feminine form of Charles. *Caraleen, Caraleena, Caraline, Caralyn, Caralyne, Caralynn, Carilyn, Carilynne, Carolan, Carolann, Carolanne, Caroliana, Carolin, Carolina, Carollyn, Carolyn, Carolyne, Carolynn, Carolynne, Karaleen, Karaleena, Karalina, Karaline, Karalyn, Karalynna, Karalynne, Karoline, Karolinka, Karolyn, Karolyna, Karolyne, Karolynn, Karolynne, Leena, Lina, Sharleen, Sharla, Sharlena, Sharlene, Sharline, Sharlyne*

Caron (Welsh) Loving, kind. (French) Pure. Form of Karen. *Caren, Carin, Carren, Carron, Caryn*

Carys (Welsh) To love. *Caris, Caryss, Carysse, Cerys*

Casey (Irish) Vigilant, watchful. *Cacey, Cacia, Cacie, Caisee, Caisey, Caisi, Caisie, Casee, Casi, Casie, Caycee, Caycey, Cayci, Caycie, Caysee, Caysey, Caysi, Kaysey, Kaysi, Kaysie, Kaysy, Kaysyee*

Casmir (Slavic) Peacemaker. *Casimira, Casmira, Casmirah, Casmyra*

Cassandra (Greek) Original prophet of doom in classical mythology. *Casandera, Casandra, Cassandre, Cassandrea, Cassandry, Cassaundra, Cassondra,*

Cassy, Kasandera, Kass,
Kassandra, Sande, Sandee,
Sandera, Sandi, Sandie,
Sandra, Sandy, Saundra,
Sohndra, Sondra, Zandra

Cassia (Greek) Cinnamon-
like spice. *Cassey, Cassi,*
Cassy, Kassi, Kassia, Kassie,
Kassy

Cassidy (Irish) Curly
headed; clever. *Cassady,*
Cassidey, Kassadey, Kassidy,
Kassodey

Cassiel (Latin) Angel of
Saturday; earthy mother.

Cassietta (African
American) Cassietta
George, "Queen of Good
Gospel Music," Grammy
Award–winning gospel
singer in 1960s and 1970s.

Cassiopeia (Greek)
Mother of Andromeda;
clever. *Cassiopia, Kassiopeia,*
Kassiopia

Castora (Spanish) Brilliant.

Catalina (Spanish) Form
of Katherine. *Catalena,*
Catalene, Catalinah, Cataline

Catava (African) Sleep.

Cate (English) Form of
Catherine.

Catera (Modern English)
Blessed, pure. (Brand
name) Model of Cadillac
car. *Katara, Katera, Katerra*

Cathay (Khitay) Name of
semi-nomadic people who
dominated northern China
from the tenth through
twelfth centuries.

Catherine (Greek) Pure.
Cait, Caitey, Caitie, Caitlin,
Caitlinn, Caitrin, Caitrine,
Caitrinn, Caitriona,
Caitrionagh, Caity, Cat,
Cataleen, Catarina, Catarine,
Cate, Cateline, Caterina,

Catey, Catha, Cathaleen,
Cathaline, Catharin,
Catharine, Catharyne,
Cathatina, Cathatyna, Cathe,
Cathee, Cathelin, Cathelina,
Cathelle, Catherin, Catherina,
Catherinn, Catheryn, Cathi,
Cathie, Cathirin, Cathiryn,
Cathleen, Cathlene, Cathline,
Cathlyne, Cathrine, Cathrinn,
Cathryn, Cathrynn,
Cathy, Cathye, Cathyleen,
Catlaina, Catlina, Catriona,
Catrionagh, Catryna, Cay,
Caye, Cazzy, Ekaterina,
Kait, Kaitey, Kaitie, Kaitlin,
Kaitlinne, Kaitrin, Kaitrine,
Kaitrinna, Kaitriona,
Kaitrionaugh, Kasienka,
Kasja, Kaska, Katarina,
Katchen, Kate, Katee, Katell,
Katelle, Katenka, Katerina,
Katerinka, Katey, Katha,
Katharine, Katharyn,
Katharyne, Kathee, Kathelina,
Katheline, Katherin,
Katherina, Katherine,
Katheryn, Katherynn,
Kathi, Kathie, Kathileen,
Kathiryn, Kathleen, Kathlene,
Kathleyn, Kathline, Kathrine,
Kathrinna, Kathryn,
Kathryne, Kathy, Kathyleen,
Kathyrine, Katica, Katie,
Katina, Katinka, Katka,
Katla, Katlaina, Katleen,
Katoushka, Katrena,
Katrina, Katrine, Katriona,
Katrionaugh, Katryna,
Katushka, Katy, Katya, Kittee,
Kittie, Kitty, Trina, Trine,
Trinette, Yekaterin, Yekaterina

Catori (Native American)
Spirit.

Cavanaugh (Middle
English) Chubby.
Cavanagh, Kavanagh,
Kavanaugh

Caylin (American) Form
of Caitlin. *Caylean, Caylen,*
Caylena, Caylene

Ceara (Irish) Ruddy; dark;
spear. *Caera, Chiara, Ciar,*
Ciara, Ciaran, Ciarra,
Cieara, Ciera, Cierra, Kiara,
Searra, Siara, Sierra

Cecania (German)
Freedom.

Cecilia (Latin) Blind one;
the sixth; feminine form
of Cecil. *C'Ceal, Cacelie,*
Ceceley, Cecelia, Cecely,
Cecile, Cecilee, Ceciliane,
Cecilie, Cecilija, Cecilla,
Cecille, Cecily, Cecilya,
Cecilyann, Cecyle, Cecylia,
Ceil, Cele, Celia, Celie,
Cicely, Cile, Cilia, Cilka,
Cilla, Cilly, Cissie, Kikelia,
Kikylia, Sacilia, Sasilia,
Sasilie, Seelia, Seelie, Seely,
Sela, Selia, Sesilia, Sessaley,
Sesseelya, Sessile, Sessilly,
Sessily, Sheila, Sile, Sileas,
Silke, Sissey, Sissie, Sissy

Celandia (Greek) Swallow.
Celandinah, Celandine

Celena (Greek) Form of
Selena. *Caleena, Celeanah,*
Celeena, Celeenah, Celene,
Celina

Celeste (Latin) Heavenly.
Cela, Celeena, Celena, Celesse,
Celesta, Celesteen, Celesteene,
Celestena, Celestene, Celestia,
Celestiel, Celestijna, Celestina,
Celestine, Celestyn, Celestyna,
Celestyne, Celia, Celie,
Celina, Celinda, Celine,
Celinka, Celinna, Celisse,
Celka, Celleste, Celyna,
Cesia, Cesya, Salena, Saleste,
Salestia, Salina, Seleena,
Selena, Selene, Seleste,
Selestia, Selestina, Selestine,
Selestyna, Selestyne, Selinda,
Seline, Selyna, Selyne, Silesta,
Silestena, Silestia, Silestijna,
Silestina, Silestyna, Silestyne,
Tinka, Zelena

Celica (Brand name) Model
of Toyota car.

Centola (Arabic) Light of knowledge.

Cerelia (Greek) Goddess of the harvest. (Latin) Relating to spring. *Cerella, Ceres, Sarelia, Sarillia*

Ceridwen (Welsh) Poetic goddess. *Kerridwyn*

Cerise (French) Cherry; cherry red. *Cerisa, Cerisse, Charisse, Cherise, Sarese, Sherise*

Cettina (Italian) Blessed, happy; bringer of joy.

Chablis (French) Dry white wine. *Chablea, Chablee, Chabley, Chabli, Chablie*

Chadee (French) From Chad. *Chadae, Chadai, Chaday, Chaddae*

Chai (Hebrew) Life. *Chae, Chaeli, Chaella, Chaia, Chay*

Chaka (Arabic) Chakra; energy center. (Hebrew) Life. *Chayka*

Chalan (Peruvian) Horse trainer.

Chalcedony (Greek) Quartz; mystical stone.

Chalee (English) Meadow on the ledge; form of Shelee.

Chalice (French) Goblet. *Chalie, Chalisse, Challis, Challyce*

Chalina (Spanish) Form of Rose. *Chalin, Chalinah, Chaline, Challain*

Chanah (Hebrew) Grace; variation of Hannah. *Chaanach, Chaanah, Chana, Chanach, Chanaiana, Channa, Cheyanne, Cheyenne, China, Chyna, Chynna, Connie*

Chance (Old French) Church official or chancellor. *Chancey*

Chandelle (French) Candle. *Chandal, Chandale, Chandela, Chandellah*

Chandler (English) Candlemaker. *Chandlar, Chandlier, Chandlor*

Chandra (Sanskrit) Of the moon. (Hindi) Goddess Devi, foe of evil. *Candi, Candy, Chanda, Chandani, Chandara, Chandrama, Chandria, Chandy, Chante, Chaundra, Cinda, Cindi, Cindy, Cinthia, Cyndi, Cynthia*

Chanel (French) Canal; channel; perfume. *Chanell, Chanelle, Channelle, Chenelle, Shanel, Shanell, Shanelle, Shannel, Shannelle, Shenelle, Shynelle*

Channing (English) Wise. *Chane, Chanin, Channin*

Chantal (Old French) Stone or singer. *Chandler, Chantale, Chantalle, Chantel, Chantele, Chantell, Chantelle, Chantrell, Chauntel, Shantal, Shantalle, Shantel, Shantell, Shantelle, Shontel, Shontelle*

Chapa (Native American) Superior.

Chapawee (Native American) Industrious.

Chardonnay (French) White wine. *Chardonai, Chardonay, Chardonee, Chardonnai*

Charis (Greek) Kindness. *Chareece, Charie, Charise, Charrys*

Charisma (Greek) Grace; beauty; kindness. *Carisa, Carisma, Carissa, Carrie, Carry, Chareesse, Charis, Charisa, Charise, Charissa,*

Charisse, Charysse, Cherish, Cruz, Karas, Karis, Karisma, Karisse, Sherisa

Charity (Latin) Loving and benevolent. *Caridad, Carissa, Carita, Caritas, Chareese, Charis, Charissa, Charisse, Charita, Charitee, Charitey, Charitye, Chariza, Charty, Cherri, Cherry, Cordia, Cordie, Karita, Sharitee, Sharitey, Sharity, Sharitye*

Charla (French) Form of Charlene. *Char, Charlae, Charlai*

Charlene (English) Form of Caroline. *Charlaine, Charlean, Charleen, Charline, Charlynne*

Charlotte (French) Little and womanly; feminine of Charles. *Carlotta, Charlet, Charlette, Charlot, Charlotta*

Charmaine (French) Form of Carmen. *Charmagne, Charmaigne, Charmain, Charmane, Charmeine*

Charu (Hindi) Charming.

Chase (French) Hunter. *Chace, Chaice, Chason, Chasse*

Chastity (Latin) Purity, innocence. *Chasaty, Chasida, Chasity, Chassity, Chasta, Chastina, Chastine, Chastitee, Chastitey, Chiquita*

Chay (Old German) Man. (Irish) Fairy dwelling.

Chaya (Hebrew) Life. *Chava, Chavah*

Chelle (English) Form of Michelle.

Chelsea (Old English) River landing place. *Chalsie, Chelde, Chellsie, Chelsa, Chelsee, Chelseigh, Chelsey, Chelsi, Chelsie, Chelsy, Kelsey, Kelsie, Kelsy*

Chen (Chinese) Dawn.

Chen-Chio (Chinese) Meaning unknown.

Chen-Tao (Chinese) Meaning unknown.

Chenoa (Native American) White dove. *Chenee, Chenna, Chenoah*

Chepi (Native American) Fairy.

Cher (French) Dearest. *Cher, Sher, Shere*

Cheridah (Latin) Charity, kindness.

Cheriss (French) Precious. *Charisha, Cherish, Cherrish*

Cheryl (French) Beloved. *Charalin, Charalyn, Charalynne, Charelin, Charelyn, Charelynn, Charilyn, Charilynn, Cher, Cheralin, Cheralyn, Chere, Cherelle, Cherée, Cheri, Cherie, Cherilin, Cherilynn, Cherilynne, Cherralyn, Cherri, Cherrilin, Cherrilyn, Cherry, Cherrylene, Cherrylin, Cherryline, Cherrylyn, Cheryle, Cherylin, Cheryline, Cheryllyn, Cherylyn, Cora, Corey, Cori, Corrie, Cory, Sharelyn, Sharelynne, Sharilynn, Sher, Sheralin, Sheralynne, Sherelle, Sherey, Sheri, Sherice, Sherie, Sherilin, Sherralin, Sherrill, Sherrilyn, Sherry, Sherryl, Sherrylene, Sherryline, Sherryll, Sherrylyn, Sheryl, Sheryle, Sherylin, Sherylyn*

Chesna (Slavic) Peaceful. *Chesnah, Chesney, Chessna, Chessnah, Chezna*

Cheyenne (Native American) Courage. *Chana, Chayan, Chayanne, Cheyanna, Cheyanne, Chiana, Chianna, Chyanne,*

Shayan, Shayanne, Shyann, Shyanne

Chhaya (Hindi) Shadow.

Chika (Japanese) Near and dear. *Chikah, Chikako, Chikara*

Chilali (Native American) Snowbird. *Chilalea, Chilalee, Chilalei, Chilaly*

Chimalis (Native American) Bluebird.

China (Chinese) Fine porcelain. *Chinah, Chine, Chinea, Chinna*

Chinara (Nigerian) God receives. *Chinira, Chinirah, Chynira*

Chinshu (Japanese) Calm place.

Chinue (African) God's own blessing.

Chione (Egyptian) Daughter of the Nile.

Chipo (African) Gift.

Chiquita (Spanish) Little one. *Chaquita, Chica, Chikata, Chiquitta*

Chitralekha (Indian) Beautiful design.

Chitrali (Sanskrit) Beautiful lady.

Chitrangda (Hindi) Portrait. *Chitra*

Chiyo (Japanese) Thousand years; eternal.

Chloe (Greek) Blooming. *Chloie, Cloea, Cloee*

Cho (Japanese) Butterfly. (Korean) Beautiful. *Choe*

Cho Hee (Korean) Beautiful and joy.

Chon (Korean) Heaven.

Chorei (Japanese) Transparent spirituality.

Chosposi (Native American) Bluebird eye.

Chow (Chinese) Summer.

Christabel (French) Beautiful Christian. *Christabela, Christabelah, Christobel, Chrystobelle*

Christina (Greek) Anointed; feminine of Christian. *Chrissta, Chrisstan, Christa, Christan, Christeen, Christeena, Christel, Christen, Christena, Christene, Christian, Christiana, Christiane, Christianna, Christie, Christin, Christine, Christini, Christinn, Christmar, Christyna, Chrystal, Chrystalle, Chrystee, Chrystel, Chrystelle, Chrystina, Chrystle, Crissey, Crissie, Crissy, Crista, Cristal, Cristel, Cristelle, Cristen, Cristena, Cristie, Cristin, Cristina, Cristine, Cristiona, Crysta, Crystal, Crystena, Crystene, Crystie, Crystina, Crystine, Crystyna, Khristeen, Khristena, Khristina, Khristine, Khristya, Kirsten, Kirstin, Krista, Kristeen, Kristel, Kristen, Kristijna, Kristin, Kristina, Kristine, Krysta, Krystal, Krystka, Krystle, Teena, Teyna, Tina, Tiny*

Christy (English) Of Christ; form of Christine. *Chrissti, Chrisstie, Chrissty, Christi, Cristi, Cristy, Kristi, Kristy*

Chu Hua (Chinese) Chrysanthemum.

Chumani (Native American) Dewdrops. *Chumanee, Chumaney*

Chun (Chinese) Spring.

Chun Hei (Korean) Justice.

Chung Ae (Korean) Noble and love.

Chung Cha (Korean) Noble and daughter.

Chyou (Chinese) Autumn.

Cian (Irish) Ancient. *Ciann, Cien*

Ciannait (Irish) Ancient. *Ciana, Ciandra, Cianna*

Cinderella (English) Fairytale princess. *Cindella, Cinderela, Cinderelah, Cinderele*

Cinnabar (Greek) Red; mineral.

Citrine (Middle English) Reddish-yellow. (Latin) *Citrus.*

Claire (Latin) Bright. *Clair, Claireen, Clairene, Claireta, Clairette, Clairey, Clairice, Clairinda, Clairissa, Clairita, Clairy, Clara, Clarabel, Clarabelle, Claral, Clare, Clarene, Claresta, Clareta, Claretta, Clarey, Clari, Claribel, Claribella, Claribelle, Clarice, Clarie, Clarinda, Clarine, Clarisa, Clarissa, Clarisse, Clarita, Claritza, Clarrie, Clarry, Clary, Claryce, Clayre, Clayrette, Clayrice, Clayrinda, Clayrissa, Clerissa, Cliara, Clorinda, Klaire, Klara, Klaretta, Klarissa, Klaryce, Klayre, Kliara, Klyara*

Clancy (Irish) Red-headed fighter. *Clancey, Clancie, Clansi, Clansy*

Clarissant (Scottish) In Arthurian legend, sister of Gawain.

Claudette (French) Lame; feminine form of Claude. *Claudella, Claudelle, Claudetta, Claudey, Claudia, Claudie, Claudina, Claudine, Claudy, Cleta, Clodia, Clyde, Klaudia, Klodia*

Clay (German) Adhere; mortal.

Clementine (Latin) Mild; clemency; giving mercy; feminine form of Clemens. *Clem, Clemence, Clemency, Clementia, Clementina, Clementya, Clementyn, Clementyna, Clemmie, Clemmy, Klementijna, Klementina*

Cleopatra (Greek) Her father's fame. *Kleopatra*

Cleotha (African American) Cleotha Staples was a popular American gospel singer and member of The Staple Singers.

Clinique (Brand name) Estée Lauder cosmetics brand.

Clio (Greek) Praise. *Clea, Cleon, Cleone, Cleonie, Cleopatra, Cleta*

Clodagh (Irish) The river Clody named for a local female deity. *Cloda*

Cloris (Greek) Blooming; flower goddess. *Chloris*

Clotho (Greek) Weaver.

Coco (Spanish) Diminutive form of Soccoro. French pet name. (Brand name) Chanel cosmetics brand. *Cocoa*

Colette (Greek) Victory of the people. (French) Victorious. Diminutive of Nicole. *Coleta, Cosette*

Colleen (Irish) Girl; feminine form of Cole. *Celena, Celina, Celine, Clemmie, Coleen, Colene, Collena, Collene, Collie, Colline, Colly, Kolleen, Kolline*

Colomba (Latin) Dove. *Collie, Colly, Colombe, Colum, Columbia, Columbine*

Comfort (Latin) Strengthen.

Compassion (Latin) Sympathy.

Concepción (Latin) Conception; pure. *Cetta, Chiquin, Chita, Concetta, Concha, Conchata, Conchissa, Conchita*

Concetta (Italian) Pure. *Conceta, Concheta, Conchetta*

Concordia (Latin) Peace, harmony. *Concord, Concorde*

Condwiramurs (Scottish) In Arthurian legend, wife of Percival.

Constance (Latin) Faithful. *Connie, Constant, Constantia, Constantine, Constanza, Constanze*

Contessa (Italian) Royalty; feminine form of Count.

Cookie (Latin) Cook's occupation. *Cooke*

Cora (Greek) Heart; maiden. *Corabel, Corabella, Corabelle, Corabellita, Coralee, Coralia, Coralie, Coralyn, Corazon, Coree, Corella, Corena, Corene, Corentine, Coretta, Corey, Cori, Corie, Corilla, Corin, Corina, Corine, Corinne, Corisa, Corissa, Corita, Corlene, Correen, Corrella, Correlle, Correna, Correnda, Correne, Correy, Corri, Corrie, Corrina, Corrine, Corrissa, Corry, Corynna, Corynne, Coryssa, Kora, Korabell, Kore, Koreen, Koretta, Korey, Korilla, Korina, Korinne, Korry, Koryne, Korynna, Koryssa*

Coral (Latin) Rock. *Coralee, Coralena, Coralia, Coralie, Coraline, Corallina, Coralline, Coraly, Coralyn, Coralyne, Creola, Koral, Koralie, Korall, Koralline*

Cordelia (Latin) Rope maker. (Irish) Daughter of the sea. Feminine of Cordell. *Cordelie, Cordella, Cordelle, Cordey, Cordi, Cordie, Cordy, Delia, Delie, Della, Kordelia, Kordella, Kordelle*

Corky (Latin) Lively, buoyant. (English) Hill; hallow.

Corliss (Old English) Cheerful and generous; feminine form of Carl or Carlisle. *Corlee, Corless, Corley, Corlie, Corly*

Cornelia (Latin) Horn; feminine form of Cornelius. *Corelie, Cornalia, Corneelija, Cornel, Cornela, Cornelija, Cornell, Cornella, Cornelle, Cornelya, Cornie, Korneelia, Korneelya, Kornelia, Kornelija, Kornelya, Neal, Neel, Neely, Nela, Nelia, Nell, Nella, Nellie, Nelly*

Corrie (Irish) Form of Corey.

Corrina (Latin) Spear; form of Corinne; feminine of Corin. *Carinna, Carinne, Coreen, Coreene, Coren, Corrianne, Corrienne, Corrinda, Corryn, Coryn, Corynn, Corynne, Karinne, Karynna, Korin*

Cosette (French) Form of Nicole. *Cosete, Cosett, Cosetta, Cosettah*

Cotovatre (English) From *The Legend of King Arthur*, name of a lake.

Courage (English) Heart; confidence; valor.

Courtesy (French) Polite, gracious; respect.

Courtney (Old English) Courtly, courteous. *Cordney, Cordni, Cortenay,* Corteney, Cortie, Cortland, Cortnee, Cortneigh, Cortney, Courtenay, Courteneigh, Courteney, Courtland, Courtlyn, Courtnay, Courtnee, Courtnie, Courtny, Kordney, Kortney, Kortni, Kourtenay, Kourtnee, Kourtneigh, Kourtney, Kourtnie*

Cressida (Greek) Gold.

Cricket (American) Loud insect of the night.

Crisiant (Welsh) Like a crystal.

Crystal (Latin) Brilliant glass. *Cristal, Cristale, Kristal, Krystal*

Cundrie (Scottish) In Arthurian legend, women who condemned Percival.

Curran (Irish) Heroine. *Curin, Curina, Curinna*

Cybill (Greek) Fortuneteller, soothsayer. *Cybil, Cybille, Sibyl*

Cyd (Greek) Public hill.

Cydney (French) From Saint-Denis. *Cidney, Cydne, Cydnee, Cydnei, Cydnie, Sydney*

Cynara (Greek) Thistle. *Cinara, Cinarah, Cynarah*

Cynthia (Greek) Moon. *Cinda, Cindee, Cindeigh, Cindi, Cindie, Cindy, Cinnie, Cinny, Cinta, Cinthia, Cintia, Cinzia, Cyn, Cynda, Cyndee, Cyndi, Cyndia, Cyndie, Cyndra, Cyndy, Cynnie, Cynthea, Cynthie, Cynthya, Cyntia, Cytia, Kynthia, Kynthija, Sindee, Sindi, Sindy, Sindya, Sinnie, Sinny, Sintia, Synda, Syndee, Syndi, Syndy, Syntha, Synthee, Syntheea, Synthia, Synthie, Synthya*

Cyra (Persian) Throne; sun; feminine form of Cyrus. *Cira, Cyrah, Cyrena, Cyrene, Cyrina, Cytherea, Cytheria, Kyra*

Cyrilla (Greek) Noble. *Cerelia, Cerella, Cirila, Cirilah*

Cyzarine (Russian) Royalty. *Cyzars, Czarina*

D

Da Brat (American) Rapper born Shawntae Harris.

Da-Shin (Chinese) Peaceful heart.

Da-Xia (Chinese) Hero.

Daba (Hebrew) Kind words.

Dabria (Latin) Name of an angel.

Dacey (Irish) From the South. *Dacee, Daci, Dacia, Dacie, Dacy, Daicee*

Daelen (English) Form of Dale. *Daelan, Daelin, Daelon, Daelyn, Daelyne, Daleena, Dalehna, Dalena, Dalenna, Dalennah*

Daeshawna (American) Combination of Dae and Shawna. *Daeshauna, Daeshawn, Daeshona, Daishauna*

Daffodil (French) Flower. *Daffey, Daffie*

Dagen (Hebrew) Corn; grain. *Daegan, Daegon, Dagan, Dagana, Dagon*

Dagmar (Danish) Joy of the land. (German) Glorious. *Dagmara, Dagmarah, Dagmaria, Dagmariah, Dagmarya, Dagmaryah*

Dagna (Scandinavian) Day. *Dagnah, Dagnana, Dagnanna, Dagne, Dagnee, Dagney, Dagnia, Dagniah, Dagnie, Dagny*

Dahlia (Scandinavian) Valley. *Dahliah, Dahlya, Dalia*

Dai (Japanese) Great. *Dae, Day, Daye*

Dainin (Buddhist) Graciously shining.

Daisy (Latin) Day's eye. *Daisee, Daisey, Daisi, Daisie, Dasee, Dasey, Dasi, Dasie, Dasy, Deisi, Deissy, Deisy*

Daiya (Polish) Present. *Daia, Daiah, Daya, Dayah*

Dakota (Native American) Friend. *Dakoda, Dakotah, Dakottah, Takota*

Dale (German) Valley dweller. *Dael, Daela, Dahl, Dail, Daila, Daile, Dalena, Dalene, Dalina, Daline, Dallon, Dayl, Dayle*

Dalia (Hebrew) Branch. *Daelia, Dahlia, Dailia, Daleah, Daleia, Daliah, Dalialah, Daliyah*

Dallas (American) Place name. *Dallace, Dallis, Dalyce, Dalys, Dalyss*

Dalmace (Latin) Area in Italy. *Dalma, Dalmassa, Dalmatia*

Dalton (English) Town in the valley. *Dalltan, Dallten, Dalltin, Dallton, Daltyn, Delton*

Damalis (Greek) Calf. *Damalas, Damali, Damalla, Damallah*

Damaris (Greek) Gentle. *Damar, Damara, Damarius, Damary, Damarylis, Damarys, Damarysa, Damaryss, Dameressa,*

Dameris, Damiris, Dammaris, Dammeris, Damris, Damriss, Damrissa, Demara, Demaras, Demaris, Demariss, Demarys, Demaryse, Demaryss, Demarysse

Dame (German) Lady.

Damia (Greek) Goddess of the forces of nature. *Damiah, Damya, Damyah*

Damiana (Greek) Tamer. *Damianah, Damianna, Damiannae, Damiona*

Damita (Spanish) Baby princess. *Dameeta, Dameetah, Dametia, Dametiah, Dametra, Dametrah, Damitah, Damyta, Damytah*

Dana (English) Bright as day. *Daena, Daenah, Daina, Danae, Danah, Danaia, Dane, Danean, Daneana, Danella, Danice, Danna, Dayna*

Dania (Hebrew) God's judgment. *Daniah, Daniya, Danya*

Danica (Latin) Morning star. *Danee, Daney, Danie, Danika, Danne, Dannee, Danney, Dannie, Dannii, Danny, Dannye, Dany*

Danice (American) Combination of Danielle and Janice. *Danisah, Daniss, Danissa, Danysah*

Danielle (Hebrew) Judged by God. *Danae, Danal, Danala, Danalle, Daneal, Daneala, Daneale, Daneel, Daneela, Daneil, Daneila, Daneille, Danele, Danell, Danella, Danelle, Dani, Dania, Daniah, Daniela, Daniele, Daniella, Danja, Danna, Danni, Dannia, Danya, Danyae, Donella, Donnelle*

Dannon (American) God is my judge; form of Daniel. *Daenan, Daenen, Dainon, Danaan, Danon*

Danuta (Hebrew) God has judged. (Polish) Little deer; also used as boy's name.

Dao-Ming (Chinese) The right path.

Daphne (Greek) Laurel tree. *Daffi, Daffy, Daffye, Dafnee, Dafney, Dafni, Dafnie, Dafny, Daphane, Daphaney, Daphanie, Daphany, Dapheney, Daphna, Daphnee, Daphney, Daphni, Daphnie, Daphnis, Daphny*

Dara (Hebrew) Pearl of wisdom. *Dahra, Dahrah, Daira, Dairah, Darah, Darja, Darra*

Daralis (English) Cherished. *Daralice*

Darby (Irish) Free person. *Darb, Darbe, Darbea, Darbee, Darbi, Darbia, Darbiah, Darbiana, Darbie, Darbra, Darbye*

Darcelle (French) Form of Darcy. *Darcela, Darcelah, Darcell, Darselle*

Darcie (Irish) Dark girl. (French) Of the fortress. *Darcea, Darcee, Darcey, Darci, Darcia, Darciah, Darcy, Darsea, Darsee, Darsey, Darsi, Darsie, Darsy*

Darena (American) Famous and loved.

Daria (Greek) Wealthy. *Dari, Darian, Dariane, Dariele, Dariya, Darrelle, Darria, Darriah, Darya*

Darice (Persian) Queenly. *Dareece, Darees, Dareese, Daricia, Dariciah, Darisa, Darissa, Darycia, Darys, Darysa, Darysah, Daryse, Darysia*

Darlene (French) Little darling. *Darelle, Darla, Darlah, Darlean, Darlecia, Darlee, Darleen, Darleena, Darleenah, Darleene, Darlen, Darlena, Darlenah, Darlenne, Darli, Darlie, Darlina, Darlinah, Darline, Darling, Darlis, Darlita, Darly, Darlyna, Darlynah, Darlyne, Darlynne, Darryl, Daryl, Darylle*

Darnell (English) Hidden nook. *Darnel, Darnela, Darnelah, Darnele, Darnella, Darnellah, Darnelle, Darnyell, Darnyella, Darnyelle*

Darshana (Hindi) Sight; observation. *Darsha, Darshina, Darshna*

Daru (Hindi) Pine tree. *Daroo, Darua, Darue*

Darva (Slavic) Honey bee.

Daryl (English) Area in France. *Darel, Darrell, Darrelle, Darryl, Darrylin, Darrylyn, Darylin*

Daryn (Greek) Gifts. (Irish) Great. *Darin, Darina, Darinah, Daron, Daryna, Darynah, Daryne, Darynn, Darynne*

Dasha (Greek) Gift of God. *Dashae, Dashah, Dashenka*

Davan (Hebrew) Beloved one. *Dava, Daveigh, Davina*

Davida (Scottish) Cherished friend. *Davia, Daviane, Davidine, Davina, Davonna, Davynn*

Davine (Scottish) Friend; darling. *Davannah, Davean, Davee, Daveena, Davene, Daveon, Davey, Davi, Daviana, Davin, Davineen, Davinia, Davinna, Davria, Devean, Deveen, Devene, Devine*

Daw (Thai) Stars.

Dawn (English) Daybreak. *Dawana, Dawanah, Dawandra, Dawandrea, Dawanna, Dawannah, Dawin, Dawina, Dawna, Dawnah, Dawne, Dawnee, Dawnetta, Dawnisha, Dawnlin, Dawnlynn, Dawnn, Dawnna, Dawnnah, Dawnya*

Day (American) Light and hope. *Dey*

Daya (Hebrew) Bird. *Dayah*

Dayana (Arabic) Divine.

Dayla (Hebrew) To draw water. *Daylea, Daylee*

Dayton (English) Sunny town. (American) Place name. *Daytonia*

Dea (Greek) Goddess.

Deana (English) Valley. *Deane, Deanna, Deena, Dene, Denna*

Debbani (Arabic) Gray.

Deborah (Hebrew) Bee. *Deb, Debbea, Debbee, Debbera, Debberah, Debbey, Debbi, Debbie, Debbora, Debborah, Debbra, Debbrah, Debby, Debbye, Debea, Debee, Debera, Deberah, Debi, Debie, Debo, Debora, Deboran, Deborrah, Debra, Debrah, Debrea, Debrha, Debria, Debroah, Deby, Devera, Devora, Devorah, Devorit, Dobra*

Dee (Welsh) Dark. *Dea, Deah, DeeDee, Didi*

Deepa (Hindi) Light.

Deidra (Irish) Fear. *Dedra, Deidra, Deirdra, Diedre*

Deila (Old Norse) Quarrel, fight. (French) Place name; a part of land "La Delle" in Normandy.

Deiondre (African American) Valley. *Deandra*

Deja (French) Before. *Daeja, Daija, Daijon, Daja, Dajan, Dajona, Dajone, Déja, Dejae, Dejaena, Dejah, Dejana, Dejanae, Dejanah, Dejanai, Dejanay, Dejane, Dejanea, Dejanee, Dejanna, Dejannaye, Dejon, Dejonae, Dejonee, Dejonna*

Deka (African) Pleasing. *Dekah*

Delaney (Irish) Child of a competitor. *Delaine, Delayna, Delayne*

Delbin (Greek) Dolphin; name of a flower.

Delfina (Spanish) Dolphin. *Delfeena, Delfi, Delfie, Delfin, Delfinah, Delfine, Delfyn, Delfyna, Delfynah, Delfyne, Delpha, Delphe, Delphi, Delphina, Delvina*

Delia (Greek) Place name; pet form of Bedelia. *Dehlia, Delea, Deleah, Deli, Deliah, Deliana, Delianne, Dellia, Delliah, Dellya, Delya, Delyah*

Delicia (African American) Delight. *Daleesha, Dalisia, Delesia, Delice, Delyse*

Delight (Old French) Emotion.

Delilah (Hebrew) Delicate. *Dalialah, Dalila, Daliliah, Delila, Delilia, Delilla, Delyla, Delylla, Lila, Lilah*

Delinda (Latin) Anointed. *Gundelinda*

Della (Greek) Visible. (German) Noble. *Adela, Adella, Del, Dela, Dell, Delle, Delli, Dellie, Dells*

Delling (Scandinavian) Scintillating.

Delmar (Latin) Sea.
Delma, Delmah, Delmarah,
Delmare, Delmaria

Delpha (Greek) Derived
from Philadelphia. *Delphe,*
Delphia

Delphine (Greek) Dolphin;
place name. *Delphina,*
Delphinah, Delphinia,
Delphiniah, Delphinie,
Delphyna, Delphyne, Delvina,
Delvinah, Delvine, Delvinia,
Delviniah, Delvyna,
Delvynah, Dolphina,
Dolphinah, Dolphine,
Dolphyn, Dolphyna, Dolphyne

Delsie (English) God is my
oath. *Delcea, Delcee, Delsa,*
Delsea, Delsee, Delsey, Delsi,
Delsia, Delsy, Delza

Delta (Greek) The
fourth. *Deltah, Deltar,*
Deltare, Deltaria, Deltarya,
Deltaryah, Delte, Deltora,
Deltoria, Deltra

Delu (African) The only
girl.

Delwyn (English) Proud
friend. *Delwin*

Demelza (Old English)
Fort on a hill. *Demi, Demie*

Demetria (Greek) Goddess
of the harvest. *Deetra,*
Deitra, Demee, Demeetra,
Demeetrah, Demeta,
Demeter, Demeteria,
Demetra, Demetri,
Demetrias, Demetrice,
Demetriona, Demetris,
Demetrius, Demey, Demi,
Demia, Demiah, Demie,
Demii, Demma, Demmee,
Demmi, Demmie, Demmy,
Demy, Detria, Dymeetra,
Dymetra, Dymitrah,
Dymitria, Dymitriah,
Dymytria, Dymytrya,
Dymytryah

Denise (French) In mythol-
ogy, a follower of Dionysus,
the god of wine. *Danice,*
Danise, Denece, Deneece,
Deneesha, Deneise, Denese,
Denesse, Deni, Denice,
Denicy, Deniece, Deniese,
Deniesha, Denisha, Denishia,
Denisse, Denize, Dennice,
Denyce, Denys, Denyse,
Dineese, Dinice, Dynice,
Dynise, Dynyce

Denita (English) God is my
judge; form of Danielle.
Danett, Danis, Daniss,
Danita, Danitra, Danitrea,
Danitria, Danitza, Daniz,
Denitta

Denna (Hebrew) Valley.
Dane, Deana, Deeyn, Dena,
Denaé, Denah, Denai,
Denay, Dene, Denea, Denee,
Deneé, Deney

Denver (American) Place
name; green valley. *Denvor*

Dericia (African American)
Athletic.

Derika (German) Ruler
of the people. *Derekah,*
Derekiah, Derikah, Derikia

Derora (Hebrew) Running
streams. *Derorice, Derorit,*
Drora, Drorah, Drorit,
Drorlya

Derry (Irish) Redhead.
Deree, Derey, Deri, Derie,
Derree, Derrey, Derri,
Derrie, Dery

Deryn (Welsh) Bird. *Deron,*
Derren, Derrin, Derrine,
Derron

Desdemona (Greek)
Misery. *Desdemonda,*
Desmona

Desiree (Latin) Crave.
(French) Hoped for. *Desea,*
Desee, Desey, Desi, Desideria,
Desiderio, Desie, Désir,

Desira, Desirah, Desirai,
Desire, Desireah, Désirée,
Desirey, Desray, Desree,
Dessie, Dessirae, Dessire,
Dessiree, Desy, Desyrae,
Desyrai, Desyray, Dezi,
Dezia, Dezzia, Dezzie

Desma (Greek) Pledge.
Desmé

Despina (Greek) Young
lady. *Despoina*

Desta (Ethiopian) Happy.
Destah, Desti, Destie, Desty

Destiny (French) Fate.
(Ethiopian) Happy.
Desta, Destah, Destaney,
Destani, Destania, Destanie,
Destannee, Destanney,
Destanni, Destannia,
Destannie, Destanny,
Destany, Destenee, Desteni,
Destenia, Destenie, Desteny,
Desti, Destiana, Destie,
Destin, Destine, Destinee,
Destinée, Destiney, Destini,
Destinie, Destinne, Destinni,
Destinnia, Destinnie, Destnie,
Desty, Destyn, Destynia,
Destyniah, Destynie, Destyny,
Destynya, Destynyah

Deva (Hindi) Celestial
spirit. *Deava, Deavah,*
Deeva, Deevah, Devah, Diva,
Divah, Dyva, Dyvah

Devaki (Hindi) Black.

Deval (Hindi) Divine.
Devee, Devi, Devika

Devene (Scottish) Beloved.
Devean, Deveen

Devon (English) From
Devonshire. *Deaven, Devan,*
Devana, Devanna, Deven,
Devenne, Deveyn, Devin,
Devinne, Devion, Devione,
Devionne, Devondra, Devone,
Devoni, Devonn, Devonne,
Devvon, Devyn, Devynn

Devona (English) Defender.
Devonda, Devonnah

Dextra (Latin) Flexible. *Dekstra, Dex, Dextrah, Dextria*

Dhanishta (Indian) Star. *Dhani*

Dhanya (Indian) Great.

Dhara (Hindi) Earth. *Dharinee, Dharti*

Dharma (Hindi) Ultimate law of all things. *Dharmetta*

Dia (Spanish) Day.

Diamond (English) Brilliant. *Damonica, Diaman, Diamandi, Diamanta, Diamante, Diamantina, Diamantra, Diamend, Diamemn, Diamon, Diamonda, Diamondah, Diamonde, Diamonia, Diamoniqua, Diamonique, Diamont, Diamonta, Diamonte, Diamontina, Dimond, Dimonda, Dimondah, Dimonde, Dimonte*

Diana (Latin) Divine. *Daiana, Daianna, Deahanne, Deane, Deann, Deanna, Deanne, Dee-Ann, Deeane, Deeann, Deeanne, Déanne, Di, Diaan, Diaana, Diaanah, Diaane, Diahann, Diahanna, Dian, Dianah, Dianalyn, Dianarose, Dianatris, Dianca, Diandra, Diandre, Diandrea, Diane, Dianelis, Diani, Diania, Dianiah, Dianie, Dianiella, Dianielle, Dianita, Diann, Dianna, Diannah, Dianne, Diantha, Dianthah, Dianthe, Dianya, Dianyah, Dianys, Didi, Dihan, Dihana, Dihanah, Dihane, Dihann, Dihanna, Dihanne, Dyan, Dyana, Dyanne, Dyanthah, Dyanthe, Dyanthia, Dyanthiah, Dyanthya, Dyanthyah*

Diantha (Greek) Divine flower. *Diandre, Dianthe, Dianthia*

Diara (African) Gift.

Didina (French) Beloved.

Dido (Latin) Mythical queen of Carthage.

Diella (Latin) Worshipper of God. *Dielle*

Dierdre (Irish) Sorrowful. *Dede, Deeddra, Deedra, Deedrah, Deedrea, Deedri, Deedrie, Deerdra, Deerdrah, Deerdre, Deidra, Deidrah, Deidre, Deidrea, Deidrie, Deirdra, Deirdre, Deirdree, Derdre, Didi, Didra, Diedra, Diedre, Dierdra, Diérdre, Dierdrie, Dydree, Dydri, Dydrie, Dydry, Dyerdre*

Dillian (Latin) Worshipped one. *Dilli, Dilliana, Dilliane, Dilliannah, Dillianne, Dylane, Dylian, Dyliana, Dylianah, Dyliane, Dyllian, Dylliana, Dylliane, Dyllianne, Dyllianna, Dylliannah, Dyllianne, Dylyan, Dylyana, Dylyanah, Dylyann, Dylyanna, Dylyannah, Dylyanne*

Dilys (Welsh) Faithful. *Dylis, Dyllis, Dylys*

Dimaia (American) Daughter of Maia.

Dinah (Hebrew) Judgment. *Deanna, Deena, Dena, Dina, Dinna, Dinnah, Dyna, Dynah, Dynna, Dynnah*

Dindrane (Scottish) In Arthurian legend, sister of Percival.

Dionne (Greek) Daughter of heaven. *Deonee, Deonia, Deonne, Deonyia, Dion, Diona, Dionah, Diondra, Diondrea, Dione, Dioney, Dioni, Dionie, Dionis, Dionna, Dionte, Diony, Dyon, Dyona, Dyonah, Dyone, Dyonee, Dyoney, Dyoni, Dyonie, Dyonne, Dyony*

Dionyza (Shakespearean) Character from *Pericles*.

Dior (French) Golden. *Diora, Diorah, Diore, Diorra, Diorrah, Diorre, Dyor, Dyora, Dyorah, Dyorra, Dyorrah, Dyorre*

Diotama (Greek) Great math teacher in Ancient Greece.

Dipti (Hindi) Brightness.

Dirran (Arabic) Intelligent; logical.

Diva (Latin) Goddess. *Devine, Diveena, Divina, Divinah, Divinia, Diviniah, Diviniea, Dyveena, Dyvina, Dyvinah, Dyvinia, Dyvyna, Dyvynah, Dyvynia, Dyvyniah*

Divinity (English) Divine. *Divina, Divinia*

Divonah (Hebrew) South. *Dimona, Dimonah, Divona*

Divya (Hindi) Heavenly.

Dixie (American) Southern girl. *Dix, Dixee, Dixey, Dixi, Dixon, Dixy, Dyxee, Dyxey, Dyxi, Dyxie, Dyxy*

Diza (Hebrew) Joyous. *Ditza, Ditzah, Dizah, Dyza, Dyzah*

Djab (French-Creole) Devil.

Dobara (Science fiction) Character from *Star Trek: The Next Generation*.

Dodie (Hebrew) Beloved. *Doda, Dode, Dodea, Dodee, Dodey, Dodi, Dodia, Dodiah, Dody, Dodya, Dodyah*

Doe (Middle English) Female deer; nickname for almost any *D* name. *Dee, Dee Dee, Didi*

Doli (Native American) Bluebird. (African) Doll. (American) Sorrowful. Form of Dolores.

Dolores (Latin) Lady of sorrows. *Delores, Deloria, Deloris, Dolley, Dolly, Dolora, Dolorcitas, Dolorita, Doloritas, Dorrie*

Domani (Italian) Tomorrow.

Dominique (French) Belonging to God. *Dom, Domeneka, Domeneque, Domenicah, Domenicka, Domeniga, Domenika, Domeniqua, Domeniquah, Domina, Dominah, Domineca, Domineka, Domineque, Dominga, Domini, Dominia, Dominiah, Dominica, Dominicah, Dominick, Dominicka, Dominikah, Dominiqua, Dominiquah, Dominixe, Domino, Dominoque, Dominuque, Dominyika, Domique, Domka, Domnica, Domnicah, Domnicka, Domnika, Domonica, Domonice, Domonika, Domyna, Domyno*

Donatella (Italian) Gift. *Donatha, Donathia, Donathiah, Donathya, Donathyah, Donato, Donatta, Donetta, Donette, Donita, Donnette, Donnita, Donte*

Donelle (Irish) World leader.

Donna (Latin) Lady. *Dona, Donae, Donah, Donail, Donalda, Donaldina, Donalea, Donalisa, Donay, Dondi, Dondra, Dondrea, Dondria, Donelda, Donella, Donellia, Doni, Donia, Donnae, Donnah, Donnai, Donnalee, Donnalen, Donnay, Donnaya, Donne, Donnell, Donni, Donnica, Donny, Dontia, Donya*

Donoma (Native American) Sight of the sun.

Dora (Greek) Gift. *Dorah, Doral, Doralia, Doraliah, Doralie, Doralin, Doralina, Doraline, Doralisa, Doraly, Doralyn, Doralyna, Doralynah, Doralyne, Doralynn, Doralynne, Doran, Dorana, Dorchen, Dore, Dorece, Doreece, Dorelia, Dorella, Dorelle, Doresha, Doressa, Doretta, Dori, Dorie, Dorielle, Dorika, Doriley, Dorilis, Dorinda, Dorindah, Dorion, Dorita, Dorlin, Doro, Dorree, Dorrey, Dorri, Dorrie, Dorry, Dory, Dorynda, Doryndah*

Dorcas (Greek) Gazelle. *Dorcia, Doreka*

Doreen (French) Golden girl. *Doreana, Doreanah, Doreena, Doreenah, Doreene, Dorena, Dorenah, Dorene, Dorin, Dorina, Dorine, Doryn, Doryna, Dorynah, Doryne*

Doria (Greek) From the sea. *Doriah, Dorria, Dorrya, Dorryah, Dorya, Doryah*

Dorian (Greek) Sea; from Doris. *Dorean, Doreane, Doriana, Doriane, Doriann, Dorianna, Dorianne, Dorin, Dorina, Dorinah, Dorriane*

Doris (Greek) Of the sea. *Dore, Doreece, Doreese, Dori, Dorice, Dorisa, Dorise, Dorreece, Dorreese, Dorris, Dorrise, Dorrys, Dorryse, Dory, Dorys*

Dorothy (Greek) Gift of God. *Dasya, Do, Doa, Dolley, Dolly, Doortje, Dorathee, Dorathey, Dorathie, Dorathy, Dordei, Dordi, Dorefee, Dorethie, Doretta, Dorifey, Dorika, Doritha, Dorka, Dorle, Dorlice, Dorlisa, Doro, Dorofey, Dorolice, Dorosia, Dorota, Dorotea, Dorothea, Dorothee, Dorothey, Dorothi, Dorothie, Dorottya, Dorte, Dortha, Dorthy, Doryfey, Dosi, Dossie, Dosya, Dot, Dotea, Dotee, Dotey, Doti, Dotie, Dotson, Dott, Dottea, Dottee, Dottey, Dotti, Dottie, Doty*

Dorrit (Greek) Dwelling. (Hebrew) Generation. *Dorit, Dorita, Dorite, Doritt, Doritte, Dorrite, Doryt, Doryte, Dorytt, Dorytte*

Dory (American) Form of Doris. *Dore, Dorey, Dorie, Dorri*

Dreama (English) Dreamer. *Dreamah, Dreamar, Dreamara, Dreemar*

Dree (Scottish) Suffering.

Dresden (German) People of the Riverside forest.

Drew (Greek) Courageous. *Drewa, Drewee, Drewia, Drewie, Drewy, Dru, Drue*

Drina (Spanish) Form of Alexandrine. *Dreena, Drena, Drinah, Dryna*

Dristi (Hindi) Sight.

Drucilla (Greek) Innocent. *Drewcela, Drewcella, Drewcila, Drewcilla, Drewcyla, Drewcylah, Drewcylla, Drewcyllah, Drewsila, Drewsilah, Drewsilla, Drewsillah, Drewsyla, Drewsylah, Drewsylla, Drewsyllah, Drucela, Drucella, Drucey, Druci, Drucie, Drucill, Drucillah, Drucy, Drucyla, Drucylah, Drucyle, Drucylla, Drucyllah, Drucylle, Druscila, Druscilla, Druscille, Drusey, Drusie, Drusila, Drusilla, Drusy, Drusylah, Drusyle, Drusylla, Drusyllah, Drusylle*

Duaa (Arabic) Prayer to God. *Dua*

Duenna (Spanish) Protector of friends. *Duena, Duenah, Duennah*

Duff (English) Baker.

Dularee (Hindi) Beloved daughter.

Dulcie (Spanish) Sweet. *Delcina, Delcine, Delsine, Douce, Douci, Doucie, Dulce, Dulcea, Dulcebela, Dulcee, Dulcey, Dulci, Dulcia, Dulciana, Dulciane, Dulciann, Dulcianna, Dulcianne, Dulcibel, Dulcibell, Dulcibella, Dulcibelle, Dulcie, Dulcina, Dulcine, Dulcinea, Dulcy, Dulse, Dulsea, Dulsee, Dulsey, Dulsi, Dulsia, Dulsiana, Dulsibell, Dulsie, Dulsine, Dulsy*

Dumi (African) The inspirer.

Durene (Latin) Enduring. *Dureen, Dureena, Durina, Durine*

Dusana (Russian) Spirit, soul. *Dusa, Dusanka, Duska*

Duscha (Russian) Sweetheart. *Duschah, Dusha*

Dustin (German) Valiant fighter. (English) Brown rock. *Dust, Dustain, Dustan, Dustean, Dusteana, Dusteanah, Dusteane, Dusteena, Dusteenah, Dusten, Dustina, Dustinah, Dustine, Dustion, Duston, Dustyn, Dustyna, Dustynah, Dustyne, Dustynn*

Dusty (English) Dusty place. *Dustea, Dustee, Dustey, Dusti, Dustie*

Duvessa (Irish) Dark beauty.

Duyen (Vietnamese) Charm and grace.

Dyani (Native American) Deer. *Dianee, Dianey, Diani, Dianie, Diany, Dyanee, Dyaney, Dyanie, Dyany*

Dylan (Welsh) Sea. *Dylaan, Dylana, Dylane, Dylanee, Dylanie, Dylann, Dylen, Dylin, Dyllan, Dylynn*

Dyllis (Welsh) Sincere. *Dylis, Dylissa, Dylissah, Dyllys, Dyllysa, Dyllyse, Dylys, Dylysa, Dylysah, Dylyse, Dylyss, Dylyssa, Dylyssah*

Dymphna (Irish) Patron saint of the mentally ill. *Dympna*

Dysis (Greek) Sunset.

E

Eadda (English) Wealthy; successful. *Eada, Eadah, Eaddah*

Earlene (Irish) Pledge; feminine form of Earl. *Earla, Earlean, Earleen, Earline, Erla, Erleen, Erlene, Erlenne, Erlina, Erlinda, Erline*

Earna (English) Eagle.

Eartha (Old English) Earth.

Easter (American) From the holiday. *Eastan, Eastera, Easterine, Easteryn*

Easton (English) From East town.

Eathelin (English) Noble waterfall.

Ebba (German) Strength; return of the tide.

Ebere (African) Mercy.

Ebony (Greek) Hard wood. *Ebanie, Ebonee, Ebonie, Ebonique*

Ecaterina (Romanian) Innocent.

Edana (Irish) Ardent. *Edan, Edanah*

Edda (Old English) Rich. *Eda*

Edeline (English) Kind. *Edelin, Edelyn, Edolina, Edoline*

Eden (Hebrew) Delight. *Edan, Edena, Edene, Edie, Edin, Edyn*

Edena (Hawaiian) Delightful. (Babylonian) Plain. (Hebrew) Delight. *Eden, Edene, Edenia, Edin, Edna, Edon, Edona, Edyne*

Edeva (English) Expensive gift. *Eddeva, Eddeve, Edevah*

Edith (Old English) Rich gift. *Eadith, Ede, Edetta, Edette, Edita, Editha, Edithe, Editta, Edyta, Edyth, Edythe*

Edla (Swedish) Noble.

Edlen (English) Waterfall.

Edna (Hebrew) Pleasure; rejuvenation. *Adna, Ednah, Ednita*

Edria (Hebrew) Mighty. *Edra, Edreah, Edriah, Edrya*

Edrice (English) Prosperous ruler. *Edris, Edriss, Edrisse, Edrys*

Edwina (German) Prosperous friend; heir's ax. *Edweena, Edwena, Edwine, Edwinna, Edwyna, Edwynna*

Effie (Greek) Well spoken; short form of Euphemia. *Efea, Effi, Effy, Efi, Ephie*

Efrata (Hebrew) Honored. *Efratah*

Efrosini (Hebrew) Fawn or bird.

Egeria (Greek) She who gives encouragement.

Eido (Japanese) Illuminating way.

Eileen (Greek) Light. *Alene, Eileene, Eilena, Eilene, Eilina, Eiline, Eillen, Eilyn, Eleen, Elene, Ilene*

Eilis (Gaelic) Noble; kind.

Eir (Scandinavian) Goddess of healing.

Eira (Welsh) Snow. *Eirah, Eyra, Eyrah*

Ekta (Hindi) Unity.

Ekua (African) Born of Wednesday.

Elaine (French) Form of Helen. *Alaine, Alana, Elain, Elaina, Elana, Elayne, Elena, Laine, Laney*

Elam (Hebrew) Highlands.

Elani (Greek) Light.

Eleanor (Greek) Mercy. *Elana, Elanie, Elanor, Elanore, Eleanora, Eleanore, Elenor, Elenore, Eleonor, Eliana, Elianore, Elinor, Elinore, Ellenor, Ellie, Ellinor, Ellinore, Elynor, Leonora, Leonore, Nell*

Electra (Greek) Bright; the shining one. *Electrah, Elektra*

Eleora (Hebrew) The Lord is my light.

Elfriede (German) Peaceful ruler. *Elfreda, Elfredda, Elfreeda, Elfreida, Elfreyda, Elfrida*

Eliann (Hebrew) My God has answered. *Eliana, Liana*

Elif (Turkish) Slim and tall.

Eligia (Italian) Chosen one.

Elise (French) Consecrated by God; form of Elizabeth. *Alise, Alysa, Alyse, Alyssa, Alysse, Eilis, Eilise, Elisa,*

Elisee, *Elisha, Elisie, Elissa, Elisse, Ellice, Ellise, Ellyce, Ellyse, Ellyze, Elyci, Elyse, Elyssa, Elysse, Lise*

Elita (French) Special one. *Ellita, Ellitia, Ellitie, Ilida, Lida*

Elizabeth (Hebrew) Consecrated to God. *Aliza, Bess, Beth, Betsy, Bette, Bettie, Betty, Elisabeth, Eliza, Ellie, Elsa, Elsbet, Elsbeth, Else, Elspet, Elspeth, Isabel, Isabella, Isabelle, Libby, Lisbeth, Liz, Liza, Lizzie*

Elke (Greek) Protector of mankind; form of Axelia. *Elki, Ilki*

Ella (Old German) All. *Elah, Ellah, Ellia, Ellie*

Elladan (Science fiction) Character from J. R. R. Tolkien's *The Lord of the Rings.*

Elle (French) Woman; girl. *El, Ele*

Ellen (English) Light; form of Helen. *Elen, Elin, Ellan, Ellene, Ellin, Ellyn, Ellynn, Ellynne, Elyn*

Ellery (English) Elder-tree island. *Elarie, Elery, Ellarie, Ellerie*

Ellis (English) Form of Elias. *Elis, Ellys, Elys*

Elma (Greek) Amiable.

Elmina (English) Noble. *Almina, Elminah, Elmyna, Elmynah*

Elodie (Greek) Marshy, white blossom. *Elodee, Elodi, Elodia, Elody*

Eloise (French) Intelligent, smart. *El, Ell, Elois, Eloisa, Elouise*

Elora (American) Short form of Elnora. *Ellora, Elorah*

Elsa (Hebrew) My God is a vow.

Elu (Native American) Full of grace.

Elvira (Spanish) Form of German for "close." *Elva, Elvera, Elvie, Elvina, Elvyra*

Elvita (Spanish) Truth.

Elysia (Greek) Blissful. *Elishia*

Emani (Arabic) Believer. *Amani, Amoni, Emane, Emanee, Emanie, Emoni, Emonie, Imani, Imoni*

Emanuelle (Hebrew) God is with us. *Emanuel, Emanuela, Emmanuella, Emmanuelle, Manuella*

Ember (French) Form of Amber. *Emberlee, Emberly*

Emeraude (French) Emerald.

Emery (German) Industrious leader. *Emeri, Emerie, Emerre*

Emiline (Old German) Labor. *Emaline, Emelyn, Emmaline, Emmeline, Emmiline, Emmilyne, Emylin, Emyln*

Emily (Latin) Eager. *Em, Emalee, Emeli, Emelia, Emeline, Emely, Emil, Emile, Emilee, Emileigh, Emilia, Emilie, Emiliee, Emilly, Emmaly, Emmie, Emmilee, Emmilie, Emmilly, Emmily, Emmy, Emmye, Emmylee, Emylee*

Emlyn (Welsh) Brave and noble warrior. *Emlin*

Emma (German) All-embracing. *Emmet, Emmett, Emmie, Emmot, Emmott*

Emmanaia (Science fiction) Name from gaming fiction.

Emme (English) Form of Emma.

Emmylou (German) Whole or complete.

Ena (Irish) Form of Helen. *Enah, Enna*

Enat (Irish) Little.

Endora (Hebrew) Fountain. *Endorah, Endorra, Endorrah*

Enedina (Greek) Warm; indulgent.

Engracia (Spanish) Graceful. *Engrace, Engrasia*

Enid (Welsh) Soul.

Ennis (Irish) Sole; only choice.

Enola (Native American) Magnolia.

Enriqua (Spanish) Ruler.

Enya (Scottish) Jewel; blazing. *Enia, Eniah, Enyah*

Enye (Hebrew) Grace.

Enza (Latin) Citizen or descendent of Laurento.

Eos (Greek) Dawn.

Epiphany (Greek) Manifestation. *Ephana, Epifani, Epifanie*

Eppie (Greek) Well spoken of. (English) Diminutive of Euphemia or Hephzibah. Also used as an independent name. *Eppy*

Epua (Swahili) Clear away or remove.

Erasma (Greek) Loveable. *Erasmah*

Erato (Armenian, Greek) Muse of erotic poetry.

Erela (Hebrew) Angel. *Erella, Erellah*

Eres (Welsh) Beautiful.

Erica (Scandinavian) Ever-powerful; honorable ruler. *Ericca, Ericka, Erika, Erikah, Errica*

Erin (Irish) Western island. *Earin, Earrin, Eran, Eren, Erian, Erinn, Erinna, Errin, Eryn, Erynn, Erynna*

Eris (Greek) Goddess of strife.

Ermine (Latin) Noble. (German) Soldier. Form of Hermina. *Erma, Ermin, Ermina, Erminda, Erminie*

Ernestine (Old German) Earnest; vigorous. *Earnestine, Erna, Ernaline, Ernesia, Ernesta, Ernestina, Ernesztina, Ernie*

Escama (Spanish) Merciful. *Escame*

Eshe (Swahili) Life. *Eisha, Esha, Eshah*

Esme (Latin) Esteem. *Esma, Esmee, Esmie*

Esmerelda (Spanish) Emerald. *Esmaralda, Esmarelda, Esmeralda, Esmiralda, Esmirelda*

Esperanza (Spanish) Hope. *Esparanza, Esperance, Esperansa, Esperanta, Esperenza*

Essence (Latin) The embodiment; spirit of; that which is. *Essencee, Essences, Essenes, Essense, Essynce*

Estee (English) Short form of Estelle. *Estey, Esti, Estie, Esty*

Estelle (Latin) Star. *Estee, Estel, Estela, Estele, Estelina, Estell, Estella, Esthella, Estie, Stella*

Esterina (Greek) Strong and vital.

Esther (Persian) Star. *Essie, Esta, Ester, Esthur, Eszter, Ettie, Hester, Hesther, Hettie*

Estila (Latin) Column.

Estrella (French) Star. *Estrela, Estrele, Estrell, Estrelle*

Etaina (Celtic) She who shines.

Etenia (Native American) Wealthy.

Eternal (Latin) Without beginning or end.

Eternity (American) Everlasting.

Ethana (Hebrew) Strong. *Ethanah, Ethena, Ethenah*

Ethel (Old English) Noble. *Adele, Ethelbert, Ethelda, Ethelred*

Ethereal (Greek) Lightness.

Etienne (French) Form of Stephan.

Etoile (French) Star. *Etoila, Etoilah, Etoyle*

Etsu (Japanese) Delight.

Etta (Old German) Little. *Etka, Etke, Ettie, Etty, Itta*

Ettard (Scottish) In Arthurian legend, lover of Pelleas.

Eudana (Science fiction) Character from *Star Trek: Voyager.*

Eudora (Greek) Good gift. *Eudor, Eudorah, Eudore*

Eugenia (Greek) Well born. *Eugenie, Eugina, Evgenia*

Eulalia (Greek) Fair of speech. *Eula, Eulalee, Eulalie, Eulia*

Eun (Korean) Silver. *Euna, Eunah*

Eun Ae (Korean) Grace with love.

Eun Kung (Korean) Grace and honor.

Eun Mi (Korean) Grace and beauty.

Eun Sun (Korean) Graceful and good.

Eunice (Greek) Victorious. *Eunise, Euniss, Eunyce, Unice*

Euphemia (Greek) Spoken well of. *Effam, Eufemia, Euphan, Euphemie, Euphie*

Euphrosyne (Greek) Joy.

Euporia (Greek) She who has a beautiful voice.

Eusebia (Greek) Pious.

Eustacia (Latin) Tranquil. *Eustasia, Eusticiah, Stace, Stacie*

Eustolia (Greek) Agile.

Euterpe (Greek) Muse of the flute.

Evadne (Greek) A water nymph.

Evangeline (Greek) Messenger of good news. *Evangaline, Evangalyne, Evangelina, Evangelyn*

Evania (Greek) Form of Evan. *Evana, Evanna, Evany*

Evanthe (Greek) Flower. *Evantha*

Evarista (Greek) Excellent one.

Eve (Hebrew) Life. *Ava, Ev, Eva, Evander, Evie, Evita, Evy, Ewa*

Evelyn (English) Hazelnut; form of Eve. *Avalina, Avaline, Avelina, Aveline, Evalina, Evalyn, Eveleen, Evelina, Eveline, Evette*

Ever (Scottish) Forever.

Everest (English) Mountain.

Everilda (English) The slayer of the boar. *Everlid*

Evian (French) Place name; town in France famous for Evian springwater. *Evan*

Evonne (French) Young archer. (Scandinavian) The wood of the yew tree. *Evanne, Evenie, Evenne, Eveny, Evon, Evone, Evoni, Evonna, Evonnie, Evony, Evyn, Eyvone, Ivonne, Vonni, Vonnie, Vonny, Yvonne*

Ewa (Polish) Life.

Eyota (Native American) Greatest one. *Eyotah*

Ezri (Hebrew) Helper. *Ezra, Ezria, Ezriah, Ezryah*

F

Fabiana (Italian) Bean farmer. *Fabianah, Fabianna, Fabiannah, Fabienna, Fabiennah, Fabienne, Fabyana, Fabyanah, Fabyanna, Fabyannah*

Fabiola (Latin) Form of Fabia. *Fabiolah, Fabiole, Fabyola*

Fabrizia (Italian) Craftswoman. *Fabriziah, Fabrizya, Fabrizyah*

Fadila (Arabic) Generous. *Fadilah, Fadyla*

Fai (Chinese) Brilliant light.

Faiga (Germanic) Bird.

Faina (English) Happy. *Fainah, Faine, Fayna, Fenna*

Faith (Latin) Trust. *Faeth, Faethe, Faithe, Faithful, Fayth, Faythe, Fidelity*

Faizah (African) Victory. *Faiza, Fayza, Fayzah*

Fala (Native American) Crow.

Faline (Latin) Catlike. *Falena, Falene, Falin, Falina*

Fallon (Celtic) Of a ruling family. *Fallan, Fallen, Fallenn, Fallenna, Fallona, Fallonah, Fallonya, Fallonyah, Falon*

Falynn (English) Beautiful fairy. *Faelyn, Faelynn, Failyn, Failynn, Faylinn, Faylynne, Felyn*

Fanchone (French) Freedom. *Fanchon*

Fang (Chinese) Fragrant, sweet-smelling.

Fang Hua (Chinese) Fragrant flower.

Fanny (English) Free; from France; nickname for Frances. *Fanci, Fancia, Fancie, Fanette, Fania, Fannia, Fannie*

Fanta (African) Beautiful day.

Fantasia (Latin) Imagination. *Fantasy, Fantasya, Fantaysia, Fantazia, Fiantasi*

Faren (English) Wanderer. *Faran, Farana, Farane, Fare, Farin, Farine, Faron, Faronah, Faryn, Feran, Ferin, Feron*

Farica (German) Chief of peace. *Faricah, Faricka, Farika, Fariqua, Fariquah, Farique, Faryca, Farycah, Farycka, Faryque*

Farida (Arabic) Unique.

Farrah (Old English) Beautiful. *Farah, Farra, Farria, Farriah, Farrya, Farryah, Farya, Faryah, Fayre*

Farran (Irish) Adventurous. *Farrahn, Farrand, Farren, Farrin, Ferran, Ferrin, Ferron, Ferryn*

Fatima (Arabic) Daughter of the prophet. *Fatema, Fathma, Fatime, Fattim, Fatyma, Fatymah*

Fatin (Arabic) Captivating.

Faustine (Latin) Fortunate. *Fausta, Faustah, Fausteen, Faustyne*

Fawiza (Indian) Successful.

Fawn (Latin) Young deer. *Faun, Fauna, Faunah, Faunia, Fauniah, Fauny, Faunya, Faunyah, Fawna, Fawnah, Fawne, Fawnia, Fawniah, Fawnna, Fawny, Fawnya, Fawnyah*

Faxon (German) Long-haired. *Faxan, Faxin, Faxine, Faxyne*

Fay (Old French) Fairy. *Fae, Fai, Faie, Faya, Fayah, Fayana, Faye, Fayette, Fei, Fey, Feya, Feyah, Feye*

Fayla (Nigerian) Lucky. *Faiola, Faiolah, Fayola, Fayolah, Feyla*

Fayyim (Indian) Strong.

Fe (Spanish) Trust.

Feather (English) Part of a bird.

February (English) The second month.

Fedra (Greek) Splendid one.

Feena (Irish) Small fawn. *Feana, Feanah, Feenah*

Felberta (English) Brilliant.

Felicia (Latin) Fortunate; happy; feminine of Felix. *Falica, Falisa, Felice, Feliciana, Felicita, Felicity, Felisca, Felissa, Felisse, Feliza, Felyce, Philicia, Phylice, Phylicia*

Femi (Egyptian) Love. *Feme, Femia, Femiah, Femie, Femmi, Femmie, Femy, Femyah*

Fenella (Irish) Form of Fionnula. *Fenell, Fenellah, Fenelle, Finellah*

Fenna (Irish) Fair-haired. *Fena, Fenah, Finah, Fyna*

Feodora (Russian) God's gift. *Fedora, Fedorah, Fedoria, Fedorra, Feodorrah*

Fern (Old English) Leafy plant. *Fearn, Fearne, Ferna, Ferne, Ferni, Fernly, Firn, Firne, Furn, Furne, Fyrn, Fyrne*

Fernley (English) From the fern meadow. *Fernlee, Fernlei, Fernleigh, Fernlie*

Feronia (Latin) Goddess of springs and woods.

Fiala (Czech) Violet flower. *Fialah, Fyala, Fyalah*

Fidelity (Latin) Faithful. *Fidea, Fideah, Fidel, Fidela, Fidelah, Fidele, Fidelia, Fideliah, Fidelio, Fidella*

Fifine (French) He shall add. *Feefeem, Fefe, Fefi, Fefie, Fiffi, Fiffy, Fifi, Fifina, Fifinah*

Fila (Persian) Lover. *Filiah, Filya, Fylia, Fyliah, Fylya, Fylyah*

Filia (Greek) Friend. *Filiah, Fylia*

Filipina (Polish) Lover of horses. *Felipa, Felipe, Felippa, Filipa, Filippina, Filpina, Philippa*

Filma (German) Veiled. *Filmah, Fylma, Fylmah*

Filmena (Greek) Love song. *Filemon, Filomenah, Filomene, Filomina, Filominah, Filomyna,*

Filomyne, Fylomena, Fylomenah, Fylomina, Fylomine, Fylomyna, Fylomyne

Filotea (Greek) She who loves God.

Finola (Irish) White-haired. *Fionnula*

Fiolla (Science fiction) Character from *Star Wars*. *Fiola*

Fiona (Old English) White. *Feeona, Feeonah, Feonia, Feoniah, Feonnee, Fieonne, Fione, Fionn, Fionna, Fionnah, Fionnea, Fionni, Fionniah, Fyona, Fyoni, Fyoniah*

Fiorella (Italian) Little flower. *Fiorelle*

Fiorenza (Italian) Flower.

Fira (English) Fiery. *Firah, Fyra, Fyrah*

Flannery (Celtic) Sheet of metal; flat land. *Flan, Flanna, Flanneree, Flannerey, Flanneri, Flannerie*

Flavia (Latin) Blond, golden hair. *Flaviah, Flavianna, Flavianne, Flaviar, Flavien, Flavienne, Flaviere, Flavya, Flawia, Flawya*

Fleta (English) Swift, fast. *Fleeta, Fletah, Flita, Flitah*

Fleur (French) Flower. *Fleure, Fleuree, Fleuret, Fleurett, Fleuretta, Fleurettah, Floretta, Florettah, Florette, Flouretta, Flourette*

Floreal (French) Flowers.

Florence (Latin) Blooming flower; flourishing. *Fleur, Flo, Flor, Flora, Florentia, Florenz, Floria, Florida, Florie, Floris, Florrie, Flory, Floryn, Flossie, Flower*

Florian (Latin) Blossoming. *Florann, Floren, Floriana, Florianna*

Flower (English) Plant.

Fola (African) Honor. *Floah*

Foluke (Yoruban) Given to God. *Foluc, Foluk*

Fonda (Spanish) Earth; grounded; profound. *Fondah, Fondea, Fonta, Fontah*

Fontanna (French) Fountain. *Fontaina, Fontainah, Fontaine, Fontana, Fontannah, Fontanne, Fontayn, Fontayna, Fontaynah, Fontayne, Fountain, Fountanne*

Forrest (French) Forest. *Forreste, Forrestt, Forrie*

Fortitude (Latin) Strength; courage.

Fortuna (Latin) Fortune. *Fortunah, Fortunata, Fortunate, Fortunia, Fortuniah, Fortunya, Fortunyah*

Fortune (French) Given to luck. *Fortoona, Fortunee, Fortunne*

Fosette (French) Dimpled. *Foset, Fosete, Fosett*

Fotina (Greek) Light. *Fotinia, Fotinya, Fotyna*

Franca (Latin) Free. (French) Place name; from France. Form of Frances. *Franc, Francka, Francki, Franka, Frankah, Franke, Frankee, Frankia, Frankyah*

Frances (Old French) Free; androgynous name, although Frances is generally used for girls and Francis for boys. *Fanny, Fran, Francene, Francesca, Franceska, Francess,*

Francesta, Francine, Francisca, Franny

Frederica (German) Peaceful ruler. *Federica, Feriga, Fredalena, Fredaline, Fredericka, Frederika, Frederina, Frederique, Fredith, Fredora, Fritzi, Fritzie*

Freedom (English) Liberty.

Freya (Scandinavian) Goddess of love, fertility, and beauty. *Frey, Freyah*

Frida (Spanish) Peaceful ruler; nickname for Frederica. *Fridah, Frideborg, Fryda, Frydah, Frydda, Fryddah*

Frieda (German) Peace. *Freda, Fredie, Freida, Freide, Freyda, Freydah, Friedah, Friede, Winifred*

Friera (Spanish) Sister.

Frigg (Norse) Beloved.

Frodina (German) Wise friend. *Frodinah, Frodine, Frodyn, Frodyna*

Fronde (Latin) Leafy branch.

Fukayna (Egyptian) Intelligent.

Fulla (German) Full. *Fula, Fulah, Fullah*

Fulvia (Latin) Blond.

Fuyo (Japanese) Peony.

Fynballa (Irish) Fair. *Finbalah, Finballa, Finballah, Fynballah*

G

Gabele (French) Short form of Gabrielle. *Gabale, Gaball, Gabel, Gabell*

Gabor (Hungarian) God is my strength. *Gabora, Gaborah, Gabore*

Gabriela (Hebrew) Feminine version of Gabriel. *Gabby, Gabi, Gabriele, Gabriella, Gabrielle, Gaby, Galia, Galya, Gavra, Gavrila*

Gaea (Greek) Earth. *Gaia, Gaiah, Gaiea, Gaya, Gayah*

Gaeriel (Science fiction) Character from *Star Wars*; hero of God.

Gaetana (Italian) From Gaeta. *Gaetan, Gaetanah, Gaetane, Gaetanna, Gaetanne, Gaitana, Gaitanah, Gaitane, Gaitann, Gaytana, Gaytane, Gaytanne*

Gage (French) Promise. *Gaig, Gaige, Gayg, Gayge*

Gaia (Greek) Earth. *Gaioa, Gaya*

Gail (Irish) Stranger. (Old Norse) To sing. *Gael, Gaela, Gaell, Galatea, Gale, Gayle, Gaylia*

Gala (English) Joyful. *Galah, Galla, Gallah*

Galen (English) Festive. *Gaelen, Gaellen, Galane, Galean, Galleene, Gallen, Galyn, Galyne, Gaylaine, Gaylyn*

Gali (Hebrew) Hill; fountain. *Gailee, Gallea, Galy*

Galiana (German) Haughty. *Galayna, Galianah, Galiane, Galiena*

Galilahi (Native American) Attractive.

Galina (Greek) Full of light. *Galaina, Galainah, Galaine, Galinah, Galine, Galinka, Gallin, Gallina, Galyna, Galynah*

Galya (Hebrew) God shall redeem. *Galia, Gallia, Gallya*

Gana (Hebrew) Garden. *Ganah, Gania, Ganiah, Ganice, Ganit, Ganyah*

Ganesa (Hindi) Forunate. *Ganesah, Ganessa, Ganessah*

Ganieda (Scottish) In Arthurian legend, Merlin's sister.

Gardenia (English) Flower. *Deenia, Gardeen, Gardeena, Gardeene, Gardin, Gardina, Gardinia, Gardyn, Gardyna, Gardynia*

Garland (French) Wreath. *Galrlynde, Garlan, Garlana, Garlanah, Garlinda, Garlinde, Garlon, Garlyn, Garlynd*

Garnet (Latin) Red seed. *Garnetah, Garnete, Garnett, Garnetta, Garnettah, Garnette, Granata, Grenata, Grenatta*

Garyn (English) Spear carrier. *Garan, Garen, Garin, Garryn*

Gasha (Russian) Good. *Gashka*

Gatha (Hindi) Song.

Gauri (Hindi) White. *Gori, Gowri*

Gay (French) Merry. *Gae, Gaea, Gai, Gaia, Gaye*

Gayatri (Hindi) Mother of the Vedas; goddess.

Gaynelle (African American) Happy. *Gaynell*

Gayora (Hebrew) Valley of the sun.

Gazelle (Latin) Graceful. *Gazella*

Geela (Hebrew) Joy.

Geena (American) Nobility. *Geana, Geeandra, Geina, Gen, Gena, Geneene, Genelle, Genette, Jeena, Jena*

Gefjun (Scandinavian) She who gives wealth. *Gefion, Geffion*

Gelasia (Greek) Laughter.

Gelilah (Hebrew) Rolling hills. *Gelalia, Gelalya, Gelila, Geliliya*

Gelsey (Persian) A variety of jasmine (*Gelsemium*). *Gelsi, Gelsy*

Gelya (Russian) Angelic.

Gemini (Greek) Twin. *Gemelle, Gemina, Geminia, Geminine, Gemmina*

Gemma (pronounced with a soft *g*, as in *gemstone*) (Latin) Precious stone. *Gem, Gema, Gemah, Gemee, Gemmah, Gemmey, Gemmia, Gemmy, Jemma, Jemmsa*

Genene (Scottish) God is gracious. *Geanine, Geannine, Genine, Gineen, Ginene, Jeanine*

Genesee (Native American) Beautiful valley.

Genesis (Latin) Birth. *Genes, Genesia, Genesys, Genicis, Genisis, Genisys, Genysis, Genysys, Jenesis, Yenesis*

Geneva (French) Juniper berry. *Geneve, Genevia, Genevie, Genneeva, Genneevah, Genny, Ginneva, Gyniva, Gynniva, Gynnivah*

Genevieve (Welsh) White wave. *Genavee, Genaveve, Genevie, Geniveve, Gineveve, Ginevieve, Ginevive, Guinevieve, Guinivive*

Genice (American) Form of Janice. *Genece, Genesa, Genis, Genise*

Genji (Chinese) Gold.

Gentle (American) Kind. *Gentil, Gentille, Gentylle*

Geona (Hebrew) Glorification. *Geonit*

Georgia (Greek) Farmer; feminine version of George. *Georgea, Georgeanne, Georgeen, Georgeena, Georgette, Georgiana, Georgianna, Georgie, Georgienne, Georgina, Georgine, Georgy, Gerda, Gina, Giorgia, Gruzia, Jirca, Jirina, Jirka, Jorgina*

Geraldine (German) Hard spear; feminine version of Gerald. *Geralda, Geraldeen, Geraldene, Geraldyne, Gereldine, Gerhardine, Geri, Gerri, Gerrie, Gerry*

Gerda (Norwegian) Protector. *Gerdah, Gerta*

Germain (English) Bud. *Germaine, German, Germine, Germyn, Jarman, Jermain, Jermaine, Jermana, Jermayne, Jermyn*

Gertrude (German) Adored warrior. *Gerd, Gerda, Gert, Gerta, Gerte, Gertie, Gerty, Jera, Jerica, Trude, Trudi, Trudie, Trudy, True, Truta*

Gervaise (French) Strong. *Gerva, Gervaisa, Gervayse, Gervis*

Geva (Hebrew) Hill. *Gevah*

Gevirah (Hebrew) Queen. *Gevira*

Ghada (Arabic) Young woman. *Gada, Gadah, Ghadah*

Ghislaine (French) Sweet; pledge.

Giacinta (Italian) Form of Hyacinth. *Gyacinta, Gyacynta*

Giacobba (Hebrew) Substitute. *Giacoba, Giacobah, Giacobbah, Gyacoba*

Gialia (Italian) Youthful. *Giala, Gialana, Gialietta*

Gianina (Italian) God is good. *Giacinthia, Gianetta, Gianna, Giannine*

Gig (English) Horse-drawn carriage.

Giladah (Hebrew) Hill of testimony. *Galat, Geela, Gila, Gili, Gilia*

Gilana (Hebrew) Joy. *Gila, Gilah, Gilanah, Gilane, Gilania, Gilenia, Gylan, Gylana, Gylanah, Gylane*

Gilberte (French) Shining pledge. *Gilberta, Gilbertina, Gilbertine, Gill, Gillie*

Gilda (Irish) Servant of God. (English) Gold-coated. *Gildah, Gilde, Guilda, Guildah, Guylda, Guyldah, Gylda, Gyldah*

Gill (Latin) Youthful. *Gili, Gilli, Gillie, Gilly, Gyl, Gyll*

Gilla (Hebrew) My joy is in the Lord. *Gila, Gilah, Gilana, Giliah*

Gillian (Latin) Graceful; blessing; form of Juliana. *Gilian, Giliane, Gilliana, Gillianah, Gillianne, Gillien, Gillyan, Gillyana, Gillyanah*

Gilora (Science fiction) Character from *Star Trek: Deep Space Nine.*

Gina (Hebrew) Garden. *Geena, Gena, Ginat, Ginia*

Ginger (Latin) Flower. *Gin, Ginja, Ginjah, Ginjar, Ginjer, Gynger, Gynya, Gynyah*

Gioia (Italian) Joy. *Gioya, Joya*

Giordana (Italian) Descending. *Giadana, Giadanah, Giadanna, Giodana, Giodanna, Giordanah, Giordanna, Giordannah, Gyodana, Gyodanna*

Giovanna (Italian) God is good. *Giovana, Giovanah, Giovannah, Giovanne, Giovannica, Giovona, Giovonah, Giovonnah, Gyovana, Gyovanna*

Giselle (English) Sword pledge. *Ghisele, Gigi, Gisela, Giseli, Gisella, Gizela, Gizella, Gizelle, Gysell, Gyselle*

Gita (Hebrew) Good. *Geeta, Ghita, Gitah, Gitel, Gitka, Gittel, Gyta, Gytah*

Gitana (Spanish) Gypsy. *Gipsy, Gitane, Gitanna, Gypsy, Jeetanna*

Gitel (Hebrew) Good. *Gitele, Gitell, Gitelle, Gytelle*

Githa (English) Gift. *Getta, Githah, Gittah, Gytha, Gythah*

Giuseppina (Hebrew) He shall add. *Guiseppina, Josephine*

Gladys (Welsh) Version of Claudia. *Glad, Gladdys, Gladiss, Gladuse, Gladyce, Gladyss, Gleda, Gleddis, Gleddys*

Glafira (Greek) Fine, elegant.

Glen (Irish) Secluded wooded valley. *Glena, Glenda, Glenetta, Glenn, Glenna, Glenne, Glyn, Glynis, Glynn, Glynnis*

Glenys (Welsh) Holy. *Glenice, Glenis, Glenise, Glenyss*

Gloria (Latin) Glory. *Glora, Glorea, Gloriah, Gloriana, Glorianne, Gloriela, Gloriella, Glory, Glorya, Gloryah*

Gobinet (Irish) Mouth. *Gobnait, Gobnat, Gobnet, Gubnet*

Godiva (Old English) Gift of God. *Godivah, Godyva, Godyvah*

Golda (Old English) To shine. *Gaoldarina, Goldarine, Goldee, Golden, Goldi, Goldia, Goldie, Goldina, Goldy, Goldyah*

Goma (Swahili) Joyful dance. *Gomah*

Goneril (Shakespearean) Character from *King Lear.*

Gopi (Hindi) Cowherd girl.

Gotzone (Spanish) Angel.

Grace (Latin) Graceful, blessing. *Gracey, Gracie, Graice, Graise, Grase, Graza, Grazia, Grazina, Greice, Greyse*

Grainne (Irish) Goddess of grain. *Grainnia, Grania, Granna*

Gratia (Latin) Grateful. *Gratiana*

Grayson (English) Bailiff's child. *Graison, Grasien, Gray, Graysen*

Graziella (Italian) Form of Grace. *Graziel, Graziela, Graziele, Graziell, Grazielle, Graziosa, Grazyna*

Greer (Greek) Watchful. *Grear, Gregoria, Gregorina, Grier, Gryer*

Greta (Greek) Precious jewel. *Grata, Gratah, Greata, Greatah, Greet, Gret, Gretah, Gretha, Grieta, Gryta*

Gretchen (German) Little pearl. *Gretchan, Gretchin, Gretchon, Gretchun, Gretchyn, Margaret*

Gretel (German) Form of Margaret. *Gretell, Grethel, Gretill, Gretyl*

Grid (Norse) Wife of Odin.

Griselda (German) Gray warrior. *Chriselda, Gris, Grisa, Griseldis, Grishilda, Grishilde, Grizelda, Selda, Zelda*

Gro (Norse) Gardener.

Guadalupe (Spanish) River of black stones. *Guadalup, Guadelupe, Guadlupe, Guadulupe, Gudalupe*

Guanyin (Chinese) Goddess of Mercy.

Gudrun (Scandinavian) Battler. *Gudren, Gudrin, Gudrina, Gudrine, Gudrinn, Gudrinna, Gudrinne, Gudruna*

Guia (Spanish) Guide.

Guila (Italian) Form of Julia. *Giula, Giulia, Giullia*

Guinevere (Irish) White wave; French version is Genevieve. *Guenevere, Guenn, Gwen, Gwendaline, Gwendolen, Gwendoline, Gwendolyn, Gwenith, Gwenn, Gwenne, Gwenyth, Gwyn, Gwyndolyn, Gwyneth, Gwynne, Jennifer*

Gunda (Scandinavian) Warrior. *Gundah, Gundala, Gunta*

Gunhilda (Scandinavian) Woman warrior. *Gunhilde, Gunilda, Gunilla, Gunnhilda*

Gunjana (Indian) Buzzing of a bee.

Gunnvor (Scandinavian) Cautious in war. *Gunver, Gunvor*

Gunwanti (Indian) Virtuous.

Gurice (Hebrew) Lion cub. *Gurit*

Gurley (Australian) Willow. *Gurlea, Gurlee, Gurleigh, Gurli*

Guro (Norse) Divinely inspired; wisdom.

Gustava (Latin) Majestic. *Gus, Gussi, Gussie, Gussy, Gusta*

Gustey (English) Windy. *Gustea, Gustee, Gustie, Gusty*

Gwyneth (Welsh) Happiness. *Gwenith, Gwynith, Gwynneth*

Gyo Shin (Japanese) Heart of dawn.

H

Habiba (Arabic) Loved one. *Habibah, Habibeh, Habibi, Haviva, Havivah, Hebiba*

Habika (African) Sweetheart.

Hachi (Native American) River. *Hachee, Hachie, Hachy*

Hadara (Hebrew) Beauty. *Hadarah, Hadaria, Hadariah, Hadarit, Hadarya, Hadaryah, Haduraq*

Hadassa (Hebrew) Myrtle. *Hadas, Hadassah, Haddasa, Haddasah*

Hadiya (Swahili) Gift. *Hadia, Hadiyah, Hadya*

Hadley (English) Meadow of heather. *Hadlea, Hadlee, Hadleigh*

Hafwen (Welsh) Pleasant summer. *Hafwena, Hafwenah, Hafwin, Hafwyn*

Haidee (Greek) Modest. *Haidey, Haidi, Haidy, Haydee, Haydie*

Haiden (English) Hedged valley. *Haden, Hadyn, Haeden, Haidn, Haidyn*

Haimi (Hawaiian) Seeker.

Haiwee (Native American) Dove.

Hakue (Japanese) Pure blessing.

Hala (African) Form of Halla. *Halah, Halya, Halyah*

Haley (Norse) Hero. (Irish) Wise one. *Haile, Hailey, Hale, Haleh, Haleigh, Haleigha, Hali, Halley, Halli, Hallie, Hally, Haylee, Hayley, Hollis*

Halia (Hawaiian) In loving memory. *Halea, Haleeah, Halya, Halyah*

Haliaka (Hawaiian) Leader. *Haliakah, Halyaka, Halyakah*

Halima (Arabic) Gentle. *Haleema, Haleemah, Haleima, Halimah, Halime, Helima, Helyma, Helymah*

Halimeda (Greek) Loves the sea. *Halimedah, Halymeda, Halymedah*

Hallam (German) From the hills.

Halle (Scandinavian) Heroine. *Halla, Hallah, Halliah, Hallya, Hallyah*

Halona (Native American) Fortunate. *Hallona, Hallonah, Halonah, Haloona, Haona*

Halsey (Old English) From Hall's island. *Halsea, Halsie*

Halston (English) Stone town.

Hama (Japanese) Beach.

Hana (Japanese) Flower. *Hanae, Hanidea, Hanka*

Hanako (Japanese) Flower child.

Hanele (Hebrew) Compassionate. *Hanall, Hanalle, Hanel, Hanela, Hanelah*

Hania (Hebrew) Resting place. *Haniah, Haniya, Hannia, Hanniah*

Hanifa (Arabic) True believer. *Haneefa, Hanifah, Hanyfah*

Hannah (Hebrew) God is merciful; graceful one. *Channa, Hana, Hania, Hanita, Hanka, Hanna, Hanne, Hannele, Hanni, Hannia, Hanniah, Hannicka, Hannya, Honna*

Hansa (Hindi) Swan. *Hansika, Hansila*

Happy (English) Happy. *Happea, Happee, Happey, Happi, Happie*

Haralda (Scandinavian) Army ruler. *Harelda, Hareldah, Heralda, Heraldah*

Harhsa (Hindi) Joy.

Hariel (Hebrew) Ruler of animals.

Harley (English) Rabbit pasture. *Harlee, Harleen, Harleigh, Harlie, Harly*

Harlow (English) Mound of the people.

Harmony (Greek) Harmony. (Old English) Soldier. *Harmene, Harmeni, Harmon, Harmone, Harmonee, Harmonei, Harmoney, Harmoni, Harmonia, Harmoniah, Harmonie, Harmonya, Harmonyah*

Harper (Old Norse) Whaler. *Harp, Harpo*

Harpreet (Punjabi) Devoted to God. *Harprit*

Harriet (French) Ruler of the household; feminine form of Harry. *Etta, Etty, Happy, Hariot, Harrie, Harrietta, Harriette, Harriott, Hatsee, Hatsey, Hatsie, Hatsy, Hattie, Hatty, Hetty*

Haru (Japanese) Spring.

Hasana (Swahili) She arrived first. *Hasanna, Hasna, Hassana, Hassna*

Hasia (Hebrew) Protected by God. *Hasiah, Hasya, Hasyah*

Hasina (Swahili) Good. *Haseena, Haseenah, Hasinah, Hassina, Hasyna*

Hava (Hebrew) Life. *Chaba, Chaya, Chayka, Eve, Havah, Havvah, Kaija*

Haven (Dutch) Harbor. *Hagan, Hagen, Havan, Havis, Hazen, Hogan*

Haviva (Hebrew) Beloved. *Havelah, Havi*

Hawa (African) Desire.

Haya (Japanese) Quick; light. (Arabic) Humble. *Haia, Haiah, Hayah*

Hayfa (Arabic) Shapely. *Haifa, Haifah, Hayfah*

Hazel (Old English) Hazel tree. *Haize, Haizelah, Haizell, Haizella, Haizellah, Haizelle, Haslett, Hayzal, Hayzaline, Hazall, Hazela, Hazella, Hazlet, Hazlit*

Hea Jung (Korean) Graceful and noble.

Hea Woo (Korean) Graceful girl.

Heather (English) Heath or shrub. *Heath, Heathar, Heatherlee, Heatherly, Hethar, Hether*

Heavenly (American) Spiritual. *Heaven, Heavenleah, Heavenlee, Heavenlei, Heavenli, Heavenlie, Heavyn, Heavynlie, Heven, Hevenley*

Heba (Hebrew) Gift from God. *Hebah*

Hebe (Greek) Youth. *Hebee, Hebey, Hebi, Hebia, Hebie, Heby*

Hecate (Greek) Mythical witchcraft goddess.

Hecuba (Greek) Mother of Paris and Hector.

Hedda (German) Battler. *Heda, Hedah, Hedaya, Heddah*

Hedia (Hebrew) God's voice. *Hedaya, Heddah, Hediah, Hedley, Hedu, Hedya*

Hedva (Hebrew) Joy.

Hedwig (Old English) Hidden weapon. *Havoise, Hedda, Heddy, Hedvick, Hedvicka, Hedvig, Hedvige, Hedvika, Hedwiga, Hedwyg, Hedwyga, Hedy, Hendvig, Hendvyg, Jadviga*

Hedy (Greek) Sweet. *Heddi, Heddie, Hede, Hedee, Hedey*

Hee Won (Korean) Garden.

Heera (Indian) Diamond.

Hei Ryung (Korean) Graceful and bright.

Heidi (German) Noble and serene; version of Adelheid or Hedwig. *Haidee, Hede, Hedee, Heida, Heidea, Heidee, Heidey, Heidy, Heydy, Hidea, Hidee, Hidey, Hiede, Hiedi, Hydi*

Heidrun (Norse) Goat who supplies mead for the gods.

Hekenu (Egyptian) In mythology, falcon-headed god.

Hekt (Egyptian) Goddess of birth and fertility.

Hela (Norse) Goddess of the underworld.

Helen (Greek) Torch. *Eileen, Elaine, Elayne, Eleanor, Elena, Elene, Elinor, Galina, Helaine, Helena, Helene, Helina, Hellen, Jelena, Jelika, Lena, Lenny, Lenora, Nelly*

Helice (Greek) Spiral. *Helicia, Heliciah, Helyce, Helycia*

Heliotrope (Latin) Flower; faithfulness.

Helma (German) Short for Wilhelmina. *Halma, Halmah, Helmah, Helme*

Heloise (French) Form of Louise. *Heloisa, Heloisah, Heloysa*

Helsa (Dutch) Form of Elizabeth. *Helsah, Helse, Helsiah, Helsie*

Hema (Hindi) Snow.

Henna (Hindi) Tree or shrub of the Middle East, having fragrant red or white flowers. (English) Rule. *Hena, Henaa, Henah, Heni, Henia, Henka, Hennah, Henny, Henya*

Henrietta (German) House ruler; feminine form of Henry. *Enrica, Enriqueta, Hendrike, Henriette, Henrika, Henriot, Henriqueta, Henriquetta, Henryetah, Henryette, Hetty*

Hepziba (Hebrew) My love is with her. *Chepziba, Eppie, Hefzia, Hefziba, Hephziba, Hephzibah, Hepsibah, Hepsie,* *Hepzi, Hepzia, Hepzibah, Hetta, Yetta, Yettie*

Hera (Greek) Queen; jealous. *Herah, Heria, Heriah, Herya, Heryah*

Herlinda (German) Pleasant, sweet.

Hermia (Greek) Messenger. *Hermilda, Herminia, Hermita*

Hermina (Latin) Noble. *Hermalina, Hermia, Herminna*

Hermione (Greek) Earthy; feminine form of Hermes, the messenger of the gods. *Hemine, Herma, Hermia, Hermina, Hermine, Herminna*

Hermosa (Spanish) Beautiful. *Hermosah*

Hero (Greek) Defender.

Hertha (Old English) Earth. *Eartha, Erda, Ertha, Heartha, Hearthea, Heartheah, Hearthiah, Hearthyah, Herta, Hertah, Herthah, Herthia, Herthiah, Herthya, Herthyah, Hirtha*

Herzeloyde (Scottish) In Arthurian legend, Percival's mother.

Hester (Dutch) Star. (Latin) Form of Esther. *Hessi, Hessie, Hessye, Hestar, Hestarr, Hesther, Hetta, Hetti, Hettie, Hetty*

Hestia (Greek) Goddess of the hearth. *Hestea, Hesti, Hestiah, Hestie, Hesty, Hestya, Hestyah*

Heta (Native American) Racer. *Hetah*

Hiawatha (Native American) Creator of rivers. *Hiawathah, Hyawatha, Hyawathah*

Hibah (Arabic) Gift. *Hyba, Hybah*

Hila (Hebrew) Praise. *Hilla, Hillah, Hillel, Hillela, Hilly*

Hilary (Greek) Cheer. *Hilaire, Hilar, Hilaria, Hill, Hillari, Hillary, Hilleree, Hillerie, Hillery, Hilliard, Hilly, Ilario, Laris*

Hilda (German) Warrior. *Hilde, Hildegard, Hildegarde, Hildegaurd, Hildegaurda, Hildegaurde, Hildie, Hildred, Hildy, Hyldaagaurde, Hyldaaguard, Hyldagard, Hyldagarde, Hyldegarde, Hyldeguard, Hyldeguarde*

Hildemare (German) Splendid. *Hildemar, Hildemara, Hyldemar, Hyldemare*

Hilma (German) Protected. *Hilmah, Hylma, Hylmah*

Hina (Japanese) Sunshine.

Hinda (Hebrew) Doe. *Hindah, Hindey, Hindie, Hindy, Hynda, Hyndah*

Hiolair (Irish) Happy.

Hippolyta (Greek) Freer of horses. *Hippolyte*

Hiriko (Japanese) Generous. *Hiroko, Hiryko, Hyryko*

Hisa (Japanese) Long lasting. *Hisae, Hisah, Hisay, Hysa*

Hisolda (Irish) Fair.

Hiten (Hindi) Meaning unknown.

Ho Sook (Korean) Goodness and purity.

Hoa (Vietnamese) Flower. *Ho, Hoah*

Hollace (Old English) Near the holly bush. *Holice, Holisa, Holisah, Holissah, Holles, Holless, Hollice, Holliss, Hollyce, Hollys, Hollyse, Hollyss, Hollyssa*

Holly (Old English) Holly bush. *Holea, Holeah, Holee, Hollei, Holleigh, Holli, Hollie, Hollye, Hollyn, Holy*

Honesty (Latin) To be truthful. *Honesta, Honestah, Honestee, Honestey, Honestia, Honestie*

Honey (English) Sweet. (German) Familiar alternative to "darling" or "dear." *Honig, Honalee, Honea, Honeah, Honee, Honi, Honia, Honiah, Honnea, Honnee, Honney, Honni, Hony*

Hong (Vietnamese) Pink; rosy.

Honor (Latin) Dignified. (French) Nobleman. *Honner, Honnor, Honora, Honorah, Honore, Honoria, Honorin, Honorine, Honour, Honourah, Nora, Norah, Noria, Norry*

Honovi (Native American) Strong deer. *Honovee, Honovey, Honovie, Honovy*

Hope (Old English) Faith.

Horatia (Latin) Keeper of the hours. *Horacia, Horaciah, Horacya, Horacyah*

Hortense (Latin) Gardener. *Hartencia, Hartinsia, Hortensia, Hortensiah, Hortensya, Hortensyah, Hortenxia, Hortinzia, Ortensia*

Hosea (Hebrew) Salvation. *Hosia, Hosiah*

Hoshi (Japanese) Star. *Hoshee, Hoshey, Hoshie, Hoshiko, Hoshiyo, Hoshy*

Hua (Chinese) Blossom.

Huberta (German) Bright mind. *Hubertah, Hubertia, Hubertiah, Hubertyah*

Hui fang (Chinese) Nice flower.

Humbleness (Latin) Virtue.

Humility (Latin) Virtuous trait. *Humiliah, Humillia, Humilliah, Humylia, Humyliah, Humylya, Humylyah*

Huong (Vietnamese) Flower.

Hurit (Native American) Beautiful.

Huyana (Native American) Rain falling.

Hwa Young (Korean) Eternal beauty and prosperity.

Hy (English) Life.

Hyacinth (Greek) Blue crystal. *Cintha, Cinthia, Cinthie, Hyacintha, Hyacinthia, Hyacinthie, Hyacintie, Hyacynth, Jacinda, Jacinta, Jacinthe, Jacynth, Jancintha*

Hydra (Greek) Water snake.

Hye (Korean) Graceful.

Hye Su (Korean) Graceful and beautiful.

Hyun Joe (Korean) Wise and respectful.

Hyun Ok (Korean) Wise and jade.

I

Iafa (Hebrew) Strong and beautiful.

Ianira (Greek) Enchantress. *Ianirah, Ianyra*

Ianthe (Greek) Violet flower. *Iantha, Ianthia, Ianthina, Ianthya, Ianthyah, Ianthyna, Iolanda, Iolande, Iolanthe*

Ibi (Indigenous) Earth.

Iblis (English) Character from Arthurian legend, wife of Lancelot.

Iccha (Indian) Wise.

Icess (Egyptian) Form of Isis. *Ices, Icesis, Icesse, Icey, Icia, Icis, Icy, Isis*

Ida (Old German) Youthful. *Idah, Idaia, Idal, Idalee, Idalia, Idalis, Idaly, Idamae, Idana, Idania, Idanna, Idarina, Idarine, Idaya, Idda, Ide, Idella, Idena, Idetta, Idette, Idys, Iida, Ita, Yda, Ydah*

Idalia (Greek) Sun. *Idaliah, Idalya, Idalyah*

Idalis (English) Happy, noble laborer. *Idalesse, Idalise, Idaliz, Idallas, Idallis, Idelis, Idelys*

Idara (Latin) Well-organized woman.

Ideh (Hebrew) Praise.

Idelia (German) Noble. *Ideliah, Idelya*

Idelle (Welsh) Form of Ida. *Idela, Idelah, Idele, Idell, Idella, Idil*

Idina (Old English) Variation of Edina.

Idit (Hebrew) Choicest.

Idonea (Scandinavian) Eternal youth. *Idonia, Idony, Idun*

Idoya (Spanish) Pond; where the Virgin Mary is worshipped.

Iesha (American) Woman; form of Aisha. *Ieaisha, Ieasha, Ieashe, Ieesha, Ieeshia, Ieisha, Ieishia, Iescha, Ieshah, Ieshea, Iesheia*

Igraine (Scottish) In Arthurian legend, mother of Arthur.

Iha (Indian) Wish, desire.

Ikia (Hebrew) God is my salvation. *Ikaisha, Ikea, Ikeesha, Ikeeshia, Ikeia, Ikeishia, Ikeshia, Ikeyia, Ikiah, Ikiea, Ikiia, Ikya, Ikyah*

Ilana (Hebrew) Tree. *Alana, Alanna, Allana, Ilaina, Ilainah, Ilainie, Ilanah, Ilaney, Ilani, Ilania, Ilanit, Ilanna, Ileanne, Ileinah, Ileinee, Ileyna, Ileynah, Ileyni, Ileynie, Illana, Illani, Illanie, Illanna, Illannah, Illeana*

Ilaria (Italian) Form of Hilary.

Ilda (German) Heroine in battle.

Ilena (Greek) Form of Helena. *Ileanne, Ileen, Ileena, Ileenah, Ileina, Ilina, Ilinee, Ilini, Ilyna, Ilynah, Ilyni, Ilynie*

Ilene (Irish) Light. *Eileen, Helen, Ilean, Ileane, Ileanne, Ileen, Ileine, Ilyne*

Ilisa (Scottish) Consecrated to God; form of Elisa. *Ilicia, Ilisah, Ilissa, Ilissah, Illisa, Illissa, Illysa, Ilysa, Ilyssa, Ilyza*

Ilsa (German) Consecrated to God. (English) Noble; derived from Elizabeth. *Ilisa, Ilise, Ilse*

Ima (Japanese) Now; the present. *Imah*

Imala (Native American) Strong-minded. *Imalah*

Imam (African) Chief.

Iman (Arabic) Believer.

Imelda (German) Battle. *Imalda, Imeldah, Melda, Ymelda*

Imena (African) Dream. *Imenah, Imene*

Imogene (Latin) Image; last born. *Emogen, Emogene, Imagene, Imagina, Imajean, Imogen, Imogenia, Imogine, Imogyn, Imojean, Imojeen, Innogen, Innogene*

Ina (Irish) Pure. *Ena, Inanna, Inanne*

Inari (Finnish) Lake. *Inaree, Inarie, Inary*

India (Hindi) From India. *Indea, Indeah, Indee, Indeya, Indi, Indiah, Indie, Indiya, Indya*

Indiana (American) Place name. *Indeana, Indeannah, Indiannah, Indianne*

Indira (Hindi) God of heaven and thunderstorms; goddess Lakshmi. *Indiara, Indra, Indre, Indyra, Indyrah*

Indu (Hindi) Moon.

Ines (Spanish) Gentle. *Inesa, Inesita, Inessa, Inez*

Infiniti (Brand name) Luxury car brand. *Infinity*

Ingrid (Scandinavian) Hero's daughter; derived from Ing, god of fertility. *Inga, Inge, Inger, Ingmar, Ingrede*

Innis (Irish) Island. *Innes*

Integrity (Latin) Completeness; purity.

Iola (Greek) Dawn. *Iolah, Iole*

Iolana (Hawaiian) To soar like an eagle, hawk. *Iolanah, Iolane, Iolann, Iolanna*

Iolite (Greek) Violet; water sapphire; path to enlightenment.

Iona (Greek) Flower name; purple jewel. *Ione, Ioney, Ioni, Ionia, Iyona*

Iras (Hebrew) Flower. *Iriss, Irisse, Irys, Iryssa, Irysse*

Irem (Turkish) Garden in heaven.

Irene (Greek) Peace. *Erina, Ireene, Irena, Irenea, Ireneah, Irina*

Iria (English) Lady.

Iriel (Hebrew) God is my light.

Iris (Greek) Goddess of the rainbow. *Irisa, Irisha, Irissa, Irita, Irys, Irysa, Iryssa*

Irma (German) Whole. *Erman, Ermingarde, Irmah, Irmin, Irmina, Irmingarde, Irminia*

Irmine (Latin) Noble. *Irmina, Irminah, Irmyne*

Isabeau (French) Consecrated to God; form of Elizabeth.

Isabel (Spanish) Consecrated to God; form of Elizabeth. *Isabal, Isabeli, Isabella, Isabelle, Isbel, Iseaabal, Ishbel, Isobel, Issabel, Issie, Izabel, Izabele, Izabella*

Isela (Hebrew) Devoted to God. (German) Pledge. *Gisela, Isel*

Ishara (Hindi) Rich.

Ishi (Japanese) Rock. *Ishiko, Ishiyo, Shiko, Shiyo*

Isidore (Greek) Gift of Isis, the Egyptian goddess associated with fertility. *Dora, Dorie, Dory, Isadora, Isadorya, Isidor, Isisdora, Izadora, Izadorah, Izadore, Izzy*

Isis (Egyptian) Supreme goddess. *Isiss, Isys*

Ismaela (Hebrew) God will hear. *Ismaila*

Ismena (Greek) Wise. *Ismenah, Ismenia, Ismenya*

Isoke (African) Satisfying gift. *Isoka, Isokah*

Isolda (Old English) Fair. *Isault, Isolad, Isolde, Izolde, Yseult*

Isra (Iranian) Rainbow.

Israt (Arabic) Delight.

Istas (Native American) Snow.

Istra (Nordic Mythology) Norse counterpart of Psyche, Cupid's wife.

Itala (Italian) From Italy. *Italea, Italeah, Italei, Italie, Italo, Italus, Italy, Italya, Italyah*

Ituha (Native American) Sturdy oak.

Itzel (Spanish) Protected. *Itchel, Itesel, Itsel, Itssel, Itza, Itzallana, Itzell*

Iva (Hebrew) God's great gift. (Japanese) Yew tree. *Ivah*

Ivana (Hebrew) God is gracious. *Ivania, Ivanka, Ivanna, Ivannah, Ivannia*

Iverna (Latin) From Ireland. *Ivernah*

Ivette (French) Archer. *Ivet, Ivete, Iveth, Ivetha, Ivett, Ivetta*

Ivory (Latin) White as elephant tusks. *Ivoory, Ivoree, Ivorey, Ivori, Ivorine, Ivree*

Ivria (Hebrew) From the other side of the river. *Ivriah, Ivrit*

Ivy (Old English) Vine. *Ive, Ives, Ivey, Ivi, Ivie, Ivye*

Iyana (Hebrew) Form of Ian. *Iyanah, Iyannah, Iyannia*

Iyanla Origin and meaning unknown.

J

Ja (Hawaiian) Fiery. *Jah*

Jacey (Greek) Familiar form of Jacinta. *Jacci, Jaci, Jacia, Jaciah, Jaciel, Jaciela, Jaciele, Jacy, Jaycie*

Jacinta (Greek) Attractive. *Jacant, Jacent, Jacenta, Jacentah, Jacente, Jacintah, Jacinte, Jacinth, Jacintha, Jacinthia, Jacinthby, Jacintia*

Jacoba (Latin) Feminine of Jacob. *Jacobea*

Jacqueline (French) Supplanter, substitute; feminine form of Jacob or James. *Jackee, Jackelyn, Jackey, Jackie, Jacklin, Jaclyn, Jacquelyn, Jacquetta, Jacqui, Jacquith, Jaklyn*

Jada (Hebrew) Wisdom. *Jayda*

Jade (Spanish) Stone of the loins. *Ijada, Jadae, Jadah, Jadda, Jaddah, Jadea, Jadeah, Jadeann, Jadee, Jadera, Jadienne, Jaed*

Jadwiga (Polish) Refuge in war.

Jae (Latin) Jaybird. *Jaey, Jai*

Jae Hwa (Korean) Respect and beauty.

Jael (Hebrew) Goat. *Jaele, Jaelea, Jaelee, Jaelei, Jaeleigh, Jaeley, Jaeli, Jaely, Jahlia, Jahlie, Jailey, Jaili*

Jaen (Hebrew) Ostrich.

Jaffa (Hebrew) Beautiful. *Jafra, Yaffa*

Jaha (Swahili) Proud. *Jahida, Jahidah*

Jahnavi (Hindi) Ganga River in India.

Jaimie (French) I love. *Jaemey, Jaemi, Jaemia, Jaemiah, Jahmey, Jahmi, Jahmie, Jaime, Jaimea, Jaimeah, Jamee, Jamey, Jamie*

Jaira (Hebrew) God teaches. *Jahra*

Jakeisha (Swahili) Life. *Jakeishia*

Jakki (American) Substitute; familiar form of Jacqueline. *Jacki, Jakea, Jakee, Jaketah, Jakete, Jakevah, Jakevia, Jaki, Jakia, Jakie, Jakke, Jakkea, Jakkee, Jakkie, Jakky, Jaky*

Jakushitsu (Japanese) Tranquil space.

Jala (Arabic) Clear. *Jalah*

Jalaja (Sanskrit) Lotus.

Jale (Turkish) Hoarfrost.

Jaleh (Persian) Dew.

Jalena (Latin) Temptress. *Jalaine, Jalana, Jalina*

Jama (Sanskrit) Daughter. *Jamah, Jamia*

Jamelia (Arabic) Beautiful. *Jamealah, Jameale, Jameall*

Jameson (Hebrew) Supplanter; form of James.

Jamila (Arabic) Beautiful. *Jahmeala, Jahmela, Jahmil, Jahmillah, Jahmille, Jahmyla, Jahmylla, Jaimila, Jaimille, Jaimyla, Jamal, Jameale, Jamelah*

Jamini (Sanskrit) Wife of Yama.

Jamuna (Hindi) Holy river Yamanu.

Jana (Hebrew) Gracious, merciful. *Jaana, Jaanah, Janah, Janalee, Janalisa, Janna, Janya, Janyah*

Janan (Arabic) Heart.
Jananee, Jananey, Janani, Janania, Jananiah, Jananie, Janann, Jananni, Janany

Jane (Hebrew) God is gracious; feminine form of John. *Gianina, Giovanna, Jain, Jan, Janet, Janeth, Janey, Janice, Janie, Janina, Janis, Janith, Janna, Jannie, Janot, Janyce, Jayne, Jina, Jo Ann, Joan, Joann, Joanna, Joanne, Johanna, Joni, Jovanna, Juana, Juanita, Seonaid, Sheena, Shena, Sine, Sinead*

Janel (French) God is gracious; form of Jane. *Jaenel, Jaenela, Jaenell, Jainel, Janelis, Janell, Janella, Janellah, Janielle, Janille, Jannell, Jannella, Jannelle, Jaynele, Jaynelle*

Janese (Hebrew) God is gracious; form of Jane. *Janesey, Janess, Janesse, Janis*

Janet (Hebrew) God is gracious. *Jan, Janete, Janett, Jannet*

Jania (Hebrew) God's gracious gift. *Jainia, Janiah, Janina*

Janica (Hebrew) God is gracious; form of Jane. *Janycka*

Janice (Hebrew) God is gracious. *Janece, Janeice, Janeise, Janis*

Janine (French) God is gracious. *Janean, Janeene, Janene, Jenine*

Jany (Hindi) Fire.

Jardena (Spanish) Garden. *Jardan, Jardana, Jardanah, Jardane, Jardania, Jarden, Jardene, Jardenia, Jardin, Jardina, Jardine, Jardyn, Jardyna, Jardyne, Jardynia*

Jariah (Hebrew) Splendid.

Jarita (Arabic) Earthen water jug. *Jara, Jareata, Jareatah, Jareet, Jareeta, Jareetah, Jaretta, Jari, Jaria, Jariah, Jarida, Jarika, Jarina, Jaryte, Jarytte, Jaytta*

Jarvia (German) Skilled with a spear. *Jarviah, Jarvya, Jarvyah*

Jasia (Polish) God is gracious. *Jasya, Jazia, Jaziah*

Jasmine (Persian) Form of flowering olive. *Jasmain, Jasmaine, Jasman, Jasmane, Jasmeet, Jasmin, Jasmina, Jasmit, Jassmain, Jassmaine, Jassmit, Jesmin, Jessamine, Jessamyn, Yasmin, Yasmine*

Jasper (English) Jem stone. *Jaspere*

Jatara (Hebrew) God is gracious. *Jatarah, Jataria*

Jaya (Hindi) Victory. *Jaea, Jaia, Jaiah, Jayah*

Jayani (Hindi) Sakti (power, energy) of Ganesha.

Jaylene (English) Blue jay. *Jaeleen, Jailen, Jaylena*

Jazz (American) Musical style popularized in the early and mid-1900s. *Jaz, Jazee, Jazey, Jazi, Jazie, Jazy, Jazzee, Jazzey, Jazzi, Jazzie, Jazzy*

Jeanne (Scottish) God is gracious. *Janine, Jannette, Jean, Jeane, Jeanette, Jeaneva, Jeania, Jeanice, Jeanie, Jeanine, Jeannie, Jeen, Jeene, Jennette*

Jedda (Australian) Beautiful girl. *Jeda*

Jedida (Hebrew) Beloved.

Jelena (Russian) Light; form of Helen. *Jelaina, Jelainah, Jelaine, Jelana, Jelanah, Jelane, Jelayna, Jelean, Jeleane, Jeleen, Jeleene, Jelene, Jelin, Jelyna, Jelynah, Jelyne*

Jemima (Hebrew) Dove. *Gemima, Gemimah, Gemma, Jamima, Jamin, Jem, Jema, Jemimah, Jemma, Jemmie, Jemyma, Jemymah, Mimi, Yemimah*

Jenay (Hebrew) Small bird. *Janea, Janee, Janée, Jena, Jenai, Jenea, Jennae, Jennay, Jennaye*

Jendan (African) To give thanks. *Jenden*

Jendayi (African) Give thanks.

Jenell (German) Knowledge; understanding; kindness. *Genell, Jenall, Jenalle, Jenel, Jenela, Jenelah, Jenele, Jenella, Jenille, Jennel, Jennele, Jennell, Jennille, Jinelle*

Jenna (Welsh) Fair. *Jena, Jenah*

Jennifer (Old Welsh) White wave. *Jen, Jenafar, Jenet, Jenifer, Jenna, Jennafar, Jennett, Jenni, Jennie, Jennifar, Jenny, Jenyfer, Jinny*

Jenova (Hebrew) God is Jehovah.

Jensine (Welsh) White wave; white phantom; form of Jennifer. *Jeni*

Jeong (Korean) Sentiment; pure. *Jyo*

Jeraldine (German) Brave spear carrier. *Jeraldeen, Jeraldinah*

Jerica (German) Mighty warrior ruler. *Jericah, Jericka*

Jerolyn (German) Mighty with a spear; form of Geraldine. *Jeralyn, Jerelyn, Jerri, Jeryl, Jerylin*

Jersey (English) From a section of England.

Jerusha (Hebrew) Inheritance. *Jerushah, Yerusha*

Jesen (Scandinavian) Autumn.

Jessalin (Hebrew) Wealthy one from the pool. *Jessalina, Jessalinah*

Jessamine (Persian) Wealthy. *Jessamin, Jessamyn*

Jesse (Hebrew) Wealth. *Jescie, Jesea, Jesee, Jesey, Jesie, Jess, Jessé, Jessea, Jessee, Jessey, Jessia, Jessie, Jessy*

Jessica (Hebrew) Wealthy one. *Jessa, Jessaca, Jessalyn, Jessca, Jessi, Jessia, Jessicka, Jessika, Jessyca, Jessye*

Jette (English) Jet-black mineral. *Jeta, Jetah, Jetia, Jetiah, Jetje, Jett, Jettah, Jetti, Jettia, Jettie, Jetty*

Jewel (Old French) Priceless gem. *Bijoux, Jewal, Jewele, Jewelei, Jeweleigh, Jeweli, Jewelie, Jewell, Jewelle, Jewely, Juel, Juela, Juele*

Jezebel (Hebrew) Impure. *Jesabel, Jesabela, Jesabelah, Jesabele, Jesabell, Jesabella, Jesabellah, Jesabelle, Jessabel, Jessebelle, Jez, Jezebela, Jezebelle*

Jiana (American) Graceful. *Jianah, Jianna, Jiannah*

Jibon (Hebrew) Life. *Jibona, Jibone, Jybon*

Jill (English) Form of Jillian. *Jil, Jyl, Jyll*

Jillian (Latin) Youthful. *Jilian, Jiliana, Jilianah, Jiliane, Jiliann, Jilianna, Jiliannah, Jilleen, Jilliana, Jilly, Jilyann, Jilyanna, Jilyannah, Jyllian*

Jimena (Hebrew) Substitute. *Jimi*

Jimin (Japanese) Compassionate.

Jin (Japanese) Tender. *Jyn*

Jin Ae (Korean) Treasure and love.

Jin Kyong (Korean) Truth.

Jing Wei (Chinese) Small bud.

Jira (African) Related by blood.

Jirakee (Australian) Waterfall cascade. *Jirakie, Jyrakee*

Jivanta (Hindi) Creating. *Jivantah*

Jiya (Indian) Meaning unknown.

Jizelle (German) Promise. *Gizele, Gizell*

Jo Beth (English) Combination of Jo and Beth. *Jobeth, Joebeth, Joebetha, Joebethe, Johbeth, Johbetha, Johbethe*

Jo Dee (American) Combination of Jo and Dee; form of Judith. *Jode, Jodea, Jodele, Jodell, Jodevea, Jodey, Joedee, Joedey, Joedi, Joedie, Joedy, Johdea, Johdee, Jowdie*

Joakima (Hebrew) The Lord will judge.

Joan (Hebrew) God is gracious. *Joaneil, Joanmarie, Joannanette, Joayn, Joen, Joenah, Joenn, Jonni*

Joanna (English) God is gracious; form of Joan. *Jaonah, Jhoana, Jo-Ana, Joahna, Joananna, Joandra, Joanka, Joanne, Joayna, Joenna*

Joaquina (Hebrew) God will establish. *Joaquinah, Joaquine, Joaquyn, Joaquyna, Joaquynah, Joaquyne*

Jimena (Hebrew) Substitute.

Jobey (Hebrew) Afflicted. *Jobea, Jobee, Jobi, Jobia, Jobie, Jobina, Jobitt, Jobitta, Jobrina, Jobya, Jobye*

Joccoaa (Latin) Witty. *Jocoaa*

Jocelyn (Old English) Just one. *Joceline, Jocelyne, Jocie, Josalin, Joscelin, Joscelyne, Joseceline, Joslin, Joslyn, Jossie, Justa, Justina, Justine*

Jocosa (Latin) Gleeful.

Jody (Hebrew) God will increase; form of Joseph, for girl or boy. *Jodee, Jodi, Jodie, Johdea, Johdee, Johdey, Johdi, Johdie, Johdy, Jowdee, Jowdey, Jowdi, Jowdy*

Joelle (Hebrew) The Lord is God. *Joela, Joelah, Joele, Joeli, Joelia, Joelie, Joell, Joella, Joellah, Joellen, Joelly, Jowele, Jowell, Jowelle, Joyelle*

Joey (American) God is gracious; familiar form of Jo.

Johanna (German) God is gracious; form of Joan. *Johan, Johanah, Johanka, Johann, Johonna, Jonna, Joyhanna, Joyhannah*

JoJo (American) Nickname.

Jolanta (Greek) Violet flower. *Joland, Jolanda, Jolande, Jolander, Jolanka, Jolánta, Jolante, Jolantha, Jolanthe*

Jolene (Hebrew) God increases. *Jolean, Joleen, Joleene*

Jolie (French) Pretty. *Joli, Joline, Jolli, Jollie, Jolly, Joly, Jolye*

JoMei (Japanese) Spreads light.

Jonelle (Hebrew) She is gracious to God. *Jonele, Jonell*

Joni (American) Form of Joan. *Joncee, Joncey, Jonci, Joncie, Jone, Jonee, Joney, Jonie, Jonilee, Jony*

Jonina (Hebrew) Dove. *Jona, Joneen, Joneena, Joneene, Joninah, Jonine, Jonnina, Jonyna, Jonynah*

Joo Mi (Korean) Meaning unknown.

Jora (Hebrew) Autumn rain. *Jorah, Jorai, Joria, Joriah*

Jordan (Hebrew) Descender. *Jordana, Jordane, Jordanna, Jordea, Jordee, Jordi, Jordian, Jordie, Jordin, Jourdain, Jourdan*

Josephine (Hebrew) He shall increase; feminine version of Joseph. *Fifi, Giuseppina, Jo, Joette, Josefa, Josefina, Josefine, Josepha, Josephe, Josetta, Josette, Josey, Josie*

Josie (Hebrew) God will increase; form of Josephine. *Joesey, Josey, Josi, Josia, Josiah, Jossie, Josy, Josye*

Joss (German) Joyous; form of Jocelyn. *Jocalin, Jocalina, Jocalyn, Jocelina, Jocelinah, Jocelinn, Jocelle, Jocelynne, Joci, Jocia, Jocilyn, Jocilynn, Jocinta, Joscelin, Josilin, Jossalin*

Jovanna (Latin) Majestic. *Joevana, Jonvonah, Jouvan, Jovado, Joval, Jovan, Jovann, Jovannah, Jovannia, Jovanniah, Joviana, Jovina, Jovon, Jovonda, Jovone, Jovonia, Jovonn, Jovonnah, Jowan, Jowana, Jowanna*

Jovi (Latin) Joyful. *Jovee, Jovey*

Joy (Latin) Rejoice. *Joi, Joia, Joice, Jovita, Joyah, Joye, Joyeeta, Joyella, Joyeuse, Joyia, Joyous, Joyvina*

Joyce (Latin) Joyous. *Joice, Joise, Joycee, Joycey, Joycia, Joyciah, Joyicie, Joyse, Joysel*

Judith (Hebrew) Praised. *Giuditta, Jude, Judett, Judetta, Judette, Judi, Judie, Judine, Judit, Judita, Judite, Juditha, Judithe, Juditt, Juditta, Juditte, Judy, Judyta, Judyth, Judytt, Judytte, Jutka, Siobhan, Siubhan, Yehudith*

Juhy (Hindi) Flower. *Juh, Juhi*

Juice (American) Nickname.

Julia (Latin) Youthful; feminine version of Julius. *Giulia, Giulietta, Jeuleah, Jewelea, Jeweleah, Jewelia, Jeweliah, Joletta, Joliette, Juelea, Jules, Juli, Juliah, Juliana, Julianna, Julianne, Julica, Julie, Juliea, Julija, Julina, Juline, Julita, Juliya, Julya*

Juliet (French) Youthful; form of Julia. (Shakespearean) Character from *Romeo and Juliet. Jewelett, Jeweletta, Jewelette, Jeweliet, Jeweliete, Jewelyet, Jewelyette, Jewlyett, Jolet, Jolete, Juelet, Juelett, Julliet, Julliete, Jullietta, Julyeta, Julyetah, Julyetta, Julyettah*

Julitta (Spanish) Youthful; form of Julia. *Juleet, Juleetah, Juleete, Julet, Juleta, Juletah, Julit, Julitt, Julittah, Julitte, Julyta*

Jumana (Arabic) Pearl. *Jumanah*

Jun (Chinese) Truthful.

June (Latin) Young. *Juen, Juin, Juine, Juna, Junel, Junell, Junella, Junelle, Junett, Junetta, Junette, Juney, Junia, Juniata, Juniet, Junieta, Junilla, Junille, Junina, Junine, Junita, Junn, Juno, Junula*

Jung (Korean) Righteousness.

Juniper (Latin) Juniper berry.

Juno (Latin) Queen.

Justa (Latin) Just. *Giustine, Justill, Justine*

Justice (Latin) Form of Justus. *Justys, Justyse*

Justina (Italian) Just, righteous; form of Justus. *Justean, Justeane, Justeen, Justeene, Justein, Justeine, Justena, Justeyn, Justeyna, Justeynah, Justeyne, Justinah, Justinna*

Jyoti (Hindi) Light; flame. *Jioti*

Jysella (Science fiction) Character from *Star Wars.*

K

Kaatje (Dutch) Pure.

Kabibe (African) Little lady.

Kabira (African) Powerful.

Kacela (African) Hunter.

Kacey (Irish) Brave. *Casey, Casie, K. C., K. Cee, Kace, Kacee, Kaci, Kacy, Kasey, Kasie, Kaycee, Kaycie, Kaysie*

Kachelle (English) Stove tile; form of German Kachel.

Kachine (Native American) Sacred dancer. *Cachina, Kachena, Kachina, Kachinah*

Kaci (Irish) Brave. *Kacy*

Kacia (Greek) Thorny. *Kaycia, Kaysia*

Kacondra (African American) Bold. *Condra, Connie, Conny, Kacon, Kacond, Kaecondra, Kakondra, Kaycondra*

Kacy (American) From the initials K. C.

Kade (English, Scottish) Barrel; from the wetlands.

Kadejah (Arabic) Trustworthy. *Kadija, Kadijah*

Kaden (American) Charismatic. *Caden, Kadenn*

Kadence (French) Rhythmic flow of sounds.

Kadenza (Latin) Cadence; dances. *Cadenza, Kadena, Kadence*

Kadie (American) Virtuous. *Kadee*

Kadiea (Arabic) Powerful.

Kadija (African) Prophet's wife. *Kadee*

Kadin (Arabic) Companion.

Kadisha (Hebrew) Holy. *Kadischa, Kadiza*

Kady (English) Sassy. *Cady, K. D., Kadee, Kadie, Kaydie, Kaydy*

Kaede (Japanese) Maple leaf.

Kaela (English) Keeper of the keys; pure. *Kaelah, Kaeleah*

Kaelin (Irish) Rejoicer; waterfall; pool; pure; impetuous. *Kaelan, Kaelen, Kaelinn, Kaelynne, Kaeylynn, Kaylin*

Kaelyn (American) Combination of Kae and Lynn. *Kaelin, Kailyn, Kay-Lynn*

Kaethe (Greek) Pure.

Kagami (Japanese) Mirror.

Kahlila (Arabic) Beloved, sweetheart; from Khalil.

Kai (Hawaiian) Sea. (Native American) Willow tree.

Kaia (Greek) Earth. *Kaiah*

Kaida (Japanese) Little dragon.

Kaie (Celtic) Combat.

Kaija (Finnish) Pure. (Greek) Earth.

Kaila (Hebrew) Laurel; crown. *Kail, Kailah, Kala, Kalae, Kalah*

Kailani (Hawaiian) Sky. *Kaelana, Kaelanah, Kaelanee, Kaelani*

Kailas (Hindi) Home of the Lord.

Kailey (American) Spunky; laurel; crown. *Kaili, Kailie, Kalee, Kaylee, Kaylei*

Kaili (Hawaiian) Deity. (American) Crown.

Kailyn (American, English) Laurel tree; keeper of the keys.

Kaimana (Hawaiian) Diamond. *Kaemana, Kaemanah, Kaiman, Kaimanah*

Kaimi (Hawaiian) Seeker.

Kainda (African) Hunter's daughter.

Kairi (Greek) Opportunity.

Kairos (Greek) Goddess from Jupiter.

Kaisa (Swedish) Pure. *Kaisah, Kaysa, Kaysah*

Kaitlyn (Celtic) Little darling; pure hearted. *Caitlin, Caitlyn, Kailyn, Kait, Kaitlan, Kaitland, Kaitlin, Kaitlynn, Kaitlynne, Katie, Katlan, Kaydee*

Kaiya (Japanese) Forgiveness. *Kaiyah, Kaiyia*

Kajal (Hindi) Eyeliner.

Kajol (Hindi) Eyeliner.

Kajsa (Swedish) Pure. *Kaisa*

Kakra (Ghanese) Younger of twins.

Kala (Hindi) Black; royal; time. *Cala, Kalah, Kalla, Kallah*

Kalama (Hawaiian) Flaming torch.

Kalani (Hawaiian) Heavens. *Kalana, Kalauni, Kaloni, Kaylanie*

Kalanit (Hebrew) Flower.

Kalare (Latin) Bright; clear.

Kalauni (Tongan) Crown. *Kalauney*

Kalea (Arabic) Sweet; bright. *Kahlea, Kahleah, Kailea, Kaileah, Kallea, Kalleah, Kaylea, Kayleagh, Khalea, Khaleah*

Kalei (American) Sweetheart. *Kahlei, Kailei, Kallei, Kaylei, Khalei*

Kaleigh (Hebrew) Beloved. (Arabic) Sweetheart. *Kalea*

Kalena (Hawaiian) Chaste. *Kaleena*

Kalene (Czech) Flower. (Gaelic) Thin piece of land. (Polish) Flowering plant.

Kalet (French) Beautiful energy. *Kalay, Kalaye*

Kaley (Hawaiian) Hesitating. (American) Crown; form of Kelly; energetic. *Kalee, Kaleigh, Kalleigh*

Kali (Hindi) The black one; form of Hindi goddess Devi. (Hawaiian) Hesitating. (Greek) Beauty. *Kala, Kalli*

Kalia (Hawaiian) Beauty.

Kalidas (Greek) Most beautiful. *Kaleedus, Kali*

Kalie (Dutch) Keeper of the keys; pure. *Kali*

Kalifa (African) Chaste, holy. *Kalifah*

Kalika (Greek) Rosebud. *Kalyca*

Kalila (Arabic) Beloved. *Cailey, Cailie, Caylie, Kailey, Kaililah, Kaleah, Kalela, Kalie, Kalilah, Kaly, Kay, Kaykay, Kaylee, Kayllie, Kyle, Kylila, Kylilah*

Kalin (Irish) Pure; form of Caleb.

Kalina (Hawaiian) Unblemished. *Kaline, Kalinna, Kaylynna*

Kalinda (Hindi) Sun. (Sanskrit) Mountains. *Kaleenda, Kalin, Kalindi, Kalynda, Kalyndi*

Kalisa (American) Pretty and loving; combination of Kay and Lisa. *Caylisa, Kaleesa, Kalisha, Kaykay, Kaylisa, Kaylssa*

Kaliska (Native American) Coyote that chases deer.

Kalista (Greek) Most beautiful one.

Kaliyah (Arabic) Darling, sweetheart. *Kahlilah*

Kallan (American) Loving. *Kall, Kallen, Kallun*

Kalle (Finnish) Strong.

Kalli (Greek) Castle, fortress. *Callie, Kali, Kalie, Kalley, Kallie, Kally*

Kallie (Cambodian) Best.

Kallima (American) Butterfly.

Kalliope (Greek) Beautiful voice. *Calli, Calliope, Kalli, Kallyope*

Kallista (Greek) Pretty; bright-eyed. *Cala, Calesta, Calista, Callie, Callista, Cally, Kala, Kalesta, Kalista, Kalli, Kallie, Kally, Kallysta, Kalysta*

Kalliyan (Cambodian) Best.

Kallolee (Hindi) Happy. *Kalloleigh, Kalloli, Kallolie*

Kalona (German) Amish town.

Kaloni (Hawaiian) Sky. *Kalonee, Kalonia*

Kalonice (Greek) Beauty's victory.

Kalpana (Sanskrit) Imagination.

Kalyca (Greek) Rosebud.

Kalyn (American) Loved. (Arabic) Keeper of the keys. (English) Laurel tree. *Calynn, Calynne, Kaelyn, Kaelynn, Kalen, Kalinn, Kallyn, Kalyna*

Kama (Sanskrit) Love. *Kamah, Kammah*

Kamakshi (Hindi) Goddess Parvati.

Kamala (Hindi) Lotus. *Camala, Kam, Kamalah, Kamali, Kamilla, Kammy*

Kamalei (Hawaiian) Beloved child. *Kamalea, Kamaleah*

Kamali (Rhodesian) Spirit protector. *Kamalie*

Kamana (Hindi) Desire.

Kamaria (Swahili) Like the moon. *Kamaarie, Kamar, Kamara, Kamariah*

Kamballa (Australian) Young woman. *Kambala, Kambalah*

Kambo (African) Must work for everything.

Kambrea (Latin) From Wales.

Kambria (Latin) Girl from Wales. *Cambria, Kambra, Kambrie, Kambriea, Kambry*

Kamea (Hawaiian) Precious one. *Kam, Kamaya, Kamea, Kameo, Kammie, Maya, Mea*

Kameko (Japanese) Tortoise-child; symbol for long life.

Kameli (Hawaiian) Honey. *Kamely*

Kamella (Hungarian) Young ceremonial attendant.

Kameron (American) Variant of Cameron; crooked nose; kind. *Kamren, Kamrin, Kamron*

Kami (Shinto) Above; God. (Slavic) Young attendant. *Cami, Cammie, Cammy, Kamelia, Kamille, Kammie, Kammy*

Kamila (Arabic) Perfect. (Slavic) Noble.

Kamilah (Arabic) Perfect one. *Camilla, Kamilla*

Kamilia (Slavic) Fragrant evergreen tree with fragrant flowers. *Kam, Kameela, Kamela, Kamella, Kamila, Kamilla, Kamillah, Kammy, Kamyla, Milla*

Kamin (Japanese) Joyful.

Kamna (Hindi) Desire.

Kamryn (American) Crooked nose. *Cameron*

Kanaka (Indian) Gold.

Kanakabati (Indian) Fairy tale.

Kanani (Hawaiian) Beautiful. *Kana, Kanan, Kananie, Kanany*

Kanara (Hebrew) Tiny bird; lithe. *Kanarit, Kanarra*

Kanchana (Greek) White; pure. *Candace*

Kandace (Greek) Charming; glowing. *Candace, Candie, Candy, Dacie, Kandi, Kandice, Kandiss*

Kande (African) First-born daughter.

Kandice (English, Greek) Brilliant; white; clarity; pure. *Kandis, Kandyce*

Kandra (American) Light. *Candra*

Kane (Japanese) Two right thumbs. *Cathan, Kain, Kaine*

Kaneesha (American) Dark-skinned. *Caneesha, Kaneesh, Kaneice, Kaneisha, Kanesha, Kaneshia, Kaney, Kanish, Nesha*

Kanene (African) Little important thing.

Kanesha (African American) Spontaneous. *Kaneesha, Kaneeshia, Kaneisha, Kanisha, Kannesha*

Kanga (Australian) Short for kangaroo; jumpy.

Kani (Hawaiian) Sound. *Cani, Kanee, Kanie, Kany*

Kanika (Egyptian) Black cloth. *Kanica*

Kanisha (American) Pretty. *Kaneesha, Kanicia, Kenisha, Kinicia, Koneesha*

Kaniya (Hindi) Virgin. (Thai) Young lady. (Native American) Form of Niya, meaning "champion."

Kannitha (Cambodian) Angel.

Kanoni (African) Little bud.

Kansas (Native American) Derived from Kansa, meaning "people of the south wind." (American) Place name.

Kantha (Hindi) Hindi god Lord Shiva; recreation; wife.

Kanti (Native American) Sings.

Kanushi (Hindi) Meaning unknown.

Kanya (Asian) Young lady. *Kanja, Kanjah, Kanyah*

Kaori (Japanese) Fragrant, beautiful girl.

Kaoru (Japanese) Fragrant.

Kaprece (American) Capricious. *Caprice, Kapp, Kappy, Kapreece, Kapri, Kaprise, Kapryce, Karpreese*

Kapua (Hawaiian) Blossom.

Kapuki (African) First girl in the family.

Kara (Greek) Pure. *Karan, Karen, Karyn, Kasen, Kasia, Kassia, Katja, Katoka, Katrien, Kaysa*

Karan (American) Sweet melody.

Karana (Greek) Pure.

Karasi (African) Life and wisdom.

Karayan (Slavic) Dark one.

Karbie (American) Energetic. *Karbi, Karby*

Kareela (Australian) Southern wind. *Karela, Karelah, Karella, Karellah*

Karel (American) Form of Carol. (German) Farmer. (English) Strong. *Karell, Karelle*

Karen (Greek) Pure. *Caren, Carin, Caron, Caronn, Carren, Carrin, Carron, Carryn, Caryn, Carynn, Carynne, Karan, Kare, Kareen, Karenna, Kari, Karin, Karina, Karon, Karron, Karryn, Karyn,*

Keren, Kerran, Kerrin, Kerron, Kerrynn, Keryn, Kerynne, Taran, Taren, Taryn

Karena (Scandinavian) Pure one. *Kareina, Karenah, Karrana, Karranah*

Karenza (Cornish) Loving, affectionate. *Karanza, Karanzah, Karensia, Karensiah*

Kari (Turkish) Flows like water. *Cari, Carrie, Kary, Keri, Kery*

Karian (American) Daring. *Kerian*

Karida (Arabic) Untouched, virginal. *Kareeda, Karidah, Karita, Karyda*

Karima (Arabic) Giving. *Kareema, Kareemah, Kareima, Kareimah, Karimah*

Karin (Greek) Pure. *Karen, Karine, Karinne, Karyn*

Karis (Greek) Graceful. *Karese, Karice, Karise, Karisse, Karyce*

Karise (Latin) Dearest one.

Karishma (Hindi) Miracle.

Karissa (Greek) Love; grace. *Carissa, Krissy, Sissa*

Karka (Hindi) Crab.

Karla (German) Strong; womanly. *Carla, Karlah, Karlia, Karlie, Karrla*

Karlee (Latin) Womanly; strong. *Karley, Karli, Karlie, Karly*

Karleen (American) Witty; combination of Karla and Arleen. *Karlene, Karline, Karly*

Karli (Turkish) Covered with snow. *Karlie*

Karlotta (German) Pretty; form of Charlotte. *Karlota, Karlotte, Lotta, Lottee*

Karly (Latin) Strong voiced. *Carly, Karlee, Karlie, Karlye*

Karlyn (Greek) Little and womanly.

Karma (Sanskrit) Action. *Carma, Carmah, Karmah, Karmana*

Karmaine (French) Form of Charmaine. *Karmain, Karmane, Karmeine*

Karmel (Hebrew) Garden. *Karmela, Karmelah, Karmele*

Karmen (Latin) Song. *Carmen, Karmin, Karmine*

Karmina (Hebrew) Song; songstress.

Karmiti (Native American) Trees. *Karmitey, Karmitie, Karmity*

Karna (African) Horn of an animal.

Karolina (Polish) Little and strong; form of Carolina. *Karaline, Karalyn, Karalynna, Karalynne, Karla, Karleen, Karlen, Karlene, Karli, Karlie, Karlina, Karlinka, Karo, Karoline, Karolinka, Karolyn, Karolyne, Karolynn, Karolynne*

Karrie (English) Melody, song.

Karrington (Welsh) Rocky town. *Carrington*

Karsen (American) Anointed one. *Carsen, Carson, Karson*

Karuna (Hindi) Merciful.

Karya (Hindi) Effect; product.

Karyan (Armenian) Dark one.

Karyn (English) Pure; form of Katherine. *Karan, Karen, Karon*

Kasa (Native American) Fur-robe dress.

Kasandra (Greek) Helper of men.

Kasey (Irish) Vigiliant; alert. *Casey, Kaci*

Kashmir (Sanskrit) Place name. *Cashmere, Cashmir, Kash, Kashmere*

Kasi (Hindi) Illuminating. *Casey, Kaci, Kass, Kassi, Kassie*

Kasia (Polish) Pure; from Katherine.

Kasie (Irish) Brave.

Kasinda (African) Born to a family with twins.

Kasmira (Old Slavic) Demands peace. *Kasamira, Kazamira*

Kasra (Persian) Character in *Shahnameh* the eleventh-century *Epic of Kings* by Firdowski.

Kassandra (Greek) Capricious. *Cassandra, Kasandra, Kass, Kassandrah, Kassie*

Kassia (Polish) From Katherine.

Kassidy (Celtic, Gaelic) Clever. *Cassidy, Cassir, Kasadee, Kassydi*

Kassie (Irish) Prophet; unheeded prophetess.

Kat (American) Pure; from Catherine.

Kata (Japanese) Worthy.

Katalin (Hungarian) Pure.

Katarina (Greek) Pure. (Latin) Virginal. *Katareena, Katarena, Katarinna, Kataryna, Katerina, Katyrna*

Katarra (Science fiction) Character from *Star Wars*.

Katarzyna (Czech) Pure.

Katchi (American) Sassy. *Catsby, Cotchy, Kat, Kata, Katchie, Kati, Katshi, Katshie, Katshy, Katty, Kotchee, Kotchi, Kotchie*

Kate (Greek) Pure, virginal. *Cait, Caitie, Cate, Catee, Catey, Catie, Kait, Kaite, Kaitlin, Katee, Katey, Kathe, Kati, Katie, Katy*

Katelin (Irish) Pure, virginal. *Caitlin, Kaitlin, Kaitlynne, Kat, Kate-Lynn, Katelynn, Katline*

Katelyn (Celic, Gaelic) Pure beauty.

Katen (Irish) Pure, virginal.

Kateri (German) Pure; form of Katherine.

Katerina (Slavic) Pure.

Katherine (Greek) Pure. *Cara, Caren, Cari, Carin, Carrie, Carry, Caryn, Kara, Karan, Karen, Kari, Karin, Karina, Karon, Karrie, Karry, Karyn, Katarina, Kate, Katharine, Katheryn, Kathreen, Kathryn, Kathy, Katie, Katina, Katrin, Katrina*

Kathleen (Celtic) Little darling. *Cathaleen, Cathaline, Cathleen, Kathaleen, Kathaleya, Kathaleyna, Kathaline, Kathelina, Katheline, Kathie, Kathlene, Kathlin, Kathline, Kathlyn, Kathlynn*

Katia (Slavic) Pure. *Kateeya, Kati, Katya*

Katima (American) Powerful daughter.

Katina (Greek) Pure; unsullied.

Katiuscia (English, Irish) Pure.

Katlin (Irish) Pure. *Katlyn, Katlynn*

Katoka (Hungarian) Pure.

Katrice (American) Graceful. *Katreese, Katrese, Katrie, Katrisse, Katry*

Katriel (Hebrew) God is my crown. *Katriele, Katriella, Katriellah, Katrielle*

Katrin (German) Pure.

Katrina (German) Pure. *Katreena, Katreynah, Katryna, Kaytrina*

Katyayani (Hindi) Goddess Durga.

Kaula (Polynesian) Prophet.

Kaulauna (Hawaiian) Famous. *Kaula, Kaulani*

Kausalya (Hindi) Highly skilled.

Kaveri (Hindi) Sacred river of India.

Kavi (Hindi) Poet.

Kavindra (Hindi) Mighty poet.

Kavita (Hindi) Poem.

Kawena (Hawaiian) Rosy reflection in the sky. *Kawana, Kawona*

Kay (Hebrew) Crown of laurels. *Caye, Kaye*

Kaya (Native American) Wise child. (Japanese) Resting place. *Kaea, Kaja, Kayah, Kayia*

Kaydence (American) Musical.

Kayla (Hebrew) Crown of laurels. *Kaila, Kailyn, Kay, Kaylah, Kaylene, Kayln, Kaylynn*

Kaylana (American) Combination of Kay and Lana.

Kaylee (American) Combination of Kay and Lee. *Chaeli, Kayleigh*

Kayleen (American) Pure lass. *Kaylean, Kayleane, Kayleene, Kaylen*

Kayley (American) Bright; beautiful. (Irish, Scottish, English) Slender; keeper of the keys. (Arabic) Laurel. *Kay, Kaylee, Kayli, Kaylie*

Kaylin (American) Pure; keeper of the keys. *Kaylyn, Kaylynn*

Kazanna (Hindi) Treasure. *Kasanna, Kazi, Kazy, Kizzy*

Kazia (Hebrew) Plant with cinnamon-like bark.

Keahi (Hawaiian) Flames; fire.

Keaira (Gaelic) Little dark one.

Keala (Hawaiian) Path.

Keandra (Hawaiian) Water baby. *Keandrah, Keandre*

Keanna (Irish) Beautiful. *Keana, Keanah, Keanne, Keenan*

Keanu (Hawaiian) Cool mountain breeze.

Keara (Irish) From a saint's name. *Kearah, Kearia, Kearra*

Keaton (English) Where hawks fly. *Keatan, Keatin, Keeten, Keeton, Keitan, Keiton*

Kedma (Arabic) Toward the east.

Keedera (Science fiction) Character from *Star Trek: Deep Space Nine.*

Keegan (Irish) Small and fiery; bright flame.

Keeley (Irish) Lively; aggressive; beautiful. *Kealee, Kealey, Keali, Kealie*

Keelia (Irish) From Keely.

Keelin (Irish) Slender; fair.

Keelty (Gaelic) From the woods.

Keely (Gaelic) Beautiful and graceful. *Kealy, Keel, Keelan, Keeler, Keeley*

Keen (Gaelic) Brave.

Keena (Celtic) Brave. *Keenah, Keenya, Keina, Keinah, Keyna*

Keeya (African) Garden flower.

Kefira (Hebrew) Young lioness.

Kehinde (Yoruban) Second of twins.

Kei (Japanese) Rapture; reverence.

Keiki (Hawaiian) Child. *Keikanne, Kiki*

Keiko (Japanese) Adored one.

Keilah (Hebrew) Citadel. *Keila*

Keilana (Hawaiian) Adored one. *Kealanah, Keilanah, Keilani*

Keilantra (African American) Princess of the night sky; magical. *Keil, Keilei*

Keir (Celtic) Black.

Keira (Celtic) Black-haired.

Keisha (African) Favorite. *Keasha, Keesha, Keeshah, Keicia, Keishah, Keshia, Keysha, Kicia*

Keishla (African) Her life.

Keita (Celtic) Forest. *Keiti*

Keitha (Gaelic) Female warrior.

Kekona (Hawaiian) Second born.

Kelby (German) Place by the flowing water. *Kelbea, Kelbeigh, Kelbey, Kellbie*

Kelcie (Scottish) Brave; ship island. *Chelsea, Kelcy, Kellsey, Kelsee, Kelsey, Kelsy*

Kelda (Scandinavian) Clear mountain spring. *Kel, Kell, Kelley, Kelly*

Kele (Native American) Sparrow hawk. *Kelea, Keleah*

Kelila (Hebrew) Regal woman. *Kalula, Kayla, Kayle, Kaylee, Keluila, Kelulah, Kelylah, Kyla, Kyle*

Kelis (American) Beautiful.

Kella (Irish) Warrior.

Kellan (Gaelic) Warrior princess. *Kelleen, Kellene, Kellyn, Kellynn*

Kellen (Irish) Powerful.

Kelly (Irish) Church; warrior; wood; holly; farm by the spring. *Kel, Kelli, Kellie*

Kellyn (Irish) Powerful.

Kelsey (Scandinavian) Ceol's island; beautiful island; from the ship's island; shipping harbor. *Kelcie, Kels, Kelsi, Kelsie, Kelson, Kelsy, Kelton*

Kelsi (Scottish) Brave; ship island. *Chelsea, Kelcy, Kellsey, Kelsee, Kelsey, Kelsie, Kelsy*

Kember (American) Zany. *Kem, Kemmie, Kimber*

Kempley (English) From a meadowland; rascal. *Kemplea, Kempleigh, Kemplie, Kemply*

Kenadia (American) Chief.

Kenda (English) Child of clear, cool water. *Kendi, Kendie, Kendy, Kennda, Kenndi, Kenndie, Kenndy*

Kendall (Celtic) Ruler of the valley. *Ken, Kendal, Kendalia, Kendaline, Kendel, Kendell, Kendra, Kenna, Kenni, Kenny, Kindall, Kindell*

Kendis (African American) Pure.

Kendra (Anglo-Saxon) Understanding; knowledge. *Kendrah, Kenna, Kennie, Kindra, Kinna, Kyndra*

Kenia (Hebrew) Animal horn. *Keneah*

Kenisha (American) Gorgeous woman.

Kenley (English) Royal meadow. *Kenlea, Kenleah, Kenlee, Kenli, Kenlie*

Kenna (Celtic, Gaelic) Handsome.

Kennedy (Irish) Chief with helmet. *Kennedi*

Kennice (English) Beautiful. *Kaneese, Kanese, Kanice, Kena, Kenah, Kenenza, Kenni, Kennise*

Kennis (Gaelic) Beautiful.

Kennita (American) Chief with helmet.

Kensington (English) Place name. *Kensi, Kensy, Kenzi, Kenzington, Kenzy*

Kenya (African) Place name. *Keenya, Kennya, Kenyetta*

Kenyangi (Ugandan) White egret.

Kenyatta (East African) Musician.

Kenyon (English) Blond; white-haired.

Kenzie (Scottish) Light-skinned. *Kenzea, Kenzee, Kenzey, Kenzy*

Keola (Hawaiian) Life.

Kepa (Basque) Stone.

Kera (Celtic, Gaelic) Pure.

Keran (Armenian) Wooden post.

Kerani (Hindi) Sacred bells. *Kerana, Keranee, Keraney, Kerania*

Keren (Hebrew) Animal's horn. *Keron, Kerran, Kerren, Kerrin*

Kerensa (Cornish) Love.

Kern (Celtic) Dark-haired child.

Kerry (Gaelic) Ciara's people; dark eyes. *Keri, Kerri, Kerrie, Kerrin, Kerwin*

Kerryn (American) Dusky and pure.

Kerstin (German) Christian. *Kersten, Kerston, Kerstyn*

Kerzi (Turkish) Meaning unknown.

Kesare (Spanish) Long-haired.

Kesha (American) Laughing. *Kecia, Kesa, Keshah*

Keshet (Hebrew) Rainbow. *Kesheta, Keshetah, Keshete, Keshett*

Keshia (African) Favorite.

Keshon (African American) Happy. *Keshann, Keshaun, Keshawn, Keshonn, Keshun*

Kesi (Swahili) Born during troubled times. *Kesee, Kesey, Kesie*

Kesia (African) Favorite. *Kessia, Kessiah, Kessya*

Kessie (Ghanese) Fat at birth. *Kessey*

Kestra (Science fiction) Character from *Star Trek: The Next Generation*.

Ketaki (Indian) Monsoon flower.

Ketifa (Arabic) Flower. *Ketifah, Kettifa, Kettifah, Ketyfa*

Ketika (Hindi) Meaning unknown.

Ketina (Hebrew) Girl. *Keteena, Keteenah, Ketinah*

Keturah (Hebrew) Fragrance.

Ketzia (Hebrew) Surface; cinnamon-like bark.

Kevina (Gaelic) Lively; from Kevin. (Irish) Beautiful. *Kevine, Kevinne, Kevyn, Kevynn, Kevynne*

Kevlyn (American) Handsome child; form of Kevin.

Kevyn (Irish) Beautiful. *Kevan, Keven, Kevon, Kevynn*

Keyah (African) In good health.

Keyanna (American) Living with grace.

Keyla (American) Living with grace. *Keylon*

Kezia (Hebrew) Cassia; cinnamon. *Keesha, Keisha, Keishia, Keshia, Ketzia, Keziah, Kezzy, Lakeisha*

Khadijah (Arabic) Prophet's first wife; trustworthy. *Khadaja, Khadajah, Khadije, Khadijia*

Khalidah (Arabic) Immortal. *Khali, Khalidda, Khalita*

Khanh (Vietnamese) Meaning unknown.

Khara (Latin) Dearest. *Cara*

Khety (Egyptian) Meaning unknown.

Khina (Greek) Goose; nesting. (Iranian) Sweet voice.

Kia (African) Hill.

Kiah (Australian Aboriginal) From the beautiful place.

Kiana (Hawaiian) Moon goddess. *Kianah, Kiane*

Kiandra (English) From Kendra.

Kianga (African) Sunshine.

Kianna (Irish) Ancient. *Kiana, Kiani*

Kiara (Celtic) Small; dark.

Kiaria (Japanese) Fortunate.

Kiarra (Irish) Small; dark.

Kichi (Japanese) Fortunate.

Kiden (African) Female born after three boys.

Kiele (Hawaiian) Gardenia; fragrant blossom. *Kielee, Kieleigh, Kieley, Kielie*

Kiera (Irish) Dusky; dark-headed; dark; black. *Kiearra, Kieran, Kyra*

Kiersten (Scandinavian) Anointed.

Kieu (Vietnamese) Meaning unknown.

Kiho (African) Fog.

Kijana (African) Youth.

Kiki (Spanish) Short for names beginning with K.

Kiku (Japanese) Chrysanthemum. *Kiko*

Kilana (Science fiction) Character from *Star Trek: Deep Space Nine*.

Kilenya (Native American) Coughing fish.

Kiley (Irish) Good-looking; from the straits. *Kielea, Kielee, Kielei, Kieley, Kieli, Kielia, Kielie*

Kilia (Hawaiian) Heaven. *Killia, Killiah, Kylia, Kyliah*

Killian (Irish) Little warrior. (Gaelic) Fierce. *Kilean, Kilian, Kiliane, Kilien, Killiean, Killien, Killion, Kyllien*

Kim (Old English) Chief. *Kemble, Kimball, Kimbell, Kimble, Kimmey, Kimmi, Kimmy, Kym*

Kimana (Native American) Butterfly. *Kimanah, Kimani, Kimannah, Kimanne, Kymana*

Kimatra (Hindi) Seduce. *Kim*

Kimber (English) Leader. *Kim, Kimball, Kimberley, Kimberly*

Kimberley (Old English) Land belonging to Cyneburg; royal fortress; meadow. *Kim, Kimberlee, Kimberly, Kimby, Kimmi, Kimmie, Kimmy, Kymberly*

Kimi (Japanese) She who is without equal. *Kimee, Kimmi*

Kimimela (Native American) Butterfly.

Kimn (English) Ruler.

Kimora (Chinese) Meaning unknown.

Kin (Japanese) Golden.

Kina (Hawaiian) From China. *Kinah, Kyna*

Kindness (Anglo-Saxon) Warm-hearted, considerate.

Kineks (North American) Rosebud.

Kineta (Greek) Active one. *Kinetah, Kinete, Kinett, Kinetta*

Kinfe (African) Wing.

Kinipela (Hawaiian) Wave.

Kinsey (English) Offspring. *Kensey, Kinnsee, Kinnsey, Kinnsie, Kinsee, Kinsie, Kinzee*

Kioko (Japanese) Meets world with happiness. *Kioka, Kiyo*

Kiona (Native American) Brown hills. *Kionah, Kionna, Kyona, Kyonah*

Kione (African) Someone who comes from nowhere.

Kipling (English) Cured salmon. *Kiplin*

Kipp (English) High hill. *Kip, Kyp*

Kippi (Old Norse) Tied together.

Kira (Persian) Sun. (Latin) Light. (Japanese) Sunlight. (Science fiction) Character from *Star Trek: Deep Space Nine*. *Keera, Kera, Kiera, Kierra, Kiria, Kiriah, Kirra, Kirya*

Kirabo (African) Gift from God.

Kiral (Turkish) Supreme chief.

Kiran (Hindi) Ray of light. *Kearan, Kearin, Kearon, Keeran, Kiranpal*

Kirana (Hindi) Ray of light.

Kirby (Anglo-Saxon) From the church town. *Kerby, Kirbee, Kirbey, Kirbie*

Kiri (Cambodian) Mountain. *Kiree, Kirey*

Kirima (Eskimo) A hill.

Kirit (Hindi) Crown.

Kiros (African) King.

Kirra (Celtic) Dark lady.

Kirsi (Hindi) Amaranth blossoms. *Kirsie*

Kirsten (Greek) Christian; stone church. *Kier, Kiersten, Kirsti, Kirstie, Kirstin, Kirsty, Kristi, Kristine*

Kirtana (Hindi) Praise.

Kirti (Hindi) Fame.

Kisa (Russian) Kitty. *Kisah, Kiska, Kysa, Kysah*

Kisha (Slavic) Rainfall. *Keshah*

Kishi (Native American) Night. *Kishee, Kishey, Kishie*

Kiska (Russian) Pure.

Kismet (English) Fate; destiny. *Kismat, Kismeta, Kismetah, Kismete, Kismett*

Kissa (Ugandan) Born after twins. *Kissah, Kisser, Kyssa, Kyssah*

Kita (Japanese) North.

Kitra (Hebrew) Crowned. *Kitrah*

Kitty (Latin) Little cat. *Kit, Kittee, Kittey, Kitti, Kittie*

Kitu (Hindi) Meaning unknown.

Kiwa (Japanese) Born on the border.

Kiya (Australian) Always returning; pretty girl; form of Kylie. *Kya*

Kiyoshi (Japanese) Quiet child.

Kizzy (Hebrew) Cinnamon. *Kissee, Kissie, Kiz, Kizzie*

Klara (Hungarian) Bright and famous. *Klari, Klarice, Klarika, Klarissa, Klarisza, Klaryssa*

Klarika (Hungarian) Brilliant.

Klarissa (German) Bright-minded. *Clarissa, Klarisa, Klarise, Klarissah*

Klavdia (Slavic) Lame one.

Klementyna (Polish) Mild; merciful. *Clemence, Clementine, Klementina*

Kludia (French) Form of Claudia.

Knowledge (Middle English) To confess, to recognize.

Kochava (Hebrew) Star.

Koemi (Japanese) Smiling. *Koemey, Koemie, Koemy*

Koffi (Swahili) Born on Friday. *Kaffi, Koffe, Koffie*

Koge (Japanese) Fragrant flower.

Kogen (Japanese) Wild, untamed source. *Kogyn*

Kohana (Japanese) Little flower.

Koko (Native American) Night.

Koleyn (Australian) Winter. *Kolein, Koleina*

Kolfinnia (Scandinavian) White. *Kolfinia, Kolfiniah, Kolfinna*

Kolina (Greek) Pure.

Kolora (Australian) Lake. *Kolorah, Kolori, Kolorie*

Kolton (English) Coal town.

Komal (Hindi) Tender. *Komala*

Komala (Hindi) Delicate.

Kona (Hawaiian) Lady. *Konia*

Konane (Hawaiian) Lunar glow.

Konstance (Latin) Loyal. *Constance, Kon, Konstanze*

Kora (Greek) Companion; maiden. *Korah, Kore, Korra*

Kordell (Latin) Warm-hearted. (Welsh) Sea jewel. (French) Rope maker. (English) From Cordell.

Koren (Greek) Maiden. *Kori, Korin, Korrie, Korry*

Kori (Greek) Girl.

Korina (Greek) Strong-willed; small girl. *Corinna, Koreena, Korena, Korinna, Koryna*

Kortney (English) Courteous.

Kory (American) Hollow.

Kosma (Greek) Universe; harmony. *Cosma*

Kostya (Slavic) Faithful.

Koto (Japanese) Harp.

Kourtney (English) From the court; dignified. *Courtney, Kortnee, Kortni, Kourtnie, Kourtny*

Kozue (Japanese) Tree branches.

Kreeli (American) Sweet and charming.

Krisalyn (American) Beautiful bearer of Christ.

Krista (Czech) Christ-bearer; short for Christina. *Khrista, Krysta*

Kristal (English) Clear; brilliant; glass.

Kristen (Greek) Bright-eyed; follower of Christ. *Christen, Cristen, Kristin*

Kristi (Greek) Anointed follower of Christ.

Kristina (Greek) Anointed; Christ-bearer. *Christina, Krista, Kristie, Krysteena*

Kristine (Greek) Christ-bearer.

Kristy (Greek) Christ-bearer.

Kristyn (Greek) Christian; anointed; form of Kristen.

Kriti (Hindi) Work of art.

Krupa (Hindi) Meaning unknown.

Krupali (Hindi) Meaning unknown.

Krysta (Czech) Christian; anointed.

Krystal (American) Clear, brilliant glass. *Cristalle, Cristel, Crysta, Crystal, Crystalle, Khristalle, Khristel, Khrystalle, Khrystle, Kristel, Krys, Krystalle, Krystalline, Krystelle, Krystie, Krystle, Krystylle*

Krysten (Greek) Anointed follower of Christ.

Krystina (Greek) Anointed.

Krystyn (Scandinavian) Christian; anointed.

Ksena (Polish) Praise to God.

Kshama (Hindi) Forgiveness; patience; a form of the Hindu goddess Devi.

Kuhuk (Hindi) Meaning unknown.

Kuma (Japanese) Bear.

Kumani (African) Destiny.

Kumari (Sanskrit) Woman. *Kumaree, Kumarey, Kumaria, Kumariah*

Kumberlin (Australian) Sweet. *Cumberlin, Cumberlyn, Kumberlina, Kumberline, Kumberlyne*

Kumi (Japanese) Long; continued beauty.

Kumiko (Japanese) Braid. *Kumi*

Kumud (Hindi) Lotus. *Kumuda*

Kunani (Hawaiian) Beautiful. *Kunanee, Kunaney*

Kuniko (Japanese) Child from the country.

Kunti (Hindi) Mother of Pendavas.

Kura (Japanese) Treasure house.

Kuri (Japanese) Chestnut. *Curi, Kurey, Kurie, Kury*

Kuron (African) Thanks.

Kusum (Indian) Flower.

Kuyen (Native American) Moon.

Kwanita (Native American) God is gracious.

Kwashi (African) Born on Sunday.

Kya (African) Diamond in the sky. *Kia*

Kyara (Irish) Little and dark.

Kyla (Irish) Lovely. (Old English) Narrow; narrow channel. (Yiddish) Crown. *Ky, Kylah, Kylea, Kylee, Kyleigh, Kylene*

Kylar (English) Chapel; shelter. *Kyler, Kylor*

Kyle (Irish) Narrow land; handsome.

Kylee (Celtic) Crown; from Kyla.

Kyleigh (Irish) Narrow land.

Kylene (Irish) Little piece of land.

Kylia (American) Narrow land.

Kylie (Aborigine) Boomerang. *Kay, Kayle, Kayleigh, Leigh*

Kyna (Gaelic) Wise. *Cyna, Cyne, Kyne*

Kynan (Welsh) Chief.

Kynthia (Greek) Born under the sign of cancer. *Cinthia, Cynthia*

Kyoko (Japanese) Mirror. *Kyoka*

Kyra (Greek) Noble. *Kyrea, Kyree, Kyrie, Kyry*

Kyrene (Greek) Lord; ruler. *Kirena, Kirenah, Kirene*

Kyria (Greek) Ladylike. *Kyrea, Kyree, Kyrie, Kyry*

Kyrielle (French) French verse.

Kyung Mi (Korean) Honored and beauty.

Kyung Soon (Korean) Honored and mild.

L

L'Oréal (French) Cosmetics brand name.

Laah (Hebrew) Weary.

Laasya (Hindi) Dance.

Labana (Hebrew) Moon; whiteness; frankincense. *Labahna, Labanah*

Labdhi (Native American) Heavenly power.

Labrenda (Old Norse) Sword. *Labrenna, Labrennah, Labrinda, Labrindah*

Lacey (Latin) Cheerful. *Laci, Lacie, Lacy, Laicee, Laicey, Layce*

Lachandra (American) Moon. *Lachanda, Lachandah, Lachandrah*

Lachelle (African American) Sweetheart. *Lachel, Lachell, Laschell, Lashelle*

Lachesis (Latin) Fury.

Lachianina (Celtic, Gaelic) From the land of the lake. *Lachianinah, Lachlanie, Lachlany, Lachyanina, Lachyaninah*

Lacienega (Spanish) Swamp, marsh.

Lacole (Italian) Victory of the people. *Lacola, Lacolla, Lacollah, Lecole, Lecolla*

Lacrecia (Latin) Wealthy. *Lacricia, Lacriciah, Lacrycia, Lacryciah*

Lacy (Greek) Happy. *Lace, Lacie, Lase, Laycee*

Lada (Slavic) Goddess of love and fertility. *Ladah, Ladia, Ladiah*

Ladan (American) Bright as day.

Ladancia (French) Morning star. *Ladanciah, Ladancya, Ladanika, Ladanikah*

Ladawn (English) Sunrise.

Ladonna (Spanish) Woman. *Ladona, Ladonah, Ladonia, Ladonnah, Ladonnia, Ladonniah*

Ladye (English) Lady.

Lae (Laos) Dark.

Lael (Hebrew) Of God.

Laela (Hebrew) Dark beauty; night. (Arabic) Born at night. *Lael, Laele*

Laetitia (Latin) Joy. *Lateaciah, Lateacya, Latycia, Leticia, Letisia, Letzyiah*

Laguna (American) Place name; water-loving. *Lagunah*

Lahela (Hawaiian) Innocent lamb. *Lahelah*

Lahoma (Native American) People.

Laikana (Tongan) Lilac. *Laelaka, Laelakah, Lailakah, Laylaka*

Laila (Arabic) Night. (Hebrew) Dark beauty. *Laili, Laleh, Layla, Laylah, Leila*

Lailie (Hebrew) Born during light.

Laima (Slavic) Luck.

Laine (English) Bright one. *Laene, Lain, Lane, Layne*

Lainey (English) Sun ray. *Lainie*

Laisa (Biblical) Place name; form of Elasa, located north of Jerusalem.

Laisha (Hebrew) A lion.

Lajerrica (English) Powerful ruler.

Lajessica (Hebrew) Wealthy. *Lajesika, Lajessicah, Lajessika, Lajessykah*

Lajli (Hindi) Humble. *Lajita*

Lajuana (American) God is gracious. *Lajuanah, Lajuanna, Lajuannah, Lawanah*

Laka (Hawaiian) Docile.

Lake (English) Body of water.

Lakeisha (Swahili) Favorite one. *Lakeesha, Latasha, Latonya, Latoya, Lawanna*

Laken (American) From the lake.

Lakendra (African American) Knowing, understanding. *Lakandra, Lakendrah, Lakendrya*

Lakeshia (American) Joyful. *Keishia, Lakaisha, Lakeesha, Lakeishah, Lakezia, Lakisha*

Laketa (African American) Woods. *Laketha, Laketta, Lakettah, Lakette*

Lakia (Arabic) Treasure. *Lakiah, Lakyah*

Lakin (African American) Found treasure.

Lakota (Native American) Friend.

Laksha (Hindi) White rose.

Lakshmi (Hindi) Lucky omen. *Lakshmie, Laxmi*

Lakyle (Gaelic) Half wood.

Lala (Slavic) Tulip. *Laella, Laellah, Laila, Lalah*

Lalage (Greek) Talkative. *Lallie, Lally*

Lalaine (American) Helpful; hardworking.

Lalan (Hindi) Nurturing.

Lalasa (Hindi) Love. *Lalassa, Lalassah*

Laleh (Arabic) From Leila.

Lali (Greek) Well spoken. *Laily, Lallea*

Lalika (Hindi) Beautiful woman.

Lalima (Hindi) Redness.

Lalisa (English) Noble; kind.

Lalita (Hindi) Variety; beauty. *Lai, Lala, Lali, Lalitah, Lalite, Lalitte*

Lalitamohana (Hindi) Attractive, beautiful.

Lalitya (Indian) Lovely, charming.

Lalo (Latin) To sing a lullaby.

Lama (Arabic) Darkness of lips.

Lamees (Arabic) Soft to the touch.

Lamis (Arabic) Soft. *Lamisa, Lamisah, Lamissa, Lamissah, Lamys*

Lamora (French) Honor. *Lamorah*

Lamya (Arabic) Dark.

Lan (Vietnamese) Flower. *Lang*

Lana (Polynesian) To float. *Lan, Lanae, Lanna, Lannette, Lanny*

Lanai (Hawaiian) Terrace; veranda.

Lanakila (Hawaiian) Triumph.

Landen (English) Rough land.

Landon (English) Grassy plain.

Landrada (Spanish) Counselor.

Landry (English) Rough road.

Lane (Middle English) Narrow road. *Laine, Layna, Layne*

Lanelle (African American) Narrow road. *Lanela, Lanelah, Lanell*

Lanette (American) Beautiful. *LaNet, LaNett, Lanetta, LaNette*

Laney (English) Path, roadway.

Lang (Scandinavian) Tall one.

Langley (English) Long meadow. *Langlee, Langli, Langlie, Langly*

Lani (Hawaiian) Sky; heaven. *Lanni, Lannie*

Lanikai (Hawaiian) Heavenly sea.

Lann (Irish) Blade.

Lanna (English, Irish) Good-looking, beautiful.

Lanni (Irish) Attractive.

Lansing (American) Place name. *Lanseng*

Lantha (Greek) Purple flower. *Lanthe, Lanthia, Lanthina*

Lanza (Italian) Noble and eager.

Lapis (Egyptian) Lapis lazuli; gemstone.

Laquanna (African American) Outspoken. *Kwanna, LaQuanna, LaQwana, Quanna*

Laqueta (African American) Quiet one.

Laquetta (English) Wildflower. *Etta, Quetta*

Laquiesha (American, English) Joyful, happy. *Laquisha*

Laquinta (African American) Fifth.

Laquita (African) Fifth.

Lara (Latin) Well known; name of a nymph. *Laralaine, Laramae*

Laraine (Latin) Sea bird. *Lareine, Larene, Loraine*

Larby (American) Pretty; form of Darby. *Larbee, Larbey, Larbi, Larbie*

Lareina (Greek, Spanish) Seagull; flies over water; queen. *Larayna, Larayne, Lareine, Larena, Larrayna, Larreina*

Lari (English) Crowned with laurel. *Laree, Larey, Larian, Larie, Larriann, Larrie*

Laria (Greek) The stars are mine.

Lariel (Hebrew) Lioness of God. *Lariele, Lariell, Lariella, Lariellah*

Larina (Greek) Seagull.

Larissa (Greek) Cheerful one. *Lareesa, Lareese, Laris, Larisa, Larresa*

Lark (English) Bird. *Larke, Larkin, Lirkin*

Larmina (German) Love. *Larminah, Larmine, Larmyn*

Larsen (Scandinavian) Laurel crowned. *Larson, Larssen, Larsson*

Larue (French) Street. *LaRue*

Larya (Slavic) Crowned with laurel.

Lasar (Irish) Red-haired. *Lasara, Lasarah, Lazer*

Lashawn (African American) God is gracious.

Lashonda (American) God is gracious. *Lala, Lasha, Lashanda, LaShanda, LaShounda*

Lassie (Irish) Young girl, maiden.

Lasthenia (Latin) Herb of Pacific coast of North and South America; golden fields. (Greek) Natural philosopher; one of Plato's female students.

Lata (Hindi) Vine.

Latanya (African American) Fairy queen.

Latara (Irish) Rocky hill. *Latarah, Latarya, Tara*

Latasha (American) Beauty. *Latacha, LaTasha, Latayshah, Latisha*

Latavia (Arabic) Pleasant. *Lataviah*

Lateefah (North African) Gentle; pleasant. *Lateefa, Latifa, Latiffa*

Latifah (African) Elegant. *Lateefa, Latifa, Latiffe, Latifuh*

Latika (Hindi) Small creeper.

Latina (English) Little one. *Lateenah, Latinah, Latyna, Latynah*

Latisha (Latin) Great joy. *Laeticia, Laeticiah, Laetitia*

Latona (Greek) Goddess name. *Latonah, Latonea, Latonia, Leto*

Latonya (African American) Praised woman. *Latonia, LaToya, Tonya*

Latoya (African American, American, Spanish) Praised woman; victorious one. *Latoia, LaToyah, Latoyah, Latoyia, Toyah*

Latreece (American) Go-getter. *Latreese, Letrice*

Latrice (American) Weary; bringer of joy. *Latrecia, Latresh, Trice, Tricey*

Laudine (Scottish) Widow.

Laudomia (Italian) Praise the house. *Laudomiah*

Laura (Latin) Laurel leaves; honor; fame; spirit. *Lauranne, Laure, Laureen, Laurel, Lauren, Laurena, Lauretta, Laurette, Laurie, Laurien, Lauriette, Laurin, Lauryn, Lor, Lora, Lorene, Lorenza, Loretta, Lorette, Lori, Lorin, Lorina, Lorita, Lorna, Lorry, Loryn*

Laurel (English) Crowned with laurel. *Laural, Laurell, Laurella, Laurelle, Lorel, Lorell, Lorella, Lourelle*

Lauren (French) Crowned with laurel. *Laryn, Lauran, Laurene, Lauryn, Laurynn, Lawren, Loren, Lorin, Lorren, Loryn*

Laurentia (Latin) Form of Lauren.

Laurinda (Latin) Crowned with laurel; praise.

Lausanne (Scottish) Lake Geneva.

Lavada (American) Friendly and creative.

Lavani (Hindi) Grace. *Laboni, Lavanee, Lavaney*

Lavanya (Hindi) Grace.

Lave (Italian) Burning rock.

Laveda (Latin) Innocent one. *Lavella, Lavetta, Lavette, Levita*

Lavender (English) Purple-flowering plant. *Lavenda*

Laverne (French) From the alder grove; springlike. *La Verne, Lally, Verna, Verne*

Lavey (Hebrew) Joined, attracted; from Levi.

Lavi (Hebrew) Lion.

Lavina (Latin) Woman of Rome. *Lavania, Lavena, Lavenah, Lavyna*

Lavinia (Latin) Purity. *Lavin, Lavine, Leveniah, Lovina*

Lavita (African American) Life. *Laveeda, Lavitah*

Lavonn (American) Wood. *Lavaughan, Lavaughn, Lavon, Lavone, Lavonna, Lavonnah, Lavonne*

Lawanda (American) Little wanderer. *LaWanda, Lawandah, Lawonda*

Lawann (Thai) Purity. *Lawane*

Lawrence (Latin) Crowned with laurel.

Laxmi (Hindi) Meaning unknown.

Layaleeta (Australian) Ocean. *Laialeeta*

Layla (African) Dark beauty; born at night. *Laela, Laila, Lala, Laya, Laylah, Laylie, Leila*

Layna (Greek) Light; truth. *Laenah, Laina, Lainah, Laynie*

Lazalea (Greek) Ruling eagle. *Lazaleah, Lazalee, Lazaley*

Le (Chinese) Joy. *Lei, Ley*

Lea (Hebrew) Meadow. *Aleah, Aleia, Leaha, Lyah*

Leah (Hebrew) Weary. *Lea, Leatrice, Lee, Lia, Liah*

Leala (French) Loyal one. *Lealah, Lealia, Lealie*

Leandra (Greek) Lion woman. *Leandrea, Leanndra, Leeandra*

Leane (English) Gracious plum.

LeAnn (English) Light; form of Helen.

Leann (Latin) Youthful.

Leanna (English) Graceful willow. *Leana, Leeann, Leeanne, Leianna, Liana, Lianne*

Leanne (English) Graceful plum.

Leanore (English) Torch. *Lenorah, Lenore, Leonora, Leonore*

Leatrix (American) Weary; bringer of joy.

Leauna (Latin) Young deer.

Leba (Yiddish) Beloved.

Lecea (American) Of noble birth.

Lecia (Latin) Happy. *Leecia, Leeciah, Leecy, Leecya*

Leda (Greek) Mother Creator. *Ledah, Leyda, Lida, Lidah, Lita*

Ledah (Hebrew) Birth. *Leda*

Ledell (Greek) Spartan queen.

Lee (Old English) Glade. (Gaelic) Poet. (English) Sheltered from the storm.

(Irish) Poetic. (Chinese) Plum. *Lea, Leanne, Leeanne, Leigh Anne, Leigh, Li, Ly*

Leeann (English) Light; beautiful; woman.

Leeba (Hebrew) Heart.

Leelea (Sanskrit) Meaning unknown.

Leena (Russian) Illumination. *Lena, Lina*

Leetefa (Arabic) Delicate flower, sensitive. *Ketifa, Lateiffa, Latifa, Latifah*

Leewan (Australian) Wind. *Leewana, Leiwanah, Leywana, Liwana*

Leeza (Hebrew) Devoted to God. *Leesa*

Lehana (African) One who refuses.

Lehua (Hawaiian) Sacred.

Lei (Chinese) Flower bud.

Leia (Hebrew) Weary.

Leighanna (English) Gracious; poetic.

Leighna (American) Illustrious.

Leiko (Japanese) Arrogant.

Leila (Arabic) Dark as the night. *Laila, Layla, Leilia, Lela, Lila, Lillah, Lyla*

Leilana (Hawaiian) Heavenly flowers.

Leili (Hebrew) Night. *Lailie, Laylie, Leilie*

Leire (Hebrew) Wished for. *Leira, Leyra, Leyrah*

Leisel (German) Place in the district of Birkenfield in Rhineland-Palatinate.

Lela (Spanish) Lofty.

Leli (Swiss) From the high tower. *Lely, Lelya, Lelyah*

Lella (Latin) Lily.

Lemuela (Hebrew) Devoted to God. *Lemuelah, Lemuella, Lemuellah*

Lena (Hebrew) Dwelling. *Lenore, Leonne, Leonora, Leonore, Lina*

Lenci (Hungarian) Light. *Lencee, Lencey, Lencia, Lencie*

Lene (Norwegian) Illustrious.

Leni (Latin) Shining light. *Lenie, Lennee, Lenni, Leny*

Lenka (Slavic) Illumination.

Lenna (German) Strength of a lion. *Lenda, Lennah*

Lenora (Spanish) Brave as a lioness; from Leona.

Lenore (Greek) Light. *Lenor, Lenora*

Lenya (Russian) Lion.

Leola (Latin) Lion. *Leona, Leonarda, Leontine, Leontyne*

Leolani (Hawaiian) Tall.

Leoma (German) Brave woman.

Leona (German) Lioness. *Leonia, Leonie, Leonissa, Leonissah*

Leonani (Hawaiian) Beautiful voice.

Leonora (Greek) Light.

Leontyne (French) Like a lion.

Leopolda (Old German) Bold leader. *Leopoldine*

Leora (Hebrew) Light. *Leeora, Leorah, Liora, Liorah*

Leosa (Science fiction) Character from *Star Trek Voyager.*

Leotie (Native American) Flower of the prairie.

Lequoia (Native American) From the Sequoia tree.

Lera (Russian) Strong, brave. *Lerah, Leria, Leriah*

Lerato (African) Love.

Lesa (American) Consecrated to God.

Lesh (French) To restrain.

Lesley (Scottish) Gray fortress. *Lesle, Lesli, Leslie, Lesly, Leslye, Lezlie*

Leslie (Scottish) Dweller in the gray castle. (Old English) Small meadow. *Lee, Les, Lesley, Lesly*

Leta (Latin) Joy. (Swahili) Bringer. (Greek) Small with wings. *Leeta, Lita*

Letha (Greek) Forgetful; oblivion. *Leda, Leitha, Leithia, Leta, Lethia*

Lethia (Greek) Forgetfulness.

Leticia (Latin) Joy; gladness. *Letecia, Letisha, Letitia, Lettice, Tiesha*

Letitia (Latin) Joy. *Laetitia, Latasha, Laticia, Leetice, Leta, Letice, Leticia, Letizia, Letty, Letycia, Ticia, Tish*

Letricia (Latin) Noble. *Letriciah, Letricya*

Levana (Latin) Rising sun. *Levanna, Livana, Livna*

Levia (Hebrew) Combined forces.

Lewa (African) Beautiful.

Lewana (Hebrew) Moon. *Lewanna*

Lexi (Greek) Protector of mankind. *Lexia, Lexie, Lexsis, Lexus, Lexuss, Lexxus*

Lexine (Hebrew) Helper and defender of mankind.

Lexis (English) Protector of mankind.

Lexus (Brand name) Make of car. *Lexorus, Lexsis, Lexxus*

Leya (Spanish) Loyalty. *Leyah*

Leyna (Old German) Little angel. *Lenya, Leyns*

Leyza Origin and meaning unknown.

Li (Chinese) Pretty; powerful.

Li Hua (Chinese) Pear blossom.

Li Mei (Chinese) Pretty rose.

Li Ming (Chinese) Pretty and bright.

Lia (Hebrew) Dependence. *Li, Liah*

Liadan (Irish) Gray lady.

Lian (Chinese) Graceful willow. *Leane, Leanne, Liane*

Liana (Hebrew) Vine; to bind; youth. *Leana, Liane, Lianna, Lianne*

Liani (Spanish) Daughter of the sun; form of Elaina.

Liannaka (Dutch) Bringer of peace; hope. *Anna, Lan, Lani, Lanna*

Libba (Hebrew) Consecrated to God; from Elizabeth. *Libbi*

Libby (Hebrew) Consecrated to God. *Libi, Lybbi*

Libe (Hebrew) Love. *Liba, Libbe, Libbeh, Libi*

Liberty (English) Freedom. *Libby*

Libra (Latin) Scales; equality.

Licha (Spanish) Nobility.

Licia (Latin) Happy.

Lida (Russian) Beloved by all. *Leedah, Lidah, Lyda*

Lidia (Greek) From Lydia, an ancient Asian land. *Lydia*

Lidiva Origin and meaning unknown.

Lidwina (Scandinavian) Friend of the people.

Lien (Chinese) Lotus. *Lien Hua*

Lieneke (Dutch) Goddess of joy.

Liese (German) Beloved by God. *Lieselotte, Liesl*

Liesel (German) Dedicated and gracious. *Leesel, Leezel, Leizl, Liesa, Liesl, Lisel, Lisl*

Lieu (Vietnamese) Willow tree.

Lil' Kim (American) Rapper born Kimberly Denise Jones.

Lila (Arabic) Night.

Lilac (Sanskrit) Lilac blossom; blue-purple.

Lilah (Arabic) Night.

Lilia (Slavic) Lilac. *Lileah, Lyleah, Lylia*

Liliana (Latin) Lily flower. (English) Flower; innocence, purity; beauty.

Lilianna (Latin) Gracious lily.

Liliha (Hawaiian) Angry; disregard.

Lilika (Greek) Lily flower.

Lilike (Hungarian) Lily flower.

Lilis (Hebrew) Spirit of the night. *Lilisa, Liliss, Lilisse, Lillis, Lyliss*

Lilith (Arabic) Of the night; night demon. *Lily, Lilyth*

Lilka (Polish) Warrior maiden.

Lillian (English) Combination of Lily and Ann. *Lilian, Liliana, Lilias, Lillia, Lillianne, Lilyanne*

Lilliana (Latin) Lily flower.

Lillias (Latin) Lily.

Lilo (Hawaiian) Generous one. *Lilow*

Lilovarti (African) Joyfulness.

Liluye (Native American) Singing hawk while soaring.

Lily (Latin) A flower. *Lil, Lili, Lilia, Lilian, Liliana, Lilianne, Lilias, Lillie, Lilly, Lily Ann, Lis*

Limber (African) Joyfulness.

Lin (Chinese) Beautiful; jade. *Linn, Lynn*

Lina (Greek) Tender; light of spirit. *Lena, Linah*

Linaeve (American) Tree of song.

Linda (Spanish) Pretty. *Belinda, Lin, Linden, Lynda*

Lindie (Spanish) Beautiful. *Lindey, Lindi, Lindy, Lyndi, Lyndy*

Lindley (English) Pasture.

Lindsay (Old English) Linden Tree Island. *Lindsey, Lindy, Lindzee, Linsey, Lyndsay, Lyndsey, Lyndsy, Lynsey*

Linette (Middle French) Linnet bird; flaxen. *Lanette, Linet, Linnet, Lynette*

Ling (Chinese) Tinkling pieces of jade.

Linh (Vietnamese) Gentle spirit.

Linne (English) Waterfall.

Linnea (Scandinavian) Lime tree. *Lin, Linayah, Linea, Linnay, Lynnea*

Linore (Greek) From Lenore.

Liolya (Russian) Shining light. *Liolia, Lioliah, Lyolya*

Liona (Italian) Lioness.

Liora (Hebrew) Light. (English) Laurel tree.

Lirit (Hebrew) Musical grace. *Lirita, Lirite, Lyrit, Lyrite*

Lis (Scandinavian) Consecrated to God. *Lys*

Lisa (Hebrew) Consecrated to God. *Lisetta, Lisette, Liza*

Lisabet (English) God of plenty; form of Elizabeth.

Lisanor (Scottish) In Arthurian legend, a damsel.

Lisbet (Hebrew) From Elizabeth.

Lise (German) Consecrated to God.

Lisea (Hebrew) Consecrated to God. *Lesa*

Liseli (Native American) Meaning unknown.

Lisette (French) Devoted to God. *Lissette*

Lisimba (African) Lion.

Lisle (French) Of the island.

Lisolette (Scandinavian) Little and strong; form of Caroline; form of Liselette.

Lita (Latin) Light.

Litonya (Native American) Hummingbird darting.

Litsa (Greek) One who brings good news.

Litzy (Scandinavian) Devoted to God.

Liv (Norwegian) Life. *Leev*

Livana (Greek) Goddess. *Livania, Livanna, Livanya*

Livanga (African) Think before you act.

Livi (Latin) Olive branch; peace.

Livia (Hebrew) From Olivia.

Livvy (Greek) From Oliver.

Lixue (Chinese) Pretty snow.

Liz (English) Consecrated to God; form of Elizabeth. *Lis, Lizzi, Lizzy*

Liza (Hebrew) Consecrated to God. *Leeza, Lizah, Lyza*

Lizbeth (Hebrew) From Elizabeth.

Lizeth (Hebrew) Devoted to God.

Lizette (English) God of plenty; form of Elizabeth.

Lizina (Slavic) Consecrated to God. *Lyzina, Lyzinah*

Llamrei (Scottish) In Arthurian legend, Arthur's horse.

Llawella (Welsh) Leader. *Lawella*

Llewellyn (Welsh) Like a lion.

Lluvia (Spanish) Rain.

Loan (Vietnamese) Meaning unknown.

Loba (African) To talk.

Locke (Old English) Stronghold.

Lockett (French) Keepsake. *Locket, Lockete, Locketta, Lockettah*

Loe (Hawaiian) King.

Logan (Scottish) Little hollow. *Logun*

Lois (Hebrew) Better. (French) Renowned fighter (German) Warrior. *Loes*

Lokapela (Hawaiian) Beautiful rose.

Lokelani (Hawaiian) Small red rose.

Loki (Scandinavian) Trickster god.

Lola (Spanish) Strong woman. *Lolita*

Lolaksi (Hindi) Sakti (power, energy) of Ganesha.

Lolita (Spanish) Manly; form of Carlos. *Loleeta, Loleetah, Loletah*

Lolotea (African) Gift. *Lolotee, Loloti, Lolotie*

Lolovivi (African) Love is sweet.

Lomasi (Native American) Pretty flower.

Lona (English) Lioness; ready for battle. *Lonee, Lonna*

London (English) Fortress of the moon.

Loni (English) Lion.

Lonikie (Dutch) Pretty one.

Lonna (Slavic) Light.

Lora (Latin) Laurel-crowned. *Lorra, Lorrah*

Lorand (Hungarian) Crowned with laurel. *Lorant*

Lore (Basque) Flower. *Lorre*

Lorelei (German) From the Rhine River.

Lorelle (American) Form of Laurel.

Lorena (English) Crowned with laurel. *Loren, Lorren, Lorron, Lorryn, Loryn*

Lorene (American) Small victories.

Loretta (English) Small, wise one. *Lauretta, Lorretta*

Lori (Latin) Crowned with laurel. *Laurie, Loree, Lorie, Lory*

Lorinda (Latin) Crowned with laurel. *Larinda, Lorenda*

Loring (French) Famous in war.

Loris (Dutch) Clown. *Chloris, Loriss, Lorysse*

Lorna (Celtic) Of Lorne. *Lorenah*

Lorraine (Old German) Where Lothar dwells. *Loretta, Lorette, Lori, Lorna, Lorne, Lorrie, Lorry*

Losa (Polynesian) Rose. *Losana, Lose*

Losira (Science fiction) Character from *Star Trek*.

Lotta (Latin) Petite beauty.

Lotte (German) Little and strong; old-fashioned; from Charlotte. *Lottee, Lotti, Lotty*

Lottie (Latin) Petite beauty.

Lotus (Greek) Dreamlike; lotus flower.

Louanna (German) Gracious warrior.

Louhi (Finnish) Mythology; goddess of death; snake.

Louisa (German) Fights with honor.

Louise (Old German) Warrior maiden. *Aloysia, Eloisa, Eloise, Lisette, Liusadh, Lois, Loise, Lou, Louisa, Louisiana, Loyce, Lu, Luana, Luane, Luisa, Luise, Lulie, Lulu, Luwana, Ouisa, Ouise*

Lourdes (French) Place name; section of France where Virgin Mary was seen. *Lordes, Lordez*

Louvain (Belguim) Place name.

Love (Old English) Loved one. *Lovie, Luv*

Lovette (English) Little loved one.

Lovey (American) Loved one. *Lovie*

Lowri (Welsh) Crowned with laurels.

Luana (German) Graceful battle maiden. (Hawaiian) Content; peaceful.

Luba (Russian) Lover. *Liba, Lubah, Lyuba*

Luca (Italian) Bringer of light.

Luce (Latin) Light.

Lucetta (French) Bringer of light; illumination.

Lucia (Italian) Light.

Luciana (Italian, Latin) Illumination; light.

Lucie (French) From Lucille.

Lucille (Latin) Light. *Loucil, Loucile, Loucille, Lucile, Lucyl, Lusille*

Lucina (German) Goddess of childbirth. *Lucena, Lucinah, Lucyna*

Lucinda (Latin) Bringer of light. *Lucinda, Lucinde, Lukene*

Lucine (Armenian) Moon.

Lucky (American) Fortunate; light. *Luckie*

Lucrece (Latin) Bringer of light.

Lucretia (Latin) Riches. *Lucrece, Lucrezia, Lucy*

Lucy (Latin) Light. *Lou, Lu, Luce, Lucette, Lucia, Luciana, Lucianna, Lucianne, Lucida, Lucie, Lucienne, Lucile, Lucille, Luz, Luza*

Ludmila (Czech) Loving people. *Lidmila, Ludmilla, Ludmillah, Lyudmila*

Luella (Old English) Elfin. *Loella, Louella, Luelle*

Luisa (Spanish) Warrior; form of Louis. *Louisa, Luisah, Luiza, Luysa*

Lujuana (Spanish) Renowned warrior. *Lu*

Luka (Latin) Light.

Lukina (Ukrainian) Graceful and bright.

Lula (Arabic) Pearl.

Lulani (Hawaiian) Heaven's peak.

Lulu (African, Arabic) Pearl.

Lumina (Latin) Of the light; glowing.

Luna (Latin) Moon. *Lune, Lunetta*

Lundy (Scandinavian) By the island. *Lundee, Lundi, Lundrea*

Lunette (French) Little moon.

Lupe (Latin) Wolf.

Lupita (Spanish) From Guadalupe.

Lurleen (German) Place name. *Lura, Lurlene, Lurline*

Lux (Spanish) Light.

Luyu (Native American) Wild dove.

Luz (Spanish) Light. *Luzi, Luzie*

Ly (Vietnamese) Reason.

Lyanne (Greek) Melodious. *Liann, Lianne, Lyan, Lyana, Lyaneth, Lyann*

Lycorida (Greek) Twilight; form of Lycoris.

Lycoris (Greek) Twilight.

Lydia (Greek) Woman from Persia; beauty. *Lidia, Lydie*

Lydie (Greek) Maiden from Lydia, Greece.

Lykaios (Greek) Wolfish, of a wolf, wolflike.

Lyla (French) From the island. *Lila, Lilah*

Lyle (French) From the island. *Lile*

Lyn (American) Beautiful.

Lynda (American, English) Beautiful. *Linda, Lindi, Lynde, Lynn*

Lynde (English) From the hill of linden trees.

Lyndon (English) Flexible.

Lyndsay (English) From Linden Tree Island. *Lindsay, Lyndsey*

Lynelle (American) Pretty. *Linelle, Lynel*

Lyneth (Welsh) Beautiful one.

Lynette (English) Bird; little beauty. *Linett, Lynet, Lynnet*

Lynley (English) Meadow near the brook.

Lynn (Anglo-Saxon) Cascade.

Lynna (English) Waterfall.

Lynnea (Latin) Pretty.

Lynsey (American) From the linden tree.

Lynton (English) Town near the brook.

Lynx (American) Wild cat. *Linx*

Lyonesse (Irish) Little lion.

Lyra (Greek) Song; expression of emotion.

Lyric (Greek) Melodic word. *Liric, Lirick, Lirique, Lyrec*

Lyris (Greek) Harp; lyre. *Liris, Lirisa, Lirise, Lyre*

Lysa (German) From Lisa.

Lysandra (Greek) One who is freed. *Lisandra, Lisandrah, Lysanna*

Lysette (American) Pretty little one. *Lysett*

Lysia (Hebrew) Consecrated to God.

M

M. C. Lyte (American) Rapper born Lana Michele Moorer.

Mab (Gaelic) Joy, happiness; intoxicating one; queen in legend. *Mabinna, Mabley, Mave, Mavis*

Mabel (Latin) Lovable. *Amabel, Mabel, Mabella, Mabil, Mabry, Maibelle, Maybelle, Maybelline*

Mabyn (Welsh) Ever young.

Macalla (Australian) Full moon. *Macala, Macalah*

Macaria (Greek) Daughter of Hercules and Deianara; blessed. *Macariah, Macaryah*

Macayle (Hebrew) Who is like God; form of Michaela.

Macha (Native American) Aurora.

Machi (Japanese) Ten thousand.

Machiko (Japanese) Child of Machi; fortunate one.

Mackenna (Irish) Child of the handsome one. *Makena, Makenah, Makenna, Mikenah*

Mackenzie (Irish) Child of the wise leader. *Mackensi, Mackenze, Mackenzey, Mackenzi, Mykenzie*

Macra (Greek) Long-living. *Macrah*

Macy (Polish) Sea of bitterness. *Mace, Macey, Macie*

Mada (English) High tower. *Madah, Madda, Maddah, Maida*

Madalena (Greek) From Madeline; high tower; jaunty. *Madaleyna, Madalyna, Madelayna, Madelen, Madeleyna, Madelyna*

Maddox (Welsh) Lucky. *Maddax, Maddee, Maddux*

Madeira (Spanish, Portuguese) Sweet wine; island off the African coast.

Madelia (Greek) High tower.

Madeline (Greek) High tower. (Hebrew) Woman from Magdala; form of Magdalene. *Lena, Lene, Madalena, Madalynn, Maddalena, Maddie, Maddy, Madelaine, Madeleine, Madelon, Madelyn, Madelynne, Madigan, Madleen, Madlin, Mady, Mae, Magda, Magdalen, Magdalena, Magdalene, Magdaline, Maigarena, Maighdlin, Mala, Malina, Marleen, Marlena, Marlene, Marline, Matty, Maudlin, May, Mayalen*

Madge (Greek) Pearl. *Madgie*

Madhavi (Hindi) Creeper with beautiful flowers; springtime.

Madhu (Hindi) Honey.

Madhul (Hindi) Sweet.

Madhulika (Hindi) Nectar.

Madhur (Hindi) Sweet.

Madhuri (Hindi) Sweet girl; sweet; sweetness.

Madison (English) Good; child of Maud. *Maddison, Maddy, Madissen, Madisyn*

Madja (Danish) Meaning unknown.

Madonna (Latin) My lady.

Madra (Spanish) Mother. *Madonna, Madraye, Madre, Madreah, Madrona*

Mae (English) Flower; month of May. (Latin) Great. *May*

Maegan (Irish) Pearl.

Maeko (Japanese) Truthful child.

Maemi (Japanese) Honest child.

Maeron (Irish) Bitter.

Maeryn (Gaelic) Bitter.

Maeve (Irish) Joyous. (Celtic) Queen. (Greek) Goddess of song. (Latin) Purple flower. *Maeva, Maive, Mave, Mayve*

Magan (Hindi) Absorbed. (Teutonic) Power. (Greek) Competent. *Magahn, Magana*

Magara (Rhodesian) Child who constantly cries.

Magda (Hebrew) High tower; one who is elevated.

Magdalen (Greek) High tower. (Hebrew) Woman from Magdala. *Magdala, Magdalena, Magdalene, Magdalina, Magdalone, Magdelena, Magdelina*

Magena (Hebrew) Covering; protection. (Native American) Coming moon. *Magenna*

Maggie (English) Pearl. *Maggi, Maggy*

Magna (Latin) Strength. (Norse) Large. *Magnea, Magnilda*

Magnolia (Latin) Flower; flowering tree. *Magnole, Magnolea*

Maha (African) Beautiful eyes.

Mahal (Polynesian) Love. *Mahala, Mahalah*

Mahala (Hebrew) Woman; tenderness; marrow. (Hawaiian) Woman; tenderness. (Native American) Woman. (Arabic) Powerful. *Mahalar, Mahalia, Mahela, Mahelia, Mehala*

Mahalath (Arabic) Lyre.

Mahalia (Hebrew) Affection. *Mahaliah, Mehaliah*

Mahari (African) Forgiver.

Mahdi (African) Expected one.

Mahdis (Persian) Moonlike.

Mahima (Hindi) Greatness.

Mahina (Hawaiian) Moon.

Mahira (Hebrew) Energy. *Mahirah, Mahyra*

Mahita (Hindi) Honorable.

Mahla (Hebrew) Polished. *Mahlah*

Mahogany (English) Dark wood. *Mahagonie, Mahoganey, Mahogony*

Mahola (Hebrew) Dance.

Mahsa (Persian) Like the moon.

Mahubeh (Arabic) Good greeting; good fortune; form of Mahubah.

Mahwah (Native American) Beautiful.

Mai (Japanese) Brightness. (Native American) Coyote. (Vietnamese) Flower. *Maie*

Maia (Greek) Mother; nurse. (English) Maiden. *Maea, Maiah, Maya*

Maida (Old English) Maiden. *Mady, Maidel, Maidie, Maidy, Mayda*

Maik (Hawaiian) Now.

Maiko (Japanese) Child of Mai.

Mailee (English) From the wished-for-one's meadow. *Marilea, Marilia, Maryleigh*

Maili (Polynesian) Gentle breeze.

Maille (Gaelic) Sea of bitterness; form of Molly.

Maimi (Japanese) Smile of truth. *Maimee, Maymee*

Maimun (Arabic) Lucky.

Maina (Hindi) Bird.

Maine (French) Mainland. *Mayne*

Maire (Irish) Bitter. *Mair, Maira, Mairah, Mayr, Mayre*

Mairead (Scottish) Pearl. *Maired, Mared*

Mairi (Gaelic) Sea of bitterness; version of Mary.

Mairwen (Welsh) Fair; version of Mary.

Maisha (African) Life.

Maisie (Gaelic) Pearl. *Maesee, Maesey, Maesi, Maesie, Maesy, Maisee, Maisey, Maisi, Maisy, Maize, Maizie, Margaret, Marjorie, Maysie, Mazee, Mazey, Mysie*

Maitane (English) Dearly loved. (Spanish) Darling; beloved.

Maitea (Spanish) Love. *Maite, Maitena*

Maitland (English) Meadow. *Maitlande, Mateland, Matelande, Matylande, Maytland*

Maitryi (Hindi) Friendship. *Maitri*

Maizah (African, Arabic) Discerning.

Maj (Swedish) Pearl.

Maja (Arabic) Splendid. *Majid, Majida, Majyd*

Majondra (Spanish) Meaning unknown. *Jondra, Maj, Majie*

Maka (Native American) Earth.

Makaila (American) Who is like God.

Makaio (Hawaiian) Gift of God.

Makala (Hawaiian) Shrub.

Makana (Hawaiian) Gift.

Makani (Hawaiian) Wind. *Makanee, Makanie*

Makara (Hindi) Born under Capricorn.

Makayla (American) Who is like God. *Micaelah, Micaele, Micala, Michaela*

Makeena (American) Child of the wise; from McKenna.

Makelina (Hawaiian) From Magdelene.

Makiko (Japanese) Child of Maki.

Makya (Native American) One who hunts eagles.

Mala (Greek) High tower; form of Magdelene.

Malachite (English) Precious gem.

Malaika (African) Angel.

Malana (Hawaiian) Light.

Malania (Greek) Dark-haired. *Melanian, Mellani, Mellenie, Melonia*

Malati (Hindi) Small, fragrant flower; jasmine flower. *Malti*

Malavika (Hindi) From Malva.

Malaya (Filipino) Free. *Malae, Malaia, Malaine, Malayna*

Malca (Hebrew) Queen. *Malcah, Malka*

Maleah (Hawaiian) Bitter.

Malha (Hebrew) Queen. *Maliah, Miliah*

Mali (Southeast Asian) Flower; smart; funny; lucky. *Mal, Malee, Maley, Malie, Malley, Mallie, Maly*

Malia (Hawaiian) Calm and peaceful. *Maylia*

Maliha (Hindi) Strong; beautiful. (Arabic) Pretty; good-looking. *Hala, Malha, Mali*

Malika (Arabic) Queen; princess. (Slavic) Industrious. (Sanskrit) Garland. *Malak, Malik, Malikah*

Malila (Native American) Salmon going fast upstream.

Malin (Scandinavian) Woman from Magdela.

Malina (Hebrew) Tower. (Native American) Soothing. *Malinah, Malini, Malinna, Malyna*

Malinda (Greek) Gentle. *Malindah, Malynda, Malyndah*

Malinza (Science fiction) Character from *Star Wars*.

Malise (Celtic) Black; dark.

Malissa (Greek) Honey bee.

Malka (Hebrew) Queen. *Malkah, Malkeh, Malkya*

Malkia (African) Queen.

Mallika (Hindi) Jasmine. *Malika*

Malloren (American) Laurel of bad luck.

Mallory (French) Without good fortune. (German) Army counselor. *Mal, Malin, Mallorey, Mallorie, Mally, Malori, Malory*

Mallow (Irish) By the river Allo.

Malti (Hindi) Small, fragrant flower.

Malu (Hawaiian) Peacefulness.

Malva (Greek) Tender. *Malvah*

Malvina (Scottish) Armored chief. *Mal, Mally, Malva, Malvie, Mel, Mellen, Melly, Melvina, Melvine, Mevin*

Mamie (English) Bitter. *Mamee, Mamey, Mami, Mamy*

Mamiko (Japanese) Child of Mami.

Mamta (Hindi) Mother's love for child; wife of sage Asija.

Mana (Japanese) Sensitive. *Manah, Manal, Manali*

Manar (Arabic) Guiding light. *Manaar, Manara*

Manasa (Hindi) Mind.

Manasi (Hindi) Born of the mind. *Manasie*

Manavi (Hindi) Wife of Manu.

Manchu (Chinese) Purity.

Manda (Spanish) Warrior. *Mandakini*

Mandana (Persian) Everlasting.

Mandara (Hindi) Mythical tree; calm.

Mandeep (Hindi) Light of heart.

Mandel (German) Almond. *Mandell*

Mandelina (American) Lovable.

Mandisa (African) Sweet.

Manette (French) Little wished for.

Mangaia (Polynesian) Peace. *Mangaea, Mangaiah*

Mangena (Hebrew) Melody.

Manhattan (American) Place name. (English) Whiskey. *Maisie, Manda, Manny*

Manisha (Hindi) Sharp intellect, genius; sagacity.

Manjari (Hindi) Sacred basil; blossom.

Manju (Hindi) Sweet.

Manjula (Hindi) Sweet.

Manjusha (Hindi) Treasure chest. (Sanskrit) Box of jewels.

Manon (French) Bitter. *Manona*

Manoush (Arabic) Sweet sun.

Mansi (Native American) Plucked flower. *Mancee, Mancey, Manci*

Manuela (Spanish) God is with us. *Manuel, Manuele, Manuelita, Manuella, Manuelle*

Manushi (Hindi) Human.

Manya (Russian) Wished for. *Mania, Maniah*

Manyara (African) You have been humbled.

Mapiya (Native American) Sky; heavenly. *Mapiyah*

Mara (Greek) Eternally beautiful. (Hebrew) Melody. *Marah, Marra*

Marabel (English) Wished for. *Marabela, Marabell, Marabelle*

Marayna (Science fiction) Character from *Star Trek: Voyager*.

Marcella (Latin) God of war; little hammer. *Marcelin, Marceline, Marcelle, Marciana, Marcie, Marclyn, Marcy*

Marcia (Latin) Martial, warlike; brave. *Marcelia, Marcey, Marchette, Marchita, Marci, Marcie, Marcille, Marcy, Marquita, Marsha, Marshe, Marsi, Marsie, Marsy, Martia, Marzia*

Mardell (English) From the meadow. *Mardela, Mardelah, Mardele*

Marden (English) From the valley marsh. *Mardana, Mardene*

Mardi (French) Tuesday.

Mareel (Science fiction) Character from *Star Trek: Deep Space Nine*.

Maren (Latin) Sea; of the sea; bitter. *Marin, Marren, Marrin*

Maretta (Hebrew) Bitter. *Marella, Mari, Mariette, Marit, Mary*

Margaret (Greek, Persian, Hebrew, Irish, Latin) Child of light; pearl; jewel. *Garet, Greta, Gretchen, Grete, Gretel, Gretle, Madge, Maergrethe, Mag, Magee, Maggie, Maggy, Mairghread, Maisie, Mamie, Marga, Margalith, Margalo, Margareta, Margaretha, Margarethe, Margarida, Margarita, Margaux, Marge, Margery, Marget, Margette, Margherita, Margiad, Margie, Margita, Margo, Margory, Margot, Margret, Marguerite, Marjoe, Marjorie, Marjory, Marta, Maymie, Meg, Meggie, Midge, Peg, Peggy, Reta, Rita*

Marge (American) Pearl. *Marg*

Margo (French) Pearl. *Margeaux, Margot*

Mari (Japanese) Ball. *Maree*

Maria (Hebrew) Bitter; the star of the sea. *Malia, Mar, Mariah, Marie, Mary, Marya, Ri*

Mariabella (Italian) Beautiful. *Mariabelle, Maribel, Maribelle, Mary*

Mariah (Hebrew) Bitter; star of the sea; God is my teacher. *Mariaha, Mariahna*

Mariam (Hebrew) Wife of Herod; bitter; mother of Jesus; wished-for child. *Mariama, Mariamne*

Marianne (French) Little; bitter. *Maire, Manya, Mara, Marian, Mariana, Mariann, Marianna, Marilyn, Marion, Marisha, Marrion, Mary, Mary-Ann, Maryanne*

Mariasha (Egyptian) Perfect one. (Hebrew) Bitter with sorrow.

Maribel (French) Beautiful. *Maribella, Maribelle*

Marice (Greek) Marsh flower. *Maryce*

Maricel (Latin) Full of grace. *Mar, Marcella, Maricelle*

Maridel (English) Beautiful; bitter.

Marie (French) Bitter. *Maree, Mary*

Mariel (German) Bitter. *Maretta, Marette, Mariella, Marielle, Marietta, Mariette*

Marietta (Italian) Little; bitter; star of the sea. *Marieta, Maryeta, Maryetta*

Marigold (Greek) Flower; mother of Jesus. *Golda, Goldie, Mari*

Marika (Dutch) Wished for. *Maricah, Marijke, Marique*

Mariko (Japanese) Child of Mari; circle.

Marilee (Greek) Bitterness; God is with us. *Marilea, Mary Lee*

Marilla (Hebrew) Wished for. *Marila, Marilah*

Marilyn (Hebrew) Descendent of Mary. *Maralyn, Marilynne, Marylynn*

Marina (Latin) Sea maiden. *Marena, Marin*

Marinette Origin and meaning unknown.

Marini (Swahili) Healthy; pretty. *Marinee, Marinie*

Marinka (Russian) Of the sea. *Marina*

Marinna (Australian) Song. *Marrinah*

Mariola (Spanish) Wild field plant from Texas.

Marion (French) Bitter; star of the sea. *Mariana, Mariano*

Mariposa (Spanish) Butterfly. *Mariposah, Maryposa*

Maris (Latin) Of the sea. *Marice, Marys, Meris*

Marisa (Spanish) Of the sea; bitter. *Marce, Maressa, Marissa, Marisse, Mariza, Marsie, Marysa, Maryssa, Merisa*

Marisol (Spanish) Sunny sea. *Marysol*

Marissa (Latin) Of the sea. *Maressa, Mari, Marina, Maris, Marisa, Marissah, Maritza, Merisa, Merrisa, Rissa*

Maritza (German) Of the sea. *Maritsa, Maritzah*

Marjani (African) Coral.

Marjeta (Czech) Pearl.

Marjolaine (French) Marjoram. *Marjolain, Marjolayn*

Marjorie (Greek) Pearl. *Marcail, Marge, Margery, Margey, Margie, Margo, Marjary, Marje, Marjorey, Marjory, Marjy*

Marla (English) Star of the sea. *Magdala, Marlah*

Marlee (Australian) Elder tree. *Marleigh, Marley, Marli, Marlie, Marly*

Marlene (Greek) Child of light; from the high tower. *Lena, Lene, Madeline, Marla, Marleen, Marlena, Marlie, Marline, Marly*

Marley (English) Marshy meadow; woman from Magdala. *Marlene*

Marliss (English) Woman of Magdala. *Marla, Marlene, Molly*

Marlo (English) Wished-for child. *Marlow, Marlowe*

Marmara (Greek) Radiant. *Marmarah*

Marna (Hebrew) Rejoice. *Marne, Marnette, Marni, Marnie, Marny*

Marnina (Hebrew) Cause of joy. *Marneena, Marnyna*

Marny (Scandinavian) From the sea.

Maroula (Greek) Wished for. *Maroulah*

Marquise (French) Noble. *Markese, Marquese*

Marquita (French) Canopy. *Marquia, Marquitta*

Marsala (Italian) Town; sweet, fortified wine.

Marsena (Hebrew) Bitterness of a bramble.

Marta (Arabic) Lady; mistress; bitter; pearl.

Martha (Aramaic) Lady; mistress; who becomes bitter; provoking. *Marella, Marta, Marth, Marthe, Marti, Martina, Martita, Marty, Masia, Mattie, Matty*

Martina (Latin) Warlike; who loves everyone; warring. *Marta, Martin, Martine, Marty, Tina*

Maru (Polynesian) Gentle.

Maruti (Hindi) Lord Hanuman.

Marvelle (French) Miracle. *Marva, Marvel, Marvell, Marvella*

Marvina (French) Famous friend. *Marvinah*

Mary (Hebrew) Bitter; rebellion. *Madonna, Mair, Maire, Mairi, Mairin, Mally, Mame, Mamie, Manette, Manon, Mara, Mare, Marel, Marella, Maren, Maretta, Mari, Maria, Marian, Mariath, Marie, Marieta, Mariette, Marija, Marika, Marilla, Mariya, Marla, Marlo, Marquita, Marya, Mash, Masha, Mashia, Maura, Maure, Maureen, May, Mayme, Maymie, Meriel, Merry, Mimi, Minette, Minnie, Minny, Miriam, Mitzi, Moira, Moire, Molly, Moya, Muire, Muriel, Polly*

Masago (Japanese) Sand. *Massago*

Masako (Japanese) Child of Masa; justice.

Matana (Hebrew) Gift. (Arabic) Blessing. *Matanah, Matania, Matannia*

Matangi (Hindi) Devi.

Mathea (Hebrew) Gift of God. *Mathia, Mattea, Matthea*

Mathilda (German) Battle maiden; strength; strong in war. *Maddie, Maddy, Maitilde, Mala, Matelda, Mathilde, Mathylda, Matilda, Mattie, Matty, Mattye, Tila, Tilda, Tillie, Tilly*

Matrika (Hindi) Mother; name of goddess. *Matrica, Matricka*

Matsuko (Japanese) Pine-tree child.

Mattea (Hebrew) God's gift. *Mattaya*

Maud (English) Strength in battle; mighty battle maiden. *Maude, Maudie, Maudine, Maudy*

Maura (Irish) Dark-skinned; bitter; dark. *Moirah*

Maureen (French) Dark; dark-haired. (Irish) Bitter. *Maura, Maurin, Maurine, Maurizia, May, Mo, Moira, Mora, Moreen, Morena, Moria, Moriah*

Mauve (French) Violet.

Maverick (English) Spirited. *Maveric, Maverik*

Mavia (Irish) Happy. *Maviah, Mavie*

Mavis (French) Small bird; song-thrush; joy. *Maeve, Maeves, Maive, Mauve, Maves, Meave*

Maxine (Latin) Greatest. *Maxeen, Maxene*

May (English) Month of May. (Hebrew) Bitter. (Latin) Great. *Mae, Mai, Maia, Maize, Maya, Maye, Mayes, Mays*

Maya (Greek) Mother. (Hindi) God's divine creative power.

Mayako (Japanese) Child of Maya.

Mayra (Australian) Wind of spring. *Maera, Maira*

Maysa (Arabic) Graceful.

Maysun (Arabic) Graceful. *Maesun, Maisun*

Mayuko (Japanese) Child of Mayu.

Mayuri (Hindi) Peahen.

Mazal (Hebrew) Lucky star. *Mazala, Mazalah*

Meade (Greek) Honey wine. *Mead, Meed, Meede*

Meadow (English) Meadow.

Meara (Gaelic) Merry, filled with mirth. *Meera, Mira*

Meckenzie (Gaelic) Daughter of the Wise Leader.

Meda (Native American) Priestess.

Medea (Greek) Ruling; goddess. (Latin) Middle child. *Madora, Media, Medora*

Medha (Hindi) Intelligence; form of the Hindu goddess Devi; goddess Saraswati.

Media (Latin) Middle child. *Mediah, Medya, Medyah*

Medilion Origin and meaning unknown.

Medora (Greek, Latin) Ruling; middle child. *Madora, Medea, Meia*

Mee (Chinese) Beautiful. *Mee-Mee, Mei*

Meena (Hindi) Precious blue stone. *Meenah, Mina, Minah*

Meenakshi (Hindi) Woman with beautiful eyes.

Meera (Hebrew) Light. *Meira, Meyra, Mira*

Megan (Greek) Mighty; strong, able; pearl; soft and gentle. *Maeghan, Margaret, Meagan, Meg, Megann, Meggie, Meggy, Meghan, Megless, Megs*

Megara (Greek) Wife of Hercules; pearl.

Megha (Hindi) Cloud.

Meghana (Hindi) Raincloud.

Mehadi (Hindi) Flower. *Mehadie*

Mehitabel (Hebrew) God is our joy. *Mehitabelle, Mehitabelle*

Mehri (Arabic) Kind; lovable; sunny. *Mehry*

Mei (Chinese) Plum. (Hawaiian) May. (Latin) Great one.

Meinwen (Welsh) Slender. *Meinwin*

Meira (Hebrew) Light.

Meiying (Chinese) Beautiful flower.

Mekell (African American) Who is like God. *Mekelle*

Mekia (Hawaiian) Eyes; member of the Royal Hawaiian Band who brought the first ukulele to the U.S. mainland.

Mela (Hindi) Religious gathering. *Mella*

Melanctha (Greek) Black flower. *Melantha*

Melanie (Greek) Dark-skinned. *Mel, Mela, Melane, Melani, Melania, Melany, Melanya, Mellie, Melloney, Melly, Melonie, Melony, Milena*

Melba (Greek) Slender. (Latin) Mallow flower. *Melva*

Meldoy (Greek) Choral song.

Melecent (Greek) Honey bee; strength. *Melicinte*

Melenna (Greek) Yellow as canary. *Melena, Melina*

Melesse (Ethiopian) Eternal. *Mellesse*

Melia (Greek) Industrious. (Hawaiian) Nymph daughter of Oceanus.

Melika (Arabic) Owner of slaves.

Melina (Latin) Bright canary yellow. *Melyna*

Melinda (Greek) Gentle one; honey. *Linda, Lindy, Malena, Malina, Malinda, Malinde, Mallie, Mally, Melina, Minda, Mindy*

Melisenda (French) Honest; diligent; sweet.

Melissa (Greek) Bee; honey bee. *Lis, Lisa, Lissa, Mel, Meli, Melicent, Melisent, Melisse, Melita, Mellie, Mellissa, Melly, Millicent, Millie, Milly, Missy*

Melitta (Greek) Honey sweet; honey bee; garden. *Carmelita, Melissa, Melita*

Melody (Greek) Song. *Mellie, Melly, Melodi, Melodie*

Melosa (Spanish) Gentle; sweet. *Melosia*

Melpomene (Greek) Tragedy. *Melpomeni*

Melrose (Latin) Sweet rose. *Melrosa*

Mena (Hindi) Mother of Menaka; wife of the Himalayas. *Meehah, Menah*

Menaka (Hindi) Celestial damsel.

Menuha (Hebrew) Tranquility.

Merane (French) Sea of bitterness. *Meirane, Meraine*

Mercedes (Latin) Ransom; virgin; merciful. (Brand name) Make of car. *Mary, Mercedees, Mercedeze, Mercedies, Mercia, Mercy*

Mercy (Middle English) Merciful; compassion; pity. *Merci, Mercia*

Meredith (Old Welsh) Protector of the sea. *Meri, Meridith, Merry*

Mereki (Australian) Peacemaker. *Merekee, Merekie*

Meri (Hebrew) Rebellious. *Meree*

Meridian (American) Perfect posture. *Meridiane*

Merit (Latin) Deserving. *Merritt, Merriwell*

Merle (French, Latin) Blackbird. *Meriel, Merl, Merla, Merlina, Merola, Merrill, Meryl, Myrle, Myrlene*

Merleen (English) Falcon. *Merlene*

Merlyn (French) Blackbird. (Welsh) Fort by the sea; falcon. *Merlin*

Meroe (Ethiopian) Former capital of Ancient Ethiopia.

Merpati (Indonesian) Dove.

Merry (Middle English) Mirthful; joyful. *Meredith, Merri, Merrie, Merrielle, Merrilee, Merrily, Merrita*

Mersadize (English) Princess. *Sadi, Sadie, Sadize*

Meryl (German) Famous. (French) Blackbird. (Irish) Shining. *Meryle*

Mesha (Hindi) Ram; born under the sign of Aries; burden; salvation.

Messina (African) Spoiler. (Latin) One in the middle. *Messena*

Meta (Latin) Ambitious. (German) Pearl. *Margaret.*

Mia (Italian) Mine. (Hebrew) Bitter. (Scandinavian) Star of the sea. *Miah*

Miakoda (Native American) Power of the moon.

Michaela (Hebrew) Like God. *Micaela, Michaelina,*

Michaeline, Michal, Michelina, Micheline, Michelle, Michelyn, Mickey, Miguela, Mikaela, Mikaeli, Mikhaeli, Nichelle, Shell, Shelly

Michelle (Italian) Like the Lord; close to God. *Michell, Michella, Michellene*

Michi (Japanese) Righteous way.

Michiko (Japanese) Child of Michi; beauty; wisdom.

Midge (Persian, Latin) Child of light.

Midori (Japanese) Green. *Madory, Midorie*

Mieko (Japanese) Already prosperous.

Miette (French) Small, sweet thing. *Miettah*

Migdana (Hebrew) Gift. *Migdanna*

Migina (Native American) Moon returning. *Migeena, Miginah*

Migisi (Native American) Eagle.

Mignon (French) Dainty; petite; delicate; graceful. *Mignonne, Migonette, Migonn, Migonne*

Mihoko (Japanese) Child of Miho.

Mika (Japanese) New moon. (Native American) Intelligent raccoon. (Russian) Child of God.

Miki (Japanese) Flower stem.

Mila (Italian) Miracle. (Russian) Dear one. *Camilla*

Milan (Italian) Place name.

Milcah (Hebrew) Queen. *Milca*

Mildred (English) Gentle adviser. *Hil, Hildred, Mil, Mildraed, Mildrid, Mildryd, Milley, Milli, Millie, Milly*

Milena (Slavic) Favored one. *Mela, Milina*

Milissa (English) Bee. *Melissa*

Millicent (English) Industrious; strength. *Melicent, Melisande, Melisenda, Melly, Mili, Millie, Millisent, Milly*

Mily (Hawaiian) Beautiful. (English) Hard-working. *Milly*

Min (Korean) Cleverness; love; smooth; fine; small.

Mina (Arabic) Place near Makkah. (German) Love. (Persian) Sky blue. *Meena, Mena, Min, Minah, Myna, Mynah*

Minako (Japanese) Child of Mina.

Minal (Native American) Fruit. *Minala, Minalah*

Minda (Hindi) Knowledge. *Mindah*

Mindel (Yiddish) Sea of bitterness.

Mindy (Greek) Gentle. *Mindee, Mindi, Mindie*

Mine (Japanese) Resolute protector.

Minerva (Latin) Goddess of wisdom; power; thinker. *Minette, Minnie, Minny*

Mingmei (Chinese) Smart; beautiful. *Mingmey*

Mink (American) Weasel-like.

Minka (Teutonic) Strong, resolute. *Minkah*

Minna (Old German) Love. (Hebrew) Bitter. *Mina, Minda, Mindy, Minetta, Minette, Minnah, Myna, Willaminna*

Minnelli (American) Last name used as first name, as in Liza Minnelli.

Minnie (Latin) Tiny. *Mini, Minnee, Minni*

Minta (Greek) Of the mint plant. *Araminta, Mint, Mintha*

Mio (Spanish) Mine. *Myo*

Mira (Latin) Wonder. (Spanish) Behold. (Hebrew) Bitter. *Mirella, Mirelle, Mirielle, Mirila, Myra, Myrilla*

Mirabelle (Latin) Wonderful; beautiful to look upon. *Marabel, Mirabel, Mirabella, Mirable*

Miranda (Latin) Extraordinary; to be admired; beautiful. *Mandy, Meranda, Mira, Myranda, Randy*

Mireil (Hebrew) God has spoken. *Mirele, Miriella*

Miremba (Ugandan) Peace.

Mireya (Hebrew) God has spoken; miracle. *Mireille, Mirielle*

Miriam (Hebrew) Bitter; rebellion. *Meryem, Mimi, Mims, Mimsie, Mirem, Miri, Mirjam, Miryam, Mitzi, Myriam*

Mirth (Old English) Happiness; mirth.

Misako (Japanese) Child of Misa.

Misha (Russian) Who is like God. *Mishan*

Missy (Old English) Young girl. *Missie, Missye, Sissy*

Misty (Old English) Covered by mist. *Mistee*

Mitena (Native American) Coming moon, new moon.

Mitexi (Native American) Sacred moon.

Mitra (Hindi) Friend; sun.

Mitsuko (Japanese) Child of Mitsu.

Mitzi (German) Strong willed. *Mitzee, Mitzey*

Miwa (Japanese) Beautiful harmony.

Miya (Japanese) Sacred house. *Miyah*

Miyoko (Japanese) Beautiful generations; child of Miyo.

Miyuki (Japanese) Silence of deep snow.

Mnemosyne (Greek) Goddess of mercy.

Moana (Hawaiian) Ocean. *Moanah*

Modestus (Latin) Modest one.

Modesty (Latin) Modest one. *Desty, Modesta, Modeste, Modestia, Modestine, Modestus*

Modron (Scottish) In Arthurian legend, a goddess.

Moesha (African American) Drawn out of the water.

Mohini (Hindi) Most beautiful; enchantress. *Mohinee*

Moira (Irish) Bitter; great. *Maire, Mary, Maura, Moyra*

Mollie (Irish) Bitter. *Maili, Mary, Molly*

Momoko (Japanese) Child of Momo.

Mona (Arabic) Peaceful. (Irish) Noble. (Greek) Solitary. *Monica*

Monet (Greek) Solitary. *Monae, Monay*

Monica (Latin) Adviser; counselor. *Mona, Monca, Monique*

Monique (French) Wise. *Mon, Mone, Monee, Moneeqe, Moneeque, Moni, Moniqe*

Monisha (Hindi) Solitary life; Lord Krishna.

Monroe (Irish) From the red marsh. *Monrow*

Montana (Spanish) Mountain, mountainous. *Montanah*

Moon (Korean) From the moon; letters. *Moone*

Moon Unit (American) Universal appeal.

Mopsa (English) Shepherdess.

Mora (Spanish) Sweet berry.

Morasha (Hebrew) Inheritance. *Morash*

Morgan (Welsh) Enchantress half-sister of Arthur; white sea; bright; dweller by the sea. *Morgana, Morgane, Morganica, Morganne*

Morgance (Celtic) Sea dweller.

Morgandy (Celtic) Little one from the edge of the sea.

Morgause (Scottish) In Arthurian legend, the half-sister of Arthur who married Lot.

Morgen (German) Morning.

Moria (Hebrew) My teacher is God. *Moriah, Moriel, Morit, Moryah*

Morie (Japanese) Bay.

Morit (Hebrew) Teacher. *Moritt, Moritta*

Morvydd (Scottish) In Arthurian legend, the twin sister of Sir Ywain.

Moselle (Hebrew) Drawn from the water. (French) White wine. *Mosela, Mosella, Moses, Mosheh, Mozelle*

Mouna (Arabic) Wish, desire.

Mridul (Hindi) Soft. *Mridula*

Mrinalini (Hindi) Lotus.

Mukul (Hindi) Soul; bud.

Muluk (Indonesian) Praised highly. *Muluka*

Muna (Arabic) The Lord is with you. (Irish) Noble.

Muncel (African American) Strong and willing.

Mungo (Irish) Loveable.

Muriel (Arabic) Myrrh. (Irish) Sea-bright. (Latin) Angel of June. *Meriel, Muireall, Murial*

Murphy (Irish) Sea warrior. *Murffie, Murphey*

Muse (Greek) Nine daughters of Mnemosyne and Zeus; guiding spirit.

Musetta (Old French) Ballad. *Musa, Muse, Museta, Musette*

Musidora (Greek) Beautiful music. *Musidorah*

Mutsuko (Japanese) Child of Mutsu.

Mya (Burmese) Emerald.

Mychau (Vietnamese) Great. *Mah Chow*

Myda (Greek) Wet, damp; moldy.

Myer (Hebrew) Light. *Myar*

Myfanwy (Welsh) Sweet woman; beloved one.

Myiesha (Arabic) Life's blessing.

Mykala (English) Who is like God.

Myla (English) Merciful. *Milla, Millah*

Myoki (Japanese) Wondrous joy.

Myra (Latin) Aromatic shrub. *Miranda, Myrah, Myrra*

Myrna (Gaelic) Beloved. *Merna, Mirna, Moina, Morna, Moyna, Muirne*

Myrtle (Greek) Flower; symbol of victory; tree. *Mert, Mertice, Mertle, Mirtle, Myrta, Myrtia, Myrtice, Myrtilla, Myrtis*

N

Nabila (Arabic) Born to nobility. *Nabeela, Nabilah, Nabyla, Nabylah*

Nachine (Spanish) Hot, fiery. *Nachina, Nachinah, Nachyna, Nachyne*

Nadda (Arabic) Generous. *Nada, Nadah*

Nadezda (Czech) One with hope.

Nadia (French) Hopeful. *Nada, Nade, Nadeen, Nadene, Nadi, Nadie, Nadina, Nadine, Nadja, Nady, Nadya*

Nadie (Russian) From Nadia.

Nadine (Slavic) Hope. *Nada, Nadeen, Nadezhda, Nadia, Nadie, Nadina, Nadya, Nata*

Nadira (Arabic) Precious; rare; pinnacle. *Nadirah, Nadra, Nadyra, Nadyrah*

Naeva (French) Evening. *Naeve, Nahvon*

Nafeeza (Arabic) Precious thing. *Naf, Naffo, Naffy, Nafiza*

Nafuna (African) Delivered feet first.

Nagida (Hebrew) Prosperous. *Nagda, Nagdah, Nagyda*

Nagihan (Turkish) Meaning unknown.

Nahid (Arabic) Venus, goddess of love and beauty; one with full, round breasts.

Nahimana (Native American) Mystic.

Nahoko (Japanese) Child of Naho.

Naia (Greek) Flowing.

Naida (Greek) Water nymph. *Naia, Naiad, Naiia, Nayad, Nyad*

Nailah (African) Succeeding. *Naila, Nayla*

Naimah (Arabic) Living a soft, enjoyable life. *Maima, Naeemah, Naima*

Naina (Hindi) Eyes.

Nairi (Armenian) Land of rivers. *Naira, Naire, Nairee, Nairia*

Nairne (Scottish) From the narrow river glade.

Naiyah (Greek) Water nymph.

Naja (African) Stoic and strong. *Najah*

Najila (Arabic) Brilliant eyes. *Najilah*

Najwa (African American) Passionate.

Nakeisha (African American) Her life. *Nakeasha, Nakeesha, Nakeysha*

Nakia (Egyptian) Pure; faithful. *Nakea*

Nala (African) Successful. *Nalah, Nalo*

Nalani (Hawaiian) Calmness of the skies. *Nalanee, Nalaney, Nalanie, Nalany*

Nalanie (Hawaiian) Heaven's calm.

Nalini (Sanskrit) Lovely.

Nallely (Hawaiian) Heaven's calm.

Namazzi (Ugandan) Water.

Nami (Japanese) Wave. *Namee, Namie, Namiko, Namy*

Namrata (Hindi) Modesty.

Nan (English) Gracious. *Nanice, Nann, Nanon*

Nanako (Japanese) Child of Nana.

Nanami (Japanese) Seven beauties; seven seas.

Nancy (Hebrew) Full of grace. *Nan, Nana, Nance, Nancee, Nanice, Nanine, Nanny, Nansee, Nansey*

Nanda (Hindi) Sakti (power, energy) of Ganesha.

Nandalia (Australian) Fire. *Nandalee, Nandalei, Nandali, Nandaly*

Nandini (Hindi) Bestower of joy; daughter.

Nandita (Hindi) Happy.

Nanette (French) Gracious. *Nanete, Nanett, Nanetta, Ninette*

Nani (Greek) Charming. *Nanee, Nanie*

Nanna (Hebrew) Graceful one.

Nantale (Ugandan) Clan totem is a lion.

Naoko (Japanese) Child of Nao.

Naomi (Hebrew) Pleasant one; above all, beauty. *Mimi, Mims, Mimsy, Naoma, Noami, Nomi, Omie*

Napea (Latin) Of the valley.

Napua (Hawaiian) Flowers.

Nara (Old English) Near one. (Gaelic) Joyous. (Native American) Place name. *Narah, Nera*

Narcissa (Greek) Self-love. *Narcisse*

Narcisse (French) Daffodil. *Narci, Narcis, Narcissa, Narcissey, Narcissie, Narsee, Narsey, Narsis*

Narda (Latin) Fervently anointed.

Narella (Greek) Bright one. *Narelle, Rell, Relle, Relly*

Nari (Japanese) Thunder. *Naree, Naria, Nariah, Narie*

Nariko (Japanese) Thunder.

Narkaesha (African) Pretty.

Narmada (Indian) River.

Nascha (Native American) Owl.

Nasha (African) Born during the rainy season.

Nashaly (African) Born during the rainy season.

Nashwa (Egyptian) Wonderful feeling. *Nashy*

Nasia (Latin) From Natalie.

Nasiche (Ugandan) Born during the locust season.

Nasnan (Native American) Surrounded by song.

Nastasia (Greek) Form of Anastasia. *Nastasha, Nastassa, Nastassia*

Nasya (Hebrew) Miracle. *Nasia, Nasiah, Nasyah*

Nata (Native American) Speaker. *Natah, Natia, Natka*

Natala (Slavic) Born on Christmas. *Natalah*

Natalia (Italian) Born on Christmas.

Natalie (Latin) Birthday; child born at Christmas. *Nastassia, Natalee, Nataleigh, Natalia, Nataline, Natalja, Nataly, Natalya, Natasa, Natasha, Natashi, Natashia, Natassia, Nathalia, Nathalie, Natividad, Natosha, Natty, Nettie, Netty, Noel, Noelle, Novella, Talia, Tallie, Tally, Tasha, Tosh, Tosha*

Natane (Native American) Daughter.

Natania (Hebrew) Gift of God. *Natanja, Natanjah, Natanya, Nathania*

Nataniella (Hebrew) Gift of God. *Natania, Natanielle, Nathania, Nathanielle*

Natara (Arabic) Sacrifice. *Natarah, Nataria, Natarya*

Natasha (Greek) Rebirth; from Anastacia. *Nahtasha, Nastia, Natasa, Natashah*

Natesa (Hindi) Dance lord.

Nathaly (French) Birthday, especially the birth of Christ.

Natira (Science fiction) Character from *Star Trek*.

Natsuko (Japanese) Child of Natsu.

Nature (Latin) Essence. *Naturee, Naturia, Naturiah, Naturie*

Nautica (English) Meaning unknown.

Nava (Hebrew) Beautiful. *Navah, Naveh, Navit, Navita*

Navdeep (Hindi) Meaning unknown.

Naveena (Indian) New.

Navila (Arabic) Born to nobility.

Nawar (Arabic) Flower.

Nayana (Hindi) Eye.

Nayeli (Native American) He who wrestles. *Nayela, Nayelli, Nayla*

Nayely (Arabic) Highness; grace.

Nayoko (Japanese) Child of Nayo.

Naysa (Hebrew) Miracle of God.

Nazirah (Arabic) Equal; like.

Neala (Gaelic) Champion. *Nealah, Neela, Neila, Neilla, Nela, Niela, Nila*

Nebta (Egyptian) Meaning unknown.

Neci (Latin) Intense, fiery.

Necia (Latin) Fiery; passionate. *Necee, Neciah, Necie*

Neda (Slavic) Born on Sunday; sanctuary. *Ned, Neddy, Nedjelko, Nedo, Nerida*

Nedda (English) Prosperous guardian. *Neddah, Neddi, Neddie, Neddy*

Nediva (Hebrew) Noble and generous.

Nedra (Latin) Awareness.

Neeharika (Hindi) Dewdrops.

Neelam (Hindi) Sapphire.

Neelja (Hindi) Meaning unknown.

Neely (Irish) Form of Nelia. *Neela, Neeley, Neeli, Neelia*

Neema (Hindi) Prosperous.

Neena (Hindi) Mighty. *Neana, Neenah*

Neerja (Hindi) Lotus flower.

Neeta (Hindi) Upright.

Nefertiti (Egyptian) The beautiful woman has come.

Neferu (Egyptian) Meaning unknown.

Neha (Hindi) Rain.

Neith (Egyptian) Divine mother.

Neiva (Spanish) Snow.

Nekeisha (American) Form of Nakeisha. *Nechesa, Nekeesha, Nekeysha, Nekysha*

Nekia (Arabic) Pure. *Nakeia, Nakia, Nakiea, Nakiya, Nekeya, Neya*

Nelda (English) By the alder tree. (Irish) Champion. *Neldah, Nell, Nellda, Nellie*

Nelia (Gaelic) Champion. *Nelah, Neleah, Nellea, Nellia*

Nell (Greek) Stone. *Nelle*

Nelleke (Dutch) Horn.

Nellie (Greek) Bright one. *Nela, Nelda, Nelia, Nelina, Nelita, Nella, Nellis, Nellwyn, Nelly*

Nellis (Greek) Light.

Nellwyn (English) Nellie's friend. *Nellwin, Nellwinn, Nelwinn, Nelwyn*

Nelly (Greek) Stone.

Nenet (Arabic) Goddess of the deep. *Neneta, Nenete, Nennet, Nennett*

Neola (Greek) Youthful.

Neoma (Greek) New moon. *Neona*

Neorah (Hebrew) Light.

Nerhim (Turkish) Meaning unknown.

Neria (Hebrew) Lamp of God; angel. *Neriah*

Nerice (American) Powerful woman.

Nerin (Greek) One from the sea.

Nerina (Greek) Sea nymph. *Nerine, Neryn*

Nerissa (Latin) Daughter of the sea. *Narissa, Neressa, Nerisa, Nerisse*

Nerita (Spanish) Sea snail.

Neroli (Italian) Orange blossom. *Nerole, Nerolia, Nerolie, Neroly*

Nerys (Welsh) Lady. *Nereece, Neris, Nerise, Neriss, Nerisse, Neryse*

Nessa (Old Norse) Headland. *Nesa, Nessie, Nissa*

Netis (Native American) Trustworthy. *Netisa, Netissa, Netissah, Nettys*

Netta (Hebrew) Plant or shrub. *Netah, Netia, Nettah, Nettia*

Neva (Spanish) Covered with snow. *Nevea, Nevia, Nevita*

Nevada (Latin) Snowy. *Nevedah*

Nevaeh (American) *Heaven* spelled backward.

Nevala (Science fiction) Character from *Star Trek*.

Neveah (Slavic) Butterfly.

Neviah (Hebrew) Forecaster.

Nevina (Irish) Saint worshipper. *Neveena, Neveene, Nevenah, Nevene*

Neylan (Turkish) Fulfilled wish. *Neilani, Neilania, Neilany, Nelana*

Neysa (Greek) Pure.

Nguyet (Vietnamese) Little one.

Nhi (Vietnamese) Little one.

Nhu (Vietnamese) Everything according to one's wishes.

Nhung (Vietnamese) Velvet.

Nia (Swahili) Purpose. *Neya, Niah*

Nichelle (African American) Victorious maiden. *Nichele, Nishele*

Nichole (Greek) Victorious.

Nicia (Greek) Victorious army. *Nicanor*

Nickan (Persian) Goodness of grandparents.

Nicki (Greek) From Nicole. *Nicky*

Nickita (Russian) Victorious people.

Nicole (Greek) Victorious people. *Colette, Collette, Cosette, Lacole, Nicci, Nichelle, Nichola, Nichole, Nickie, Nicky, Nicola, Nicolette, Nicoline, Nika, Nikki, Nikole, Nikolia, Nyki, Nykki, Nykky, Nykole, Nyky*

Nidha (Asian) Sleep; night.

Nidia (Latin) Nest. *Nidi, Nidiah*

Nidra (Hindi) Form of the Hindu goddess Devi.

Niesha (African American) Pure.

Nieve (Spanish) Snowy.

Nigella (Latin) Dark night. *Nige, Nigela, Nigelah, Nigele*

Nijole (Slavic) Form of Nicole.

Niju (Hindi) Pansophist. *Nij*

Nika (Russian) Born on Sunday. *Nikah, Nikka, Nyka, Nykah*

Nike (Greek) Victory.

Niki (English) Victorious people. *Nicky, Nicole*

Nikita (Greek) Unconquered, victorious people. *Nickeeta, Nikeeta, Nikitte, Niquita*

Nikki (American) From Nicole.

Nikole (English) Victorious people.

Nile (Egyptian) From the River Nile.

Nilgun (Turkish) Meaning unknown.

Nilima (Hindi) Blueness.

Nilini (Hindi) Perpetuator of the Kuru race.

Niloufer (Hindi) From the heavens.

Nimah (Arabic) Blessing; loan. *Nima*

Nimeesha (African) Princess.

Nimisha (Hindi) Meaning unknown.

Nimmi (Hindi) Meaning unknown.

Nimue (English) Full of life, vibrant; form of Vivian.

Nina (Spanish) Girl; grace. *Ninette, Ninon, Ninya*

Nineve (English) Full of life, vibrant; form of Vivian.

Ninon (French) Form of Annie. *Ninona, Ninonah*

Niobe (Greek) Fern.

Nira (Hawaiian) Of the loom. (Hebrew) Plow.

Niradhara (Hindi) Meaning unknown.

Niral (Hindi) Meaning unknown.

Nirguna (Hindi) Meaning unknown.

Nirmala (Hindi) Pure; immaculate.

Nirupa (Hindi) Decree; command.

Nirvana (Hindi) Deep silence; ultimate bliss. *Nirvahna, Nirvanah, Vana*

Nirvelli (Native American) Water child.

Nisha (Hindi) Night.

Nishi (Japanese) West. *Nishee, Nishey, Nishie, Nishy*

Nishtha (Indian) Devotion.

Nisi (Hebrew) Emblem.

Nissa (Scandinavian) Elf, fairy. *Nissah, Nissan, Nisse, Nissi, Nissim*

Nita (Native American) Bear.

Nitara (Hindi) Deeply rooted. *Nitarah, Nitarra, Nitarrah*

Niti (Hindi) Meaning unknown.

Nitika (Native American) Angel of precious stone.

Nitsa (Greek) Light.

Nitu (Hindi) Meaning unknown.

Nituna (Native American) My daughter.

Nitya (Hindi) Goddess.

Nityapriya (Indian) Ever pleasing.

Nitza (Hebrew) Bud from a flower.

Nitzana (Hebrew) Blossom. *Nitza, Nizana*

Nivea (Latin) Snow; reflecting the snow-white color.

Nivedita (Indian) Surrendered.

Niverta (Hindi) Meaning unknown.

Nixie (German) Water sprite. *Nixee, Nixey, Nixi, Nixy*

Niyati (Hindi) Fate.

Nizana (Hebrew) Flower bud. *Nitzana, Nitzania, Zana*

Noble (Latin) Honorable one.

Noelani (Hawaiian) Beautiful girl from heaven. *Noelanee, Noelania, Noelanni*

Noeline (Latin) Form of Noel. *Noeleen, Noelleen, Noelline*

Noella (French) Christmas. *Noel, Noele, Noelle, Nowele*

Noemi (Hebrew) Pleasantness.

Nohely (Latin) Christmas. *Noheli*

Noire (Greek) Verdent; blooming.

Nokomis (Native American) Grandmother.

Nola (Latin) Of noble birth.

Noletta (Latin) Unwilling. *Noleetah, Noleta, Nolita*

Nollie (English) Familiar form of Magnolia. *Nolle, Nolley, Nolli, Nolly*

Nona (Latin) Ninth. *Nonah, Nonee, Noney, Noni, Noniah*

Nonnita (Celtic) Named for Saint Nonn; mother of Saint David of Wales. (Latin) Ninth. *Non, Nonee, Nonh, Noni, Nonie, Nonna, Nonyah*

Noor (Aramaic) Form of Nura. *Noora, Noorah, Noorie, Nour*

Nora (Greek) Bright one; honor; light. *Norah, Noreen, Norina, Norine*

Norberta (German) Blond hero.

Nordica (German) From the north. *Norna*

Norell (Scandinavian) From the north. *Norele, Norella, Norellah, Norelle*

Nori (Japanese) Doctrine. *Noree, Norey, Noria, Norie*

Noriko (Japanese) Doctrine child; child of Nori.

Norina (English) Light.

Norleen (Irish) Honest. *Norlean, Norlein, Norline, Norlyne*

Norma (Latin) Model. *Normie*

Normandy (French) Place name.

Notburga (German) Meaning unknown.

Noura (Arabic) Inner light. *Nourah*

Nova (Latin) New. *Noova, Novah, Novia*

Novella (Latin) Newcomer. *Novela, Novelah, Novele, Novelle*

Novia (Spanish) New; girlfriend. *Noviah, Novya*

Novyanna (Spanish) Lovely. *Novie, Novy*

Noy (Hebrew) Decoration.

Noya (Arabic) Beautiful; ornamented.

Nozomi (Japanese) Hope.

Nu (Vietnamese) Girl. *Nue*

Nuala (Celtic) White-haired. *Nualah, Nula*

Nubia (Egyptian) From Nubia.

Nuna (Native American) Land.

Nura (Arabic) Light. *Noora, Noura, Nuriah*

Nuray (Turkish) White moon.

Nurhan (Turkish) Meaning unknown.

Nuria (Hebrew) God's fire. *Noor, Noura, Nur, Nuriah, Nuriel*

Nusa (Hungarian) Grace.

Nuttah (Native American) My heart.

Nya (Irish) Champion. *Neale, Neil, Niall, Nyah*

Nyasia (Irish) Champion.

Nydia (Latin) Refuge, nest. *Nidia, Nidiah, Ny, Nydiah, Nydie, Nydya*

Nyeki (African) Second wife.

Nyla (Greek) Winner. *Nila, Nylah, Nyle, Nylea*

Nyoko (Japanese) Gem; treasure.

Nyree (Maori) Sea. *Niree, Nyra, Nyrie*

Nysa (Greek) New beginning. *Nisa, Nissa, Nyssa*

Nyssa (Greek) Beginning.

Nyx (Greek) Night. *Nix*

O

Oba (Nigeria) Ancient river goddess. *Obah*

Obelia (Greek) Pillar of strength. *Obeliah, Obelya, Obelyah*

Obsession (Old English) Product name; to be obsessed; compulsive.

Oceana (Greek) From the sea. *Oceanah, Oceane, Oceania, Oceanna, Oceanne*

Octavia (Latin) Eighth child. *Occtavia, Octave, Octaviana, Octavie, Ottavia, Tave, Tavi, Tavia, Tavie*

Oda (Norse) Small, pointed spear. *Odah*

Odda (Scandinavian) Rich. *Oddah, Oddia, Oddiah*

Ode (African) Born during travel. *Odee, Odey, Odi, Ody*

Odea (Greek) Walker by the road. *Odee*

Odeda (Hebrew) Strong. *Odeada, Odeadah, Odedah*

Odele (Hebrew) Wealthy; melody. *Odel, Odell, Odelle*

Odelette (French) Form of Odele. *Odelatt, Odelatta, Odelattah, Odelet*

Odelia (German) Little wealthy one; praise God. *Odeliah, Odelinda, Odella, Odellah, Odilia*

Odella (German) Little wealthy one. *Odela, Odelah, Odelyn*

Odera (Hebrew) Plough.

Odessa (Greek) Odyssey, journey, voyage. *Odesa, Odessah, Odessia, Odissa, Odissah*

Odetta (French) Melody. *Odeta, Odetah*

Odette (French) Happy home. *Oddete, Oddett*

Odil (French) Rich.

Odina (Latin) Mountain. *Odeane, Odeen, Odeena, Odeenah*

Ofa (English) Name of a king.

Ofelia (Greek) Helper. *Ofeelia, Ofellia, Ofilia, Ophelia*

Ofira (Hebrew) Gold. *Ofara, Ofarrah, Ophira, Ophyra*

Ohanna (Armenian) God's gracious gift. *Ohana, Ohanah, Ohannah*

Ohio (Native American) Large river.

Ohnicio (Irish) Honor.

Oihane (Spanish) From the forest.

Oistin (Latin) Venerable.

Ojal (Hindi) Vision.

Okal (African) To cross.

Okapi (African) Animal with a long neck.

Okelani (Hawaiian) From heaven. *Okalana, Okalanah, Okalanea, Okalani*

Oki (Japanese) Ocean-centered. *Okie*

Oksana (Russian) Glory be to God. *Oksanochka*

Ola (Hawaiian) Well-being. *Olah*

Olalla (Greek) Sweetly spoken. *Olallah*

Olathe (Native American) Beautiful. *Olanth, Olantha, Olanthye*

Olayinka (Yoruban) Honors surround me.

Olba (Aboriginal) Red ochre.

Olcay (Turkish) Meaning unknown.

Oldina (Australian) Snow. *Oldeena, Oldeenah, Oldenia, Oldyn*

Olen (Russian) Deer. *Olian, Olien, Oliene, Olyan*

Olesia (Polish) Helper and defender of mankind.

Olga (Russian) Holy. *Olgah, Olgy, Olva*

Oliana (Hawaiian) Oleander. *Oliann, Olinah, Olyan*

Olina (Hawaiian) Joyous. *Olinah, Olyna, Olynah*

Olinda (German) Protector of property. *Olindah, Olynda*

Olisa (Native American) God. *Olisah, Olysa, Olysah*

Olive (Old Norse) Kind one. (Latin) Olive tree. (Old French) Peace. *Liv, Livvy, Livy, Nola, Nollie, Olivette, Olivya, Ollie, Olly, Olva*

Olivia (Latin) Form of Olive. *Livia, Oliviah, Olivianne, Olivya*

Olwen (Welsh) White footprint. *Olwene, Olwenna, Olwin, Olwyna*

Olympia (Greek) Of Mount Olympus; heavenly. *Olimpie, Olympe*

Oma (Hebrew) Reverent. (German) Mother. (Arabic) Commanding. *Omah*

Omaira (Arabic) Red. *Omara, Omari, Omaria*

Omaka (Maori) Place where the stream flows.

Omana (Sanskrit) Giver of life.

Omega (Greek) Great.

Ona (Lithuanian) Graceful one. *Onah*

Onaedo (African) Gold.

Onaona (Hawaiian) Sweet smell.

Onawa (Native American) Awake. *Onawah, Onowa, Onowah*

Ondine (Latin) Water sprite. *Ondene, Ondin, Ondyn*

Ondrea (Slavic) Strong, courageous. *Ohndria, Ondri, Ondria, Ondriannah*

Oneida (Native American) Eagerly awaited. *Oneidah, Onida, Onidah*

Onella (Hungarian) Torch light. *Ondela, Onelah, Onellah*

Oni (Native American) Born on holy ground. *Onee, Oney, Onnie, Ony*

Onida (Native American) Expected one.

Onora (Irish) Version of honor. *Onorah, Onoria, Onorina, Onorine*

Ontario (Native American) Beautiful lake. *Ontaryo*

Ontibile (African) God is watching over me.

Onur (Turkish) Honor.

Onyx (Greek) Dark black; precious stone.

Oola (Aboriginal) Red lizard. (Irish) Apples. *Ulla*

Oona (Gaelic, Latin) Unity. *Ona, Oonagh, Oonaugh, Oonie*

Opa (Native American) Owl. *Opah*

Opal (Sanskrit) Jewel. *Opala, Opalah, Opalia, Opell*

Opaline (French) Jewel; precious stone.

Ophelia (Greek) Useful; wise. *Ofelia, Ofilia, Ophelie, Phelia*

Ophira (Greek) Gold. *Oprah*

Oprah (Hebrew) Light; runaway. *Opra*

Ora (Spanish) Gold. *Orabel, Orabele, Orabell*

Oralee (Hebrew) Lord is my light. *Areli, Oralea, Oraleah, Oralei*

Oralia (Latin) Golden; light. *Ora, Orah, Oral, Oralee, Oralie, Orel, Orelda, Oria, Oriole, Orlena, Orlene, Orlie, Orly, Orpah*

Orana (Australian) Welcome. *Oranah, Oranna, Orannah*

Orane (French) Rising.

Orchid (Latin) Flower.

Orea (Greek) Mountains. *Oreah, Oreal, Oria*

Orenda (Native American) Magic power. *Orendah*

Oria (Latin) From the Orient. (Latin) Dawn, sunrise. (Irish) Golden.

Oriana (Latin) Dawn. (Greek) East. *Oralia, Orane, Orania, Orelle, Orlanna*

Orianna (Latin) Golden; dawning. *Orienne*

Oriel (French) Golden; angel of destiny. *Oriela, Oriellah, Orielle*

Orina (Russian) Form of Irene. *Orinah, Oryna, Orynah*

Orinda (Teutonic) Fire serpent. *Orenda, Orendah, Orindah*

Oriole (Latin) Fair-haired. *Oriola, Oriolah, Orioll, Oriolla*

Orla (Latin) Golden woman. *Orlagh, Orlah*

Orlanda (Latin) Bright sun. *Orlandah, Orlantha, Orlie*

Orlantha (German) From the land.

Orlena (Latin) Golden. *Orlana, Orleana, Orleanah, Orleene*

Ormanda (German) Of the sea. *Orma, Ormandah, Ormandea*

Ornella (Italian) Flowering ash tree.

Ornice (Irish) Pale. *Orna, Ornah*

Orpah (Hebrew) Neck; skull. *Orpa, Orphie*

Orsa (Latin) Bear. *Orsah, Orse*

Orseline (Latin) Bearlike. *Orsalin, Orsalina, Orsaline, Orsalyn*

Ortensia (Latin) Gardener; farmer. *Hortense*

Orva (French) Golden. *Orvah*

Orwina (Hebrew) Bear friend. *Orwin, Orwinah, Orwine, Orwyn*

Osana (Spanish) Health.

Osanna (Latin) Praise the Lord. *Osanah, Osannah*

Osen (Japanese) One thousand. *Osena, Osenah*

Osita (Spanish) Divinely strong. *Ositah, Osithe, Osyta*

Osma (Latin) God's servant. *Osmah, Ozma*

Oswalda (English) God's power. *Osvalda, Oswaldah*

Othelia (Spanish) Rich. *Othilia*

Otilie (Czech) Lucky heroine. *Otila, Otilah, Ottili, Otyla*

Otylia (Polish) Rich. *Otilia, Ottylya, Otylyah*

Ouida (French) Warrior woman.

Ova (Latin) Egg.

Ove (Norse) Spear's point.

Owena (Welsh) Well born. *Owenah, Owina*

Oz (Hebrew) Strength. *Ozz*

Ozora (Hebrew) Strength of the Lord.

P

Paavana (Hindi) Pure.

Paavani (Hindi) Ganges River.

Pabiola (Latin) Humble.

Paca (Spanish) Frenchman. *Paka*

Paciana (Latin) Peaceful woman.

Padgett (Greek) Wisdom. *Padget, Paget, Pagett, Pagette*

Padmani (Sri Lankan) Blossom. *Padmanee, Padmaney, Padmanie, Padmany*

Pagan (Latin) From the country. *Pagen, Pagon, Pagun, Pagain*

Page (French) Intern. *Paige, Payge*

Paisley (Scottish) Patterned fabric. *Paislay, Paislee, Paizley, Pazley*

Paiton (English) Warrior's town. *Paiten, Paityne, Peiton, Peityn*

Paka (African) Kitten.

Pala (Native American) Water. *Palah, Palla, Pallah*

Palakika (Hawaiian) Version of Frances. *Farakika*

Palila (Hawaiian) Bird. *Palilah, Palyla, Palylah*

Pallas (Greek) Another name for Athena, goddess of the arts, goddess of wisdom. *Palace, Pallas, Pallassa*

Palma (Latin) Palm tree. *Pallma, Palmar*

Palmer (English) Palm tree. *Palima, Pallma, Pallmara, Pallmyra, Palma, Palmira, Palmyra, Pammimirah*

Paloma (Spanish) Dove. *Palloma, Palometa, Palomita, Peloma*

Pamela (Greek) Honey. *Pam, Pamala, Pamalia, Pamelia, Pamelina, Pamella, Pamilia, Pamilla, Pammela, Pammi, Pammie, Pammy*

Pana (Native American) Partridge. *Panah, Panna, Pannah*

Panambi (African) Butterfly.

Pancha (Spanish) Free. *Pac, Panchah, Panchitta*

Pandita (Hindi) Scholar.

Pandora (Greek) All gifted. *Panda, Pandorra, Panndora*

Panphila (Greek) She loves all. *Panfila, Panfyla, Panphyla*

Pansy (English) Flower. *Pansea, Pansee, Pansey, Pansie*

Panya (African) Mouse. *Pania, Paniah, Panyah*

Paola (Italian) Form of Paula. *Paoli, Paolina, Paoline*

Papina (Native American) Vine growing on an oak tree. *Papinah, Papyna*

Paramita (Sanskrit) Perfect. *Paramitah, Paramyta, Paramytah*

Paris (French) Place name. *Parisa, Parris, Parrish*

Parker (English) Park keeper. *Park, Parke*

Parma (Indian) Foremost.

Parnel (French) Rock. *Parnela, Parnelah, Parnele, Parnell, Parnella*

Parthenia (Greek) Virginal. *Parthania, Parthena, Parthenie, Parthina, Parthine, Pathania, Pathena, Pathenia, Pathina*

Parvani (Hindi) Hindu goddess Devi.

Parvati (Sanskrit) Mountain climber. *Parvatee, Parvatey, Parvatia, Parvatie*

Pascale (French) Child of Easter; feminine version of Pascal. *Pascalette, Pascaline, Pascalle, Paschale*

Pasha (Greek) Sea. *Pascha, Pasche, Pashal, Pashel*

Passion (Latin) Passion. *Pashion, Pashonne, Passionette*

Pasua (African) Born by cesarean section.

Patam (Sanskrit) City. *Patem, Patim, Pattam, Pattim*

Paterekia (Hawaiian) Aristocrat.

Patia (Spanish) Leaf. *Patiah, Patya, Patyah*

Patience (English) Patience. *Paciencia, Patient*

Patricia (English) Noble. *Pat, Patreece, Patreice, Patria, Patric, Patrica, Patrice, Patricka, Patrizia, Patsy, Patti, Pattie, Patty, Tricia, Trish, Trisha*

Paula (Latin) Small. *Paola, Paolina, Paule, Pauleen, Paulene, Pauletta, Paulette, Paulie, Paulina, Pauline, Paulita, Pauly, Paulyn, Pavla, Pavlina, Pavlinka, Pola, Polcia, Pollie, Polly*

Pausha (Hindi) Name of the lunar month of Capricorn.

Pavana (Hindi) Wind. *Pavani*

Pax (Latin) Peace.

Paxton (Latin) Peaceful town. *Paxtin, Paxtynn*

Paz (Hebrew) Gold. *Paza, Pazia, Paziah, Pazice, Pazit, Paziya, Pazya*

Peace (English) Peaceful.

Pearl (Latin) Pearl; jewel. *Pearla, Pearle, Pearleen, Pearlena, Pearlette, Pearley, Pearline, Pearly, Perl, Perla, Perle, Perlette, Perley, Perlie, Perly*

Pedzi (African) Last child.

Pela (Hawaiian) Pretty. *Bela*

Pelagia (Greek) Ocean; sea-dweller. *Pelage, Pelageia, Pelagie, Pelegia, Pelgia, Pellagia*

Pelenakino (Hawaiian) Strong as a bear. *Peresekila, Peresila, Perisila*

Peliah (Hebrew) God's miracle. *Pelia*

Pelika (Hawaiian) Peaceful; version of Freda. *Ferida*

Pelipa (Native American) Lover of horses.

Pelulio (Hawaiian) Emerald. *Berulo*

Pemba (African) Meteorological power.

Penda (African) Beloved. *Pendah, Pendana*

Penelope (Greek) Bobbin weaver. *Lopa, Pela, Pelcia, Pen, Penelopa, Penina, Penine, Penna, Pennelope, Penni, Penny, Pinelopi, Piptisa, Popi*

Peninah (Hebrew) Coral. *Peni, Penie, Penina, Penini, Peninit*

Penny (Greek) Form of Penelope. *Penee, Penney, Penni, Pennia*

Peony (English) Flower. *Peoni, Peonie*

Pepita (Spanish) Familiar form of Josephine. *Pepa, Pepitah, Pepite, Pepitta*

Peridot (French) Fairytale; gemstone.

Perilla (Latin) Plant with leaves used in cooking. *Perila, Perilah, Perillah, Peryla*

Perlita (Italian) Pearl. *Perleta, Perlitta, Perlyta, Perlytah*

Permelia (Latin) Sweetness. *Parmelia*

Perry (French) Pear tree. *Peri, Perrey, Perri, Perrie*

Persis (Latin) From Persia. *Perssis*

Petronella (Latin) Roman clan name. *Pernel, Pernelle, Peronel, Peronelle, Petrina, Petronelle, Petronia, Petronilla, Pier, Pierette*

Petula (Latin) Sassy. *Petulah*

Petunia (English) Flower. *Petune, Petuniah*

Phedra (Greek) Bright. *Faydra, Fedra, Phadra, Phaedra, Phedre*

Phemie (Scottish) Form of Euphemia. *Phemee, Phemey, Phemi, Phemia*

Philana (Greek) Lover of mankind. *Philanna, Philina, Phillane, Phylana*

Philadelphia (Greek) City; brotherly love. *Philli, Phillie*

Philberta (English) Brilliant. *Filberta, Philbertah, Philberte*

Philippa (Greek) Lover of horses. *Philipa, Philippine, Phillipina, Pippa*

Philomela (Greek) Lover of songs. *Filomela, Philomelah, Phylomela, Phylomelah*

Philomena (Greek) Beloved. *Filomena, Philomene, Philomina*

Phoebe (Greek) Brilliant. *Pheabe, Phebe, Pheby, Phobe*

Phyllis (Greek) Green tree branch. *Philis, Phillis, Philliss, Phillys, Phylis, Phyllida, Phylliss*

Pia (Latin) Pious. *Peah, Piah*

Pinquana (Native American) Fragrant.

Piper (English) Pipe player. *Pyper*

Pippi (French) Rosy-cheeked. *Pipi, Pippey, Pippie, Pippy*

Pirene (Greek) Daughter of the river god Achelous.

Pisa (Italian) Place name.

Pita (African) Fourth daughter. *Peeta, Peetah*

Pixie (English) Tiny. *Pixee, Pixi, Pixy*

Placida (Spanish) Calm. *Plasida*

Pleasance (English) Pleasure. *Pleasant, Pleasants, Pleasence*

Plena (Latin) Abundant.

Pocahontas (Native American) Capricious.

Poeta (Italian) Poetry. *Poetah, Poetree, Poetri, Poetry*

Polly (English) Form of Molly. *Pauleigh, Pollee, Polley, Polli, Pollie, Pollyann, Pollyanna, Pollyanne*

Pollyam (Hindi) Goddess of the plague.

Pomona (Latin) Apple. *Pomma, Pommah, Pomme*

Poppy (Latin) Flower. *Poppi*

Porter (Latin) Gatekeeper. *Portie*

Portia (Latin) Roman clan name. *Porcha, Porscha, Porsche, Porschia, Porsha*

Posy (English) Small bouquet of flowers. *Posee, Posey, Posie*

Pragyata (Hindi) Wisdom.

Prarthana (Hindi) Prayer.

Prashanti (Hindi) Peace.

Pratima (Hindi) Image.

Precious (American, Latin) Dear.

Preeti (Hindi) Love.

Preita (Finnish) Most loving one.

Prema (Hindi) Love.

Premila (Sanskrit) Loving girl. *Premilla, Premillah, Premylla*

Prerana (Hindi) Encouragement.

Presley (English) Priest's meadow. *Preslea, Preslee, Preslie, Presslie*

Preyasi (Hindi) Beloved.

Pribislava (Czech) To help glorify. *Pribena, Pribka, Pribuska*

Prima (Italian) First one. *Primalia, Primetta, Primina, Priminia, Primula*

Primavera (Italian) Spring.

Primrose (English) First rose.

Princell (English) Royal title. *Prin, Princesa, Princessa*

Priscilla (Latin) From ancient times. *Cilla, Cyla, Prisca, Priss, Prissy, Silla*

Prisma (Greek) Cut glass. *Prusma*

Pritha (Hindi) Mother of Pandavas.

Priti (Hindi) Satisfaction; renowned wife of Pulastya/Sukha.

Pritika (Hindi) Beloved. *Priyal, Priyam*

Priya (Hindi) Loved one, darling. *Priyal, Priyam, Priyanka, Priyasha, Priyata, Priyati*

Priyanka (Hindi) Dear one.

Promise (Latin) Pledge. *Promis, Promisi, Promiss, Promyse*

Prospera (Latin) Prosperous. *Prosperitie*

Providence (English) Providence.

Prudence (Latin) Foresight. *Pru, Prudy, Prue*

Prunella (French) Color of a plum. *Prunela, Prunell, Prunellah*

Psyche (Greek) Soul. *Psyke, Syche*

Ptolema (Greek) Meaning unknown.

Pua (Polynesian) Flowering tree. *Puah*

Puakai (Hawaiian) Ocean flower. *Puakea, Puakeah, Puakiah*

Pualani (Hawaiian) Beautiful flower. *Pualanee, Pualaney, Pualanie, Pulania*

Pulkita (Hindi) Meaning unknown.

Puma (Spanish) Mountain lion.

Pundari (Hindi) Meaning unknown.

Punita (Hindi) Pure.

Purandhri (Hindi) Beautiful woman.

Purity (English) Unsullied, clean. *Pure, Puritee, Puriti, Puritie*

Purnima (Hindi) Night of the full moon.

Purva (Hindi) Elder.

Purvaja (Hindi) Elder sister.

Purvi (Hindi) East.

Purvis (French) Provide.

Pusti (Hindi) Nourishment; form of the Hindu goddess Devi; wife of Ganapati.

Pyhrrha (Greek) Red.

Pyrena (Greek) Fiery. *Pirena, Pirenah, Pyrene*

Pythia (Greek) Prophet. *Pithea, Pithia, Pithiah, Pythea*

Q

Qadira (Arabic) Wields power. *Kadira*

Qamra (Arabic) Moon. *Kamra*

Qatai (Arabic) Conclusive. (Science fiction) Character from *Star Trek: Voyager*.

Qitarah (Arabic) Aromatic. *Qeturah, Quetura, Queturah*

Quan (Chinese) Goddess of compassion.

Quanah (Native American) White coral beads. (English) Queenly. *Kwanda, Kwandah, Quandah, Qwanda*

Quanella (African American) Sparkling. *Kwannie, Quanela*

Quanesha (African American) Singing. *Kwaeesha, Kwannie, Quaneisha, Quanisha*

Quanika (American) Combination of Quan and Nika; joyful. *Kwantina, Kwantynna, Quantinna, Quantyna, Quawanica*

Quantina (American) Brave queen. *Kwantynna, Quantinna, Quantyna*

Quarralia (Australian) Star. *Quaralia, Quaraliah, Quaralyah, Quarralian*

Quarrtulain (Indian) God's mercy.

Quartilla (Latin) Fourth.

Quartz (German) Jewel, gem; crystalline.

Quasar (Indian) Meteorite.

Qubilah (Arabic) Agreement. *Quabila, Quabyla*

Queena (English) Queen. *Queen, Queenation, Queeneste, Queenette, Queenie, Quenny*

Queisha (American) Contented child. *Queshia, Queysha*

Quella (English) Pacify. *Quela, Quele, Quellah*

Quenby (Scandinavian) Womanly. *Quenbee, Quenbey, Quenbi, Quenbie, Quinbee, Quinbie, Quinby*

Querida (Spanish) Beloved. *Queridah, Queryda, Querydah*

Questa (French) Hunter. *Kesta, Quest, Questah*

Queta (Spanish) Home ruler. *Keta, Quetta, Quettah*

Quiana (American) Gracious; queen; form of Hannah. *Qiana, Qianna, Quiyanna*

Quianna (American) Grace. *Qianna, Quiana, Quiyanna*

Quillen (Spanish) Woman of the heights.

Quinby (Scandinavian) Living like royalty. *Quenby, Quin, Quinbie, Quinnie*

Quinceanos (Spanish) Fifteenth child. *Quin, Quince, Quincee, Quincy*

Quinci (English) Fifth son's estate. *Quincy*

Quincylia (American) Popular, fifth child. *Cylia, Quince, Quincy*

Quinella (Latin) Girl who is as pretty as two. *Quinel, Quinela, Quinn*

Quinn (Gaelic, Greek) Wise; queen; fifth born. *Quin, Quina, Quinah*

Quintessa (Latin) Essence. *Quinn, Quintessenz, Tess, Tessa*

Quintina (Latin) Fifth. *Quin, Quinetta, Quinette, Quinta, Quintana, Quintessa, Quintona, Quintonice*

Quirina (Latin) Contentious.

Quirita (Latin) Citizen.

Quisha (African American) Beautiful mind. *Keisha, Kesha, Key*

Quita (Latin) Peaceful. *Keeta, Keetah*

Quiterie (French) Tranquil.

Quorra (Italian) Heart.

R

Raama (Hebrew) One who trembles. *Raamah, Rama, Ramah*

Raanana (Hebrew) Fresh. *Ranana*

Rabab (Arabic) Pale cloud. *Rababa*

Rabiah (Arabic) Breeze. *Rabi, Rabia, Raby*

Rachav (Hebrew) Big baby. *Rachev*

Rachel (Hebrew) Little lamb, ewe; one with purity. *Chelle, Chellie, Rachael, Rachele, Rahel, Rah'zell, Raquel, Ray, Raychel, Shelley, Shellie, Shelly*

Radella (Old English) Elfin adviser. *Radela, Radelia, Radellah, Railiah*

Radha (Hindi) Favorite friend. *Radhah*

Radhika (Hindi) Form of the Hindu goddess Devi; fifth sakti (power, energy); wife of Krishna.

Radinka (Slavic) Active.

Radmilla (Slavic) Worker for the people. *Radmila, Radmilah, Radmile, Radmille*

Rae (Scottish) Grace. (English) Doe. (German) Wise protection. *Raeann, Raelene, Ray, Raye, Rayette*

Raeka (Spanish) Beautiful; unique. *Rae*

Raelene (French) Royal temptress. *Raelean, Raeleen, Railean, Raileen, Raileene*

Raelin (Celtic) Meaning unknown. *Rae, Raelyn*

Raeni (Jamaican) Queen.

Rafa (Hindi) Happy. *Rafah, Raffa*

Rafaela (Spanish) God heals; feminine version of Raphael. *Rafa, Rafaelia, Rafaella, Rafella, Rafelle, Raffaela, Raffaele, Raphaella, Raphaelle, Refaela, Rephaela*

Ragamaya (Sanskrit) Beloved.

Ragini (Hindi) Melody.

Ragnhild (Norse) One who is wise in battle. *Ragnhilda, Ragnhilde, Ragnilda, Ranilida, Renilda, Renilde*

Rahab (Hebrew) Proud; quarrelsome.

Rai (Japanese) Trust.

Raidah (Arabic) Leader. *Raida, Raidah, Rayda, Raydah*

Raimy (African) Compassionate. *Raimee*

Rain (Latin) Ruler. *Raina, Raine, Rana, Rane, Ray, Rayne, Reign, Rein*

Rainbow (English) Array of bright colors. *Rainbeau, Rainbo*

Rainelle (English) Combination of *rain* and *elle*. *Rainell*

Rainfreda (German) Advice. *Rainfrida, Rainfridah*

Raissa (Old French) Thinker. (Russian) Rose. (Greek) Rose. *Raisa*

Raizel (Hebrew) Rose. *Rayzel, Razel*

Raja (Arabic) Anticipation. *Raga, Ragya, Rajya*

Rajni (Hindi) Dark of the night. *Rajani*

Rakel (Hebrew) Ewe.

Rakhil (Hindi) Lamb.

Raksha (Hindi) Moon; protection.

Raku (Japanese) Pleasure.

Raleigh (English) Field of birds. *Raileigh, Railey, Raley, Rawleigh, Rawley*

Ralphina (English) Wolf counselor; feminine form of Ralph. *Ralphine*

Rama (Hebrew) Highly praised. *Ramah*

Ramla (Egyptian) One who predicts the future.

Ramona (Spanish) Wise protector. *Mona, Ramiele, Ramonah, Ramonda, Ramonna, Raymona*

Ramose (Latin) Branches. *Ramosa, Ramosah*

Ramya (Hindi) Elegant, beautiful.

Ran (Scandinavian) Goddess of the sea.

Rana (Spanish) Frog. *Rana, Ranah, Raniyah, Ranna, Ranya*

Ranait (Irish) Graceful. *Ranaita, Ranaite, Ranayte*

Randa (Arabic) Tree. *Randah*

Randi (English, American) Wolf shield; form of Randall. *Rande, Randea, Randeen*

Rane (Norwegian) Queen; pure. *Rain, Raine, Ranie*

Ranger (English) Protector of the forest.

Rangi (Maori) Sky. *Rangia, Rangy*

Rani (Hindi) Queen.

Ranielle (African American) God is my judge; form of Danielle.

Raniyah (Arabic) Gazing. *Raniya*

Ranjana (Hindi) Delightful. *Ranjanah*

Ranjita (Hindi) Adorned.

Ranveig (Scandinavian) Housewife. *Rannaug*

Rapa (Hawaiian) Moonbeam. *Rapah*

Raphaella (Hebrew) Healed by God. *Rafaella*

Rashawna (Irish) God is gracious. *Rashawn, Rashawnah, Rashawne, Roshauna*

Rashida (African) Righteous. *Rasheda, Rasheddah, Rasheeda, Rasheida, Rashidah*

Rasia (Greek) Rose. *Rasine, Rasya*

Rasika (Hindi) Connoisseur.

Rasine (Polish) Rose. *Roisine*

Rasna (Hindi) Tongue.

Ratana (Thai) Crystal. *Rana, Ranya, Ratania, Rattana*

Rati (Hindi) Hindu goddess Devi.

Ratri (Hindi) Night. *Ratree, Ratrey, Ratria, Ratry*

Raula (French) Wolf. *Raole, Raulla, Raulle*

Ravva (Hindi) Sun. *Rava, Ravah, Ravvah*

Raven (English) Dark-haired; wise; bird. *Ravan, Rave, Ravin*

Rawnie (Gypsy) Lady. *Rawna, Rawnee, Rawney*

Raya (Hebrew) Friend. *Raeah, Raia, Rayah*

Rayanne (American) Grace; combination of Ray and Anne. *Rayann*

Rayelle (English) Lamb.

Raylene (French) Counselor; form of Raymond. *Raylina*

Rayma (German) Wise protection. *Ray*

Raymonde (German) Wise protector. *Raemond, Raimond, Ratmay, Raymae*

Rayna (Hebrew) Pure, clean. *Raina, Rana, Rane, Rania, Renait, Renana, Renatia, Renatya, Renina, Rinatia, Rinatya*

Razi (Hebrew) My secret. *Raziah, Raziela, Razilia, Razille*

Raziya (African) Agreeable.

Rea (English) Manly. *Raya, Rhia, Ria*

Reanna (German) Mighty grace. *Reana, Reanah, Reane, Reian, Reyanah*

Reba (Hebrew) Fourth; square; stooped.

Rebecca (Hebrew) Bound, tied. *Becca, Becha, Becka, Becky, Bekki, Reba, Rebakah, Rebeca, Rebeccah, Rebeckah, Rebeka, Rebekah, Rebekka, Rebequa, Rebeque, Ree, Reeba, Riba, Rifka, Riva, Rivca, Rivka, Rivy*

Rechaba (Hebrew) Rider of horses. *Rechabah*

Reena (Hindi) Peaceful. *Reen, Reene*

Reese (Welsh) Enthusiastic. *Ree, Reece, Rees, Rere*

Reet (Greek) Pearl. *Reeta, Reete, Reit, Reite*

Regan (Irish, Scottish) King's heir. *Reagan, Reagin, Reagon*

Regina (Latin) Queenly. *Gina, Rain, Raina, Rane,*

Rani, Regan, Reggie, Rein, Reina, Reine, Rexy, Reyna, Rina

Rei (Japanese) Gratitude. *Rey*

Reidun (Norwegian) Nest-lovely.

Reiko (Japanese) Child of Rei; gratitude.

Reilley (Irish) Rye. *Rielly, Riley*

Rekha (Hindi) Straight line. *Reka*

Reman (Hindi) Meaning unknown.

Remington (English) Town of the raven.

Remy (French) From Rheims. *Remi*

Ren (Japanese) Waterlily.

Rena (Hebrew) Peace; joyous song. *Reena, Rinah, Rinne*

Renata (Latin) Reborn. *Renate, Renée, Renette*

Rene (Greek) Peaceful. *Reene, Renee, Renne*

Renee (French) Born again. *Renata, Renay, Rene, Renelle, Reney, Reni, Renia, Renie, Renni, Rennie, Renny*

Renita (Latin) To be firm. *Reneeta*

Rennefer (Egyptian) Weaver.

Renni (Hebrew) Song. *Renney*

Renora (Japanese) Compassion. (Science fiction) Character from *Star Trek: Deep Space Nine*.

Renuka (Hindi) Mother of Parasurma.

Rere (Polynesian) Watchful one. *Reree*

Reseda (Latin) Healing one. *Reseada, Reseeda, Resida, Residah*

Reshma (Hindi) Silky.

Resi (Greek) Harvester. *Resee, Ressi, Ressy*

Reta (African) Shaking. *Rhetah, Rita, Ryta*

Retha (Greek) Best. *Reatee, Reati, Reaty, Retey*

Reubena (Hebrew) Behold. *Reubina, Reuvena, Rubena, Rubina*

Reva (Latin) Renewed strength. *Reava, Reeva, Reevah, Revia*

Revati (Hindi) Wife of Balarama.

Revaya (Hebrew) Satisfaction. *Revaia, Revayah*

Revelation (Latin) Lacy; insight.

Rewa (Polynesian) Slender. *Rewah*

Rexana (Latin) God's gracious queen. *Rexanna, Rexannah, Rexanne*

Reyhan (Turkish) Sweet-smelling flower. *Reihan, Reihana, Reihane, Reyhane*

Rhea (Greek) Stream. (Latin) Poppy. *Rea, Ria*

Rhedyn (Welsh) Fern. *Readan, Readon, Rheaden, Rheden, Rheedin*

Rhiamon (Welsh) Witch. *Rhianon*

Rhiannon (Welsh) Mythological nymph. *Rheanna, Rheanne, Rhiana, Rhiann, Rhianna, Rhiannan, Rhianon, Rhuan, Riana, Riane, Rianna, Rianne, Riannon, Rianon, Riona*

Rhoda (Greek) Rose. *Rhodah, Rhodia, Rhodie, Rodie, Roe*

Rhodanthe (Greek) Rose.

Rhodelia (Greek) Rosy-cheeked. *Rhodeliah, Rodelia, Rodelya, Rodelyah*

Rhonda (Celtic) Good spear. *Rhonnda, Ronda*

Rhonwen (Welsh) Slender; fair. *Ronwen, Roweena, Roweina, Rowena, Rowina*

Rhoswen (Gaelic) White rose.

Rhu (Hindi) Pure.

Rhysati (Science fiction) Character from *Star Wars*.

Ria (Spanish) Mouth of a river. *Rhia, Rhiah, Rhya, Rya*

Riana (Irish) Honorable.

Riane (Gaelic) Little king.

Riannon (Welsh) Great queen, witch, or goddess. *Rianne*

Ricarda (Italian) Powerful ruler; feminine version of Richard. *Rica, Ricca, Richarda, Richel, Richela, Richele, Richella, Richelle, Richenda, Richenza, Ricki, Rickie, Ricky, Riki, Rikki, Rikky*

Riccadonna (Italian) Rich lady. *Ricadona, Ricadonna, Riccadonah, Rickadonah*

Richael (Hebrew) Innocence of a lamb. (Irish) Name of a saint. *Ricael, Rikael*

Richelle (German) Powerful ruler. (English) Brave one. *Ricarda, Ricky, Rikki*

Rickena (Czech) Meaning unknown.

Rickma (Hebrew) Woven. *Ricma, Ricmah, Ryckma, Rycma*

Rida (Arabic) Favored by God. *Ridah, Ryda*

Riddhi (Hindi) Will follow.

Rieko (Japanese) Child of Rie.

Rigoberta (Spanish) Ridge.

Rihana (Arabic) Sweet basil.

Rika (Swedish) Ruler. *Rhica, Rhicca, Rhika, Rique*

Rikako (Japanese) Child of Rika.

Riku (Japanese) Land. *Rikuya*

Riley (Gaelic) Valiant. *Reilly, Ryley, Ryly*

Rima (Hindi) White antelope. *Rheyma, Rhimah*

Rimona (Hebrew) Pomegranate.

Rimu (Polynesian) Red pine tree. *Rymu*

Rina (Hindi) Queen. *Reena, Riena*

Rinako (Japanese) Child of Rina.

Rinda (Scandinavian) Ancient mythological figure. *Rind*

Rini (Japanese) Little bunny.

Ripley (English) From the shouter's meadow.

Risa (Latin) Laughing one. *Risé, Risë*

Risako (Japanese) Child of Risa.

Risha (Hindi) Born in the month of Taurus. *Rishah, Rysha, Ryshah*

Rishabh (Hindi) Octave note.

Rishona (Hebrew) First.

Rissa (Greek) Sea fairy. *Rissah, Rysa, Rysah, Ryssa*

Rita (Greek) Pearl; precious. *Reeta, Reta, Rheta, Rhetta*

Ritsa (Greek) Defender of humankind. *Ritsah, Rytsa*

Ritu (Hindi) Season.

Riva (French) River. *Reeva, Reva, Ria, Rive, Rivi, Rivy*

Rivka (French) Shore. *Rivka, Ryvam, Ryvka*

Riza (Greek) Harvester. *Rieser, Rizah, Rizza*

Rizpah (Greek) Hope. *Ritzpa, Rizpa*

Roana (Spanish) Reddish-brown skin. *Roannah*

Roberta (English) Bright; famous. *Bert, Berta, Berthe, Bertie, Bobbi, Bobbie, Bobby, Robbin, Robin, Robina, Robinette, Robyn, Ruperta*

Robin (English) Queen of morning. *Robbin, Robbyn, Robyn*

Rochelle (French) From the little rock. *Rochella, Rochette*

Rocio (Italian) Dewdrops. *Rocyo*

Roderica (German) Famous one. *Roderika*

Roesia (French) Rose. *Rodica, Rodicia, Rohesia*

Rogan (Gaelic) Red-haired. *Roan*

Rohana (Hindi) Sandal-wood. *Rohanna, Rohena*

Rohini (Hindi) Star. *Rohiney, Rohiny, Rohyni*

Roisin (Latin) Rose. *Roisina, Roisine, Roysyn*

Rokeya (Polynesian) Dawn. *Rokey*

Rolanda (German) From the famous sea. *Rolande, Rollande, Rolonda*

Romana (Italian) From Rome. *Roma, Romy*

Romia (Hebrew) Highly praised. *Romiah, Romya*

Rona (Gaelic) Covenant; oath.

Ronalda (Old Norse) Mighty.

Roni (Hebrew) Happy. *Ronie, Ronilie, Rony, Ronye*

Roniya (Hebrew) God's happiness. *Ronia, Roniah, Roniyah*

Ronnell (African American) Feminine version of Ron. *Ranell, Ronell, Ronelle*

Rory (German) Form of Roderick; famous ruler; red. *Rorie, Rorrie, Rorry*

Rosa (Irish) Noted protector; rose; pink.

Rosalba (Latin) White rose. *Rosalbah*

Rosalind (Spanish) Pretty rose. *Rosalia, Rosalinda, Rosaline, Rosalyn, Rosalynde, Rose-Lyn, Roseline, Roselyn, Rosey, Rosilind, Roslin, Rozalan*

Rosalynda (Spanish) Beautiful. *Rosalinda*

Rosamund (German) Garden of flowers. *Rosamond, Rosamonde, Rosamunda, Rosamunde*

Rosanne (Latin) Gracious rose. *Rosanna, Roseanna, Roseannah, Rosehannah, Rozanna, Rozanne*

Rosaria (Italian) Rosary. *Rosariah, Rosarya, Rozaria, Rozarya*

Rose (Latin) Flower. *Chara, Charo, Rasia, Roanee, Roanna, Rois, Rosa, Rosabell, Rosalee, Rosaleen, Rosalia, Rosalie, Rosamund, Rosebud, Rosella,*

Roselle, Rosellen, Rosemarie, Rosemary, Rosemonde, Rosena, Rosetta, Rosette, Rosey, Rosie, Rosina, Rosita, Roslin, Rosly, Rosmund, Roz, Rozamund, Rozsi

Roselani (Hawaiian) Heavenly rose. *Roselana, Roslaney*

Rosemary (English) Bitter rose; fragrant herb.

Roshin (Japanese) Dewdrop mind.

Roshni (Hindi) Light.

Rosita (Spanish) Rose. *Rositah, Rozetah*

Roslin (French) Little red-haired one. *Rosalind, Rosalinda, Rosalinde, Rosalyn, Rose-Lynn, Roslyn, Rosselin*

Rossalyn (Scottish) From the Cape. *Rosaline, Rosalyne, Rossalin*

Roula (Greek) Rebel. *Roulah*

Rowan (English) From the rowan tree; tree with red berries.

Rowena (Welsh) Red-haired; rugged. *Rowana*

Roxanne (Persian) Brilliant one. *Rox, Roxana, Roxane, Roxann, Roxanna, Roxie, Roxy*

Royanna (English) Gracious queen. *Roiana, Roianna, Royana, Royanne*

Ruby (French) Red gem. *Rubee, Rubia, Rubie, Rubina*

Ruchi (Hindi) Luster; beauty. *Ruchee, Ruchie, Ruchy*

Ruchika (Hindi) Meaning unknown.

Ruchira (Hindi) Beautiful.

Rudelle (French) She is famous. *Rudele, Rudell, Rudella*

Rudrani (Hindi) Wife of Shiva.

Rue (Latin, Greek) Herb; regret. *Ruey*

Ruffina (Italian) Red-haired. *Rufina, Rufiniah*

Rui (French) Regal. *Ru*

Rukan (Arabic) Steadfast. *Rukann*

Rukiya (Swahili) Rising. *Rukiyah*

Rukmini (Hindi) Wife of Lord Krishna. *Rukminy*

Rumer (English) Gypsy. *Roumar, Rumar, Rumor*

Rumiko (Japanese) Child of Rumi.

Runa (Scandinavian) Secret lore.

Rupa (Hindi) Silver.

Rupal (Hindi) Beauty.

Rupali (Hindi) Beautiful.

Ruri (Japanese) Emerald. *Ruriko*

Rusty (English) Tawny. *Ruste, Rustey, Rustie*

Ruta (Hawaiian) Friendly. *Rutah*

Ruth (Hebrew) Compassionate friend. *Ruthanne, Ruthie*

Ryan (Gaelic) Little king. *Rian, Ryanne, Ryen*

Ryba (Czech) Fish.

Ryesen (English) Rye.

Ryo (American) River.

Ryoko (Japanese) Child of Ryo.

S

Saada (Hebrew) One who gives support. *Saadah*

Saamiya (Arabic) Elevated; exalted; lofty.

Saba (Greek) Woman of Sheba. *Sabah*

Sabana (Latin) From the open plain.

Sabara (Hebrew) Thorny cactus. *Sabarah, Sabarra*

Sabbatha (Latin) Child born on Sunday. *Sabbathe*

Sabeans (Hebrew) Captivity; conversion; old age.

Sabiha (Arabic) Forenoon; beautiful.

Sabina (Latin) Sabine woman. *Bienchen, Biene, Bini, Sabienne, Sabine, Sabinna, Sabiny, Sabse, Saidhbhin, Savina*

Sabirah (Arabic) Patient.

Sabita (Hindi) Sun; sweet; form of Savita.

Sabiya (Arabic) Morning east wind. *Sabaya, Sabayah, Sabyah*

Sable (English) Dark-brown color fur; black. *Sabel, Sabela, Sabelle*

Sabola (Egyptian) Prophetess.

Sabra (Arabic) To rest. (Hebrew) Thorny cactus. *Sabe, Sabera, Sabrah*

Sabrina (Latin) From the border land. *Sabreena, Sabrena, Sabrinna*

Sachi (Hindi) Wife of Indrid. (Japanese) Bliss. *Sachee, Sachey, Sachie, Sachy, Sashi, Sashie*

Sachiko (Japanese) Bliss; child of Sachi.

Sacrifice (Old English) To make sacred.

Sada (Japanese) Pure one. *Sadda, Saddah, Sadea, Sadel*

Sadah (Arabic) Good fortune; from Zada.

Sadb (Gaelic) Meaning unknown.

Sade (Nigerian) Honor confers a crown.

Sadhana (Hindi) Patience.

Sadie (English) Princess. *Sade, Sadee, Sady, Sadye, Shaday*

Sadira (Arabic) Ostrich returning from water.

Sadiya (Arabic) Lucky. *Sadia, Sadiah, Sadya, Sadyah*

Saeko (Japanese) Child of Sae.

Saeran (Welsh) Irish saint.

Safa (Arabic) Innocent. *Safah, Saffa*

Safak (Turkish) Meaning unknown.

Safara (African) Her place.

Saffi (Danish) Wisdom. *Saffee, Saffia, Saffie, Safi*

Saffron (English) Yellow flower. *Saffrone, Safron*

Safiya (African) Pure.

Saga (English) Journey.

Sagara (Hindi) Ocean. *Sagarah*

Sage (French) Wise one; from the sagebrush plant; prophet. *Saige*

Sagira (Egyptian) Little one.

Sagittarius (Latin) Archer.

Sahana (Indian) Raga.

Sahara (Arabic) Moon. *Shahar*

Saheli (Hindi) Friend. *Sakhi, Sakina*

Sahiba (Hindi) Lady.

Sahila (Hindi) Guide.

Sahirah (Egyptian) Clean, pristine.

Sahyko (Native American) Mink.

Sai (Japanese) Talented. *Saiko*

Saida (Arabic) Fortunate one. *Saeda, Saida, Sayda*

Saidah (African) Happy, fortunate.

Saige (English) Wise one. *Sage.*

Sailia Origin and meaning unknown.

Sailor (English) Mariner. *Sailer, Sailie, Saylor*

Saima (Arabic) Fasting woman.

Saisha (Sanskrit) Meaningful life. *Saesha*

Saiun (Japanese) Colorful sky. *Saiun.*

Saja (Arabic) Calm.

Sajili (Hindi) Decorated.

Sajni (Hindi) Beloved.

Sakae (Japanese) Wealthy. *Sakai, Sakay*

Sakari (Native American) Sweet. *Sakara, Sakaria*

Sakhi (Asian) Woman friend.

Saki (Japanese) Cloak; rice wine. *Sakee, Sakia, Sakya*

Sakiko (Japanese) Child of Saki.

Sakima (Native American) King; for a boy or girl.

Sakina (Hindi) Friend.

Sakinah (Arabic) God-inspired peace of mind; tranquility. *Sakina*

Sakti (Hindi) Energy; goodness. *Saktee, Saktia, Sakty*

Sakuko (Japanese) Child of Saku.

Sakuna (Native American) Bird. *Sakunah*

Sakura (Japanese) Cherry blossoms.

Sakurako (Japanese) Child of Sakura. *Sakurah*

Sala (Hindi) Sacred tree. *Salah, Salla*

Salal (English) Plant.

Salali (Native American) Squirrel. *Salalee, Salalei, Salaleigh*

Salama (Egyptian) Peaceful.

Sale (Hawaiian) Princess. *Saarai, Sera*

Saleema (Arabic) Peaceful.

Salena (Indian) Moon; salt. *Salean, Salenah*

Salene (French) Dignified one.

Salette (English) Little princess. *Salete, Salett, Saletta, Salettah*

Salia (English) Princess.

Salihah (African) Correct.

Salimah (Arabic) Safe, healthy.

Salina (Latin) By the salt water; solemn. *Saleena, Salena*

Sally (Spanish) Saviour. *Sal, Salaidh, Salli, Sallie, Sallye*

Salma (Spanish) Ambitious.

Saloma (Hebrew) Peace. *Salome.*

Salome (Hebrew) Welcome; peace.

Saloni (Hindi) Dear, beautiful.

Salote (Polynesian) Lady.

Salsa (Cuban) Dance.

Salvadora (Spanish) Saved. *Salvadorah*

Salvia (Latin) Strong. *Sallvia, Salviana, Salviane, Salvinah*

Salwa (Arabic) Solace, comfort. *Salva*

Samala (Hebrew) Her name is God. *Samalah, Sammala, Sammalah*

Samantha (Aramaic) Listens well. *Sam, Sammi, Sammy*

Samara (Hebrew) Ruled by God. (Latin) Seedling. *Samora*

Samatha (Hebrew) Listener of God.

Sameh (Hebrew) Listening. *Samaiya*

Sami (Arabic) Praised. *Samee, Samey, Samie, Sammee*

Samiah (Arabic) Exalted.

Samicah (Hebrew) Meaning unknown. *Samika*

Samiksha (Hindi) Overview; analysis.

Samira (Arabic) Entertaining. *Samire, Samyre*

Samirah (Arabic) Entertaining companion.

Samma (Arabic) Sky, skye. *Ma, Sa, Samm*

Sammy-Jo (Hebrew) God is good; God has heard.

Sampriti (Hindi) Attachment.

Samta (Hindi) Meaning unknown.

Samuela (Hebrew) Her name is God. *Samella, Samielle, Sammila, Samuella*

Samularia (Latin) Sweet one forever. *Lari, Laria, Sammy*

Samye (Tibetan) Place of first Buddhist monastery built in Tibet. Forest; thinkers; unexpected.

Sana (Hebrew) Lily. *Sanaa, Sanah*

Sanako (Japanese) Child of Sana.

Sanam (Persian) Lover.

Sananda (Hindi) Happiness. *Sanansah*

Sancha (Spanish) Holy. *Sanchia*

Sanchali (Indian) Movement.

Sanchay (Hindi) Collection. *Sandhaya, Sandhya*

Sanchaya (Indian) Meaning unknown.

Sancho (Spanish) Holy. *Sancha*

Sancia (Latin) Holy.

Sandia (Spanish) Watermelon.

Sandora (English) Defender of mankind. *Alexandra, Sandrine, Sandy*

Sandra (Greek) Helper and defender of mankind. *Sandrah, Saundie, Saundra*

Sandrine (Greek) Helper and defender of mankind. *Sandreen, Sandrene, Sandrin*

Sandya (Hindi) Sunset time; name of a god. *Sandiha*

Sang Hee (Korean) Benevolence and pleasure.

Sangita (Hindi) Musical.

Saniya (Hindi) Moment in time.

Sanjana (Indian) Gentle.

Sanjna (Hindi) Wife of the sun.

Sanjula (Hindi) Beautiful. *Sanjushree, Sohni*

Sanna (Scandinavian) Truth. *Sana*

Sanne (American) Lily. *Sanneen, Sanneena*

Sanrevelle (Portuguese) Meaning unknown. *Rev, Revelle, Revla, San*

Sansana (Hebrew) Palm tree leaf. *Sansanah*

Santana (Spanish) Saintly. *Santanne, Santina*

Santavana (Hindi) Hope. *Santavanah*

Santillana (Spanish) Soft-haired. *Santillanah*

Santina (Spanish) Little saint.

Sanura (Egyptian) Kitten. *Sanurah*

Sanya (Sanskrit) Born on a Saturday. *Sanyah*

Sanyogita (Hindi) Meaning unknown.

Sanyukta (Hindi) Union. *Sanjukta*

Saoirse (Celtic) Freedom.

Sapata (Native American) Dancing bear. *Sapatah*

Sapna (Hindi) Dream.

Sapphira (Greek) Blue jewel. *Saphira, Sapphire*

Sappho (Greek) First known woman poet; poetry.

Sarab (Arabic) Dream.

Sarah (Hebrew) Princess; lady. *Sadey, Sadie, Sairne, Sara, Sarene, Sarett, Sari, Sarina, Sarine, Sarita, Sarri, Sarrie, Sary, Zara, Zarah, Zaria*

Sarahi (Hebrew) Princess.

Sarai (Hebrew) Quarrel-some. *Sari*

Saraid (Celtic) Excellent.

Saranu (Sanskrit) Fast run-ner. *Saran, Sarana, Saranah*

Sarasvati (Hindi) Goddess.

Saravati (Hindi) River.

Sarea (Hebrew) Name of an angel.

Saree (Arabic) Most noble. *Sarie, Sary*

Sari (Hebrew) Princess. *Saree, Sarey, Sarie, Sarree, Sarrey, Sarri*

Sariah (Hebrew) My princess.

Saricia (Science fiction) Character from *Star Wars*.

Sarika (Hindi) Thrush.

Saril (Turkish) Flowing water. *Sarila, Sarill, Sarille, Saryll, Sarylle*

Sarina (Latin) Serene, calm. *Sareena, Sarena, Sarrie*

Sarisha (Hindi) Charming.

Sarita (Hindi) Stream; river. *Sareatta, Sareeta, Sareete*

Sarmistha (Hindi) Daughter of Vrsaparvan.

Saroja (Hindi) Born near a lake.

Saronna (African American) Princess. *Sarona, Saronah, Saronnah*

Sarotte (French) Princess.

Saryu (Hindi) River Sharayu in Ramayana.

Sasa (Japanese) Assistant. *Sasah*

Sasha (Russsian) Defender of mankind; form of Alexander. *Sacha, Sachie, Sascha, Sasheen, Sashy*

Sashenka (Russian) Defender and helper of mankind.

Sashi (Hindi) Moon. (Japanese) To cut, to stab.

Sasilvia (Hawaiian) From Silvia.

Saskia (Slavic) Protector of mankind.

Sasona (Hebrew) Happy. *Sasonah*

Sass (Irish) Bright. *Sas, Sasi, Sassi*

Sasthi (Hindi) Meaning unknown.

Satara (Irish) Princess from the rocky hill. *Satarah, Sataria, Satarya, Sataryah*

Satin (French) Smooth fabric. *Saten*

Satinka (Native American) Magic dancer.

Sato (Japanese) Sugar. *Satu*

Satoko (Japanese) Child of Sato.

Satoria (African American) Bird. *Satori, Satory, Satorya, Satoryah*

Saturnia (Latin) Planting. *Saturna, Saturne, Saturniah, Saturnya*

Satyavati (Hindi) Mother of Vyasa.

Sauda (Swahili) Dark-skinned. *Saudah*

Saumya (Hindi) Mild.

Saundarya (Hindi) Meaning unknown.

Savana (Spanish) Treeless plain.

Savanna (Spanish) From the open plain Savannah. *Sava, Savana, Savanah*

Savarna (Hindi) Daughter of the ocean.

Savea (Scandinavian) Swedish nation.

Savina (Russian) Sabine woman. *Saveena, Savyna*

Savita (Hindi) Sun.

Savitri (Hindi) Form of the Hindu goddess Devi; fourth sakti (power, energy).

Sawa (Japanese) Swamp. *Sawah*

Sawni (Native American) Echo. *Sawnee, Sawney, Sawny*

Sawsan (Arabic) Great-smelling flower.

Sawson (Arabic) Lily. *Sawsen, Sawsin, Sawsyn*

Saxon (Latin) Large stone; swordsman.

Sayana (Hindi) Fourteenth-century commentator on the Vedas; tropical.

Sayo (Japanese) Born at night. *Saio*

Sayoko (Japanese) Child of Sayo.

Scarlet (Middle English) Deep red. *Scarlett, Scarlette, Scarlit, Scarlitt*

Schmetterling (German) Butterfly.

Scholastica (Latin) Scholar.

Schuyler (Dutch) Shield; scholar. *Schuylar, Schyler, Skiler, Sky, Skye*

Scota (Latin) Irish woman.

Scout (French) Scout; watchman.

Seanna (Celtic) God's grace. *Shauna, Shaune, Shawna, Shawnie, Shawnna, Shawny, Shay, Siana*

Searlait (French) Petite.

Season (Latin) Planting time.

Sebastianne (Latin) Revered one. *Sebastiana, Sebastiane*

Sebastiona (French, Italian, Latin) Venerable, revered; form of Sebastian.

Sebille (English) Fairy.

Sebrina (English) Princess.

Secilia (Latin) Unseeing. *Sasilla, Seciliah, Sesilia, Sesiliah*

Secunda (Latin) Second-born child. *Seconda, Secondah, Secondia*

Seda (Armenian) Forest voices. *Sedah*

Seema (Greek) Sprout. (Hindi) Limit; border.

Sefika (Turkish) Meaning unknown.

Seina (Spanish) Innocent.

Seiran (Welsh) Bright. *Seiryan*

Sekai (African) Laughter.

Seki (Japanese) Wonderful. *Seka, Sekah, Sekee*

Sela (Hebrew) Rock. *Cela, Celia, Selah, Selia*

Selby (English) Of the manor house farm. *Selden, Seldon, Selwin, Selwyn*

Selena (Greek) Moon. *Celena, Celene, Celia, Celie, Celina, Sela, Selene, Selia, Selina, Selinda, Sellie, Selly, Sena*

Selima (Arabic) Peace. *Selema, Selemmah*

Selina (Greek) Moon.

Selma (Scandinavian) Divinely protected. *Salmah, Selle, Sellma, Zelma*

Sema (Greek) Divine omen.

Semele (Latin) Once.

Semine (Danish) Goddess of sun, moon, and stars. *Mina, Mine, Semina*

Semira (African) Fulfilled. *Semirah*

Semra (Turkish) Meaning unknown.

Sen (Vietnamese) Lotus flower.

Sena (Greek) Guest. *Senah, Senia, Senya*

Senalda (Spanish) Sign, symbol. *Sennah*

Senga (Scottish) Purity. *Sengah*

Senja (Finnish) Meaning unknown.

Sennett (French) Wise one. *Senet, Senta*

Senona (Spanish) Lively.

Senta (German) Assistant.

Seona (Scottish) God is gracious. *Seonah, Seonia, Seoniah*

September (Latin) Seventh moon.

Septima (Latin) Seventh born. *Septimma, Septyma*

Sequoia (Native American) Giant redwood tree.

Sera (Latin) Heavenly, winged angel.

Serafina (Latin) Heavenly, winged angel.

Seraphina (Hebrew) Afire; angel; seraph. *Sarafina, Sera, Serafina, Serafine, Seraphim, Seraphine*

Serena (Latin) Peaceful one; calm. *Sarina, Serenah, Serene, Serenna, Serina*

Serenity (English) Peaceful disposition. *Serenitee, Serenitie*

Serica (Greek) Silky. *Sarica, Saricah, Saricka*

Serilda (German) Armed maiden of war. *Sarilda, Sarildah*

Serina (Latin) Serene, calm. *Sereena, Serin, Serinah, Serreena, Serrin, Serrina*

Serwa (African) Jewel.

Sesen (African) To wish for more.

Sesha (Hindi) Serpent who symbolizes time.

Setsu (Japanese) Faith.

Settimia (Australian) Meaning unknown.

Sevati (Hindi) White rose.

Seve (Breton) Meaning unknown. *Seva*

Sevita (Hindi) Beloved.

Sexburth (Anglo-Saxon) Meaning unknown.

Sezen (Turkish) Meaning unknown.

Sezja (Russian) Protector.

Shaba (Spanish) Rose. *Shabah, Shabana, Shabanah*

Shada (Native American) Pelican. *Shadae, Shadea*

Shadrika (English) Ruler of the shadows. *Shadreeka, Shadreka, Shadrica*

Shadya (Arabic) One who sings. *Shadia, Shadiah*

Shae (English, Irish) Gift; fairy palace. *Shay, Shea*

Shaelyn (Irish) From the fairy palace pool. *Shaelean, Shaeleen, Shaeleena*

Shahina (Arabic) Falcon bird. *Shahean, Shaheen, Shaheena, Shahi*

Shaila (Hindi) Stone, mountain. *Shailah, Shayla*

Shailaja (Hindi) Meaning unknown.

Shaili (Hindi) Style.

Shaina (Hebrew) Beautiful. *Shane, Shania, Shayna, Shayne*

Shaine (Hebrew) Beautiful. *Shaina, Shana, Shanie, Shanna, Shay, Shayna, Shaynah*

Shaka (Hindi) Divine woman. *Shakah, Shakha, Shakia*

Shakila (African) Pretty.

Shakina (African) Beautiful one.

Shakira (Arabic) Grateful. *Shakeera, Shakeerah, Shakeira, Shakera, Shakyra, Skakarah*

Shako (Native American) Mint.

Shalana (Irish) Attractive. *Shalain, Shaland, Shalane, Shalaun*

Shalini (Hindi) Modesty.

Shalisa (Hebrew) Honey bee. *Shalesa, Shalese, Shalice, Shalise*

Shalom (Hebrew) Peace.

Shalot (Scottish) Character in Arthurian legend that inspired Tennyson's poem "The Lady of Shalott."

Shamara (Arabic) Ready for battle. *Shamarah, Shamari, Shamarra*

Shamira (Hebrew) Protector. *Shamirah, Shamyra*

Shamita (Hindi) Peacemaker.

Shammara (Arabic) He girded his loins. *Shammarah*

Shana (Hebrew) God is gracious. *Shanae, Shanah, Shanaia, Shannah*

Shanata (Hindi) Peaceful.

Shandra (African American) God is gracious. *Shandrah*

Shandy (English) Rambunctious. *Shandee, Shandey, Shandi*

Shanequa (American) From Moniqua; adviser.

Shanessa (Irish) God is gracious. *Nessa*

Shani (Swahili) Marvelous.

Shania (Native American) I'm on my way.

Shanice (English) God is gracious. *Shaneece, Shaneese, Shaniece*

Shanida (English) Prosperous. *Shaneeda, Shaneedah, Shanyda*

Shanika (Hindi) Gracious; beautiful. *Shaneca, Shaneecah, Shanica*

Shaniqua (American) Adviser; form of Moniqua.

Shanita (Native American) Bear. *Shaneeta, Shaneetah, Shaneta*

Shaniya (Native American) I'm on my way.

Shanley (Gaelic) Child of the old hero. *Shanlea, Shanlee, Shanleigh, Shanli*

Shanna (Hebrew) God is gracious; form of Shannon; lovely. *Shanah, Shanea, Shannah*

Shannelle (French) Channel. *Chanel, Channel, Schannel, Shanel, Shanelly, Shannel*

Shannon (Irish) Wise one; river name. *Shan, Shanen, Shanon*

Shantah (Hindi) Peace; a god. *Shanta, Shanti*

Shantana (Spanish) Saint. *Shantania, Shantanna, Shantanne, Shantenah*

Shantay (French) Enchanted.

Shante (Hindi) Rest, peace.

Shanteca (Greek) Harvester. *Shantecca, Shanteka, Shantika*

Shantell (Africa American) Song. *Chantel, Shantal, Shantel*

Shantelle (American) Stormy place. *Shantel, Shanty, Telle, Telly*

Shanti (Hindi) Peaceful, tranquil.

Shantia (Greek) God's gracious princess. *Shantiah, Shantida, Shantya, Shauntia*

Shantina (American) Warrior princess. *Tina*

Shanton (French) We sing.

Shantora (Latin) Victorious. *Shantoree, Shantorey, Shantori, Shantory*

Shappa (Native American) Red thunder. *Shapah, Shappah*

Shaquana (African American) Truth in life.

Shara (Hebrew) Princess. *Sharae, Sharah, Sharra, Sharray*

Sharay (Hebrew) My song, my lord. *Ray, Shay*

Sharda (Hindi) Meaning unknown. *Shardah*

Sharenne (Hebrew) From the graceful plains. *Sharenah, Sharenna, Sharennah*

Shari (Hebrew) Beloved. *Shary, Sherry*

Sharice (French) Precious. *Shareece, Shariece, Sharise, Sharyce*

Sharik (African) Child of God. *Sharike, Sharique, Sharyque*

Sharis (Hebrew) Flat plain.

Sharmaine (Latin) Song. *Sharmain, Sharmane, Sharmayne, Sharmine*

Sharman (English) Fair share. *Charman, Charmane*

Sharmila (Hindi) Protected one.

Sharmistha (Hindi) Wife of Yayat.

Sharon (Hebrew) Princess. *Charon, Shara, Sharee, Sharen, Shari, Sharonda, Sharron, Sharry, Sharyn, Sherri, Sherry*

Sharseia Origin and meaning unknown.

Sharvani (Hindi) Goddess.

Shasa (African) Precious water.

Shashi (Hindi) Moon; moonbeam.

Shasmecka (African) Princess. *Shas*

Shasta (Native American) Three.

Shatara (Irish) From the rocky hill. *Shatarah, Shataria, Shatarra, Shatarrah*

Shateque (African American) Follower.

Shatoria (African American) God's gracious victory. *Shatoriah, Shatorya*

Shauna (Irish) God is gracious; feminine form of Shaun. *Shaunna, Shawna*

Shawanna (German) Wanderer. *Shawana, Shawanah, Shawannah*

Shawmbria (American) Combination of Shawn and Bria.

Shawn (Hebrew) God is gracious. *Shaun, Shaunna*

Shawndelle (Irish) God is gracious to her. *Shaundell, Shawndele*

Shawnee (Irish) God's gift. *Sean, Shawn, Shawna*

Shawnnessy (Irish) God is gracious. *O'Shaughnessy, Saughnessy, Seannesy*

Shay (Irish) Stately one. *Shaye*

Shayla (Irish) Fairy palace. *Shaela, Shaila, Shaylah*

Shaylee (Irish) Fairy princess of the field. *Shaleigh, Shaylea, Shaylie, Shealee*

Shayna (Hebrew) Beautiful.

Shayndel (Yiddish) Beautiful.

Shea (Irish) Fairy palace. *Shae, Shay*

Sheba (Hebrew) From Sheba. *Chebah, Sheeba, Sheebah*

Sheena (Irish) God's gracious gift. *Sheenah*

Sheera (Hebrew) Song.

Sheetal (Hindi) Cool.

Sheha (Irish) From the boundary. *Shehah*

Sheila (Latin) Blind. *Selia, Sheela, Sheelah, Sheilagh, Sheilah*

Shela (Celtic) Musical.

Shelagh (Gaelic) Blind.

Shelah (Hebrew) Request.

Shelbi (English) Sheltered town. *Shelbee, Shelbie, Shelby, Shellbey*

Sheldon (English) From the farm on the ledge. *Shelden*

Shelley (English) From the ledge meadow; form of Michelle. *Sheli, Shelli, Shellie, Shelly*

Shenandoa (Native American) Beautiful star girl. *Shenandoah*

Shenara Origin and meaning unknown.

Shenna (Irish) Shining. *Shena, Shenae, Shenea*

Sheona (Irish) She is unity. *Sheonah*

Shepry (American) Friendly and honest mediator.

Shera (Hebrew) Light-hearted. *Sheera, Sheerah, Sherah*

Sheri (Hebrew) From Sharon. *Sherri, Sherrie*

Sheridan (English, Irish, Scottish) Untamed; the wild one. *Sheridin, Sheridon*

Sherill (English) Bright. *Cheril, Cherrill, Cheryl, Sherelle, Sheril, Sherrill, Sheryl*

Sherilyn (American) Combination of Sherry and Lyn.

Sherine (Hebrew) From Sharon.

Sherise (Greek) From Charisse.

Sherlyn (American) His song, his plain.

Sherri (Hebrew) Beloved. *Sherry*

Sheryl (English) Charity. *Cherie, Cheryl, Sherri, Sherry*

Sheyla (English) Gift of God.

Shian (Native American) Tribal name. *Shianne*

Shika (Japanese) Deer. *Shikah*

Shikah (Japanese) Gentle deer.

Shikha (Bengali) Flame.

Shiloh (Hebrew) His gift. *Shilo*

Shima (Native American) Mother.

Shin (Korean) Belief.

Shina (Japanese) Virtue; good. *Shinah, Shine*

Shinko (Japanese) Faith.

Shira (Hebrew) Song. *Shirah, Shiri*

Shirley (English) Country meadow. *Sherey, Sherlie, Shir, Shirl, Shirlee, Shirleen, Shirleigh, Shurl, Shurlie*

Shirlyn (English) Bright meadow.

Shivani (Indian) Goddess Parvati.

Shobha (Hindi) Attractive. (Sanskrit) Brilliance.

Shobhna (Hindi) Ornamental; shining.

Shobi (Hebrew) Glorious.

Shoko (Japanese) Child of Sho.

Shoshannah (Hebrew) Rose. *Shosha, Shoshana, Shoshanah, Shoshanna*

Shradhdha (Hindi) Faith, trust.

Shreya (Hindi) Auspicious.

Shri (Hindi) Luster.

Shridevi (Hindi) Goddess.

Shrijani (Hindi) Creative.

Shruti (Hindi) Hearing.

Shu (Chinese) Kind, gentle.

Shubha (Hindi) Meaning unknown.

Shubhada (Indian) Giver of luck.

Shulamit (Hebrew) Tranquil.

Shyann (French) Form of Cheyenne. *Chayanne, Sheyenne*

Shyla (Hindi) Goddess. *Shila, Shy, Shylah*

Shylah (Celtic) Loyal to God; strong. *Shy, Shyla*

Shysie (Native American) Silent little one.

Sian (Welsh) God's gracious gift.

Sibel (Turkish) Meaning unknown. *Sibella, Sibilla, Sibylla, Siebel*

Sibley (Greek) Prophetess. *Cybil, Cybill, Sib, Sibbi, Sibby, Sibeal, Sibille, Sibyl, Sibylle, Sybil, Sybille, Sybilline, Sybyl*

Sibongile (African) Thanks.

Sibyl (Latin) Wise; seer; prophetic. *Sibelle*

Siddhi (Hindi) Achievement; daughter of the god Daksha.

Sidone (African American) It is heard.

Sidonia (Italian) From Sidonia. *Sydania, Syndonia*

Sidonie (French) Flower.

Sidra (Latin) Like a star. *Sidrah, Sydra*

Sieglinde (German) Victory.

Sienna (Italian) Reddish brown.

Sierra (Spanish) Saw-tooth mountain range. *Cierra, Searah, Searrah, Siera, Sierrah, Sierre*

Signa (Scandinavian) Signal, sign. *Signe, Signey, Sygney*

Signild (Scandinavian) Meaning unknown.

Sigourney (French) Daring king.

Sigrid (Old Norse) Winning adviser. *Sigrath, Sigurd, Sigwald*

Sigrun (Scandinavian) Secret victory. *Sygrun*

Siham (Arabic) Arrows. *Syham*

Sihu (Native American) Flower. *Syhu*

Sika (African) Money.

Sila (Turkish) Homesick.

Sile (Scottish) Youthful; the blind one; the sixth.

Sileas (Latin) Youth.

Silei (Samoan) Meaning unknown.

Silke (German) Blind.

Silvana (Latin) Forest.

Silver (English) White.

Silvia (Latin) Woodland maid. *Silva, Silvana, Silvie, Sylva, Sylvana, Sylvia, Sylvie, Sylwia, Zilvia*

Sima (African) Treasure, prize.

Simba (Swahili) Lion.

Simone (Hebrew) One who hears. *Simona*

Simoni (Hindi) Obedient.

Simran (Hindi) God's gift.

Sine (Gaelic) God's gracious gift.

Sinead (Irish) Gracious.

Siobhan (Gaelic) God is gracious.

Siran (Armenian) Alluring.

Sirena (Greek) Siren.

Sirisha (Hindi) Flower.

Siroun (Armenian) Lovely.

Sirvat (Armenian) Rose.

Sissy (American) From Cecilia; familiar name for "sister." *Cissee, Cissey, Cissy, Sis, Sissi, Sissie*

Sistine (Italian) Spiritual. *Sisteen, Sisteene*

Sitara (Sanskrit) Morning star.

Sitembile (African) Trust.

Siusan (Scottish) Lily.

Siv (Norwegian) Kinship; wife of Thor. *Seev*

Siyanda (African) We are growing.

Skyla (English) Sky; sheltering. *Sky, Skylah*

Skylar (English) Eternal life; strength; love and beauty. *Schuyler, Skieler, Skilar, Skiler, Sky, Skye, Skyla, Skylie, Skylor, Skyrah*

Smita (Hindi) Smiling. *Susmita*

Smridhi (Hindi) Meaning unknown.

Smriti (Hindi) Recollection. (Hindi) Form of the Hindu goddess Devi.

Snana (Native American) Jingles like bells.

Sneh (Hindi) Love.

Sneha (Hindi) Affection.

Snigdha (Hindi) Soft.

Snøfrid (Scandinavian) Meaning unknown.

Snow (American) Frozen rain. *Sno*

Snowy (American) White; pure.

Sofi (Greek) Wisdom. *Sofia, Sofie, Sophia, Sophie*

Sofiel (Spanish) Wise; angel of fruits and vegetables.

Sojourner (Old French) To stay for a time; name of former slave-turned-equal-justice-advocate, Sojourner Truth.

Sokanon (Native American) Rain.

Solace (Latin) Comfort.

Solada (Thai) Listener.

Solana (Spanish) Sunshine. *Solande, Solanna, Solena, Solinda*

Solange (French) Rare jewel. *Solangia*

Soledad (Spanish) Solitary; health.

Soleil (French) Sun.

Solita (Latin) Alone. *Soleata, Soleeta, Soleita, Solitah, Solite, Solyta*

Solosolo (Samoan) Dry.

Somatra (Hindi) Excelling the moon.

Sommer (German) Summer season. *Somara, Somer, Sommar*

Sona (Hindi) Gold.

Sonakshi (Hindi) Golden eye.

Sonal (Hindi) Golden. *Sonali*

Sondra (Greek) Helper; defender of mankind.

Sonia (Russian) Wisdom. *Sonja, Sonya*

Sonika (Hindi) Golden.

Sonja (Scandinavian) Wisdom. *Sonjae, Sonjia*

Sonnenschein (German) Sunshine.

Sonora (Spanish) Pleasant-sounding.

Sonya (Latin) Wisdom. *Sonnya*

Soo (Korean) Excellence; long life.

Soo Min (Korean) Gentle spirit.

Soo Yun (Korean) Perfect lotus blossom.

Soon Bok (Korean) Mild and gentle blessed.

Sophie (Greek) Wisdom. *Sadhbh, Sofi, Sofia, Sofie, Sophia, Sophronia, Sophy, Zofka*

Sophronia (Greek) Foresighted.

Sora (Native American) Chirping songbird.

Sorano (Japanese) Of the sky. *Sora*

Soraya (Arabic) Princess.

Sorcha (Gaelic) Bright.

Sorilbran (English) Smart.

Sorley (Scandinavian) Viking.

Sorrel (French) Bitter; from the tree. *Sorel, Sorie, Sorrell*

Sosanna (Irish) Lily. *Sosanah, Sosanna, Sosannah*

Soshannah (Hebrew) Lily.

Sosie (French) Double; look alike.

Souzan (Arabic) Fire.

Soyala (Native American) Winter solstice.

Sparrow (English) Bird.

Speranza (Italian) Hope. *Speranca*

Spica (Latin) Name of a star.

Spirituality (Greek) Spiritual; significance of life.

Spodumene (Greek) Burnt to ashes; ash-gray.

Spring (English) Spring season.

Sraddha (Hindi) Faith; wife of Shiva.

Srilata (Hindi) Creeper.

Sripada (Hindi) Noble footprint. *Sripata*

Srishti (Hindi) Creation; nature.

Sruti (Hindi) Ability to hear.

Stacia (Greek) One who shall rise again. *Staci, Stacy, Stasia, Stasya, Tasia*

Star (American) Star. *Starr*

Stardust (American) Dust from a star.

Starleen (English) Star.

Stefania (Greek) Crown. *Fannie, Fanny, Stef, Stefa, Stefanie, Steffi, Steffie, Stefka, Stepania, Stepha, Stephana, Stephania, Stephanie, Stephannie, Stephanya*

Stella (Latin) Star. (French) Form of Estella. *Star, Starla, Starling, Starr, Stela, Stellar*

Stephaney (Greek) Crowned.

Stesha (Greek) Crowned one.

Stockard (English) From the yard of tree stumps. *Stockerd, Stockyrd*

Storm (English) Stormy weather; tempest. *Storme, Stormie, Stormy*

Subhadra (Hindi) Wife of Arjuna, a hero of the epic *Mahabharata*.

Subhaga (Hindi) Fortunate person.

Subhangi (Hindi) Fortunate person.

Subhuja (Hindi) Auspicious. *Apsara*

Suchi (Hindi) Radiant glow.

Suchitra (Hindi) Beautiful.

Sudevi (Hindi) Wife of Krishna.

Sudha (Hindi) Nectar.

Sudie (English) Lily.

Sugar (English) Sugar; sweet.

Sujata (Hindi) Of noble birth, well bred.

Sukanya (Hindi) Comely.

Suki (Japanese) Beloved. *Sukie*

Suksma (Hindi) Fine.

Sukutai (African) Hug.

Sula (Icelandic) Large sea bird; peace.

Sultan (African) Ruler.

Sulwyn (Welsh) Bright as the sun.

Suma (Egyptian, Japanese) To ask.

Sumana (Hindi) Flower.

Sumanna (Hindi) Good natured.

Sumati (Hindi) Wisdom.

Sumayah (Arabic) Pride.

Sumehra (Arabic) Beautiful face.

Sumey (Asian) Flower. *Sumy*

Sumi (Japanese) Clear, refined.

Sumitra (Indian) Good friend; mother of Lakshamana.

Summer (English) Summer season. *Samar, Somar, Sumar*

Sun (Korean) Goodness.

Sun Hi (Korean) Goodness and happiness.

Sun Jung (Korean) Goodness and noble.

Sundarai (Hindi) Beautiful.

Sundeep (Punjabi) Light; enlightened. *Sundip*

Sunee (Hindi) Good thing.

Sunflower (American) Flower.

Sunila (Hindi) Blue.

Sunita (Hindi) Daughter of the god Dharma. *Sunrita*

Suniti (Hindi) Good principles.

Sunniva (English, Scandinavian) Gift of the sun.

Sunshine (American) Sunlight.

Suparna (Hindi) Leafy.

Suprabha (Hindi) Radiant.

Supriti (Hindi) True love.

Supriya (Hindi) Beloved.

Surabhi (Hindi) Wish-yielding cow.

Suravinda (Hindi) Beautiful. *Yaksa*

Surotama (Hindi) Auspicious. *Apsara*

Suruchi (Hindi) Good taste.

Surupa (Hindi) Beautiful.

Surya (Hindi) Sun.

Susan (Hebrew) Lily. *Soos, Soozie, Sosana, Sue, Sue Anne, Sue Ellen, Suisan, Sukey, Sukie, Susanna, Susannah, Susanne, Suse, Susette, Susi, Susie, Susy, Suzanna, Suzanne, Suzette, Suzie, Suzy, Zsa Zsa*

Sushanti (Hindi) Peace.

Sushma (Hindi) Beautiful woman.

Sushmita (Hindi) Smiling. *Susmita*

Susie (French) From Susan. *Susey, Susi, Susy, Suze, Suzi, Suzie, Suzy, Suzy Q*

Susila (Hindi) Wife of Lord Krishna; clever in amorous sciences.

Suvarna (Hindi) Golden.

Suvrata (Hindi) Child of god Daksa.

Suzana (English) Lily. *Suzanna, Suzannah, Suzenna, Suzzanna*

Suzette (French) Little lilly. *Susette*

Svea (Scandinavian) Swedish nation. *Svay*

Sveta (Slavic) Bright light.

Svetlana (Russian) Star. *Svetochka.*

Swarupa (Hindi) Truth.

Swati (Indian) Name of a star.

Sweta (Hindi) Fair complexioned.

Sybella (Greek) Prophetess; oracle.

Sybil (Greek) Prophet. *Sibel, Sibyl, Syb, Sybill, Sybille, Sybyl*

Sydelle (Hebrew) Princess.

Sydney (French) From the city of Saint-Denis. *Sid, Siddie, Sidell, Sidne, Sidney, Sidoney, Sidonia, Syd, Sydel, Sydell, Sydny*

Sydni (French) Contradiction of Saint-Denis. *Sidney, Sydnee*

Syeira (Gypsy) Princess.

Syesha (American) Variant of Saisha.

Sylvia (Latin) From the forest. *Syl, Sylvea*

Symona (American) It is heard.

Symone (French) God is heard. *Simon, Simona, Simone, Symona*

Symphony (English) Concordant in sound. *Symfoni, Symphanie, Symphany, Symphoni, Symphonie*

Syna (Greek) Two together.

Synnove (Scandinavian) Sun gift.

Syrida Origin and meaning unknown.

Syshe (Yiddish) Street.

Szitakota (Slavic) Dragonfly.

T

Taa (Native American) Seed.

Taahira (Arabic) Pure, chaste.

Taalah (Origin unknown) Young palm tree.

Taanach (Hebrew) Who humbles thee.

Taariq (Swahili) Morning star.

Taban (Irish) Genius.

Tabassum (Arabic) Smiling.

Tabia (Swahili) Talented. *Tabya*

Tabina (Arabic) Follower of Muhammad.

Tabitha (Greek, Hebrew, Native American) Gazelle; roebuck; tiara. *Tabatha, Tabbi, Tabbie, Tabby*

Tabora (Arabic) Plays a small drum.

Taborri (Native American) Voices that carry. *Tabby, Taborah*

Tacey (English) Silent, calm. *Tace, Tacita, Taicee, Taici*

Taci (American) Strong, healthy.

Tacincala (Native American) Deer. *Tawi*

Tacita (Latin) To be silent. *Taceta, Tacetah, Tasita, Taycita*

Tacy (Latin) Silence.

Tadako (Japanese) Child of Tada.

Tadewi (Native American) Wind.

Tadi (Native American) Wind.

Tadita (Native American) Runner.

Taffy (Welsh) Beloved. *Taffea, Taffee, Taffey, Taffi, Tafy*

Tahirah (Arabic) Chaste, pure. *Taheera, Tahira*

Tahiti (Polynesian) Rising sun. *Tahitia, Tahity*

Tahlia (Hebrew) Morning dew. (American) Combination of Tai and Lia.

Tahnee (English) Little one.

Tahzai Origin and meaning unknown. *Tahzay*

Tai (Vietnamese) Talent. *Tie, Tye*

Taido (Japanese) Gentle way.

Taifa (African) Nation, tribe.

Tailynn (American) Combination of Tai and Lynn.

Taima (Native American) Crash of thunder. *Taimah, Taimi, Taimy*

Taina (Spanish) Gracious; from Anna.

Taini (Native American) Returning moon.

Tainn (Native American) New moon.

Taipa (Native American) To spread wings.

Tais (Greek) Bound. *Taisa, Tays, Taysa*

Taite (English) Pleasant and bright. *Tait, Tayt, Tayte*

Taja (African) To mention. *Teja, Tejal*

Tajsa (Polish) Princess; born at Christmas.

Taka (Japanese) Tall, honorable. *Takah*

Takako (Japanese) Child of Taka.

Takala (African) Corn tassel. *Takalah*

Takara (Japanese) Treasure; precious object. *Takarah, Takaria*

Taki (Japanese) Waterfall. *Takie, Taky*

Takia (Arabic) Worshipper. *Taki, Tikia, Tykia*

Takira (American) Sun.

Takiyah (North African) Pious, righteous.

Takoda (Native American) Friend to all.

Tala (Native American) Stalking wolf. *Talah*

Talaitha (African American) Inventive. *Taleetha, Taleta, Taletha, Talith, Talitha, Tally*

Talasi (Native American) Corn-tassel flower.

Tale (African) Green.

Taleebin (Australian) Young. *Taleabin, Taleebina, Taleebine, Taleebyn*

Taleen (Armenian) Meaning unknown. *Tal, Taline, Talyn*

Talia (Hebrew) Dew from heaven. (Greek) Blooming. *Tahlia, Tai, Tali, Tally, Talya, Talyah*

Talieya (Greek) Blooming.

Taline (Armenian) Monastery.

Talisa (African American) Consecrated to God. *Talesa, Talisha*

Talisha (African American) Damsel arise.

Talitha (Aramic) Angel who escorts the sun on its daily course. *Taleetha, Taleta, Taletha, Talith*

Taliyah (Greek) Blooming. *Taliya*

Tallis (French) Forest. *Taleece, Talice, Talise, Taliss*

Tallulah (Native American) Leaping water. *Tallie, Tallula, Tally, Talula, Talulah*

Tallya (Greek) Blooming.

Tallys (French) Forest.

Talma (Native American) Thunder. *Talmah*

Talon (English) Claw. *Taelon, Taelyn, Talen, Tallon*

Talor (Hebrew) Morning dew. *Talorah, Talore*

Tam (Vietnamese) Heart.

Tama (Japanese) Jewel. *Tamaa, Tamah, Tema*

Tamaka (Japanese) Bracelet. *Tamakah, Tamaky*

Tamali (Hindi) Tree with very dark bark.

Tamanna (Hindi) Desire. *Tamana, Tamanah*

Tamar (Russian) Twelfth-century Gregorian queen. *Tamour*

Tamara (Hebrew) Palm tree, spice. *Tamar, Tamarah, Tamarind, Tamary, Tamika*

Tamasha (African) Pageant.

Tamassa (Hebrew) Form of Thomasina. *Tamasa, Tamasine*

Tamatha (American) Dear Tammy.

Tamber (American) Music pitch.

Tambre (English) Great joy; music. *Amber, Tambur*

Tambrey (American) Immortal. *Tambree*

Tameka (Arabic) Twin.

Tamesis (Greek) Goddess of the river.

Tamia (English) Palm tree; form of Tamara.

Tamika (African American) People.

Tamiko (Japanese) Child of Tami.

Tamila (American) Combination of Ta and Mila.

Tamira (African American) Spice or palm tree.

Tamitha (Hebrew) Twin.

Tamiya (Hebrew) Form of Tammy.

Tamma (Hebrew) Perfect.

Tammy (Hebrew) Perfect one. *Tammie, Tammye*

Tamra (Hebrew) Spice or palm tree. *Tamora, Tamorah*

Tamrika (American) Combination of Tammy and Erika.

Tamsyn (Native American) Benevolent. *Tamsa, Tamsan, Tamsen, Tamsin*

Tamya (American) Palm tree; form of Tamara.

Tamyra (African American) Spice or palm tree. *Tamirah*

Tan (Vietnamese) New.

Tana (Slavic) Fairy queen. *Tanah*

Tanaka (Japanese) Dweller.

Tanasha (African American) Strong willed, persistent. *Tenyasha*

Tanashia (Origin unknown) Born on Christmas.

Tanaya (Hindi) Child of mine.

Tandice (African American) Team.

Tandra (English) Form of Tandy.

Tandy (English) Team. *Tandee, Tandey, Tandi*

Tanesha (African) Strong. *Tanish, Tanisha, Tannesha*

Taney (Japanese) Valley. *Tahnee, Tahney, Tahni, Tanie*

Taneya (Russian) Fairy queen.

Tangerine (English) From Tangers.

Tangia (American) Angel.

Tanginika (African American) Lake goddess.

Tani (Japanese) Valley. (Melanesian) Sweetheart. (Tonkinese) Youth. (Andalusian) Bull that charges randomly. *Tangee*

Tania (Slavic) Fairy queen of Tatiana. *Tanya*

Taniel (African American) Feminine form of Daniel.

Tanika (Hindi) Rope.

Tanisha (African American) Born on Monday.

Tanissa (American) Combination of Tania and Nissa.

Tanith (Greek) Goddess of love.

Taniya (English) Fairy queen. *Tania, Taniyah, Tanya, Tonya*

Tanner (English) Leather worker. *Tanner*

Tansy (Greek) Immortality; flower name. *Tansee, Tansey, Tansi*

Tanu (Hindi) Body; slim.

Tanuja (Hindi) Daughter.

Tanushi (Hindi) Beauty.

Tanvi (Hindi) Delicate girl.

Tanya (Russian) Fairy princess. *Tan, Tani, Tania, Tatiana, Tatjana*

Tanzi (English) Immortal.

Tao (Vietnamese) Peach.

Tapanga (African) Sweet; unpredictable. *Pangi, Tata*

Tapi (Hindi) Meaning unknown.

Tapti (Hindi) River.

Tara (Celtic) Rocky hill; tower. *Taria, Taryn*

Tarala (Hindi) Honeybee.

Tarana (African) Born during the day.

Taraneh (Arabic) Melody, song. *Taran, Tarana*

Tarangini (Indian) River.

Tarannum (Hindi) Melody.

Tararia (Spanish) Form of Teresa.

Tarcisia (Greek) Valiant.

Taree (Japanese) Arching branch.

Tareva-Chine' (Native American) Beautiful eyes. *Tu-Sha*

Taria (English) Crown.

Tarian (Welsh) Coat of arms.

Tariana (African American) Holy hillside.

Tariel (Origin unknown) Angel of summer.

Tarika (Hindi) Star. *Tarikah, Taryka*

Tarin (Irish) Form of Tara. *Taron, Tarren, Tarrin, Tarryn*

Tarisai (African) Look, behold.

Tarja (Arabic) Stave of a poem. (Finnish) Wealthy.

Tarjani (Indian) First finger.

Tarne (Australian) Salty water. *Tarnee, Tarni, Tarnie, Tarny*

Tarquinia (Italian) Place name.

Tarra (Australian) Creek.

Tarsha (Native American) Tan.

Tarsila (Greek) Valiant.

Taruna (Sanskrit) Young girl.

Taryn (Greek) Queen. *Tarin*

Tasanee (Thai) Beautiful view.

Taseem (Indian) Salute of praise.

Tasha (Greek) Born on Christmas; short for Natasha. *Tacha, Tashe, Taska, Tysha*

Tashi (Asian, English) Prosperity; born on Christmas.

Tasia (Greek) Resurrection. *Tasya, Tasyah*

Tasmine (American) Twin. *Tasmin, Tasmyn, Tasmyne*

Tassilyn (American) Mythological name.

Tasya (Slavic) Resurrection.

Tate (English) To be cheerful; windy; great talker.

Tatiana (Russian) Fairy queen. *Tanya, Tatania, Tatia, Tatianna, Tatiannia, Tatie, Tattianna, Tatyana, Taynanna*

Tatum (English) Cheerful, bringer of joy. *Tait, Taite, Taitum, Tat, Tayte*

Tatyana (Latin) Fairy queen; silver-haired. *Tatyanah, Tatyannah*

Taura (Latin) Bull; from Taurus, a sign of the zodiac. *Taurah, Taural, Taurya*

Tauret (Egyptian) Goddess of pregnant women.

Tavia (Latin, Old English) Great. *Taiva, Tavah, Taves, Tay*

Tavie (Scottish) Twin. *Tavee, Tavey, Tavi*

Tavita (Latin) Eighth.

Tawana (Native American) Tan hide. *Tawan, Tawanne, Towanna*

Tawanda (German) Slender, young.

Tawnie (English) Little one; yellowish-brown. *Tahnee, Tauni, Tawny*

Taya (English) From Taylor. *Taia, Tayah, Tiya*

Tayce (French) Silence.

Tayen (Native American) New moon.

Tayla (English) Tailor. *Taila, Taylah*

Taylar (French) To cut. *Tayla, Taylara, Tayllar, Tayller*

Taylor (English) Tailor. *Tailor, Tay, Tie*

Tayna (English) Tailor.

Tazanna (Native American) Princess.

Tazara (African) Railway line.

Tazu (Japanese) Stork; longevity. *Taz, Tazi, Tazoo*

Tea (Spanish) Princess; aunt.

Teagan (Irish) Attractive, beautiful. *Taegan, Teagen, Teaghin, Tegan*

Teal (English) Greenish-blue color; duck. *Teala, Teel, Teele*

Tebeth (Hebrew) Good; goodness.

Teca (Slavic) Summer. *Tecah, Teka*

Teddi (English) God-given; form of Theodora. *Tedde, Teddey*

Tedra (Greek) Outgoing. *Teddra, Tedera, Tedrah*

Teena (Latin) Little one. *Teenah, Teenia*

Tehya (Native American) Precious.

Teigra (Greek) Tiger.

Teishymn Origin and meaning unknown.

Tejal (Hindi) Lustrous.

Tejana (Spanish) Texan female.

Teji (Hindi) Enlightment.

Tekla (Greek) Divine fame. *Thekla*

Tekli (Polish) Famous for God.

Teleri (Welsh) From the River Tyleri.

Telissa (American) Combination of Talia and Aisha.

Telma (Greek) Ambitious.

Telyn (Welsh) Harp.

Tema (Hebrew) Righteous; palm tree.

Temima (African American) Whole; honest.

Temina (Hebrew) Honest.

Temira (Hebrew) Tall. *Temora, Timora*

Temis (Greek) She who establishes order.

Temperance (Latin) Moderate.

Tempest (French) Storm. *Tempestt, Tempist, Tempyst*

Tena (English) Anointed; follower of Christ.

Tenaya Origin and meaning unknown.

Tendai (African) Be thankful to God.

Tender (American) Sensitive.

Tendra (Science fiction) Character from *Star Wars*.

Teness (American) Meaning unknown.

Tenille (American) Combination of Te and Nellie. *Teneille, Tenneal, Tennielle, Tennille*

Tenley Origin and meaning unknown.

Tennen (Japanese) Natural.

Teotista (Greek) Drunk with the love of God.

Tera (English) High hill.

Terah (Latin) Earth, hillside.

Teranika (Celtic) Earth's victory.

Terceiro (Spanish) Born third.

Terehasa (African) Blessed.

Tereixa (Galician) Reaper. *Thereasa*

Terena (Latin) Earthly. *Terenna, Terrena, Terrenna*

Terentia (Greek) Guardian.

Teresa (Spanish) Harvester. *Taresa, Taressa, Theresa, Tressa*

Terhi (Finnish) Acorn.

Teri (English, Greek) Harvester; form of Teresa. *Tere, Terri, Terrie*

Terin (Latin) Yellow singing bird; ash-colored.

Terpsichore (Greek) Dancing.

Terra (Latin) Earth. *Tera, Terry*

Terrelle (German) Thunder ruler. *Terele, Terell, Terella, Teriel*

Terri (Greek) Harvester. *Teri, Terre, Terrey, Tery*

Terrwyn (Welsh) Valiant.

Terrylyn (American) Combination of Teri and Lyn.

Tertia (Latin) Third. *Ters, Tersh, Tersha, Tersia*

Teryl (English) Bright and vivacious.

Tesia (Polish) Loved by God.

Tess (Greek) Fourth-born. *Tes, Tese, Tessie*

Tessa (Italian) Countess. *Tesa, Teza*

Tessica (American) Wealthy harvester. *Tesica, Tessika*

Tetisheri (Egyptian) Matriarch of Egyptian royal family of the late seventeenth and early eighteenth centuries.

Tetsu (Japanese) Iron. *Tetsoo*

Tevy (Cambodian) Angel. *Tevee, Tevey, Tevi*

Texcean (Spanish) From Texas. *Tex*

Thaddea (Greek) Appreciative. *Thada, Thadda, Thaddeah*

Thadine (Hebrew) Praised. *Thady, Thadyne*

Thaisa (Greek) Bond. *Thais*

Thalassa (Greek) From the sea. *Thalassah*

Thalia (Greek) Blooming; plentiful. *Taylee, Taylie, Thalius*

Than (Vietnamese) Death; brilliant.

Thana (Arabic) Gratitude. *Thaina, Thaynah*

Thandie (Zulu) Beloved. *Thandee, Thandey, Thandi, Thandy*

Thandiwe (African) Loving one.

Thao (Vietnamese) Respectful of parents.

Thara (Arabic) Wealth.

Thea (Greek, Laos) Goddess; sort. *Teah, Teeah, Theah, Theeah, Tiah*

Theala (Science fiction) Character from *Star Wars*.

Thelma (Greek) Nursing. *Telma*

Thema (African) Queen. *Themah*

Themis (Greek) Goddess of justice.

Themista Origin and meaning unknown.

Theodora (Greek) Gift of God. *Dora, Fedora, Feodora, Tedra, Teodora, Theda, Thedora, Theodosia, Theone, Theophania, Theophilia, Theora*

Theodosia (Greek) God-given.

Theola (Greek) Divine.

Theone (Greek) Godly. *Theona, Theonah, Theonie*

Theophilia (Greek) Loved divinely.

Thera (Greek) Wild.

Theresa (Greek) Reaper. *Teresa, Teressa, Teri, Terri, Terry, Tess, Tessa, Tessica, Tessie, Tessy, Therese, Toireasa, Tracey, Tracie, Tracy, Tressa*

Therese (French) From Theresia.

Thi (Asian) Poetry. *Thia, Thy, Thya*

Thirza (Hebrew) Sweet-natured; cypress tree. *Thyrza, Tirza, Tyrza*

Thisbe (Greek) Where the doves live.

Thistle (English) Thistle.

Thomasa (Greek) Twin. *Tammy, Tamsen, Tamsin, Tamson, Thomasina, Thomasine, Thomassa, Tomasina, Tommie, Tommy*

Thora (Old Norse) Thunder. *Thordia, Tora*

Thorborg (Scandinavian) Thunder.

Thordis (Scandanavian) Thor's spirit. *Thordia, Thordisa, Thordisah, Thordise*

Thracia (Greek) Place name.

Thu (Asian) Autumn.

Thuraya (Arabic) Stars and planets.

Thurid (Scandinavian) Wife of Thorstein the Red; viking.

Thuy (Vietnamese) Pure.

Thy (Asian) Poetry.

Thyra (Greek, Scandinavian) Shield-bearer. *Thira*

Thyrrni (Scandinavian) Loud.

Tia (Spanish, Greek) Aunt; princess. *Tiana, Tianna*

Tiana (Greek) Princess. *Tianna, Tyana*

Tiara (Latin) Crowned. *Teara, Tiarra, Tyara*

Tiaret (African) Lioness.

Tiarra (Hebrew) Crowned.

Tiegan (Aztec) Little princess in the big valley. *Tiegs, Tiegy*

Tien (Vietnamese) Fairy.

Tienette (Greek) Crowned with laurel. *Tien, Tiena*

Tiera (Latin, Spanish) Land; Earth.

Tierney (Irish) Noble. *Tierany, Tiernan, Tiernee, Tyernee*

Tierra (Spanish) Earth; land.

Tiesha (Latin) Joy; form of Leticia.

Tieve (Celtic, Gaelic) Hillside.

Tifara (Hebrew) Happy. *Tifarah, Tifarra, Tifarrah*

Tiffany (French) Appearance of God. *Fanny, Tifanee, Tifany, Tiff, Tiffani, Tiffanie, Tiffie, Tiffy, Tiphany*

Tigerlily (Asian) Tigerlily; flower. (American) Lily; tiger.

Tilda (French, German) Mighty in war; maid of battles.

Tillie (German) Might, power.

Timandra (Greek) Daughter of hero Tyndareus.

Timberly (African American) Tall ruler.

Timera (Hebrew) Palm tree. *Tamara, Tamyra*

Timotha (English) To honor God.

Timothea (Greek) Honoring God. *Timaula, Timi*

Tina (Spanish) Majestic.

Tinble (English) Bell sounds. *Tynbal, Tynble*

Tineka-Jawana (African) Meaning unknown.

Ting (Chinese) Slim; graceful.

Tinisha (American) Born on Christmas.

Tinker (Irish) Traveling metalsmith.

Tiombe (African) Shy.

Tionne (Science fiction) Character from *Star Wars*.

Tiponya (Native American) Owl poking the hatching egg. *Tiponi*

Tipper (Irish) Water pourer.

Tira (Scottish) Land.

Tirza (Hebrew) Kindness. *Thirza, Tirzah*

Tisha (Latin) Form of Patricia; joyful. *Tesha, Ticia, Tishah*

Titania (Greek) Giant. *Tita*

Titian (Greek) Red-gold.

Tiva (Native American) Dance.

Tivona (Hebrew) Lover of nature. *Tibona, Tivonah, Tivone*

Toakase (Tonga) Woman of the sea. *Toa*

Tobi (Hebrew) God is good. *Tobey, Tobie, Tobit*

Tocarra (American) Combination of To and Cara.

Toki (Japanese) Hopeful. *Tokee, Tokey, Toko*

Tokiko (Japanese) Child of Toki.

Tola (Polish) Priceless. *Tolah, Tolla*

Tolena (French) Meaning unknown. *Toley*

Tolia (Polish) Worthy of praise.

Tolinka (Native American) Coyote's ear.

Tomai (Greek) Honoring Thomas.

Tomi (Japanese) Rich. *Tomee, Tomey, Tomie*

Tomiko (Japanese) Child of Tomi.

Tomo (Japanese) Intelligent. *Tomoko*

Tona (Greek) Flourishing. (Latin) Praiseworthy.

Toni (French) Worthy of praise. *Tonee, Toney, Tony, Tonye*

Tonya (Latin) Worthy of praise. *Tonnyah, Tonyia*

Topanga (Native American) Where the mountain meets the sea.

Topaz (Latin) Yellow gemstone. *Topaza, Topazz, Tophaz*

Tora (Japanese) Tiger. (Hebrew) Law. *Torah, Torra, Torrah*

Toral (Hindi) Folk heroine.

Toreth (Welsh) Abundant.

Tori (Japanese) Bird. *Torree, Torri, Torrie, Torry, Tory*

Torie (American) Victorious.

Toril (Scandinavian) Female warrior. *Torill, Torille*

Torlan (Welsh) From the river.

Tosca (Latin) From Tuscany, Italy.

Tosha (English) Born on Christmas. *Toshea, Toshia*

Toshi (Japanese) Mirror image. *Toshee, Toshey, Toshy*

Tosia (Latin) Inestimable.

Totie (English) Gift of God.

Tourmaline (Asian) Name of a gemstone.

Tova (Hebrew) Good. *Tovah, Tove*

Toyah (Scandinavian) Toy.

Toyo (Japanese) Plentiful.

Traci (English) Brave; summer. *Tracee, Traice, Traicey, Traici, Traicie, Traicy*

Tracy (French) Path, road. *Tracey*

Trang (Vietnamese) Intelligent; beautiful.

Tranquilia (Spanish) Calm, tranquil.

Tranquility (Latin) God-inspired peace of mind; devout.

Trava (Czech) Spring grasses. *Travah*

Treasa (Celtic) Strong.

Trella (Spanish) Star; from Estrella.

Tresa (Greek) Harvester; the third.

Tressa (Greek) Reaping life's rewards. *Tresa, Tresah, Trisa*

Treva (Celtic) Prudent. *Treve*

Trevina (Irish) Prudent. *Trevanna, Treveane*

Triana (Greek) Pure. *Trianna*

Tricia (Latin) Noble woman.

Trifine (Greek) Delicate. *Trifena, Trifene, Triffena, Trifin, Trifina*

Trifosa (Greek) She who delights in God.

Trilby (Italian) One who sings; musical trills. *Trilbee, Trilbey, Trillbi*

Trilochana (Indian) Lord Shiva.

Trina (Greek) Fire; full of spirit; perfect. *Treena, Trin, Trinah*

Trind (Swedish) Pure.

Trinh (Vietnamese) Pure.

Trini (Latin) Trinity.

Trinity (Latin) Holy three. *Trin, Triniti, Triny*

Trish (American) From Patricia.

Trisha (Latin) Of noble descent.

Trishna (Hindi) Thirst; form of the Hindu goddess Devi.

Trista (Latin) Sorrowful. *Tristah, Tristal, Tristia*

Tristan (Latin) Bold. *Tristiana, Tristiane, Tristianna*

Tristana (Latin) Sad.

Tristessa (Latin) Sad woman.

Triveni (Hindi) Three sacred rivers.

Trixie (American) Bringer of joy.

Troy (French) Place name. *Troi, Troya, Troye*

Tru (English) From Truly. *True*

Truda (Polish) Warrior woman.

Trude (German) From Gertrude.

Trudel (Dutch) Form of Trudy. *Trudela, Trudelah, Trudele, Trudell*

Trudie (English) Strong; spear.

Trudy (English) Beloved. *Truda, Trudi, Trudia, Trudie*

Trula (German) True.

Trupti (Hindi) Satiatedness.

Trusha (Hindi) Thirst.

Tryamon (English) Fairy princess.

Tryna (Greek) Third. *Tryane*

Tryne (Dutch) Pure. *Trine*

Tryphena (Latin) Dainty.

Tu (Chinese) Jade.

Tuesday (English) Day of the week.

Tuhina (Hindi) Dewdrop. *Tuhinah*

Tula (Teutonic) Form of Gertrude.

Tulasi (Hindi) Sacred plant; basil.

Tulia (Spanish) Destined for glory.

Tullia (Irish) Peaceful. *Tulliah, Tullya, Tullyah*

Tully (Irish) At peace with God. *Tulee, Tulei, Tuley, Tuli, Tulie, Tulli, Tuly*

Turquoise (French) Precious stone. *Turkois, Turkoise, Turquois*

Tusnelda (German) She who fights giants.

Tusti (Hindi) Peace; happiness; form of the Hindu goddess Devi.

Tuwa (Native American) Earth.

Tuyen (Vietnamese) Angel.

Twila (English) Creative. *Twyla*

Twyla (English) Third.

Tyanne (American) From Tyrus and Anne. *Ty*

Tydfill (Welsh) Meaning unknown.

Tyesha (African American) Duplicitous. *Tesha, Tisha, Tyeisha, Tyiesha, Tyisha*

Tyler (English) Tailor. *Tylar, Tyller, Tylor*

Tyna (Czech) Form of Kristina. *Tynae, Tynia*

Tyne (English) River.

Tynice (American) Meaning unknown.

Tyra (Scandinavian) God of battle. *Thyra, Tyraa, Tyrah*

Tyree (Irish) Island off Scotland.

Tyrell (African American) Thunder; ruler.

Tyrina (African American) Meaning unknown.

Tyronica (African American) Goddess of battle.

Tzila (Hebrew) Protection.

Tziporah (Hebrew) Bird.

Tzippa (Hebrew) Bird.

Tzofit (Hebrew) Hummingbird.

Tzvia (Hebrew) Deer or gazelle.

U

Ualani (Hawaiian) Heavenly rain. *Ualana, Ualanah, Ualaney, Ualanie, Ualanya*

Uberta (Italian) Bright.

Uchenna (African) God's will.

Udaya (Hindi) Dawn.

Udele (English) Wealthy. *Uda, Udela, Udell, Udella, Udelle*

Udiya (Hebrew) Fire of God. *Udia, Udiyah, Uriela, Uriella*

Ugolina (German) Intelligent. *Hugolina, Ugolin, Ugoline, Ugolyne*

Uinise (Polynesian) Fair victory.

Ujila (Hindi) Bright light. *Ujala, Ujjala, Ujvala*

Ujwala (Hindi) Bright, lustrous.

Ula (Irish) Sea jewel. (Scandinavian) Inherited estate. *Eula, Oola, Ulla, Ullah*

Ulima (Arabic) Wise. *Uleema, Ulema, Ulymah*

Ulla (German) Willful. *Ulah, Ullah*

Ulrika (German) Wolf ruler. *Ulrica, Ulrike*

Ultima (Latin) Last, endmost. *Ultimah*

Ultreia (Gaelic) Meaning unknown.

Ulu (African) Second-born girl.

Ululani (Hawaiian) Heavenly inspiration.

Ulva (German) She-wolf; brave.

Uma (Hindi) Mother; name for the Hindu goddess Devi. *Umah*

Umali (Hindi) Generous.

Umay (Turnish) Hopeful. *Umai*

Umayma (Arabic) Little mother.

Umeko (Japanese) Child of the plum blossom. *Ume, Umeki*

Umina (Australian) Sleeping child. *Uminah, Umyna, Umynah*

Umm (Arabic) Mother.

Una (Latin) One; unity; wholeness. *Juno, Oona, Oonagh, Unah*

Unaiza (Arabic) Meaning unknown.

Undine (Latin) Of the wave; mythology; water spirits. *Onde, Ondinah, Ondine, Unda, Undyna*

Undurra (Australian) Silver tree with yellow flowers. *Undura, Undurah*

Unega (Native American) White.

Unity (English) Oneness; together. *Unitea, Unitee, Unyt, Unytee*

Unn (Scandinavian) She who is loved. *Un*

Unnati (Hindi) Progress.

Unni (Norse) Modest.

Uny (Latin) Unity; together.

Upala (Hindi) Beach.

Urania (Greek) Heavenly; muse of astronomy. *Uraina, Urainia, Uraniya, Uranya*

Urbana (Latin) From the city. *Urbani, Urbanna, Urbannia*

Urbi (African) Princess. *Urbia, Urby*

Uriah (Hebrew) God is light. *Uria*

Uriana (Greek) Unknown. *Rhianna, Riana, Rianna*

Urika (Native American) Useful. *Ureka, Urica, Urikah, Uriqua*

Urit (Hebrew) Light. *Urice, Urita, Uritah, Urith*

Urmila (Hindi) Wife of Lakshmana.

Ursula (Latin) Little bear. *Orsa, Orsola, Ursa, Ursie, Ursola, Ursule, Urzula*

Ursulina (Spanish) Little bear.

Urvasi (Hindi) Most beautiful of Apsaras.

Usagi (Japanese) Moon. *Usa*

Usdi (Native American) Baby.

Usha (Hindi) Dawn. *Ushah, Ushas*

Ushi (Chinese) Ox.

Ushmil (Hindi) Warm. *Ushria*

Ut (Vietnamese) East.

Uta (German) Fortunate maid of battle. *Ute*

Utah (Spanish) Mountain dweller. *Utar*

Utina (Native American) Woman of my country. *Utahna, Uteana, Uteena, Utinah, Utona, Utyna*

Uttara (Hindi) Mother of Pariksit.

Uwimana (African) Daughter of God.

Uzza (Arabic) Mighty. *Uza, Uzah, Uzzah*

V

Vachya (Hindi) To speak. *Vachia, Vachiah*

Vada (Hebrew) Rose. *Vaida, Vay*

Vail (English) From the valley. *Val, Vale, Valle, Vayle*

Vailea (Polynesian) Water that talks. *Vaileah, Vailee, Vaileigh*

Vaishali (Hindi) Ancient city of India.

Vala (English) Chosen. *Valah, Valla, Vallah*

Valborg (Swedish) Powerful mountain.

Valda (Old Norse) Spirited warrior. *Valdah, Valma, Valmah*

Valencia (Latin) Bravery. (Spanish) Place name. *Valancia, Valean, Valecia, Valeen, Valeenah, Valence*

Valene (Latin) Strength. *Valensha, Valentia, Valenzia, Valina, Valinicia, Vallan*

Valentine (Latin) Good health. *Val, Valeda, Valentiane, Valentina, Valentyna, Valina, Vally, Valtina*

Valerie (Latin) Strong. *Val, Valarie, Valeria, Valerian, Valery, Vallerie, Vallie, Vally*

Valeska (Polish) Glorious ruler. *Valeskah*

Valisa (Latin) Wild one. *Vall, Vallie*

Valkyrie (Scandinavian) Fantastic. *Valkee, Valkie, Valkry*

Vallonia (Latin) Acorn. *Valloniah, Vallonyah, Valonah, Valonya*

Valma (Welsh) Mayflower. *Valmah, Valmai, Valmar*

Valonia (Latin) Of the vale. *Lonia, Loniah, Vallon, Valona*

Valora (Latin) Valorous. *Valoria, Valorie, Valory, Valorya*

Van (Dutch) Form of Von.

Vanaja (Hindi) Daughter from the forest. *Vanaia, Vanajah*

Vandana (Hindi) Worship.

Vanecia (Latin) Goddess of beauty and love. *Vanetia, Vanicia, Venecia, Venetia, Venezia, Venice, Venise, Venize*

Vanessa (Greek) Butterfly. *Nessa, Nessie, Nessy, Vanna, Vannia, Vannie, Vanora, Venissa*

Vanetta (Dutch) Little one of nobility. *Vaneta, Vanetah, Vanett, Vanettah*

Vani (Hindi) Alternate name for goddess Saraswati; knowledge. *Vanie, Vany*

Vania (Hebrew) God is gracious. *Vanea, Vaneah, Vaniah, Vannie*

Vanika (Hindi) Small forest.

Vanita (Hindi) Woman.

Vanja (Scandinavian) Version of John; grace. *Vanjah*

Vanjan (Hindi) Meaning unknown.

Vanka (Russian) Favored by God. *Vancan, Vankah, Vankia*

Vanna (Asian, Greek) Golden colored; God's gift. *Vana, Vannaugh*

Vanni (Italian) Graceful. *Vania, Vaniah, Vanie*

Vanora (Scottish) White wave. *Vannora*

Vanya (Russian) Gracious gift of God. *Vania, Vanja, Wania, Wanja, Wanya*

Varana (Hindi) River. *Varanah, Varanna*

Varda (Hebrew) Rose. *Vadit, Vardah, Vardia, Vardice, Vardina, Vardis, Vardit*

Varsha (Hindi) Rain. *Varisha, Varshah*

Varuni (Hindi) Hindi goddess of wine and alcohol.

Vasanta (Hindi) Spring. *Vasantah, Vasante*

Vasavi (Hindi) Mental daughter of the Pitrs.

Vashti (Persian) Beautiful. *Vassy*

Vasiliki (Greek) Basil.

Vasudha (Hindi) Earth.

Vasumati (Hindi) Apsara of unequalled splendor.

Vatsala (Sanskrit) Affectionate.

Vea (Latin) Leader.

Veda (Hindi) Knowledge, wisdom. *Devis, Vedad, Vedah, Veed, Veeda, Vida, Vita*

Vedette (French) From the guard tower. (Italian) Scout. *Vedett, Vedetta*

Vedi (Sanskrit) Knowledge.

Veena (Hindi) Musical instrument; Beena.

Vega (Arabic) Falling star. *Vegah*

Vela (Latin) Star. *Velah, Vella, Vellah*

Velika (Slavic) Great. *Velikah, Velyka*

Velinda (African American) Combination of prefix Ve- and Linda; form of Melinda. *Valinda*

Vellamo (Finnish) Rocking motion. *Velamo*

Velma (Greek) Protector. *Valma, Vellma, Vilma, Vylma*

Velvet (English) Fabric.

Venecia (Italian) Place name.

Venetia (Italian) From Venice. *Veneta, Venetiah*

Venetta (English) Newly created. *Veneta, Venette*

Venice (Latin) Place name.

Venus (Greek) Goddess of love. *Venis, Venussa, Venys*

Vera (Latin) True. (Slavic) Faith. *Vere, Verena, Verenia, Verin, Verina, Verine, Verouska*

Verda (Latin) Young. *Virdinia, Viridis*

Verdad (Spanish) Truth. *Verdada*

Verena (Teutonic) Defender. (Latin) Truthful. *Vereena, Verene, Verina, Verine, Veruchka, Veruschka, Verushka, Veryna*

Vernice (Latin) Brings victory. *Vernese, Vernessa, Vernis, Vernise, Vyrnesse*

Verity (Latin) Truth. *Verita, Veritie*

Veronica (Latin) True image. *Nica, Nicky, Ron, Ronica, Ronnie, Véronique*

Verran (Welsh) Short one.

Veruca (Latin) Wart.

Verushka (Russian) Meaning unknown.

Vesna (Slavic) Spring; resurrection.

Vesper (Latin) Evening. *Vespera, Vesperah*

Vesta (Latin) Guardian of the sacred fire. *Vestah*

Vestal (Latin) Chaste, pure.

Veta (Spanish) Intelligent. *Veeta, Vetah, Vitta*

Vevay (Welsh) White wave. *Veva, Vevae*

Vevila (Gaelic) Woman with a melodious voice. *Vevilla, Vevillia*

Vevina (Latin) Sweet lady. *Vevin, Vevinah*

Vibhuti (Hindi) Great personality.

Victoria (Latin) Victory. *Torey, Tori, Toria, Torri, Vic, Vicki, Vickie, Vicky, Victoire, Victorienne, Victory, Viktoria, Vitoria*

Vida (Hebrew) Beloved. *Veda, Veeda, Veida, Vidette, Vieda, Vita, Vitia*

Vidette (Hebrew) Dearly loved. *Vidett*

Vidonia (Latin) Vine; branch. *Vidonyah*

Vidya (Hindi) Wisdom; knowledge.

Vienna (Latin) From wine country. (Austrian) Place name. *Venia, Vennia, Vienne*

Viera (Slavic) Truth; faith.

Vigdis (Scandinavian) Goddess of war.

Vigilia (Latin) Alert. *Vigiliah, Vigula, Vijiliah*

Vilette (French) Small town. *Vietta, Vilet, Vileta, Vilett, Viletta, Vylette*

Vilhemina (Russian) Resolute protector. *Vilhelmine, Vilhlmin, Vylhelmina*

Vimala (Hindi) Pure; sakti (power, energy) of the Gayatri Devi.

Vina (Spanish) From the vineyard. *Vinah, Vinna, Vinnah*

Vinata (Hindi) Humble; mother of Garuda.

Vinaya (Hindi) Good behavior; modesty.

Vincentia (Latin) To conquer. *Vincenta, Vincentena, Vincentina, Vincentine, Vincetta, Vinia, Vinnie*

Vineeta (Hindi) Unassuming; humble.

Vinna (Spanish) From the vine. *Vinnia, Vinniah, Vynna*

Viola (Scandinavian) Violet.

Violet (Latin) Violet. *Viola*

Vira (Spanish) Blond-haired. *Virah, Vyra*

Virgilia (Latin) Strong. *Virgilla*

Virginia (Latin) Chaste; maiden. *Gina, Ginger, Ginia, Ginni, Ginny, Jinny, Virgie, Virginie, Virgy*

Virgo (Latin) Virgin.

Viridis (Latin) Youthful and blooming. *Virdis, Virida, Viridia, Viridiana*

Virsila (Czech) Little she-bear.

Visala (Hindi) Celestial Apsara.

Visolela (African) Imagination. *Visolelah, Vysolela*

Vita (Latin) Life. *Verta, Vitas, Vitia*

Viveka (German) Little woman; of the strong fortress. *Vivica*

Vivian (Latin) Living, lively. *Vibiana, Viv, Viveca, Viviana, Vivianne, Vivie, Vivien, Vivienne, Vivyan, Vivyen, Vyvyan*

Viviefont (Latin) Lively.

Vixen (Latin) Female fox. *Vyxen*

Voleta (Greek) Veiled one. *Voletta, Volette, Volettie*

Volumnia (Shakespearean) Character from *Coriolanus*.

Vonda (Hebrew) Admired. *Vondah*

Vondra (Czech) Woman's love. *Vondrah*

Vorsila (Greek) Little bear. *Vorsilla, Vorsula, Vorsulah*

Vrida (Spanish) Green. *Vridah, Vryda*

Vrinda (Hindi) Virtue and strength.

Vyoma (Hindi) Sky. *Vioma, Viomah, Vyomah, Vyomika*

W

Wachiwi (Native American) Dancing girl.

Wadd (Arabic) Beloved. *Wad*

Wade (American) Campy.

Wafa (Arabic) Faithful. *Wafiyya, Wafiyyah*

Wahalla (Old Norse) Immortal. *Walhalla*

Waheeda (Hindi) Beautiful. (Arabic) Single. *Wahidah*

Waida (German) Warrior. *Waidah, Wayda, Waydah*

Wainani (Hawaiian) Beautiful water. *Wainanee, Wainanie, Wainany*

Waja (Arabic) Noble. *Wagiha, Wagihah, Wahija, Wajan, Wajihah*

Wakana (Japanese) New blooms. *Wakanah*

Wakanda (Sioux) Inner magical power. *Wakenda*

Wakeisha (Swahili) Life. *Wakeshia, Wakesiah, Wakeysha*

Walada (Arabic) Giving birth. *Walad, Walidah*

Walanika (Hawaiian) True image; version of Veronica. *Walonika, Welonika*

Walburga (Anglo-Saxon) Mighty defender; fortress. *Walburg*

Walda (German) Strong protection. *Wallda, Welda, Wellda*

Walentya (Polish) Healthy.

Waleria (Polish) Strong. *Waleriah, Walerya, Waleryah, Walleria*

Walida (Arabic) Newborn. *Wallidah*

Walker (English) Last name. *Walliker, Wallker*

Wallis (English) From Wales. *Walice, Wallie, Walliss, Wally, Wallys*

Waltraud (Teutonic) Rule strength.

Wamika (Hindi) Sky.

Wamil (Indian) Good looking.

Wanaao (Hawaiian) Sunrise.

Wanda (German) Wanderer. *Vanda, Wandis, Wenda, Wendeline, Wendy*

Wandy (German) Wandering. *Wandee, Wandey, Wandi, Wandie, Wandis*

Waneta (English) Fair complexion. (Native American) Charger. *Wanetta, Wanette, Wanita*

Wangari (African) Leopard.

Wanika (Hawaiian) God's gracious gift. *Waneeka, Wanikah*

Wanisha (American) Pure.

Wannetta (English) Little pale one. *Wanetah, Wannetah, Wannette, Wonitta*

Wapeka (Native American) Skillful. *Wapekah*

Wapin (Native American) Sunrise.

Waratah (Australian) Red flowering tree. *Waratah, Warrata, Warratah*

Warda (Teutonic) Guardian. *Wardah*

Waseme (African) Good-looking.

Washi (Japanese) Eagle. *Washee, Washie*

Wasila (English) Healthy. *Wasilla, Wasylla, Wasyllah*

Wasula (Native American) Bad hair.

Wateka (Native American) Meaning unknown.

Wattan (Japanese) Homeland. *Watan*

Wauna (Native American) Snow goose. *Waunah*

Wava (Latin) Stranger. *Wavah, Wavia, Wavya*

Waverly (English) To wave; from the aspen trees. *Waverley*

Wawetseka (Native American) Pretty woman.

Waynette (English) Wagon maker. *Wainete, Wainetta, Wainettah*

Waynoka (Native American) Clean water. *Wainoka, Wainokah*

Weayaya (Native American) Setting sun.

Wednesday (American) Born on Wednesday.

Weeko (Native American) Pretty girl. *Weiko, Weyko*

Weetamoo (Native American) Lover. *Weatamoo, Weetamoe, Weetamore, Wetemoo*

Wendelle (English) Wanderer. *Wendalina, Wendaline, Wendall*

Wendy (English) Fair. *Wenda, Wenday, Wendee, Wendi, Wendie, Wendye, Windy*

Weslee (English) Form of Wesley. *Weslea*

Whaley (English) Whale meadow. *Whalee, Whaleigh, Whali, Whalia, Whalie*

Whitley (English) White field. *Whitelea, Whitlea, Whitlee, Whitly, Whittley, Witlee*

Whitney (English) From the white island. *Whitnee, Whitnie, Whitny, Whittney*

Whoopi (English) Excitable.

Widjan (Arabic) Ecstasy.

Wihtburth (Anglo-Saxon) Meaning unknown.

Wila (Hawaiian) Faithful. *Wilah, Willah, Wyla, Wylah*

Wilda (English) Willow. *Willida, Wylda*

Wileen (German) Determined guardian. *Wileane, Wileene, Wilin, Wilyn, Wyleen, Wyleene*

Wilfreda (English) Peaceful will; feminine version of Wilfred.

Wilhelmina (German) Feminine version of William; will and helmet. *Wiletta, Wilette, Wilhelmine, Willa, Willamina, Willimina*

Willa (Teutonic) Fierce protector. *Billie, Billy, Guillelmine, Guillemette, Helma, Mina, Minnie, Minny, Vilhelmina, Vilma, Wihelma, Wilhelmina, Wilhemine, Will, Willamina,*

Willette, Willie, Willy, Wilma, Wilmette, Wyla

Willabelle (French) Willful one. *Wilabel, Wilabele, Willabela, Wylabell, Wylabelle*

Willow (English) Freedom; tree. *Willo*

Wilma (German) Protector. *Wilmette, Wilmina, Wylma*

Wilona (English) Desired. *Wilo, Wiloh, Wilonah, Wylona*

Wilva (Teutonic) Determined. *Wilvah, Wilvar, Wylva, Wylvah*

Winda (Swahili) Hunt. *Windah, Wynda*

Winema (Native American) Female chief. *Winemah, Wynema*

Winifred (English) Friend of peace. *Fred, Freddie, Freddy, Win, Winn, Winni, Winnie, Winny, Wyn*

Winna (African) Friend. *Winnah, Wyna, Wynah, Wynna*

Winnipeg (Canadian) Muddy water. *Winipeg, Wynipeg*

Winola (German) Enchanting friend. *Winolah, Wynola*

Winona (Sioux) First-born daughter. *Wanona, Wenona, Winonah*

Winsome (English) Pleasant and attractive.

Winter (English) Winter. *Winters, Wynter*

Wira (Polish) Blond-haired. *Wiran, Wyra, Wyrah*

Wisconsin (Native American) Long river. *Wisconsyn*

Wisdom (English) Wisdom; discerning.

Wisia (Latin) Victory. *Wicia, Wiciah, Wisiah, Wysia*

Wislawa (Polish) Meaning unknown.

Woorak (Australian) Honeysuckle. *Wooraka*

Worsola (Latin) Little she-bear. *Worsolah, Worsula*

Wrenn (English) Small bird.

Wyanet (Native American) Beautiful. *Wianet, Wianete, Wianetta, Wyanett*

Wyetta (African American) Feminine version of Wyatt.

Wynflæd (Anglo-Saxon) Meaning unknown.

Wynn (Welsh) Fair. *Weeny, Win, Winn, Winnie, Winny, Wyn, Wynne, Wynnie, Wyonna*

Wynonah (Native American) First-born. *Wenona, Wenonah, Winona, Winonah, Wynnona*

Wyome (Native American) Big field.

Wyoming (Native American) Broad plains. *Wyoh, Wyomia, Wyomiah*

Wyuna (Australian) Clear water. *Wyunah*

X

Xalbadora (Spanish) Savior.

Xanadu (American) Place name; an idyllic, exotic, fictional place. *Zanadu*

Xandria (Greek) Defender of man; version of Alexandra. *Xandra, Zandra*

Xandy (Greek) Protector of man. *Xandi*

Xantha (Greek) Blond; yellow. *Xana, Xanna, Xanne, Xanth, Xanthe, Xanthia, Xanthie, Xanthippe, Xanthis, Zanthie*

Xantippi (Greek) Light-colored horse. *Xantippie, Zanthippe, Zantippe*

Xara (Arabic) Shining flower.

Xavia (Basque) New house.

Xaviera (Arabic) Bright. (Basque) New house. *Xavière*

Xenia (Greek) Hospitable. *Xena*

Xenobia (Greek) Jewel of my father.

Xenosa (Greek) Stranger. *Xenos, Xenosah, Zenos, Zenosa, Zenosah*

Xerena (Latin) Tranquil. *Seren, Xeren, Xerenah, Xerene, Zyrenah*

Xevera (Spanish) Owns a new house.

Xiang (Chinese) Fragrant. *Xeang, Xyang, Ziang, Zyang*

Xianthippe (Greek) Form of Xanthe, wife of Socrates.

Xiao (Spanish) Meaning unknown.

Xiao-Niao (Chinese) Small bird.

Xiao-Xing (Chinese) Morning star.

Ximena (Hebrew) Heroine; He heard.

Xin (Chinese) Elegant; beautiful.

Xina (English) Little. *Xeena, Xeenah, Xinah, Zeena*

Xiomara (Spanish) Ready for battle. *Xiomy*

Xiu Mei (Chinese) Beautiful plum.

Xuan (Vietnamese) Spring. *Xuana, Zuan, Zuanah*

Xuxa (Hebrew) Lily. *Xuxah*

Xya (Latin) Trembling. *Xia, Zia, Ziah, Zya, Zyah*

Xylia (Greek) Wood dweller. *Xyla, Xylina, Xylona*

Xylona (Greek) From the forest. *Xileana, Xyleena, Xylina, Zylina, Zylona*

Xylophia (Greek) Lover of the forest. *Xilophia, Xilophiah, Xylophila, Zilophia, Zylophiah*

Xyza (Gothic) By the sea.

Y

Yaa (African) Born on Thursday. *Ya*

Yaara (Hebrew) Honeycomb. *Yaari, Yaarit, Yara*

Yachi (Japanese) Good luck. *Yachiko, Yachiya*

Yachne (Hebrew) Gracious. *Yachna, Yachnee*

Yadira (Hebrew) Friend, companion.

Yadra (Spanish) Mother.

Yael (Hebrew) Mountain goat. *Jael, Yaala, Yaalat, Yaela, Yaella*

Yaffa (Hebrew) Beautiful. *Yaffah*

Yagoona (Australian) Today. *Yagoonah*

Yaki (Japanese) Broiled; baked.

Yakira (Hebrew) Dear. *Yakara, Yakirah, Yakyrah, Yekarah*

Yaksha (Hindi) Sister of Daksha.

Yale (English) Fertile moor. *Yaile, Yayle*

Yalika (Native American) Spring flowers. *Yalyka*

Yaluta (Native American) Talking woman. *Yalutah*

Yama (Japanese) Mountain.

Yamilla (Slavic) Merchant. *Yamila, Yamile, Yamille, Yamyla, Yamyll*

Yaminah (Arabic) Right and proper. *Yamina, Yamuna, Yemina*

Yamini (Hindi) Night. *Yamni*

Yamuna (Hindi) Sacred river. *Juamana, Yamunah*

Yanaba (Native American) Brave. *Yanabah*

Yanaha (Native American) She confronts an enemy. *Yanaba*

Yang (Chinese) Sun.

Yanira (Hebrew) To understand.

Yara (Australian) Seagull. *Yarah, Yarnah, Yarra, Yarrah*

Yaravi (Inca) Song of love and death. *Yara, Yari*

Yardena (Hebrew) To descend. *Jardena, Yardenah*

Yardeniya (Hebrew) God's garden. *Jardenia, Yardenia*

Yardley (English) Open-minded. *Yardlee, Yardleigh, Yardli, Yardlie, Yardly*

Yarenna Origin and meaning unknown.

Yarmilla (Slavic) Merchant.

Yashawini (Indian) Successful lady.

Yashila (Indian) Famous.

Yashna (Hindi) Prayer. *Yashnah*

Yashona (Hindi) Rich.
*Yaseana, Yashauna,
Yashawna, Yeseana, Yeshauna,
Yeshawna, Yeshona*

Yasmine (Persian)
Flowering olive. *Yasmeen,
Yasmeena, Yasmin, Yazmin,
Yazmyn*

Yasu (Japanese) Tranquil.
Yazoo

Yatra (Hebrew) Good.
Yatvah

Yauvani (Hindi) Full of
youth.

Yavonna (Hebrew) Beautiful.

Yayoi (Japanese) March.

Ydel (Hebrew) Praise. *Yidel*

Ye (Greek) Kind.

Yeardley (English) Home
enclosed in a meadow.
*Yeardlee, Yeardleigh, Yeardli,
Yeardlie, Yeardly*

Yedda (English) Singing.
Yeda, Yeddah, Yetta

Yei (Japanese) Flourishing.

Yejide (Yoruban) Image of
her mother.

Yelena (Russian) Light.
Yalena

Yen (Chinese) Desired. *Yeni,
Yenie, Yenih, Yenny*

Yenene (Native American)
Wizard poisoning a sleep-
ing person.

Yenta (Hebrew) Ruler at
home. *Yentel, Yentele, Yentil*

Yeo (Korean) Mild. *Yee*

Yepa (Native American)
Snow girl. *Yepah, Yeppa,
Yeppah*

Yera (Australian) Joyful.
Yerah, Yerra, Yerrah

Yesenia (Arabic) Flower.

Yesmin (Turkish) Jade.

Yesmina (Hebrew) Right
hand; strength.

Yetty (African American)
Ruler of the household.

Yeva (Russian) Live-giving.

Yildiz (Turkish) Star.

Yilla (Australian) Cicada.
Yila, Yilah, Yillah

Yin (Chinese) Silver.

Ylwa (Scandinavian) She-
wolf. *Ylva*

Yo-Yo (American) Rapper
Yolanda Whittaker.

Yoana (Hebrew) God's gift.

Yogini (Hindi) One who
can control their senses;
feminine form of yogi, one
practiced in yoga.

Yogita (Hindi) One who
can concentrate.

Yoi (Japanese) Born in the
evening. *Yoy*

Yoki (Native American)
Bluebird. *Yokee, Yokie, Yoky*

Yoko (Japanese) Positive.

Yolanda (Greek) Violet
flower; modest. *Eolande,
Iolande, Iolanthe, Jo, Jolanda,
Jolaunda, Landa, Yo, Yolande,
Yolantha*

Yolie (Greek) Violet flower.
Yola, Yolee, Yoly

Yoluta (Native American)
Seed. *Yolutah*

Yomaris (Spanish) I am the
sun. *Maris, Marisol*

Yon (Burmese) Rabbit.
Yonnah

Yona (Hebrew, Native
American) Dove.

Yoninah (Hebrew) Dove.
Yonina

Yori (Japanese) Honest.
Yoriko, Yoriyo

Yoshiko (Japanese) Child of
Yoshi. *Yoshyko*

Young (English) Newly
begun; fresh.

Young Il (Korean)
Prosperity; everlasting and
superior.

Young Mi (Korean)
Prosperity; eternal and
beautiful.

Young Soon (Korean)
Prosperity; eternal and
mild.

Yovela (Hebrew) Rejoicing.
Yovelah, Yovella, Yovelle

Ysanne (Spanish) Dedicated
to God. *Ysanda, Ysann,
Ysannah*

Ysolde (English) Lover of
Tristan.

Yu (Chinese) Jade.

Yudelle (Hebrew) Praised;
admired. *Yudela, Yudelah,
Yudeliah, Yudellah*

Yuka (Japanese) Snow;
lucky.

Yukako (Japanese) Child of
Yuka.

Yukiko (Japanese) Snow
child.

Yula (Russian) Young; form
of Julia. *Yulenka, Yuliya,
Yulya*

Yulan (Chinese) Jade orchid.
Ulan

Yumi (Japanese) Beauty.

Yumiko (Japanese) Child of
Yumi.

Yun (Chinese, Korean)
Melody.

Yun Hee (Korean) Lotus
flower and pleasure.

Yuri (Japanese) Lily. *Yuriko, Yury*

Yuriko (Japanese) Child of Yuri.

Yusra (Arabic) Rich. *Yusrivva, Yusrvvah*

Yutsuko (Japanese) Child of Yutso.

Yvette (Teutonic) Yew; archer. *Ivon, Ivona, Yvo, Yvonne*

Yvonne (French, Greek) Archer. *Yvetta, Yvette, Yvone*

Z

Zaafirah (Arabic) Victorious; successful.

Zaanannim (Hebrew) Movings; person asleep.

Zabana (Native American) Savannah; meadow.

Zabel (Slavic) Consecrated to God.

Zabia (African) First-born.

Zabrina (American) Fruitful desert flower. *Zabreena, Zabryna*

Zacharee (Hebrew) God is remembered.

Zaci (African) God of fatherhood.

Zada (Syrian) Lucky one. *Sada, Zaiada, Zayda*

Zadhiya (Japanese) Meaning unknown.

Zadie (English) Princess.

Zafaran (Arabic) Spice.

Zafina (Arabic) Victorious. *Zafinah, Zafyna, Zafynah*

Zagir (Russian) Flower.

Zagros (Greek) Sweet, feminine.

Zahara (Arabic) Shining, luminous. *Zahar, Zaharah, Zahra*

Zahari (Hebrew) Blossom; flower the bright dawn.

Zahava (Hebrew) Golden. *Zahavah, Zehava, Zehavi, Zeheva, Zehuva*

Zahidah (Arabic) Ascetic; abstentious.

Zahira (Arabic) Brilliant illumination. *Zahirah, Zahyra*

Zahra (Arabic, Swahili) White; flowers. *Sahra, Zahrah, Zara, Zarah*

Zahwa (African) Flower.

Zahwah (Arabic) Pretty.

Zaida (Arabic) Fortunate one. *Sada, Zada, Zai, Zayda*

Zaide (Hebrew) Elder. (Arabic) Wealthy. *Saidee, Zaidee, Zaidey*

Zaila (African) Female.

Zaina (Arabic) Beautiful.

Zainab (Scandinavian) Beautiful.

Zair (Hebrew) Little; afflicted; in tribulation.

Zaira (Arabic) Rose. *Zahirah, Zaire, Zi, Zizi*

Zaire (African) Place name. *Zayaire*

Zakia (Hebrew) Bright, pure.

Zakiya (African) Smart, intelligent.

Zale (Greek) Sea strength. *Zaile, Zayle*

Zalia (Hebrew) Sea strength.

Zalika (African) Well born.

Zaltana (Native American) High mountain.

Zama (Latin) Came from Zama.

Zambda (Hebrew) Meditation.

Zan (Hebrew) God is gracious. (Chinese) Support; praise.

Zana (Hebrew) Graceful lily. *Zanah*

Zanaide (Greek) Devoted to God.

Zanda (English) Beautiful girl; independent.

Zandra (Greek) Defender of mankind. *Andra, Andria, Zandria*

Zane (Arabic) Beloved.

Zaneta (Spanish) God's gift. *Zanetta*

Zanette (French) God is gracious.

Zanita (Greek) Long teeth. *Zaneta, Zanetta, Zanette, Zanitt*

Zankhana (Hindi) Deep desire.

Zanna (Latin) Lily. *Zana, Zanah, Zannah*

Zanoah (Hebrew) Forgetfulness; desertion.

Zanta (African) Beautiful; girl. *Santa, Santah*

Zanthe (Greek) Light blond. *Zanth, Zanthi, Zanthie, Zanthy*

Zanubiya (Arabic) Name of great Syrian queen.

Zaqaria (Indian) Meaning unknown.

Zara (Hebrew, Arabic) Dawn; princess. *Zarah, Zari, Zarry*

Zaray (Arabic) Beautiful flower.

Zarda Origin and meaning unknown.

Zareah (Hebrew) Leprosy; hornet.

Zareen (Hebrew) Golden.

Zarela (Spanish) Meaning unknown.

Zarephath (Hebrew) Ambush of the mouth.

Zaretan (Hebrew) Tribulation; perplexity.

Zaria (Arabic) Rose. *Zari, Zariah*

Zariel (American) Lion princess.

Zarifa (Arabic) Moves with grace. *Zarifah*

Zarina (African) Golden. *Zareana, Zareena, Zarine*

Zarita (Spanish) Princess. *Zareate, Zareeta, Zaritte*

Zarna (Hindi) Meaning unknown.

Zarola (Arabic) Hunter.

Zasha (Russian) Pet form of Alexander. *Sasha*

Zasu (African) Meaning unknown.

Zati (Hebrew) Olive tree. *Zatthu*

Zavannah (English) Savannah; meadow.

Zavia (English) Bright; new house.

Zaviera (Spanish) Owner of the home.

Zavrina (American, English) Princess. *Sabrina*

Zawadi (African) Gift.

Zay (Arabic) Lucky.

Zayit (Hebrew) Olive. *Zayita*

Zaylin (American) Meaning unknown. *Aylin, Zayla*

Zayna (Arabic) Beauty.

Zayra (Hebrew) Princess.

Zaza (Hebrew) Golden. *Zazah, Zehavit*

Zdebka (Russian) Meaning unknown.

Zdenek (Czech) One from Sidon; winding sheet. *Zdenka*

Zea (Latin) Wheat. *Sea, Seah, Siah, Zeah*

Zeanes (Hebrew) Meaning unknown.

Zebina (Greek) One who is gifted.

Zee (Hebrew) Wolf. *Zeela, Zella, Zelmora, Zelnora*

Zeeba (Persian) Beautiful.

Zehava (Hebrew) Golden. *Sehari, Sehava, Zehuva, Zohar*

Zeitia (Galician) Meaning unknown.

Zelda (German) Woman warrior. *Selda, Zeldah*

Zelek (Hebrew) Shadow; noise of him who licks; laps.

Zelenka (Czech) Little innocent one. *Selen, Zelen*

Zelia (Greek) Zeal. *Selia, Selya, Selyah, Zeliah*

Zelinda (German) Shield of victory. *Segelinde*

Zeljka (Slavic) Wish.

Zella (Hebrew) Wise and peaceful.

Zelma (German) Divinely protected.

Zelotes (Hebrew) Zealous.

Zelpha (Hebrew) Dignified. *Zilpha*

Zemaraim (Hebrew) Wool; pith.

Zemil (Hebrew) Joyous melody.

Zena (Greek) Alive.

Zenaide (Greek) One who has devoted her life to God. *Zenaida, Zenayda*

Zenda (Arabic) Womanly. *Senda, Sendah*

Zenevieva (Irish) Pale.

Zenia (Greek) Hospitable. *Xenya, Zeniah*

Zenobia (Greek) Of Zeus. *Zena, Zenina, Zenna, Zenobie, Zenovia, Zinovia*

Zenon (Greek) Stranger. *Xenon*

Zenzi (German) Growing.

Zeolia (English) Meaning unknown.

Zeph (Hebrew) Treasured by God.

Zephan (Irish) Saint.

Zephaniah (Hebrew) The Lord has hidden. *Sephanee, Sephaney, Zephanee, Zephania*

Zephath (Hebrew) Beholds; covers.

Zequinha (Spanish) Meaning unknown.

Zera (Greek) Wolf. *Sera, Zerah*

Zerdali (Turkish) Wild apricot. *Zerdalia*

Zeredah (Hebrew) Ambush.

Zeresh (Hebrew) Misery; strange.

Zerlinda (Hebrew) Beautiful dawn. *Serline, Zerleene, Zerlina*

Zeruah (Hebrew) Meaning unknown.

Zeta (Greek) Investigator; researcher. *Sita, Zitah*

Zethel (Hebrew) Meaning unknown.

Zeuti (Greek) Meaning unknown.

Zeva (Greek) Sword. *Serah, Zevia*

Zevida (Hebrew) Gift. *Zevuda, Zevyda*

Zeynee (Turkish) Ornament.

Zez (Hebrew) Meaning unknown.

Zhalore (Hebrew) Meaning unknown.

Zhen (Chinese) Purity. *Zenn, Zhena, Zhenah, Zhenna*

Zhengqiu (Chinese) Precious.

Zhenya (Russian) Of noble birth.

Zhi (Chinese) Wisdom.

Zhijuan (Chinese) Precious; beautiful.

Zi (Chinese) Graceful.

Zia (Hebrew, Latin) To tremble; kind of grain. *Zea, Ziah*

Ziahon (Hebrew) Meaning unknown.

Ziarre (American) Goddess of the sky.

Ziazan (Armenian) Rainbow.

Zibiah (Hebrew) Doe.

Zigana (Hungarian) Gypsy girl.

Zila (Hebrew) Shadow. *Zilah, Zilla, Zillah, Zylia*

Zilli (African) My shadow. *Zili*

Zilya (Russian) Harvester. *Zylyah*

Zima (Polish) Winter.

Zina (African) Name. *Zena, Zinah, Zine, Zinnie*

Zinaida (Greek) Of Zeus. *Zenais, Zina*

Zinnia (English) Flower. (Latin) Colorful flowers. *Zin, Zina, Zinia, Zinnya, Zinya*

Ziona (Hebrew) Sign. *Zinoah, Zyona, Zyonah*

Zippora (Hebrew) Bird. *Zeporah, Zipporah*

Zisel (Hebrew) Sweet. *Zysel*

Zita (Hebrew, Persian) Seeker; virgin.

Zitala (Native American) Bird. *Zitkalah*

Zizi (Hungarian) Dedicated to God.

Zoe (Greek) Life. *Zoé, Zoë, Zoee, Zoey*

Zofia (Polish) Wisdom. *Zofey*

Zohreh (Persian) Happy. *Zohra*

Zoila (African) Child.

Zoisite (Austrian) Type of mineral.

Zola (Italian) Ball of earth.

Zoleen (Hebrew) Meaning unknown.

Zona (Latin) Prostitute.

Zonda (Hebrew) Defender of mankind.

Zone Origin and meaning unknown.

Zonta (Native American) Honest, trustworthy.

Zora (Slavic) Golden dawn. *Zarya, Zohra, Zoradah, Zorah, Zoranna, Zori, Zoriana, Zorie, Zorina, Zorry*

Zosima (Greek) Lively.

Zotia (Polish) One with wisdom. *Zosia*

Zov Origin and meaning unknown.

Zsa Zsa (Hungarian) Rose; lily. *Zsusanna, Zsuzsanna*

Zuette (French) Yew. *Zuet, Zueta*

Zula (Hebrew) Brilliant; ahead.

Zuleika (Arabic) Fair-haired. *Zuleyka*

Zulema (Arabic) Peace. *Zulima*

Zuriaa (Spanish) White; light-skinned.

Zuriel (Hebrew) God is my rock.

Zurine (Spanish) White.

Zuza (Czech) Graceful lily.

Zuzana (Slavic) Rose. *Zuzanna*

Zylphia (American) Victorian.

Boy Names

A

Aabha (Indian) Light.

Aaron (Hebrew) Shining light. (Arabic) Messenger. *Aahron, Aaran, Aaren, Aarin, Aaronn, Aarron, Aaryn, Aeron, Aharon, Ahran, Ahren, Ahron, Aranne, Aren, Arin, Aron, Aronne, Arran, Arron, Haroun, Harun*

Aban (Irish) Little king. *Abban, Abbana, Abben, Abbin, Abbon*

Abbas (Hebrew, Arabic) Father. *Ab, Abba, Abbe, Abbey, Abbie, Abo*

Abbott (Arabic) Father. *Abad, Abba, Abbe, Abboid, Abbot, Abby, Abot*

Abdiel (Hebrew) Servant of God.

Abdulaziz (Arabic) Slave of God. *Adelazim, Adulazaz*

Abdullah (Arabic) God's servant. *Abadalan, Abdaga, Abdala, Abdela, Abduala, Abdulha, Abdulla, Adbulahi*

Abeeku (African) One who is born on Wednesday.

Abel (Hebrew) Breath. *Abeles, Abell, Abi, Able, Ablius, Adal, Avel*

Abelard (German) Resolute. *Abalard, Abelardo, Abelhard, Abilard, Adalard, Adelard*

Abhay (Hindi) Fearless. *Abhaya*

Abheek (Indian) Fearless.

Abhijit (Hindi) Victorious. *Abhijeet*

Abhorson (Scottish) Lives by the river. *Abhor*

Abi (Turkish) Elder brother. *Abbe, Abbey, Abe, Abee, Aby*

Abijah (Hebrew) God is my Father.

Abner (Hebrew) Father of light. *Ab, Abbey, Abby, Avner*

Abraham (Hebrew) Father of a multitude. *Abe, Aberham, Abhiram, Abie, Abra, Abrahaim, Abrahame, Abrahamo, Abrahan, Abraheem, Abrahem, Abrahim, Abrahin, Abrahm, Abrahon, Abram, Abramo, Abran, Alibaba, Avraham, Avram, Avrom, Braham, Bram, Ibrahim*

Abrahsa (Hebrew) Father.

Absolom (Hebrew) My father is peace. *Absalon, Abselon, Absolum*

Abtin (Persian) Fereidoun's father.

Abukakar (Egyptian) Noble.

Abuna (Arabic) Our father.

Acacio (Hebrew) The Lord holds.

Acar (Turkish) Bright. *Accerlee, Ackerli, Acklea, Akerly*

Accalon (Scottish) Lover of Morgan Le Fay.

Ace (Latin) Unity. *Acer, Acey, Acie*

Achachak (Native American) Spirit.

Achan (Biblical) He who troubleth.

Achilles (Greek) Mythical Trojan war hero. *Achill, Achille, Achillea, Achilleo, Achilleus, Achylle, Akil, Akilles*

Achuta (Hindi) Untouchable.

Ackley (Old English) Meadow of oaks. *Acklea, Ackleah, Ackli, Akleigh*

Acton (Old English) Town with many oaks. *Actan, Actun, Actyn*

Acura (American) Luxury automobile brand.

Adahy (Native American) Lives in the woods. *Adahi*

Adair (English) Oak tree ford. *Adaire, Adare, Adayre, Addaire, Addare, Addyre*

Adalai (Hebrew) Refuge of God. (Arabic) Just. *Adlai*

Adalbert (Old German) Noble. *Adalberto, Berto*

Adalgiso (Old German) Noble hostage.

Adam (Hebrew) Earth. *Ad, Adamec, Adamek, Adamik, Adamo, Adams, Adamson, Adan, Adao, Adas, Addam, Addams, Addem, Addie, Addis, Addison, Addy, Ade, Adem, Adham, Adhamh, Adie, Adnet, Adnon, Adnot, Adom*

Adan (Irish) Warm. *Aden, Adian, Adin, Adon, Adun, Adyn, Aedan, Aidan, Aiden*

Adar (Hebrew) Noble. *Addair, Addar, Addare*

Adare (Irish) From the ford of the oak tree.

Addai (Hebrew) Man of God.

Addison (Old English) Adam's son. *Addisen, Addisun, Addoson, Addyson, Adison, Adisson, Adyson*

Adelbert (Old German) Famous for nobility. *Albert, Delbert*

Adelfried (Old German) He who protects the descendants.

Adelino (Old German) Noble.

Adelmio (Old German) Of noble birth.

Adelmo (Old German) Noble protector.

Ademaro (Old German) Glorious in battle.

Adeodatus (Latin) Given by God.

Adger (Old English) Happy spear. (Scottish) Oak tree ford. *Adair, Adar, Agar, Ager*

Adham (Arabic) Black.

Adie (German) Noble; kind; often used as a nickname. *Addie, Addy, Adolph*

Adin (Hebrew) Delicate. *Addyn, Adyn*

Adir (Hebrew) Magestic; noble. *Adeer*

Aditya (Hindi) Lord of the sun.

Adiv (Hebrew) Polite. *Adeev, Adev*

Adler (German) Eagle. *Addla, Addlah, Addlar, Addler, Adlar*

Adley (Hebrew) Just. *Adlea, Adlee, Adlie*

Adli (Hebrew) Just, wise. *Adlai, Adlea, Adlee, Adler, Adlie*

Admon (Hebrew) Red peony.

Adnan (Arabic) Peasant. *Adnaan, Adnane*

Adney (English) Dweller on the island. *Adnee, Adni, Adny*

Adolph (German) Noble wolf. *Addof, Adolf, Adolfo, Adolfus, Adolphe, Adolphus*

Adon (Hebrew) Lord. *Adonie, Adonys*

Adoni (Australian) Sunset. *Adonee, Adoney*

Adonis (Greek) Handsome mythological figure. *Adonai, Adonyse, Andonis*

Adred (Science fiction) Character from *Star Trek: Deep Space Nine*.

Adri (Indian) Rock. *Adree, Adrey*

Adrian (Greek) Rich. (Latin) Dark one. *Adarian, Adorjan, Adrain, Adreian, Adreyan, Adriane, Adriann, Adrianne, Adriano, Adrianus, Adrien, Adrien, Adrion, Adrionn, Adrionne, Adron, Adryan, Adryn, Adryon, Hadrian, Hadrianus*

Adriel (Hebrew) Of God's flock. *Adrial, Adriall, Adriell, Adryel*

Aeary (Irish) Scholar.

Aegeon (Shakespearean) Character from *The Comedy of Errors*.

Aemiliano (Latin) Rival. *Emilio*

Aemilius (Latin) Eager. *Aimil, Aymil, Emelen, Emelio, Emil, Emilan, Emile,*

Emiliano, Emilianus, Emilio, Emilion, Emilyan, Emlen, Emlin, Emlyn, Emlynn

Afi (African) Born on Friday. *Kofi*

Afram (African) River in Ghana.

Africa (Latin) From Africa. *Afrate, Afro*

Afton (Celtic) From the Afton River. *Afton, Aftan, Aftin, Aftyn*

Agamemnon (Greek) King of Mycenae who led the Greeks in the Trojan War.

Agapetus (Spanish) Beloved.

Agatho (Italian) Catholic saint and pope from Sicily. *Agathe*

Aglovale (Arthurian) Knight of the Round Table.

Agravaine (Arthurian) Knight of the Round Table and nephew of King Arthur.

Agrippa (Hebrew) One who causes great pain at birth. *Agripah, Agrypa, Agryppa, Agryppah*

Ahab (Hebrew) Uncle.

Ahanu (Native American) He laughs.

Ahearn (Celtic) Lord of the horses. *Ahearne, Aherin, Ahern, Aherne, Aheron, Aheryne, Hearn*

Ahir (Turkish) Last.

Ahmad (Arabic) To praise. *Achmad, Achmed, Ahamad, Ahamada, Ahamed, Ahmaad, Ahmaud, Ahmed, Amad, Amahd, Amed*

Ahmik (Hebrew) Strength of God's flock.

Ahren (Old German) Eagle.

Ahura (Hindi) Lord.

Aidan (Irish) Little fiery one. *Aiden, Aidun, Ayden, Aydin*

Aiken (Old English) Made of oak. *Aicken, Aikin, Ayken*

Ailani (Hawaiian) Chief.

Aimon (Spanish) Homebody. *Aimond, Aymon, Eamon, Edmund, Haimon, Heman*

Aitan (Hebrew) Strong.

Ajatashatru (Hindi) Without enemies.

Ajax (Greek) Eagle.

Ajay (Hindi) Conqueror. *Aj, Aja, Ajae, Ajai, Ajaye, Ajaz, Ajee, Ajit*

Akaash (Hindi) Sky. *Aakash, Akasha*

Akamu (Hawaiian) Red earth. *Adamu, Akanah*

Akbar (Arabic) Powerful. *Akbara*

Akecheta (Native American) Fighter. *Akechetah*

Akeem (Hebrew) God will establish. *Ackeem, Akeam, Akiem*

Akemi (Japanese) Beautiful dawn. *Ackemy, Akemee*

Akim (Hebrew) The Lord will judge. *Achim, Achym, Ackeem, Ackime, Ahkiem, Ahkyem, Akee, Akima*

Akira (Scottish) Anchor. (Japanese) Distinct. *Akihito, Akio, Akiyo, Akyrah*

Aksel (Old German) Father of peace. *Aksell, Ax, Axe, Axel*

Akshay (Hindi) Indestructible. *Akshaj, Akshaya*

Akule (Native American) Looks up.

Al-Ashab (Arabic) Gray.

Aladdin (Arabic) Servant of Allah. *Aladan, Aladdan, Aladdyn, Aladen*

Alam (Hindi) Whole world. *Aalam, Alame*

Alamo (American) Famous battle.

Alan (Gaelic) Handsome. *Ailan, Ailin, Alain, Alean, Allan, Allen, Allon, Alun*

Alarbus (Shakespearean) Character from *Titus Andronicus*.

Alaric (German) Noble ruler. *Alarick, Alarico, Alarik, Aleric, Allaric, Allarick, Alric, Alrick, Alrik*

Alastair (Scottish) Defender of mankind; version of Alexander. *Alaisdair, Alaistair, Alaister, Alasdair, Alastaire, Alasteir, Alaster, Alastor, Aleister, Alistair, Alistaire, Alister, Allaistar, Allastair, Allaster, Allastir, Allysdair, Alystair*

Alban (Latin) White. *Albain, Albany, Albean, Albein, Alben, Albin, Albion, Alby*

Albert (German) Noble, bright; famous. *Adelbert, Ailbert, Al, Albertine, Alberto, Albertus, Albie, Albrecht, Alby, Albyrt, Albyrte, Alvertos, Aubert, Bert, Bertel, Bertie, Berty, Elbert*

Albin (English) White. *Alben, Albene, Albenik, Albeno, Albinson, Auben, Aubin*

Albrecht (German) Noble; intelligent. *Adelbert, Albert, Alberto*

Alcander (Greek) Manly; strong. *Alcandor, Alcindor, Allcander*

Alcibiades (Shakespearean) Character from *Timon of Athens*. (Greek) Violent force; Athenian general and politician during the Peloponnesian War. *Alkibiades*

Alcott (Old English) Old cottage. *Alcot, Alkot, Allkot, Allkott, Walcot, Walcott*

Alden (Middle English) Old friend. *Aldan, Aldean, Aldin, Aldon, Aldwin, Aldyn, Elden*

Alder (Middle English) Type of birch tree. (English) Revered one. *Aldair, Aldare, Aldus, Elder*

Aldo (English) Old and wise. *Alda, Aldous, Alds, Aldus*

Aldrich (Old English) Old king. *Aldred, Aldren, Aldric, Aldrick, Aldridge, Aldrige, Aldrin, Aldritch, Aldrych, Alldric, Alldrich, Alldrick, Alldridge*

Aleixo (Greek) Defender.

Alem (Arabic) Wise man. *Alerio, Alim*

Aleron (French) Knight. (Latin) Winged.

Aleser (Arabic) Lion.

Alexander (Greek) Protector of mankind. *Alakesander, Alec, Aleck, Alejandro, Alejo, Alek, Aleks, Aleksander, Aleksey, Alesandro, Alessandro, Alex, Alexandre, Alexas, Alexei, Alexio, Alick, Alik, Alkeos, Alyc, Alyck, Alyk, Alysander, Iksander, Ixsander, Sacha, Sander, Sanders, Sandie, Sandor, Sandro, Sandy, Sasha, Xander*

Aleyn (English) Fisher king in Arthurian legend.

Alfonso (Old German) Noble and ready. *Affonso, Alfio, Alfons, Alfonse, Alfonsus, Alfonza, Alfonzo, Alonso, Alonzo, Alphonse, Alphonsus*

Alford (English) From the old ford.

Alfred (Old English) Wise counsel. *Ailfrid, Alf, Alfeo, Alfie, Alfredo, Alfric, Alfrid, Allie, Elfred, Fred, Freddie*

Alger (German) Noble warrior. *Aelgar, Algar, Allgar, Elgar, Elger*

Algernon (French) Mustachioed. *Algenon, Algie, Algin, Algon*

Algot (Scandinavian) Meaning unknown.

Ali (Arabic) Greatest; exalted. (Muslim) Protected by God. *Aly*

Alice (Old German) Of good cheer.

Alim (Arabic) Wise; learned. *Alem*

Alistar (Greek) Man's defender. *Alastair, Alastor, Aleister, Alistaire, Allistar, Allister, Aly*

Allard (Old English) Noble and brave. *Alard, Ellard*

Allen (Scottish) Handsome. *Alan, Allan, Alleyne, Alyn*

Allston (Old English) Al's town. *Alston, Alton*

Almas (Muslim) Diamond.

Alo (Native American) Spiritual guide.

Aloysius (Old German) Famous warrior. *Ablois, Aloess, Alois, Aloisio, Alosius, Aloys, Lewis, Louis, Ludwick, Ludwig, Lutwick*

Alpha (Greek) Superior; excellent. (African) Leader. *Alfa, Alfah, Alphah*

Alphaeus (Hebrew) Changing. *Alfeus*

Alphus (Hebrew) He who follows after. *Alfaeus, Alfeos, Alfeus, Alpheaus, Alphoeus*

Alpin (Welsh) Attractive. *Alpyn*

Alroy (Spanish) King. *Alroi*

Alston (English) From the old place. *Allston, Alsdon, Alstan, Alsten, Alstin, Alstun, Alstyn*

Altair (Arabic) Bird. (Greek) Star. *Altayr*

Alton (Old English) From the old town. *Alten, Altown*

Alva (Hebrew) His highness. *Alvah, Alvan*

Alvar (English) Warrior. *Albaro, Allvar, Alvara, Alvaro, Alvarso*

Alvertos (Old English) Shepherd. *Adalverto, Alvert, Alvertis, Alvertos*

Alvin (Old English) Elf wine. *Albin, Aloin, Aluin, Alvan, Alven, Alwyn*

Alvis (Old Norse) All wise. *Alviss, Elvis*

Alwin (Teutonic) Beloved by all. *Ailwyn, Alwan, Alwyn*

Alzen (Science fiction) Character from *Star Trek: Voyager*.

Amadeus (Latin) Love of God. *Amadeo, Amadis, Amado, Amandus, Amedeus*

Amal (Hebrew) Labor. (Arabic) Hope. *Amahl*

Amando (Latin) Loves God. *Amand, Amandio, Amandus, Amaniel*

Amanin (Science fiction) Character from *Star Wars*. *Amanaman*

Amar (Greek) Immortal. *Amarande, Amare, Amaree, Amari, Amario, Amarjit, Amaro*

Amari (Arabic) Builder. *Amerion*

Amaros (Arabic) Moon. *Amaraja, Amaraji, Amaral, Amaran, Amarand, Amarant, Amarapa, Amarbir, Amarco, Amarcus, Amard, Amardad, Amardev, Amardip, Amardit, Amardo, Amare, Amaree, Amareet, Amareh, Amaren, Amares, Amaresa, Amaresh, Amarfis, Amargi, Amari, Amaria, Amariah, Amarian, Amariea, Amaril, Amarin, Amario, Amariy, Amarja, Amaro, Amarok, Amaron, Amaroo, Amaroq, Amarri, Amarsa, Amarth, Amarti, Amaru, Amarya*

Amator (Latin) Lover.

Ambrose (Greek) Immortal. *Ambie, Ambroise, Ambros, Ambrosi, Ambrosio, Ambrosius, Emrys*

Amedeo (Italian) Painter (1884–1920) known for the use of graceful, elongated lines.

Amerigo (Italian) Industrious. *Americo, Americus*

Ames (Latin) Loves. (French) Friend.

Amherst (English) Place name.

Amiel (Hebrew) The Lord of my people. *Ammiel, Amyel*

Amiens (Shakespearean) Character from *As You Like It*. (French) Place name.

Amin (Arabic) Honest, trustworthy. *Amen, Amyn, Amynn*

Amir (Arabic) Princely. *Aamer, Aamir, Ameer, Amire, Amiri, Amyr*

Amit (Hindi) Boundless; endless. *Amitan, Amreet, Amrit, Amryt*

Amon (Hebrew) Trustworthy; faithful. *Amman, Ammen, Ammyn, Amun, Eammon, Eamon*

Amory (Latin) Loving; for boy or girl. *Ameree, Amerie, Amery, Ammeri, Ammori, Amor, Amorie, Emery, Emory*

Amos (Hebrew) Troubled. *Amose, Amous*

Amram (Hebrew) Father of Aaron and Moses. *Amarien, Amrem, Amrym*

Amund (Scandinavian) Divine protection. *Amondo*

An (Chinese) Peace. *Ana, Anah*

Anacletus (Greek) Calling forth. *Anakletos, Cletus*

Analu (Hawaiian) Manly.

Anand (Hindi) Bliss. *Ananda, Anant, Ananth*

Ananias (Hindi) God will hear. (Biblical) Cloud of the Lord.

Anastasius (Greek) Reborn. *Anas, Anastacio, Anastacios, Anastagio, Anastas, Anastase, Anastasi, Anastasio, Anastasios, Anastice, Anastisis, Athanasius*

Anath (Hebrew) Answer.

Anatole (Greek) East. *Anatol, Anatoley, Anatoli, Anatolio, Anatoliy, Anatoly, Anitoly*

Anay (Hindi) Radha's husband.

Ancel (German) Deity. *Ancell, Ancelot, Ansel, Anselm*

Anderson (Swedish) Son of Andrew. *Anders, Andersen, Andy*

Andrew (Greek) Valiant; courageous. *Aindrea, Anders, Andery, Andie, Andonis, Andor, Andrae, Andre, Andreas, Andrei, Andres, Andrews, Andros, Andru, Andrue, Andrzej, Andy, Antero, Audrew, Drew*

Andrily Origin and meaning unknown.

Andromeda (Greek) Constellation in the Northern Hemisphere.

Angel (English) Messenger. *Ange, Angel, Angelico, Angell, Angelo, Angil, Angyl, Anjel, Anjelo*

Angus (Gaelic) Superb or unique. *Aeneas*

Anicetus (Old French) Unconquerable. *Aniceta, Anicetta, Anniceta, Annicetta*

Anker (Greek) Manly. *Ankur*

Ankhhaf (Arabic) Oldest son of Pharaoh Seneferu; high-ranking religious and political adviser of Khafre. *Ankh Haf*

Annan (Celtic) From the stream. *Annon, Annun*

Annas (Hebrew) High priest. *Ananias, Anis, Anish*

Anoop (Hindi) Incomparable; best. *Anup*

Ansari (Arabic) Helper.

Anselm (Old German) Deity. *Ancell, Ancelot, Ansel, Anselme*

Anson (English) Son of a nobleman. *Ansen, Ansonia, Ansun, Hansen, Hanson*

Anstice (Greek) Resurrected.

Antenor (Greek) Elder of Troy.

Anterus (Roman) Saint.

Anthony (Latin) Priceless. (Greek) Flourishing. *Anathony, Anfernee, Anothony, Antajuan, Antanee, Antanie, Antavas, Antenee, Anthan, Anthany, Anthey, Anthjuan, Anthney, Anthone, Anthonee, Anthoney, Anthonie, Anthonio, Anthonou, Anthoy, Antione, Antjuan, Antoine, Anton, Antoni, Antonio, Antonius, Antony, Antuan, Tonio, Tony*

Antigonus (Greek) Like the ancestor. (Shakespearean) Character from *The Winter's Tale.*

Antiochus (Shakespearean) Character from *Pericles.*

Antipholus (Shakespearean) Character from *The Comedy of Errors.*

Antonio (Spanish) Worthy of praise.

Anwar (Arabic) Bright one. *Anward*

Apemantus (Shakespearean) Character from *The Life of Timon of Athens.*

Apenimon (Native American) Worthy of trust.

Apollo (Greek) Manly. *Apolinario, Apollos, Apolo, Apolonio, Appollo, Polo*

Apostolos (Greek) Disciple. *Apostul*

Aquarius (Latin) Constellation, the Water Bearer; eleventh sign of the Zodiac.

Aquila (Latin) Strong as an eagle. *Acquilla, Aquil, Aquilas, Aquiles, Aquilino, Aquilla, Aquille, Aquillino*

Ara (Arabic) Opinions. *Arah*

Aragorn (Fiction) Character from *The Lord of the Rings* by J. R. R. Tolkien.

Arali (African) Basement of the earth.

Aram (Assyrian) High place. *Aramia, Arra, Arram, Arum*

Aramis (French) Fictional swordsman. *Airamis, Aramys*

Arandis (Science fiction) Character from *Star Trek: Deep Space Nine*.

Arash (Arabic) Hero.

Arcadicus (Latin) Of or pertaining to Arcadia; pastoral. *Arcadia, Arcadian, Arcadien*

Archangelo (Latin) Principal angel. *Arcangello, Arcangelo*

Archelaus (Greek) Ruler of the people.

Archer (English) Bowman. *Archar, Archor*

Archibald (English) Bold prince. *Arch, Archaimbaud, Archambault, Arche, Archi, Archibaldo, Archibold, Archie, Archy, Arkady, Arky*

Archidamus (Shakespearean) Character from *The Winter's Tale*.

Archimedes (Greek) To think about first. *Archim*

Arda (Turkish) Meaning unknown.

Ardalan (Persian) Hurried.

Ardell (Latin) Eager. *Ardel*

Arden (Latin) Passionate; for boy or girl. *Ardan, Ardelia, Ardene, Ardian, Ardie, Ardin, Ardis, Ardn, Ardon*

Arel (Hebrew) Lion of God.

Arend (Dutch) Form of Arnold.

Ares (Greek) God of war.

Aretino (Italian) Attacker. *Aretin, Aretine, Artyno*

Argus (Greek) Bright.

Ari (Hebrew) Lion eagle. *Arie, Arius, Arri, Ary, Arye*

Arian (English) Enchanted.

Aries (English) Constellation. *Ares, Arie, Ariez, Aryes*

Arion (Greek) Enchanted; poet who was rescued by dolphins after being thrown into the sea. (Hebrew) Melodious. *Arian, Arien, Ario, Arione, Aryon*

Aristide (Greek) Descended from the best. *Aristedes, Aristeed, Aristidis, Aristo*

Aristotle (Hebrew) Lion. *Arelk, Arey, Aristito, Aristokles, Aristotelis*

Arizona (Spanish) Good oak.

Arjay (American) Phonetic spelling of R. J.

Arje (Dutch) Form of Adrian.

Arjun (Sanskrit) White one. *Arjen, Arjin, Arjuna, Arjune*

Arland (German) Famous throughout the land. *Arleigh, Arlen, Arles, Arlie, Arliss, Arlo, Arly, Arlyss*

Arledge (Old English) Lives at the hare's lake. *Arlidge, Arlledge*

Arley (Old English) From the hare. *Arleigh, Arlie, Harleigh, Harley, Harly, Hartley*

Arlo (Old English) From the protected town. *Harlow*

Armand (German) Warrior; form of Herman. *Armad, Arman, Armanda, Armando, Armands, Armanno, Armaude, Armenta, Armon, Armond, Armondo, Herman, Hermann*

Armani (African) Faith.

Armstrong (Old English) Strong-armed warrior. *Armston*

Arnold (German) Eagle and powerful. *Arnald, Arnaldo, Arnaud, Arnault, Arndt, Arne, Arnel, Arnell, Arness, Arnie, Arno, Arnoll, Arnot, Arnulfo*

Arnon (Hebrew) Rushing stream; also girl's name. *Arnan, Arnen, Arnin*

Arnulfo (Spanish) Eagle. *Nuflo, Nulfo*

Arrigo (Italian) Estate ruler. *Enrico*

Arrio (Spanish) Belligerent. *Ario, Arryo, Aryo*

Arsenio (Greek) Masculine. *Areseny, Arsen, Arseneo, Arsenius, Arsenyo, Arsinio, Arsinyo*

Arslan (Arabic) Lion hero.

Artemis (Greek) Goddess of the moon and hunting.

Arthur (Welsh) Bear hero. *Art, Arta, Artair, Arte, Artek, Arth, Arthor, Artie, Artur, Arturis, Arturo, Arty, Aurthar, Aurther, Aurthur, D'Artagnan*

Aruiragus (Latin) Melodies. (Shakespearean) Character from *Cymbeline*.

Arun (Hindi) Dawn, sun.

Arundel (Old English) He who dwells with eagles. *Arundle*

Arvid (Scandinavian) Eagle's tree.

Arvin (English) Friend. *Arv, Arvie, Arvis, Arvy, Arwen, Arwin*

Arwed (Swedish) Eagle of the woods.

Arwen (English) Noble, royal; muse. Character from *The Lord of the Rings* by J. R. R. Tolkien.

Asa (Hebrew) Healer. *Asaa, Asah, Ase, Assa*

Asad (Arabic) Most prosperous one. *Asadel, Asadour, Asael, Azad*

Aseem (Hindi) Limitless. *Asim*

Asher (Hebrew) Fortunate. *Anschel, Asha, Ashar, Ashbel, Ashe, Asherman, Ashor, Ashur, Asser*

Ashkii (Native American) Sacred child.

Ashley (Old English) Ash tree; for boy or girl. *Ash, Ashby, Ashe, Asheley, Ashelie, Ashford, Ashlan, Ashleigh, Ashlen, Ashlie, Ashlin, Ashling, Ashlinn, Ashlone, Ashly, Ashten, Ashton, Aslan*

Ashraf (Arabic) Honorable.

Asija (Hindi) Great sage.

Asker (Turkish) Soldier. *Aske*

Asmodel (Greek) Angel of patience; guardian of April ruling the Zodiac sign of Taurus.

Asphar (Hebrew) Pool in the desert.

Aster (Greek) Star.

Astin (English) Form of August. *Asten, Aston*

Asuman (Hindi) Lord of vital breaths.

Asvin (Hindi) God of medicine.

Atash (Persian) Fire.

Athan (Greek) Immortal. *Ateef, Athen, Athin, Athon, Athons*

Athanasios (Greek) Noble.

Atharvan (Hindi) Knower of the Arthara vedas.

Athelstan (Old English) Noble stone.

Athol (Scottish) Place name; New Ireland; coming from Ireland. *Affol, Athal, Athalton, Athil, Atholton*

Athos (Greek) Zeus.

Atilla (Hungarian) Beloved father. *Atalik, Atila, Attal, Attila, Attilio*

Atlantis (Greek) Last island.

Atlas (Greek) Mythical Titan who supported the earth on his back.

Atley (English) From the meadow. *Atlea, Atlee, Atleigh, Atli, Attleah, Attley, Attlie*

Atohi (Native American) Woods.

Atticus (Latin) From Athens.

Attilio (Italian) Little father. *Atilio, Atilla, Attila, Attilah*

Atul (Hindi) Matchless.

Atwell (English) Lives by the spring.

Aubrey (English) Elfin king. *Alberik, Auberon, Aubree*

Auburn (Latin) Fair. *Alban, Aubin*

Audie (English) Old friend. *Auden, Audi, Audiel, Audley, Audy*

Audio (American) Sound.

Audric (French) Wise ruler. *Audrick, Audrik, Audryc*

August (Latin) Exalted. *Agosto, Agustin, Augie, Augusta, Auguste, Augustina, Augustine, Augustus, Gus, Gussie, Gussy, Gusta*

Augwynne (Science fiction) Character from *Star Wars*.

Aulii (Hawaiian) Delicious.

Aurek (Polish) Golden hair.

Aurelius (Latin) Golden one. *Areliano, Aurek, Aurel, Aurele, Aurelian, Aurelio, Aurey, Auryn*

Auriga (Latin) Wagoner.

Austin (Latin) Useful. *Austan, Austen, Austun, Austyn*

Autolocus (Greek) He who is wolf; self-luminous. (Shakespearean) Character from *A Winter's Tale*. *Autolycus, Autolykos*

Avel (Greek) Breath.

Avenau (French) Oat pasture. *Avena, Aveneil, Aveneill, Avenell, Avenil, Avenill*

Averill (Old English) Boar warrior. *Averel, Averell, Averiel, Averil, Averyl, Averyll, Avrel, Avrell, Avryll, Everil, Everill, Haverhill, Haverl*

Avery (English) Counselor. *Avary, Averey, Averi, Averie, Avrey, Avry*

Avicus (German) Honorable.

Avis (Latin) Bird. *Avice*

Avon (Welsh) River in England.

Avonmore (Irish) From the great river.

Awan (Native American) Somebody. *Awen, Awin, Awon*

Awarnach (Old English) From Arthurian legend; giant.

Axel (Swedish) Divine source of life. *Aksel, Axell, Axil, Axill, Axl, Axtel, Axyle*

Ayers (English) Heir to a fortune.

Aylward (English) Awesome guardian. *Ailward*

Ayman (Arabic) Lucky, fortunate. *Aymeen*

Azad (Arabic) Independent. *Asad, Azzad*

Azar (Persian) Fire.

Azariah (Hebrew) Servant of Nego. *Abednego*

Azeem (Arabic) Defender. *Aseem, Asim, Azim, Azzeem*

Azen (Science fiction) Character from *Star Trek: Voyager*.

Azure (Biblical) He who assists; also girl's name.

B

Babyface (American) One with a baby face; singer whose real name is Kenneth Edmonds.

Badal (Hindi) Cloud.

Baden (Welsh) From Baddon. *Badan, Baddan, Badden, Baddon, Bade, Badin, Badon, Badyn, Baedan, Baede, Baeden, Baedin, Baedon*

Badr (Arabic) Full moon. *Badar*

Badrick (English) Ax ruler. *Badric, Badryck, Badryk, Brdryc*

Bae (Korean) Inspiration.

Bahram (Persian) Name of a Persian King. *Bairam*

Bail (English) Form of Vail. *Bale, Balle, Bayl, Bayle*

Bailey (French) Berry clearing. *Bailea, Bailio, Baily, Baley*

Bain (Irish) Lives near the pale bridge; bridge over white water. *Bainbridge, Bainbrydge, Baine, Banbrigge, Bayn, Bayne, Baynn*

Bairre (Irish) White; fair.

Baker (English) Occupational surname. *Backstere, Baecere, Bakir, Bakker, Bakory, Bakr, Bax, Baxley, Baxter*

Bala (Hindi) Young strength.

Balaaditya (Indian) Young son.

Balachandra (Indian) Young moon.

Balaji (Hindi) Lord Venkatesh; name of Vishnu.

Balavan (Hindi) Powerful.

Balázs (Greek) Royal.

Balder (English) Bold, courageous army. (Norse) Mythological son of Odin. (Swedish) God of light. *Baldhere, Baldier, Baldr, Baldur, Baudier*

Baldev (Hindi) Full of strength. *Balbir, Balduf*

Baldric (German) Brave ruler. *Baldrick, Baldryc, Baldryck, Baudrey, Baudric*

Baldwin (German) Bold friend. *Baden, Baduouin, Baldwyn, Maldwyn, Win, Wyn*

Balin (Hindi) Mighty warrior. *Bali, Baline, Balyn, Baylen, Baylin, Baylon, Blyne, Valin*

Ballard (Old English) Dancing song. *Balard, Balerd, Ballad, Ballerd*

Ballentine (English) Strength, valor.

Ballinamore (Irish) From the great river.

Baltasar (German, Spanish) Protect the king; one of the three wise men. *Baldasare, Baldassare, Balshazar, Baltazar, Balthazar, Balthazzar, Baltsaros, Belshazzar*

Banagher (Irish) Pointed hill.

Banan (Irish) White. *Banen, Banin, Banon, Banyn*

Bancroft (Old English) Bean field. *Bancrofft, Bank, Bankey, Bankroft, Banney*

Bane (Hawaiian) Long-awaited child. *Baen, Baene, Ban*

Banefre Origin and meaning unknown.

Banji (African) Second born of twins.

Banjo (American) Musical instrument.

Banke (Hindi) Lord Krishna.

Banko (Japanese) Everlasting. (Shakespearean) Character from *MacBeth*. *Banquo*

Banner (Scottish) Flag bearer. *Banna, Bannar, Bannor, Banny*

Banzan (Japanese) Indestructible mountain.

Baptiste (Greek) Baptizer; named for John the Baptist. *Baptista, Baptysta, Battista*

Baradine (Australian) Small kangaroo. *Baradin, Baradyn, Baradyne*

Barak (Hebrew) Lightning bolt. *Barrack, Barrak, Baruch*

Baran (Russian) Ram. *Baren, Barran, Barren*

Barbaras (Hebrew) Meaning unknown. *Barabba*

Barber (Latin) Beard. *Barbour*

Barclay (Old English) Birch meadow. *Barchiel, Barclae, Barcley, Barklay, Barkleigh, Barkley, Barkli, Barksdale, Berkeley, Berkley*

Bardalph (English) Ax-wielding wolf, ferocious. *Bardawulf, Bardolf, Bardolfe, Bardolph, Bardow, Bardowl, Bardulf, Bardulph, Barwolf*

Barden (English) Barley valley. *Baedan, Baird, Bairdan, Bairdyn, Bardon, Bayrdan*

Bardshaw Origin and meaning unknown.

Baris (Turkish) Peaceful. *Barris, Barrys, Barys*

Barker (English) Tanner of leather. *Barger, Barkker, Barklea, Barkly, Berbicarius, Berbicis, Bercher, Berger*

Barlow (English) Bare hillside. *Barloe, Barlowe, Barrlow, Barrlowe*

Barnabas (Hebrew) Son of prophecy. *Bama, Barn, Barnabe, Barnabie, Barnabus, Barnaby, Barnebas, Barnes, Barney, Barnie*

Barnett (Old English) Noble man. (German) Mighty as a bear. *Barnet, Barnete, Barnette, Baronette, Barr, Barret, Barrett*

Baron (German) Nobleman; derived title. *Baaron, Barin, Baronie, Barron, Baryn, Beron*

Barric (English) From the barley or the grain farm. *Barrick, Barrik, Baryc, Baryck, Baryk, Beric, Berric, Berrick, Beryc, Beryk*

Barry (Irish) Spear thrower. (Welsh) Son of Harry. *Bari, Barie, Barrett, Barrie, Barrington, Barris, Barrymore, Berry*

Bartholomew (Hebrew) Furrow. *Bart, Bartel, Barth, Barthol, Bartholemew, Bartlett, Bartley, Bartold, Bartolomeo, Bartolomeu, Barton, Bat, Bertol, Tholy, Tolly*

Bartram (Danish) Glorious raven. *Barthram, Bertram*

Baruch (Hebrew) Blessed. *Boruch*

Basam (Arabic) Smiling. *Basem, Basim, Bassim*

Basil (Greek) Royal. (Arabic) Brave. *Basia, Basile, Basilia, Basilo, Bazyli, Vasilis, Vasily*

Basim (Arabic) Smiling. *Basaam, Basam, Basant, Baseem, Basem, Bassam, Bassem, Bassim*

Basir (Turkish) Intelligent; discerning. *Bashar, Basheer, Basyr, Bechir*

Baso (Sephardic) Glass. (Basque) Woods.

Bassanio (Shakespearean) Character from *The Merchant of Venice*.

Bassett (Old French) Short, low. *Basse, Basset*

Bassianus (Shakespearean) Character from *Titus Andronicus*.

Bassui (Japanese) High above average.

Batai (Science fiction) Character from *Star Trek: The Next Generation*.

Bates (Greek) One who walks or haunts. (Hebrew) Son of Talmai.

Bayard (Old French) Bay horse. (English) Reddish-brown hair. *Baeyard, Baiardo, Baird, Baiyard, Bayardo, Bayerd, Baylen, Bayless, Baylor, Bayrd*

Baz (Afghanistan, Pakistan) Eagle.

Beacan (Irish) Small. *Beacen, Becan, Becen, Becin, Becon, Becyn*

Beacher (Old English) Dweller by the beech tree. *Beach, Beachy, Beech, Beecher, Beechy*

Beardsley (Old English) Beard; wood.

Beasley (English) Field of peas. *Beaslea, Beasli, Peaslee, Peasley*

Beau (French) Beautiful. *Beaumont, Beauregard, Beaux, Bo*

Beck (Swedish) Brook. *Beckett, Bek*

Beckman (Swedish) Someone who lives near a stream.

Bede (Old English) Prayer.

Bedir (Turkish) Full moon. *Bedwyn, Bedyr*

Bedivere (Welsh) In the Arthurian legend, he returns Excalibur to the Lady of the Lake. *Bedevere, Bedver, Bedwin*

Bedrich (Czech) Peaceful ruler. *Fredrick*

Behdad (Persian) Given honor.

Behruz (Persian) Good day. *Behrooz*

Bela (Hebrew) Destruction. *Béla, Belah, Belay, Beldon*

Belar (Science fiction) Character from *Star Trek: Deep Space Nine.*

Belarius (Shakespearean) Character from *Cymbaline.*

Beldon (Old English) Beautiful pasture. *Balidyn, Belden, Beldin, Belidon, Bellden, Belldin, Belldon, Belldyn*

Bellamy (Old French) Handsome friend. *Belami, Belamie, Belamy, Bell, Bellamey, Bellamie*

Belmiro (Portuguese) Good looking. *Belmirow, Belmyro, Belmyrow*

Beltran (Spanish) Bright raven.

Belveder (Italian) Beautiful. *Belvedear, Belvydear, Belvydere*

Bemossed (Native American) Walker.

Bemus (Greek) Platform. *Bemis*

Benaiah (Hebrew) Yahweh has created.

Bence (Hungarian) Victor.

Benedict (Latin) Blessed. *Benecio, Benedick, Benedikt, Benedix, Benito*

Benen (Irish) Blessed.

Benjamin (Hebrew) Son of my right hand. *Ben, Bengamen, Benji, Benjie, Benjy, Bennie, Bennjamin, Benny, Benson, Benyamin*

Benjiro (Japanese) Enjoys peace.

Bennett (Latin) Anglicized version of Benedict. *Benet, Benett, Benette, Benit, Benitt, Benn, Benner, Bennet, Bennette, Benoit, Bentley, Benyt, Benytt*

Benson (Hebrew) Ben's son. *Bennsan, Bennsen, Bennsin, Bennsyn, Bensen, Bensin, Benssen, Bensson, Bensyn*

Bentfield Origin and meaning unknown.

Bentley (Old English) From the moor. *Bentlea, Bentleah, Bentlee, Bentleigh, Bentlie*

Benvenuto (Italian) Welcome.

Benvolio (Latin) Happy face. (Shakespearean) Character from *Romeo and Juliet.*

Beowulf (Anglo) Intelligent wolf.

Bergen (German) Mountain dweller. *Bergan, Berger, Bergin*

Berk (Turkish) Solid, firm. *Berc, Berck, Berke*

Bernal (German) Strong as a bear. *Bernaid, Bernald, Bernaldo, Bernhold, Bernold, Bernolle, Burnal*

Bernard (German) Bold as a bear. *Barend, Barn, Barnard, Barnardine, Barney, Barnie, Barnum, Barny, Berend, Bern, Bernardo, Bernd, Berndt, Berne, Bernhard, Bernhardt, Bernie, Bjorn*

Bernstein (German) Amber; the bear's stone. *Bernsteen, Bernsteyn, Berstein*

Berthold (German) Bright, illustrious; brilliant ruler. *Bertin, Bertold, Burthold*

Berto (Spanish) Bright flame. *Burto, Robert*

Bertram (German) Bright. *Bert, Bertil, Bertol, Bertold, Bertolt, Berton, Bertraim, Bertramus, Bertrem*

Bertrand (German) Bright shield. *Bertrando, Bertranno, Burtrand*

Bethuel (Hebrew) House of God. *Bethel*

Bevin (Irish) One with a sweet song; son of Evan. *Bevan, Bevis*

Bharat (Hindi) India; universal monarch.

Bhudev (Hindi) Lord of the earth.

Bickford (English) Ax-man's ford. *Bickforde, Bycford, Byckford, Bykford*

Bidziil (Native American) He is strong.

Big Daddy Kane (American) Rapper Antonio Hardy.

Bijan (Persian) Hero. *Bihjan, Byjan*

Bilis (Phillipino) Swift.

Bing (Chinese) Soldier; ice.

Bingham (German) Kettle-shape hollow. *Bing, Binga, Binge, Binghampton, Binghamton*

Biondello (Italian) Shield. (Shakespearean) Character from *The Taming of the Shrew.*

Birch (Old English) White; birch tree. *Berch, Berche, Birche, Birk, Birkee, Birket, Birkett, Birkey, Birkhead, Birkhed, Birkit, Birky, Burch, Byrch, Byrche*

Birchard Origin and meaning unknown.

Birkey (English) Island with birch trees. *Berk, Berkee, Berki, Birky*

Bishop (English) Bishop. (Greek) Overseer. *Bish, Bishup*

Bjorn (Scandinavian) Bear. *Beorn, Bjame, Bjami, Bjarne, Bjomolf, Bjorne*

Blaan (Gaelic) Yellow; Scottish saint. (Irish) Thin, lean. (English) River. *Bla, Blane, Blaney, Blayn, Blayne, Blayney*

Blackburn (English) Black brook. *Blackbern, Blackberne, Blackburne*

Blade (English) Knife, sword; glory. *Bladen, Bladon, Bladyn, Blae, Blaed, Blaid, Blaide, Blayd, Blayde*

Blaine (English) Source of a river. (Irish) Thin, lean. *Blain, Blane, Blaney, Blayne*

Blair (Irish) Plain. *Blaire, Blare, Blayr, Blayre*

Blaise (French) Stammerer. *Blais, Blaisot, Blasi, Blasien, Blasius, Blayze, Blazej*

Blake (Old English) Fairhaired. *Blaec, Blaek, Blakely, Blanchard, Blanco, Blayk*

Blaz (Old German) Unwavering protector.

Blaze (American) Flame. (English) Trail mark made on a tree. (Latin) Stutter. *Blayse, Blayz, Blayze, Blayzz, Blazen, Blazer*

Bleoberis (Scottish) Knight in Arthurian legend.

Blue (American) Color.

Boaz (Hebrew) Swift; strong. *Boas, Booz, Bos, Boz*

Boden (Old French) Herald. *Bodain, Bodein, Bodene, Bodin, Bodine, Bodyn, Bodyne*

Bogart (German) Strong as a bow. *Bogar, Bogey, Bogie, Bogy*

Bonar (French) Gentle. *Bona, Bonar, Bonnar*

Bond (English) Tiller of the soil. *Bondie, Bondon, Bonds, Bondy*

Boniface (French) Good fate. *Bonifacey, Bonifacio, Bonifacius, Bonifaco, Bonifacy, Bonifaz*

Bono (American) All good. *Bonus*

Booker (Old English) Beech tree. *Bookie, Bookker, Books, Booky*

Boone (Latin) Good. *Bon, Bone, Bonne, Boon, Boonie, Boony*

Booth (Old English) Hut. *Boot, Boote, Boothe, Bothe*

Borachio (Italian) Lightning. (Shakespearean) Character from *Much Ado About Nothing*.

Borak (Arabic) Lightning; Al Borak was the legendary horse that bore Muhammad from Earth to the seventh heaven. *Borac, Borack*

Borden (Old English) Near the boar's den. (Old French) Cottage. *Bordan, Bordin, Bordon, Bordyn*

Borg (Old Norse) From the castle. *Borc, Borge*

Boris (Russian) Fight. *Boriss, Borja, Borka, Borris, Bors, Borya, Boryenka, Borys*

Borna (Persian) Youthful one.

Bors (Russian) Fighter. *Borys*

Boston (American) Place name. *Bostan, Bosten, Bostin*

Boswell (Old French) Forested town. *Bos, Boswel, Bosworth, Bozwell*

Botan (Japanese) Peony. *Boten, Botin, Boton, Botyn*

Boult (Shakespearean) Character from *Pericles*.

Boutros (Arabic) Small rock; form of Peter. *Badrosian, Bedros, Botros, Boutro, Butras, Butrus*

Bowen (Welsh) Son of Owen. *Bohan, Bohannon, Bowan, Bowden, Bowie, Bowin, Bowon, Bowyn, Bowynn*

Boyce (French) Woodland. *Boice, Boise, Boycey, Boycie, Boyse*

Boyd (Irish) Blond. *Boid, Boydan, Boyde, Boyden, Boydin, Boydon, Boydyn*

Boyet (Shakespearean) Character from *Love's Labour's Lost*.

Brabantio (Shakespearean) Character from *Othello*.

Bradburn (English) Broad stream. *Bradbern, Bradberne, Bradborne, Bradbourn, Braddborne*

Braden (Irish) Brave. *Bradden, Bradin, Bradine, Bradun, Braedan, Braeden, Braedon, Brayden, Breden*

Bradley (Old English) Broad meadow. *Brad, Braddlea, Braddlee, Braddleigh, Braddley, Braddli, Braddlie, Braddly, Bradford, Bradlay, Bradleigh, Bradlie, Brady, Braid*

Brady (Irish) Spirited one. *Bradye, Braedee, Braedey, Braedie, Braiden, Braidy*

Bram (Irish) Raven. *Bramdon, Brame, Bramm, Bramston, Bran*

Bramha (Hindi) Third major deity.

Bramwell (English) Bramble well. *Bramwel, Bramwele, Bramwyll, Branwell*

Branch (Latin) Extension.

Branco (Portuguese) Pale.

Brandeis (German) Dweller on a burned clearing. *Brandis*

Brandon (Old English) Fiery hill. *Bran, Brand, Branden, Branford, Brant, Brendan, Brenden, Brennan, Brennen, Brent*

Brant (English) Marked by fire. *Brand, Brandt, Brannt, Brante, Branton*

Brasil (Irish) Brave. *Brasill, Brasyl, Brazil, Brazille, Brazyl*

Braulio (Italian) Meadow on the hillside. *Braili, Brauli, Brauliuo*

Brawley (English) Meadow on the hillside. *Brawlea, Brawlee, Brawleigh, Brawli, Brawlie, Brawly*

Braxton (English) Brock's town. *Braxston, Braxten, Braxtyn, Brox*

Breck (Irish) Freckled. *Brecken, Brek, Brexton*

Brendan (Irish) Little raven. *Brannan, Breandan, Bren, Brenden, Brenn, Brenndyn, Brennen, Bryn*

Brent (Old English) Steep hill. *Brendt, Brente, Brentson, Brentt*

Brenton (English) Steep hill. *Brentan, Brentton, Brentun, Brentyn*

Breri (English) A messenger.

Brett (Irish) Native of Brittany. *Bhrett, Brente, Bret, Bretlin, Brette, Bretton, Brit, Britt*

Brewster (Old English) Brewer. *Brew, Brewer, Brewstar*

Brian (Irish) Strong. *Brainao, Briand, Briann, Brianne, Briano, Briant, Briaun, Brien, Bryan, Bryant, Bryon*

Briar (English) Shrub or small tree. (French) Heather. *Brier, Brierly*

Brice (Welsh) Alert. *Bricen, Brise, Brisen*

Brick (English) Bridge. *Bric, Brickman, Brik, Bryc*

Brigham (Old English) One who lives near a bridge. (Old French) Soldier. *Brigg, Briggs, Bringham*

Brighton (English) From the bright town. *Breighton, Bright, Brightin, Bryton*

Brinley (Old English) Tawny. *Brin, Brinlea, Brinlee, Brinlei, Brinleigh, Brinli, Brinlie, Brinly, Brynlea, Brynlei, Brynleigh*

Brock (Old English) Badger. *Braxton, Broc, Brocke, Brockett, Brockleah, Brockley, Brockly, Brocleigh, Brocton, Brok, Broque*

Broderick (English) Broad ridge. *Brod, Brodderrick, Broddy, Broderic, Broderyk, Brodrick, Brodrig, Brodrik, Rick, Roderick*

Bromley (Old English) Brush-covered meadow. *Bromlee, Bromleigh, Bromli, Bromlie, Bromly, Bromwell, Bromwood*

Bronco (Spanish) Rough, unbroken horse.

Bronislaw (Polish) Weapon of glory. *Bronislav, Bronyslav, Bronyslaw*

Bronson (German) Brown's son. (English) Color; son of the dark man. *Berowne, Bronnson, Bronsen, Bronsin, Bronsonn, Broun, Brown, Bruin, Bruins, Bruno*

Bronwen (Welsh) Dark and pure. *Bronwyn*

Bronze (Italian) Metal; yellowish to copper-brown.

Brook (Old English) Stream; brook. *Brooc, Brooke, Brooker, Brookes, Brookin, Brooks, Broox*

Brooklyn (Modern English) Beautiful brook.

Bruce (French) Thicket. *Brooce, Broose, Brucey, Brucy, Brue, Bruis, Bruse*

Bruno (German) Brown-haired. *Brunon, Bruns*

Bryant (Irish) High, noble. *Briant, Brient*

Bryce (English) Son of a nobleman. *Brice, Brycen, Bryceton, Bryse, Bryson, Bryston*

Buckley (Old English) Meadow of deer. *Buck, Bucklee, Buckleigh, Buckli, Bucklie, Buckly, Buckminster, Buckner, Bucky, Buclea, Buclie, Buklee*

Bud (Old English) Herald. (German) To puff up. *Budd, Buddie, Buddy*

Buddha (Buddhist) Wise one.

Buford (English) Ford near the castle. *Burford*

Bukka (Hindi) Heart; loving; sincere.

Bun B (American) Rapper Bernard Freeman.

Burdette (English) Small bird. *Berdet, Berdett, Berdette, Burdet, Burdette*

Burgess (Old English) Free citizen; shopkeeper. *Bergen, Bergess, Birgess, Burg, Burges, Burgiss, Byrgess*

Burhan (Arabic) Proof.

Burke (German) Castle. *Berc, Berk, Birk, Birke, Bourke, Burk, Byrk, Byrke*

Burle (English) Knotted wood. (German) Boundary line. *Berl, Burl, Burleigh, Burley, Byrl, Byrle*

Burne (Old English) Brook. *Beirne, Bern, Burney, Burns, Byrne*

Burr (Swedish) Youth. *Bur, Burral, Burrol*

Burt (Old English) Fortress; bright flame. *Bert, Berton, Burton*

Buster (Old English) One who breaks things. *Busta, Bustar*

Butch (American) Manly. *Butcher*

Buzz (Irish) Village in the woods. *Busby, Buzzy*

Byrd (English) Like a bird. *Berd, Bird, Birdie, Byrdie*

Byron (French) Cottage. (English) At the cowshed. *Beyron, Birin, Biron, Buiron, Byran, Byren, Byrom*

C

Cabal (French) Joined by a secret. (English) Arthur's dog in legend of King Arthur. *Cafall*

Cable (Old French) Rope. *Cab, Cabe, Cabel, Cabell*

Cade (Old English) Round. (Welsh) Pure. (French) Cask. Short form of Cadence. *Caden, Caide, Caiden, Cayden, Codey, Codi, Codie, Cody, Coty, Kade, Kaden, Kayde*

Cadell (Welsh) Battler. *Cadel, Caidel, Caydel, Cedell*

Cador (Scottish) In Arthurian legend, Arthur's nephew.

Caedmon (Irish) Wise warrior. *Cadman*

Caelan (Irish) Victorious people. *Caelen, Cailean, Cailin, Calan, Caley*

Caelum (Latin) Celestial. *Caellum, Caelus, Chaelus*

Caesar (Greek) Long-haired; hairy. (Latin) Fine head of hair. (Shakespearean) Character from *Julius Caesar*. *Caesarae, Caesare, Caesario, Caeser, Casa, Casarius, Caseare, Cesar, Czar, Kaiser*

Cage (English) Enclosed space.

Cahil (Turkish) Naive.

Cahir (English) Warrior.

Cai (Welsh) Form of Gaius. *Cae, Caio, Caw, Cay*

Cain (Hebrew) Craftsman; spear. *Caine, Chaim, Connie, Kain, Kaine, Kane*

Cairn (Welsh) Landmark made of mound of stones. *Cairne, Carn, Cayrn, Cayrnes*

Cairo (Arabic) Capital of Egypt. *Cayro, Kairo*

Caithness (Scottish) River valleys by fertile farm and croft land. (Shakespearean) Character from *Macbeth*.

Caius (Latin) Rejoice; form of Gaius. *Cai, Caio, Cais, Kay, Kaye, Keye, Keyes, Keys*

Cajetan (Italian) From Gaeta; form of Gaetan. *Cajetano, Kajetan, Kajetano*

Calbraith Origin and meaning unknown.

Calder (Old English) River of stones. (Irish) Lives near stony river. *Caldre, Caulder*

Caldwell (Old English) Cold spring. *Cadmus, Cadwell*

Caleb (Hebrew) Faithful; dog; bold. *Cal, Cale, Cleve, Cliff, Colby*

Calen (Scottish) Victorius people. *Caelan, Calin, Clean*

Calhoun (Old English) Warrior. (Irish) Narrow woods. *Calhaun, Callhoun, Colhoun, Colquhoun*

Caliban (Shakespearean) Character from *The Tempest*.

Callahan (Irish) Decendant of Callachen. *Calaghan, Callaghan, Kallaghan, Kallahan*

Callis (Latin) Chalice. *Calliss, Kallis, Kallys, Kallyss*

Callistus (Latin) Chalice. (Greek) Most lovely. *Calisto, Calix, Calixte, Calixto, Calleas, Callice, Callinicus, Callis, Calliste, Callixtus, Callys, Callyx*

Callum (Irish) Dove. *Callam, Callim, Callym, Kallum*

Calogrenant (Scottish) Knight in Arthurian legend.

Calvert (Old English) Shepherd. *Calbert, Calvex*

Calvin (Latin) Bald. *Calvine, Calvino, Calvyn, Kalvin, Vinnie*

Camden (Scottish, Irish) Winding valley. *Camdin, Camdon, Camdyn*

Cameron (Old English) Bent nose. *Camaeron, Camedon, Camm, Camren, Camron, Camry, Camryn, Camyron, Kameron, Kamrey*

Camillo (Latin) Free-born child; noble; masculine of Camille. *Camillus, Camilo, Camilus, Kamillo, Kamilo*

Campbell (French) Beautiful field. (Irish) Crooked mouth. *Camp, Campbel*

Canaan (French) Church official; large gun. *Cannen, Cannin, Canning, Cannyn*

Cancer (Greek) Sign of the zodiac; crab.

Candide (Latin) Sincere. *Candid, Candida, Kandide*

Candidius (Latin) Pure; sincere. (Shakespearean) Character from *Antony and Cleopatra*.

Canice (Irish) Handsome.

Canna (Sanskrit) Renowned.

Canon (French) Official of the church. *Cannan, Canning, Cannon, Kanon*

Canute (Scandinavian) Knot. *Cnut, Knut, Knute*

Canyon (Latin) Canyon. *Cannyon, Canyan, Canyin, Kanyon*

Caphis (Shakespearean) Character from *Timon of Athens*.

Cappi (Gypsy) Meaning unknown. *Cappie, Cappy, Kappi*

Capricornus (Latin) Horned goat; constellation of the Zodiac. *Cap*

Capucius (Latin) Ambassador. (Shakespearean) Character from *Henry VIII*.

Capulet (Shakespearean) Character from *Romeo and Juliet*.

Caradoc (Welsh) Love. *Caradoq*

Carden (Irish) From the black fortress. (Old English) Wool carder. *Card, Cardew, Cardin, Cardon*

Carew (Latin) Chariot; run. *Carewe, Crew, Crewe, Rew*

Carey (Irish) Dark ones; near the castle. *Carrey, Cary*

Carl (Old German) Free man; form of Charles. *Carel, Carlisle, Carlito, Carlos, Carlyle, Caroll, Carrlos, Carroll, Caryl, Karel, Karl*

Carleton (Old English) Carl's town. *Carlson, Carlton, Carston*

Carlow (Irish) Quadruple lake. *Carlo, Carlowe, Carolo, Charlo, Karlo*

Carlyle (Old English) Carl's island. *Carl, Carley, Carlile, Carlisle, Lisle, Lyle*

Carmelo (Hebrew) From the garden. (Italian) Fruitful orchard. *Carmel, Carmeli, Carmello, Karmel, Karmello, Karmelo*

Carmine (Italian) Song. *Carman, Carmen, Carmi, Carmin, Carmino, Karman, Karmen*

Carnelian (Latin) Red gemstone.

Carnell (English) Defender of the castle. *Carnel, Karnel, Karnell*

Carolus (French) Strong. (Scandinavian) Freeman. (Old German) Man. *Caroll,*

Carrol, Carroll, Cary, Caryl, Caryll

Carpus (Hebrew) Fruit; fruitful.

Carrick (Irish) Rocky cliff or cape.

Carroll (Irish) Champion. *Carel, Carolo*

Carson (Scandinavian) Son of marsh-dwellers. *Carsen, Carsyn, Carvell*

Carsten (Greek) Anointed. (German) Follower of Christ. *Cristian, Cristiano, Karsten, Kristen, Kristian*

Carter (Old English) Cart driver. *Cartier, Cartrell*

Carvell (Old English) Wood carver. (French) Swampy dwelling. *Carvel, Carvil, Carville*

Carver (English) Wood carver. *Carvar, Carvor, Karver, Karvor*

Casey (Irish) Brave. *Case, Casee, Cassi, Cozzi, Cozzy*

Cashlin (Irish) Little castle. *Cashlind, Cashlyn, Kashlin, Kashlyn*

Cashmere (Kashmir) Peacemaker; luxurious fabric from Kashmir.

Casimir (Slavic) Peacemaker. *Cace, Cacey, Casey, Casimeer, Casimer, Casimiro, Casmir, Casmire, Cayce, Caycey, Caz, Kasey, Kasimir, Kasimiro, Kazimierz, Kazimir*

Caspar (Persian) Keeper of the treasure. *Casper, Cass, Gaspar, Gaspard, Gasparo, Gasper, Jasper, Kaspar, Kasper*

Cassidy (Irish) Clever; curly haired. *Casidy, Cassidee, Cassidi, Kassidy*

Cassius (Latin) Vain. *Cash, Casius, Cass, Cassian, Cassio*

Castor (Greek) Beaver. *Caster, Castorio, Kaster, Kastor*

Catcher (Old English) One who catches, as in a ball.

Cathal (Irish) Strong; wise. *Cathel, Cathol, Kathal, Kathol*

Cato (Latin) All knowing. *Caton, Cayto, Kaeto, Kato*

Cavalon (English) In Arthurian legend, the name of a king.

Cawley (Scottish) Ancient. (English) Cow meadow. *Cawlea, Cawli, Kawlee, Kawley*

Cecil (Latin) Blind. *Cece, Cecile, Cecilus, Cecyl*

Cedar (English) Cedar tree.

Cedric (Welsh) Gift of splendor. (Old English) War leader. *Caddaric, Ced, Cedrick, Cedrik, Cedro, Cedrych, Cerdric, Chadrick, Kedrick, Sedrick, Sedrik*

Celesto (Latin) Heavenly. (Italian) High; lofty. *Célestine, Celestino, Celindo, Celsius, Celso, Celsus, Selestine, Selestino, Silestino*

Cemal (Arabic) Attractive.

Centaurus (Greek) Mythical beast.

Cepheus (Latin) Small rock. *Cephas, Cephus*

Cerdic (Welsh) Beloved. *Caradoc, Caradog, Ceredig, Ceretic*

Cerek (Polish) Lordly.

Cerimon (Shakespearean) Character from *Pericles*.

Cerny (Czech) Black.

Cetus (Latin) Constellation; whale.

Chad (Old English) Warlike. *Chaddie, Chadric, Chadrick, Chadwick, Chadwyck*

Chaim (Hebrew) Life; masculine form of Eve. *Cahya, Cahyim, Cahyyam, Cain, Chai, Chaika, Chaimek, Chayim, Chaym, Chayme, Chayyim, Haim, Haym, Hayvim, Hayyim, Hy, Hyman, Hymen, Hymie, Manny*

Chainey (French) Oak tree. *Chalney, Chaney, Chany, Cheney*

Chalmers (Scottish) Son of the Lord. *Chalmer, Chalmr, Chamar, Chanarr*

Chancellor (Old French) Secretary. *Chancelor, Chancey, Chanse, Chanseler, Chansellor, Chantz, Chanze, Chaunce, Chauncey, Choncey*

Chander (Hindi) Moon. *Chand, Chandan, Chandara, Chandony*

Chandler (French) Candlemaker. *Chan, Chand, Chandlor*

Chandra (Hindi) Bright, radiant.

Chane (Swahili) Dependable. *Chaen, Chain, Chayn, Cheyn*

Channing (Old English) Knowing. (Old French) Cannon. *Canal, Cannon, Canon, Chann, Channe, Channon*

Chante (Jamaican) Song. *Chant, Chanthar, Chatra, Shantae*

Chapman (English) Merchant. *Chap, Chapmen, Chappy, Chopmin*

Charles (Old English) Manly. *Carel, Carlo, Charlemagne, Charley, Charlie, Charlot, Charls, Chars, Chas, Chaz, Chick, Chico, Chip, Chuck, Karol, Karolek, Karolik, Karoly*

Charon (Greek) Fierceness.

Chase (Old French) Hunter. *Chace, Chasen, Chayce, Chayse*

Chata (African) Ending.

Chatam (Native American) Hawk.

Chatan (Hebrew) Groom.

Chatham (English) Warrior's home. *Chathem, Chathim, Chathom, Chathym*

Chatillon (English) Character from *As You Like It*.

Chauncey (Latin) Chancellor. *Chauncee, Chauncy, Chaunesy, Chod*

Chavez (Spanish) Dreammaker.

Chayton (Native American) Falcon.

Cheech (American) Nickname of comedian Richard Anthony Marin of Cheech and Chong.

Chen (Chinese) Great.

Cheney (French) From the oak forest. *Chenee, Cheni, Chenie, Cheny*

Cherokee (Native American) People of a different speech. *Cherokey, Cheroki, Cherokie, Cheroky*

Chesmu (Native American) Gritty.

Chester (Latin) Camp. *Ches, Chess, Cheston*

Cheveyo (Native American) Spirit warrior.

Chevy (French) Knight. (Old English) Hunt. *Cheval, Chevalier, Chevall, Chevie, Chevrolet*

Cheyenne (Native American) Red people. *Chayan, Chayann, Shayan, Shayanne*

Chiamaka (African) God is splendid.

Chike (African) Power of God.

Chikezie (African) Well made by God.

Chilton (Old English) Farm by the spring. *Chil, Chill, Chilly*

Chimon (Japanese) Wisdom gate.

Chin Ho (Korean) Precious and goodness.

Chipper (English) Form of Chip. *Chipman, Chipp, Chyp*

Chiron (Greek) Wise teacher. *Kiron*

Chivalry (Old French) Knightliness; gallantry.

Chogan (Native American) Blackbird.

Chotan (Japanese) Deep pool.

Christian (Greek) Anointed. *Chrestian, Christiaan, Christiano, Christianos, Cristian, Cristobel, Karstan, Kristian, Kristo, Krystian, Krystiano*

Christopher (Greek) Christ bearer. *Chris, Christ, Christion, Christo, Christof, Christop, Christoper, Christoph, Christophe, Christos, Christpher, Cristo, Cristobal, Cristoforo, Cristopher, Cristy, Kester, Kristo, Kristof, Kristofer*

Christovao (Swedish) Christ bearer.

Chuck (American) Nickname of Charles. *Chuckey, Chucki, Chucky, Chuk*

Chudamani (Indian) Jewel adorned by the gods.

Chung (Chinese) Intelligent; wise one. (Vietnamese) Common.

Chung Hee (Korean) Righteous and pleasure.

Churchill (English) Lives near the church hill. *Churchil*

Ciaran (Irish) Small and dark-skinned. *Carra, Ceirnin, Kern, Kerr, Kerry, Kerwin, Key, Kiernan, Kieron, Kirwin*

Cicero (Latin) Historian. *Cecero, Ciceron, Ciro*

Cid (Spanish) Lord. *Cidd, Cyd, Cydd*

Ciel (French) From heaven.

Cipriano (Spanish) From Cyprus. *Ciprian, Ciprien, Cyprian, Cyprien, Siprian, Siprien, Sipryan*

Ciqala (Native American) Little one.

Circinus (French) Constellation designated by eighteenth-century astronomer Nicolas-Louis de Lacaille.

Cirrillo (Italian) Lordly. *Cirilio, Cirilo, Cyrilo, Cyryllo, Cyrylo*

Cisco (Spanish) Free; form of Francis and Francisco. *Francesco, Frisco, Paco, Pancho*

Clachas (English, Shakespearean) Character from *Troilus and Cressida.*

Claiborne (Old English) Born of the earth. *Claiborn, Claibourn, Claibourne, Clayborn, Clayborne, Claybourne, Clayton*

Clancy (Irish) Offspring of a redheaded soldier. *Clan, Clancey, Claney*

Clarence (Latin) Clear. *Claran, Clarance, Clarendon, Clarens, Claron, Clarons, Claronz, Clarrance, Clarrence, Klarance, Klarenz*

Clark (Old English) Cleric. *Clarke, Clarkson, Clerc, Clerk*

Claude (Latin) Lame. *Claidianus, Claud, Claudan, Claudell, Claudido, Claudie, Claudien, Claudino, Claudio, Claudius, Claudon, Clodito, Clodo, Clodomiro, Cloyd, Clyde, Colt, Klaudio*

Claus (Greek) People of victory; diminutive of Nicholas. *Claes, Clause, Klaus*

Clay (German) Adhere. *Clayland, Klay*

Clayborne (English) Brook near the clay pit. *Claeburn, Claibern, Claiborn, Claybourne*

Clayton (English) Town built on clay. *Claiton, Cleyton, Clyton, Klayton*

Cleavant (English) Steep bank; cliff. *Cleevant, Cleeve, Cleevont*

Cleavon (English) Cliff. *Clavin, Cleavan, Cleaven, Clyvon*

Clement (Latin) Merciful. *Clem, Clemendo, Clemens, Clemente, Clementino, Clementius, Clements, Clemmie, Clemmons, Clemmy, Clemon, Klemens, Klement, Klementos, Kliment*

Cleomenes (English) Character from *Hamlet* and *Julius Caesar*.

Cleon (Greek) Famous one. *Clem, Colin, Collin, Cullen*

Cletus (Greek) Illustrious. *Cleatus, Cleotis, Cletis, Cleytus*

Cleveland (Old English) Land near the hill. *Cleaveland, Cleavland, Cleavon, Cleon, Cleve, Clevon, Clive*

Clifford (Old English) Hill. *Cleiv, Clifton, Clint, Clinton, Cliv, Clive, Cliven, Clyff, Clyfford, Clyford, Clyve*

Clinton (English) Hill town. *Clindon, Clinten, Clyndon, Clynton*

Cloten (English, Shakespearean) Character from *Julius Caesar*.

Clovis (German) Famous warrior; form of Louis. *Clodoveo, Clothilde, Clotilde, Clovio, Clovisto, Clovito*

Clyde (Welsh) Heard from afar. *Cloyd, Clydell*

Cochise (Native American) Wood.

Cody (Irish) Descendant of a helpful person. *Coddy, Codell, Coedy, Cohen, Kodey*

Coeus (Greek) Mythical name; father of Leto.

Cohn (Greek) Victory of the people. *Cailean*

Cola (American) Soft drink.

Colar (French) Victorious people.

Colbert (German) Seaman. (Old English) Renowned mariner. *Colvert, Culbert*

Colborn (Old English) Cold brook. *Colbourn, Colbourne, Colburn, Collborn, Collbourn, Collburn*

Cole (English) Coal. *Coal, Col, Colie, Kol*

Colin (rish) Youth. (Greek) Victor. Short form of Nicholas. *Coilin, Colan, Collins, Colyn*

Collier (English) Miner. *Colier, Collie, Collyer, Colyer*

Colm (Irish) Of Saint Columba. (Latin) Dove. Short for Columba or Columban. *Callum, Collumbano, Colombain, Colum, Columbano, Columbanus, Columkille*

Colman (Latin) Form of Coleman. *Colmann*

Colson (English) Triumphant people.

Colter (Old English) Colt herder. *Coltrane, Coulter*

Colton (English) Coal town. *Coleton, Colton, Colsten, Colston, Colten, Coltin, Kolt, Kolton*

Columbus (Latin) Dove. *Colobo, Colombé*

Colville (Native American) Tribe located in eastern part of the state of Washington. (French) Place name; derived from Colville-Sur-Mer in Normandy, France. (Science fiction) Character from *Dr. Who. Colvile, Colvill*

Coman (Arabic) Noble. *Comin, Comyn*

Cominius (Shakespearean) Character from *A Midsummer Night's Dream.*

Conall (Irish) Friendship. *Conal, Connall, Connell*

Conan (Gaelic) Wise. *Con, Conant, Condon, Conin, Conn, Conon*

Confucius (Chinese) Philosopher.

Cong (Chinese) Intelligent.

Conlan (Irish) Hero. *Colen, Colin, Conlon, Conlyn*

Conner (Irish) Desire. *Conners, Connor, Conor, Konnor, O'Conner, O'Connor*

Conrad (Old German) Brave counsel. *Con, Conrado, Conroy, Cort, Curt, Konrad, Kurt, Rad*

Constantine (Latin) Constant; steadfast. *Constans, Constant, Constantin, Constantino, Constantinos, Constantius, Constanz, Costa, Konstantin, Konstantio, Konstanz*

Constanzo (Italian) Constant; firm.

Conway (Welsh) River. *Conwy*

Cook (English) Cook. *Cooke, Cooki, Cookie, Cooky*

Coolio (American) Rapper Artis Leon Ivey Jr.

Cooper (Latin) Cask. (Old English) Barrel maker. *Coop, Kuper*

Copper (Old English) Mineral; reddish-brown.

Corbin (Old French) Raven. *Corben, Corbet, Corbett, Corbie, Corbit, Corbitt, Corbyn, Corvin, Corwan, Corwin, Corwyn, Korbin, Korbyn*

Cordaro (Spanish) Form of Cordero. *Coradaro, Cordara, Cordarro, Corrdare*

Cordell (Latin) Rope. *Cord, Cordale, Cordas, Corday, Cordelle, Kordell, Kordelle*

Corey (Scottish) Mountain glen.

Corin (Latin) Spear. *Coren, Corrin, Cyran, Koren, Korin, Korrin*

Cormack (Irish) Chariot driver. *Cormac, Cormic, Cormick*

Cornelius (Latin) Horn; hornblower. *Carnell, Corneille, Cornel, Cornelio, Cornelious, Cornell, Cornelus, Corney, Cornilius, Kornelious, Kornelis, Kornelius, Neal, Neel, Neely, Neil*

Corrado (Italian) Bold; sage counselor. *Corradeo*

Corrigan (Irish) Spearman. *Carrigan, Corigan, Corrigun, Korrigan*

Corrin (Irish) Spear carrier. *Corren, Corryn, Korrin, Korryn*

Cort (German) Bold. *Corte, Corty, Court, Kort*

Cortez (Spanish) Courteous; form of Curtis. *Coretes, Curtice, Curtis, Curtiss, Kortes, Kortez*

Cortney (English) Form of Courtney. *Cortnay, Cortne, Kortney*

Corvette (American) Model of Chevrolet car.

Corvus (Latin) Raven.

Corwin (English) Heart's companion. *Corwinn, Corwyne, Corwynne, Korwynn*

Corydon (Greek) Battle-ready; lark. *Coridon, Coryden, Coryell*

Cosimo (Greek) Perfect universe. *Cosmé, Cozmo, Kosmo*

Costante (Latin) Firm; constant. *Constant*

Costard (Shakespearean) Character from *Love's Labour's Lost.*

Coty (French) Old house. *Cote, Cottee, Cotti, Cotty*

Courtland (Old English) King's land. *Cortland, Court*

Courvoisier (French) Brand of liqueur developed by Emmanuel Courvoisier and his associate Louis Gallo in the Parisian suburb of Bercy; cognac of Napoleon.

Coyne (French) Modest. *Coy, Coyan, Coye*

Craig (Irish) Crag. *Craigh, Craigie, Craik, Cruz, Cyrus, Kraig*

Crandall (English) Valley of cranes. *Crandal, Crandell*

Cranmer (Shakespearean) Character from *Henry V.*

Crawford (Old English) Ford of the crows. *Crawfurd*

Creighton (Old English) Town near a creek. *Cree, Creigh, Crichton*

Crispin (Latin) Curly. *Crepin, Crespen, Crespin, Crippen, Crisp, Crispen, Crispian, Crispino, Crispo, Crispus, Crisspin, Krispen*

Crocker (English) God feeds them.

Crockett (Middle English) Crook. *Crock, Crocket, Croquet, Croquett, Krock*

Crofton (Irish) Town with cottages. *Krofton*

Cromwell (Shakespearean) Character from *Henry VIII.* (Old English) Winding stream.

Cronus (Greek) Titan; mythical father of Zeus. *Cronan*

Crosby (Scandinavian) Shrine of the cross. *Crosbee, Crosbi, Cross*

Cruz (Spanish) Cross bearer. *Cruzito*

Ctirad (Czech) Meaning unknown.

Cuba (Spanish) Country.

Culhwch (Scottish) In Arthurian legend, Arthur's nephew.

Cullen (Irish) Handsome. *Culea, Cullan, Culley, Culli, Cullinan, Cully, Culy*

Cupid (English) Cherub. (Latin) Desire, passion; god of love. (Shakespearean) Character from *Henry VIII.*

Curan (Irish) Hero. (Shakespearean) Character from *Timon of Athens. Curon, Curran, Curren, Currin, Curron, Curry*

Curio (English) Gentleman attending the duke. (Shakespearean) Character from *King Lear.*

Currier (Old English) Churn. *Curran, Curren, Currer, Currey, Currie, Curry*

Curtis (Latin) Court. (Old French) Courteous. *Curtys, Kurt, Kurtis, Kurtiss*

Custennin (Irish) Mythological giant.

Cuyler (Irish) Chapel.

Cyd (Greek) Public hill; form of Sydney. *Cydney*

Cygnus (Latin) Northern constellation; swan.

Cymbeline (Shakespearean) Character from *The Taming of the Shrew.*

Cynan (Welsh) Chief. *Cinan, Cinon, Cynin, Cynon*

Cyprian (Latin) From the Island of Cyprus. *Ciprian, Ciprien, Cyprien, Cyprryan*

Cyril (Greek) Lordly. *Cerek, Cerel, Ciril, Cirilio, Cirillo,*

Cirilo, Cy, Cyra, Cyrill, Cyrilla, Cyrille, Cyrillus, Kiril, Kyril

Cyrus (Persian) Sun. *Ciro, Cy*

D

D'Angelo (American) Form of Dangelo.

Dabeet (Indian) Warrior.

Dabir (Arabic) Tutor. *Dabar, Dabor, Dabyr*

Dabney (French) From Aubigny, France. *Dabnee, Dabnie, Dabny*

Dacey (Irish) Southerner. *Dace, Daci, Daicey, Daycy*

Dacian (English) Of the Nobility. (Irish) Southener.

Dack (English) From the French town Dax.

Dada (African) Curly haired. *Dadah, Dadi*

Daegan (Irish) Black-haired. *Daegen, Daigin, Daygen, Daygun*

Daelen (English) Small valley; alternate form of Dale. *Daelan, Daelin, Daelon, Daelyn, Daelyne*

Daemon (Greek) Form of Damian. *Daemen, Daemin, Daemiyn, Daemyen*

Daequan (American) Form of Daquan. *Daekwaun, Daekwon, Daequon*

Daeshawn (American) Combination of Da and Shawn. *Daesean, Daeshun, Daishawn, Daishown*

Daeshim (Korean) Great mind.

Dafydd (Welsh) Form of David. *Dafid, Dafidd, Fayd*

Dag (Scandinavian) Day. *Daeg, Dagget, Dagmar, Dagney, Dagny, Dailey, Daily, Daley, Day, Daymond, Dayton, Deegan*

Dagan (Hebrew) Grain. *Daegan, Daegon, Dagen, Dageon, Dagin, Dagon, Dagyn*

Dagobert (German) Bright day. *Dagbert, Dogoberto*

Dagonet (English) In *The Legend of King Arthur*, he is Arthur's fool.

Dai (Japanese) Big.

Dai-In (Japanese) Hidden greatness.

Daido (Japanese) Great way.

Dailan (English) Pride's people. (Irish) From the Dale. Unseeing. *Daelan, Daelen, Daelin, Dailan, Dailen, Dalain, Dalan, Dalen, Dallen, Dallin, Dalon, Dalyn*

Daire (Irish) Wealthy.

Dakarai (African) Happy. *Dakairi, Dakar, Dakara, Dakaraia, Dakari, Dakarri*

Dakin (English) One who comes from Denmark; form of Danish. *Daine, Dane*

Dakota (Native American) Friend. *Dakkota, Dakoata, Dakodah, Dakodas, Dakottah, Dekot, Dkotha, Dokata, Dokcota, Dokotta*

Dalbert (German) From a bright place. *Dalbiret, Dalburt, Dalbyrt*

Dale (Old English) Valley. (German) Valley dweller. *Dal, Daley, Dalibor, Dallan, Dallen, Dallin, Dallon, Dalton, Daly, Dawley, Dayle*

Dalit (Hebrew) To draw water.

Dallas (Irish) Skilled. *Dalieass, Dall, Dalles, Dallus, Dallys, Dalys, Dellis*

Dallin (English) Pride's people. (Irish) From the dale. *Dallen, Dallon*

Dalman (Australian) Bountiful place. *Dailman, Dallmen, Dalmin, Dalmon*

Dalphin (French) Dolphin. *Dalphine, Delphin, Delphyn, Dolphine*

Dalston (English) From Dougal's place. *Dalis, Dallston*

Dalton (English) From the valley. *Dalaton, Dalltan, Dallten, Dalltin, Dallton, Dalltyn, Dalt, Daltan, Dalten, Daltin, Daltyn, Delton*

Dalvin (English) Form of Delvin. *Dalven, Dalvon, Dalvyn*

Dalziel (Scottish) Small field. *Dalzil, Dalzyel, Dalzyl*

Damarcus (American) Combination of Da and Marcus. *Damacus, Damaquez, Damarcue, Damarquis*

Damasus (Greek) From Damascus. *Damaskenos, Damaskinos*

Damek (Czech) Earth. *Damick, Damicke, Damik, Damyk*

Damerae (Jamaican) Boy of joy.

Damien (Greek) Tamer. *Daemien, Daimen, Damaiaon, Damaien, Daman, Damaun, Damayon, Dame, Damean, Damen, Damian, Damiane, Damiann, Damiano, Damianos, Damián, Damie, Damienne, Damieon, Damiion, Damine, Damionne, Damiyan, Damiyon, Damján, Dammion, Damon, Damyen, Damyin, Damyon, Damyyn, Daymian, Dema, Demyan*

Dan (Vietnamese) Yes. *Dahn, Danh, Dann*

Dana (Norse) From Denmark. *Daen, Dain, Daina, Danah, Dane, Dayn, Dayna, Dene*

Dandin (Hindi) Holyman. *Dandan, Danden, Dandon, Dandyn*

Dandre (French) Combination of De and Andre. *Dandrae, Dandras, Dandray, Dandrea*

Daniel (Hebrew) God is my judge. *Dacso, Dainel, Dan, Dan'l, Dana, Danal, Danek, Danel, Danick, Danieal, Danieko, Dániel, Daniël, Danielius, Daniell, Danielo, Daniels, Danielson, Danik, Danika, Danil, Danila, Danile, Danilka, Danilo, Daniyal, Danna, Dannal, Danni, Dannial, Dannick, Danniele, Danniell, Danno, Danny, Danukas, Danyck, Danyl, Danylo, Dasco, Deniel, Doneal, Donois, Eoniel, Nelo*

Danior (Gypsy) Born with teeth. *Danyor*

Danladi (African) Born on Sunday. *Danladee, Danladey, Danladie, Danlady*

Dannon (American) Form of Danno. *Daenan, Dainon, Danaan, Danen*

Danso (African) Trustworthy.

Dante (Latin) Enduring one. *Danatay, Danaté, Dant, Dantae, Dantay, Danté, Dantee, Danton, Darte, Dauntay, Dauntaye, Daunté, Dauntrae, Duran, Durant*

Dantreil (American) Combination of Dante and Darell. *Dantrel, Dantrey, Dantril, Dantyrell*

Danuta (Hebrew) God has judged. (Polish) Little deer; also used as girl's name.

Danzel (Cornish) Form of Denzell. *Danzell*

Dara (Cambodian) Stars. *Darah*

Darby (Irish) Free man. *Dar, Darbey, Debey, Derbe, Derbee, Derbi, Derbie, Derby*

Darcy (Irish) Dark. *D'Arcy, Daray, Darce, Darcel, Darcey, Darci, Darcie, Darcio, Darsey, Darsy*

Dard (Greek) Son of Zeus.

Dardo (Greek) Astute.

Dareh (Persian) Wealthy. *Dare*

Dario (Spanish) Well off. *Daryo*

Darius (Persian) King. (Greek) Wealthy. *Dairus, Daria, Darian, Darien, Darieus, Darioush, Dariuse, Dariush, Dariuss, Dariusz, Darreus, Darrias, Darrios, Darriuss, Darrus, Darryus, Darus, Daryos, Daryus, Derrious, Derris, Derrius*

Darnell (English) Hidden peace. *Dar, Darn, Darnall, Darneil*

Darod (Science fiction) Character from *Star Trek: Voyager.*

Darrell (Old French) Beloved. *Dahrll, Dare, Daril, Darl, Darleen, Darlen, Darlin, Darly, Darlynn, Daroyl, Darral, Darrall, Darrel, Darril, Darrill, Darrilo, Darrol, Darryl, Darryle, Darryll, Daryell, Daryl, Daryll, Darylle, Derrell, Derryl, Deryl*

Darren (Old English) Rocky hill. *Daren, Darin, Darra, Darran, Darrience,*

Darrin, Darrion, Darryn, Darun, Dearron

Darshan (Sanskrit) Being able to see clearly. *Darshaun, Darshen, Darshin, Darshon*

Dartmouth (English) Port's name; Ivy League college.

Dartun (English) Deer town. *Dartel, Dartin, Darton, Dartrel*

Darvell (English) Eagle town. *Darvel, Darvelle, Darvyl, Darvyle*

Darwin (Old English) Beloved friend. *Darwen, Darwyn, Darwynn, Derwin, Derwynn*

Dashiell (French) Page boy.

Dathan (English) Beloved gift of God. *Dathen*

Dattatreya (Hindi) Son of the god Atria.

David (Hebrew) Beloved. *Dabi, Daevid, Daevyd, Dafydd, Daived, Daivid, Daivyd, Dauid, Dav, Dave, Daved, Daveed, Davey, Davi, Davida, Davidd, Davidde, Davide, Davidek, Davido, Davidson, Davie, Davina, Davis, Davison, Davita, Davood, Davoud, Davy, Davyd, Davydas, Davydd, Davyde, Davyson, Dawed, Dawes, Dawid, Dawit, Dawson, Dawud, Dawyt, Dayvid, Deved, Devi, Devid, Devidd, Devidde, Devlin, Devod, Devyd, Devydd, Devydde, Dewey, Dewi*

Davin (Scandinavian) Bright Finn. *Daevin, Davan, Davon, Davyn, Dawan, Dawin, Dayvon, Deavan, Deaven*

Davonte (American) Combination of Davon and Te. *Davonnte, Davontea, Davonti, Dovontee*

Davood (Persian) Beloved.

Dawson (English) Son of David. *Dawsan, Dawsen, Dawsin, Dawsyn, Dayson*

Dax (French) Town in southwestern France that dates to before Roman occupation. (English) Water. (Science fiction) Character from *Star Trek: Deep Space Nine*.

Dayton (Old English) Bright town. *Daeton, Daiton, Daythan, Daython, Daytona, Daytonah, Daytonn, Deyton*

Deacon (Greek) Messenger. *Deakin, Declan, Deicon, Deke, Deycon*

Dean (Old English) Valley. *Deane, Deen, Deene, Dene, Deyn, Deyne, Dino, Dyn, Dyne*

Deandre (American) Strong. (English) Courageous, valiant man. *Dandrae, Dandras, Dandray, Dandre, Deandrae, Deandres, Deandrey, Deeandre, Deiandre, Deyandre, Dondre, Dondrea*

Dearborn (English) Deer brook. *Dearborne, Dearbourne, Dearburne, Deerborn*

Debashis (Indian) Benediction of God.

Decha (Thai) Strong. *Dechah*

Declan (Irish) Man of prayer. *Daclan, Deklan, Diclan, Dyclan*

Decretas (Latin) Lord; earthly man. (Shakespearean) Character from *Antony and Cleopatra*.

Dedrick (German) Ruler of the people. *Deadric, Deddrick, Dedryk, Deedrick*

Deems (English) Judge's child. *Deam, Deim, Deym, Deyms*

Deepak (Hindi) Small lamp; kindle. *Dipak*

Deepan (Indian) Lighting up.

Deepit (Indian) Lighted.

Deicola (Latin) He who cultivates a relationship with God.

Deion (African American) God of wine and revelry. (Greek) Short form of Dennis. *Deione, Deionta, Deionte, Dion*

Deiondre (African American) Valley. *Deiondray, Deiondré*

Deiphobus (Shakespearean) Character from *Troilus and Cressia*.

Dejuan (American) Combination of De and Juan. *D'Won, Dejan, Dejun, Dijuan*

Dekel (Hebrew) Palm tree. *Dekal, Dekil, Dekyl*

Delano (French) From the elder tree grove. (Irish) Dark. *Del, Delane, Delaney, Delanio, Delayno, Dellano*

Delara (Hebrew) God has liberated me.

Dele (African American) Meaning unknown.

Delling (Scandinavian) Scintillating.

Delmon (French) Mountain. *Delman, Delmen, Delmin, Delmyn*

Delmonte (American) Brand name.

Delmore (Latin) Sea. *Delmar, Delmer*

Deman (Dutch) Man. *Demann*

Demarco (Italian) Warring. (English) Male. *D'Marco, Damarco, Demarcco, Demarcio, Demarkco, Demarko*

Dembe (African) Peace.

Demetrius (Greek) Lover of the earth. *Demeter, Demetre, Demetri, Demetrio, Demetrios, Demetris, Demitiri, Demmy, Dimitri, Dimitry, Dimity, Dmitri*

Demian (Greek) He who emerged from the vinage.

Demissie (African) Destructor.

Demont (French) Mountain. *Demonta, Demontae, Demonte, Demontre*

Dempsey (Irish) Proud. *Dempsie, Dempsy*

Dempster (English) One who judges. *Dempstar, Demster*

Denholm (Scandinavian) Home of the Danes. *Denby, Denham, Denholme, Denim*

Denley (English) Meadow; valley. *Denlea, Denlee, Denli, Denly*

Denman (English) Man from the valley. *Denmen*

Dennis (Greek) Fine wine lover. *Denis, Denit, Dennet, Dennett, Dennison, Denniston, Dennit, Denny, Dennys, Denzel, Denzell, Denzil, Dion, Tennis, Tennyson*

Denton (English) Happy home. *Dent, Denten, Dentin, Dentown*

Denver (English) Green valley. *Denvor*

Denzel (African American) Wild one. (English) Place name, near Cornwall. (Welsh) High stronghold. *Danzel, Danzell, Dennzel, Denzal, Denzall, Denzell, Denzil*

Deo (Greek) Godlike.

Deodato (Latin) He who serves God.

Derek (German) Ruler. *Derex, Derick, Derik, Derrick, Derrik, Derrike, Derry, Derych, Dirk*

Dermot (Irish) Free of envy. *Der, Dermod, Dermott, Kermit*

Deron (Hebrew) Bird; freedom. *Dereon, Deronn, Diron, Dyron*

Deror (Hebrew) Loves freedom. *Derori, Derorie*

Derry (Irish) Redhead. *Darrie, Darry, Deri, Dery*

Derward (English) Deer keeper. *Derwood, Dirward, Durward, Dyrward*

Deshawn (Irish) God is gracious. *D'Shawn, Dashaun, Dashawn, Deshon, Dushawn*

Deshi (Chinese) Virtuous. *Déshì*

Desiderio (Spanish) Desire. *Desi, Desideryo*

Desire (French) Wish.

Desmond (Latin) Society. *Des, Desi, Desmund, Dess*

Desta (Ethiopian) Happiness.

Destin (French) Fate. *Destan, Desten, Destine, Deston, Destyn*

Deuce (Latin) Two; devil.

Deusdedit (Italian) Papal name.

Devak (Indian) Divine.

Devarsi (Hindi) Sage of the Devas.

Deverell (Welsh) From the riverbank.

Devine (Irish) Ox. *Devyne, Dewine*

Devlin (Irish) Brave one. *Dev, Devland, Devlen, Devlyn*

Devon (Irish) Poet. *Deivon, Devan, Deven, Devin, Devohn, Devone, Devonn, Devonne, Divon*

Devoto (Latin) Dedicated.

Dewayne (Irish) Dark. (African American) From the wagon maker. *Dewain, Dewaine, Dewane, Dewaun, Dewaune, Dewon*

Dewei (Chinese) Of great principle.

Dewey (Welsh) Treasured one. *Dew, Dewi, Dewie, Dewy*

Dewitt (German) Blond. *Dewit, DeWitt, Dewyt, Dewytt, Wit*

Dexter (Latin) Right-handed. *Daxter, Decca, Deck, Decka, Dekka, Dex, Dextar, Dextor, Dextron, Dextur*

Dezso (Hungarian) Desired.

Dhananjay (Hindi) Arjuna, a mythic horse in a Hindi epic tale.

Dharuna (Hindi) Rishi, a Vedic poet; a popular Indian name.

Dhatri (Hindi) Son of Vishnu.

Dia (African) Champion.

Diadelfo (Greek) Brother of Zeus.

Diallo (African) Bold.

Diamano (Latin) To lose.

Diamond (English) Brilliant. *Diaman, Diamante, Diamend, Diamont, Diamund, Dimond, Dimonte*

Dian (German) From the god of wine.

Dichali (Native American) Speaks a lot.

Dickinson (English) Powerful, rich ruler. *Dick, Dicken, Dickens, Dickenson, Dickerson, Dikerson, Diksan, Dix, Dixon*

Dickran (Armenian) Ancient king. *Dicran, Dikran*

Dickson (English) Son of Dick. *Dickenson, Dikerson*

Dictino (Greek) Goddess of the ocean.

Didier (French) Desire.

Diederik (Danish) Ruler of the people. *Dierk, Dierks, Dirck, Dirk*

Diego (Spanish) Supplanter. *Diaz, Jago*

Dieter (German) Army of the people. *Deiter, Deyter*

Dietrich (German) Ever-powerful ruler. *Deitrich, Deitrica, Deke, Didric, Didrick, Diedrich, Diedrick, Diedrik, Dieter, Dieterick, Dietric, Dietrick*

Digby (Old English) Settlement near a ditch. *Digbe, Digbee, Digbey, Digbie*

Digno (Latin) Worthy of the best.

Diji (African) Farmer.

Dikembe (African American) Sports figure.

Dilip (Hindi) King; ancestor of Rama.

Dillard (English) Faithful.

Dillon (Irish) Faithful. *Dil, Dill, Dillie, Dilly, Dillyn, Dilon, Dilyn, Dilynn*

Dilwyn (Welsh) Shady place. *Dillwin, Dilwin*

Dimas (Greek) Loyal comrade.

Dimos (Spanish) Giving.

Dinesh (Hindi) Sun god.

Dinsmore (Irish) Fortified hill. *Dinmoar, Dinmor, Dinse, Dinsmoor*

Diokles (Mythology) Priest of Demeter. *Diocles*

Diomedes (Greek) Evil king.

Dionysus (Greek) Celebration. (Mythology) God of wine. *Dion, Dionesios, Dionicio, Dionisio, Dionisios, Dionusios, Dionysios, Dionysius, Dyonisius, Dyonisus*

Dior (French) Present.

Dirk (German) Form of Derek. *Derc, Dirc, Durc, Durk*

Disney (American) Brand name.

Djau (Australian) Aboriginal tribe of Australia; mouth.

Doak Origin and meaning unknown.

Doane (English) Hill dweller. *Doan*

Dobry (Russian) Good. (Polish) Good. *Dobri, Dobrie*

Doc (English) Short for doctor; seventh son of the seventh son.

Dolabella (Shakespearean) Character from *Antony and Cleopatra*.

Dolan (Irish) Dark-haired. *Dolin, Dollan, Dolyn*

Dolf (German) Noble wolf. *Dolfe, Dolff, Dolffe, Dolfi, Dolph, Dolphe, Dolphus, Dulph, Dulphe*

Dominador (Latin) To want to be loved.

Dominick (Latin) The Lord's. *Dom, Domenick, Domenico, Domingo, Dominic, Dominica, Dominik, Dominique, Dominy*

Domitus (Latin) Tamed. *Domitius*

Donahue (Irish) Dark warrior. *Donahu, Donohoe, Donohu, Donohugh*

Donalbain (Scottish) Great chief. (Shakespearean) Character from *Macbeth*.

Donald (Old English) Ruler of the world. *Don, Donal, Donaldson, Donghal, Donley, Donn, Donnally, Donne, Donnell, Donnie, Donny*

Donatien (French) Gift. *Donathan, Donathon, Donatyen*

Donato (Latin) Given. (Italian) Gift. *Donatello, Donati, Donatus*

Dong (Vietnamese) Winter.

Dong-Min (Korean) East and cleverness.

Donkor (African) Humble.

Donnelly (Irish) Dark warrior. *Donahue, Donnel, Donnell, Donner, Donovan, Donovon*

Donus (Italian) Papal name.

Dooley (Greek) Dark hero. *Doolea, Doolee, Dooleigh, Dooli, Doolie, Dooly*

Doran (Greek, Hebrew) Gift. (Irish) Stranger. *Dore, Dorin, Doron, Dorran, Dorren, Dorryn, Doryn*

Dorian (Greek) Gift. *Dorie, Dorien, Dorrian, Dorrien*

Dorjan (Hungarian) Dark man.

Dornin (Romanian) Stranger.

Dorrell (Scottish) King's doorkeeper. *Dorrel, Dorrelle*

Dorset (Old English) Tribe near the sea. *Dorsey*

Doryo (Japanese) Generosity.

Dosio (Latin) Rich.

Doud Origin and meaning unknown.

Dougal (Scottish) Dark stranger. *Doogall, Dougall, Dugal, Dughall*

Douglas (Old English) Dark water. *Doug, Dougal, Dougie, Douglass, Dougles, Dug, Dugaid, Dugald, Dugan, Duglass*

Dov (Hebrew) Bear. *Dove, Dovi, Dovid, Dovidas, Dowid*

Dover (Old English) Water.

Doyle (Old English) Dark stranger. *Doial, Doiale, Doiall, Doil, Doile, Doyal, Doyel, Doyele, Doyell, Doyelle, Doyl*

Drake (Latin) Dragon. (German) Male swan. *Draco, Drago*

Draper (English) Fabric maker. *Draeper, Draiper, Dray, Drayper, Draypr*

Draven (American) Combination of D and Raven. *Davone, Dravian, Dravion, Dravon*

Draylan (Science fiction) Character from *Star Trek: Deep Space Nine*. *Draylen, Draylin*

Dre (American) Short form of Andre. *Deandre, Drae, Dray, Dré*

Dreng (Norwegian) Hired hand.

Drew (Welsh) Wise. *Drewe*

Dries (Greek) Man warrior.

Driscoll (Irish) Interpreter. *Driscol, Dryscol, Dryscoll, Dryscolle*

Droe (Science fiction) Character from *Star Wars*.

Dromio (Shakespearean) Character from *The Comedy of Errors*.

Druce (Irish) Wise man.

Drummond (Scottish) Druid's mountain. *Drummund, Drumond, Drumund*

Dryden (English) Dry valley. *Dridan, Dridin, Dry, Drydon*

Drystan (Irish) Riot; sad.

Duane (Irish) Wagon maker. *Deune, Duain, Duaine, Duana, Duwayne, Dwain, Dwaine, Dwane, Dwayne*

Duante (African American) Wagon maker.

Dubham (Irish) Black. *Dubhem, Dubhim, Dubhom, Dubhym*

Duce (Latin) Leader.

Dudley (Old English) People's meadow. *Dud, Duddy, Dudlea, Dudlee, Dudleigh, Dudli, Dudlie, Dudly*

Duer (Irish) Heroic.

Duffy (Scottish) Dark. *Duff, Duffey, Duffie*

Dugan (English) Worthy. *Doogan, Doogen, Dougan, Dougen, Douggan, Douggen, Dugen, Duggan*

Duke (Latin) Leader. *Duk, Dukey, Dukie, Duky*

Dukker (Gypsy) Fortune-teller. *Duker*

Dulal (Hindi) Loved one.

Dulani (African) Cutting. *Dulanee, Dulaney, Dulanie, Dulany*

Dumaine (Shakespearean) Character from *Love's Labour's Lost*.

Duman (Turkish) Smoky.

Dume (African) Bull.

Duncan (Old English) Dark warrior. *Doncan, Dun, Dunc, Dunkan*

Dunham (Scottish) Brown.

Dunley (English) Hilly meadow. *Dunlea, Dunlee, Dunleigh, Dunli, Dunlie, Dunly*

Dunn (English) Brown. *Dun, Dune, Dunne*

Dunstan (English) From the fortress. *Dunsten, Dunstin, Dunston, Dunstyn*

Dunton (English) Hill town. *Duntan, Dunten, Duntin, Duntyn*

Dur (Hebrew) Stacked up.

Durand (Latin) Enduring. *Duran, Durance, Durandt, Durant, Durante, Durrant*

Durango (American) Model of Dodge truck.

Duranjaya (Hindi) Heroic son.

Duras (Science fiction) Character from *Star Trek*.

Durdanius (Shakespearean) Character from *Julius Caesar*.

Durell (Scottish) King's doorkeeper. *Durel, Durelle, Durial*

Durjaya (Hindi) Difficult to conquer.

Durko (Czech) Form of George.

Durril (Gypsy) Gooseberry. *Duril, Durryl, Duryl*

Durward (Old English) Gatekeeper. *Derward, Derwood, Durwald, Durwin, Durwood, Ward*

Dusan (Russian) God is my judge. *Dusen, Dusin, Dusyn*

Duscha (Slavic) Divine spirit.

Dushawn (American) Combination of Du and Shawn. *Dusean, Dushan, Dushane, Dushaun*

Dustin (Old English) Dark stone. *Dunston, Dustain, Dustan, Dustion, Dusty, Dustynn*

Dutch (German) From the Netherlands.

Duvie Origin and meaning unknown.

Duy (Vietnamese) Save.

Dwalin (Science fiction) Character from *Lord of the Rings*.

Dwayne (Irish) Dark. *Dawayne, Duwain, Duwan, Dwain*

Dweezil (Origin unknown) Nickname.

Dwight (Old English) Fair. *DeWitt, Dwhite, Dwite, Dwyte*

Dwyer (English) Fabric dyer.

Dyami (Native American) Eagle.

Dylan (Welsh) Sea. *Dillan, Dillon, Dyllan, Dyllon, Dylon*

Dyre (Scandinavian) Dear heart. *Dire*

Dyson (English) Short form of Dennison. *Dysen, Dysonn*

E

Ea (Irish, German) Brilliant; famous. *Eah*

Eachan (Irish) Horseman. *Eachann, Eachen, Eachon, Egan*

Eadbert (Anglo-Saxon) King.

Eagan (Irish) Very mighty.

Eamon (Irish) Form of Edmund. *Aimon, Amon, Eaman, Eamen, Eammon, Eiman, Eimon*

Ean (English, Scottish) God is gracious. *Eaen, Eann, Eonn, Eyon, Eyyn*

Earc (Irish) Red.

Earl (Old English) Nobleman. *Airle, Earland, Earld, Earle, Earlie, Early, Eorl, Erie, Erl, Erle, Errol, Erroll*

Earnest (English) Sincere. *Earnesto, Eranest, Ernist, Ernyst*

Easton (English) Eastern town. *Eason, Easten*

Eaton (English) From the estate town by the river. *Eatton, Eton*

Eben (Hebrew) Stone. *Eb, Eban, Ebenezer, Ebenn, Ebin, Ebon, Ebyn*

Eberhard (German) Strong, wild boar. *Eber, Eberardo, Ebere, Eberhardt, Evard, Everard, Everardo, Everhardt, Everhart*

Ebi (African) Good thought.

Ebner (Hebrew) Father of light. *Ab, Abbey, Abbie, Abby, Abna, Abnar, Abner, Abnor, Avner, Eb, Ebbie, Ebby, Ebner*

Ebo (Fante) Born on Tuesday.

Ebony (English) Hard wood. *Ebonee, Ebonie*

Eccelino (Italian) Like his father.

Ecio (Latin) Possessor of great strength.

Edan (Scottish) Fire. *Eadan, Eaden, Eadon*

Edbert (English) Wealthy; bright.

Eden (Hebrew) Delight. *Eaden, Eadin, Edan, Edin, Edyn, Eiden*

Edgar (Old English) Prosperous warrior. *Edek, Edgard, Edgardo, Edgarton, Edger, Edgerton, Edgy*

Edililo (Greek) He who is like a statue.

Edison (English) Son of Edward. *Eddison, Edisen, Edson, Edyson*

Edme (Scottish) Protector; form of Esme and Edmund.

Edmund (Old English) Rich warrior. *Ed, Edmand, Edmaund, Edmon, Edmond, Edmonde, Edmondo, Edmun, Ned, Ted, Teddy*

Edom (Hebrew) Of blood.

Edred (English) King.

Edric (English) Prosperous ruler. *Eddrick, Ederic, Edreese, Edrice*

Edsel (Old English) Rich. (American) Clunky car. *Edsell*

Edur (Basque) Snow. *Edure*

Edward (Old English) Rich guardian. *Eddie, Eddy, Edoardo, Edouard, Eduard, Eduardo, Edvard, Edwardo, Edwards, Edwardson, Neddie, Teddie*

Edwin (Old English) Rich friend. *Eadwinn, Edwan, Edwen, Edwon, Edwyn*

Edwy (English) Name of a king.

Efrain (Hebrew) Fruitful. *Efraine, Efrayne, Efren*

Egan (Irish) Little fire. *Egann, Egen, Egil, Egon*

Egbert (English, German) Intelligent; formidably brilliant. *Egbirt, Egburt*

Egerton (Old English) Edge. *Edgarton, Edgerton, Egeton, Egmont*

Egil (Scandinavian) Awe-inspiring. *Egyl, Eigel, Eigil*

Eglamour (Shakespearean) Character from *The Two Gentlemen of Verona*.

Egmont (German) Weapon; defender. *Egmount*

Egor (Russian) Farmer; form of George. *Igor*

Ehren (German) Honorable. *Eren*

Ehud (Hebrew) He who praises.

Eiddwen (Welsh) Fond and faithful. *Eiddweyn, Eidwin, Eyddwen*

Eiros (Welsh) Bright. *Eros*

Eisig (Hebrew) He who laughs.

Eitan (Hebrew) Strong; firm. *Eita, Eithan, Eiton*

Eknath (Hindi) Poet; saint.

Ekon (Nigerian) Strength. *Ek, Koni*

Elam (Hebrew) Highlands. *Elame*

Elan (Hebrew) Tree. (Native American) Friendly. *Elann*

Elazar (Hebrew) God has helped.

Elbert (German) Bright; famous. *Elberto*

Elbio (Celtic) He who comes from the mountain.

Elder (Old English) Old. *Alder, Eldred*

Eldon (Old English) Ella's mound. *Elden*

Eldridge (Old English) Old counsel. *Elbridge, Elderydg, Eldredge, Eldrege, Eldrid, Eldrige, Elric, Elrick*

Eldwin (English, German) Old, wise ruler; old friend. *Eldwinn, Eldwyn, Eldwynn*

Eleazar (Hebrew) God helps. *Elasar, Elazaro, Eleaser, Eliezer, Elizard*

Elek (Hungarian, Green) Defender of humankind. *Elec, Eleck*

Elenio (Greek) He who shines like the sun.

Eleutherius (Latin) Free. *Eleuthere*

Elfego (Germanic) Spirit of the air.

Elgin (English) Noble. (Irish) White. *Elgan, Elgen*

Elias (Hebrew) The Lord is God. *Eliasz, Elihu, Ellias, Ellice, Ellis, Ellison, Ellsworth, Ellys, Elyas, Elyes*

Elie (Greek) Light; form of Eleanor. *Eli*

Eliecer (Hebrew) God is his constant aid.

Elijah (Hebrew) God the Lord; the strong Lord. *Elija, Elijha, Elijiah, Elijuah, Elijuo, Eliya, Eliyah*

Elika (Hawiian, Greek) Wealthy. *Elyka*

Eliot (Hebrew) High. *Eli, Eliott, Eliud, Eliut, Elliot, Elliott, Elliotte, Ely, Elyot*

Elisaku Origin and meaning unknown.

Elisandro (Greek) Liberator of men.

Elizur (Hebrew) God is my rock.

Elkanah (Hebrew) Zeal of God. *Elkan, Elkana, Elkin*

Ellard (German) Sacred; brave. *Alard, Allard*

Ellery (Latin) Cheerful. *Elari, Elery, Ellary, Ellerey, Ellory, Elory*

Ellis (English, Greek, Hebrew) My God is Jehovah; form of Elias from Elijah. *Elis, Ellison*

Elman (German) Elm tree.

Elmer (Old English) Famous nobleman. *Almer, Ellmer, Elman, Elmo, Elmore, Ulmer*

Eloy (Latin) Chosen. *Eloi*

Elrond (Fiction) Character from *The Lord of the Rings* by J. R. R. Tolkien.

Elson (Old English) Noble one's son.

Elsu (Native American) Flying falcon.

Elton (Old English) Ella's town. *Alton, Eldon, Ellton, Elten, Elthon, Eltonia*

Elvis (Scandinavian) Wise; sage. *Elva, Elvin, Elviz, Elvys*

Elwood (English) From the old forest. *Woody*

Eman (Irish) Earnest; sincere. *Emani*

Emanuel (Hebrew) God is with us. *Emanuele, Emmanuel, Imanuel, Immanuel, Manny, Manuel*

Emaus Origin and meaning unknown.

Emeril (Portuguese) Meaning unknown.

Emerson (Old English) Emery's son. *Emersen, Emmerson, Emmyrson, Emreson, Emyrson*

Emery (German) Powerful home. *Emari, Emerich, Emerio, Emmerie, Emmery, Emmory, Emory*

Emile (Latin) Eager to please. *Aimil, Aymil, Emelen, Emelio, Emil, Emile, Emilian, Emiliano, Emilianus, Emilio, Emilion, Emilyan, Emlen, Emlin, Emlyn, Emlynn*

Eminem (American) Rapper Marshall Mathers.

Emmett (English) Hard worker; truth. *Emet, Emett, Emitt, Emmet, Emmitt, Emmot, Emmott*

Emre (Turkish) Brother. *Emra, Emreson*

Emrick (Welsh) Form on the Greek for "immortal." *Emeric, Emerick, Emric, Emris, Emryk, Emrys*

Enapay (Native American) Brave. *Enapai*

Endrikas (Lithuanian, German) Ruler of the house.

Endor (Hebrew) Fountain of youth; adorable.

Eneas (Greek) Praised. *Enneas, Ennes, Ennis*

Engelbert (Old German) Bright as an angel. *Bert, Berty, Ingelbert, Inglebert*

Engu (Japanese) Whole or complete fool.

Enki (Japanese) Postponement; god who ruled over the Abzu.

Enkil Origin and meaning unknown.

Enmei (Japanese) Bright circle.

Ennis (Greek) Mine. *Eni, Enis, Ennys*

Enoch (Hebrew) Trained and vowed; dedicated; profound. *Enoc, Enock, Enok*

Enrique (Basque) Ruler of an estate. *Enrico, Quique*

Enzi (Swahili) Powerful. *Enzy*

Eowyn (Hawaiian) God's gracious gift. *Keona, Keowynn*

Ephraim (Hebrew) Fruitful. *Efraim, Efrem, Ephrain, Ephram, Ephrem*

Equinox (Latin) Equal night.

Eran (Hebrew) Watchful; vigilant. *Eren*

Erastus (Greek) Beloved. *Eraste, Erastious, Rastus*

Ercole (Italian) Great gift. *Ercoal*

Eri (Teutonic) Vigilant.

Eriberto (Italian) Glorious soldier; form of Herbert. *Erberto*

Eric (Scandinavian) Ruler of all. *Aric, Ehrich, Erek, Ericc, Erick, Erico, Erik, Erikson, Eryc, Eryk*

Eridanus (Latin) Large southern constellation.

Eris (Greek) Goddess of strife.

Erland (English) Nobleman's land. *Earland, Erlan, Erlen*

Erling (English) Nobleman's son.

Ermanno (Italian) Man of the army; warrior. *Armand, Erman, Ermano, Erminio, Ermon, Harman*

Ernest (Old German) Vigorous. *Earnest, Earni, Earnre, Ernestino, Ernesto, Ernests, Ernestus, Ernie, Ernst*

Eros (Greek) God of love.

Errol (English) Nobleman; form of Earl. *Earland, Earle, Earleen, Early, Erie, Erle, Erleen, Erlene, Errol, Erroll, Erryl*

Erskine (Old English) Green heights. *Ersin, Erskin*

Ervin (Hungarian) Form of Irving. *Ervan, Erven, Erwan, Erwin, Erwyn, Irvin, Irving*

Eryu (Japanese) Dragon wisdom.

Esau (Hebrew) Hairy. *Esaw*

Esbern (Danish) Holy bear. *Esbirn, Esbirne, Esburn, Esburne*

Escalus (English) Ancient lord. (Shakespearean) Character from *Measure for Measure*.

Escanes (Shakespearean) Character from *Pericles*.

Eskander (Persian) Defends mankind; form of Alexander. *Alejandro, Alekanekelo, Aleksander, Aleksandr, Aleksanteri, Aleksi, Aleksy, Ales, Alexandre, Alexandrukas, Elek, Eskander, Iskender, Lyaksandro, Oles, Sandor*

Esmond (Old English) Protective grace. *Desmond, Desmund, Esmund*

Espen (Danish) Bear of the gods. *Espan, Espin*

ESPN (American) TV sports network. *Espen*

Essien (African) Sixth-born son. *Esien*

Esteban (Spanish, Greek) Crowned. *Estabon, Estefan, Estephan, Estephen, Estevan, Estevez*

Esterio (Greek) As clean and pure as heaven.

Estes (Latin) Estuary. *Eston*

Estio (Portuguese) Summer.

Etchemin (Native American) Canoe man.

Ethan (Latin) Constant. *Eathen, Efan, Eithan, Etan, Ethen, Ethon*

Ethelbert (English) Splendid.

Ethelred (English) King. (German) Noble counselor.

Ethelwolf (English) King. *Ethelwulf*

Etienne (French) Crowned. *Estienne, Etiene*

Ettore (Italian) Loyal. *Etor, Etore*

Etu (Native American) Sun. *Eetu*

Eubie Origin and meaning unknown.

Euclid (Greek) Intelligent. *Euclyd*

Eugene (Greek) Well born. *Eoghan, Eugeen, Eugen, Eugeni, Eugenio, Eugenius, Evgeny, Ezven, Gene*

Euno (Greek) Intelligent.

Eurwyn (Welsh) Gold; fair-haired.

Eusebius (Latin) Pious.

Eustace (Greek) Fruitful. *Estachy, Eustache, Eustachio, Eustachius, Eustazio, Eustis, Stace, Stacie*

Eutychian Origin and meaning unknown.

Evagelos (Greek) Evangelist. *Evangelo, Evangelos*

Evan (Irish) Young warrior. *Evaine, Evann, Evans, Evanston, Even, Evin, Evon, Evyn*

Evangelista (Greek) Good news giver; messenger of God. *Evangeleana, Evangeleanah, Evangeleane, Evangeleena, Evangeleene, Evangelia, Evangelica, Evangeline, Evangelique, Evangelista, Evangelyn, Evangelyna, Evangelynah, Evangelyne*

Evaristus (Latin) Pleasing.

Everard (Old English) Strong.

Everest (English) Name of Earth's tallest mountain.

Everett (German) Strong boar. *Everard, Everet, Everrett, Evert, Evrett*

Evzen (Slavic) Of noble birth.

Ewald (Old English) Always powerful. *Evald*

Ewert (Old English) Hearder of the ewes. *Ewart*

Ewing (English) Friend of the law. *Ewan, Ewart, Ewen*

Ezekiel (Hebrew) Strength of God. *Ezakeil, Ezeck, Ezeckiel, Ezeeckel, Ezekeyial, Ezekial, Ezekielle, Ezequiel, Eziakah, Eziechiele*

Ezio (Latin) Like an eagle.

Ezra (Hebrew) Salvation. *Esra, Ezer, Ezera, Ezrah, Ezri, Ezzret*

Ezral (Science fiction) Character from *Star Trek: Enterprise.*

F

Faas (Scandinavian) Wise counselor. *Fas*

Fabian (Latin) Bean. *Fab, Fabain, Fabayan, Fabean, Fabia, Fabiana, Fabiano, Fabien, Fabion, Fabius, Fabya, Fabyan*

Fabrizio (Latin) One with skilled hands. *Fabrizius*

Fabron (French) Blacksmith. *Fabra, Fabre, Fabriano, Fabroni, Fabryn*

Fadi (Arabic) Redeemer. *Fadee, Fadhi*

Fadoy (Ukrainian) Form of Thaddeus. *Faday, Faddei, Faddey, Faddi, Fady*

Fagan (Gaelic) Ardent. *Faegen, Faegin, Faegon, Faegyn, Fagen, Faigen, Faigin, Faigon, Faigyn, Faygan, Faygen, Faygin, Faygon, Faygyn*

Fahd (Arabic) Panther. *Fahaad, Fahad*

Fai (Chinese) Start.

Fairfax (Old English) Blond-haired. *Fair, Fairfield, Fax, Fayrfax*

Faisal (Arabic) Decisive; criterion. *Faisel, Faisil, Faisl, Faiyaz, Faiz, Faizal, Faizel, Fasel, Fasil, Faysal, Fayzal, Fayzel*

Fakih (Arabic) Smart, intelligent.

Falito (Italian) God has healed.

Falk (German) Surname relating to falconry. *Falcko, Falckon, Falcon, Falconn, Falk, Falke, Falken, Falxo, Faulco*

Falkner (English) Falconer; one who trains falcons. *Falconer, Falconner, Falconnor,*

Faulconer, Faulconner, Faulconnor, Faulkner

Fallon (Celtic) Of a ruling family.

Falstaff (English) Kingly; noble. (Shakespearean) Character from *The Merry Wives of Windsor.*

Fane (English) Glad. *Fain, Faine, Fayn, Fayne*

Fanuco (Spanish) Free.

Fanuel (Hebrew) Vision of God.

Faraji (African) Consolation. *Farajy*

Faraz (Arabic) Elevation. *Farhaz, Fariez*

Farley (Old English) Distant meadow. *Fairlea, Fairlee, Fairlei, Fairleigh, Fairley, Far, Farland, Farlay, Farlea, Farlee, Farli, Farlie, Farly, Farrleigh, Farrley*

Farnell (English) From the fern slope. *Farnal, Farnall, Farnalle, Farnel*

Farnley (English) Fern meadow. *Farnlea, Farnlee, Farnleigh, Farnli, Farnlie, Fernley, Fernlie*

Farold (English) Mighty traveler. *Farr*

Farquahar (Scottish) Dear. *Fark, Farq, Farquar, Farquarson, Farque, Farquy*

Farran (English) Wanderer. *Faron, Farron, Farrun, Farryn, Ferren, Firrin*

Farrar (Latin) Blacksmith. *Farar, Farer, Faron, Farra, Farrer, Farrier, Farron*

Farrell (Old English) Man of valor. *Faral, Farel, Faril, Farol, Farrel, Farrill, Farrow, Farryl, Farryll, Faryl, Ferol, Ferreell, Ferrel, Ferryl*

Farrow (English) Piglet. *Farow*

Faste (Norwegian) Firm.

Fath (Arabic) Victor.

Fatin (Arabic) Captivating; seducer; alluring. *Faten, Fatine, Fatyn, Fatyne*

Faust (Latin) Lucky. *Fauste, Faustis, Faustise, Faustu, Faustus, Faustyce, Faustys*

Favian (Latin) Understanding. *Favian, Favien, Favio, Favion, Favyen, Favyon*

Faxon (German) Long-haired. *Faxan, Faxen, Faxin, Faxyn*

Fazel (Persian) Learned.

Fazio (Italian) Good worker. *Fazyo*

Federico (Spanish) Peaceful ruler. *Federic, Federick, Federigo, Federoquito*

Fedro (Greek) Splendid man.

Feivel (Yiddish) Bright one. *Feyvel*

Felix (Latin) Happiness. *Felic, Felice, Felike, Feliks, Felizio, Felo, Filix, Filyx, Fliks, Fylyx*

Felton (English) Field town. *Felltun, Feltan, Felten, Feltin, Feltyn*

Fenton (English) From the settlement of the town on the moor. *Fen, Fennie, Fenny, Fentan, Fenten, Fentin, Fentun, Fentyn, Fintan, Finton*

Feodore (Russian) Form of Theodore. *Feadodor, Feador, Feaodore, Fedar, Fedinka, Fedor, Fedore, Fedya, Feedor, Feodor*

Feoras (Greek) Smooth rock.

Ferdinand (German) Courageous traveler. *Ferd, Ferde, Ferdie, Ferdinan, Ferdinandus, Ferdy, Fernandas, Fernando, Ferrando, Nando*

Fergus (Irish) Strong man. *Feargas, Fergie, Fergis, Fergun, Ferguson, Fergusson, Fergy, Furguson, Fyrgus*

Feroz (Hindi) Winner.

Ferran (Arabic) Baker. *Farran, Feran, Feren, Feron, Ferren, Ferrin, Ferron, Ferryl, Ferryn*

Ferrand (French) Gray-haired. *Farran, Farrando, Farrant, Ferand, Ferrant, Gerand*

Ferrell (Irish) Form of Farrell. *Ferel, Ferell, Ferrel, Ferrill, Ferryl*

Ferris (Latin) Iron. *Faris, Farris, Feris, Ferrel, Ferrell, Ferrice, Ferrise, Ferriss, Ferryce, Ferrys*

Feste (Latin) Festive; joyful. (Shakespearean) Character from *Twelfth Night.*

Festus (Biblical) Festive; joyful. *Festys*

Fidias (Greek) Unhurried.

Fielding (Old English) Field. *Field, Fielder, Fields*

Fifi (African) Born on Friday.

50 Cent (American) Rapper Curtis James Jackson III. *Fiddy*

Filbert (English) Brilliant. *Filberte, Filberti, Filberto, Filbirt, Filburt, Fillbert, Fillbirt, Fillburt, Fylbert, Fylbirt, Fylburt, Fyllbert, Fyllbyrt*

Filip (Scandinavian) Form of Philip. *Filipe, Filipek, Filippo, Filips, Fill, Fillip*

Filmore (English) Famous. *Fillmore, Filmer, Fyllmer, Fyllmore, Fylmer, Fylmore, Philmore*

Finch (English) Small bird.

Fineas (Irish) Form of Phineas. *Finneas, Fyneas*

Finley (Celtic) Fair-haired one. *Findlay, Finlay, Finlea, Finlee, Finleigh, Finnlea, Finnleigh, Fynlay, Fynlea, Fynley, Fynnley*

Finnegan (Irish) Fair. *Finegan, Fineghan, Finneghan, Fynegan, Fyneghan, Fynnegan, Fynneghan*

Finnian (Irish) Fair-haired. *Finian, Finley, Finn, Finnie, Finnis, Finny, Fyn, Fynn*

Fintan (Irish) From Finn's town. *Finten, Fintin, Finton, Fintyn, Fyntan, Fynten, Fynton, Fyntyn*

Fiorello (Italian) Little flower. *Fiore, Fiorelleigh, Fiorelley, Fiorelli, Fiorellie, Fiorelly, Fyorellee, Fyorellie, Fyorello, Fyorelly*

Firas (Arabic) Persistent. *Fira, Fyra, Fyras*

Firdaus (Indian) Paradise.

Firouz (Persian) Victorious.

Fischer (English) Form of Fisher.

Fiske (Swedish) Fisherman. *Fisk, Fysk, Fyske*

Fitch (English) Weasel; ermine. *Fitche, Fytch*

Fitz (English) Son; Fitz names were commonly given to the illegitimate sons of royalty. *Filz, Fits, Fitzgerald, Fitzhugh, Fitzpatrick, Fitzroy, Fyts, Fytz*

Fiz (Latin) Happy.

Flannery (Old French) Sheet of metal. (Irish) Red-haired. *Flainn, Flan, Flanan, Flanin, Flann, Flannon, Flanon, Flanyn*

Flavian (Greek) Yellow; blond. *Flavel, Flavelle, Flavien, Flavyan, Flawian, Flawiusz, Flawyan*

Flavio (Italian) Gold or blond. *Flabio, Flavias, Flavious, Flavius, Flavyo*

Flavius (Latin) Blond; yellow-haired. *Flavian*

Fleance (Italian) Son of Banquo.

Fleming (English) Native of Flanders. *Flemming, Flemmyng, Flemyng*

Fletcher (Old French) Seller of arrows. *Flecher, Fletch*

Flint (English) Hard, quartz rock. *Flinte, Flynt, Flynte*

Floke (German) Form of Volker. *Folker*

Florent (French) Flowering. *Florentin, Florentine, Florentyn, Florentyne, Florentz, Florynt, Florynte*

Florian (Latin) Flowering, blooming. *Florentin, Florentino, Florentyn, Florien, Florinio, Florion, Florrian, Florus, Flory, Floryant, Floryante*

Floritzel (Italian) Flower. *Flor, Florus*

Floyd (Welsh) Hollow. *Floid, Floyde*

Fluellen (Welsh) Like a lion.

Flurry (English) Flourishing. *Fluri, Flurie, Flurri, Flurrie, Flury*

Flynn (Irish) Son of the red-haired man. *Flin, Flinn, Flyn*

Fo-hai (Chinese) Buddha-ocean.

Fo-hsing (Chinese) Buddha-mind.

Focio (Latin) Illuminated.

Fonty Origin and meaning unknown.

Fonzie (German) Form of Alphonse. *Fons, Fonsee, Fonsey, Fonsi, Fonsie, Fonsy, Fonz, Fonzee, Fonzey, Fonzi, Fonzy*

Forbes (Irish) Prosperous. *Forbe, Forbs*

Ford (Old English) River crossing. *Forde*

Fordel (Gypsy) Forgiving. *Fordal, Fordele, Fordell, Fordelle, Fordil, Fordile*

Fordon (German) Destroyer. *Fordan, Forden, Fordin, Fordyn*

Formosus (Latin) Finely formed.

Forrest (Old French) Out of the woods. *Forest, Forestt, Forrester, Forrestt, Forster, Foryst*

Fortinbras (Scandinavian) Norwegian king. (Shakespearean) Character from *Hamlet.*

Fortino (Italian) Fortunate; lucky. *Fortin, Fortine, Fortyn, Fortyne*

Fortune (French) Fortunate. *Fortun, Fortunato, Fortuné, Fortunio*

Foster (Old French) Forest keeper. *Forster*

Fouad (Lebanese) Heart.

Fowler (English) Trapper of fowl.

Fox (English) Fox. *Foxx*

Fraco (Spanish) Weak.

Franchot (French) Nickname for Francis.

Francis (Old French) Free; androgynous name, although Francis is generally used for boys and Frances for girls. *France, Franciskus, Franco, Francys, Frannie, Franny, Franscis, Fransis, Franus, Frencis*

Francisco (Spanish) Free land. *Francesco, Fransysco, Frasco*

Francois (French) Free. *Francoise, François*

Franklin (Old French) Free man. *Francelen, Francklen, Francklin, Francklyn, Frank, Frankie, Franklyn, Franklynn*

Franz (German) Free. *Frans, Fransz, Frants, Franzen, Franzie, Franzin, Franzl, Franzy*

Frasier (French) Strawberry. *Fraizer, Fraser, Fraze, Frazer, Frazier, Frazyer*

Frayne (French) Dweller at the ash tree. *Frain, Fraine, Frayn, Frean, Freane, Freen, Freene, Frein, Freine, Freyn*

Frederick (German) Peaceful ruler. *Fred, Fredderick, Freddie, Freddy, Fredek, Frederic, Frederico, Fredricks, Fredrik, Fréderick, Frédérik, Fritz*

Freeborn (English) Child of freedom. *Freborn, Free*

Freedom (English) Liberty.

Fremont (German) Guardian of freedom. *Fremonte*

Fresco (Spanish) Fresh.

Frewin (English) Noble friend. *Freewan, Freewen, Frewan, Frewen, Frewon, Frewyn*

Frey (Scandinavian) God of weather. *Frai, Fray, Frei*

Freyr (English) He who is foremost lord. (Norse) God of peace and prosperity.

Fridmund (German) Peaceful guardian. *Frimond, Frymond, Frymund*

Frisco (Spanish) Form of Francis.

Fritz (German) Peaceful ruler. *Fritson, Fritts, Fritzl, Frizchen*

Frode (Norwegian) Wise. *Frod*

Frollo (English) In *The Legend of King Arthur*, he was killed by Arthur.

Fudoki (Japanese) Immovable; unmoving wisdom.

Fujita (Japanese) Field.

Fulbright (German) Very bright. *Fulbert, Fulbirt, Fulburt, Fulbyrt*

Fuller (Old English) One who works with cloth. *Fuler*

Fulton (Old English) Town near the field. *Faulton, Folton*

Furio (Latin) Furious.

Fynn (African) Name for the Offin River. *Fyn*

Fyodor (Russian) Gift of God. *Fydor, Fydore, Fyodore*

G

Gabai (Hebrew) Delight; adornment.

Gabriel (Hebrew) God is my strength. *Gab, Gabe, Gaberial, Gable, Gabrail, Gabriael, Gabrieal, Gabriello, Gabryel, Gavrila*

Gad (Native American) Juniper tree.

Gadi (Arabic) God is my fortune. *Gad, Gaddy, Gadie, Gadiel, Gady*

Gael (Irish) Gaelic-speaking Celt.

Gaetan (Italian) From Gaeta, region in southern Italy. *Gaetano, Gaetono*

Gage (French) Pledge. *Gager, Gaig, Gaige, Gayg, Gayge*

Gaines (English) Increase in wealth. *Gainor, Gains, Gainsborough, Gayne, Gaynes, Gaynor*

Gaino Origin and meaning unknown.

Gajendra (Hindi) Elephant king.

Gale (English) Lively. *Gail, Gaile, Gayl, Gayle*

Galen (Greek) Tranquil. *Gaelan, Gaelen, Gaelin, Gaelyn, Gailen, Galan, Galin, Galon, Galyn*

Galileo (Italian) From Galilee.

Gallagher (Irish) Eager aide. *Gahan, Gallagher*

Gallant (English) Courageous.

Galloway (Latin) From Gaul. *Gallowai, Gallwai, Gallway, Galwai, Galway*

Gallus (Shakespearean) Character from *Anthony and Cleopatra*.

Galvin (Irish) Sparrows. *Gal, Gall, Gallven, Gallvin, Galvan, Galven, Galvon, Galvyn*

Gamal (Arabic) Camel. *Gamali, Gamall, Gemal, Gemali, Jamal, Jammal, Jemaal*

Gamel (English) Old one.

Gan (Hebrew) Garden. (Chinese) Daring. (Vietnamese) Near.

Gandale Origin and meaning unknown.

Ganesh (Hindi) Hindi god.

Gangol (Indian) Precious.

Gannon (Irish) Fair complexion. *Ganan, Ganen, Ganin, Gannan, Gannen, Gannyn, Ganon, Ganyn*

Gao (Chinese) Tall; high.

Garcia (Spanish) Mighty with a spear. *Garcya, Garcyah, Garcyas, Garsias, Garsya, Garsyah, Garsyas*

Gardiner (Danish) Garden keeper. *Gard, Gardell, Garden, Gardener, Gardenner, Gardenor, Gardie, Gardiner, Gardnar, Gardnard, Gardner*

Garek (Polish) Form of Edgar. *Garak, Garok*

Garen (French) Guardian. *Garan, Garin, Garion, Garrion, Garyon*

Gareth (Norse) Enclosure. (French) Watchful. *Gar, Gareth, Garette, Garit, Garret, Garreth, Garry, Garth, Gary*

Garfield (English) Promontory. *Garfyeld*

Garion (English) Form of Garry. *Garrion, Garyon*

Garland (French) Wreath. *Garlan, Garlande, Garllan, Garlon, Garlund, Garlyn*

Garman (English) Spearman. *Garmann, Garmen, Garrman*

Garner (Latin) Granary. (French) Sentry. *Garnar, Garnier, Garnit, Garnor, Garnyr*

Garnett (Latin) Pomegranate seed; garnet stone. (English) Armed with a spear. *Garnie*

Garrett (English) Strong. *Garett, Garrard, Garret, Garretson, Garrith, Garritt, Garrot, Garyth, Gerrity, Jared, Jarod, Jarret, Jarrett, Jarrot, Jarrott*

Garrick (English) Oak spear. *Gaerick, Garic, Garick, Garik, Garreck, Garrek, Garric, Garrik, Garryck, Garryk, Garyc, Garyck, Garyk, Gerreck*

Garrison (French) Fort. *Garison, Garisson, Garris, Garryson, Garson, Garyson*

Garth (Scandinavian*)* Garden; gardener. *Garthe*

Gary (German) Spear carrier. *Gare, Gari, Garie, Garri, Garrick, Garrie, Garry, Garvey, Garvie, Garvin, Gervais, Gervase, Gervis*

Gaspar (Persian) Treasure bearer. *Caspar, Casper, Gasparas, Gaspard, Gaspare, Gaspari, Gasparo, Gasper, Gazsi, Jaspar, Jasper, Kaspar, Kasper*

Gaston (French) From Gascony. *Gascon, Gastan, Gastaun, Gasten, Gastin, Gastone, Gastyn*

Gatian (Hebrew) Family.

Gavin (Welsh) Hawk. *Gav, Gavan, Gaven, Gavinn, Gavino, Gavn, Gavohn, Gavon, Gavun, Gavynn*

Gavrie (Russian) Man of God.

Gavril (Slavic) Believer in God. *Ganya, Gavi, Gavrel, Gavriel, Gavrilla, Gavrilo, Gavryel, Gavryele, Gavryell, Gavryelle, Gavryl, Gavryle, Gavryll, Gavrylle, Gavy*

Gawain (Welsh) Courteous. *Gauvain, Gawaine, Gawayn, Gawayne, Gawen, Gwayn, Gwayne*

Gawonii (Native American) He is speaking.

Gaylord (French) Brave. *Gaelor, Gaelord, Gailard, Gaillard, Gailor, Gailord, Gallard, Gayelord, Gaylard, Gayler, Gaylor*

Geary (English) Changeable. *Gearee, Gearey, Geari, Gery*

Geb (Egytpian) Land of God.

Gedeon (Hungarian) Warrior; form of Gideon.

Geert (Germanic) Brave; strength.

Geet (Indian) Song.

Gelasius (Greek) Laughter.

Gemelo (Latin) Fraternal twin.

Gemini (Latin) Twins; sign of the Zodiac.

Gene (English) Well born. *Eugene, Gena, Genek, Genio, Genya, Gine, Jeno, Yengeny, Yevgeni, Yevgenij, Yevgeniy*

Gener (Catalan) January.

Genesis (Hebrew) Origin. *Gennesis, Ginesis, Jenesis, Jennesis*

Genjo (Chinese) Gold.

Genko (Japanese) Original silence.

Gennaro (Latin) Consecrated to God.

Genovese (Italian) From Genoa, Italy. *Geno, Genovis*

Gent (English) Gentleman. *Gental, Gentel, Gentil, Gentle, Gentyl, Gentyle*

Geode (Greek) Earthlike.

Geoffrey (German) Peace. *Gef, Geff, Geoff, Geoffery, Geoffre, Geoffri, Geoffroy, Geoffry, Geofri, Giotta, Godfrey, Gottfried, Jeff*

Geordi (Greek) Hill near meadows.

George (Greek) Farmer. *Egor, Geordie, Georg, Georges, Georgi, Georgie, Georgio, Georgius, Georgy, Giorgio, Giorgis, Goran, Jeorg, Jerzy, Jiri, Jorge, Jorgen, Jorges, Jorrin, Juergen, Jur, Jurek, Jurgen, Jurgi, Jurik, Juro, Seiorse, Yegor, Yoyi, Yura, Yurchik, Yuri, Yurik, Yurko, Yusha, Zhorka*

Geraint (English) Old. *Geraynt*

Gerald (French) Spear warrior. *Garold, Garrard, Garrod, Geraldo, Gerard, Gerardo, Geraud, Gerbert, Gerek, Gerhard, Gerhardt, Gerhart, Gerrit, Gerry, Girard, Girauld, Girault, Giraut, Jarett, Jarrett, Jerard, Jerry*

Gerard (English) Brave spearman. *Garrat, Garratt, Gearard, Gerad, Gerar, Gerard, Geraro, Gerd, Gerrard, Girad*

Gerik (Polish) Prosperous spearman. *Geric, Gerick, Gérrick*

Gerlac (German) Spear thrower. *Gerlach, Gerlache, Gerlaich*

Germain (French) Bud. *Germane, Germayn, Germayne, Germin, Germon, Germyn, Jarman, Jermain, Jermaine, Jermyn*

Germanus (Latin) Brotherly. *Germaine, German, Germano, Jermayn, Jermayne*

Geron (French) Guard.

Gersham (Hebrew) Exile. *Gersho, Gershom, Geurson, Gursham, Gurshun*

Gershon (Yiddish) Stranger in exile. *Gershoom*

Gerson (Hungarian) Stranger banished. *Gersan, Gershawn, Gerzon*

Gert (German, Danish) Fighter.

Gervasio (Spanish) Warrior. *Garvas, Gervais, Gervaise, Gervase, Gervasius, Gervaso, Gervasy, Gervayse, Gerwazy, Jarvey, Jarvis, Jervis*

Geteye (African) His teacher.

Ghadir (Arabic) Sword.

Ghalib (Indian) Excellent.

Ghazi (Arabic) Invader.

Gi (Korean) Brave.

Giacomo (Hebrew) Replaces. *Gaimo, Giacamo, Giaco, Giacobbe, Giacobo, Giacopo, Gyacomo*

Gian (Hebrew) The Lord is gracious. *Ghian, Ghyan, Gianetto, Giannis, Giannos, Gyan*

Giancarlo (Italian) Gracious; powerful. *Giancarlos, Gianncarlo, Gyancarlo*

Giannes (Hebrew) Gift from God. *Gian, Gianne*

Gianni (Italian) God is gracious. *Giani, Gianney, Gianni, Gianny, Gionni*

Gibor (Hebrew) Powerful. *Gibbor*

Gibson (English) Son of Gilbert. *Gibbon, Gibbons, Gibbs, Gibbson, Gilson*

Gideon (Hebrew) Mighty warrior. *Gedeon, Gid, Giddy, Gideone, Gydeon, Hedeon*

Gifford (English) Worthy gift. *Giff, Giffard, Gifferd, Giffie, Giffy, Gyfford, Gyford*

Gig (Spanish) Spear.

Gil (Greek) Shield bearer. (Hebrew) Happy. *Gili, Gilie, Gill, Gilley, Gilli, Gillie, Gillis, Gilly, Gyl, Gyll*

Gilbert (German) Bright desire. *Bert, Gib, Gibbes, Gibbs, Gibby, Gibson, Giggon, Gil, Gilberto, Gillett, Gillette, Gilly, Gip, Gipper, Guilbert, Wilbert, Wilbur*

Gilby (Scandinavian) Hostage's estate. (Irish) Blond boy. *Gilbee, Gilbey, Gilbi, Gilbie, Gilibee, Gillbey, Gillbi, Gillbie, Gillby, Gylbee, Gylbey, Gylbi, Gylbie, Gylby, Gyllbee, Gyllbey, Gyllbi, Gyllbie, Gyllby*

Gildas (English) Guilded.

Gilen (Basque, German) Illustrious pledge. *Gilenn, Gylen*

Giles (Greek) Shield of hides. (French) Youth. *Egedio, Egide, Egidius, Gide, Gil, Gilean, Gileon, Gilles, Gillette, Gillian, Gillis, Gyles, Jetes, Jyles*

Gilford (Old English) Ford near the wooded ravine. *Gilmore, Gilroy, Guilford*

Gilmore (Irish) Devoted to the Virgin Mary. *Gillmor, Gillmore, Gillmour, Gillmoor, Gilmoore, Gilmor, Gilmour, Gylmoor, Gylmoore, Gylmor, Gylmore*

Gines (Greek) He who produces life.

Gino (Italian) Noble born. *Ghino, Gyno*

Gioacchino (Italian) Founded by God. *Gio, Gioaccino*

Giovanni (Italian) Gift from God. *Giannino, Giovanathon, Giovann, Giovannie, Giovanno, Giovon, Giovonni, Giovonnia, Giovonnie, Givonni*

Gipsy (English) Wanderer. *Gipson, Gypsy*

Girish (Hindi) God of mountain.

Giuseppe (Hebrew) The Lord increases. *Giuseppi, Giuseppino, Giusseppe, Guiseppe, Guiseppi, Guiseppie, Guisseppe*

Glanville (French) Settlement of oak trees. *Glannville, Glanvil, Glanvill, Glanvyl, Glanvyll, Glanvylle*

Gleb (Russian) God of life.

Glen (Irish) Secluded, wooded valley. *Glean, Gleann, Glenard, Glendon, Glenn, Glennie, Glennis, Glennon, Glenny, Glenon*

Glenton (Scottish) Valley town. *Glennton, Glynnton, Glynton*

Godfrey (German) God's peace. *Giotto, Godard, Goddard, Goddenn, Godding, Godhart, Godin, Godofredo, Godrick, Godwin, Goffredo, Gotfrid, Gottfried, Gotthardt, Govert*

Goel (Hebrew) Redeemer.

Goldman (Old English) To shine. *Gold, Goldwin, Goldwyn*

Goldwin (English) Golden friend. *Goldewin, Goldewinn, Goldewyn, Goldwinn, Goldwinne, Goldwyn, Goldwyne, Goldwynn, Goldwynne*

Goliath (Hebrew) Exile. *Golliath, Golyath*

Gomda (Kiowa) Wind. *Gomdah*

Gomer (English) Good fight.

Gonzalo (Spanish) Wolf. *Consalvo, Goncalve, Gonsalve, Gonzales, Gonzalous, Gonzelee, Gonzoalos, Gonzolo*

Gopal (Hindi) Lord Krishna.

Goran (Greek) Farmer. *Gorin, Gorren, Gorrin*

Gordon (Old English) Fertilized pasture. *Gord, Gordain, Gordan, Gorden, Gordie, Gordin, Gordo, Gordonn, Gordun, Gordy, Gordyn, Gore, Gorham, Gorrell, Gorton*

Gorman (Irish) Small blue-eyed one. *Gormen*

Goro (Japanese) Fifth.

Gosheven (Native American) Leaper.

Govert (Dutch) Heavenly peace.

Gower (Old English) Crooked coastline. (French) Harness maker. *Gowar, Gowell*

Gracia (Latin) Nice; welcome.

Grady (Latin) Rank. *Gradea, Gradee, Gradey, Gradi, Gradie, Graidee, Graidey, Graidi, Graidie, Graidy, Graydee*

Graham (Latin) Grain. (English) Gray home. *Graeham, Graehame, Graeme, Grahame, Grahem, Grahim, Grahime, Grahm, Graihame, Gram, Grayham, Greyham, Greyhame*

Grand (English) Grand; superior.

Granger (French) Farm steward. *Grainger, Grange, Graynger*

Grant (French) To give. *Grandt, Grantham, Granthem*

Grantley (English) Great meadow. *Grantlea, Grantlee, Grantleigh, Grantli, Grantlie, Grantly*

Granville (French) Big town. *Gran, Granvel, Granvil, Granvile, Granvill, Granvyl, Granvyll, Granvylle, Grenville, Greville*

Gratiano (Italian) Grace. (Shakespearean) Character from *The Merchant of Venice*.

Gray (Old English) To shine. *Grai, Graydon, Graye, Grayson, Greeley, Grey, Greye, Griswold*

Grayden (English) Gray-haired. *Graden, Graeden, Graedin, Graiden*

Grayson (English) Baliff's son. *Graeson, Graison, Graysen*

Greeley (English) Gray meadow. *Greelea, Greeleigh, Greeli, Greelie, Greely*

Green (English) The color green. (Shakespearean) Character from *King Richard II*. *Greener*

Greer (Greek) Watchful. *Grear, Grier*

Gregory (Greek) Watchman. *Gero, Gragos, Graig, Greg, Greger, Gregg, Gregoire, Gregoor, Gregor, Gregori, Gregorio, Gregorios, Gregorius, Gregson, Gregus, Greig, Greis, Gries, Grig, Grigg, Grigor, Grigori, Grigson, Griogair, Grioghar, Grischa, McGregor*

Gremio (English) Enrages. (Shakespearean) Character from *The Taming of the Shrew*.

Gresham (English) From the grazeland. *Grisham*

Griffin (English) Mythological beast—half lion, half eagle—charged with watching over golden treasures. (Latin) Hooked nose. (Welsh) Red; ruddy. *Griff, Griffie, Griffith, Griffon, Griffyn, Griffynn, Gryffin, Gryffyn, Gryphon*

Griffith (Welsh) Fierce chief. *Griffeth, Griffie, Griffy, Gryffith*

Grimshaw (English) Dark woods. *Grymshaw*

Griswold (German, French) Gray forest. *Gris, Griswald, Griswaldo, Griswoldo, Griz, Grizwald, Gryswald, Gryswaldo*

Grover (English) One who tends the groves. *Grove*

Grumio (English) Enrages. (Shakespearean) Character from *The Taming of the Shrew*.

Guadalupe (Arabic) Wolf valley. *Guadalope*

Guaina (Quechua) Young.

Guard (English) Sentry; watchman.

Guiderius (Latin) Guide. (Shakespearean) Character from *Cymbeline*.

Guido (Spanish) Guide.

Guildenstern (English) Courtier. (Shakespearean) Character from *Hamlet*.

Guillermo (Spanish) Resolute; protector. *Gillermo, Gughilmo, Guilherme, Guillaume, Gwillyn, Gwilym, William*

Guinness (English) Brand of beer.

Guion Origin and meaning unknown.

Guir (Irish) Beige.

Gunnar (Old Norse) War. *Guenter, Guenther, Gun, Guner, Gunn, Guntar, Gunter, Guntero, Gunther*

Gus (Scandinavian) Short form of Anugs, Augustine, and Gustave. *Guss, Gussie, Gussy, Gusti, Gustry, Gusty*

Gustave (Swedish) Goth. *Gus, Gustaaf, Gustaf, Gustaof, Gustav, Gustava, Gustaves, Gustavius, Gustavo, Gustavs, Gustavus, Gustik, Gustus, Gusztav*

Guthrie (Irish) War hero. *Guthre, Guthree, Guthrey, Guthri, Guthry*

Guy (French) Guide. *Guie, Guyon*

Gwidon (Polish) Life. *Gwydon*

Gwyn (Welsh) Fair; blessed. *Gmynn, Gwinn, Gwinne, Gwynne*

H

Haakon (Scandinavian) Highborn. *Haaken, Hacon, Hagan, Hakan, Hako, Hakon*

Habib (Arabic) Loved one; beloved. *Habeeb, Habyb*

Hackett (French) Little hewer of wood. *Hacket, Hackit, Hackitt, Hackyt, Hackytt*

Haddad (Arabic) Blacksmith. *Hadad*

Hadden (Old English) Heath. *Haddan, Haddon, Haddyn*

Haden (English) Form of Hadden. *Hadan, Hadin, Hadon, Hadun*

Hadi (Arabic) Rightly guide. *Haddi, Hadee, Hady*

Hadley (Old English) Heather meadow. *Had, Hadlea, Hadlee, Hadleigh, Hadly, Leigh*

Hadrian (Greek) Wealthy; form of Adrian. *Hadrien, Hadrion, Hadryan, Hadryen, Hadryin, Hadryn, Hadryon*

Hadwin (English) Friend in time of war. *Hadwen, Hadwinn, Hadwyn, Hadwynne*

Hafez (Arabic) Keeper.

Hagan (Irish) Little Hugh. (German) Strong. *Haggan*

Hagar (Hebrew) Stranger. *Hager, Hagir, Hagor, Hagr*

Hagen (Irish) Young. *Hagin, Hagon, Hague, Hagun*

Haggai (Hebrew) Feast.

Hagley (Old English) Enclosed meadow. *Haglea, Haglee, Hagleigh, Hagli, Haglie, Hagly*

Hahn (German) Rooster.

Haidar (Arabic) Lion. *Haider, Haydar, Hyder*

Hailama (Hawaiian) Famous brother. *Hailamah, Hailaman, Hairama, Hilama*

Haines (English) From the vine-covered cottage. *Hanes, Haynes*

Haing (Cambodian) Cambodian American physician and actor best known for Academy Award for *The Killing Fields*.

Hakaku (Japanese) White crane.

Hakeem (Arabic) Wise. *Hakam, Hakem, Hakiem, Hakim, Hakym*

Hakon (Scandinavian) Of Nordic ancestry. *Haaken, Haakin, Haeo, Hak*

Halbert (Old English) Shining hero. *Bert, Halbirt, Halburt, Halbyrt*

Halden (Scandinavian) Half Danish. *Hal, Haldin, Haldon, Hall*

Haldor (Norse) Rock of Thor; Norse god of thunder.

Haley (Old English) Hay meadow. *Hail, Hailey, Haily, Hale, Haleigh, Halley, Hallie, Hayl, Hayle, Hayleigh, Hayley, Hayli*

Halil (Turkish) Dear friend. *Halill, Halyl*

Hall (Old English) Meeting room.

Hallam (Old English) Valley. *Halam, Hallem*

Hallan (English) Dweller at the hall. *Hailan, Halan, Halin, Haylon*

Halley (English) Meadow near the hall. *Hallee, Halleigh, Halli, Hally, Haly*

Halliwell (English) Holy well. *Haliwel, Haliwell, Halliwel, Hallywel*

Halsey (Old English) From Hal's island. *Hallsea, Hallsey, Hallsy, Halsea, Halsy*

Halton (English) Estate on the hill. *Haltan, Halten, Haltin, Haltyn*

Halvor (Norwegian) Rock. *Hainar, Hallvard, Halvar, Halvard*

Halwn (Australian) Meaning unknown.

Hamal (Arabic) Lamb. *Amahl, Amal, Hamahl, Hamel, Hamol*

Hamaliel (American) Angel of logic; August. *Humatiel*

Hamar (Scandinavian) Hammer. *Hamer, Hammar, Hammer*

Hamid (Arabic) Thankful to God. *Haamid, Hamaad, Hamadi, Hamd, Hamdrem, Hammad, Hammyd, Hammydd, Humayd, Mohammed*

Hamil (English) Scarred. *Hamel, Hamell, Hamil, Hammil*

Hamilton (Old English) Flat-topped hill. *Hamel, Hamell, Hamelton, Hamil, Hamill, Hamiltyn, Hammill, Hamylton*

Hamish (Scottish) He who supplants; form of James. *Hamysh*

Hamlet (Old German) Home. (Shakespearean) Character from *Hamlet*. *Ham, Hamlin, Hamlit, Hamlot, Hammond, Hampton*

Hamlin (German) Loves his home. *Hamblin, Hamelen, Hamlyn, Lin*

Hammet (German) Village; home. *Hammett, Hamnet, Hamnett*

Hammond (English) Village. *Hammon, Hammund, Hamond, Hamund*

Hamon (Greek) Faithful one.

Hamza (Arabic) Lion. *Hamzah, Hamze, Hamzeh, Hamzia*

Hanan (Hebrew) Grace. *Hananel, Hananiah, Johann*

Hania (Native American) Spirit warrior.

Hanley (English) High meadow. *Handlea, Handlee, Hanleigh, Hanly*

Hannes (Scandinavian) The Lord is gracious. (Hindi) Swan. *Hanes, Hanns, Hans, Hansel, Hanss, Hanus, Hanzel*

Hannibal (Old English) Steep incline. *Anibal, Han, Hanley, Hannybal, Hanybal*

Haran (Hebrew) Mountaineer.

Harbin (German) Little warrior. *Harban, Harbon, Harbyn, Haren*

Hardicanute (Norse) Hard nose.

Hardy (Old English) Good health. *Hard, Hardee, Harden, Hardey, Hardi, Hardie, Hardin, Harding, Hardley*

Hari (Hindi) Sun; Vishnu. *Harin*

Harkin (Irish) Dark red. *Harkan, Harken, Harkon, Harkyn*

Harlan (German) Flax. (Old English) Rabbit archer. *Arley, Harford, Harland, Harle, Harlea, Harlee, Harlen, Harlenn, Harley, Harlin, Harlow, Harlyn, Harlynn*

Harlem (American) Place name.

Harmendra (Indian) Moon.

Harmon (Greek) Harmony. (Old English) Soldier. (Latin) Noble. *Harm, Harman, Harmann, Harmin, Harmond, Harms, Harmyn, Hermen*

Harold (Old German) Commander. *Hal, Harild, Harolda, Harrel, Harrell, Harry, Haryld, Herald, Hereld, Herlad, Herold, Heroldo, Heronim, Herrick, Herrold, Herryck, Heryld, Hiraldo*

Harper (Old Norse) Whaler. *Harp, Harpo*

Harrison (English) Son of Harry. *Harison, Harreson, Harrisen, Harrisson*

Harry (Old English) Army ruler. (German) Ruler of the household. *Harray, Harrey, Harri, Harrie, Harris, Harrison, Hary*

Harsh (Arabic) Joy. *Harshad, Harshal, Harshi, Harshini, Harshit, Harshita*

Harshul (Hindi) Deer.

Hart (English) Stag. *Harte, Hartley, Hartman, Hartwell, Hartwig, Heart*

Hartley (English) Deer meadow. *Hartlea, Hartlee, Hartleigh, Heartley*

Hartwell (English) Deer well. *Hartwel, Hartwil, Harwell*

Haru (Japanese) Born in spring.

Harun (Arabic) Superior.

Harvey (Old German) Battle. *Harv, Harvard, Harve, Harvee, Harvie, Harvy, Herv, Herve*

Hasan (Arabic) Good-looking. *Hasain, Hasani, Hasaun, Hashaan, Hason, Hassan, Hassani, Hassian, Hassun, Heseny, Nasanni*

Haskel (English) Ash tree; form of Ezekiel. *Haskell*

Haslett (English) Hazel tree land. *Haslet, Hazel, Hazlet, Hazlitt*

Hastings (Old English) Son of the austere man. *Hastey, Hastie, Hasting, Hasty*

Havelock (Norwegian) Sea battler. *Haveloc, Haveloch, Havlocke*

Haven (Dutch) Harbor. *Haeven, Havan, Havin, Havon*

Havika (Hawaiian) Beloved.

Hawk (Old English) Falcon. *Hawke, Hawkin, Hawkins*

Hawley (English) Hedged meadow. *Hawlea, Hawlee, Hawleigh, Hawli*

Hawthorne (Old English) Where hawthorn trees grow. *Hawthorn*

Hayden (Old English) Hay field. *Haidan, Haidin, Haidn, Haydan, Haydenn, Haydin, Haydn, Haydun, Haydyn, Heydan, Heyden, Heydin, Heydn, Heydon, Heydun, Heydyn*

Hayes (Old English) Hedged area. *Hais, Haiz, Haize, Hays, Hayse, Hayz*

Haywood (Old English) Hedged forest. *Heiwood, Heywood, Woody*

Hearn (Scottish) Form of Ahearn. *Hearne, Herin, Hern, Herne*

Heathcliff (English) Cliff near a heath. *Heafclif, Heafcliff, Heaffclif, Heaffcliff,*

Heaffcliffe, Heaffclyffe, Heath, Heathclif, Heathcliffe, Heathclyffe

Heaton (English) High ground. *Heatan, Heaten, Heatin, Heatyn*

Heavy D (American) Rapper Dwight Errington Myers.

Heber (Hebrew) Partner. *Hebar, Hebor*

Hector (Greek) Anchor. *Heckter, Heckter, Hecktir, Hecktore, Hecktur, Hectar, Hektar, Hektir, Hektor, Hektore, Hektur*

Hedley (Old English) Heathered meadow. *Headleigh, Headley, Headly, Heddlea, Heddlee, Heddleigh, Heddley, Heddli, Heddlie, Hedly*

Hedwig (German) Fighter. *Heddwig, Heddwyg, Hedwyg*

Hedwyn (Welsh) Friend of peace. *Heddwin, Heddwyn, Hedwen, Hedwin*

Heinrich (German) Ruler of the household. *Heine, Heiner, Heini, Heinie, Heinreich, Heinric, Heinriche, Heinrick, Heinrik, Heynric, Heynrich, Heynrick, Heynrik, Hinric, Hinrich, Hinrick, Hynric, Hynrich, Hynrick, Hynrik*

Heinz (Hebrew) God is gracious. *Hines*

Helaku (Native American) Full of sun.

Helicanus (Shakespearean) Character from *Pericles*.

Helios (Greek) God of the sun.

Heller (German) Sun.

Hello (French) Greeting; surprise. *Halo*

Helmut (English) Helmet. *Hellmut, Hellmuth, Helmaer, Helmuth*

Hendrick (Old English) Lord's manor. *Hedric, Hedrick, Heindric, Heindrick, Hendric, Hendricks, Hendrickson, Hendrik, Hendrikus, Hendrix, Hendryc, Hendryck, Hendrycks, Hendryx, Henric, Henrik*

Henley (Old English) High meadows. *Henlea, Henlee, Henleigh, Henli, Henlie, Henly*

Hennessy (Irish) Surname.

Henoch (Yiddish) Initiator. *Enoch, Henock, Henok*

Henry (German) House ruler. *Enrico, Enrique, Enzio, Hal, Hank, Harris, Harrison, Harry, Hawke, Hawkin, Hawkins, Heinrich, Heinz, Henderson, Henke, Henny, Henri, Henriot, Henrique, Henryk, Parry, Petty*

Hephaestus (Greek) God of the crafts.

Herbert (Old English) Exalted ruler. (German) Shining army. *Bert, Bertie, Erberto, Harbert, Herb, Herbie, Heribert, Heriberto*

Hercules (Greek) Hera's glory. *Ercole, Ercolo, Ercule, Herakles, Herc, Hercule, Herculie*

Herman (German) Soldier. *Armand, Armando, Ermanno, Herm, Hermann, Hermie, Hermy, Herrick*

Hermes (Greek) Messenger. *Ermes, Hermilio, Hermite, Hermus*

Hernan (Spanish) Adventurous. (German) Peacemaker.

Herrick (German) War ruler. *Herick, Herik, Herryck, Heryc*

Herring (English) Small fish.

Hershel (German) Deer. *Hersch, Herschel, Herschell, Hersey, Hersh, Hershal, Hershey, Hertz, Herzel, Herzl, Heschel, Heshel, Hirsch, Hirschel, Hirschl, Hirsh, Hirshel*

Herve (English) Bitter. *Herv, Hervee, Hervey, Hervi, Hervie, Hervy*

Hewitt (German) Little smart one. *Hewet, Hewie, Hewlett, Hughlet*

Hezekiah (Hebrew) God is my strength. *Hazikiah, Hez, Hezeki, Hezekia, Hezekial, Hezekyah, Hezikyah*

Hiamovi (Native American) High chief. *Hyamovi*

Hickory (English) Hickory tree.

Hideaki (Japanese) Clever. *Hideo, Hydeaki*

Hiemo (Latin) Winter.

Hieronimo (Greek) Form of Jerome. *Hierome, Hieronimos, Hieronymo*

Hieronymus (Greek) Holy name. *Hieronymous*

Hilario (Spanish) Happy. (Latin) Cheerful. *Hilarius*

Hilary (Latin) Cheerful. *Hi, Hil, Hilaire, Hilery*

Hildebrand (German) Battle sword. *Hildabrand, Hildebrando, Hildo, Hildreth, Hill*

Hilel (Hebrew) Greatly praised. *Hillel, Hylel, Hyllel*

Hilmar (Swedish) Famous; noble. *Hillmar, Hilmer, Hylmar, Hylmer*

Hilton (Old English) Hill settlement. *Hillton, Hylton*

Hinto (Native American) Blue. *Hynto*

Hipparchus (Greek) Greek astronomer from the late second century B.C.E. *Hipparcos*

Hippias (Greek) Tyrant of Athens in fifth century B.C.E.; sophist; teacher of philosophy; quibbler.

Hippocrates (Greek) Horse.

Hiram (Hebrew) Noble one. *Hi, Hirom, Huram, Hy, Hyram, Hyrum*

Hiromasa (Japanese) Fair; just.

Hiroshi (Japanese) Generous. *Hyroshi*

Hisoka (Japanese) Secretive. *Hysoka*

Hitesh (Hindi) Good person.

Ho (Chinese) Good.

Hobart (Danish) Bart's Hill. (German) Bright mind; bright spirit. *Bart, Hobard, Hobarte, Hobert, Hobie, Hoebard, Hoebart*

Hodding (Dutch) Bricklayer.

Hoel (Scottish) Father of Isolde.

Hogan (Irish) Youth. *Hogen, Hogun, Hogyn, Hoin*

Hogarth (Norse) Hilltop garden. *Hoagy, Hogie*

Holata (Native American) Alligator.

Holden (Old English) Valley. *Holbrook, Holdan, Holdin, Holdon, Holdun, Holdyn*

Holgernes (Shakespearean) Character from *Love's Labour's Lost*.

Holland (French) Place name, province of the Netherlands. (Shakespearean) Character from *Henry VI*. *Holand, Hollan*

Hollis (Old English) Holy day; grove of holly trees. *Hollie, Holliss, Hollister, Holly, Hollys, Hollyss*

Holm (Norse) Island. *Holmes, Holms*

Holt (English) Forest. *Holtan, Holten, Holtin, Holton*

Homer (Greek) Promise. *Homar, Homere, Homero, Homeros, Homerus, Omero*

Honore (French) Honored one. *Honorato, Honoratus, Honoray, Honorio*

Honorius (Latin) Man of honor. (Italian) Honor.

Honovi (Native American) Strong.

Hopper (Saxon) Dancer.

Horace (Greek) Behold. (Latin) Keeper of the hours. *Horacio, Horatio, Horatius, Horazio, Orazio*

Hormisdas (Italian) Saint Hormisdas was a widower and a Roman deacon at the time of his ascension to the papal throne.

Hormoz (Arabic) Character from *Shahnameh*, eleventh-century *Epic of Kings* by the Persian poet Firdowski.

Horst (German) Thicket.

Hortensio (Italian) Garden. (Latin) Garden lover. (Shakespearean) Character from *The Taming of the Shrew*. *Hortensius*

Horton (Latin) Garden. (Old English) Gray settlement. *Hort, Hortan, Horten, Hortun, Hortyn, Orton*

Hosea (Hebrew) Salvation. *Hoseia, Hoshea, Hosheah, Hosheia*

Hoshi (Japanese) Star.

Houston (English) Town house. *Hewson, Houstan, Houstun, Houstyn, Huston, Hutcheson, Hutchinson*

Hovie (American) Legendary southern gospel singer Hovie Lister.

Howard (English) Protector of the home. *Howerd, Howie, Ward*

Howe (English) Hill. *Hough, Houghton, Howden, Howel, Howell, Howells*

Howie (English) Form of Howland. *Howee, Howey, Howy*

Hoyt (English) Small boat. *Hoit, Hoyce, Hoyle, Hoyts*

Hsin (Chinese) After ancient dynasty. (Norse) Spirit.

Huang Fu (Chinese) Rich future.

Hubert (German) Shining spirit. *Hub, Hubbard, Hubbell, Huberto, Hubie, Hubirt, Hubyrt, Hugibert, Huibert, Uberto*

Hudson (Old English) Son of Hud. *Hud, Hudsan, Hudsin, Hudsyn*

Hugh (German) Bright soul. *Hew, Huego, Huet, Huey, Hughes, Hughie, Hugi, Hugo, Ugo*

Hui K'o (Chinese) Able wisdom.

Hui-Chao (Chinese) Wise illumination.

Hulk (Old English) Heavyweight. (American) Comic character.

Humbert (German) Famous giant. *Humberto, Humbirt, Humbyrt, Umberto*

Hume (Norse) Lakeside hill; careful. *Holm, Holmes*

Humphrey (Old English) Peaceful force. *Humfrey, Humfri, Humfrid, Humfrie, Humfried, Humph, Humpherey, Humphree, Humphry, Humphrys, Humpty, Humpy, Hunfredo*

Huni (German) Peace.

Hunt (Old English) Search. *Hunta, Huntar, Hunter, Huntington, Huntley, Huntur*

Huritt (Native American) Handsome.

Hurley (Irish) Sea tide. *Hurlea, Hurlee, Hurleigh, Hurli, Hurlie, Hurly*

Hurst (English) Thicket of trees. *Hearst, Hirst, Hyrst*

Husamettin (Turkish) Sharp sword.

Hussain (Arabic) Good; small handsome one. *Hossain, Husain, Husani, Husayn, Husein, Husian, Hussan, Hussayn, Hussin*

Huston (English) Form of Houston. *Hustin*

Hutch (German) Hutch dweller. *Hutcheson, Hutchinson*

Hutton (Old English) Settlement on the bluff. *Hut, Hutan, Huten, Hutin, Huton, Hutt, Huttan, Hutten, Huttin, Huttun, Huttyn, Hutun, Hutyn*

Huxley (English) Ash-tree field. *Hux, Huxford, Huxlea,*

Huxlee, Huxleigh, Huxli, Huxlie, Huxly

Hyatt (Old English) Lofty gate. *Hayatt, Hiat, Hiatt, Hiatte, Hyat, Hyatte*

Hydrus (Greek) Lesser snake.

Hyginus (Greek) Healthy.

Hyman (Hebrew) Life; god of marriage. *Hayim, Hayvim, Hayyim, Hy, Hyland*

Hyo (Korean) Familial duty.

Hypnos (Greek) God of sleep.

Hyun-Ki (Korean) Wise.

Hyun-Shik (Korean) Clever.

Hyun-Su (Korean) Long life.

I

Iachima (Japanese) Lotus.

Iago (Latin, Spanish) Supplanter. (Shakespearean) Character from *Othello*. *Jago*

Iakobos (Greek) Supplanter. *Iakov, Iakovos, Iakovs*

Ian (Scottish) God is gracious. *Eian, Iain, Iane, Ianna, Iantha, Ianthe, Iin, Ion*

Ib (Danish) Oath of Baol.

Ibeamaka (African) The agnates are splendid.

Ibrahim (Arabic) Form of Abraham. *Ibrahaim, Ibraham, Ibraheem, Ibraheim, Ibrahiem, Ibrahiim*

Ibsen (German) Archer's son. *Ibsan, Ibsin, Ibson, Ibsyn*

Icarus (Greek) Legendary figure. *Icharus*

Ichabod (Hebrew) Departed glory. *Icobod*

Iden (English) Pasture in the wood. *Idan, Idin, Idon, Idun*

Idris (Welsh) Eager lord. *Idrease, Idrees, Idres, Idress, Idreus, Idriece, Idriss, Idrissa, Idriys, Idryss, Idys*

Ignado (Spanish) Fire. *Ignaas, Ignac, Ignacio, Ignaz, Ignazio*

Ignatius (Latin) Fiery. *Iggy, Ignace, Ignacey, Ignacius, Ignatas, Ignatios, Ignatus, Ignatys, Ignatz, Ignaze*

Igor (Scandinavian) Hero; form of George. *Igoryok*

Iham (Indian) Expected.

Ike (Hebrew) He will laugh. *Ikee, Ikey, Ikke*

Il Sung (Korean) Sincere.

Ilan (Hebrew) Tree. *Eilon, Elam, Elan, Ilon*

Ilia (Hebrew) God is Lord. *Ilija, Illia, Illya, Ilya, Ilyah*

Ilias (Greek) The Lord is my God. (Hebrew) Jehovah is God. (Arabic) Prophet's name. *Illyas, Ilyas, Ilyes*

Ilie (Slavic) The Lord is God.

Illanipi (Native American) Amazing.

Imad (Arabic) Support; pillar.

Imam (Hebrew) Short form of Immanuel.

Imhotep (Egyptian) He comes in peace.

Immanuel (Hebrew) God with us. *Emanuel, Emanuele, Emmanouil, Emmanuel, Emmanuelle, Imanol, Imanual, Imanuel, Imanuele,*

Immanual, Immanuele, Immuneal, Manny, Manoel, Manuel

Imran (Arabic) Host. *Imraan, Imren, Imrin, Imryn*

Imre (Hebrew) Well spoken. *Imray, Imri, Imrie*

In Ho (Korean) Meaning unknown.

In Su (Korean) Meaning unknown.

Inder (Hindi) Godlike. *Inderbir, Inderjeet, Inderjit, Inderpal, Inderpreet, Inderveer, Indervir, Indra, Indrajit*

Indiana (English) Land of the Indians. *Indy*

Indigo (Greek) Dark blue.

Indro (Italian) Man of the forest; woodsman.

Inerney (Irish) Steward of church lands.

Ing (German) Mythical fertility god. *Inge*

Ingelbert (German) Form of Engelbert. *Ingelberte, Ingelbirt, Ingelbyrt, Inglebert*

Ingmar (Scandinavian) Famous son. *Ingamar, Ingamur, Ingemar*

Ingram (German) Raven. *Graham, Gram, Ingham, Ingraham, Ingrem, Ingrim*

Ingvar (Scandinavian) He who is foremost. *Ingevar, Ingvarr, Yngvar*

Innis (Irish) Island. *Inis, Iniss, Inniss, Innys, Innyss*

Innocent (Latin) Harmless. (English) Innocence. *Innocenty, Innocentz, Innocenz, Innocenzyo, Inocenci, Inocencio, Inocente, Inocenzio*

Inyri (Science fiction) Character from *Star Wars*.

Ioan (Greek) God is gracious. (Hebrew) Gift from God. *Ioane, Ioann, Ioannes, Ioannikios, Ioannis, Ione, Ionel*

Ira (Hebrew) Watchful. *Irah*

Iravan (Hindi) Son of Arjuna/Uloopi.

Irin (Hebrew) Those who watch; peace.

Irmin (German) Strong. *Irman, Irmen, Irmun, Irmyn*

Ironside (Scottish) In Arthurian legend, the knight who slaughtered all the knights except Gareth.

Irving (Old English) Sea friend. *Irven, Irvin, Irvine, Irvinn, Irvon, Irvyn, Irwin, Irwyn*

Isaac (Hebrew) Laughter. *Ike, Isaack, Isaak, Isaakios, Isac, Isacco, Isak, Ishaq, Isiac, Issac, Issaic, Issiac, Itzak, Izak, Yitzchak, Zach*

Isaiah (Hebrew) Salvation of the Lord. *Isa, Isaia, Isaid, Isaih, Isaya, Isayah, Isiah, Isish, Issia, Issiah, Izaiah, Izaiha, Izaya, Izayah, Izayaih, Izayiah, Izeyah*

Isam (Arabic) Safeguard.

Ishan (Hindi) Direction. *Ishaan, Ishaun*

Ishmael (Hebrew) God will hear. *Isamael, Isamail, Ishma, Ishmail, Ishmale, Ishmeal, Ishmeil, Ishmel, Ishmil, Ismael, Ismail*

Isidro (Spanish) Gifted with many ideas. *Chidro, Isidoro*

Israel (Hebrew) Wrestled with God. *Iser, Israele, Israhel, Isreal, Isrell, Isrieal, Isrrael, Isser, Izrael*

Issey (Japanese) Fashion designer.

Ithamar (Hebrew) Island of the palm tree. *Itamar, Ittamar*

Ither (Scottish) In Arthurian legend, killed by Percival.

Itsu (Japanese) One. *Ichi*

Ivan (Russian) God is gracious. *Evan, Iván, Ivanchik, Ivann, Ivano, Ivas, Iven, Ivin, Ivon, Ivun, Ivyn*

Ives (Old English) Little archer. *Ive, Ives, Yvan, Yves, Yvo*

Ivo (German) Cut wood. *Ivonnie, Ivor, Yvo, Yvonne*

Izaak (Hebrew) Form of Isaac.

J

Jaap (Dutch) Form of Jim. *Jape*

Jabari (Swahili) Fearless. *Jababri, Jabarae, Jabare, Jabaree, Jabarei, Jabarie, Jabarri, Jabarrie, Jabary, Jabbaree, Jabbari, Jabiari, Jabier, Jabori, Jaborie*

Jabbar (Arabic) Foxer. *Jabaar, Jaber*

Jabez (Hebrew) Born in pain. *Jabar, Jabe, Jabes, Jabesh*

Jabin (Hebrew) God has created. *Jabain, Jabien, Jabon, Jabyn*

Jabir (Arabic) Comforter. *Jabiri, Jabori, Jabyr*

Jabril (Arabic) Archangel of Allah. *Jabrail, Jabree, Jabreel, Jabrel*

Jacari (American) Form of Jacorey. *Jacarey, Jacaris, Jacarre, Jacarri*

Jace (American) Moon. (Greek) Healer. *J. C., Jacee, Jaci, Jacie, Jaece, Jaecee, Jaecey*

Jacek (Polish) Lily; male. *Jaeci, Jaice, Jaicee, Jaicey, Jaici, Jaicy*

Jacen (Greek) Form of Jason. *Jaceon, Jacon, Jacyn*

Jachin (Hebrew) He who strengthens. *Jacin*

Jacinto (Portuguese) Hyacinth. *Jacindo, Jacint, Jacinta, Jacynto*

Jack (American) Form of Jacob. *Jac, Jacko, Jak, Jax*

Jackal (Sanskrit) Wild dog. *Jackel, Jackell, Jackyl, Jackyll*

Jackson (English) Son of Jack. *Jacksen, Jacksin, Jacson, Jakson*

Jacob (Hebrew) Supplanter. *Cob, Cobb, Giacobo, Giacomo, Iacovo, Iago, Jaccob, Jachob, Jacinto, Jackib, Jackob, Jaco, Jacoba, Jacobb, Jacobi, Jacobina, Jacobine, Jacobo, Jacobson, Jacopo, Jacques, Jacub, Jaecob, Jaicob, Jake, Jakob, Jakub, Jalu, Jascha, Jayme, Jeb, Jecis, Jeks, Jeska, Jocek, Jock, Jocob, Jocobb, Jokubus, Yaacov, Yacov, Yago, Yakov*

Jacques (French) Supplanter; substitute. *Jackques, Jackquise, Jacot, Jacquan, Jacque, Jacquees, Jacquel, Jacquese, Jacquess, Jacquet, Jacquett, Jacquez, Jacquis, Jacquise, Jaques, Jaquese, Jaqueus, Jaquez, Jaqueze, Jaquis, Jaquise, Jaquze, Jarques, Jarquis*

Jacy (Native American) Moon.

Jade (Spanish) Precious stone. *Jaed, Jaeid, Jaid, Jayd*

Jaden (Hebrew) God heard. *Jadan, Jadee, Jadeen, Jadenn,*
Jadeon, Jadin, Jadon, Jadyne, Jaiden, Jayden

Jadrien (American) Combination of Jay and Adrien. *Jadrian, Jaedrian, Jaidrian, Jaidrien*

Jae-Hwa (Korean) Rich.

Jaegue (German) Hunter. *Jaager, Jaeger, Jagur, Jaygur*

Jafar (Sanskrit) Little stream. *Ja'far, Jafari, Jaffar, Jaffer, Jafur*

Jagger (English) Carter. *Gagger, Jagar, Jaggar*

Jaguar (Spanish) Jaguar. *Jagguar*

Jaideep (Hindi) Light of the universe.

Jair (Spanish) God enlightens. *Jairay, Jaire, Jairo, Jayrus*

Jairus (Hebrew) My light; who diffuses light.

Jakeem (Arabic) Uplifted. *Jakeam, Jakim, Jakym*

Jalal (Hindi) Revered. *Jalaal, Jalil*

Jaleel (Arabic) Loftiness; glory. *Jalal, Jaleell, Jaleil, Jalel*

Jalen (American) Combination of Ja and Len. *Jailen, Jalaan, Jalen, Jalon, Jalone, Jalun, Jalynn*

Jamal (Arabic) Handsome. *Jaimal, Jamael, Jamala, Jamarl*

Jamar (African American) Handsome. *Jamaar, Jamaari, Jamaarie, Jamahrae, Jamair, Jamal, Jamalle, Jamara, Jamaras, Jamaraus, Jamarr, Jamarre, Jamarrea, Jamarree, Jamarri, Jamarvis, Jamaur, Jammar, Jarmar, Jarmarr, Jaumar, Jemaar, Jemar, Jimar*

Jamel (Arabic) Form of Jamal. *Jamell, Jamelle, Jamuel, Je-Mell, Jimell*

Jamen (Hebrew) Forms of Jamin. *Jaemon, Jamohn, Jamon, Jamoni*

James (Hebrew) Supplanter; substitute; patron saint of Spain. *Diego, Giacomo, Hamish, Jaemes, Jaemie, Jaemy, Jaime, Jaimes, Jaimie, Jame, Jameson, Jamesy, Jamey, Jameyel, Jameze, Jami, Jamia, Jamiah, Jamian, Jamiee, Jamiesen, Jamieson, Jamison, Jamme, Jammey, Jammie, Jammy, Jamy, Jamye, Jamze, Jan, Jay, Jaymes, Jaymie, Jim, Jimbo, Jimmie, Jimmy, Santiago, Seamus, Shamus, Sheamus*

Jamond (American) Combination of James and Raymond. *Jaemond, Jaimund, Jamod, Jamonta*

Jamsheed (Persian) From Persia. *Jamshaid, Jamshead, Jamshed*

Jan (Slavic) God is gracious. *Jahn, Jana, Janae, Jann, Jano, Jenda, Jhan, Yan*

Janica (Hebrew) God is gracious.

Janus (Latin) Passageway. *Jannese, Jannus, Januario, Janusz*

Japesh (Sanskrit) Lord of reciters.

Japhet (Hebrew) Handsome. *Japeth, Japheth, Yaphet*

Jaquan (American) Combination of Ja and Quan. *Jacquin, Jaquain, Jaquan, Jaquyn*

Jarah (Hebrew) Sweet as honey. *Jara, Jera, Jerah*

Jared (Hebrew) Descending. *Ja'red, Jahred, Jaired, Jaraed, Jaredd, Jareid, Jarett, Jariet, Jarit, Jarrett, Jarrod, Jarrot, Jerred*

Jarek (Polish) Born in January. *Januarius, Januisz, Jarec, Jareck, Jaric, Jarick, Jarik, Jarrek, Jarric, Jarrick, Jaryc, Jaryck, Jaryk*

Jarl (Scandinavian) Earl; nobleman. *Jarlee, Jarleigh, Jarley, Jarli, Jarlie, Jarly*

Jarlath (Latin) In control. *Jarlaf, Jarlen*

Jaron (Hebrew) He will sing. *J'ron, Jaaron, Jaeron, Jairon, Jarone, Jayron, Jayrone, Jayronn, Je Ronn*

Jarrell (English) Mighty spearman. *Jaerel, Jaerell, Jaerill, Jaeryl, Jaeryll, Jairel, Jairell, Jarael, Jareil, Jarelle, Jariel, Jarrel, Jarryl, Jarryll, Jayryl, Jayryll, Jerall, Jerrell, Jharell*

Jarvis (Old German) True spear. *Jaravis, Jarv, Jarvaris, Jarvas, Jarvaska, Jarvey, Jarvez, Jarvise, Jarvius, Jarvorice, Jarvoris, Jarvous, Jarvus, Jarvyc, Jarvyce, Jarvys, Jarvyse, Jervey, Jervis*

Jasbeer (Indian) Victorious hero.

Jase (Greek) Healer.

Jason (Greek) Healer. *Jaasan, Jaasen, Jaasin, Jaason, Jaasun, Jaasyn, Jaesan, Jaesen, Jaesin, Jaeson, Jaesun, Jaesyn, Jahsan, Jahsen, Jahson, Jasan, Jasaun, Jase, Jasin, Jasten, Jasun, Jasyn, Jayson*

Jasper (French) Red, brown, or yellow stone. *Jaspar, Jazper, Jespar*

Javan (Hebrew) Deceiver; one who makes sadness. (Latin) Angel of Greece. *Jaavan, Jaavon, Jaevin, Jaevon, Jaewan, Jaewon, Jahvaughan, Jahvon, Javaon, Javaughn, JaVaughn, Javen, Javian, Javien, Javin, Javine, Javion, Javionne, Javohn, Javon, Javona, Javone, Javoney, Javoni, Javonn, Javonne, Javonni, Javonnie, Javonnte, Javonta, Javontae, Javontai, Javontay, Javontaye, Javonte, Javonté, Javontee, Javontey, Javoun, Javyn, Jayvin, Jayvine*

Javed (Persian) Eternal; exempt from death.

Javier (French) Enlightened. (Spanish) New house. *Javy, Xavier, Xever*

Jawhar (Arabic) Jewel; essence.

Jax (English) God has been gracious. *Jaxon, Jaxen, Jaxsen, Jaxsun, Jaxun*

Jaxon (English) God has been gracious, has shown favor. (American) Son of Jack. *Jacksen, Jacsin, Jacson, Jakson*

Jay (Old French) Jay bird. (English) Supplanter; substitute. *Jai, Jave, Jaybird, Jeays, Jeyes*

Jay-Z (American) Celebrity born Shawn Corey Carter. *Jaze*

Jayant (Hindi) Victorious.

Jaydon (Hebrew) Form of Jaden.

Jaylen (American) Combination of Jay and Len. *Jayleen, Jaylun*

Jayvyn (African) Light spirit.

Jazz (American) Musical style popularized in the

early and mid-1900s. *Jaze, Jazzlee, Jazzman, Jazzy*

Jean (French) Form of John. *Jéan, Jeannah, Jeannot, Jeano, Jeanot, Jeanty, Jene*

Jebediah (Hebrew) Beloved by God. *Jebadia, Jebadiah, Jebadieh, Jebidia, Jebidiah, Jebidya, Jebydia, Jebydiah, Jebydya, Jebydyah, Jed, Jedadiah, Jeddediah, Jededia, Jedediah, Jedidia, Jedidiah, Jedidiyah, Yedidiah, Yedidya*

Jedrek (Polish) Strong. *Jedreck, Jedric, Jedrick, Jedrik, Jedryc*

Jeevan (Hindi) Life.

Jeeves (American) Common English term for butler.

Jefferson (English) Son of Jeff. *Gefferson, Jeffe, Jeffers, Jeffey, Jeph*

Jeffrey (Old French) Peaceful. *Geoff, Geoffrey, Godfrey, Jefarey, Jefarie, Jefary, Jeferee, Jeferey, Jeferi, Jeferie, Jefery, Jeff, Jeffaree, Jeffarey, Jeffari, Jeffarie, Jeffary, Jeffeory, Jefferay, Jefferee, Jeffereoy, Jefferey, Jefferi, Jefferie, Jefferies, Jeffers, Jefferson, Jeffery, Jeffory, Jeffrie, Jeffries, Jeffry, Joffrey*

Jelani (Swahili) Mighty. *Jel, Jelan, Jelanee, Jelaney, Jelanie, Jelany, Jelaun*

Jemond (French) Worldly. *Jemon, Jémond, Jemonde, Jemone, Jemun, Jemund*

Jenkin (Flemish) Little John. *Jenkins, Jenkyn, Jenkyns, Jennings*

Jenson (Scandinavian) Form of Janson. *Jensan, Jensin, Jenson, Jenssen*

Jenuro (Latin) Born in January.

Jeovanni (Italian) Form of Giovanni. *Jeovahny, Jeovan, Jeovanie, Jeovanny*

Jeremiah (Hebrew) Exalted of God. *Geremiah, Jaramia, Jemeriah, Jemiah, Jeramiha, Jere, Jereias, Jeremaya, Jeremia, Jeremial, Jeremias, Jeremija, Jeremya, Jeremyah, Jeri, Jerimiah, Jerimiha, Jerimya, Jerri, Jerrie, Jerry, Yirmeyah*

Jeremy (Hebrew) Chosen by God. *Dermot, Geremia, Jaremay, Jaremy, Jereamy, Jeremias, Jeremry, Jérémy, Jeremye, Jereomy, Jeriemy, Jerime, Jerimy, Jerremy, Jerry*

Jericho (Arabic) City of the moon. *Jeric, Jerick, Jericko, Jerico, Jeriko, Jerric, Jerricko, Jerrico, Jerricoh, Jerriko, Jerrycko, Jerryco, Jerryko*

Jermaine (English) Sprout. *Jarman, Jer-Mon, Jermanie, Jermiane*

Jermyn (Latin) German. *Germain, Germaine, German, Jer-Mon, Jeremaine, Jeremane, Jerimane, Jermaine, Jerman, Jermane, Jermanie, Jermanne, Jermany, Jermayn, Jermayne, Jermiane, Jermine, Jermoney, Jhirmaine*

Jerney (Slavic) Form of Bartholomew.

Jerolin (Latin) Holy. *Jerolyn*

Jerome (Latin) Sacred name. *Gerome, Jeroen, Jerom, Jérome, Jérôme, Jeromee, Jeromey, Jeromie, Jeromo, Jeromy, Jerrome, Jerromy, Jerry*

Jerrold (Spanish) Rules by the spear. *Jeraldo, Jerold, Jerrald*

Jerry (German) Mighty spearman. *Jehri, Jeree, Jeri, Jerie, Jeris, Jerison, Jerree, Jerri, Jerrie, Jery*

Jerzy (Polish) Form of George. *Jersey, Jerzey, Jerzi, Jurek*

Jesper (French) Jasperstone.

Jesse (Hebrew) Wealth. *Jescee, Jescey, Jese, Jesee, Jesi, Jesie, Jessyie, Jesy, Jezze, Jezzee, Jezzey, Jezzi, Jezzie, Jezzy*

Jesuedo (German) He who takes the lead.

Jesus (Hebrew) God will help. *Jecho, Jessus, Jesu, Jesús, Jezus, Josu, Yesus*

Jet (English) Hard, black mineral. *Jetson, Jetter*

Jethro (Hebrew) Preeminence. *Jeth, Jethroe, Jetro, Jetrow, Jettro*

Jevonte (African American) Son of Jeptheh. *Jevonta, Jevontae, Jevontaye, Jevonté*

Jiang (Chinese) Fire.

Jibade (African) Born close to royalty. *Jibad, Jybad, Jybade*

Jibben (Gypsy) Life. *Jibin*

Jibril (Arabic) Archangel of Allah. *Jibreel, Jibriel*

Jikai (Japanese) Ocean of compassion.

Jimmie (English) Form of Jim. *Jimee, Jimme, Jyme, Jymi*

Jin (Chinese) Gold.

Jin-Sang (Korean) Aid; truth and benevolence.

Jing (Chinese) Essence.

Jintao (Korean) Meaning unknown.

Jiri (Czech) Form of George. *Jirka*

Jiro (Japanese) Second son.

Jiryu (Japanese) Compassionate dragon.

Jitendra (Hindi) Conqueror.

Jiven (Hindi) Life giver. *Jivan, Jivanta, Jivon, Jyvan*

Joachim (Hebrew) God will judge. *Akim, Joakim, Joaquin, Jocheim, Jokim, Jov*

Job (Hebrew) Afflicted. *Jobe, Jobert*

Joben (Japanese) Enjoys cleanliness. *Joban, Jobin, Jobon, Jobyn*

Jodan (American) Combination of Joe and Dan. *Jodahn, Jodian, Jodin, Jodon*

Jody (Hebrew) God will increase; for boy or girl. *Jodey, Jodie, Jodiha, Joedee, Joedey, Joedi, Joedy*

Joel (Hebrew) The Lord is God. *Joël, Jõel, Joell, Joelle, Joely, Jole, Jolson, Yoel, Yohel*

John (Hebrew) God's grace. *Eoin, Hans, Hansen, Hanson, Iaian, Ian, Ivan, Jack, Jackson, Jaenda, Janco, Janos, Jansen, Janson, Jantje, Jehan, Jehann, Jenkin, Jenkins, Jenkyn, Jenkyns, Jenner, Jennings, Jens, Jense, Jentz, Jian, Jock, Jocko, Joen, Joenes, Joennes, Joenns, Johahn, Johan, Johanan, Johane, Johann, Johannan, Johannes, Johaun, Johnavon, Johne, Johnnie, Johnny, Johnsie, Johnson, Johon, Jone, Jones, Joness, Jonesy, Jonnel, Jontavious, Jovan, Juan, Juha, Juhana, Juhanah, Juhanna, Juhannah, Juho, Seain, Sean, Shane, Shawn, Zane*

Joji (Japanese) Form of George.

Jomei (Japanese) Spreads light. *Jomey*

Jonas (Hebrew) Dove. *Jonah, Jonahs, Jonass, Jonaus, Jonelis, Jonukas, Jonus, Jonutis, Jonys, Joonas, Yonah, Yonas*

Jonathan (Hebrew) God's gift. *Johnthan, Jon, Jonatane, Jonate, Jonatha, Jonathen, Jonathin, Jonathon, Jonathun, Jonathyn, Jonaton, Jonattan, Jonethen, Jonnatha, Jonnathon, Jonnathun, Jonnattan, Jonthon, Jounathon, Nat, Nate, Nathan, Yanaton*

Jons (Swedish) God is gracious.

Joost (Dutch) Just.

Joram (Hebrew) Jehovah is exalted. *Joran, Jorim*

Jordan (Hebrew) Descender. *Giordano, Jeordon, Johordan, Jordaan, Jordae, Jordain, Jordaine, Jordane, Jordani, Jordanio, Jordann, Jordanny, Jordano, Jordany, Jordayne, Jordáo, Jorden, Jordenn, Jordie, Jordin, Jordon, Jordun, Jordy, Jordyn, Jorrdan, Jory*

Joseph (Hebrew) He shall add. *Bepe, Beppe, Beppy, Cheche, Giuseppe, Iokepa, Iosef, Isoep, Jazeps, Jessup, Jo, Joe, Joey, Jooseppi, Joseba, Josef, Josep, Josephat, Josephe, Josephie, Josephus, José, Josheph, Josiah, Josias, Josie, Josip, Jóska, Joza, Joze, Jozef, Jozeph, Jozhe, Jozio, Jozka, Jozsi, Jozzepi, Jupp, Jusepe, Juziu, Keo, Osip, Pepa, Pepe, Pepito, Peppe, Pino, Seosaidh, Sepp, Yeska, Yosayf, Yosef, Yoseph, Yousef, Youssel, Yusef, Yusif, Zeusef*

Joshua (Hebrew) God of salvation. *Johsua, Johusa, Josh, Joshau, Joshaua, Joshauh, Joshawa, Joshawah, Joshia, Joshua, Joshuaa, Joshuah, Joshue, Joshuea, Joshuia, Joshula, Joshus, Joshusa, Joshuwa, Joshwa, Josiah, Jousha, Jozshua, Jozsua, Jozua, Yehosha*

Joze (Slavic) Meaning unknown.

Jozef (German) Form of Joseph. *Jozef, Jozeff*

Juan (Spanish) God is gracious; grace. (Hebrew) Gift from God. *Juanch, Juanchito, Juane, Juann, Juanun*

Judd (Hebrew) Praised. *Jud, Juda, Judah, Judas, Judda, Juddah, Juddas, Juddson, Jude, Judge, Yehuda, Yehudah, Yehudi*

Judson (English) Son of Judd.

Juhani (Finnish) God is gracious.

Julian (Latin) Youthful. (English) Love's child. *Giulo, Joles, Julas, Jule, Julean, Julen, Juleo, Jules, Juliaan, Julian, Julianne, Juliano, Julias, Julien, Juliene, Julienn, Julienne, Julio, Julion, Julious, Julius, Juliusz, Juliyo, Jullien, Jullin, Jullius, Juluis, Julyan, Julyen, Julyin, Julyo, Julyon*

Juma (Arabic) Born on a Friday. *Jimoh, Jumah*

Jun (Chinese) Truthful. *Joon, Junnie*

Jung Hee (Korean) Affection; honored and pleasant.

Junichiro (Japanese) Meaning unknown.

Junius (Latin) Young. *June, Junio, Junius, Junot*

Jussi (Finnish) Gift from God.

Justin (Old French) Justice. *Iestyn, Iustin, Jastin, Jobst, Jost, Jusa, Just, Justain, Juste, Justek, Justian, Justice, Justinas, Justinian, Justinius, Justinn, Justino, Justins, Justis, Justn, Justo, Justton, Justukas, Justun, Justus, Justyn, Ustin, Yustyn*

K

Kabil (Turkish) Form of Cain. *Kabar, Kabel, Kabieri, Kabyl, Khabir*

Kabir (Hindi) Spiritual leader.

Kabonero (African) Symbol.

Kabonesa (African) Born in hard times.

Kabos (Hebrew) Swindler.

Kabr (Hindi) Grass.

Kacy (American) Happy. *K. C., Kace, Kacee, Kacey, Kaci, Kaecey, Kaicee, Kase, Kasee, Kasy, Kaycee*

Kada (Hungarian) Meaning unknown.

Kadar (Arabic) Powerful. *Kade, Kedar*

Kade (Gaelic) Swamp.

Kadeem (African American) Newly created.

Kaden (American) Exciting. *Cade, Caden, Caiden, Caidin, Caidon, Caydan, Cayden, Caydin, Caydon, Kadan, Kadon, Kadyn, Kaiden*

Kadi (Irish) Pure. (American) Angel who presides over Friday.

Kadin (Arabic) Friend, companion. *Kadeen, Kaden*

Kadir (Arabic) Green. *Kadeer*

Kadmiel (Hebrew) God is first.

Kado (Japanese) Entrance.

Kaelan (Irish) Strong. *Kael, Kaelen, Kaelin, Kaelyn*

Kaga (Native American) Writer.

Kagan (German) Thinker.

Kahale (Hawaiian) Homebody.

Kahanu (Hawaiian) He breathes.

Kahil (Arabic) Friend; lover. *Cahil, Kahlil, Kaleel, Khaleel, Khalil*

Kahoku (Hawaiian) Star.

Kaholo (Hawaiian) Boy who runs.

Kahraman (Turkish) Hero.

Kai (Hawaiian) Ocean. (Greek) Earth. (Native American) Sea; willow tree. (Scottish) Fire. (Welsh) Keeper of the keys.

Kaid (English) Round; happy. *Caiden, Cayde, Caydin, Kaden, Kadin, Kayd*

Kaikara (Ugandan) Traditional name of God.

Kaikeapona (Hawaiian) Smooth skin.

Kailas (Indian) Abode of the Hindu god Shiva.

Kailin (Irish) Sporty. *Kailen, Kailyn, Kale, Kalen, Kaley, Kalin, Kaylen*

Kainon (Science fiction) Character from *Star Trek: Deep Space Nine.*

Kaipo (Hawaiian) Embraces.

Kaiser (German) Form of Caesar. *Kaesar, Kaisar, Kaizer, Kayser*

Kaisha (Japanese) To rewrite.

Kaj (Scandinavian) Earthy. *Kaje*

Kakumyo (Japanese) Clear awakening.

Kal-El (American) Character from *Superman.*

Kala (Hindi) Black. *Kalah*

Kalama (Hawaiian) Source of light. *Caramel, Kalam, Kalameli, Kalamelil, Kalamely, Kalan*

Kalani (Polynesian) Gallon. *Kalany, Kalonee, Kaloney*

Kalb (Arabic) Dog. *Kaleb*

Kale (Hawaiian) Strong and manly. *Kail, Kalolo, Karolo, Kayle, Kaylee, Kayley, Kaylie*

Kaleb (African) Old Testament Cain. *Caleb, Kailub, Kalaeb, Kalleb*

Kalei (Hawaiian) Joy. *Kalea*

Kaleo (Hawaiian) Pure.

Kalepa (Hawaiian) Faithful. *Kaleba*

Kalidas (Hindi) Poet; musician; slave of goddess Kali.

Kalil (Arabic) Beautiful, good friend. *Kahill, Kailil, Khalil*

Kalin (Greek) Handsome. *Kallan, Kallin, Kallon, Kallun, Kalon, Kalun, Kalyn*

Kalkin (Hindi) Tenth incarnation of God. *Vishnu*

Kalle (Scandinavian) Form of Carl.

Kallen (Greek) Handsome. *Kallan, Kallin, Kallon, Kallun, Kalon, Kalun, Kalyn*

Kalman (Hungarian) Strong and manly.

Kalpanath (Hindi) Meaning unknown.

Kalvin (Latin) Blessing; form of Calvin. *Kal, Kalvan, Kalvun*

Kamadev (Hindi) God of love.

Kamal (Hindi) Red. *Kamaal, Kamyl*

Kameron (Scottish) Crooked nose. *Kameren, Kammeron, Kammi, Kammie, Kammy, Kamran, Kamrin, Kamron*

Kamil (Arabic) Perfection. *Camillo, Kamillo*

Kamlesh (Hindi) God of lotus.

Kamon (American) Alligator. *Cayman, Caymun, Kame, Kammy, Kayman*

Kana (Hawaiian) God is my judge. *Kaniela*

Kanak (Hindi) Gold.

Kanan (Hindi) Forest.

Kanaye (Japanese) Zealous one.

Kance (American) Attractive; combination of Kane and Chance. *Cance, Cans, Kaince, Kans, Kanse, Kaynce*

Kando (Japanese) Penetrating insight.

Kane (Hawaiian) Man; eastern sky. (Irish) Honor, tribute. (Japanese) Doubly accomplished, golden man. (Scottish) Warlike. *Cain, Caine, Cane, Cathan, Kain, Kaine, Kainen, Kayne, Keyne*

Kang-Dae (Korean) Powerful and big.

Kange (Native American) Raven. *Kang, Kanga, Kangi, Kangie*

Kaniel (Hebrew) Stalk; reed. *Kan, Kani, Kanny*

Kannan (Hindi) Another name for the Hindu god Krishna. *Kanan, Kanin*

Kanoa (Hawaiian) Free.

Kant (German) Philosopher. *Cant*

Kanye (American) Rapper Kanye Omari West.

Kaori (Japanese) Strong. *Kaoru*

Kaper (American) Capricious. *Cape, Caper, Kahper, Kape*

Kapil (Hindi) Rishi, a Vedic poet.

Kaplony (Hungarian) Tiger.

Kapolcs (Hungarian) Meaning unknown.

Kapono (Hawaiian) Righteous.

Kappi (Gypsy) Form of Cappi. *Kappee, Kappey*

Karcher (German) Beautiful blond boy.

Kardal (Arabic) Mustard seed.

Kardos (Hungarian) Swordsman.

Kareem (Arabic) Charitable. *Kareem, Karim*

Karel (Czech) Man; Carl's town. *Karlicek, Karlik, Karlousek, Karol, Karoly*

Karey (Greek) Pure. (Welsh) Castle; rocky island. *Karee, Kari, Karrey, Karry*

Karif (Arabic) Fall born. *Kareef*

Karim (Arabic) Giving.

Karl (German) Man; Carl's town. *Karlen, Karlens, Karlin*

Karmel (Hebrew) Red-haired. *Carmel, Carmelo, Karmeli, Karmelli, Karmello, Karmelo, Karmi*

Karney (Irish) Wins. *Carney*

Karol (Czech) Form of Carl. *Karal, Karolek*

Karr (Scandinavian) Curly hair. *Carr*

Karsa (Hungarian) Falcon.

Karsten (Greek) Blessed, anointed one.

Kartal (Hungarian) Eagle.

Kartik (Hindi) Month.

Kartikeya (Hindi) God of war; son of Shiva and Parvati.

Kasch (German) Like a blackbird.

Kaseem (Arabic) Divides. *Kasceem, Kaseym, Kasim, Kazeem*

Kasen (Latin) Protected with a helmet. *Kasan, Kasin*

Kasey (Irish) Form of Casey. *Kasi, Kasie, Kasy, Kazy*

Kasi (African) Leaving. *Kasee, Kasey*

Kasib (Arabic) Fertile. *Kaseeb*

Kasimir (Old Slavic) Demands peace. *Casimir, Casmir, Kazimir*

Kaspar (Persian) Treasured secret. *Caspar, Casper, Kasp, Kasper, Kaspir, Kaspor*

Kass (German) Standout among men. *Cass, Kasse*

Kassidy (Irish) Clever; curly haired. *Kass, Kassidi, Kassidie, Kassie*

Kateb (Arabic) Writer.

Kateo (American) Good judgment. *Cato, Cayto, Caytoe, Kato*

Katzir (Hebrew) Reaping. *Katzeer*

Kaufman (German) Merchant. *Kauffmann, Kaufmann*

Kaul (Arabic) Trustworthy. *Kahlil, Kalee, Khaleel, Khalil*

Kauri (Polynesian) Tree. *Kaeree, Kaurie*

Kaushal (Hindi) Perfect.

Kaushik (Hindi) Sage Vishramitra.

Kavan (Irish) Good-looking. *Cavan, Kaven, Kavin*

Kavanagh (Irish) Kavan's follower. *Cavanagh, Kavenagh, Kavenaugh*

Kaveh (Persian) Hero.

Kavi (Hindi) Poet.

Kay (Welsh, German) Rejoicer; fort; joyful. *Kai, Kay, Kaye, Kaysie, Keh, MacKay*

Kayin (Yoruban) Celebrated child. *Kaiyen, Kayan*

Kaylen (Irish) Laughing. *Kaylan, Kaylin, Kaylon, Kaylyn*

Kayven (Irish) Handsome. *Cavan, Kavan, Kave*

Kazimir (Slavic) Famous destroyer of peace. *Casimir, Kaz, Kazimierz, Kazmir*

Kazuo (Japanese) First son.

Keahi (Hawaiian) Fire.

Keanan (Irish) Form of Keenan. *Keanen, Keannan*

Keandre (American) Grateful. *Keondre*

Keane (English) Sharp; bold. *Kean, Keen, Keene*

Keanu (Hawaiian) Cool breeze over the mountians. *Keahnu*

Kearn (German) Dark. *Kearn, Kearny, Kerne, Kerney*

Kearney (Celtic) Warrior. *Karney, Karny, Kearns, Kerney, Kirney*

Keary (Celtic) Father's dark child. *Care, Kear*

Keaton (English) Hawk's nest. *Keeton, Keiton, Keyton*

Keb (Egyptian) Earth. *Kebb*

Kedar (Arabic) Strong; powerful. (Hebrew) Blackness; sorrow. (Hindi) Raga, a type of Hindi music.

Keefe (Gaelic) Lovable and handsome; noble. *Keefer, Keever*

Keegan (Gaelic) Little fierce one. *Kagen, Keagan, Keegen, Kegan*

Keeland (Gaelic) Little and slender. *Kealian, Kealon, Keelan, Keilan, Keillan, Kelan*

Keeley (Irish) Handsome. *Kealey, Kealy, Keelee, Keelie, Keely, Keilie*

Keemo (Vietnamese) Friendly.

Keenan (Gaelic) Little ancient one. *Keenen, Kenan, Kienan, Kienen*

Kees (Dutch) Form of Kornelius. *Keas, Keyes*

Kegan (Celtic) Fiery.

Keir (Celtic) Dark-skinned. *Keiron, Kerr, Kieran, Kieron*

Keitaro (Japanese) Blessed.

Keith (Irish) Warrior descending. (Scottish) From the battleground. (Welsh) Forest. *Keath, Keeth, Keith*

Kekoa (Hawaiian) Warrior.

Kelan (Irish) Tiny, slender. *Caolan, Keelan, Kelen, Kelin*

Kelby (Norse) From the farm by the springs. *Kelbey, Kelbie, Kellby*

Kele (Native American) Sparrow. *Kelle*

Keled (Hungarian) Royal clan of the Scythians.

Keleman (Hungarian) Gentle, kind. *Kelemen*

Kelii (Hawaiian) Wealthy.

Kell (English) From the spring.

Kellen (German) Swamp. (Irish) Powerful. *Keilan, Kel, Kelen, Keler, Kelher, Kelin, Kell, Kellin, Kelly, Kelyn, Kylher*

Kelly (Irish) Warrior. *Kelley, Kellie*

Kelsey (Scandinavian) Island of ships. (English) Island. *Kelse, Kelsi, Kelsie, Kelso, Kelsy*

Kelton (Irish) Energetic. *Keldon, Kelltin, Kellton, Kelten, Keltin, Keltonn*

Kelvin (English) River man. (Irish) From the narrow river. (Scottish) Friend of ships. *Kel, Keloun, Kelvan, Kelven, Kelvyn*

Kem (Irish) Warrior chief. (Teutonic) To cover, veil, or hide. *Kam*

Kemal (Turkish) Highest honor. *Kemel*

Kemenes (Hungarian) Furnace maker.

Kemp (Middle English) Champion. *Kem, Kemper, Kemplen, Kempson, Kempy*

Kenan (Hebrew) Possession. *Cainan*

Kendall (Celtic) Ruler of the valley. *Ken, Kendal, Kendalia, Kendaline, Kendel, Kendell, Kendra, Kenna, Kenni, Kenny, Kindall, Kindell*

Kende (Hungarian) Name of honor.

Kendis (African American) Pure.

Kendrick (Irish) Son of Henry. (Scottish) Royal chieftain. *Kendric, Kendrik, Kendryck*

Kenelm (Old English) Brave; helmet.

Kenley (Old English) Dweller at the king's meadow. *Kenlea, Kenlee, Kenleigh, Kenlie, Kenly*

Kenn (Welsh) Clear water.

Kennard (English) Strong. *Kennair, Kennerd*

Kennedy (Gaelic) Helmeted chief. *Canady, Ken, Kennady, Kenny*

Kenneth (English) Royal obligation. (Irish) Handsome. (Scottish) Goodlooking; fair. *Ken, Kenn, Kennet, Kenney, Kenny, Kevin*

Kenrich (Welsh) Chief hero, royal ruler. *Kenley, Kennard, Kenrick, Kenway*

Kent (Old English) Border; coast; bright white. *Kennt, Kentt*

Kentaro (Japanese) Large baby boy.

Kentay (African American) Outrageous. *Keon, Keontae, Keontee*

Kentlee (English) Dignified. *Ken, Kenny, Kent, Kentlea, Kentleigh, Kently*

Kenton (Old English) From the king's estate. *Kentan, Kentin, Kenton*

Kenyon (Gaelic) Blondhaired. *Ken, Kenjon, Kenny, Kenyawn, Kenyun*

Kenzo (Japanese) Wise and three.

Keon (Irish) Well born. *Keion, Keonne, Keyon, Kion, Kionn*

Keona (Hawaiian) God's gracious gift. *Keowynn*

Kepano (Hawaiian) Crown. *Kekepana, Tepano*

Kepler (German) Loves astrology; starry-eyed. *Kappler, Keppel, Keppeler, Keppler*

Ker (English) House. (Norse) Marshland. *Keir, Kerr, Kir, Kirby*

Kerecsen (Hungarian) Falcon.

Kerem (Turkish) Noble; kind. *Kereem*

Kermit (Gaelic) Freeman. *Kerm, Kermee, Kermet, Kermey, Kermi, Kermie*

Kern (Gaelic) Dark. *Curran, Kearn, Kearne, Kearns*

Kerr (Scandinavian) Serious. *Karr, Kerre, Kurr*

Kerrick (English) King's ride. *Keric, Kerric, Keryk*

Kerry (Gaelic) Dark eyes. *Keri, Kerri, Kerrie, Kerrin, Kerwin*

Kers (Indian) Plant.

Kersen (Indonesian) Cherry.

Kerwin (Irish) Dark. *Kerwen, Kerwyn, Kirwin*

Keshav (Hindi) Krishna's name.

Keshawn (African American) Friendly. *Kesh, Keshaun, Keyshawn, Shawn*

Kesley (Irish) From the gray fortress. (Scottish) Ancient surname. *Keslee, Kesli, Kezley*

Kester (English) From the Roman camp. (Scottish) Bearing Christ.

Kestrel (English) Soars.

Ketan (Hindi) Home; banner.

Ketchum (American) Place name, Ketchum, Idaho. *Catch, Ketch, Ketcham, Ketchim*

Kettil (Scandinavian) Selfsacrificing. *Keld, Ketil, Ketti, Kjeld*

Kevat (Finnish) Spring.

Keve (Hungarian) Pebble.

Kevin (Gaelic) Gentle; lovable. *Kev, Kevan, Keven, Kevon*

Keyon (Old English) Guiding; leading. *Key, Kieon*

Khadim (Hindi) Forever. *Kadeem, Kadeen, Kahdeem, Khadeem*

Khairi (Swahili) Kingly. (Arabic) Charitable; beneficent.

Khalid (Arabic) Immortal. *Khaled*

Khalon (African American) Little king.

Khambis Origin and meaning unknown.

Khambrel (American) Articulate. *Kambrel, Kham, Khambrell, Khambrelle, Khambryll, Khamme, Khammie, Khammy*

Khan (Turkish) Prince. *Chan, Kahn, Khanh*

Khorshed (Persian) Sun.

Khortdad (Persian) Perfection.

Khoury (Arabic) Priest.

Khyber (Hindi) Place name, passage of Khyer Pass, land that links Pakistan and Afghanistan. *Kibe, Kiber, Kyber*

Kian (Irish) Archaic.

Kiefer (German) Barrel maker. *Keefer, Keifer*

Kiel (Irish) Form of Kyle. *Kiell*

Kieran (Gaelic) Small and dark-skinned. *Carra, Ceirnin, Ciaran, Kern, Kerr, Kerry, Kerwin, Key, Kiernan, Kieron, Kirwin*

Kiet (Thai) Honor. *Kyet*

Kiki (Spanish) Ruler of the household.

Killian (Irish) Strife; battle; small; fierce. (Scottish) Little warlike one. *Kelian, Kilean, Kilian, Kiliane, Kilien, Killiean, Killien, Killienn, Killion, Kyllian, Kyllien*

Kilydd (Welsh) Legendary son of Kelyddon.

Kim (Old English) Chief. *Kemble, Kimball, Kimbell, Kimble, Kimmey, Kimmi, Kimmy, Kym*

Kimberley (Old English) Land belonging to Cyneburg; royal fortress meadow. *Kim, Kimberly, Kimby, Kimmi, Kimmie, Kimmy, Kymberly*

Kin (Japanese) Golden.

Kincaid (Scottish) Vigorous. *Kincaide, Kinkaid*

King (Old English) Ruler. *Kingsley, Kingston, Kingswell*

Kinga (Hungarian) Brave warrior.

Kingsley (English) Royal nature. *King, Kings, Kingslea, Kingslee, Kingsleigh, Kingsly, Kins*

Kinnel (Gaelic) Dweller at the head of the cliff.

Kinsey (Old English) Victorious prince; child. *Kensey, Kinsie*

Kintan (Hindi) Wearing a crown.

Kipling (Middle English) One who cures salmon or herring.

Kipp (Old English) Wearing a crown; sharply pointed hill. *Kinnard, Kinnell, Kipp, Kipper, Kippy*

Kira (Gaelic) Dark.

Kiral (Turkish) King. *Kyral, Kyrol*

Kirby (English) Village of the church. *Kerbey, Kerbi, Kerbie, Kirbey, Kirbie*

Kirill (Greek) The lord. *Kiril, Kirillos, Kyril*

Kirit (Hindi) Crown, tiara.

Kiritan (Hindi) Wearing a crown. *Kiriten, Kiriton*

Kirk (Old Norse) From the church. *Kirby, Kirkland, Kirkley, Kirkus, Kirkwood, Kurk*

Kirkley (English) Church meadow. *Kerklee, Kirkleigh*

Kishi (Japanese) Knight.

Kisho (Japanese) One who knows his own mind.

Kishore (Hindi) Young.

Kit (Greek) Michievious. *Kitt*

Kix (American) Brand of cereal.

Kiyiyah (Native American) Wailing wolf.

Kiyoshi (Japanese) Quiet.

Klaus (German) Victorious people. *Claas, Claus, Klaas, Klause*

Klay (English) Reliable; immortal; clay pit. *Klaie, Klaye*

Klein (German) Small. *Kleiner, Kleinert, Kline*

Klemens (Latin) Gentle. *Klemenis, Klement, Klemet, Kliment, Klimiek*

Kliment (Czech) Gentle.

Knightley (English) Protects. *Knight, Knightlea, Knightlee, Knightlie, Knightly, Knights*

Knoton (Native American) Wind.

Knowles (English) Outdoorsman. *Knowlie, Knowls, Nowles*

Knox (Old English) From the hills. *Knoll*

Knute (Scandinavian) Knot. *Canute, Cnut, Knut*

Kobe (Hebrew) Cunning. *Kobee, Kobey, Kobi, Koby*

Kody (English) Brash. *Kodee, Kodey, Kodi, Kodie, Kodye*

Kofi (African American) Friday born.

Kogen (Japanese) Wild, untamed source.

Kohana (Native American) Fast.

Koi (Native American) Panther.

Koichi (Japanese) One light.

Kolby (English) Darkhaired. (Scandinavian) From the dark country. *Colby, Kelby, Koelby, Kohlby, Kole, Koleby, Kollby*

Koleyn (Aboriginal) Winter.

Kolos (Hungarian) Scholar.

Kolton (English) Coal town.

Konala (Hawaiian) World ruler.

Kong (Chinese) Void.

Konnor (Irish) Brilliant; version of Connor. *Konnar, Konner*

Konrad (German) Bold adviser. *Conrad, Khonred, Kord, Kort*

Konstantin (Russian) Forceful. *Konstantine, Konstantyne, Tino, Tinos*

Konstantinos (Greek) Steadfast. *Constance, Konstance, Konstant, Tino, Tinos*

Kont (Hungarian) Meaning unknown.

Kontar (Ghanese) Only child.

Korey (Irish) Lovable. *Kori, Korrey, Korrie*

Kornel (Latin) Form of Cornelius. *Korneil, Korneli, Krelis, Sonia*

Korvin (Latin) Crow. *Corvin*

Koshy (American) Jolly. *Koshee, Koshey, Koshi*

Kosmo (Greek) Likes order. *Cosmos, Kosmy*

Kostas (Russian) Loyal.

Koster (American) Spiritual. *Kost, Kostar, Koste, Koster*

Kostya (Russian) Steadfast. (Slavic) Faithful.

Kourosh (Old Persian) Sunlike. (Modern Persian) Great.

Kovan (Bohemian) Smithwork.

Kozan (Japanese) Ancient mountain.

Kozma (Greek) Decoration.

Kripa (Hindi) Has a twin sister. *Kripi*

Krischnan (Greek) Christian. *Krister*

Krishna (Sanskrit) Pleasing. *Krisha, Krishnah*

Kristoffer (Greek) Bearing of Christ. *Krist, Kristofer*

Krunal (Hindi) Meaning unknown.

Kuldeep (Hindi) Light of family.

Kulvir (Hindi) Brave soul of the community.

Kumar (Sanskrit) Son.

Kunal (Hindi) Son of emperor Ashok.

Kund (Hungarian) Name of honor.

Kurt (German) Bold counselor.

Kusagra (Hindi) King.

Kush (Hindi) Son of Rama.

Kushan (Hindi) Meaning unknown.

Kwahu (Hopi) Eagle.

Kwamin (African American) Born on Saturday. *Kwame, Kwamee, Kwami*

Kwan (Korean) Strong. *Kwane*

Kwan-Sun (Korean) Strong and goodness.

Kwau (African) Born on Thursday.

Kyan (African American) Little king. *Kyann*

Kyle (Irish) Narrows; place where cattle graze; wood; church. (Scottish) From

a narrow strait; Scottish region. *Kilen, Kyleigh, Kylen, Kyli, Kylie, Lei, Leigh*

Kyler (English) Peaceful. (Dutch) Archer. (Irish) Narrows; wood; church. *Cuyler, Kieler, Kiler, Kye, Kylor*

Kyrone (African American) Brash. *Keirohn, Keiron, Keirone, Keirown, Kirone, Kyron*

Kyros (Greek) Master.

Kyrylo (Greek) Lord.

Kyu Bok (Korean) Standard and blessed.

Kyu-Bong (Korean) Standard and omniscience.

Kyung (Korean) Honored.

Kyung-Sam (Korean) Honored and achievement.

Kyzer (American) Wild spirit. *Kaizer, Kizer, Kyze*

L

La Vonn (African American) Small one. *La Vaun, La Voun*

Laakea (Hawaiian) Holy light.

Laban (Hebrew) White. *Labaan, Laben, Lavan*

Labaron (French) Baron. *LaBaron, LaBaronne*

Label (Hebrew) Lion.

Labhras (Irish) Introspective. (Latin) Crowned with laurel. *Lubhras*

Laborc (Hungarian) Brave panther.

Labrentsis (Russian) Form of Lawrence. *Labhras, Labhruinn*

Lachlan (Scottish) Feisty. *Lachlann, Lacklan, Lackland, Laughlin, Lock, Locklan*

Ladarian (American) Combination of La and Darian. *Ladarien, Ladarrion*

Ladd (Middle English) Young man. *Lad, Laddie, Laddy*

Laderrick (American) Combination of La and Derric. *Ladarrick, Laderick, Laderic*

Ladislav (Czech) Famous ruler. *Ladislao, Ladislaus, Ladislaw*

Lado (African American) Second-born son.

Ladomér (Hungarian) Trapper.

Lael (Hebrew) Belonging to Jehovah. *Lale*

Laertes (Greek) Action-oriented.

Lafayette (French) History; French soldier. *Lafayett, Laffyette*

Lafe (American) Punctual. *Laafe, Laife, Laiffe*

Laidley (English) Path along the marshy meadow. *Laedlea, Laedli, Laydlea, Laydly*

Laionela (Hawaiian) Lion.

Laird (Scottish) Lord; landed gentry. *Layrd, Layrde*

Lake (English) Tranquil water.

Laken (African American) Treasure. *Lakin*

Lakista (African American) Meaning unknown.

Lakota (Native American) Friend. *Lakoda*

Lakshman (Hindi) Brother of Rama.

Lakshmi (Hindi) Lucky omen; Hindi goddess of beauty and wealth.

Lakshya (Hindi) Target.

Lalit (Hindi) Of great beauty, beautiful.

Lallo (Native American) Little boy.

Lam (Vietnamese) Full understanding; knowledge. *Lammie, Lammy*

Laman (Vietnamese) Happy; content.

Lamani (Tongan) Lemon. *Lamanee, Lamanie, Lamany*

Lamar (Latin) Sea. *Lamair, Lamaris, Lamarr, Lamarre, Larmar, Lemar, Lemarr*

Lamberto (Latin) Wealthy in land; brilliant. *Lambard, Lambert, Lambirt, Lammert, Landbert*

Lamech (African American) Powerful.

Lamont (Norse) Lawyer. *La Monte, Lammont, Lamond*

Lamorak (Scottish) In Arthurian legend, brother of Percival.

Lance (French) Lancer. (German) Spear. *Ancel, Lancelot, Lancelott, Lancilot, Lancylotte, Launcelot*

Lander (Middle English) Occupational name meaning "landowner"; place name, Lander, Wyoming. *Landers, Landis, Landman, Landor, Landry*

Landis (Anglo-Saxon) Rough land. *Land, Landes, Landice, Landise, Landly, Landus*

Lando (German) Famous throughout the land. (American) Masculine. *Land, Landow*

Landon (Old English) Long hill. *Landan, Landen, Landun, Landyn*

Landric (German) Ruler of the land. *Landrick, Landryc*

Landry (French) Entrepreneur. *Landre, Landree, Landri, Landrie, Landrue*

Lane (Middle English) Narrow road. *Laine, Layna, Layne*

Lang (Old English) Long. (German) Tall man. *Langdon, Langford, Langhorne, Langley, Langston, Langtry*

Langden (English) Long hill. *Lang, Langdon, Langdun*

Langford (English) Long ford. *Laingford, Langford, Lankford*

Langley (English) Long meadow. *Lainglee, Laingly, Langlea, Langly*

Langston (English) Long suffering. *Lang, Langstan, Langsten*

Lansa (Native American) Lance.

Lantos (Hungarian) Lute player.

Lanty (Irish) Lively. *Laughun, Leachlainn, Lochlainn, Lochlann*

Lantz (Yiddish) Lancer.

Lao-Tzu (Chinese) Old master; old child; Chinese philosopher who is traditionally regarded as the founder of Taoism.

Laramie (French) Pensive. *Laramee, Laramey, Larami, Laramy, Laremy*

Larenzo (Spanish) Bold and spirited. *Lorenso, Lorenz, Lorenzo*

Lariat (American) Word as a name; roper. *Lare, Lari*

Larkin (Irish) Cruel. *Lark, Larkan, Larken, Larkie, Larky*

Larnell (American) Generous. *Larn, Larndelle, Larndey, Larne*

Laron (French) Thief. *Laran, Laraun, Laren, Larin, Laronn, Laryn*

Larrimore (French) One who provides arms. *Larimore, Larmer, Larmor*

Lars (Scandinavian) Crowned with laurel. *Laris, Larris, Larse, Larson, Larz*

Laserian (Irish) Flame. *Lasairian, Lasirian*

Lassen (American) Place name, mountain peak in California. *Lase, Lasen, Lassan, Lassun*

Lassiter (American) Witty. *Lassater, Lasseter, Lassie, Lassy*

László (Hungarian) Might; fame. *Laci, Lacko, Laslo*

Latafat (Indian) Elegance.

Lateef (Arabic) Gentle man. *Latif*

Lathrop (English) Home-loving. *Lathe, Lathrap, Latrope, Laye, Laythrep*

Latimer (Middle English) Interpreter. *Lattimore, Latymer*

Lauaki (Polynesian) Best.

Laughlin (Irish) Servant.

Launcelot (French) Romantic. *Lance, Lancelott, Launce*

Laurence (Latin) Glorified. *Larence, Laurance, Laurans, Laure, Lauree, Lauri,*

Laurrie, Lawree, Lawri, Lawry, Lorence, Lorry, Lowri, Lowrie

Laurent (French) Martyred. *Laurynt*

Lavan (Hebrew) White.

Lavaughn (African American) Perky. *Lavan, Lavon, Lavonn, Levan, Levaughn*

Lavesh (Hindi) Crumb.

Lavrenti (Russian) Form of Lawrence. *Laiurenty, Lavik, Lavro*

Lawler (Gaelic) Soft-spoken. *Lawford, Lollar, Loller*

Lawrence (Latin) Laurel crown. *Labhras, Larkin, Larry, Lars, Larson, Laughton, Laurence, Laurens, Laurent, Lauritz, Lawford, Lawler, Lawley, Lawrance, Lawry, Lawson, Lawton, Lon, Lonnie, Lorcan, Loren, Lorenz, Lorenzo, Lorin, Loring, Lorne*

Lawson (Old English) Son of Lawrence.

Layton (Old English) One from the meadow farm. *Lay, Layland, Leigh, Leighton*

Lazarus (Hebrew) God's helper. *El'azar, Laszlo, Lazar, Lázár, Lazaro, Lazre*

Leander (Greek) Lion man. *Leandre, Leandro, Liander*

Lear (German) Of the meadow. *Leare, Leere*

Leavery (American) Giving. *Leautree, Leautri, Leautry, Levry, Lo, Lotree, Lotrey, Lotri, Lotry*

Leben (Yiddish) Life. *Laben, Lebon*

LeBron (African American) King.

Lech (Polish) Glory of the Poles. *Lecholsaw, Leslaw, Leszek*

Lee (Old English) Glade. (Gaelic) Poet. (Chinese) Plum. *Leigh*

Leggett (French) Messenger. *Legate, Leggitt, Liggett*

Legolas (Old English) Highest angel.

Lehel (Hungarian) Breathes.

Lei (Chinese) Thunder. *Ley*

Leif (Old Norse) Beloved. *Leaf, Lief*

Leighton (English) Meadow; farm. *Laeeton, Laeton, Laiton, Laytan, Leighten, Leightun, Leiton, Leyton*

Leith (Scottish) Wide river. *Leathan*

Lél (Hungarian) Bugler.

Leland (Old English) From the meadowland. *Leeland, Leighlon, Leiland, Lelan, Lelond*

Lemar (Grench) Form of Lamar. *Lemario, Lemarr, Limar, Lymar*

Lemuel (Hebrew) Devoted to God; belonging to God. *Lemmie, Lemmy, Lemy*

Len (Native American) Flute. (German) Courage. (American) Like a lion. *Lenny*

Lencho (Spanish) Form of Lawrence. *Lenci, Lenzy*

Lenno (Native American) Man.

Lennon (Gaelic) Cloak; little cape. *Lenin, Lenn, Lennen*

Lennor (Gypsy) Summer. *Lenor*

Lennox (Scottish) Amid the elms; from the field of elm trees. *Len, Lenix, Lennie, Lenox*

Lensar (English) With his parents. *Lendar*

Leodegrance (French) Lion.

Leofrido (Teutonic) He who brings peace to his village.

Leon (Greek) Lion. *Leo, Leonato, Leone, Leonidas, Leosko*

Leonard (German) Lion-hearted. *Len, Lenard, Lénárd, Lennard, Lennart, Lennie, Lenny, Leo, Leó, Leon, Leonárd, Leonardo, Leonhard*

Leonel (English) Little lion. *Leaonal, Leaonell, Leinal, Leonell*

Leonidas (Greek) One who is bold as a lion. *Leonid, Leonidis*

Leopold (Old German) Bold leader. *Leopoldo, Leupold, Luitpold*

Leor (Hebrew) I have light.

Lequinton (American) Combination of Le and Quinten. *Lequentin, Lequinn*

Leron (Arabic) Song is mine. *Lerone, Liron, Lirone, Lyron*

Leroy (Old French) King. *Lee, Leroi, Roy*

Les (Scottish) Form of Leslie. *Less, Lessie*

Leshem (Hebrew) Precious stone.

Leslie (Scottish) Low meadow. *Leslea, Lesley, Lesly, Lezly*

Lesta (Russian) From town of Leicester. *Leisti*

Lester (Latin) Legion camp. *Leicester*

Lev (Hebrew) Heart. *Leb, Leva, Levko*

Levar (American) Soft-spoken. *Levarr*

Levente (Latin) Rising. (Hungarian) Being. *Lavant, Lavante, Levent*

Leverett (French) Baby rabbit. *Lev, Leveret, Leverit, Leveritt*

Levi (Hebrew) United. *Lev, Levey, Levin, Levon, Levy*

Lewis (Welsh) Form of Llewellyn. *Lew, Lewie, Lewy*

Lex (English) Defender of mankind. *Lexi, Lexie, Lexin*

Li (Chinese) Strength.

Li-Liang (Chinese) Powerful.

Liam (Irish) Unwavering protector. *Lliam, Lyam*

Lian (Irish) Guardian. *Lyan*

Liang (Chinese) Excellent; good. *Lyang*

Libero (Portuguese) Freedom. *Liberio*

Libor (Czech) Freedom. *Libeck, Libek, Liborek*

Liko (Chinese) Buddhist nun.

Lil Jon (American) Rapper Jonathan Mortimer Smith.

Lincoln (Old English) Home by the pond. *Linc, Link*

Lind (Old English) Linden tree. *Lindberg, Lindell, Linden, Lindley, Lindon, Lindt, Linely, Linford, Linton, Lyndon*

Lindberg (German) Mountain of linden trees. *Lin, Linbert, Linburt, Lind, Lindbert, Lindburg, Lindie, Lindy, Lydburgh, Lyndberg, Lyndbirt, Lyndbyrt*

Lindell (English) Valley of linden trees. *Lindall, Lindel, Lyndall, Lyndell*

Lindsay (English) Linden tree island. *Lindsee, Lindsey, Lindsy, Lyndsay, Lyndsey*

Linley (English) Flax meadow. *Linlea, Linli, Linly, Lynly*

Lino (Portuguese) Form of Laudalino.

Linus (Greek) Flax. *Linas, Line, Lines*

Lionel (French) Fierce. (Latin) Little lion. *Leonel, Li, Lion, Lionell, Lonell, Lonnell, Lye, Lyon, Lyonel, Lyonell*

Lipót (Hungarian) Brave.

Lisandro (Spanish) Liberator.

Lisiate (Polynesian) Brave king.

Lisimba (African American) Harmed by a lion.

Little Wayne (American) Rapper Dwayne Michael Carter Jr.

Litton (Old English) Hillside town. *Lyten, Lyton, Lytton*

Livingston (English) Leif's settlement. *Livingstone*

LL Cool J (American) Rapper James Todd Smith.

Llewellyn (Old English) Ruling. *Lewellen, Lewellin, Llewelin, Llewelleyn*

Lloyd (Old Welsh) Gray-haired. *Floyd, Loyd*

Llyr (Welsh) Sea.

Loaghaire (Irish) Calf herder; shepard. *Laoghaire*

Lochlain (Irish) Land of lakes. *Loche, Lochee, Lochlann, Locklynn*

Locke (English) Fort. *Lock, Lockwood*

Loe (Hawaiian) King.

Loffe (Swedish) Lone descendant.

Logan (Scottish) Little hollow.

Loholt (Scottish) In Arthurian legend, knight of the Round Table.

Loikanos (Greek) Man from Lucania, an area in southern Italy. *Lukianos*

Lokesh (Hindi) Lord Brahma.

Lokni (Native American) Raining through the roof.

Lombardi (Italian) Winner. *Bardi, Bardy, Lom, Lombard, Lombardy*

Lon (Gaelic) Fierce. *Lonny*

Lonato (Native American) Flint.

London (English) Fierce ruler of the world. *Londen, Lunden*

Long (Vietnamese) Dragon.

Lono (Hawaiian) God of farming.

Loota (Native American) Red. *Lootah*

Loránd (Hungarian) Brave warrior. *Lóránt*

Lorcan (Irish) Little fierce one. *Lorcen, Lorcin, Lorcon*

Lord (English) Lord; noble title.

Loredo (Spanish) Smart; cowboy. *Lorado, Loredoh, Lorre, Lorrey*

Loren (Latin) Hopeful; winning. *Lorin, Lorrin*

Lorenzo (Spanish, Italian) Bold; spirited. *Larenzo, Loranzo, Lore, Lorence, Lorenso, Lorentz, Lorenz, Lorrie, Lorry*

Lorimer (Latin) Harness maker. *Lorrimer, Lorrymer, Lorymer*

Lõrinc (Hungarian) Laurentian.

Loring (German) Famous in war.

Loritz (Dutch) Laurel. *Lauritz, Laurytz, Lorytz*

Lorne (Latin) Grounded. *Lorn*

Lot (Hebrew) Furtive; hidden; covered. *Lott*

Lothar (German) Form of Luther. *Lotair, Lotarrio, Lothair, Lotharrio*

Loudon (American) Enthusiastic. *Lewdan, Lewdin, Lewdon, Louden, Lowdan, Lowden, Lowdin, Lowdon, Lowdyn*

Louis (German) Famed warrior. *Chlodwig, Clovis, Lajos, Lew, Lewes, Lewie, Llewellyn, Lodovico, Lou, Louie, Lu, Ludvig, Ludwig, Luigi, Luis, Luthias*

Louvain (English) Vanity. *Louvayn, Louvin*

Lowell (English) Young wolf. *Lowel*

Loyal (English) Faithful. *Loial, Loy, Loye, Lyall*

Loys (American) Loyal. *Loyce, Loyse*

Lubomir (Polish) Lover of peace. *Lubomyr*

Luc (French) Light; laidback. *Lucca, Luke*

Luca (Italian) Form of Lucius. *Lucah*

Lucan (Irish) Light.

Lucas (Latin) Bringer of light. (Greek) Patron saint of doctors, artists, and creatives. *Lucca, Luces, Luka, Lukas, Luke, Lukes, Lukus*

Lucian (Latin) Soothing. *Lew, Lucyan, Luiz, Lushun, Luyciyan*

Lucius (Latin) Light. *Luca, Lucan, Lucca, Luce, Lucian, Luciano, Lucias, Lucien, Lucio*

Lucky (American) Lucky. *Luckee, Luckey, Luckie*

Ludacris (African American) Rapper born Christopher Bridges.

Ludlow (English) Hill of the leader. *Ludlowe*

Ludomir (Czech) Famous people. *Ludek*

Ludoslaw (Polish) Glorious people.

Ludovic (Slavic) Smart; spiritual. *Luddovik, Lude, Ludovik, Ludvic, Vick*

Ludvig (Scandinavian) Famous warrior.

Ludwig (German) Famous fighter. *Ludwik, Lugweg, Lugwige*

Lugono (African) Sleep.

Luigi (Italian) Form of Louis. *Luise*

Luister (African) One who listens.

Luke (English) Bringer of light. *Luc, Luca, Lucais,*

Lucan, Lucas, Luchas, Lucian, Luciano, Lucien, Lucius, Luckas, Luka, Lukács, Lukas, Lukian, Lukyan

Lukman (North African) Forecaster.

Lulani (Hawaiian) Pinnacle of heaven. *Lulanee, Lulanie, Lulany*

Lundy (Scottish) Child born on Monday. *Lundee, Lundey, Lundi, Lundie*

Lunn (Irish) Strong; warlike. *Lon, Lonn, Lun*

Lunt (Scandinavian) From the grove. *Lont*

Lusk (English) Hearty. *Lus, Luske, Luskee, Luskey, Luski, Lusky*

Luther (German) Warrior. *Lotario, Lothaire, Lutera, Luthar*

Lyall (Scottish) Loyal. *Lyal*

Lykaios (Greek) Wolfish; of a wolf; wolflike.

Lyle (Old French) Island. *Lisle, Lyell, Lysle*

Lyman (Middle English) From the meadow. *Leaman, Leyman*

Lynch (Irish) Mariner. *Linch*

Lyndal (English) Valley with lime trees. *Lindal, Lyndell*

Lyndall (English) Nature lover; valley of lime trees. *Lynd, Lyndal, Lyndell*

Lyndon (Old English) Linden tree. *Linden, Lindon*

Lynn (English) Verbose; waterfall. *Lin, Linn, Lyn, Lynne*

Lynton (English) Town of nature lovers; town with lime trees. *Linton*

Lyon (Latin) Shining one. (French) Place name.

Lyre (Old English) Harp; lyre.

Lyron (Hebrew) Form of Leron.

Lysander (Greek) Liberator; emancipation. *Lisander*

Lyulf (German) Combative. *Lyulfe, Lyulff*

M

Maarten (Dutch) Fondness of war.

Mablevi (African American) Do not deceive.

Mabon (Welsh) Son, or knight, in Arthurian legend.

Macabee (Hebrew) Hammer. *Maccabee, Mackabbe*

Macalla (Australian) Full moon. *Macal, Macalah*

Macario (Spanish) Happy. *Macareo, Makario*

Macartan (Irish) Son of Artan.

Macbeth (Scottish) Son of Beth. (Shakespearean) Character from *Macbeth*.

Macduff (Scottish) Son of the Blackman. (Shakespearean) Character from *Macbeth*.

Mace (Latin) Aromatic spice. (Old English) Medieval weapon used by a knight. *Macer, Macie*

Mackenzie (Gaelic) Son of the wise leader. *Kenzie, Mackenzy, Mackie, Mackinzie, Max*

Mackinley (Irish) Educated. (Scottish) Son of Kinley. *Mackinlea, Mackinly*

Maclean (Irish) Son of Leander. (Scottish) Son of the servant of John. *Maclain, Macleane, McLain, McLaine*

Macmorris (Irish) Son of Morris.

Macon (Middle English) To make. *Macen, Macomb, Makon*

Macy (Old French) Matthew's estate. *Mace, Maceo, Macey, Maci, Macie*

Madai (Hebrew) Measure; judging; garment.

Madan (Hindi) Cupid. *Madden, Maddin, Maddyn, Maden, Madin, Madyn*

Maddock (Old Welsh) Champion; good fortune. *Maddox, Maddy, Madoc, Madock, Madog, Madox, Maidoc*

Maddox (English) Giving. *Maddocks, Maddy, Madox*

Madhav (Hindi) Krishna.

Madison (Old English) Son of a mighty warrior; son of Maud. *Maddison, Maddy*

Madock (American) Giving. *Madac, Maddock, Maddy*

Maemi (Japenese) Honest child.

Magan (Indian) Engrossed.

Magar (Russian) Groom's attendant. *Magarious, Magne*

Magee (Irish) Practical; lively; son of Hugh. *MacGee, MacGhee, Mackie, Maggy, McGee*

Magic (Latin) Supernatural. *Magik, Magikos, Magique*

Magnar (Polish) Strength; warrior.

Magne (Norse) Fierce warrior.

Magnus (Latin) Great one. *Maghnus, Magnes, Magnum, Magnuson, Magnuss, Manius, Manus*

Maguire (Irish) Subtle. *MacGuire, McGuire*

Mahabahu (Indian) Indian warrior.

Mahabala (Hindi) Strength.

Mahammed (Arabic) Form of Muhammad. *Mahamad, Mahamed*

Mahan (American) Cowboy. *Mahahn, Mahand, Mahen, Mayhan*

Mahatma (Sanskrit) Great soul.

Mahavira (Hindi) Son of Priyavrata.

Mahdi (African) Expected one. (Arabic) Guided to the right path. *Mahde, Mahdee, Mahdy*

Mahesh (Hindi) Great ruler; Lord Shiva.

Mahkah (Native American) Earth.

Mahmood (Arabic) Form of Muhammad. *Mahamoud, Mahmoud, Mahomet*

Mahpee (Native American) Sky.

Maidoc (Welsh) Fortunate. *Maedoc, Maidock*

Maik (Hawaiian) Now.

Main (Welsh) Slender. *Mainess, Mane, Maness*

Maitland (Old English) Dweller in the meadow.

Maitreya (Hindi) Sage.

Majid (Arabic) Great, glorious. *Majd, Majdi*

Major (Latin) Greater; military rank. *Majeur, Majorie, Majors*

Makaio (Hawaiian) Gift of god. *Makayo*

Makalo (African) Wandering.

Makan (Hawaiian) Wind. *Makani, Makanie, Makany*

Makayla (Hebrew) Who is like God.

Makepeace (Old English) Peacemaker.

Makis (Hebrew) Gift from God. *Makys*

Makoto (Japanese) Sincere; honest.

Maksim (Russian) Greatest. *Maxim*

Malachi (Hebrew) Messenger of God. *Malachai, Malachy, Malaji, Malaki, Maleki*

Malchidiel (Latin) Fullness of God; Angel of March.

Malcom (Scottish) Disciple of Saint Columbia. (Arabic) Dove. *Colm, Mal, Malcolm, Malkalm, Malkelm, Malkolm*

Maleagant (Scottish) In Arthurian legend, he was a villainous knight.

Malik (Arabic) Master. *Maalik, Malek, Malic, Maliq*

Mallin (English) Strong; little warrior; rowdy. *Malen, Malin, Mallan, Mallen, Mallie, Mally*

Mallory (French) Wild spirit. (German) Army counselor. *Mal, Mallie, Malloree, Mallrie, Malory*

Mallow (Irish) By the river Allo.

Malo (Hawaiian) Winner.

Maloney (Irish) Religious; serves Saint John. *Mal, Malone, Malonie, Malony*

Malvolio (Spanish) Steward.

Mamillius (Latin) Young prince.

Mamoru (Japanese) Earth. *Mamo*

Manavendra (Hindi) King; king among men.

Manchu (Chinese) Pure.

Manco (Peruvian) King.

Mandala (Chinese) Flowers. *Manda, Mandela*

Mandar (Hindi) Tree of heaven; flower.

Mandeep (Punjabi) Mind full of light. *Mandieep*

Mandek (Polish) Army man.

Mandel (German) Almond. *Mandee, Mandela, Mandell, Mandie*

Mander (English) From me. *Mandar*

Mandhatri (Hindi) Prince.

Manfred (German) Man of peace. *Manferd, Manford, Mannfred, Manny, Mannye*

Manik (Hindi) Ruby; gem.

Manish (Hindi) Intellect; god of mind.

Manley (Old English) Man of the meadow. *Manly, Manning, Mansfield*

Manmohan (Hindi) Pleasing.

Manning (Old English) Son of the hero. *Man, Mann*

Mannix (Celtic) Monk. *Manix, Mann, Mannicks*

Manoj (Hindi) Born of mind.

Mansfield (English) From a field by a small river. *Manesfeld, Mans, Mansfeld, Mansfielde*

Mansour (Arabic) One who triumphs.

Mansukh (Hindi) Pleasing.

Mansur (Arabic) Divinely aided. *Mansoor, Mansour*

Manu (African) Second-born son. (Hawaiian) Bird. (Hindi) Lawmaker.

Manuel (Spanish) God is with us. *Mani, Manni, Mannuel, Manny, Mano, Manolo, Manual, Manuale, Manuell, Manuelo*

Manus (American) Strong willed. *Manes, Mann, Mannas, Mannes, Mannis, Mannus*

Manville (English) Hero's village. *Mandeville, Manvel*

Manzo (Japanese) 10,000-fold-strong; third son.

Mapiro (Chinese) Millet. *Mapirah*

Mar (Latin) Sea.

Marcade (Latin) Warlike.

Marcel (French) Little hammer. *Marcellino, Marcellinus, Marcello, Marcellus, Marcelo, Marchello, Marselo*

Marcellus (Latin) Martial; warlike. *Marcel, Marcelis, Marsellus, Marsey*

March (Latin) Walk forth.

Marcin (Polish) Warlike.

Marco (Italian, Spanish) Warring. *Marc, Mark, Marko*

Marcus (Latin) Warlike. *Marcas, Marckus*

Marden (Old English) From the valley with the pool. *Madrin, Mardon*

Mardian (French) Tuesday.

Mardonio (Persian) Male warrior.

Marek (Polish, Slavic) Warlike.

Mareo (Japanese) Rare, uncommon.

Margarelon (Latin) Son of a king.

Mariano (Italian) Bitter; sea of bitterness. *Maryano*

Marid (Arabic) Rebellious. *Maryd*

Marin (French) Ocean-loving. *Maren, Marine, Marino, Maryn*

Marinos (Greek) Of the sea; sailor. *Marina, Marinka, Mariono, Marynos, Marynus*

Marinus (Latin) Of the sea. *Marino*

Mario (Hebrew) Bitter; king-ruler. *Mariana, Marion*

Marius (Latin) Sailor. *Marious*

Marjun (Spanish) Contentious. *Marhwon, Marwon, Marwond*

Mark (Latin) Warlike; hammer; defender. *Marc, Marceau, Marcel, March, Marco, Marcos, Marcus, Marek, Marilo, Marius, Márk, Markie, Markis, Marko, Markó, Markos, Marks, Markus, Márkus, Marky, Marque, Marquette, Marquis, Marus, Marx*

Markandeya (Hindi) Sage.

Markham (English) Homebody. *Marcum, Markhum, Markum*

Marland (English) From the march. *Merle*

Marley (English) Secretive. *Marlee, Marleigh, Marly*

Marlin (Hebrew) Bitter; fish. *Marlen, Marllin*

Marlon (Old French) Little hawk. *Marlan, Marlin, Marlis, Marlo, Marly, Marlyn, Marlys*

Marlow (Old English) From the hillside lake. *Marlo, Marlowe*

Marmaduke (Celtic) Leader of the seas. *Duke, Marmadook, Marmahduke*

Maro (Japanese) Myself. *Marow*

Marót (Slavic) Moravian.

Marquel (American) Form of Marcellus. *Marqueal, Marquelis, Marquil, Marquille*

Marques (African American) Noble. (Portuguese) Warlike. *Markes, Marqes, Marqis, Marquess, Marquez, Marquis*

Marrock (English) Knight thought to be a werewolf. *Marrok*

Mars (Latin) Bold warrior; Roman god of war.

Marsden (Old English) Field near water. *Marden, Mardyth, Marland, Marley, Marsdon, Marston, Marwood*

Marsh (English) Handsome. *Marr, Mars, Marsch, Marsey*

Marshall (French) Keeper of the horses; military title. *Marschall, Marsh, Marshal, Marshe, Marshell*

Marston (English) From the farm by the pool; town near the marsh. *Marsdon, Marstan, Marsten*

Martin (English) Warrior of Mars, warlike, warring. *Maartan, Maartin, Mart, Martain, Marten, Martie, Martine, Marton, Marty, Mertin*

Martino (Italian) Warlike. *Martiniano*

Martir (Greek) He who gives a testament of faith. *Martyr*

Martius (Latin) Warring.

Marvel (French) To wonder; admire. *Marvell, Marvil, Marvill, Marvyl, Marvyll*

Marvin (English) Beautiful sea; good friend; lover of the sea. *Marv, Mervin, Mervyn, Merwin, Merwyn, Murvyn, Myrvyn, Myrwyn*

Masahiro (Japanese) Wise. *Masahyro*

Masakazu (Japanese) First son of Masa.

Masamba (Chinese) Leaves. *Masambah*

Masao (Japanese) Vibrant.

Masato (Japanese) Justice.

Masatoshi (Japanese) Meaning unknown.

Mashama (African) Surprising. *Mashamah*

Mashawn (African American) Vivacious. *Masean, Mashaun, Mayshawn*

Maska (Native American) Strong. *Maskah*

Maslin (Old French) Little twin; little Thomas. *Maslan, Maslen, Maslyn*

Mason (French) Stoneworker. *Mase, Masen, Masin, Masoon, Masun, Masyn*

Masoud (Arabic) Happy; lucky. *Masood, Masoud, Masud*

Massey (English) Doubly excellent. *Maccey, Masey, Massi*

Massimo (Italian) Greatest. *Masimo, Massey, Massimiliano, Massimmo*

Matai (Hebrew) Gift of God. *Massey, Máté, Mateo, Mateus, Mathe, Mathern, Matheu, Mathew, Mathias, Matia, Matias, Mats, Matt, Matteo, Matthäus, Mattheson, Mattheus, Matthew, Matthews, Matthias, Matthieson, Matthuas, Mattias, Mattieu, Mattison, Matty, Mátyás, Matyus, Matze, Mayhew*

Matanga (Hindi) Sage; adviser to the Hindu goddess Devi.

Máté (Croatian) Gift from God.

Mateo (Greek) Devoted to God. *Matteo*

Mateus (Polish) Form of Matthew. *Matejs, Mateusz*

Mather (Old English) Strong army.

Matheson (English) Son of God's gift. *Mathesen, Mathisen, Mathison, Mathysen, Mathyson*

Matheus (German) Form of Matthew. *Matheau, Matheu*

Mathias (German) Gift of God. *Mathies, Mathyes, Matt, Matthias*

Matlal (Aztec) Dark green; net.

Matlock (American) Rancher. *Lock, Mattlock*

Mats (Scandinavian) Gift from God. *Matias, Matthew, Matthias, Matts, Matz*

Matthew (Hebrew) God's gift. *Matt, Matteo, Matthias, Mattias*

Mattison (Hebrew) Son of Matt; worldly. *Matisen, Matison, Mattysen, Mattyson, Matysen, Matyson*

Matusalén (Hebrew) Symbol of longevity.

Mauli (Hawaiian) Black.

Maurice (Latin) Darkskinned; like a Moor. *Maryse, Mauricio, Maurizio, Maury, Meuriz, Morets, Morey, Moritz, Moriz, Morrell, Morrie, Morris, Morrison, Morry, Morse, Moss, Murray*

Maurizio (Italian) Dark. *Marits, Maritza, Moritz, Moritza, Moritzio*

Mauro (Latin) Form of Maurice. *Mauer, Maurio*

Maury (Italian) Darkskinned; Moor. *Amaury, Maure, Mauro*

Maverick (American) Wildly independent. (English) Nonconforming. *Maveric, Maverik, Maveryck, Mavric, Mavrick, Mavrik*

Max (Latin) Greatest. *Mac, Mack, Maks, Maksim, Massimiliano, Maxa, Maxey, Maxfield, Maxie, Maxim, Maximilian, Maximiliano, Maximilien, Maximino, Maximo, Maximus*

Maxfield (English) Mack's field. *Macfield, Makfield*

Maxwell (English) Capable. (Latin) Great. (Scottish) Mack's well. *Maxwel, Maxwill*

Mayer (English) Headman; mayor. (Hebrew) One who brightens. (Latin) Great. *Mayor, Mayr, Meier, Meir, Meyer, Myer, Myerson*

Maynard (Anglo-Saxon) Remarkable strength;

powerful; brave. *Mainard, Maynhard*

Mayo (Irish) Nature-loving; yew tree. *Maio, Maioh, Mayes, Mayoh, Mays, Moy*

Mayon (Hindi) Black God. *Maion, Mayan, Mayun*

Mayua (South American) Violet.

Mazin (Arabic) Proper. *Mazen, Mazon*

Mcaffie (Scottish) Charming. *Mac, MacAfee, Mack, Mackey, McAffee, McAffie*

Mcauliffe (Irish) Bookish. *Macaulif, Macauliff*

Mccauley (Scottish) Son of righteousness. *Macauley, Mccaulay*

McCoy (Irish) Son of Hugh. *McCoi*

McKay (Scottish) Son of Kay. *Macai, Mackay, Makkai*

McKinley (Scottish) Son of Kinley. *MacKinley*

Mead (Old English) Meadow. *Meade, Meed, Meid*

Meallan (Irish) Sweet. *Maylan, Meall*

Mecaenus (Shakespearean) Character from *Antony and Cleopatra*.

Medárd (Hungarian) Great; strong.

Megyer (Hungarian) Pearl. *Magyar*

Mehdi (Hindi) Flower.

Mehetabel (Hebrew) Favored by God; God is doing good. *Hetty, Hitty, Mehitabel, Mehitabelle, Metabel*

Mehmet (Arabic) Form of Mahomet. *Mehemet*

Mehul (Hindi) Rain. *Mukul*

Meka (Hawaiian) Eyes.

Melancton (Greek) Black flower. *Melanchthon*

Melborn (English) From the mill stream. *Melbourne*

Melbourne (English) Mill stream. *Mel, Melborn, Melbourn, Melburn, Melburne*

Melburn (English) From the mill stream. *Melburne, Milburn, Milvourn*

Meldon (English) From the hillside mill. *Melden, Meldin, Meldyn*

Melik (Slavic) His kingdom; his counselor.

Melor (English) Old English hillside; town by the mill. *Mel*

Melun (Greek) Dark-skinned.

Melvin (Celtic) Chief. *Mal, Malvin, Mel, Mell, Melvyn*

Memphis (Egyptian) One who comes from Memphis.

Menas (Shakespearean) Character from *Antony and Cleopatra*.

Mendel (Middle English) Repairman. *Mel, Menachem, Menahem, Mendal, Mendell, Mendelssohn, Mendie, Mendy, Mendyl*

Menecrates (Shakespearean) Character from *Antony and Cleopatra*.

Menelaus (Shakespearean) Character from *Troilus and Cressida*.

Menteith (Shakespearean) Character from *Macbeth*.

Menw (Celtic) Mythological wizard.

Menyhért (Hungarian) Royal; light.

Mercer (Middle English) Storekeeper. *Merce*

Mercury (Italian) God of invention. (Latin) God of trade.

Mercutio (Shakespearean) Character from *Romeo and Juliet*.

Meredith (Old Welsh) Protector of the *sea*. *Meri, Merideth, Meridith, Merry, Merydeth, Merydith, Merydyth*

Merit (Latin) Deserving of good fortune. *Merritt*

Meriweather (Latin) Fair weather. *Meriwether*

Merlin (Celtic) Sea; falcon; sea hill. *Marlen, Marlin, Marwin, Merle, Merlyn, Merv, Mervin*

Merrick (English) Ruler of the sea. *Mere, Meric, Merik, Merrack, Merrick*

Merrill (Irish) Bright sea. (French) Famous. *Meril, Merle, Merral, Merrel, Merrick, Merton, Meryl, Myril, Myrl*

Merton (English) From the farm by the sea. *Mert, Mertan, Merten, Mertin, Murton*

Mervin (Irish) Form of Marvin. *Mervan, Merven, Mervine*

Meshach (Hebrew) That draws with force.

Messala (Italian) Supporter of Brutus.

Mesut (Turkish) Happy.

Mete (Slavic) Gentle. (Greek) Pearl. *Mette*

Meyer (German) Farmer. *Mayeer, Mayer, Meier, Myer*

Mica (Hebrew) Prophet. (Latin) Mineral. *Micah, Micajah, Michah*

Michael (Hebrew) Who is like God. *Meikel, Micah, Micha, Michail, Michau, Michel, Michelangelo, Michele, Michiel, Mick, Mickey, Mickie, Micky, Midge, Miekel, Miguel, Mihal, Mihály, Mihon, Mikas, Mike, Mikel, Mikey, Mikhail, Mikhos, Mikkel, Mikó, Mischa, Mitch, Mitchell*

Michelangelo (Italian) God's angel; messenger; artist. *Michel, Michelanjelo, Mikalangelo, Mikel, Mikelangelo*

Michio (Japanese) Man with the strength of 3,000.

Mickey (Irish) Who is like God. *Mickee, Micki, Myckee, Mycki, Myckie, Mycky, Mykee, Mykie, Myky*

Midas (Greek) Mythological king.

Miguel (Portuguese) Like the Lord. *Migeul, Migueil, Miguelly, Myguell*

Mihaly (Hebrew) He who is like God. *Mihai, Mihail, Mihaly*

Mihir (Hindi) Sun.

Mikal (Native American) Racoon. *Mika, Myka*

Mikasi (Native American) Coyote.

Mikhail (Russian) Godlike; graceful. *Mika, Mikey, Mikkail, Mykhey*

Miklos (Czech) Form of Nicholas.

Miko (Finnish) One who is like God. *Mikko*

Miksa (Hungarian) Similar to God. *Miks, Myksa*

Milán (Hungarian) Kind. *Milano, Millen*

Miles (English) Merciful. (German) Soldier. (Irish) Servant. *Mila, Milah, Milan, Miles, Myles*

Milford (English) Mill by the ford. *Millford, Myllford*

Milind (Hindi) Honeybee.

Millard (Old English) Caretaker of the mill. *Milard, Millerd, Millurd*

Miller (Old English) One who mills. *Mills, Millson*

Milo (German) Soft-hearted. *Milos, Mye, Mylo, Mylos*

Miloslav (Russian) Peace celebration.

Milton (Old English) From the mill town. *Melton, Milt, Milten, Milty*

Miner (Latin) Youth. *Myner*

Minesh (Hindi) Meaning unknown.

Ming (Chinese) After a dynasty.

Minki (Korean) Meaning unknown.

Minoru (Japanese) Fruitful.

Miroslav (Slavic) Famous. *Mirek, Miroslaw*

Misu (Native American) Rippling brook. *Mysu*

Mitali (Hindi) Friend.

Mitchell (American, English, Hebrew) He who is like God. *Mitch, Mitchel, Mitchelle, Mitchill, Mitshell, Mytchil*

Mitesh (Hindi) One with few desires.

Mladen (Slavic) Forever in youth.

Moby (Fiction) Great white whale; *Moby Dick* by Herman Melville.

Mog (Indian) High lord.

Mohamed (Arabic) Praiseworthy; glorified. *Mohamid, Mohammad, Mohammed, Mohamud, Muhammod*

Mohan (Hindi) Charming; fascinating.

Mohanan (Irish) Believer. *Mon, Monaghan, Monehan, Monnahan*

Mohe (Native American) Elk.

Mohin (Hindi) Attractive.

Mohit (Hindi) Ensnarled by beauty.

Mohsen (Arabic) Son; child.

Mojag (Native American) Never silent.

Moke (Hawaiian) Drawn from the water.

Momus (Greek) God of mockery and fault-finding.

Monk (Irish) Form of Monahan.

Monroe (Irish) Mouth of the Roe River; wheel-wright. *Monro, Munro, Munroe*

Montague (French) Steep mountain; residence name. *Mont, Montagew, Montagu, Montegue*

Montana (Spanish) Mountain. *Montaine, Montanna, Montano*

Montano (Latin) Mountain. *Montaine, Montana, Montanus*

Montaro (Japanese) Big boy. *Montero*

Monte (English) Wealthy man's mountain. *Montay, Montee, Monti, Monty*

Montego (Spanish) Mountainous.

Montel (Spanish) Mountain. *Montele, Montelle*

Montenegro (Spanish) Black mountain.

Montgomery (French) Mountain hunter. (English) Rich man's mountain. *Mongomerey, Monte, Montey, Montgomerie, Montgomry, Monty, Mountgomery*

Montraie (African American) Fussy. *Montray, Montraye*

Montrell (French) Royal mountain; from Montreal, Quebec. *Montrel, Montrelle*

Montrose (French) High and mighty. *Montroce, Montros*

Moore (French) Dark; moor. *Moar, Moor, More*

Mór (Hungarian) Moorish. *Moore, Móric*

Mordecai (Hebrew) Warrior. *Mordechai, Mordy, Mort, Morty*

Mordock (Science fiction) Character from *Star Trek: The Next Generation.*

Mordred (Latin) Painful; son of King Arthur.

Moreland (English) From the moors; marshlands. *Mooreland, Moorland, Moorlande, Morland, Morlande*

Morgan (Irish) Lives by the sea.

Morholt (Scottish) In Arthurian legend, prince killed by Tristan.

Moriarty (Irish) Sea warrior; expert seaman.

Morio (Japanese) Forest.

Morley (English) English moor; meadow. Outdoors loving. *Lee, Moorley, More, Morlee, Morleigh, Morly, Morrie, Morrs, Morry*

Moroni (Arabic) Place name. *Maroney, Maroni, Marony, Moroney, Morony*

Morpheus (Greek) God of dreams.

Morris (Latin) Dark-skinned. *Maurice, Morrie, Morrison, Morry, Morse, Moss*

Morrison (English) Son of Morris. (Scottish) Son of the servant Mary. *Morrisen, Morrysen, Morryson*

Mortimer (French) Still water. *Mort, Mortemer, Morty, Mortymer*

Morton (Anglo-Saxon) City on the moor. *Mort, Morten, Morty, Mortyn*

Morven (Old English) Child of the sea. *Morvan, Murvin*

Moses (Hebrew) Drawn out of the water. *Moe, Moey, Moishe, Mose, Moshe, Mosheh, Mosie, Moss, Mosya, Moyes, Moyse*

Motega (Native American) New arrow. *Motegan*

Mowgli (Fiction) Character from *The Jungle Book* by Rudyard Kipling.

Mozart (Italian) Breathless. *Mozar*

Mu-nan (Japanese) Man who never turned back.

Mugen (Japanese) Infinity.

Muhammad (Arabic) Praised one. *Ahmad, Ahmet, Amad, Amed, Hamad, Hamid, Hammed, Mahmoud, Mehemet, Mehmet, Mohamad, Mohamed, Mohamet, Mohammad, Mohammed, Muhammed*

Mukasa (Ugandan) God's chief administrator. *Mukasah*

Mukki (Native American) Child.

Mukta (Hindi) Pearl.

Mukul (Hindi) Bud.

Mukunda (Hindi) Form of Lord Krishna; freedom giver.

Mulder (American) Of the dark. *Muldyr*

Mull (Middle English) Grinder. *Muller, Müller*

Mumtaz (Arabic) Excellent; conspicuous.

Mun Hee (Korean) Educated.

Munir (Arabic) Sparkling; brilliant; shining. *Munira, Munirah*

Murat (Turkish) Wish come true.

Murdad (Persian) Immortality; angel of July.

Murdock (Scottish) Victorious at sea. *Merdock, Merdok, Murdoch, Murdock, Murdok, Murtagh*

Murfain (American) Bold spirit. *Merfaine, Murf, Murfee, Murfy, Murphy*

Murphy (Irish) Sea warrior. *Merfee, Murphee, Murphey, Murphi, Murphie, Murphree*

Murray (Celtic) Sailor. *Moray, Muray, Murrey, Murry*

Mustafa (Arabic) Chosen one. *Mostafa, Mostafah, Mostaffa, Mustafe, Mustaffa, Mustafo, Mustofo*

Mustanen (Finnish) Black.

Mutius (Shakespearean) Character from *Titus Andronicus.*

Muzaffer (Turkish) Meaning unknown.

Mykelti (African American) He who is like God.

Mykola (Greek) Victory of the people.

Myles (English) Merciful. (Irish) Servant. (Latin) Soldier. (Greek) Inventor of the corn mill.

Myrle (American) Able. *Merl, Merle, Myrie, Myryee*

Myron (Greek) Sweet oil.

Myung-Ki (Korean) Cleverness and energy.

N

Naayantara (Hindi) Star of our eyes.

Nabarun (Indian) Morning sun.

Nabendu (Hindi) New moon.

Nabil (Arabic) Noble. *Nabiel, Nabill, Nabyl, Nabyll*

Nabucodonosor (African) God protects my reign.

Nabulung (African American) Do not receive.

Nachiketa (Hindi) Ancient rishi (Vedic poet); fire. *Nachik*

Nachman (Hebrew) Comforter. *Menachem, Menahem, Nacham, Nachmann, Nahum*

Nachmanke (Hebrew) Compassionate one; one who comforts.

Nachum (Hebrew) Comfort. *Nabum, Nachman, Nechum, Nehum*

Nada (Arabic) Generous. *Nadah*

Nadav (Hebrew) Noble; generous one. *Nadiv*

Nadidah (Arabic) Equal to anyone.

Nadim (Hindi) Friend. *Nadeem, Nadym*

Nadir (Hebrew) Pledge. *Nader*

Nadisu (Hindi) Beautiful river. *Nadysu*

Naeem (African American) Benevolent. *Naem, Naim, Naiym, Naym, Nieen*

Naftali (African) Runs in woods. *Naphtali, Neftali, Nefthali, Nephtali, Nephthali*

Nagel (English) Smooth. *Naegel, Nageler, Nagelle, Nagle, Nagler*

Nagesh (Hindi) Lord Shiva.

Nagid (Hebrew) Ruler. *Nagyd*

Nahele (Hawaiian) Forest.

Nahir (Hebrew) Light. *Nahar, Naheer*

Nahum (Hebrew) Comforter. *Naum*

Nailah (Arabic) Successful. *Naila, Nayla, Naylah*

Naimish (Hindi) Meaning unknown.

Nairne (Scottish) From the narrow river glade. *Nairn, Nayrn, Nayrne*

Naji (Arabic) To save. *Nagi, Naj, Najae, Najee, Najie, Najiee, Najih, Najy*

Najib (Arabic) Distinguish; high born. *Najeeb, Najyb, Nejib, Nejyb, Nageeb, Nagib*

Nakia (Arabic) Pure. *Nakai, Nakee, Nakeia, Naki, Nakiah, Nakii*

Nakul (Hindi) Name of one of the Pandavas.

Nalan (Hindi) Lotus.

Nalani (Hawaiian) Heaven's calm.

Nam-Kyu (Korean) Southern.

Namdev (Hindi) Poet; saint; form of Lord Vishnu.

Namid (African) Star dancer. *Namyd*

Namir (Hebrew) Leopard. *Namer, Namyr*

Nan Shin (Japanese) Gentle mind; natural mind.

Nanda (Sanskrit) Joy.

Nandin (Hindi) The delightful; follower of Shiva. *Nandyn*

Nándor (Hungarian) Short for Ferdinand. *Nandor*

Nangila (African) Born while parents were traveling. *Nangilah, Nangyla*

Nansen (Swedish) Son of Nancy. *Nansan, Nansin, Nanson*

Nantan (Native American) Spokesman. *Nanten, Nantin*

Naoko (Japanese) Direct.

Napoleon (Italian) Fierce one from Naples. (African American) Lion in a new city. *Leo, Leon, Nap, Napoleone, Nappie, Nappy*

Narayana (Hindi) Vishnu; refuge of man.

Narciso (Latin) Lily; daffodil.

Narcissus (Greek) Self-love. *Narcisse, Narcisus, Narcyssus, Narkissos*

Nard (Persian) Chess game.

Naresh (Hindi) Ruler of men.

Narik (Science fiction) Character from *Star Trek: The Next Generation.*

Narrie (Australian) Bush fire. *Narree, Narrey, Narri, Narry*

Narsi (Hindi) Poet; saint.

Nartana (Hindi) Makes others dance.

Nasario (Spanish) Dedicated to God. *Nasar, Nasareo, Nassario, Nazareo, Nazarlo, Nazaro, Nazor*

Nash (Old English) Cliff. *Nashe*

Nashoba (Native American) Wolf. *Neshoba*

Nasim (Arabic) Fresh. *Naseem, Nassim, Nasym*

Nasser (Arabic) Winning. *Naser, Nasir, Nasr, Nassar, Nasse, Nassee, Nassor*

Nassir (Arabic) Protector. *Nas, Nasir*

Natal (Spanish) Form of Noel. *Natale, Natalie, Natalino*

Natan (Hebrew) God has given. *Natain, Nataine, Naten*

Nataraj (Sanskrit) King of dance.

Nathan (Hebrew) Form of Nathaniel. *Naethan, Naethin, Naethun, Naethyn, Naithon, Nate, Nathann, Nathean, Nathin, Natthan, Nethan*

Nathaniel (Hebrew) Gift of God. *Naethanael, Naethanial, Nafanael, Nafanail, Nafanyl, Nafanyle, Naithanael, Naithanyael, Naithanyal, Nat, Natan, Nataniel, Nataniele, Nate, Nathan, Nathanae, Nathanael, Nathanal, Nathaneal, Nathaneil, Nathanel, Nathanial, Nathanie, Nathanni, Nathanualm, Nathanyal, Nathel, Nathon, Natt, Natthanyal, Natty, Nayfanial, Naythaneal, Naythanial, Naythanielle, Nithanial, Nithanyal, Nothanial, Nothaniel, Nothanyal, Nothanyel, Thaniel*

Nato (American) Gentle. *Nate, Natoe, Natoh*

Naum (Hebrew) Comforter.

Navarro (Spanish) Plains. *Navara, Navaro, Navarra, Navarre*

Navdeep (Sikh) New light. *Navdip*

Naveen (Hindi) New, modern. *Naven, Navin, Navyn*

Nayan (Hindi) Eye.

Nayland (English) Island sweller. *Nailan, Nailand, Naylan*

Nazaire (French) From Nazareth. *Nasareo, Nasarrio, Nazar, Nazario, Nazarius, Nazaro*

Neal (Gaelic) Champion. *Neale, Neel, Neely, Neil, Neill, Nels, Nial, Niall, Niel, Niels, Niles, Nils, O'Neill*

Nebraska (Native American) Flat water; place name. *Neb*

Nectarios (Greek) Sweet nectar; immortal man. *Nectaire, Nectarius, Nektario, Nektarios, Nektarius*

Ned (English) Prosperous guardian. *Nedd, Neddie, Neddyn, Nedrick*

Nedes (Old English) Necessity.

Nedim (Turkish) Meaning unknown.

Nedrun (American) Difficult. *Ned, Nedd, Neddy, Nedran, Nedro*

Neel (Hind) Blue. *Neelendra, Neelmani*

Neelambar (Indian) Blue sky.

Neema (Swahili) Born during prosperous times.

Neeraj (Hind) Born in water.

Nehemiah (Hebrew) God's compassion. *Nechemia, Nechemiah, Nechemya, Nechemyah, Nemiah, Nemo*

Nehru (East Indian) Canal.

Neil (Irish) Champion. *Neal, Neale, Neall, Nealle, Nealon, Neihl, Neile, Neill, Neille, Neils, Nels, Nial, Niall, Nialle, Niel, Niels, Nigel, Niles, Nilo*

Neilan (Irish) Champion.

Nek (Italian) Meaning unknown. *Neko*

Neka (Native American) Wild goose. *Nekah*

Nektarios (Greek) Nectar. *Nectarios*

Nelek (Polish) Like a horn. *Nelik*

Nellie (English) Short for Nelson; singing. *Nell, Nellee, Nelli, Nells, Nelly*

Nelo (Spanish) Form of Daniel. *Nello, Nilo*

Nels (Scandinavian) Champion; form of Neil. *Nelse*

Nelson (Old English) Son of a champion; son of Neil. *Nealsan, Nealsen, Nealson, Nealsyn, Neelsan, Neelsen, Neelsin, Neelson, Neelsun, Neelsyn, Neilsan, Neilsen, Neilsin, Neilson, Neilsun, Nellie, Nelly, Nels, Nelsin, Nelsun, Nelsyn, Neylsan, Neylsen, Neylsin, Neylson, Neylsun, Neylsyn, Nilsan, Nilsen, Nilson, Nilsson, Nilsun, Nilsyn, Nylsan, Nylsen, Nylsin, Nylson, Nylsun, Nylsyn*

Nemesio (Spanish) Justice. *Nemo, Nimi*

Nemuel (Hebrew) God's sea. *Nemuele, Nemuell, Nemuelle*

Neo (Greek) New.

Neper (Spanish) New city.

Neptune (Latin) Roman god of the sea. *Neptunne, Neptuno*

Nereus (Greek) Of the sea. *Nereo*

Nero (Latin) Strong. *Neron, Nerone, Niro*

Neron (Spanish) Strong; stern. *Nerone, Nerron*

Nerville (French) Village by the sea. *Nervil, Nervile, Nervill, Nervyile, Nervyle, Nervyll*

Nery (Hebrew) Form of Nuri. *Neri*

Nesbit (English) Curve in the road. *Naisbitt, Naisbyt, Naisbytt, Nasbit, Nesbitt, Nesbyt, Nesbytt, Nisbet, Nisbett, Nysbet, Nysbett,*

Nysbitt, Nysbyt, Nysbytt

Nesim (Turkish) Meaning unknown.

Nesip (Turkish) Meaning unknown.

Nesto (Spanish) Serious.

Nestor (Greek) Traveler; wisdom. *Nest, Nesta, Nestar, Nester*

Nevada (Spanish) Covered in snow. *Navada*

Nevan (Irish) Little saint; holy. *Nefan, Neven, Nevon, Nivon*

Neville (French) From the new farmland. *Nev, Nevelson, Nevil, Nevile, Newland*

Nevin (German) Nephew. (Irish) Servant of the saints. *Neffe, Nefin, Nevins, Nevyns, Nivyn, Nyvin*

Newboyd (English) New tree.

Newbury (English) Surname; renewal. *Newberry, Newbery, Newborough, Newburgh, Newburry*

Newell (Old English) From the manor; kernel. *Newall, Newbold, Newgate, Newland, Newlin, Newton*

Newlyn (Old Welsh) Pool. *Newl, Newlin, Newlynn, Nule*

Newman (Old English) Newcomer. *Neiman, Neimann, Neimon, Neuman, Neumann, Newmen, Newmie, Numan, Numen*

Newt (English) New. *Nauton, Newton, Newtown*

Niagara (Native American) Place name.

Niao-Ka (Chinese) Bird's nest.

Nicandro (Spanish) Man who excels. *Nicandreo, Nicandrios, Nicandros, Nikander, Nikandreo, Nikandrios*

Nicholas (Greek) Victorious people. *Claus, Cole, Colet, Colin, Klaas, Klas, Klaus, Miklós, Nicanor, Nicc, Nicco, Niccolas, Niccolo, Nichelas, Nichele, Nichlas, Nichol, Nicholai, Nicholas, Nicholaus, Nicholos, Nichols, Nicholson, Nick, Nickita, Nicklaus, Nicko, Nicky, Niclasse, Nico, Nicodemus, Nicol, Nicola, Nicolai, Nicolao, Nicolas, Nicole, Nicoll, Nicolo, Nicolson, Nicos, Nikita, Nikki, Niklaus, Niko, Nikola, Nikolai, Nikolaos, Nikolas, Nikolaus, Nikolie, Nikolos, Nikos, Niles, Nils, Nixon, Nycholas, Nyck, Nyk, Nykolus*

Nicodemus (Greek) Victory of the people. *Nicodemo, Nikodema*

Nicola (Italian) Form of Nicholas. *Nickola, Nicolá, Nikolah*

Niels (Scandinavian) Victorious. *Neels, Niel*

Nigan (Native American) In the lead. *Nigen*

Nigel (Latin) Dark one. *Niegal, Niegel, Nigal, Nigale, Nigele, Nigell, Nigiel, Nigil, Nigle, Nijel, Nygal, Nyigel, Nyjil*

Nihar (Hindi) Mist; fog; dew.

Nika (African) Ferocious. *Nica, Nicka, Nikka, Nycah*

Nikan (Native American) My friend.

Nike (Greek) Victory. *Nyke, Nykee, Nykie*

Nikhil (Russian) Victor.

Niki (Hungarian) Form of Nicholas. *Nikia, Nikkie, Niky*

Nikiti (Native American) Smooth. *Nikity, Nikyti, Nykiti*

Nikos (Greek) Victor. *Nicos, Niko, Nikolos*

Nila (Hindi) Blue. *Nilah, Nyla, Nylah*

Nilay (Hindi) Home; heaven.

Nile (English) Smooth. *Ni, Niles, Niley, Nyles, Nyley*

Nils (Danish) Champion.

Nilsson (Swedish) Form of Nelson.

Nima (Arabic) Blessing.

Nimai (Hindi) Name of Lord Krishna. *Nimay*

Nimbus (Latin) Rain cloud; halo.

Nimesh (Hindi) Meaning unknown. *Nimish*

Nimrod (Hebrew) Renegade. *Nimrodd, Nymrod*

Ninacolla (Chinese) Flame of fire.

Ninian (Gaelic) Fifth-century saint.

Nino (Italian) God is gracious. *Ninoshka*

Ninyun (American) Spirited. *Ninian, Ninion, Ninyan, Nynyun*

Niraj (Hindi) Lotus flower.

Niramitra (Hindi) Son of pandava Sahadeva.

Niran (Thai) Eternal. *Niron, Niryn*

Niranjan (Hindi) Name of a river; goddess Durga; night of the full moon.

Nirav (Hindi) Quiet, without sound.

Nirel (Hebrew) God's field. *Nir, Nira, Niria, Niriel, Nyree*

Nishad (Hindi) Seventh note on the Indian musical scale. *Ni*

Nishan (Armenian) Sign. *Nishon, Nyshan*

Nisi (Hebrew) Emblem.

Nissan (Hebrew) Miracle. *Nisan, Nissim, Nissin, Nisson*

Nitesh (Hindi) Heartbeat of the earth.

Nitis (Native American) Good friend. *Netis*

Nitya-Sundara (Hindi) Good-looking.

Nixon (English) Son of Nick. *Nixan, Nixen, Nixum, Nyxen*

Nizam (Arabic) Leader. *Nyzam*

Njord (Old Norse) Man of the north.

Noadiah (Hebrew) God assembles.

Noah (Hebrew) Comfort; wanderer. *Noa, Noach, Noam, Noe, Noel*

Noble (Latin) Honorable one; well born. *Nobel, Nobile*

Nocona (Native American) Wanderer. *Nokoni*

Nodin (American) Wind. (Native American) Windy day.

Noe (Spanish) Peace; rest. *Noeh, Noey*

Noel (French) Christmas. *Natal, Natale, Noël, Noell, Nole, Noli, Nowel, Nowele, Nowell*

Nohea (Hawaiian) Handsome. *Noha, Nohe*

Noi (Laos) Small. *Sanoi*

Nokonyu (Native American) Katydid's nose. *Noko, Nokoni*

Nolan (Irish) Renowned; noble. (Scottish) Famous; champion. *Nolen, Nolin, Nolyn, Nowlan*

Nollie (Scandinavian) Form of Oliver. *Noll, Nolly*

Nona (Latin) Ninth.

Noor (Hindi) Light.

Norb (Scandinavian) Innovative. *Norberto, Norbie, Norbs, Norby*

Norbert (German) Blond hero. *Bert, Norbie, Norbrit, Norburt, Norby, Northbert, Northburt, Northbyrt*

Nordin (Nordic) Handsome. *Nord, Nordan, Norde, Nordee, Nordeen, Nordun*

Norman (English) Man from the north. *Norm, Normal, Normand, Normen, Normie, Normin, Normon, Normy, Normyn, Norris, Norville*

Norris (English) Northerner. *Nore, Norice, Noris, Norreys, Norrie, Norriss, Norry, Norrys*

North (Old English) From the north. *Northcliff, Northrup, Norton, Norvin, Norward, Norwell, Norwin, Norwood, Norwyn, Nowles*

Northcliff (English) Northern cliff. *Northclif, Northcliffe, Northclyf, Northclyfe, Northclyff, Northclyffe*

Northrop (English) Northern farm. *North, Northrup*

Norton (English) Northern town. *Nort, Nortan, Norten*

Norval (Scottish) Northern village. *Norvel*

Norvell (English) North well. *Norval, Norve, Norvil, Norvile, Norvill, Norville, Norvyl, Norvylle*

Norvin (English) Northern friend. *Norvyn, Norwin, Norwyn*

Norwin (English) Friendly. *Norvin, Norwen, Norwind, Norwinn, Norwyn, Norwynn*

Noy (Hebrew) Beauty; decoration.

Numa (Arabic) Kindness. *Numah*

Nun (Egyptian) God of the ocean.

Nuncio (Italian) Messenger. *Nunzi, Nunzio*

Nuri (Arabic) Fire. *Noori, Nur, Nuriel, Nuris, Nurism, Nury*

Nuriel (Hebrew) Light of God. *Nooriel, Nurah, Nuria, Nuriya, Nuriyah, Nurya, Nuryel*

Nuru (African) Light; born in daylight.

Nuys (American) Place name, Van Nuys, California. *Nies, Nyes, Nys*

Nwa (African) Son.

Nye (Middle English) Island dweller.

Nyék (Hungarian) Borderlands.

Nyle (Old English) Island. *Nyal, Nyl, Nyles, Nyll, Nylle*

O

Oakley (Old English) From the oak meadow. *Oakes, Oakie, Oaklee, Oakleigh, Oakly, Oklie*

Obadiah (Hebrew) Servant of God. *Obadia, Obe, Obed, Obie*

Obedience (American) To obey.

Obelia (Greek) Pillar of strength; needle.

Obelix (Greek) Pillar of strength. *Obelius*

Oberon (German) Bear heart. *Auberon, Auberron, Obaron, Oberahn, Oberone, Oburahn*

Obert (German) Wealthy. *Obirt*

Obiajulu (African American) Heart is consoled.

Obsidian (English) Glassy black volcanic rock.

Ocean (Greek) Sea. *Oceane, Oceanus*

Oceana (Greek) From the sea.

Ochen (Ugandan) One of the twins.

Octavius (Latin) Eighth child. (Shakespearean) Character from *Antony and Cleopatra* and *Julius Caesar.* *Octavia, Octavian, Octavio, Octavus, Oktávián, Tavie, Tavy*

Octha (English) From Arthurian legend, an enemy of Arthur.

Oda (Norse) Small pointed spear.

Odakota (Native American) Friend.

Oddvar (Norse) Spear's point. *Odd*

Odea (Greek) Walker by the road.

Oded (Hebrew) Strong. *Odeda*

Odele (Greek) Wealthy; melody.

Odell (English) Otter. (Irish) Surname. (Scandinavian) Little wealthy one. *Odall, Ode, Odele, Odie, Odyll*

Odessa (Greek) Odyssey; journey; voyage.

Odette (English) Wealthy one. (German) Elfin spear. (Greek) Melody.

Odhran (Irish) Pale green.

Odil (French) Rich.

Odilon (French) Wealthy.

Odin (Norse) Head god in Norse mythology. *Odan, Oden*

Odina (Latin) Mountain.

Odion (Nigerian) First of twins.

Odis (German) Wealthy. *Otis*

Odo (French) Name of a bishop. (Scandinavian) Rich. (Science fiction) Character from *Star Trek: Deep Space Nine. Audo, Oddo, Odoh*

Odolf (German) Prosperous wolf. *Odolfe, Odolff, Odolph, Odulf*

Odon (Hungarian) Wealthy protector; keeper of the fief.

Odran (Irish) Pale green. *Odren, Odrin, Odron, Odryn*

Odysseus (Greek) Full of wrath.

Offa (English) King.

Ogden (Old English) From the oak valley. *Den, Denny, Ogdan, Oggie*

Ogilvy (Scottish) From the high peak. *Gil, Gilie, Gilly, Ogilvie*

Ogima (Native American) Chief. *Ogimah, Ogyma, Ogymah*

Oguz (Hungarian) Arrow.

Ohanna (Armenian) God's gracious gift.

Ohanzee (Native American) Shadow. *Ohanze*

Ohio (Native American) Large river.

Oihane (Spanish) From the forest.

Oisin (Irish) Little deer.

Oistin (Latin) Venerable. (Irish) Majestic. *Oistan, Oisten*

Oja (African) He came of a hard birth.

Ojal (Hindi) Vision.

Okal (African) To cross.

Okalani (Hawaiian) Heaven.

Okan (Turkish) Meaning unknown.

Okapi (African) Animal with a long neck. *Okapie, Okapy*

Oke (Hawaiian) Divine strength. *Oscar*

Okelani (Hawaiian) From heaven.

Oki (Japanese) Ocean-centered.

Okie (American) From Oklahoma. *Okee, Oki, Oky*

Okoth (African) Born when it was raining.

Oksana (Russian) Glory be to God.

Ola (Yoruban) Wealthy. *Olah, Olla, Ollah*

Olaf (Old Norse) Talisman; ancestor. *Olav, Olen, Olie, Olin, Olof*

Olajuwon (Yoruban) Wealth and honor are God's gift. *Olajowuan, Olajuwa, Olajuwan, Oljuwoun, Olujuwon*

Olan (Scandinavian) Royal ancestor. *Illee, Olin*

Olander (Sweish) From the land of Oland.

Olathe (Native American) Beautiful.

Olayinka (Yoruban) Honors surround me.

Olcay (Turkish) Meaning unknown.

Oldrich (Czech) One with riches and power. *Olda, Oldra, Oldrisek, Olecek, Olik, Olouvsek*

Oleg (Slavic) One who is holy. *Olag, Olig*

Oleksandr (Russian) Form of Alexander. *Olek, Olesandr, Olesko*

Oleksiy (Greek) Defender.

Oleos (Spanish) Holy oil used in church. *Leo*

Olesia (Polish) Helper and defender of mankind.

Olga (Russian) Holy.

Oliana (Hawaiian) Oleander.

Olier (French) Meaning unknown.

Olin (Old English) Holly. *Olinda, Olney*

Olindo (Spanish) Protector. *Olinda*

Oliver (Old Norse) Kind one. (Latin) Olive tree. (French) Peace. *Noll, Nolly, Olivero, Olivier, Olley, Ollie, Olly*

Oliwa (Hawaiian) Form of Oliver. *Olliva, Ollyva*

Olwen (Welsh) White footprint.

Olympe (French) Olympian.

Olympia (Greek) Of Mount Olympus; heavenly.

Oma (Arabic) Commander. (Hebrew) Cedar tree. (Irish) Olive color.

Omaha (Native American) Above all others upon a stream.

Omana (Hindi) Woman.

Omar (Arabic) Long-lived; highest; follower of the prophet. (Hebrew) He who speaks; bitter. *Omer, Omir*

Omarjeet (Hindi) Meaning unknown.

Omega (Greek) Great.

Omprakash (Indian) Light of God.

Omrao (Italian) King.

Omri (Hebrew) Sheaf of corn.

On (Chinese) Peace.

Ona (Lithuanian) Graceful one.

Onaedo (African) Gold.

Onan (Turkish) Wealthy.

Onani (African) Quick look. *Onanee, Onanie, Onany*

Onaona (Hawaiian) Sweet smell. *Onaonah*

Onawa (Native American) Awake.

Ond (Hungarian) Tenth child.

Ondrea (Slavic) Strong; courageous.

Oneida (Native American) Eagerly awaited.

Onelia (Hungarian) Torch light.

Onenn (Breton) Meaning unknown.

Oni (Native American) Born on holy ground.

Onida (Native American) Expected one.

Onofre (Spanish) Defender of peace.

Onslow (Arabic) Hill of the passionate one. (English) From the zealous one's hill.

Ontibile (African) God is watching over me.

Oona (Irish) Unity; one.

Opa (Native American) Owl.

Ora (Spanish) Gold.

Oral (Latin) Speaker; word. *Oreel, Orel, Oriel, Orrel, Orrell*

Oralee (Hebrew) Lord is my light.

Oran (Irish) Green. (Scottish) Pale-skinned. *Oram, Oren, Orin, Orran, Orren, Orrie, Orrin*

Orane (French) Rising. (Irish) Green.

Orbán (Hungarian) City dweller; educated man. *Orbó, Oros*

Orde (Latin) Beginning. *Ordell*

Orea (Greek) Mountains.

Orelious (Latin) Gold. *Orelius*

Oren (Hebrew, Gaelic) Ash tree; pale; pine tree. *Orono, Orren*

Orenda (Native American) Magic power.

Orestes (Greek) Leader. *Oresta, Oreste*

Oria (Latin) From the Orient.

Oriel (Old French) Golden; angel of destiny.

Orien (Latin) The Orient; east. *Oreon, Ori*

Orinda (Teutonic) Fire serpent.

Oringo (African) He who likes the hunt.

Oriole (Latin) Fair-haired.

Orion (Greek) Son of fire. (Mythology) Orion the hunter was placed in the sky as a constellation. *Orien, Oris*

Örkény (Hungarian) Frightening man.

Orlan (English) From the pointed hill. (German) Renowned in the land.

Orlando (Latin) Bright sun. *Lando, Orlanda, Orly*

Orlantha (Old German) From the land.

Orleans (French) Golden.

Orli (Hebrew) Light is mine.

Orly (Hebrew) Light.

Orma (African) Free men.

Orman (Old English) Spearman.

Ormand (German) Serpent.

Ormanda (German) Of the sea.

Ormond (English) Kind-hearted. *Ormand, Ormande, Orme, Ormon, Ormund, Ormunde*

Ormos (Hungarian) Like a cliff.

Ornice (Hebrew) Cedar tree.

Oro (Spanish) Gold.

Orrick (English) From the ancient oak tree. *Oric, Orick, Orreck, Orrik*

Orrin (Greek) Mountain. *Orest, Orestes*

Örs (Hungarian) Hero.

Orson (English) Ormond's son. (French) Little bear. *Orsen, Orsin, Orsini, Sonny*

Orville (French) From the golden village. *Orval, Orvalle*

Osama (Arabic) Lionlike.

Osanna (Greek) Praise.

Osaze (Hebrew) Favored by God. *Osaz*

Osbert (Old English) Inspired; divine. *Osborn, Osborne, Osman, Osmar, Osmen, Osmond, Osmund, Ossie, Osted, Ostric*

Osborn (English) Divine warrior. (German) Divine bear. *Orburn, Osbourne, Osburne*

Oscar (Old Norse) Divine spear. *Osgood, Oskar, Oszkár*

Osgood (English) Goth of the Heavens. *Osgude, Ozgood*

Osias (Greek) Salvation.

Osip (Hebrew) God will multiply; God shall add.

Osma (Latin) God's servant.

Osman (Arabic) Tender youth. *Osmen, Osmin*

Osmany Origin and meaning unknown.

Osmond (Old English) God; protector. *Osmund*

Osric (English) Divine ruler.

Ossian (Irish) Fawn.

Ossie (English) God's divine power.

Osten (German) East. *Ostin, Ostyn*

Oswald (Old English) Divinely powerful. *Ossie, Oswald, Oswaldo, Oswall, Oswell, Ozzie*

Oswin (Old English) God; friend. *Osvin, Oswinn, Oswyn, Owwynn*

Oszlár (Hungarian) Meaning unknown.

Othello (Italian) Prosperous. (Shakespearean) Character from *Othello*.

Othi (Romany, Gypsy) Meaning unknown.

Otieno (African) Born at night.

Otis (German) Wealthy. (Greek) One who hears well. *Otello, Otho, Otilio*

Otto (German) Wealthy.

Ouida (French) Warrior.

Ove (Norse) Awe; spear's point.

Overton (English) Upper town.

Ovid (Latin) Lamb.

Ovidio (Spanish) Shepherd. *Ovido*

Owen (Irish) Born to nobility; warrior. *Ewan, Ewen, Owaine, Owan, Owayne, Owens, Owin, Owine, Owyn*

Oxford (Old English) From where the oxen ford. *Oxon, Oxton*

Oya (Native American) Strength.

Oz (Hebrew) Strength. *Ozzie, Ozzy*

Ozan (Turkish) Meaning unknown. *Özcan*

Ozaner (Turkish) Meaning unknown.

Ozor (Hungarian) Ethnic group.

Özséb (Hungarian) Pious.

Ozsvát (Hungarian) Deity; might.

P

Pablo (Spanish) Borrowed. *Pable, Paublo*

Pacey (English) Born on Easter or Passover. *Pace, Paice, Payce*

Packard (Old English) One who packs.

Paco (Native American) Bald eagle. (Spanish) Free. (Italian) Pack. *Packo, Pacorro, Pako, Panchito, Paquito*

Paddy (Irish) Nobleman. *Paddee, Paddey, Paddi, Paddie, Padi, Pady*

Paden (Scottish) Royal.

Padraig (Irish) Nobleman. *Padraic*

Page (French) Young attendant. *Padgett, Paggio, Paige, Payg, Payge*

Paki (Egyptian) Witness.

Pal (Scandinavian) Small. *Paall, Pall*

Palani (Hawaiian) Free man. *Palanee, Palaney, Palanie, Palany*

Pallaton (Native American) Fighter.

Pallav (Hindi) Young shoots and leaves.

Pallu (Hebrew) Admirable; hidden.

Palmer (Old English) Palm-bearing pilgrim. *Pallmer, Palmar*

Palti (Hebrew) My escape. *Paltiel*

Pancho (Spanish) Tuft; plume. *Panchito*

Pancrazio (Italian) Supreme ruler; all powerful.

Pandarus (Latin) Gifted.

Pandita (Hindi) Scholar.

Pandya (Hindi) Meaning unknown.

Pankaj (Hindi) Lotus flower.

Panos (Greek) Rock.

Panthea (Greek) Of all the gods.

Paolo (Italian) Small.

Parag (Hindi) Pollen.

Paramartha (Hindi) Great entity.

Paras (Hindi) Touchstone.

Paris (French) Place name. (Italian) Lover. (Greek) Character in mythology. *Paras, Paree, Pares, Parese, Parie, Parys*

Parker (Old English) Cultivated land. *Park, Parke, Parkley, Parks*

Parlan (Gaelic) Ploughman; farmer. *Parlen, Parlin, Parlon, Parlyn*

Parnab Origin and meaning unknown.

Parr (Old English) From the stable.

Parry (Welsh) Son of Harry. *Paree, Parey, Pari, Parie, Parree, Parrey, Parri, Parrie, Pary*

Parsifal (English) Valley piercer.

Parth (Hindi) Name given to Arjun by Lord Krishna. *Partha, Parthey*

Pascal (French) Born at Easter. *Pace, Pascale, Pascali, Pascall, Pascalle, Pascha, Paschal, Paschalis, Pascoe, Pascoli, Pascow, Pasqual, Pasquale*

Patamon (Native American) Raging. *Pataman, Patamen, Patamin, Patamyn*

Patch (American) Small rock.

Patern (Breton) Meaning unknown. *Padarn, Padern*

Patrick (Latin) Noble one. *Paddy, Padraic, Padraig, Padruig, Pakelika, Pat, Paterson, Patric, Patrice, Patricio, Patricius, Patrickk, Patrik, Patrique, Patrizio, Patrizius, Patryc, Patryck, Patryk, Pats, Patsy, Patterson, Pattison, Pattrick, Rick, Ricky*

Patroclus (Greek) Character in *Iliad* by Homer. (Shakespearean) Character from *Troilus and Cressida*.

Patwin (Native American) Man. *Patwyn*

Pau (Hebrew) Howling; sighing.

Paul (Latin) Little one. *Oalo, Pablo, Paolo, Pasko, Pauley, Paulia, Paulin, Paulis, Paull, Paulle, Paulo, Paulot, Pauls, Paulus, Pauly, Pavel, Pavlo, Pavlos, Pawl, Pawley, Pál, Pol, Powell*

Paulo (African) Place of rest.

Paulos (German) Small.

Pavel (Slavic) Little. *Paavel, Paval, Pavil, Pavils, Pavlik, Pavlo, Pavol*

Pavlos (Slavic) Little.

Pavo (Slavic) Little.

Paxton (Teutonic, Old English) Trader; town of peace. *Packston, Paxon, Paxtan, Paxten, Paxtin, Paxtum, Paxtyn*

Paytah (Native American) Fire. *Pay, Payta*

Payton (Old English) Warrior's estate. *Paiton, Pate, Peaton*

Pázmán (Hungarian) Right; man.

Peabo (African) Peaceful.

Peace (Latin) Peace; tranquility.

Peder (Greek) Stone. *Peadair, Peadar, Peader, Pedey*

Pedro (Spanish) Rock. *Pedrin, Petronio*

Peers (English) Rock. *Peerus*

Peja (Slavic) Very dear.

Pekelo (Hawaiian) Stone. *Pekeio, Pekka*

Pelagius (Latin) Sea.

Pell (Old English) Scarf. *Pelham, Pelton*

Pelleas (English) Fisher king.

Pellegrin (Hungarian) Pilgrim.

Pello (Greek) Stone; Peru. *Piarres*

Pelton (English) From the farm by a pool. *Peltan, Pelten, Peltin*

Pembroke (Welsh) From the headland; rocky hill. *Pembrok, Pembrook*

Penda (English) King. (African) Beloved.

Penley (Old English) Enclosed meadow. *Penlea, Penlee, Penleigh, Penli, Penlie, Penly, Penn*

Penn (Old English) Enclosure. *Pen, Penna*

Penrod (German) Esteemed commander. *Penn, Pennrod, Rod*

Pentele (Hungarian) Merciful; lion.

Per (Swedish) Small rock.

Percival (Old French) Pierce the veil. *Parsefal, Parsifal, Perce, Perceval, Percheval, Perci, Percy*

Percy (French) Piercing the valley. *Pearcey, Pearcy, Percee, Percey, Perci, Percie, Piercey, Piercy*

Peregrin (Latin) Falcon. *Pelgrim, Pellefrino, Peregrin, Peregrine, Peregryn, Peregryne*

Pericles (Greek) Famous Greek orator. *Perycles*

Peril (Latin) Trial or test.

Pernell (French) Little rock. *Pernall, Perren*

Perry (Middle English) Small rock. *Parry, Peree, Perey, Peri, Perian, Perianne, Perie, Perin, Perree, Perrey, Perri, Perrie, Perrin, Perrye, Pery, Pierrey*

Persepolis (Persian) Place name, southern Iran.

Perseus (Greek) Son of Danae and Zeus.

Perth (Celtic) Thorny bush. *Pirth, Pyrth*

Peter (Latin) Rock, stone. *Parkin, Parkinson, Parle, Parnell, Peadair, Peat, Peate, Peater, Peder, Pedro, Peer, Peet, Peit, Peite, Peiter, Pelle,*

Per, Perkin, Perkins, Pero, Perrin, Pete, Péter, Peterke, Peterson, Peterus, Petey, Peti, Petie, Petò, Petr, Petri, Petrie, Petronio, Petrus, Petúr, Peyt, Piaras, Pierce, Piero, Pierre, Piers, Pierson, Piet, Pieter, Pietor, Pietro, Piotr, Pit, Piter, Piti, Pjeter, Pyete, Pyeter, Pyotr, Pytor

Petrucio (Shakespearean) Character from *The Taming of the Shrew.*

Peyton (Irish) Warrior's town. *Peyt, Peyten, Peython, Peytonn*

Phares (Biblical) Of a great house; bursting through.

Phelan (Gaelic) Little wolf.

Philander (Greek) Lover of mankind. *Filander, Fylander, Phylander*

Philario (Italian) Friend.

Philemon (Greek) Kiss. *Phila, Philamin, Philamina, Philamine, Philamyn, Phileman, Philemon, Philmyn, Philmyne, Phlmin, Phylmine, Phylmon, Phylmyn*

Philip (Greek) Horse lover. *Felipe, Filbert, Filip, Filippo, Phelps, Phil, Philby, Philip, Philipe, Philippos, Philipson, Phillip, Phillipa, Phillips, Philly, Philo, Phipps, Phyleap, Phyleep, Pilib, Pippo*

Philo (Greek) Loving. (Latin) Lover of horses. *Filo, Fylo, Phylo*

Philostrate (Greek) Master.

Philotus (Greek) Servant to Tinon.

Phinneaus (Hebrew) Oracle. *Phineas, Pinchas*

Phoenix (Greek) Mystical bird; purple. *Phenix, Pheonix, Phynix*

Phornello (African) Succeed.

Phuoc (Vietnamese) Good luck. *Phuc*

Phuong (Vietnamese) Destiny.

Pierce (English) Rock. *Pearce, Pears, Piercy, Piers*

Pierre (French) Rock. *Peirre, Piere, Pierrot*

Piers (English) Stone, rock. *Peers*

Pierson (Old English) Son of Peter. (Irish) Stone. *Pearson, Pierrson, Piersen, Piersson, Piersum, Pyerson*

Pilan (Native American) Supreme essence. *Pillan, Pyllan*

Pindarus (Shakespearean) Character from *Julius Caesar.*

Pino (Italian) Lover of horses.

Pisano (Italian) Sculptor.

Piusz (Hungarian) Pious. *Pious, Pius*

Piyush (Hindi) Nectar.

Placido (Latin) Tranquility. *Placide, Placidio, Placidus, Placyd, Placydius, Placydo*

Platinum (Latin) Silver-white precious metal.

Plato (Greek) Strong shoulders. *Platan, Platen, Platin, Platon, Platun, Platyn*

Platon (Greek) Broad-shouldered.

Platt (French) Ground without slope. *Platte*

Pluto (Greek) God of the dead; God of the underworld; ninth planet from the sun.

Plutus (Greek) God of wealth.

Polixenes (Slavic) People.

Polk (Scottish) From the pool or pit; eleventh U.S. president. (Slavic) People.

Polo (African) Alligator. *Pollo*

Polonius (Shakespearean) Character from *Hamlet.*

Ponce (Spanish) Fifth.

Pongor (Hungarian) All might. *Pongrác*

Pontain (Malaysian) Place name.

Pontius (Latin) Marine; belonging to the sea; fifth.

Pontus (Hebrew) Sea god.

Porfio (Spanish) Purple.

Porter (French) Gatekeeper; carrier. *Port, Porteur, Portie, Porty*

Poseidon (Greek) God of the sea.

Powa (Native American) Wealthy. *Powah*

Powell (English) Alert. (Old Welsh) Son of Howell. *Powal, Powall, Powel, Power, Powers, Powil*

Prabhakar (Hindi) Cause of luster.

Prabhu (Hindi) Great.

Prabodh (Indian) Consolation.

Pradeep (Hindi) Light.

Praful (Indian) Blooming.

Prakash (Hindi) Light.

Pramsu (Hindi) Scholar.

Pranav (Hindi) Om or Aum; sacred syllable for Om.

Pranay (Hindi) Love, romance.

Prasata (Hindi) Father of Draupad.

Prassana (Hindi) Cheerful.

Pratap (Hindi) Glory; dignity; majesty.

Pratik (Hindi) Symbol.

Pratyush (Hindi) Meaning unknown.

Pravat (Thai) History.

Praveen (Hindi) Proficient.

Pravin (Hindi) Capable. *Prawyn*

Prem (Hindi) Love.

Prentice (Middle English) Apprentice. *Prent, Prentis, Prentise, Prentiss, Prentyc, Prentyce, Prentys*

Preston (Old English) Dweller at the church; priest's settlement. *Prescott, Presley, Prestan, Presten, Prestin, Priest, Priestley, Priestly*

Prewitt (Old French) Valiant one. *Prewet, Prewit, Prewitt, Prue, Pruit, Pruitt*

Priam (Greek) King of Troy.

Price (Old Welsh) Urgent one. *Pryce*

Primel (Breton) Meaning unknown. *Primael, Privel*

Primo (Italian) First one. *Preemo, Premo, Prime*

Prince (Latin) Royal son. *Prins, Prinse, Prinze*

Prithu (Hindi) First Ksatriya; son of Vena.

Privrata (Hindi) Son of Satarupa.

Proculeius (Italian) Friend of Caesar.

Prometheus (Greek) Forethought.

Prosper (Latin) Fortune. *Prospero*

Proteus (Greek) Sea god.

Pryor (Latin) Head of the priory. *Prior, Pry*

Ptolemy (Greek) Star cluster. *Ptolemäus*

Pundarik (Hindi) White.

Purujit (Hindi) Conqueror of many.

Pusan (Hindi) Sage.

Putnam (Old English) From the sire's estate. *Putnem, Putney, Putnum*

Q

Qabic (Arabic) Able. *Quabic, Quabick, Quabyc, Quabyk*

Qabil (Arabic) Able.

Qadim (Arabic) Ancient.

Qadir (Arabic) Talented. *Qadar, Qadeer, Quadeer*

Qamar (Arabic) Moon. *Quamar, Quamir*

Qasim (Arabic) Provider.

Qeb (Egyptian) Father of the earth.

Qimat (Hindi) Valued.

Qing-Nan (Chinese) Younger generation.

Quaashie (African American) Ambitious.

Quaddus (African American) Bright.

Quade (Latin) Fourth. *Quaid, Quaide*

Quadrees (African American) Four. *Kwadrees, Quadrhys*

Quan (Vietnamese) Dignified.

Quan Van (Vietnamese) Authorized.

Quanah (Native American) Good-smelling.

Quang Tu (Vietnamese) Clear.

Quannell (African American) Strong willed. *Kwan, Kwanell, Kwanelle, Quan, Quanelle, Quannel*

Quant (Latin) Knowing his worth. *Quanta, Quantae, Quantal, Quantay, Quantea, Quantey, Quantez*

Quantavius (American) Combination of Quan and Octavius. *Quantavian, Quantavin, Quantavous, Quatavius*

Quarren (African American) Tenacious. *Kwarohn, Kwaronne, Quaronne, Quarron*

Quashawn (African American) Tenacious. *Kwashan, Kwashaun, Kwashawn, Quasean, Quasha, Quashaan, Quashan, Quashaun, Quashie, Quashy*

Quasim (Arabic) He who divides goods among his people.

Qudamah (Arabic) Courage. *Qudam, Qudama*

Qued (Native American) Decorated robe.

Quelatikan (Native American) Blue horn.

Quenby (Scandinavian) Form of Quimby. *Quenbey, Quenbi, Quenbie, Quenvee*

Quennel (Old French) Dweller by the oak tree. *Quenal, Quenall, Quenel, Quennal, Quennall, Quennel*

Quentin (Latin) Fifth-born child. *Quent, Quenten, Quenton, Quint, Quintilian, Quintin, Quinto, Quinton, Quintus*

Quick (American) Fast; remarkable.

Quico (Spanish) Short for many Spanish names; high rank. *Paco*

Quigley (Irish) Maternal side. *Quiggly, Quiggy, Quiglee, Quigly*

Quillan (Irish) Cub. *Quill, Quillen, Quillon*

Quimby (Norse) Woman's house. *Quenby, Quin, Quinby*

Quinby (Scandinavian) From the queen's estate.

Quincy (French) Estate belonging to the fifth son. *Quin, Quince, Quincey*

Quindarius (American) Combination of Quinn and Darius. *Quindarious, Quindarrius, Quinderious, Quindrius*

Quinlan (Irish) Well shaped, athletic. *Quindlen, Quinley, Quinlin, Quinly*

Quinn (Irish) Fifth son's estate. *Quin, Quyn, Quynn*

Quintavius (African American) Fifth child. *Quint*

Quinto (Spanish) Home ruler. *Quiqui*

Quiqui (Spanish) Friend short for Enrique. *Kaka, Keke, Quinto, Quiquin*

Quirin (English) Magic spell.

Quirinus (Latin) Roman god of war.

Quito (Spanish) Lively. *Kito*

Qunnoune (Native American) Tall.

Quoitrel (African American) Equalizer. *Kwotrel, Quitrelle*

Quon (Chinese) Bright.

Qusay (Arabic) Distant. *Quassay*

R

Raashid (Arabic) Wise man.

Rab (Scottish) Bright; fame. *Rabbie*

Rabbit (Old English) Long-eared; hare; clover flower.

Rabi (Arabic) Breeze. *Rabbi, Rabee, Rabeeh*

Racham (Hebrew) Compassionate. *Rachaman, Rachmyel, Raham*

Rad (Scandinavian) Helpful; confident. *Raad, Radd, Raddy*

Radbert (English) Intelligent. *Rad, Radbirt, Radd, Raddburt*

Radburn (English) Red brook. *Radbern, Radborn, Radbourn*

Radcliff (Old English) Red cliff. *Rad, Radcliffe, Radclyf, Radclyffe, Radford, Radley, Radnor*

Radek (Czech) Famous ruler. *Radacek, Radan, Radik, Radko, Radouvsek, Radovs*

Radford (English) Helpful. *Rad, Radferd*

Radley (English) Red meadow. *Radlea, Radlee, Radleigh, Radly*

Radman (Slavic) Joy. *Raddman, Radmen, Radmon*

Radnor (English) Red stone. *Radnore, Rednor*

Radomér (Hungarian) Happy; peace.

Radomil (Slavic) Happy. *Radomyl*

Radoslav (Czech) Happy and glorious.

Radwan (Arabic) Delight. *Radwen, Radwin, Radwon*

Rae (Old English) Doe. *Rai, Ray*

Raeburn (Teutonic) Dweller by the stream.

Raeshon (American) Form of Raeshawn; brainy. *Rashone, Rayshawn, Reshawn*

Rafa (Hebrew) Cure. *Rapha*

Rafael (Hebrew) God has healed. *Rafel, Rafello, Raffaello, Raphael*

Rafat (Indian) Elevation.

Rafferty (Irish) Prosperous. *Rafe, Rafer, Raferty, Raff, Raffer, Raffi, Raffy*

Rafi (Arabic) Exalted; form of Raphael. *Rafee, Rafey, Rafil, Rafy*

Raghnall (Irish) Powerful judgment. *Rognvaldr*

Ragin (Hindi) Advice.

Ragnar (Norse) Wise leader. *Rainer, Rayner, Raynor*

Rahman (Arabic) Compassionate. *Rahmati, Rahmen, Rahmin, Rahmon*

Rahn (American) King's adviser. *Rahnney, Rahnny*

Rahotep (Egyptian) Ruler.

Rahul (Arabic) Wolf counselor. (Hindi) Son of Lord Buddha.

Raidon (Japanese) Thunder god.

Raimy (African American) Compassionate. *Raimee*

Rainart (German) Great judgment. *Rainhard, Rainhardt, Reinart, Reinhard, Reinhardt, Reinhart*

Raine (English) Wise ruler. *Rain, Rainey, Raini, Rains, Raney, Rayne*

Rainier (Latin) Ruler. *Rainar, Rainer, Raner, Reinar*

Raivata (Hindi) Manu, the creator of mankind.

Raj (Hindi) King. *Rajan, Rajani*

Rajab (Muslim) Seventh month of the Muslim lunar calendar. *Ragab*

Rajanikant (Hindi) Sun; lord of the night.

Rajeev (Arabic) Spring.

Rajendra (Hindi) God.

Rajesh (Hindi) King.

Rajiv (Sanskrit) Striped. (Hindi) Lotus flower. *Rajeev*

Rakeem (Punjabi) Form of Raheem. *Rakeim, Rakeime, Rakem*

Rakesh (Hindi) Lord of the night; sun.

Rakin (Arabic) Respectable. *Rakeen, Rakyn*

Raleigh (Old English) Dweller by the deer meadow. *Lee, Leigh, Rawley, Rawls, Rawly*

Ralph (Old English) Wolf; wise counsel. *Raff, Raffi, Ralf, Ralfston, Ralfstone, Ralston, Ralstone, Ralstyn, Raoul, Raul, Rolf, Rolph*

Ram (Hindi) Lord Rama. *Ramie*

Ramadan (Arabic) Ninth month at the end of the Muslim year. *Rama*

Raman (Hindi) Cupid.

Ramanan (Hindi) Godlike. *Ramanjet, Ramanjot*

Ramanuja (Hindi) Saint.

Rambert (German) Strong. *Rambirt, Ramburt*

Rambures (Shakespearean) Character from *Henry V.*

Ramesh (Hindi) Ruler of Rama.

Rami (Arabic) Loving. *Rame, Ramee, Ramey, Ramih*

Ramiro (Basque) Great judge. *Ramero, Ramirez, Ramyro*

Ramon (Geman) Mighty protector. *Raymon, Remon, Romone*

Ramsden (English) Valley of rams. *Ramsdan, Ramsdin, Ramsdon, Ramsdyn*

Ramsey (Old English) Ram's land. *Ramsay, Ramsee, Ransden*

Rance (French) Kind of Belgian marble. *Rancel, Rancell, Ransel, Ransell*

Rancul (Argentinian) Plant from the grasslands.

Randal (English) Secretive. *Randahl, Randall, Randel, Randey, Randull*

Randolph (Anglo-Saxon) Shield; wolf. *Dolf, Dolph, Ran, Rand, Randal, Randall, Randell, Randie, Randl, Randle, Randolf, Randy, Rankin, Ranulf*

Ranen (Hebrew) Joyous. *Ranin, Ranon, Ranun*

Ranger (French) Dweller in the field. *Rainger, Raynger*

Rangle (American) Cowboy. *Ranglar, Rangler*

Rani (Hebrew) My song. *Ranee, Raney, Ranie, Roni*

Ranieri (Italian) Form of Ragnar. *Raneir, Ranier, Rannier*

Ranjan (Hindi) Entertaining.

Ranjeet (Hindi) Victor in war.

Ranjit (Hindi) Delighted one.

Ransford (Old English) Raven's ford.

Ransley (Old English) Raven's meadow. *Ransleigh, Ransly*

Ransom (Old English) Son of the shield. (Latin) Redeemer. *Rance, Rankin, Ransome, Ranson*

Rantidev (Hindi) Devotee of Narayana.

Raphael (Hebrew) Healed by God. *Rafael, Rafaelle, Rafaello, Rafal, Rafe, Rafer, Raff, Rafferty, Rafi, Raph*

Rashaan (Arabic) Young gift of god.

Rasheed (Arabic) Form of Rashad. *Rashead, Rashed, Rasheid, Rhasheed*

Rashid (Swahili) Wise adviser. *Rasheed, Rasheid, Rasheyd*

Rashne (Persian) Judge.

Rashon (African American) Newly created. *Rachan, Rashaan, Rasham, Rashan, Rashawn, Reshaun, Reshawn*

Rastus (Greek) Loving one.

Ratri (Hindi) Night.

Raul (French) Wolf counselor.

Raven (Old English) Bird. *Ravan, Raveon, Ravey, Ravon, Ravone, Ravyen, Revon*

Ravi (Hindi) Benevolent; sun god. *Rav, Ravee*

Ravid (Hebrew) Wander. *Ravyd*

Ravindra (Hindi) Protector of ravens.

Ravinger (Old English) Ravine. *Ravi, Ravinia*

Rawdan (English) Hilly; adventurous. *Rawden, Rawdin, Rawdon*

Rawleigh (American) Form of Raleigh. *Rawlee, Rawli*

Rawlins (Old English) Son of a little wise wolf. *Rawlings, Rawlyn, Rawson*

Ray (French) Kingly. *Rayce, Raydell, Rayder, Raydon, Rayford, Raylen, Raynell*

Rayburn (Old English) From the deer stream. *Rayborn, Raybourne, Rayburne*

Rayce (American) Counselor. (English) Race. *Racee*

Rayden (Japanese) Form of Raiden. *Raydun, Rayedon, Reyden*

Rayhan (Arabic) Favored by God. *Raehan, Raihan, Rayhaan*

Raymond (Old English) Worthy protector. *Raimund, Raimundo, Ramon, Raymund, Rayner, Reamonn, Wray*

Raynard (French) Wise; bold; courageous. *Raynard, Raynor, Reinhard, Reinhart, Renard, Renaud, Rey, Reynart, Reynaud, Reyner, Rinehart*

Rayne (English) Form of Raine. *Rayn, Rayno*

Razi (African American) Secret. *Raz, Raziel*

Read (Old English) Red-haired; reed. *Reade, Reading, Reed, Reid*

Reagan (Irish) Kingly. *Ragan, Raghan, Reagen, Reegen, Regan*

Redford (Old English) From the red ford. *Red, Redd, Redding, Redfield, Redgrave, Redman, Redwald*

Redmond (German) Adviser. *Radmond, Radmund, Redmond, Redmund*

Redpath (English) Red path. *Raddpath, Radpath, Reddpath*

Reece (Old Welsh) Enthusiastic. *Rase, Reace, Rett, Rhett, Rhys, Rice, Riece*

Reed (English) Red-haired. *Read, Reede, Reid, Rheed*

Reilly (Irish) Form of Riley. *Reilea, Reiley, Reili, Reily*

Reese (Welsh) Ardent one. *Rhys, Ries, Riess*

Reeve (Middle English) Bailiff. *Reave, Reeves*

Regan (Gaelic) Little king. *Rayghun, Reagan, Reagen, Regen, Regent, Regino*

Reginald (Old English) Powerful one. *Raghnall, Reg, Reggie, Reggy, Regnauld, Reinald, Reinhold, Reinwald, Renato, Renault, Rene, Reynold, Reynolds, Rinaldo*

Regis (Latin) Kingly, regal. *Reggis*

Regō (Hungarian) Meaning unknown.

Rehan (Arabic) Flower.

Rehor (Czech) To awaken. *Harek, Horik, Rehak, Rehorek, Rehurek*

Rei (Japanese) Law.

Reinaldo (Spanish) Form of Reynold. *Rainaldo, Raynoldo, Reinaldos, Renaldo, Reynoldo, Rinaldo*

Reinhart (German) Brave-hearted. *Reinhard, Reinhardt, Rhinehard, Rhinehart*

Reinhold (German) Wise, powerful ruler.

Rembrandt (Dutch) Sword adviser. *Rem*

Remi (French) Fun-loving. *Remee, Remey, Remmy, Remy*

Remington (Old English) From the raven's home. *Remme, Remmie, Remmy, Remy*

Remus (Latin) Swift oars-man. *Remas*

Renard (Teutonic) Counsel hard.

Rendor (Hungarian) Police-man. *Rendar, Render, Rendir*

Renee (Latin) Reborn. *Renato, Rene, René, Rennie, Renny*

Renfred (English) Lasting peace. *Ranfred, Ranfryd, Ronfred, Rynfryd*

Renfrew (Old Welsh) From the still waters. *Renfred, Renshaw, Renton, Rinfro*

Renny (Gaelic) Small but mighty.

Renzo (Latin) Form of Lawrence. *Renz, Renzy, Renzzo*

Reuben (Hebrew) Behold, a son. *Ben, Benny, Reubin, Reuby, Reuven, Rube, Ruben, Rubin*

Reuel (Hebrew) Friend of God.

Rex (Latin) King. *Rei, Rexer, Rexford, Roi*

Reyes (Spanish) King. *Rey, Reyce*

Reyhan (Arabic) Favored by God. *Reihan, Reyham*

Reynaldo (Spanish) Counselor; ruler.

Reynold (English) Knowledgeable tutor. *Ranald, Ranold, Reinhold, Renald, Renale, Rey, Reye, Reynolds*

Rez (Hungarian) Copper.

Reza (Slavic) Reaper. *Resi*

Rezin (Hebrew) Pleasant. *Rezan, Rezen, Rezi, Rezon*

Rezsö (Hungarian) Meaning unknown.

Rhett (English, Welsh) Stream. *Rhet, Rhette*

Rhodes (Greek) Field of roses. (English) Lives near the crucifix. *Rhoades, Rhodas, Rodas*

Rian (Irish) Little king. *Rhian, Rion*

Riberto (German) Brilliant.

Richard (English) Rich and powerful ruler. *Dick, Dickie, Dicky, Ricard, Ricardo, Rich, Richardson, Richart, Richerd, Richman, Richmond, Rick, Rickard, Ricker, Rickert, Rickie, Rickward, Ricky, Rikkert, Riocard, Ritchie, Rocco*

Richman (English) Powerful. *Richmen, Richmun, Rychmen, Rychmun*

Rick Ross (American) Rapper William Leonard Roberts.

Rico (Spanish) Noble ruler. *Reco, Reko, Ricko, Rikko, Riko*

Rider (Old English) Horseman. *Ryder*

Ridge (English) From the ridge. *Ridgy, Rig, Rigg*

Ridgley (English) By the meadow's edge. *Ridgeleigh,*

Ridgeley, Ridglea, Ridglee, Ridgleigh

Ridley (Old English) Reed clearing; cleared wood. *Riddley, Ridlea, Ridleigh, Ridly*

Rience (Scottish) In Arthurian legend, King of Many Isles.

Rigby (Old English) Valley of the ruler. *Rigbie, Rigbye, Rygby*

Rigel (Arabic) Foot; star in the constellation Orion.

Rikard (German) Powerful ruler.

Rikin (Hindi) Meaning unknown.

Riley (Gaelic) Valiant. *Rhyley, Riely, Ryley*

Rimon (Arabic) Pomegranite.

Ring (German) Ring. *Ringling, Ringo, Ryng*

Ringo (Japanese) Apple; peace be with you. *Ryngo*

Rio (Spanish) River. *Reo*

Riordan (Gaelic) Poet. *Rearden, Reardon*

Ripley (Old English) Dweller in the noisy meadow. *Rip, Ripleigh, Rypley*

Ris (English) Outdoorsman. *Rislea, Rislee, Risleigh, Riz*

Rishab (Hindi) Musical note Re.

Rishawn (American) Combination of Ri and Shawn. *Rishan, Rishaun, Rishon, Rishone*

Rishi (Hindi) Sage. *Ryshi*

Rishley (Old English) From the wild meadow. *Riston*

Rishon (Hebrew) First.

Ritch (American) Leader. *Rich, Richey, Ritchal, Ritchard, Ritchardt, Ritcherd, Ritchi, Ritchyrd*

Ritchell (Vietnamese) Nasty; gross. *Ratchell, Ritchel*

Ritchie (English) Form of Richie. *Ritchee, Ritchey, Ritchy*

Ritter (German) Knight. *Ritt, Rittar*

Rivalen (English) Tristan's father.

Rivan (Science fiction) Character from *Star Wars*.

Rivers (English) River; by the riverbank. *Rio, Rivar, Rive, River, Riviera, Rivor*

Riyad (Arabic) Gardens. *Rian, Riyadh*

Rizal (Hindi) Bringer of good news. *Rizzy*

Roald (Teutonic) Fame; power.

Roam (American) Wanderer. *Roamey, Roma, Rome*

Roan (English) From the rowan tree. (Irish) Little red-haired one. *Rhoan, Roen*

Roarke (Irish) Famous ruler. *Rorke, Rourke, Ruark*

Robert (Old English) Bright; famous. *Bert, Berty, Bob, Bobby, Dob, Dobbs, Rab, Rabbie, Rhobbie, Riobard, Rob, Robbee, Robben, Robbey, Robbi, Robbie, Robbins, Robby, Rober, Róbert, Roberto, Robertson, Robey, Robin, Robinson, Roby, Rubert, Rupert, Tito*

Robi (Hungarian) Shining with fame.

Robin (English) Famous brilliance.

Robson (English) Sterling character. *Robb, Robbon, Robsen*

Rocco (Italian) Rest. *Roc, Rock, Rok, Rokka, Roko*

Rochester (Old English) Rock fortress. *Roche, Rocho, Rock, Rockee, Rocker, Rocki, Rockley, Rockne, Rockwell, Rocky, Rokey, Rokie*

Rockleigh (English) Dependable; outdoorsy. *Rocklee, Rockley, Roklee*

Rockwell (English) From the rocky spring. *Rockwelle*

Roden (English) Red valley. *Rodan, Rodon, Rodyn, Roeddon*

Roderick (German) Famous one. *Broderick, Rick, Ricky, Rod, Rodd, Roddy, Roderich, Rodman, Rodmond, Rodney, Rodrick, Rodrigo, Rodrigue, Rory*

Rodger (German) Form of Roger. *Rodge, Rodgir, Rogy*

Rodman (Old English) Famous.

Rodney (Old English) Famous one's island. *Rhodney, Rod, Roddy*

Rodolf (Dutch) Famous wolf.

Rodrigo (Spanish) Form of Roderick. *Roderigo, Rodrigue*

Roe (English) Small deer. *Roebuck*

Rogan (Gaelic) Red-haired. *Roan*

Rogelio (Spanish) Beautiful one.

Roger (German) Famous spearman; quiet. *Rodger, Rodgers, Rodiger, Rog, Rogerio, Rogers, Rudiger, Rüdiger, Ruggiero, Rutger*

Rohan (Hindi) Sandlewood. (Irish) Red-haired one.

Rohit (Hindi) Red color. *Rohyt*

Roi (French) Form of Roy.

Roja (Spanish) Red. *Rojay*

Roka (Japanese) Wave.

Rókus (Hungarian) Meaning unknown.

Roland (German) From the famous land. *Orlando, Rodhlann, Roland, Rolando, Rollan, Rolland, Rollin, Rollins, Rollo, Rolly, Rolt, Rowe, Rowland*

Roldan (English) Powerful; mighty.

Rolf (German) Kind adviser. *Rolfee, Rolfie, Rolph*

Rollie (English) Form of Roland. *Roley, Rolli, Rollo, Rolly, Rolo*

Rollins (German) Dignified. *Rolin, Rolins, Rollin, Rolyn*

Romain (French) Roman. *Romaine, Romayn*

Roman (Hebrew) Strong; powerful. (Latin) Place name, Rome, Italy; from Rome. *Romano, Romanos, Romula, Romulos, Romulus*

Romeo (Italian) Pilgrim to Rome; romantic lover. (Shakespearean) Character from *Romeo and Juliet*. *Romain, Roman, Rome*

Romulus (Latin) Citizen of Rome. *Romano, Romolo, Romulo*

Romy (Italian) Form of Roman. *Romee, Romi, Rommie, Rommy*

Ronak (Hindi) Embellishment.

Ronald (Old Norse) Mighty. *Naldo, Renaldo, Ron, Ronan, Ronnie, Ronny, Ronoldo, Rynaldo*

Ronan (Celtic) Pledge.

Rondell (Welsh) Grand. *Ronde, Rondel*

Roni (Hebrew) Shout for joy; my song of joy.

Ronin (Japanese) Samurai without a master.

Rooney (Gaelic) Red-haired. *Roon, Roone, Rune*

Roosevelt (Dutch) Field of roses. *Rooseveldt, Rosevelt*

Rooster (American) Animal; loud.

Rory (Gaelic) Red king. *Rorey, Rori, Roric, Rorie, Ruaidhri, Rurik*

Roscoe (Old Norse) From the deer forest. *Rosco, Roskie, Rosko*

Rosencrantz (Shakespeare) Character from *Hamlet*.

Roshan (Hindi) One who emanates light.

Roshaun (African American) Shining light. *Rashon, RoShawn*

Roshean (American) Combination of Ro and Sean. *Roshain, Roshawn*

Rosling (Scottish) Redhead; explosive. *Roslin, Rozling*

Ross (Scottish) From the peninsula. (French) Red-haired. (English) Wood. (German) Rose-colored. *Rossano, Rosse, Roswald*

Roswald (German) Mighty horse. *Roswalt*

Roswell (English) Rose spring. *Roswel, Roswelle, Rozwell*

Roth (German) Red-haired. *Rauth, Rothe*

Rouvin (Hebrew) Behold, a son.

Rowan (Old English) Tree with red berries. *Rowe, Rowell, Rowen, Rowley, Rowson*

Rowley (English) Unevenly cleared meadow. *Rawleigh, Rowlea, Rowlee, Rowlie, Rowly*

Rowtag (Native American) Fire.

Roy (Old French) Regal one. *Roi, Royal, Royale, Royall, Roye*

Royal (French) Of the king; regal.

Royce (English) Son of the king. *Roial, Roice, Royse*

Ruben (Hebrew) Behold, a son.

Ruchir (Hindi) Beautiful.

Rudd (English) Ruddy. *Reed*

Rudeger (German) Friendly. *Rudger, Rudgyr, Rudigar, Rudiger, Rudy*

Rudolph (German) Wolf. *Dolph, Raoul, Rodolf, Rodolfo, Rodolphe, Rolf, Rollin, Rollo, Rolph, Rudi, Rudie, Rudolf, Rudy*

Rudyard (Old English) From the red gate. *Ruddy, Rudy*

Rufus (Latin) Red-haired one. *Rufe, Ruff, Rufford, Ruphus*

Rugby (English) From the raven's estate. *Rugbee, Rugbi, Rugbie*

Ruggerio (Italian) Famous warrior. *Ruge, Rugerio, Rugger*

Ruhollah (Persian) Spirit of Allah.

Runako (African American) Handsome.

Rune (English) Rune. (German) Secret. (Scandinavian) Secret lore.

Rupert (French) Famous; bright. *Ruepert, Rupirt*

Rupesh (Hindi) Lord of beauty.

Rush (French) Red-haired. *Rousse, Rusk, Ruskin, Rust*

Russel (French) Red-haired; foxlike. *Roussell, Rusell, Russ, Russell, Russill, Rusti, Rusty*

Rustin (French) Form of Rusty. *Ruston, Rustyn*

Rutherford (Old English) From the cattle ford. *Rutherfurd, Rutherfyrd, Ruthren*

Ryan (Gaelic) Little king. *Rhine, Rhyan, Rhyne, Rian, Ry, Ryane, Ryanne, Ryen, Ryun*

Ryder (English) Horseman. *Rydar*

Rylan (Old English) Dweller in the rye field. *Rycroft, Ryland, Ryle, Ryman, Ryton*

Rylee (Irish) Form of Riley. *Rillie, Ryele, Ryelle*

Ryo (Spanish) River; Rio Grande. *Rio*

Ryogi (Japanese) Defender of nobility. *Ryoji*

Ryoichi (Japanese) First son of Ryo.

Ryons (Irish) Kingly. *Ryon*

Ryozo (Japanese) Third son of Ryo.

Ryuichi (Japanese) First son of Ryu.

Ryzard (Polish) Brave ruler; variant of Richard.

S

Saad (Hebrew) Assistance. *Daadya, Saadia, Saadiah, Saadyah*

Saahdia (Aramic) Helped by the Lord. *Saadya, Seadya*

Saarik (Hindi) Bird. *Saariq, Sareek, Sareeq, Sariq*

Sabene (Latin) Optimist. *Sabe, Sabeen, Sabin, Sabyn, Sabyne*

Saber (French) Sword. *Sabar, Sabe*

Sabinian (Latin) Name of an ancient Roman clan. *Sabin, Sabine, Sabino*

Sabir (Arabic) Sword. *Sabre, Sabyr*

Saburo (Japanese) Third son.

Sacchidananda (Indian) Total bliss.

Sacha (Russian) Helper and defender of mankind. *Sascha, Sasha*

Sachchit (Hindi) Truth; consciousness.

Sachet (Indian) Animated.

Sachiel (Hebrew) Angel of water.

Sachin (Hindi) Lord Indra.

Saddam (Arabic) Powerful ruler.

Sadi (Turkish) Meaning unknown. *Sadie, Sady*

Sadik (Turkish) Truthful.

Sadler (English) Practical. *Sadd, Sadlar, Sadlur*

Safak (Turkish) Second month of Islamic calendar. *Safer, Safyr*

Sagar (Hindi) King. *Samrat, Satyavrat*

Sagaz (Spanish) Clever. *Saga, Sago*

Sage (English) Wise; herb. *Saje*

Sagittarius (Latin) Constellation of the southern hemisphere; archer; sign of the Zodiac.

Sagiv (Hebrew) Mighty; with strength.

Sagremore (Scottish) In Arthurian legend, knight of the Round Table.

Sahadev (Hindi) Prince.

Sahale (Native American) Above.

Sahen (Hindi) Falcon.

Sahib (Hindi) Sir.

Said (Arabic) Happy. *Daied, Saeed, Saiyid, Sayeed, Sayid, Syed*

Saigon (American) Rapper Brian Daniel Carenard.

Sakima (Native American) King; for a boy or girl.

Salah (Arabic) Form of Sala.

Salim (African American) Peace. *Saleem, Salem, Salima, Saliym, Salom, Salym, Selim*

Salisbury (English) Born in the willows. *Salisberry, Salisbery, Saulisbury, Saulsberry, Saulsbery, Saulsbury*

Salman (Czech) Form of Solomon. *Salmaan, Salmaine, Salmin, Salmon, Salmun*

Saloman (Hebrew) Peaceful. *Salamon, Salmon, Salomi, Salomon, Schlomo, Shalom, Shlomo, Sholem, Solom, Soloman, Solomon*

Salter (English) Salt seller. *Salt*

Salvador (Spanish) Savior. *Sal, Salvatore, Sauveur*

Sam (Hebrew) To hear. *Samho, Samm, Sammie, Sammy, Samo, Samouel, Samu, Samuel, Samuele, Samuello, Sem, Shmuel*

Samien (Arabic) To be heard.

Samir (Hindi) Wind.

Sammon (Arabic) Grocer.

Sampath (Hindi) Meaning unknown.

Samson (Hebrew) Like the sun; his ministry. *Sam, Sammy, Sampson, Sanson, Sansone*

Samudra (Hindi) Lord of the ocean.

Samuel (Hebrew) Heard God; asked God. *Sam, Samael, Samaru, Samauel, Samaul, Samel, Samelle, Sameul, Sammail, Sammie, Sammy, Samuele, Samuello, Samuelson, Samuru, Sauko, Saumel, Schmuel, Shem, Shemuel, Zamuel*

Sanat (Hindi) Lord Brahma.

Sanborn (English) One with nature. *Sanborne, Sanbourn, Sandy*

Sandeep (Hindi) Lighting the way.

Sanders (Middle English) Alexander's son. *Sander, Sanderson, Sands, Sandy, Saunders, Saunderson*

Sandhurst (English) From the sandy thicket; undaunted. *Sandhirst*

Sandon (Old English) From the sandy hill.

Sandor (Hungarian) Helper and defender of mankind.

Sanford (Old English) Dweller at the sandy ford. *Sanborn, Sandford, Sandy*

Sang Kyu (Korean) Aid and standard.

Sanjay (Hindi) Protector. *Sajo, Sanjai, Sanjaya, Sanje, Sanjye*

Sanjeev (Hindi) Love; life. *Sanjiv*

Sanjog (Hindi) Coincidence.

Sankara (Hindi) Auspicious.

Santiago (Spanish) Supplanter. *Chago, Diego, Santi, Santyago*

Santino (Spanish) Form of Santonio. *Santion*

Santo (Italian) Saint. *Santos*

Santosh (Hindi) Contentment.

Sapan (Hindi) Dream.

Sarasvan (Hindi) Meaning unknown.

Sarat (Hindi) Sage; autumn.

Sargent (French) Military man. *Sargant, Sarge, Sargeant, Sergent*

Sarkis (Russian) Protector.

Sarngin (Hindi) Name of God.

Sarojin (Hindi) Lotuslike. *Sarojun, Sarojyn*

Sarosh (Persian) Prayer.

Saswata (Hindi) Meaning unknown.

Satayu (Hindi) Brother of Amavasu and Vivasu.

Satch (French) Small bag. *Satchel*

Satrujit (Hindi) Son of Vatsa.

Saturn (Latin) Mythology: god of agriculture; sixth planet from the sun.

Saturnin (Spanish) From planet Saturn; melancholy. *Saturnino*

Satyen (Hindi) Lord of truth.

Saudeep (Hindi) Meaning unknown.

Saul (Hebrew) Asked for. *Sauly, Shaul, Sol, Solly*

Saunak (Hindi) Sage.

Saurabh (Hindi) Fragrance.

Sauron (Fiction) Character from *The Lord of the Rings* by J. R. R. Tolkien.

Saverio (Italian) Owner of the new house.

Sawyer (Middle English) Woodsman. *Saw, Sayer, Sayers, Sayre, Sayres*

Saxon (English) Germanic tribe. *Sax, Saxan, Saxe, Saxen, Saxin, Saxxon*

Sayer (Welsh) Carpenter. *Say, Sayers, Sayre, Sayres*

Scanlon (Irish) Devious. *Scan, Scanlin, Scanlun, Scanne*

Scarus (English) Friend to Marc Antony.

Schae (American) Safe; careful. *Schay*

Schaffer (German) Watchful. *Schaefer, Schaffur, Schiffer, Shaffer*

Schmidt (German) Hardworking blacksmith. *Schmid, Schmit, Schmitt, Schmydt, Schmyt*

Schneider (German) Stylish. *Sneider, Snider*

Schuyler (Dutch) Shield; scholar. *Ciel, Sky, Skye, Skylar, Skyler*

Scott (Old English) From Scotland. *Escott, Scot, Scottie, Scotty*

Scout (American) First explorer.

Scully (Scottish) Town crier; herald. *Scullee, Sculley, Scullie*

Seabert (Old English) Sea-glorious. *Sea, Seabirt, Seabright, Seabrook, Seabury, Seberg, Sebert, Seebirt, Seibyrt, Seybirt*

Seal (American) Water; natural; singer.

Seamus (Gaelic) Replacement; bonus. *Seamas, Seemus, Semus*

Sean (Celtic) God's grace. *Seann, Shaun, Shawn, Sian, Siôn*

Searles (English) Fortified. *Searl, Searle, Serles, Serls*

Seaton (English) From the farm by the sea. *Seatan, Seaton, Seeten, Seetin, Seeton, Seton, Setun, Setyn*

Sebastian (Latin) Revered one. *Bastian, Bastien, Sebastien, Sebastion, Sebestyén, Sebo, Sepastiano*

Sebes (Hungarian) Fast.

Sedgley (American) Classy. *Sedg, Sedge, Sedgely, Segdeley*

Sedgwick (English) From the place of swords; defensive. *Sedgewick, Sedgewyck, Sedgwyck*

Seferino (Spanish) Flying in the wind. *Cerfirino, Sebarino, Sephirio, Zefarin, Zefirino, Zephir, Zephyr*

Seff (Hebrew) Wolf.

Seger (English) Sea spear; sea warrior; singer. *Seager, Seegar, Seeger, Sega, Segar, Segur, Sigar*

Segwarides (Scottish) In Arthurian legend, knight of the Round Table.

Seif (Arabic) Sword of religion. *Seyf*

Seiichi (Japanese) First son of Sei.

Seiko (Japanese) Force; truth.

Selby (English) From a village of mansions. *Selbey, Shelbey, Shelbie, Shelby*

Seldon (English) From the willow valley. *Selden, Seldyn, Sellden, Shelden*

Selestino (Spanish) Heavenly. *Celeste, Celestino, Celey, Sele, Selestyna*

Seleucus (Latin) Shaken; beaten by the waves.

Selim (Turkish) Peace.

Selvon (American) Gregarious. *Sel, Selman, Selv, Selvaughn, Selvawn*

Selwyn (English) Friend from the mansion. *Selwin, Selwinn, Selwynn, Selwynne*

Sem (Netherlands) Meaning unknown.

Semih (Turkish) Meaning unknown.

Sempronius (Latin) Kinsman to Titus.

Semyon (Russian) Listener.

Senach (Gaelic) Meaning unknown.

Senajit (Hindi) Victory over army.

Sencer (Turkish) Meaning unknown.

Sener (Turkish) Bringer of joy.

Senichi (Japanese) First son of Sen.

Senior (French) Older. *Sennyur, Senyur, Sinior*

Senne (Dutch) Wise.

Sennett (French) Wise. *Senet, Senett, Senit, Senitt, Sennet, Sennit*

Senon (Spanish) Given life by Zeus. *Senan, Senen, Senin, Sennon*

Septimus (Latin) Seventh-born son. *Septimous*

Seraphim (Hebrew) Burning ones; angels; ardent. *Sarafin, Saraphim, Serafim, Serafin, Serafino, Seraphimus*

Serge (Latin) Attendant. *Serg, Sergei, Sergio, Sergius, Sirgio, Sirgios*

Sergeant (French) Officer, leader. *Sarge, Sargent*

Sergei (Russian) Good-looking. *Serge, Sergeeo, Sergeoh, Sergyo*

Servan (Breton) Meaning unknown.

Sesame (Greek) Plant bearing small, flat seeds. (American) Children's television show, *Sesame Street*. *Sesamey, Sessame, Sessamee*

Seth (Hebrew) Appointed one. *Set, Sethan, Sethe, Sethia, Shet*

Seton (English) From the sea town.

Seung (Korean) Successor; winning.

Seven (American) Number. *Sevene, Sevin*

Severin (English) River in England. (French) Severe. *Saverino, Seve, Severyn, Sevrin, Sverinus*

Severinus (Latin) Severe. *Severen*

Sevilin (Turkish) Beloved. *Sevilan, Sevilen, Sevilon, Sevilyn*

Seward (Old English) From the sea. *Seaward, Seeward, Severn, Sewell, Sewerd, Sward*

Sewell (English) Seaward. *Seawel, Seawell, Seewel, Seewell, Sewel, Seywell*

Sextus (Latin) Born sixth. *Sextys, Sixtis, Sixtus*

Seymour (French) Marshy land near the sea; prayer. *Seamoor, Seamor, Seamore, Seamour, Seemoore, Seemore, Seymore, Si, Sy*

Seyton (Shakespearean) Character from *Macbeth*.

Sezni (French) Old; wise. *Sane, Senan*

Shade (English) Secretive. *Shadee, Shadey, Shady, Shayd*

Shadow (English) Mystique. *Shade, Shadoe*

Shadrach (Arabic) Survived. *Shad, Shadd, Shadrack, Shadreck, Shadryack*

Shafir (Hebrew) Handsome. *Shafeer, Shafer, Shefer*

Shah (Arabic) King.

Shailen (Hebrew) Gift.

Shailesh (Hindi) God of mountain, Himalaya.

Shakar (Arabic) Grateful.

Shakil (Arabic) Attractive. *Shakeel, Shakill, Shakille, Shaqueel, Shaquil, Shaquille*

Shakir (Arabic) Grateful.

Shalabh (Hindi) Easy.

Shalin (Hindi) Cotton plant; modest.

Shaman (Native American) Holy man. *Schamane, Shamain, Shamon, Shayman*

Shamus (Irish) Supplanter. *Schaemus, Shamus, Shamuss, Shemus*

Shane (Irish) God is gracious. *Shaene, Shain, Shay, Shayne*

Shankar (Hindi) He who gives happiness.

Shannon (Irish) Old. *Shana, Shanan, Shane, Shanen, Shann, Shannan, Shannen, Shanon*

Shantanu (Hindi) King.

Shante (American) Poised. *Shantae, Shantay*

Shaquille (African American) Handsome. *Shakeel, Shaq, Shaquil, Shaquill*

Sharad (Hindi) Autumn. *Sharid, Sharyd*

Sharif (Arabic) Honest; honorable; noble. *Seif, Shareef, Sharife, Shariff*

Shashi (Hindi) Moon; moonbeam.

Shashwat (Hindi) Everlasting.

Shaun (Irish) God's gift. *Schaun, Schaune, Shaughan, Shawn, Shawne*

Shaw (Old English) Grove. *Shawe*

Shea (Irish) Hawklike; stately. *Shae, Shai, Shay, Shaye*

Sheehan (Gaelic) Little peaceful one. *Sheen*

Shelby (English) Village on the ledge; ledge estate. *Shel, Shelbe, Shelbee, Shelbey, Shelbi, Shelbie*

Sheldon (English) Protected hill. *Sheldan, Sheldin, Sheldun, Shelton*

Shelley (Old English) Clearing on a bank; ledge estate. *Sheileigh, Shell, Shelli, Shelly*

Shen (Chinese) Spiritual; deep-thinking.

Shepherd (Old English) One who herds sheep. *Shep, Shepard, Shepley, Shepp, Sheppard*

Shepley (English) From the sheep meadow. *Sheplea, Shepleigh, Shepply, Shipley*

Sherborn (English) From the bright, shiny stream. *Sherborne, Sherbourn, Sherburn, Sherburne*

Sheridon (Irish) Wild one. *Sharidan, Sheridan, Sheridon, Sheridyn, Sherr, Sherydon, Shuridun*

Sherlock (Old English) White-haired. *Sherloc, Sherlocke, Shurlock*

Sherman (Old English) Wool cutter. *Scherm, Scherman, Sherborne, Sherm, Shermie, Shermon, Sherwin, Shurman*

Sherrick (Irish) Surname; already gone. *Sherric, Sherrik, Sherryc, Sherryck, Sherwynne*

Sherwood (Old English) Bright forest. *Sharwood, Sherwoode, Shurwood*

Shevon (African American) Zany. *Shavonne, Shevaughan, Shevaughn*

Shilah (Native American) Brother.

Shiloh (Hebrew) Peaceful. *Shile, Shilo, Shy, Shye*

Shimon (Hebrew) Providing well.

Shin (Korean) Belief, faith, and trust.

Shin-Il (Korean) Belief, faith, trust, and superiority.

Shing (Chinese) Victory.

Shinichi (Japanese) First son of Shin.

Shipley (Old English) From the deep meadow. *Shipton*

Shiro (Japanese) Fourth-born son.

Shiv (Hindi) Lord Shiva.

Shivendu (Hindi) Pure moon.

Shoichi (Japanese) First son of Sho.

Shontae (African American) Hopeful. *Shauntae, Shauntay, Shawntae, Shontay, Shontee, Shonti, Shontie, Shonty*

Shishir (Hindi) Winter.

Shuichi (Japanese) First son of Shu.

Shulamith (Hebrew) Peaceful. *Shulamit*

Shunichi (Japanese) First son of Shun.

Shunnar (Arabic) Pleasant.

Shyam (Hindi) Form of Lord Krishna.

Shylock (Hebrew) Banker.

Siamak (Persian) Bringer of joy; great emperor Sia.

Sid (French) From Saint-Denis, France. *Cyd, Sidd, Siddie, Siddy, Syd, Sydd*

Siddel (Old English) From the wide valley. *Siddell, Sidwell, Sydell*

Sidwell (English) From the broad well. *Siddwal, Siddwall, Siddwell, Sydwel*

Sierra (Spanish) Dangerous. *Seesee, Seirrah, Serra, Siera, Syera*

Sigbjorn (Old Norse) Victory bear.

Sigebryht (Anglo-Saxon) Victory; bright.

Sigfried (Teutonic) Victory, peace. *Siegfred, Sig, Sigfred, Sigfredo, Sigfrid*

Sigge (Scandinavian) Victory, peace.

Sigmund (Teutonic) Victory shield; victory protector. *Siegmund, Siffre, Siggy, Sigismond, Sigismundo, Sigvard, Ziggy*

Sigurd (Old Norse) Victorious guardian. *Sigord, Sjure, Syver*

Silas (Latin) Wood. *Sias*

Siler (English) Meaning unknown. *Syler*

Silvano (Italian) Forest. *Silvan, Silvani, Silvia, Sylvan*

Silvester (Latin) Woodman. *Sil, Silas, Silvanus, Silvestre, Sly, Syl, Sylvester, Sylvestro, Szilveszter*

Silvio (Latin) Belonging to the forest; silver. *Silvan, Silvin*

Silvius (Latin) Forest dweller.

Simba (African) Lion. *Sim, Simbah, Symba, Symbah*

Simeon (English) Hear; listen. *Seameon, Seemeon, Simion, Simione*

Similien (French) Surname.

Simon (Hebrew) He who hears. *Semjén, Shimon, Sim, Simeon, Siomonn*

Simonides (Greek) King of Pentapolis.

Simpson (Hebrew) Simplistic. *Simpsen, Simpsun, Simson, Sympsen, Sympsin*

Sinan (Turkish) Spearhead.

Sinbad (German) Sparkling prince. *Sinbald, Sindbad, Synbald*

Sinclair (French) Saint Clair. *Sinclaire, Sinclar, Sinclare, Synclare*

Sindri (Old Norse) Glittering.

Singh (Hindi) Lion.

Sinjon (French) Saint John.

Sisyphus (Greek) From mythology; cruel king.

Sivan (Hebrew) Ninth month on the ecclesiastical calendar and third month of the civil year on the Hebrew calendar. *Syvan*

Sivney (Irish) Satisfied. *Sivneigh, Sivnie*

Siward (English) General. (Irish) Surname.

Skeet (Middle English) Speedy. *Skeat, Skeeter, Skeets*

Skipp (Old Norse) Ship owner. *Skip, Skipper, Skippy*

Skjøld (Scandinavian) Meaning unknown.

Sklaer (Dutch) Protective. *Skilar, Skye, Skyeler*

Skye (English) Sky; sheltering. *Sky, Skyy*

Skyzoo (American) Rapper Gregory Skyler Taylor.

Slade (Old English) Child of the valley. *Slaid, Slaide, Slayd, Slayde*

Slate (English) Fine-grained rock.

Slevin (Gaelic) Mountaineer. *Slavan, Slavon, Slawin, Slevan*

Sloan (Gaelic) Warrior. *Sloane, Slone*

Smith (English) Blacksmith. *Smithe, Smits, Smitty, Smyth, Smythe*

Snehal (Hindi) Friendly.

Snoop Dogg (American) Rapper Cordozar Calvin Broadus Jr.

Snorre (Scandinavian) Form of Snorri; Snorri Sturluson was a celebrated twelfth-century Icelandic historian and politician.

Snowden (Old English) From the snow-covered hill. *Snow, Snowdun*

So (Vietnamese) First-born; smart.

Socrates (Greek) Philosophical; brilliant. *Socratez, Socratis, Sokrates*

Sofronio (Greek) Self-controlled. *Sophronio*

Soham (Hindi) Presence of divinity in the soul.

Sohrab (Persian) Ancient hero.

Sol (Latin) Sun. *Soll, Solly*

Solan (Latin) Soul seeker. *Solen, Solon, Solyn*

Solanio (Italian) Friend to Antonio.

Solinus (Greek) Duke of Ephisus.

Solomon (Hebrew) Peaceful; perfect. *Salamon, Sol, Soloman*

Solt (Hungarian) Name of an honor.

Sølve (Scandinavian) Meaning unknown.

Sólyom (Hungarian) Falcon.

Som (Indian) Sun.

Soma (Hungarian) Kind of berry.

Somerby (English) From the summer village. *Somerbie, Somersby, Sommersby*

Somerly (Irish) Summer sailor. *Somerled, Sommerleigh, Sorley*

Somerton (English) Summer estate. *Summerton*

Sommar (English) Summer. *Somer, Somers, Somm, Sommars, Sommer*

Sonnagh (Welsh) Mound; rampart.

Soren (Danish) Thunder; war. *Sorren, Soryn*

Sorrel (French) Bitter; from the tree. *Sorre, Sorrell, Sorrey*

Soteria (Greek) Salvation.

Soterios (Greek) Saviour.

Spalding (English) Divided field. *Spaulding*

Sparky (Latin) Ball of fire; joyful. *Spark, Sparkee, Sparkey, Sparki, Sparkie*

Spaulding (English) Divided field. *Spalding, Spaldying, Spauldyng*

Speck (Old English) Small mark; surname.

Speers (English) Good with spears; swift moving. *Speares, Spears, Spiers*

Spencer (Old English) Dispenser, keeper. *Spence, Spenser*

Spider (American) Scary. *Spyder*

Spike (Old English) Long, heavy nail. *Spyke*

Spiridon (Greek) Like a breath of fresh air. *Speero, Spero, Spiridon, Spiro, Spiros, Spyridon, Spyros*

Spoonie Gee (American) Rapper Gabriel Jackson.

Srijan (Hindi) Creation.

Srikant (Hindi) Lover of wealth.

Srinath (Hindi) Meaning unknown.

Srinivas (Hindi) Abode of wealth.

Sriram (Hindi) Lord Rama.

Stacey (Latin) Stable. *Stace, Stacee, Staci, Stacie, Stacy, Stasia, Stasya, Tasia*

Staffan (Swedish) Garland.

Stafford (English) Dignified. *Staff, Staffard, Stafferd, Staffi, Staffie, Staffor*

Stamford (English) From the stony ford. *Stemford*

Stamos (Greek) Reasonable. *Stammos, Stamohs*

Stanbury (English) Fortified. *Stanberry, Stanbery, Stanburghe, Stansberry, Stansburghe, Stansbury*

Stancliff (English) From the stone cliff; prepared. *Stancliffe, Stanclyffe, Stanscliff, Stanscliffe*

Stanislaw (Latin) Camp of glory; stone clearing. *Aineislis, Stan, Stanislao, Stanislas, Stanislau, Stanislaus, Stanislav, Stanislavsky, Stasio, Sztaniszláv*

Stanley (Old English) From the rocky meadow. *Stanberry, Stanbury, Standish, Stanfield, Stanford, Stanhope, Stanleigh, Stanly, Stanmore, Stanton, Stanway, Stanwick, Stanwyck*

Stanwick (English) Born in village of stone. *Stanwic, Stanwicke, Stanwyck*

Stark (German) High energy. *Starke, Starkey*

Starr (English) Bright. *Star, Starri, Starrie*

Stavros (Greek) Crowned with wreath.

Steadman (English) Landowner; wealthy. *Steadmann, Sted, Stedmann*

Steele (English) Form of Steel. *Steale*

Stefan (German) Crown; wreath. *Stef, Stefano, Stefanos, Stefos, Stephano, Stephanos*

Stein (German) Stone. *Steen, Steinbeck, Steinberg, Steiner, Steinmetz, Steinway, Steyn, Stine, Styne*

Steinar (Scandinavian) Muse; rock. *Steanar, Steener, Steinard, Steinart, Steinhardt*

Sten (Swedish) Stone.

Stephen (Greek) Crown. *Esteban, Estevan, Etienne, Steenie, Stefan, Stefano, Steffan, Stepan, Stephan, Stephens, Stephenson, Stephon, Stevan, Steve, Steven, Stevens, Stevenson, Stevie*

Sterling (English) Genuine; valued. *Stirling*

Sterne (Middle English) Serious-minded. *Stearn, Stearne, Stern*

Stetson (English) Cowboy hat. *Steston, Steton, Stetsen, Stetzon*

Stewart (Teutonic) Keeper of the estate. *Stew, Steward, Stu, Stuart*

Stieran (Scandinavian) Wandering. *Steeran, Steeren, Steeryn, Stieren, Stieryn*

Stiles (English) Practical. *Stile, Styles*

Stillman (English) Quiet. *Stille, Stillman, Stilman*

Sting (English) Singer.

Stoke (English) Village.

Stokley (Old English) From the tree-stump meadow. *Stockley, Stockman, Stockton, Stockwell, Stokeley*

Stone (American) Stone, rock. *Stonee, Stoney, Stoni, Stonie, Stony*

Storm (English) Storm, tempest. *Storme, Stormy*

Story (Norwegian) Great. *Storr*

Stoyan (Bulgarian) To stay.

Strato (Shakespearean) Character from *Julius Caesar.*

Stratton (Scottish) Home loving. *Straton, Strattawn*

Strom (German) Stream. (Czech) Tree. (Greek) Bed.

Stroud (Old English) From the thicket. *Stod, Stroude*

Stuart (English) Careful; watchful. *Stewart, Stu*

Studs (Old English) House.

Sture (Swedish) Impudent.

Sudarshan (Hindi) Handsome. *Sudarsana*

Sudesha (Hindi) Son of Krishna; good country.

Sudeva (Hindi) Good. *Deva*

Sudhansu (Hindi) Moon.

Sudhir (Hindi) Great scholar; calm; resolute; brave.

Suk-Chul (Korean) Big and firm.

Sukarman (Hindi) Reciter of 1,000 sections of a Sanskrit hymn.

Sukru (Turkish) Grateful.

Sukumar (Hindi) Tender; handsome.

Sulaiman (African American) Peaceful. *Sulaman, Suleiman, Suleman, Suleyman, Suleyuman, Sulyman*

Sulio (Breton) Meaning unknown. *Suliag, Suliau*

Sullivan (Gaelic) Black eyes. *Sullavan, Sullevan, Sullyvan, Syllyvan*

Sully (Gaelic) To stain. *Sullea, Sullee, Sulley, Sullie*

Sumadhur (Hindi) Very sweet.

Sumantu (Hindi) Meaning unknown.

Sumati (Hindi) Wisdom.

Sumit (Hindi) Good friend.

Summit (English) Peak. *Summet, Summitt, Summyt*

Sumner (French) Summoner. *Sumenor, Sumnor*

Sun (Chinese) Bending; decreasing; goodness; sun.

Sundara (Hindi) Beautiful. *Sundar, Sundarama, Sunder*

Sunil (Hindi) Blue; sapphire.

Sunny (English) Bright disposition, cheerful. *Sonny, Sunday, Suni, Sunnee, Sunni, Sunnie, Suny*

Surány (Hungarian) Name of an honor.

Suresh (Hindi) Ruler of the gods.

Surya (Hindi) Sun. *Suria, Suriah*

Sutherland (Norse) From the southern land. *Suffield, Sundy, Sutcliff, Sutton*

Suvrata (Hindi) Child of Daksa.

Svein (Anglo-Saxon) Youth.

Sven (Scandinavian) Youth. *Svend, Svensen, Svenson, Swen, Swensen, Swenson*

Swain (Middle English) Knight's attendant. *Swaine, Swane, Swayne, Swayze*

Swapnil (Hindi) Dreamlike.

Sweeny (Gaelic) Little hero. *Sweanee, Sweanie, Sweeney, Sweeni*

Sydney (English) From Sidon. *Sy, Syd, Sydne, Sydni, Sydny*

Sylvester (English, Latin) From the forest. *Silvester, Silvestre, Silvestro, Sly*

Szabolcs (Hungarian) Meaning unknown.

Szalók (Hungarian) Meaning unknown.

Szemere (Hungarian) Small man; demolisher.

Szervác (Hungarian) Freed.

Szescõ (Hungarian) Meaning unknown.

Szevér (Hungarian) Serious; strict. *Szörény*

T

T. I. (American) Rapper Clifford Joseph Hams Jr.

Tab (German, Middle English) Brilliant; drummer. *Tabb, Tabbert, Tabby, Taber, Tabor, Taburer*

Tabansi (African American) One who endures.

Tabari (African American) After famous Muslim historian, al-Tabari. *Tabahri, Tabares, Tabarious*

Tabib (Turkish) Physician. *Tabeeb, Tabyb*

Tabor (Hungarian) Camp. *Taber, Taibor, Tavor, Tayber, Taybor*

Tadc (Celtic) Poet; philosopher.

Taddeo (Italian) Courageous; one who praises.

Tadeu (Portuguese) Given of God.

Tadi (Native American) Wind.

Tae-Hyun (Korean) Great and honor.

Taft (English) Flowing. *Tafte, Taftie*

Taher (Arabic) Pure; clean.

Tahir (Arabic) Chaste; pure. *Taheer, Taher, Tahyr*

Tai (Vietnamese) Talent; from Thailand.

Taimah (Native American) Thunder. *Taima, Taiomah, Tama, Tamah*

Tajo (Spanish) Day. *Taio*

Takeshi (Japanese) Bamboo.

Taksa (Hindi) Son of Bharata.

Taksony (Hungarian) Well fed; content; merciless; wild.

Taku (Japanese) Small; young.

Talbot (French) Reward. *Talbott, Talibot, Tallbott, Tallie, Tally, Talybott*

Talleen (Indian) Absorbed.

Talman (Hebrew) To injure; to oppress. *Tallmon, Talmen, Talmin, Talmyn*

Talon (English) Sharp claw. *Taelon, Taelyn, Talan, Talin, Talyn, Tawlon*

Talor (Hindi) Morning dew. *Taelor, Taelur*

Talos (Greek) Giant protector of Minos Island.

Tamarius (African American) Stubborn. *T'Marius, Tam, Tamerius*

Tamir (Arabic) Pure; tall; stately. *Tameer, Tamirr, Tamyrr, Tymyr*

Tancredo (Italian) Of thoughtful counsel. *Tancrede*

Tanek (Polish) Immortal.

Taner (Turkish) Seed. *Tanar, Tane, Tanery*

Tanner (Old English) Leather worker. *Tan, Tanier, Tann, Tanney, Tannie, Tanny*

Tansy (Greek) Immortal. (Native American) Name of a flower.

Tapan (Hindi) Sun.

Taras (Greek) Of Tarentum.

Tarasios (Greek) Of Tarentum. *Taras*

Tardos (Hungarian) Bald.

Tariq (Arabic) Star; path. *Tareck, Tareec, Tareek, Tareeq, Tarek, Tareke, Taric, Tarick, Tariek, Tarik, Teryk*

Tarján (Hungarian) Name of an honor.

Tarkan (Turkish) Meaning unknown.

Taro (Japanese) First-born male.

Tarun (Hindi) Young.

Tas (Hungarian) Well fed; stone.

Tate (Old English) Cheerful. (Native American) Long-winded talker.

Tathal (Welsh) Meaning unknown.

Tathan (Welsh) Meaning unknown.

Tatum (English) Cheerful. *Taitam, Taitem, Taitim, Taitom, Taitum, Taytom*

Taurin (Latin) Born under the sign of Taurus. *Taurinus*

Tavarius (African American) Misfortune; fun-loving. *Tav, Taverius, Tavurius, Tavvy*

Tavis (Scottish) Twin. *Tamsin, Tav, Tavish, Tevis*

Tavon (African American) Nature.

Tavor (Aramaic) Misfortune. *Tarvaris, Tavaris, Tavars, Tavarus, Tavores, Tavorious, Tavoris, Teverys*

Taylor (Middle English) Tailor. *Taelor, Tailor, Talor, Tay, Taylour, Taylr, Tie*

Teague (Irish) Poet; handsome. (Scottish) Philosopher. *Teak, Tadhg, Teag, Teeque, Tege, Teig*

Tearlach (Scottish) Manly. *Tearlache, Tearloc, Tearlocke, Tearlok*

Tecer (Turkish) Meaning unknown.

Tee (Gaelic) House.

Tegan (Celtic) Doe.

Teithi (Celtic) Mythical son of Gwynham.

Tej (Hindi) Splendor.

Telford (French) Works in iron. *Telfer, Telfor, Telfour*

Telo (Old French) Surname. *Teliau, Théliau, Thélo*

Tem (English) Country.

Temani (Hebrew) Of Teman. *Temanie, Temen, Temin, Temon*

Temo (Hebrew) Right hand; south.

Templeton (English) Town near the temple. *Temple, Templeten*

Tenenan (French) Meaning unknown. *Tenedor, Tinidor*

Tennessee (Native American) Meeting place. *Tennesy, Tennysee*

Tennyson (Middle English) Son of Dennis. *Tennessee, Tennison, Tenny, Tenson, Tenyson*

Terach (Hebrew) Wild goat; contentious. *Tera, Terah*

Tercan (Turkish) Meaning unknown.

Terence (Latin) Polished; tender. *Tarance, Tarence, Tarrance, Tarrence, Tarrynce, Terance, Terencio, Terentius, Teri, Terrence, Terris, Terry, Torrance*

Terje (Norse) Of Thor's spear.

Terrel (Old English) Thunderer. *Rell, Terel, Terele, Terell, Terille, Terral, Terrelle, Terrill, Terris, Tirell, Tirrill, Tyrell, Tyril*

Tétény (Hungarian) Chieftain Töhötöm.

Teulyddog (Welsh) Meaning unknown.

Tevaughn (African American) Tiger. *Tev, Tevan, Tivan, Tivaughan*

Tevin (African American) Son of Kevin. *Teavin, Teivon, Tevaughan, Tevien*

Tewdwr (Welsh) Meaning unknown.

Texas (American) Place name. *Tex, Texx*

Tezer (Turkish) Meaning unknown.

Thabit (Arabic) Firm. *Thabyt*

Thaddeaus (Latin) Courageous; praiser. *Tad, Tadda, Taddeo, Taddy, Tadeo, Tadeusz, Tadgh, Ted, Thad, Thada, Thaddaus, Thaddea, Thaddeus, Thaddeys, Thadea, Thadeus, Thadus, Thadys, Thadyus*

Thai (Vietnamese) Many; multiple.

Thaman (Hindi) Name of a god. *Thamane, Thamen*

Than (Burmese) Million. *Tan*

Thane (Old English) Attendant warrior. *Thain, Thayn, Thayne, Thine*

Thanos (Greek) Noble. *Anthanasios, Thanus, Thonasis*

Thaonawyuthe (Native American) One who interrupts. *Thaowayuthe*

Thatcher (Old English) Roof fixer. *Thacher, Thatch, Thaxter*

Theobold (German) Boldest. *Teoboldo, Thebault, Theo, Thibaud, Thibaut, Tibalt, Tybalt*

Theodore (Greek) Gift of God. *Fedor, Feodor, Fyodor, Ted, Teddy, Telly, Teodor, Teodore, Teodoro, Theodor*

Theodoric (Teutonic) Ruler of the people. *Thierry*

Theodosius (English) God giving.

Theophilus (Greek) Beloved of God. *Teofil, Theophile*

Theron (Greek) Hunter. *Therron, Theryon*

Thiago (Portuguese) Saint James.

Thiassi (Scandinavian) Ancient mythological figure. *Thiazi, Thjazi*

Thibaud (French) Rule of the people.

Thierry (Teutonic) People's ruler. *Theory, Thierry, Thiery*

Thomas (Greek) Twin. *Massey, Tamas, Thom, Thoma, Thompson, Thomson, Thos, Thumas, Tom, Tomas, Tomaso, Tomcy, Tommy*

Thompson (English) Prepared. *Thom, Thompsen, Thompsun, Thomson*

Thong (Vietnamese) Smart.

Thor (Old Norse) Thunder. *Soren, Sören, Søren, Thorbert, Thordis, Tor*

Thoralf (Scandinavian) Thunder. *Thord, Thorfinn, Thorgeirr, Thorgils, Thorgrim, Thorkell*

Thorin (Scandinavian) Form of Thor, god of thunder. *Thorrin, Thors*

Thorley (English) Thor's meadow. *Thorlea, Thorlee, Thorleigh, Thorly, Torley*

Thorndike (English) Thorny riverbank. *Thorndyck, Thorndyke*

Thorne (Old English) Thorn tree. *Thorn, Thorndyke, Thornley, Thornton*

Thorpe (Old English) From the village. *Thorp*

Thorstein (Scandinavian) Son of Thor.

Thurborn (Teutonic) Dweller by Thor's stream.

Thurlow (Old English) Thor's hill. *Terrell, Thorald, Thorbert, Thorburn,*

Thorley, Thormond, Thurber, Thurman, Thurmon, Thurmond, Torold

Thurston (Norse) Thor's stone. *Thirstan, Thirstein, Thirsten, Thirstin, Thirston, Thorstan, Thorstein, Thorsteinn, Thorsten, Thorston, Thurstain, Thursteen, Thurstin, Thurstyn, Torstein, Torsten, Torston, Turstan*

Tibalt (Greek) People's prince.

Tiernan (Celtic) Lord. *Tiarnach, Tiernam, Tierney, Tyrnan*

Tihamér (Hungarian) Likes silence.

Tilak (Hindi) Auspicious.

Timeus (Greek) Perfect.

Timoleon (Greek) I honor what I say.

Timon (Greek) Worthy. (Shakespearean) Character from *Timon of Athens*. *Timan, Timen, Timin*

Timothy (Greek) Honoring God. *Tadhg, Tiege, Tim, Tima, Timee, Timmie, Timmy, Timo, Timofey, Timok, Timon, Timontheo, Timoteo, Timoteu, Timothe, Timothee, Timotheus, Tmey, Tymmy*

Timur (Hebrew) Date; palm tree. (Russian) Conqueror. *Timarr, Timor, Timour, Tomor, Tömör, Tymar, Tymer*

Tinh (Vietnamese) Mindful; aware.

Titus (Greek) Of the giants. *Titan, Titas, Titek, Titis, Tito*

Titusz (Hungarian) Dove; honored.

Tivadar (Hungarian) Gift of God.

Tivon (Hebrew) Lover of nature.

Tobias (Hebrew) God is good. *Toben, Tobey, Tobia, Tobiah, Tobian, Tóbiás, Tobin, Tobit, Toby, Tova, Tovin*

Todd (Middle English) Fox. *Tod, Todde, Toddie, Toddy*

Tolbert (English) Bright prospects. *Talbart, Talbert, Tolbart, Tolburt, Tollee, Tolley*

Tomaj (Hungarian) Clan.

Tomer (Hebrew) Tall. *Tomar, Tomir, Tomyr*

Tomkin (Old English) Little. *Tom, Tomlin, Tompkin, Torsten*

Tomo (Japanese) Twin.

Tong (Vietnamese) Fragrant.

Tony (Latin) Praiseworthy. (Greek) Flourishing. Nickname for Anthony. *Tonee, Toney, Tonie*

Tor (Norwegian) Thunder. *Thor, Tore, Torre*

Torell (French) Small Tower. *Torail, Torel, Torrell*

Torger (Old Norse) Thor's spear.

Torin (Celtic) Chief.

Tormod (Scottish) Thunder spirit.

Torrance (Irish) From the low hills. *Torey, Tori, Torr, Torrey, Torry*

Toste (Scandinavian) Warrior.

Tostig (Old English) Name of an earl.

Tov (Hebrew) Good. *Tovi, Toviel, Toviya, Tuvia, Tuviah, Tuviya*

Townsend (Old English) From the end of town. *Town, Towne, Townes, Townie, Townley, Townsen*

Toyo (Japanese) Plentiful.

Tracy (Greek) Harvester. (Latin) Courageous. (Irish) Battler. *Trace, Tracee, Tracey, Treacy*

Trahaearn (Welsh) Strong as iron. *Trahern, Tray*

Tranter (Old English) Wagoneer.

Travis (French) Crossing. *Tavers, Traver, Travers, Traves, Travess, Travey, Travus, Travuss, Travys, Trever, Trevor*

Tremayne (Scottish) House by the stones; farm with a stone monolith. *Tramaine, Treemayne, Trem, Tremain, Tremaine, Tremane, Tremen*

Tremeur (French) Meaning unknown. *Treveur*

Trent (Latin) Torrent; rapid stream. (Old English) Dweller by the Trent. *Trant, Trante, Trente, Trentino, Trenton*

Trenus (Latin) Meaning unknown.

Trevor (Irish) Cautious. *Travar, Travir, Trefor, Trev, Trevar, Treyvor*

Trevrizent (Arthurian) Percival's uncle.

Trey (Middle English) Third-born; three. *Trae, Tray, Tre, Treye*

Trigve (Norwegian) Meaning unknown.

Tripp (Old English) Traveler. *Tryp, Trypp*

Trisanu (Hindi) Meaning unknown.

Tristan (Old Welsh, Latin) Noisy one; laborer. *Trestan, Trestyn, Trist, Tristen, Tristram, Tristyn*

Troilus (Shakespearean) Character from *Troilus and Cressida*.

Trory (African American) Red one.

Truman (Old English) Disciple. *True, Trueman, Truesdale, Trumain, Trumaine, Trumann*

Tryggvi (Scandinavian) True. *Trygg, Tryggve*

Tuathal (Celtic) Meaning unknown.

Tucker (Middle English) Tailor. *Tuck, Tucker, Tuckie, Tuckman, Tucky*

Tudfwlch (Welsh) Meaning unknown.

Tudur (Welsh) Divine gift.

Tugdual (French) Meaning unknown. *Tual, Tugal*

Tujan (French) Meaning unknown. *Tugen, Tujen*

Tuncer (Turkish) Meaning unknown.

Tung (Chinese) Universal.

Tupac (Quichua) The Lord.

Turiau (French) Meaning unknown. *Turio*

Turner (Middle English) Carpenter.

Turpin (Old Norse) Thunder. *Finn*

Turquine (Arthurian) Son of Mitrides.

Tushar (Hindi) Snow.

Tuvya (Hebrew) Goodness of God. *Tevya, Tuvia, Tuviah*

Twain (Middle English) Two pieces. *Tawine, Twaine, Twan, Twane, Tway*

Tye (Old English) Enclosed. *Tai, Tie, Tiegh, Tigh, Tighe, Tynan*

Tyee (Native American) Chief.

Tyler (Middle English) Tiler; roofer. *Tiler, Tyel, Tyle, Tylee, Tyler, Tylor*

Tymon (Greek) Honoring God. *Tayron, Tymaine, Tyman, Tymeik*

Tyne (Old English) River. *Tain, Tine*

Tyrek (Hebrew) Rock; sharp. *Ty*

Tyrell (African American) Thunder ruler. *Tyrel, Tyrelle, Tyrrel, Tyrrell*

Tyrone (Greek) King. *Tayron, Tayrone, Tirone, Tyerone, Tyron, Tyroney*

Tyson (English) Son of Ty; fiery. (French) Explosive. (German) Son of the German. *Tison, Tiszon, Tycen, Tyeson, Tysin*

Tytus (Polish) Form of Titus. *Tytan*

Tzuriel (Hebrew) God is my rock. *Tzuriya*

U

Ualtar (Irish) Ruler of the army. *Uaitcir, Ualteir*

Ualusi (Tongan) Walrus. *Ualusee, Ualusey, Ualusie, Ualusy*

Uang (Chinese) Great.

Uata (Ploynesian) Army leader. *Uate*

Uba (African American) Wealthy.

Ubadah (Arabic) He who serves God.

Ubaldus (Teutonic) Peace of mind. *Ubaldas, Uboldas, Uboldus*

Ubanwa (African) Wealth in children.

Uben (German) Practice. *Ubaldo, Ube*

Uberto (German) Bright mind.

Ubrig (German) Big. *Ubrigg, Ubryg, Ubrygg*

Ubrigens (German) Bothered. *Ubrigins, Ubrigyns*

Ubul (Hungarian) Meaning unknown.

Uchdryd (Welsh) Legendary son of Erim.

Uchtred (English) Cries. *Uchtrid, Uchtryd, Uctred, Uctrid, Uctryd, Uktred, Uktrid*

Udai (Hindi) To arrive. *Uday, Uhayan*

Udall (English) Certain; valley of trees. *Eudall, Udahl, Udawl, Yudall*

Udeh (Hebrew) Praise.

Udel (English) Yew grove. *Dell, Eudel, Uddal, Udell*

Udenwa (African) Thriving.

Udit (Hindi) Risen.

Udo (Teutonic) One with great fortune; prosperous.

Udolf (English) Wealthy wolf. *Udolfo, Udoplh*

Uehudah (Hebrew) Meaning unknown.

Ueli (Swiss) Noble ruler. *Uelie, Uely*

Ufuk (Turkish) Meaning unknown.

Ugo (Italian) Bright in mind and spirit. *Ugon*

Ugod (Hungarian) Name of a clan.

Ugor (Hungarian) Meaning unknown. *Ugron*

Ugur (Turkish) Meaning unknown.

Uhila (Polynesian) Lightning. *Uhilah, Uhyla*

Uhr (German) Disturbed.

Uhubitu (Native American) Dirty water.

Uilleach (Irish) Ready. *Uilleack, Uilleak, Uilliac, Uilliack, Uilliak, Uillyac, Uillyack, Uillyak*

Uilleam (Irish) Determined guardian. *Uilliam*

Uilleog (Irish) Small protector. *Uilioc, Uilleac, Uilliog, Uillyog*

Uiseann (Irish) One who conquers. *Uinsionn*

Uistean (Irish) Intelligent.

Ujala (Hindi) Shining. *Ujaala*

Ukel (American) Player. *Ukal, Uke, Ukil*

Ulan (African American) First-born twin. (Russian) Place name. *Ulane, Ulen, Ulin, Ulon*

Uland (Teutonic) Noble country. (African) First-born twin. *Ulande, Ulandus*

Ulani (Polynesian) Cheerful.

Ulas (German) Noble.

Ulbrecht (German) Noble; bright. *Ulbright*

Ulbrich (German) Aristocratic.

Uleki (Hawaiian) Wrathful. *Ulekee, Ulekie, Uleky, Ulesi*

Ulexite (German) Mineral; silky white crystalline discovered by G. L. Ulex.

Ulf (Teutonic) Wolf.

Ulffr (Scandinavian) Wolf-like; courageous. *Ulff, Ulv*

Ulfred (Norse) Noble.

Ulgar (German) High born.

Ulices (Latin) Wrathful; wanderer. *Uly*

Ulick (Scandinavian) Bright; rewarding mind. *Ulic, Ulyc, Ulyck*

Ulises (Latin) Wrathful.

Ull (Scandinavian) Glory.

Ulland (English) Noble lord. *Uland, Ullund*

Ullock (Irish) Nobleman.

Ulman (German) Wolf's infamy. *Ullman, Ullmann, Ulmann*

Ulmer (English) Famous wolf. *Ullmar, Ulmar*

Ulriah (German) Powerful wolf. *Ulria, Ulrya, Ulryah*

Ulrich (German) Wolf ruler. *Udolf, Ulger, Ull, Ulric, Ulrick, Ulu*

Ulrik (Scandinavian) Noble ruler.

Ulster (Scandinavian) Wolf.

Ultan (Celtic) From an old name. *Ultann*

Ultar (Scandinavian) Wolf. *Ultarr*

Ulucan (Turkish) Meaning unknown.

Ulysses (Latin) Hateful one, wounded in the thigh. *Uilioc, Ule, Ulesses, Ulises*

Umar (Arabic) Longevity. *Umair, Umayr*

Umber (French) Brown; plain.

Umberto (Italian) Famous German.

Umed (Hindi) Desire.

Umher (Arabic) Controlling.

Umi (African) Life. *Umie, Umy*

Umit (Turkish) Hope.

Unaduti (Native American) Wooly head.

Uner (Turkish) Famous.

Ungus (Irish) One victor.

Unitas (American) United.

Unkan (Japanese) Cloud valley.

Unkas (Native American) Fox. *Uncas, Wonkas*

Unni (Norse) Modest.

Unser (German) Surname. (American) Racing family.

Unten (English) Not a friend. *Untenn*

Unus (Latin) One. *Unuss*

Unwin (English) Enemy. *Unwinn, Unwyn*

Updike (Scottish) Surname.

Upendra (Hindi) Element.

Upjohn (English) Creative. *Upjon*

Upton (English) From the upper town. *Uppton, Upshaw, Uptawn, Upten, Uptown*

Upwood (English) Forest on a hill.

Uranus (Greek) Heaven.

Urban (Latin) From the city. *Urb, Urbain, Urbaine, Urbane, Urbano, Urbanus, Urben, Urbin, Urvan*

Uri (Hebrew) Light; God of light. *Uria, Uriah, Urian, Urie, Uriel, Uriell*

Urian (Greek) Heaven. *Urion*

Urias (Hebrew) Lord as my light; old-fashioned. *Uraeus, Uri, Uria, Urius*

Urien (Greek) Heaven. *Turien, Turio*

Urjasz (Polish) God is light.

Urjavaha (Hindi) Of the Nimi dynasty.

Uros (Hungarian) Little lord.

Ursan (Latin) Bear. *Urs*

Urson (French) Form of Orson. *Ursan, Ursen, Ursin, Ursine*

Urvano (Spanish) City boy. *Urbano*

Urvil (Hindi) Sea. *Ervil*

Urvine (American) Place name, form of Irvine, California. *Urveen, Urvene, Urvi*

Ury (Hebrew) Shining.

Usaid (Arabic) Laughs.

Usaku (Japanese) Moonlit.

Usamah (Arabic) Lion. *Usama*

Useni (African) Tell me. *Usene*

Usher (English) Bringer.

Usi (African) Smoke.

Ustin (Russian) Form of Justin.

Utah (American) Place name.

Utatci (Native American) Bear scratching.

Uther (English) Arthur's father.

Uthman (Arabic) Bird. *Othman, Usman*

Utsav (Indian) Feast Day.

Utt (Arabic) Wise and kind.

Uttam (Hindi) Third Manu; founding father of human beings. (Sanskrit) Best.

Utz (American) Befriends all.

Uwe (German) Universal ruler.

Uxio (Greek) Born into nobility.

Uzi (Hebrew) My strength.

Uziah (Hebrew) God is my strength. *Uzia, Uziya, Uzziah*

Uziel (Hebrew) Powerful. *Uzziel*

Uzoma (African American) Born on a trip.

Uzondu (African) Attracts others.

Uzor (Hungarian) Ethnic group. *Ozor*

V

Vachel (French) Cow tender; small cow. *Vache, Vachell, Vachelle*

Vaclav (Slavic) Great glory. *Vasek*

Vadim (Russian) Powerful ruler. *Vadik, Wadik, Wadim*

Vadin (Hindi) Educated orator. *Vaden*

Vaduz (German) Place name.

Vaesna (Cambodian) Lucky.

Vahe (Armenian) Victor.

Vaibhav (Hindi) Riches.

Vail (English, French, Latin) From the valley. *Bail, Bale, Vael, Vaiel, Vaile, Vaill, Vale, Valle, Vayel, Vayl, Vayle*

Vaino (Finnish) Wagon builder.

Vairaja (Hindi) Son of Virat. *Vaal*

Val (Latin) Strong; powerful; healthy. *Vall*

Vala (Polynesian) Loincloth.

Valdermar (German) Famous ruler. *Valdemarr, Valdimar, Valdymar, Vlademar, Waldemar*

Valen (English) Strong.

Valentin (Latin) Good health. *Valencio, Valente, Valentino, Valentyno*

Valentine (Latin) Strong. *Valentin, Valentino, Valentyn*

Valeray (French) Strong.

Valeri (Russian) Athletic, mighty. *Val, Valerian, Valerio, Valry*

Valerian (Russian) Strong leader. *Valerien, Valerio, Valerious, Valery, Valeryan, Valerie*

Vali (Scandinavian) Brave man. *Valea, Valee, Valeigh, Valey, Valie, Valy*

Valin (Hindi) Mighty soldier. *Valan, Valen, Valon, Valyn*

Valmihi (Hindi) Ant hill.

Valor (Latin) Boldness; bravery.

Valu (Polynesian) Eight.

Van (Dutch) Dyke. *Vane, Vann, Vanno, Von, Vonn*

Vance (Middle English) Dweller at the windmill. *Van, Vancelo, Vann, Vanse*

Vanda (Lithuanian) Ruling people. *Vandah, Vandele, Venda*

Vandan (Hindi) Saved. *Vanden, Vandin, Vandon, Vandyn*

Vander (Greek) Short for Evander. *Vand, Vandar, Vandir, Vandor, Vandyr, Vendar, Vender, Vendir, Vendor, Vendyr*

Vandiver (American) Quiet. *Van, Vand, Vandaver, Vandever*

Vandwon (African American) Covert. *Vandawon, Vandjuan*

Vandyke (Dutch) From the dyke. *Vandike, VanDyck*

Vane (Middle English) Wind; banner.

Vaninadh (Hindi) Husband of Saraswati, the goddess of knowledge.

Vannevar (Scandinavian) Good.

Vanslow (Scandinavian) Sophisticated. *Vansalo, Vanselow, Vanslaw*

Vanya (Russian) God is gracious. *Vanechka, Vanek, Vania, Vanja, Vanka, Vanusha, Vanyah, Wanya*

Varden (French) From the green hill. *Vardaan, Vardan, Varden, Vardin, Vardon, Vardyn, Vartan, Verdan, Verden, Verdin, Verdon, Verdun, Verdyn*

Vardhamma (Hindi) Growth. *Vardhaman*

Varen (Hindi) Superior. *Varan, Varin, Varon, Varyn*

Varesh (Hindi) God is superior.

Varick (German) Protecting ruler. *Varak, Varek, Varic, Varric, Varyc, Varyck, Varyk, Warick, Warrick*

Varil (French) Faithful. *Varal, Varel, Varol, Varyl*

Variya (Hindi) Excellent one.

Varkey (American) Boisterous.

Várkony (Hungarian) Avar, an ethnic group. *Varsany*

Varlan (American) Tough. *Varland, Varlen, Varlin*

Varma (Hindi) Faithful.

Varner (German) Surname; formidable. *Varn*

Varocher (French) Meaning unknown.

Varrius (Latin) Gentleman; servant to the duke.

Vartan (Armenian) Rose. *Varoun, Varten, Vartin, Varton, Vartyn*

Varun (Hindi) Lord of the waters. *Varan, Varen, Varin, Varon, Varoon, Varron, Varyn*

Vas (Slavic) Protective. *Vaston, Vastun, Vasya*

Vasant (Hindi) Spring season. *Vasan, Vasanth*

Vasava (Hindi) Indra.

Vashon (African American) God is gracious, merciful. *Vashaun, Vashonne, Vishon*

Vasil (Czech) Kingly. *Basil, Vasile, Vasilek, Vasili, Vasilios, Vasilis, Vasilos, Vasily, Vassily*

Vasilios (Greek) With royal blood; regal. *Vasilis, Vasily, Vassily, Wasily*

Vasin (Hindi) Rules all.

Vassil (Bulgarian) King. *Vass*

Vasu (Sanskrit) Rich boy.

Vasudev (Hindi) Form of Lord Krishna. *Vasu*

Vasuman (Hindi) Born of fire.

Vaughan (Celtic) Little, small. *Vaughn*

Vavrin (Czech) Laurel.

Vavrinec (Czech) Crowned with laurels. *Lawrence*

Vayk (Hungarian) Rich.

Vea (Polynesian) Chief. *Veamalohi, Veatama*

Veda (Sanskrit) Eternal knowledge. *Vedis*

Vedanga (Hindi) Knowledge. *Vedas*

Veejay (American) Talkative. *V. J., Vee-Jay, Vejay*

Veer (Hindi) Brave. *Vear, Veere*

Vega (Arabic) Falling star.

Vegas (Spanish) Meadows. (American) Place name. *Vega*

Veleslav (Czech) Great glory. *Vela, Velek, Velousek*

Velle (American) Tough. *Vell, Velley, Velly, Veltree*

Veltry (African American) Hopeful.

Venacio (Spanish) Glorious.

Vencel (Slavic) Wreath; glory. *Vaclav, Venceslas, Vyacheslav, Wazlaw, Wenzel*

Venec (Czech) Wreath. *Veniec*

Venedict (Russian) Blessed. *Venedikt, Venka, Venya*

Venezio (Italian) Glorious. *Venetziano, Veneziano*

Ventidius (Shakespearean) Character from *Antony and Cleopatra*.

Venturo (Italian) Lucky. *Venturio*

Verdun (French) Fort on a hill; place name. *Ferdon, Verden*

Vere (French) True. *Veir, Ver, Vir*

Vered (Hebrew) Rose. *Verad, Verid, Verod, Veryd*

Vergel (Latin) Rod bearer. *Verge, Vergel, Vergele, Vergill, Vergille*

Verges (English) Head borough.

Verile (German) Macho. *Verill, Verille, Verol, Verrill*

Verity (French) Truth.

Verlin (Latin) Blooming. (American) Spring. *Verlain, Verlan, Verlinn, Verlion, Verlon, Verlynn*

Verlyn (African American) Growing. *Velin, Verle, Verllin, Verlon, Virlie, Vyrle*

Vermont (French) Green mountain. (American) Place name.

Vern (Latin) Springlike. *Verin, Verna, Vernal, Verne, Vernie, Vernine, Vernol, Virn, Virne, Vyrn, Vyrne*

Verner (German) Defending army. *Verner, Virnir*

Vernon (French) Alder tree. (Latin) Spring. *Varnan, Verda, Vern, Vernen, Verney, Vernin, Vernun*

Verrier (French) Faithful.

Verrill (French) Faithful. *Verill, Verrall, Verrell, Verrol, Veryl*

Versey (English) Full of song.

Vertumnus (Latin) Changing. Roman mythology: god of the seasons, plant growth and gardens.

Vester (Latin) He who guards the fire.

Vesuvio (Italian) Smoke; volcano in southern Italy.

Viau (Breton) Lively. *Vial, Vital*

Vicente (Spanish) Winner. *Vic, Vincentay, Visente*

Victor (Latin) Victor; conqueror. *Vic, Vick, Victa, Victer, Victorien, Viktor, Vince, Vitorio, Vittorio, Wyctor*

Vid (German) Sylvan man. *Vida, Vidos*

Vida (Latin) Life. (Hebrew) Dearly loved.

Vidal (Spanish) Full of vitality. *Bidal, Vida, Vidale, Vidall, Videl, Videlio, Videll*

Vidar (Scandinavian) Soldier.

Vidkun (Scandinavian) Vast experience.

Vidor (Hungarian) Happy.

Vidvan (Hindi) Scholar.

Viet (Vietnamese) Destroy.

Viggo (Scandinavian) Exuberant. *Viggoa, Vigo*

Vigilius (Latin) Alert; vigilant.

Vihs (Hindi) Increase.

Vijay (Hindi) Victorious. *Bijay, Vijun*

Vijayendra (Hindi) Victorious god of the sky. *Vijendra*

Vikas (Hindi) Progress. *Vikash, Vikesh*

Vikesh (Hindi) Moon.

Vikram (Hindi) Glorious king.

Vikrant (Hindi) Brave.

Vila (Czech) Clever; resolute; mischievous. *Vilek, Vilem, Vilhelm, Vili, Viliam, Vilko, Ville, Vilmos*

Vilem (German) Determined guardian. *Vilhelm*

Viljalmr (Scandinavian) Resolute protector.

Viljo (Scandinavian) Guardian.

Villard (French) Village man.

Villiers (French) Kindhearted.

Vilmos (German) Steady soldier. *Villmos*

Vimal (Hindi) Pure. *Vima*

Vinay (Hindi) Good behavior. *Vynah*

Vincent (Latin) Conquering. *Vicenzio, Viken, Vikenti, Vikesha, Vin, Vince, Vincente, Vincenzo, Vinci, Vinco, Vinko, Vinn, Vinnie, Vinny*

Vine (English) One who works in a vineyard.

Vineet (Hindi) Unassuming.

Vinod (Hindi) Pleasing. *Vinodh, Vinood*

Vinson (English) Son of Vincent. (Latin) Conquering. *Venson, Vince, Vinnis, Vins, Vinsan, Vinsen, Vinsin, Vinsun, Vinsyn*

Vinton (English) Town of wine.

Vipin (Hind) Forest.

Vipul (Hindi) Plenty.

Viraj (Hindi) Splendor.

Virat (Hindi) Supreme being.

Vireo (Latin) Brave.

Virgil (Latin) Staff bearer. *Verge, Vergil, Vergilio, Virge, Virgie, Virgilio*

Vishal (Hindi) Immense.

Visvajit (Hindi) One who conquers the universe.

Visvakarman (Hindi) Architect; son of Yogasiddha.

Visvayu (Hindi) Brother of Amavasuand Satayu.

Viswanath (Hindi) The lord.

Vitalian (Italian) Life.

Vitaly (Greek) Life.

Vitas (Greek) Alive; vital. *Vidas, Vitalis, Vite*

Vitéz (Hungarian) Brave warrior.

Vito (Latin) Conquerer.

Vittorio (Italian) Victory. *Vitor, Vitorio, Vittore, Vittorios*

Vitus (Latin) Winning.

Vivar (Greek) Alive. *Viv*

Vivatma (Hindi) Universal soul.

Vivek (Hindi) Discerning with wisdom.

Vlade (Slavic) Prince.

Vladilen (Russian) Prince.

Vladimir (Slavic) To rule with peace; regal. *Bladimir, Valdimer, Vimka, Vlad, Vladamar, Vladamir, Vladimar, Vladimeer, Vladimere, Vladimire, Vladislav, Wolodymyr*

Vladislav (Czech) Glorious ruler. *Ladislav, Vladslau, Vladslav, Vladya*

Vlas (Russian) One who stammers.

Vojtech (Czech) Comforting soldier. *Vojta, Vojtek, Vojtresek*

Volf (Hebrew) Wolf.

Volker (German) People's guard. *Folke, Volker*

Volney (Greek) Hidden. *Volnee, Volni, Volnie*

Voltimand (English) Courtier.

Volund (Norse) Wonderful smith.

Volya (Slavic) Hopes.

Von (Scandinavian) Hope. *Vaughn, Vonn, Vonne*

Vortigem (English) In *The Legend of King Arthur*, the name of a king.

Voshon (African American) God's grace.

Vougay (Breton) Meaning unknown. *Nonna, Vouga*

Vui (Vietnamese) Cheerful.

Vul (African) Saves.

W

Waage (Scandinavian) Wagon.

Waban (Native American) East wind. *Waben, Wabin, Wabon, Wabyn*

Waclaw (Polish) Glorified.

Waco (American) Place name.

Wade (Middle English) Ford. *Wadley, Wadsworth, Waide, Wayde*

Wadell (English) Southerner. *Waddell, Wade*

Waden (American) God has heard. *Waden, Wedan*

Wadley (English) Ford meadow. *Wadlea, Wadleigh, Wadlie, Wadly*

Wadsworth (English) Homebody. *Waddsworth, Wadswurth*

Waggoner (German) Wagon maker.

Wagner (Dutch) Wagon driver. (German) Wagon maker. *Wagg, Waggner, Waggoner, Wagnar, Wargnur*

Wahib (Arabic) Giver, donor.

Wahid (Native American) Sacred. *Wabeed, Wahida, Wahyd*

Wahkan (Arabic) Unique; singular; unequalled.

Wain (English) Industrious. *Waine, Wane*

Wainwright (English) Wagon maker. *Wainright, Wainryght, Wayneright, Waynryght*

Waite (English) Protector. *Wait, Waitman, Waits, Wayt*

Wakefield (Old English) Wet field. *Waikfield, Wake, Wakeley, Wakeman*

Wakely (English) Wet meadow. *Wakelea, Wakelei, Wakely*

Wakiza (Native American) Determined warrior. *Wakyza*

Walbert (German) Protective, stodgy.

Walby (English) House near a wall. *Walbee, Walby*

Walchelim (Anglo-Norman) Meaning unknown.

Walcott (English) Lives in the Welshman's cottage. *Wallcot, Wallcott, Wolcott*

Waldemar (German) Mighty; famous. *Valdemar, Waldermar, Waldo*

Walden (Teutonic) Mighty. *Wald, Waldan, Waldi, Waldin, Waldo, Waldon, Waldy, Welti*

Waldo (Teutonic) Rule. *Waldemar, Waldemarr, Walden, Waldorf, Walfred*

Waldron (German) Mighty raven. *Waldran, Waldren, Waldrin, Waldryn*

Waleed (Arabic) Newborn. *Walead, Waled, Waleyd, Walid*

Walenty (Polish) Strong.

Waleran (Anglo-Norman) Meaning unknown.

Wales (English) Place name. *Wael, Wail, Wails, Wale, Waley, Wali, Waly*

Walford (English) Wealthy.

Walfred (German) Peaceful ruler. *Walfredd, Walfrid, Walfried, Walfrydd*

Walid (Arabic) Form of Waleed.

Walker (English) Distinctive. *Walk, Wally*

Wallace (Old English) Welshman. *Wallach, Wallas, Wallie, Wallis, Wally, Walsh, Welch, Welsh*

Waller (English) Man from Wales; smooth.

Wallis (English) Form of Wallace. *Walice, Wallise, Wallyce, Walyce*

Wally (English) Familiar form of Walter. *Walea, Wali, Waliy, Wallee*

Walmir (English) Pond of the Welsh.

Walmond (German) Mighty protector.

Walsh (English) Inquisitive. *Walls, Welce, Welch, Wells, Welsh*

Walten (German) Ruler.

Walter (German) Powerful warrior; army ruler. *Gauthier, Gautier, Ualtar, Wally, Walt, Walther, Watkins, Watson*

Walton (Old English) Dweller by the wall. *Walt, Walten, Waltin, Waltor*

Waltraut (German) Rule; strength. *Waltraud*

Walworth (English) Introvert; fenced-in farm. *Wallsworth, Walsworth*

Walwyn (English) Welsh friend. *Walwin, Walwinn, Walwynn, Walwynne, Welwyn*

Waman (Hindi) Falcon.

Wamblee (Native American) Eagle. *Wablea, Wambi, Wambleigh, Wambly*

Wanbi (Australian) Wild dingo. *Wanbee, Wanbie, Wanby*

Wang (Chinese) Kingly.

Waqar (Arabic) Talkative.

Wapi (Native American) Lucky.

Warburton (English) Fortified town.

Ward (English) To guard; watchman. *Wardell, Warden, Wardley, Warfield, Warford, Warley, Warmond, Warton, Warwick*

Wardell (English) Watchman's hill. *Wardel*

Warden (English) Watchful. *Warde, Wardie, Wardin, Wardon*

Wardford (English) Watchman's river.

Wardley (English) Careful. *Wardlea, Wardleigh, Wardli, Wardly*

Ware (English) Aware; cautious. *Wardlea, Wardleigh*

Warfield (English) Near the field of fish. *Warfyeld*

Waring (English) Dashing. *Warend, Warin, Warring*

Wark (American) Watchful.

Warley (English) Meadow near the river. *Warlea, Warlei, Warli*

Warmond (English) True guardian. *Warmon, Warmondo, Warmun, Warmund*

Warner (German) Defending army. *Werner*

Warren (German) Watchman; gamekeeper; enclosure. *Ware, Waren, Waring, Warrenson, Warrin, Warriner, Warron, Warry, Worrin*

Warrick (English) Strong leader. *Waric, Warik, Warrik, Warryck*

Warton (English) Defended town. *Warten, Wartin, Warton*

Warwen (American) Defensive. *Warn, Warwun*

Warwick (English) Settlement near the weir. *War, Warick, Warrick, Warweck, Warwyc, Warwyck, Wick*

Wasaki (African) Enemy.

Waseem (Arabic) Graceful; good-looking. *Wasseem*

Washburn (English) Bountiful; river. *Washbern, Washbie, Washborn, Washby*

Washi (Japanese) Eagle.

Washington (Old English) Town near water. *Wash, Washe, Washing*

Wasim (Arabic) Good-looking. *Wassim, Wasym*

Wassily (Russian) Royal; kingly.

Wat (English) Jolly.

Watford (English) Dam made of twigs and sticks. *Wattford*

Watkins (English) Son of Walter. *Watkin, Wattkin, Wattkyn, Wattkyns*

Watson (Old English) Son of Walter. *Watkins, Watt, Whatson*

Waverly (Old English) From the tree-lined meadow. *Waverlee, Waverleigh, Waverley, Waverlie*

Wayde (English) River crossing. *Wayd, Waydee*

Wayland (Old English) From the path land. *Way, Waylon, Weyland*

Waylon (English) Land by the road. *Wailon, Walon, Way, Whalan*

Wayman (English) Traveler. *Waymon*

Wayne (Old English) Wagon maker. *Waggoner, Wanye, Wayn, Waynell, Whayne*

Webb (English) Weaver. *Web, Weeb*

Webley (English) Weaver's meadow. *Webblea, Weblea, Weblee, Webli*

Webster (Old English) Weaver. *Webb, Weber, Webley, Webstar*

Weddel (English) Valley near the ford. *Weddell, Wedel, Wedell*

Weiss (German) White. *Weis, Weise, Weys, Weyss*

Welborne (English) Spring-fed. *Welbern, Welberne, Welburn, Welburne*

Welby (German) Farm near the well. *Weilby, Welbee, Welbey, Welbi*

Welcome (English) Welcome guest.

Weldon (English) Hill with a well. *Welden, Weldin, Weldyn*

Wellington (English) Rich man's town. *Wellinton*

Wells (Old English) From the springs. *Welborne, Welby, Weldon, Welford, Weller, Welles, Welton*

Welton (English) Town near the well. *Welltan, Wellton, Weltin, Weltyn*

Wen (Chinese) Cultured; ornamental.

Wenceslaus (Slavic) Great glory. *Vencel*

Wendell (Teutonic) Wend. *Wedel, Wendall, Wendel, Wendill, Wendle*

Wenlock (Welsh) Monastery lake. *Wenloc, Wenloch, Wenlok*

Wenzel (Slavic) Knowing. *Wensel, Wensyl, Wenzell, Wenzil*

Werner (Teutonic) Warrior. *Warin, Wernhar, Wernher*

Wesley (Old English) West meadow. *Wes, Wesleigh, Wess, Wessely, Wezley*

West (Old English) Westerly direction. *Westbrook, Westby, Westcott, Westleigh, Weston*

Westbrook (English) Brook on the west side. *Brook, Wesbrook, Westbrooke*

Westby (English) Western farmstead. *Wesbee, Wesbey, Wesbie, Westbey*

Wetherby (Old English) Ram's meadow. *Weatherbey, Weatherby*

Wetherell (English) Sheep corner. *Wetheral, Wetherel, Wetheril, Wetherill*

Whally (English) Woods near a hill. *Whalea, Whalee, Whaleigh, Whali*

Wheaton (Old English) Wheat town. *Wheatan, Wheatin*

Wheeler (Old English) Driver. *Wheelar*

Whistler (English) He who whistles.

Whit (Old English) White. *Whitby, Whitcomb, White,*

Whitelaw, Whitey, Whitfield, Whitford, Whitley, Whitlock, Whitman, Whitmoor, Whitmore, Whittaker, Whittemoore, Witmoore

Whitby (English) Farm with white walls. *Whitbea, Whitbee*

Whitcomb (English) Light in the valley. *Whitcombe, Whitcumb*

Whitey (English) White-skinned; white-haired. *Whitee, Whiti, Whity*

Whitfield (Old English) From a small field. *Whitley*

Whittaker (English) White field.

Wicasa (Native American) Sage. *Wicasah*

Wid (English) Wide. *Wido, Wyd, Wydo*

Wieslav (Slavic) One with great glory.

Wigar (Scottish) In Arthurian legend, King Arthur's armor.

Wilbert (German) Willful, bright; resolute. *Bylbert, Wilberto, Wilburt*

Wilbur (Teutonic) Bright resolve. *Wilburn, Willber, Wyllber, Wyllbur*

Wiley (English) Of the willows. *Whiley, Wilee, Wileigh, Wili*

Wilford (English) Ford by the willows. *Willford, Wylford*

Wilfred (Old English) Much peace. *Wilfrid, Wilfried, Willfred, Willfrid*

Willard (Teutonic) Bold resolve.

William (Teutonic) Valiant protector. *Guillaume,*

Guillermo, Uilleam, Uilliam, Vasili, Vasily, Vilem, Vilhelm, Viliam, Wil, Wiley, Wilford, Wilhelm, Wilkes, Wilkie, Will, Willard, Willem, Williams, Williamson, Willie, Willis, Willkie, Wills, Willy, Wilmar, Wilmer, Wilmos, Wilmot, Wilson, Wilton, Winton, Wyley, Wylkes

Willis (German) Son of William.

Willow (English) Willow.

Wilmer (German) Determined and famous.

Wilson (German) Son of William

Wilton (English) Farm by the Spring. *Wilt*

Wim (German) Strong helmet.

Winfield (German) Friend of the field.

Wingy (English) Winged like a bird. *Wingee, Wingi*

Winifred (Old English) Friend of peace. *Fred, Freddie, Freddy, Win, Winn, Winni, Winnie, Winny, Wyn*

Wink (American) Nickname of game shot host Winston Martindale.

Winog (Breton) Meaning unknown.

Winslow (Old English) From the friend's hill. *Winchell, Windsor, Winfield, Winfred, Winfrey, Wingate, Winthrop, Winton, Winward, Wynton*

Winston (Old English) Joy stone; victory town.

Winter (Old English) Winter. *Winters, Wynter*

Winthrop (Old English) Friendly.

Wirt (English) Worthy.

Wisdom (English) Wisdom; common sense.

Wise (Irish) Ardent or wise.

Wissian (English) Guide.

Wite (Scottish) Knowledge; punishment.

Witton (English) From the wise man's estate.

Wlod (Polish) Ruler.

Wohehiv (Native American) Dull knife.

Wojtek (Polish) Happy soldier.

Wokaihwokomas (North American) White antelope.

Wolcott (English) Wolf's home.

Wolf (English) Wolf. *Wolfe*

Wolfe (English) Wolf.

Wolfgang (Teutonic) Wolf strife. *Wolcott, Wolf, Wolfe, Wolfie, Woolsey*

Wolfram (Teutonic) Wolf; raven. *Walram*

Wolstan Origin and meaning unknown.

Woo (Chinese) Martial art; military.

Woodis (English) Wood; forest.

Woodrow (Old English) Forester; row of houses by a wood. *Woodie, Woodruff, Woodward, Woody*

Woodson (English) Son of Wood.

Woody (American) From Elwood. *Wood, Woodi*

Woorak (Australian) From the plain.

Wray (Scandinavian) From the corner.

Wren (Welsh) Chief.

Wright (Old English) Craftsman, carpenter.

Wu-pen (Chinese) Original consciousness.

Wulfhere (Anglo-Saxon) King.

Wulfnoth (Anglo-Saxon) Wolf.

Wulfsige (English) Victorious wolf.

Wulfstan Origin and meaning unknown.

Wuliton (Native American) Will do well. *Wulitan*

Wunand (Native American) God is good. *Wunan*

Wuyi (Native American) Soaring turkey vulture.

Wyalan Origin and meaning unknown.

Wyatt (Old English, French) Little warrior; water. *Wyatte, Wyeth*

Wybert (English) Battle bright. *Wibert*

Wyclef (English) From the white cliff.

Wylie (Old English) Enchanting. *Wiley*

Wyman (English) Fighter.

Wyndam (Old English) Field with the winding path. *Windham, Wyn*

Wynono (Native American) First born.

Wynter (American) Born during winter.

Wynton (English) Friend. *Winton*

Wynward (English) From the wine's forest. *Winward, Wynyard*

Wyome (Native American) Plain.

Wyoming (Native American) Wide plain. *Wyomia, Wyomie*

Wyson (English) Meaning unknown.

Wystan (Anglo-Saxon) Battle stone. *Winston*

Wythe (English) From the willow tree.

X

Xabat (Spanish) Savior.

Xalvador (Spanish) Savior.

Xander (Greek) Short form of Alexander. *Xande, Xzander*

Xanthus (Greek) Yellow, blond. *Xantha, Xanthe, Xanthos, Zanthius*

Xanto (Greek) Blond-haired.

Xat (American) Saved. *Xatt*

Xaver (Spanish) New home.

Xaverius (Spanish) Owner of new house. *Xaverious, Xaveryus*

Xavier (Arabic) Bright; splendid. (Spanish) New home. *Giaffar, Jaffar, Javier, Saverio, Xabier, Xaver, Xaviero, Xever, Zavey, Zavier*

Xavion (Spanish) Home.

Xaxon (American) Happy. *Zaxon*

Xayvion (African American) New house. *Savion, Sayveon, Sayvion, Xaivon, Xayveon, Zayvion*

Xebec (French) From Quebec; cold. *Xebeck, Xebek*

Xenik (Russian) Sly. *Xenic, Xenick, Xenyc, Xenyck, Xenyk*

Xeno (Greek) Strange, foreign. *Xenoes, Zene, Zenno, Zenny, Zeno, Zenos*

Xenophon (Greek) Soldier, mercenary, and Athenian student of Socrates; strange voice. *Xeno, Zennie, Zenophon*

Xerarch (Greek) Forest dweller. *Xerarche*

Xeres (Spanish) Older. *Xeries*

Xerxes (Persian) Prince, ruler, leader. *Xerk, Xerky, Zerk, Zerkes, Zerkez, Zerzes*

Xeven (Salvic) Lively. *Xyven*

Xhosas (African) South African tribe. *Xhoses, Xhosys*

Xi-Wang (Chinese) Desire; hope.

Xiaoping (Chinese) Small bottle.

Ximen (Spanish) Obedient. *Ximenes, Ximon, Ximun*

Xin (Chinese) New. *Xian, Xoan*

Xing-Fu (Chinese) Happiness.

Xipil (Aztec) Of fire.

Xob (Hebrew) Persecuted.

Xosé (Hebrew) Seated at the right hand of God.

Xuthus (Greek) Son of Helen.

Xyle (American) Helpful. *Zye, Zyle*

Xylo (Greek) Wood.

Xylon (Greek) Forester; one who lives in the forest. *Xilon, Zilon, Zylon*

Xyshaun (African American) Zany. *Xye, Zye, Zyshaun, Zyshawn*

Xyst (Greek) Portico; systematic. *Xist*

Xystum (Greek) Promenade. *Xistoum, Xistum, Xysoum*

Xystus (Greek) Promenade. *Xistus*

Xzavier (Basque) Form of Xavier. *Xzavaier, Xzavion, Xzavior, Xzvaier*

Y

Yaakov (Hebrew) Supplanter or heel. *Yanknv*

Yaar (Hebrew) Forest.

Yadid (Hewbrew) Beloved. *Yadyd*

Yadon (Hebrew) He will judge. *Yadin*

Yagel (Hebrew) Happiness. *Yagil, Yagyl, Yogil, Yogyl*

Yago (Hebrew, Spanish) Supplanter.

Yahir (Hebrew) Haughty.

Yahto (Native American) Blue.

Yahya (Arabic) God is good. *Yihya*

Yair (Hebrew) God will teach. *Jair, Jayr, Yayr*

Yakim (Hebrew) God develops. *Jakim, Jakym*

Yakov (Hebrew) Supplanter; held by the heel.

Yale (German, Old English) One who pays or produces; corner of land. *Yael, Yaell, Yail, Yaill, Yayl, Yayll*

Yamal (Hindi) One of a twin.

Yamin (Hebrew) Right hand. *Jamin*

Yan (Hebrew) God's grace. *Jannai, Yann, Yanni, Yannic*

Yancy (Native American) Yankee. *Yance, Yancey, Yank, Yankee, Yantsey*

Yanis (Hebrew) Gift from God.

Yannick (French) Gift from God.

Yannis (Greek) God is good. *John, Yannakis, Yanni, Yiannis*

Yanoach (Hebrew) Rest.

Yao (Chinese) Born on a Thursday.

Yaphet (Hebrew) Attractive. *Japhete, Japheth, Yapheth*

Yarb (Gypsy) Herb.

Yardley (English) Of the yard. *Yardlea, Yardleah, Yardlee, Yardleigh, Yardlie, Yardly*

Yarin (Hebrew) To understand.

Yaron (Hebrew) He will sing. *Jaron, Yairon*

Yas (Native American) Snow.

Yasahiro (Japanese) Peaceful.

Yasar (Arabic) Wealth; comfort; ease. *Yaser, Yasir, Yasser, Yassir*

Yasashiku (Japanese) Gentle, polite.

Yash (Hindi) Victorious glory.

Yasha (Russian) Form of Jacob. *Yascha, Yashka, Yashko*

Yashodhara (Hindi) One who has achieved fame.

Yashovarman (Hindi) Meaning unknown.

Yashpal (Hindi) Protector of fame.

Yashwant (Hindi) Glorious.

Yasin (Arabic) Prophet. *Yasine, Yasseen, Yassin, Yazen*

Yasir (Arabic) To be rich; to be easy. *Yasser*

Yasuo (Japanese) Peaceful one. *Yaso*

Yates (Middle English) Gate keeper. *Yaits, Yeats*

Yatin (Hindi) Ascetic.

Yauvani (Hindi) Full of youth.

Yazid (Arabic) Increasing; enhance. *Yazeed, Yazide, Yazyd*

Ye (Chinese) Universe.

Yechezkel (Hebrew) God strengthens. *Chaskel, Chatzkel, Kesel*

Yehoshua (Hebrew) Form of Joshua. *Yeshua, Yishua, Yoshua*

Yehudi (Hebrew) Praise God; man from Judah; Jew. *Yehuda, Yehudit, Yehudie, Yehudy*

Yemon (Japanese) Guardian.

Yen (Vietnamese) Calm.

Yeoman (English) Servant. *Yeomen, Yoman*

Yered (Hebrew) To come down. *Jered*

Yerik (Russian) Appointed by God; form of Jeremiah.

Yervant (Armenian) Armenian king.

Yeshaya (Hebrew) God lends.

Yevgeni (Russian) Noble; well born. *Yevgeny*

Yigal (Hebrew) He will redeem. *Yagel, Yigael*

Yigit (Turkish) Shall be redeemed.

Yitro (Hebrew) Plenty. *Yitran*

Yitzchak (Hebrew) Laughter. *Itzhak, Itzaac, Itzaack, Itzaak, Yitzac, Yitzaak, Yitzhak*

Yo (Chinese) Bright.

Yobachi (African American) Pray to God.

Yochanan (Hebrew) Form of John. *Yohanan*

Yogendra (Hindi) God of yoga.

Yogesh (Hindi) God of yoga.

Yogi (Japanese) One who practices yoga. (Sanskrit) Unity. *Yogee, Yogey, Yogie, Yogy*

Yohann (German) Form of Johan.

Yonas (Hebrew) Dove. *Yonah*

Yonatan (Hebrew) Gift from God.

Yong (Chinese) Brave.

Yong-Sook (Korean) Eternal and pure.

Yong-Sun (Korean) Courageous.

Yongvar (Norse) Of Ing's army. *Ingvarr*

Yorath (English) Worthy God. *Ialo, Iorwerth*

York (Old English, Celtic) Yew tree, from the farm of yew trees. *Yorke, Yorker, Yorick*

Yosef (Hebrew) God increases. *Yoseff, Yosif, Yousef, Yusef, Yusif, Yusuf, Yuzef*

Yoshi (Japanese) Better; best. *Yoshee, Yoshie*

Yoshifumi (Japanese) Respectful; good. *Yoshimitusu, Yoshiyuki*

Yotimo (Native American) Bee flying to its hive.

Yottoko (Native American) Mud from the river.

Youkioma (Native American) Flawless. *Youkeoma, Yukeoma, Yukioma*

Young Jeezy (American) Rapper Jay Jenkins.

Young-Ho (Korean) Prosperity eternal and cleverness.

Young-Ja (Korean) Forever stable.

Young-Jae (Korean) Forever prosperous.

Ysgarran (Welsh) Meaning unknown.

Yu (Chinese) Universe.

Yuan (Chinese) New.

Yucel (Turkish) Noble. *Yusel*

Yudhajit (Hindi) Victor in war.

Yukio (Japanese) Gets what he wants; God will nourish. *Yukyo*

Yul (Mongolian) From the far horizon. *Yule*

Yule (English) Christmas. *Euell, Ewell, Yul, Yull*

Yuma (Native American) Son of the chief.

Yunis (Arabic) Dove. *Younis, Younys, Yunus, Yunys*

Yurchik (Russian) Farmer; form of George. *Yura, Yuri, Yurik, Yuriy, Yurko, Yurli, Yury*

Yuri (Russian) Form of George. (Greek) Farmer. *Yuris*

Yusef (Arabic) To increase. *Jussef, Yusuf, Yusuff*

Yutaka (Japanese) Fisherman.

Yutu (Native American) Coyote hunting.

Yuval (Hebrew) Brook. *Jubal*

Yves (Teutonic) Yew; archer. *Ives, Yvan, Yvo*

Ywain (Irish) Form of Owen. *Ywaine, Ywayn, Ywyn*

Z

Zabdi (Hebrew) Form of Zabdiel. *Zabad, Zabdy, Zabi, Zavdi,*

Zabdiel (Hebrew) Gift. *Zabdil, Zabdyl, Zavdiel, Zebdiel*

Zabulon (Hebrew) To exhalt; honor.

Zaccheo (Hebrew) One God remembers. *Zaccheus*

Zachary (Hebrew) God remembers; renowned by God. *Zacarius, Zaccaria, Zach, Zachariah, Zacharias, Zacharie, Zacharyah, Zack, Zackry, Zak, Zakary, Zechariah*

Zachriel (Latin) Angel who rules over memory.

Zádor (Hungarian) Violent.

Zafer (Turkish) Victorious. *Zafar, Zafir*

Zahavi (Hebrew) Gold.

Zahin (Islam) Intelligent.

Zahur (Egyptian) Flower. *Zahair, Zahar, Zaheer, Zahi, Zahir*

Zaid (African American) Increase; growth. *Zaide, Zayd, Zayde*

Zaide (Yiddish) Elder.

Zajzon (Hungarian) Meaning unknown.

Zakai (Hebrew) Innocent; one who is pure. *Zaki, Zakkai*

Zakaria (Hebrew) Form of Zachariah. *Zakaraiya, Zakareeya, Zakareeyah, Zakariah*

Zaki (Arabic) Smart. *Zakee, Zakie, Zaky*

Zakur (Hebrew) Masculine.

Zalán (Hungarian) Thrower; hitter.

Zale (Greek) Strength from the sea. *Zail, Zaile, Zayl, Zayle*

Zalman (Yiddish) Peaceful and quiet. *Salman, Salmen, Salmin, Salmon, Salmyn, Zalmen, Zalmon*

Zamael (German) Angel of joy. *Samuel*

Zamir (Hebrew) Songbird. *Zamar, Zamer, Zamyr*

Zámor (Hungarian) Plough land.

Zan (Hebrew) Well fed. *Zann*

Zander (Greek) Defender of man. *Zanda, Zandah, Zandar, Zanders, Zandor*

Zane (Arabic) Beloved. (Hebrew) God is gracious. *Zain, Zaine, Zayne*

Zanebono (Italian) Good one.

Zani (English, Hebrew) Gift from the house.

Zaniel (Latin) Angel of Monday; zodiac sign for Libra.

Zanipolo (Italian) Little gift of God.

Zann (Hebrew) Lily.

Zanobi (Latin) Scarcely alive.

Zaránd (Hungarian) Gold.

Zareb (African American) Protector.

Zared (Hebrew) Trap.

Zarek (Polish) May God protect the king. *Zarec, Zareck, Zaric, Zarick, Zaryc*

Zarir (Parsi) Golden.

Zashawn (African American) God is gracious; merciful. *Zeshawn*

Zavad (Hebrew) Present. *Zabad*

Zayd (Arabic) To increase. *Zaid, Zayed, Ziyad*

Zayden (Hebrew) Lucky. *Zaydin*

Zayn (Arabic) Beauty.

Zazel (Latin) Angel summoned for love invocations.

Zazu (Hebrew) Movement.

Zdenek (Czech) One from Sidon; winding sheet.

Zebedeo (Aramaic) Servant of god Zeb.

Zebediah (Hebrew) Portion of the lord. *Zebadia, Zebadiah, Zebadya, Zebedya, Zubin*

Zebulon (Hebrew) Home. *Zebulen, Zebulun, Zevulum*

Zedekiah (Hebrew) Justice of the lord. *Zed*

Zedock (English) Victorian-era name.

Zeeman (Dutch) Seaman. *Zeaman, Zeman, Zemen, Ziman, Zimen*

Zefirino (Greek) Wind of spring. *Zefferino, Zefiro*

Zeheb (Turkey) Gold.

Zeke (Arabic) Memory of the lord. *Zeak, Zeake, Zek*

Zeki (Turkish) Smart.

Zekö (Hungarian) Meaning unknown.

Zelig (German) Blessed one. *Zelyg*

Zelimir (Slavic) Wishes for peace. *Zelimyr, Zelymir*

Zelipe (Spanish) Meaning unknown.

Zen (Japanese) Religious.

Zendo (Greek) One who devotes his life to God.

Zeno (Greek) Of Zeus. *Zenan, Zenas, Zenus*

Zenoa (Hebrew) Sign.

Zenobio (Greek) Strength of Jupiter.

Zenon (Spanish) Living.

Zenos (Greek) Gift of Zeus. *Zen*

Zephan (Hebrew) Treasured by God.

Zephyr (Greek) Wind. *Zephirin*

Zeren (Turkish) Meaning unknown.

Zerind (Hungarian) Serb.

Zero (Greek) Seeds. *Zerot*

Zétény (Hungarian) Meaning unknown.

Zeth (Greek) Investigator; researcher. *Zetico, Zeticus*

Zeus (Greek) Powerful one. *Zous, Zus*

Zev (Hebrew) Deer; wolf. *Zeva, Zevie, Ziva, Zivia, Zvi*

Zhong (Chinese) Second brother.

Zhu (Chinese) Wish.

Zhuang (Chinese) Strong.

Zia (Hebrew) Trembling. (Arabic) Light. *Ziah, Ziya, Zya, Zyah*

Ziff (Hebrew) Wolf.

Zig (American) Justice of the lord. *Ziggy*

Zimon (Hebrew) Form of Simon. *Ziman, Zimen, Zymene, Zymin*

Zimraan (Arabic) Praise; celebrated.

Zindel (Yiddish) Protector of mankind. *Zindil, Zyndel*

Zion (Hebrew) Sign; guarded land. *Zeeon, Zeon, Zione, Zyon*

Ziph (Hebrew) Mouthful; falsehood.

Zircon (Arabic) Mineral.

Zitkaduta (Native American) Redbird.

Zitomer (Czech) To live in fame. *Zitek, Zitousek*

Ziv (Hebrew) Very bright. *Zivan, Ziven, Zivi, Zivon, Zivu*

Ziven (Slavic) Vigorous and alive. *Zivon*

Ziya (Arabic) Splendor; light. *Ziyah, Zyam, Zyahm, Zyya*

Zobor (Hungarian) Gathering.

Zoe (Greek) Life.

Zoello (Greek) Son of Zoe. *Zoellus*

Zolta (Hungarian) Life.

Zoltán (Hungarian) Chieftain. *Zolton*

Zombor (Hungarian) Buffalo. *Zsombor*

Zomier (Hebrew) One who prunes trees. *Zomer*

Zorba (Greek) Live each day.

Zorro (Slavic) Golden dawn. *Zoro*

Zorya (Slavic) Star. *Zoria, Zoriah, Zoryah*

Zosimo (Greek) Lively. *Zoilo, Zosimos, Zosimus, Zotico, Zoticus*

Zowie (Greek) Life. *Zoi*

Zsigmond (Hungarian) Victorious defender.

Zsolt (Hungarian) Name of an honor.

Zuhayr (Arabic) Sweet; having flowers. *Zuhair*

Zuriel (Hebrew) The Lord is my rock.

Zurl (Hebrew) Rock, strength of God.

Zvi (Scandinavian) Deer. *Zwi*

Zydrunas (Slavic) Morning sky.

Zygmunt (Polish) Victorious protector.

Appendix

Online Resources

If you're more comfortable sitting at a keyboard than holding a printed book, this section is for you. The websites listed here give you access to thousands more baby names and ideas. Or if you're on the hunt for more information about a particular name, odds are good one of the sites listed can help.

Adoption.com's Baby Name Locator
baby-names.adoption.com
Find the perfect baby name for your child by searching among 5,400 popular, unique, or unusual baby names and read about their meanings, origins, and similar names.

Baby Name Addicts
babynameaddicts.com
Surf here for more than 51,000 names and growing. This site offers names with meanings, origins, popularity graphs, surveys, and more.

Baby Name Guide
babynameguide.com
This site offers lists of names by category, a personal favorites list, and the top 100 boy and girl names.

Baby Name Network
babynamenetwork.com
Here you'll find an extensive database of names searchable by gender and origin. Lists showing popularity by decade and user rating are also included.

Baby Name World
babynameworld.com
Check out this database of baby names, searchable by origin, to find the perfect baby name along with the meaning.

Baby Names Country
babynamescountry.com
In search of a baby name originating from a particular country? This is a great place to start.

Baby Names Directory
babynamesdirectory.com
This baby name directory offers baby names, their meanings, their ethnic origin, and also the most popular baby names.

Baby Names of Ireland
babynamesofireland.com
This site offers 200 popular, unusual, and exotic Irish names. Frank McCourt, Pulitzer prize–winning author of *Angela's Ashes*, helps with the pronunciation of each one and gives the meanings.

Baby Names World
babynamesworld.parentsconnect.com
Search 27,000 baby names to learn more about their origin and meaning, as well as view popularity ratings given by other parents.

Baby Names
babynames.com
Here you'll find baby names and their meanings, names listed by popularity, names from soap operas, and much more.

Baby Zone's Baby Names
babyzone.com/babynames
Baby Zone offers tips and hints to help make finding the perfect name for your baby easier.

BabyCenter's Baby Name Finder
babycenter.com/babyname
This site offers lists of names sorted by sex, ethnic origin, and number of syllables.

BabyChatter
babychatter.com
Find lists of baby names, coupons, and free stuff here.

Behind the Name
behindthename.com
This site offers a look into the history behind common first names.

Indian Baby Names
babynamesindia.com
This site offers 17,347 Indian and Hindu baby names with their meanings.

Internet Public Library's Names for Babies and Others
ipl.org.ar/ref/QUE/FARQ/nameFARQ.html
The Internet Public Library offers names for babies. You can also type in questions if you're searching for the meaning of a name.

Muslim Baby Names
muslim-names.co.uk
Check out this online database for Muslim baby names and their meanings.

Name Nerds
namenerds.com
This site is dedicated to all those who love names, those who are looking for names, or anyone who has a name.

Popular Baby Names
popularbabynames.com
Find more than 10,000 baby names from around the world here. The database includes names from major regions, religions, and languages. There are also baby formula, diaper, and food coupons; samples; and freebies.

Social Security Administration's Popular Baby Names
ssa.gov/OACT/babynames
This site features archived lists of given names in popularity ordered by gender and year of birth from the Social Security Administration.

Think Baby Names
thinkbabynames.com
This site offers baby names, information on trends, and more unusual names by cultural background. Or you can use the random baby name generator for fun when you find yourself overwhelmed by all the choices.

YeahBaby
yeahbaby.com
Here you'll find baby names and meanings, celebrity baby names, and more.

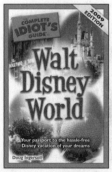